introduction to
marketing management
text and cases

introduction to marketing management

text and cases

STEWART H. REWOLDT
Professor of Marketing

JAMES D. SCOTT
Sebastian S. Kresge Professor of Marketing

MARTIN R. WARSHAW
Professor of Marketing

All of the
Graduate School of Business Administration
The University of Michigan

1969

 Richard D. Irwin, Inc., Homewood, Illinois
Irwin-Dorsey Limited, Georgetown, Ontario

First Printing, April, 1969
Second Printing, July, 1970
Third Printing, January, 1971
Fourth Printing, November, 1971

Library of Congress Catalog Card No. 69–19980

Printed in the United States of America

LEARNING SYSTEMS COMPANY—
a division of Richard D. Irwin, Inc.—has developed a
PROGRAMMED LEARNING AID
to accompany texts in this subject area.
Copies can be purchased through your bookstore
or by writing PLAIDS,
1818 Ridge Road, Homewood, Illinois 60430.

To Allison, Sara, and Alice

preface

This text is designed for a first course in marketing management. It introduces students to the approaches and problems of marketing decision making under conditions of uncertainty. The point of view taken is that of a marketing manager responsible for the planning and execution of a complete marketing program. It recognizes that marketing planning must be accomplished in the light of a changing economic, social, and legal environment which poses many constraints and requirements for the marketing manager. The text draws upon economics, the behavioral sciences, and quantitative analysis wherever these are helpful in the solution of marketing problems. No one of these "orientations" to the teaching of marketing management predominates. Rather, all are utilized in order to provide the student with all the tools available to a present-day marketing manager.

In general, an analytical rather than a descriptive approach is taken; only essential descriptive material necessary to marketing decision making is provided. The text material focuses on basic concepts and methods of analysis. By applying these to the analysis of cases the student will come to appreciate their relevance and value. The student learns marketing decision making by making marketing decisions. There is no other way to train marketing managers that works as well.

The 27 cases included present fundamental issues in marketing management. These provide students valuable experience in exercising their analytical powers and their judgment; they develop their capacity to make decisions. The cases follow each major section of text material and are designed to deepen and extend the student's understanding of the challenge the marketing manager faces in carrying out his responsibilities. Additional factual background about marketing and the environment in which it is carried on is also gained from case study.

This text is divided into seven parts. Part I introduces the student to marketing management, focuses on the planning of marketing strategy as the heart of marketing management, and stresses buyer behavior as the prime determinant of basic marketing strategy. Part II is concerned with problems and methods of demand analysis. It takes an intensive look at buyer behavior, approaches to understanding buyer behavior, and the methodology of translating marketing information into demand forecasts. Parts III through VI deal with the major decision areas of marketing management—product strategy, distribution strategy, promotion strategy, and pricing strategy. Part VII attempts to integrate strategies discussed in each of these marketing management decision areas into an overall marketing program for the firm.

Introduction to Marketing Management is shorter than some texts. It is intended for a one-semester course; hence, coverage has been limited to essentials. It is assumed that where greater depth of coverage is wanted this will be accomplished by personal input of the teacher, the use of additional readings, and the assignment of cases from other readily available sources. Our aim has been to design the book so that it is flexible and can be used in a variety of situations.

This book is the by-product of the teaching experience of the authors at both the graduate and undergraduate level. Since we have all taught the introductory marketing management course at The University of Michigan, we have had an opportunity to test both the text material and cases in the classroom and to revise these materials in the light of this experience. Our thinking about the content of this text has been much influenced by discussions with our faculty colleagues about course structure and ways it can be improved. As is undoubtedly true at most colleges and universities these days, our introductory marketing management course has been revised frequently in recent years to reflect new thinking, new concepts, new analytical approaches, and new problem materials. The most recent revision involved shortening a six-credit-hour, two-semester course into a four-credit-hour, one-semester course. This text reflects the group discussions within the marketing staff of the philosophy, content, and approach of this new course. We wish to express our sincere appreciation for these contributions of our colleagues.

We are indebted to the Graduate School of Business Administration of The University of Michigan, and particularly to its Bureau of Business Research for financial support for the collection of the case materials included in this volume. The cases were collected by several individuals working on research assignments under the supervision of the authors or of certain of our colleagues. The index of cases at the end of the book lists each of the case authors and faculty supervisors. To each we extend our hearty thanks.

We are also indebted to the many business executives who cooperated with us in our case research activities and shared their experiences in order to provide a realistic learning experience for students.

Although these individuals must go unnamed in order to protect confidential information, we nevertheless deeply appreciate their unselfish contributions.

Finally, we are indebted to our wives for their substantial contribution in providing encouragement when difficulties were encountered and in furnishing an environment conducive to the authorship task.

Ann Arbor, Michigan
March, 1969

Stewart H. Rewoldt
James D. Scott
Martin R. Warshaw

table of contents

part three: product strategy 145

5. product choice decisions 147

Decision to offer a new product. What new products to offer: *Objective of profit maximization. Profitability formula. Estimate of demand. Price estimates. Cost estimates. Life cycle estimates. Net revenue. Compound profitability formula. Resource utilization: its relationship to product planning. Utilization of production resources. Decision matrix: utilization of production resources. Example: proposed new product "X." Utilization of marketing resources. Decision matrix: utilization of marketing resources. Summary: resource utilization.* Internal development or external acquisition: *Advantages of acquiring new products by merger. Advantages of internal development. Product development and public policy.*

6. product development decisions 174

The product development process: *Characteristics of product development.* Steps in product development: *New product ideas. Preliminary evaluation. Pretesting. Test marketing. The go–no go decision. The marketing plan.* Ancillary product decisions: *Packaging. Branding. Warranty policy. Product service.* Organization for product development.

part four: distribution strategy 247

7. the distribution structure 249

The institutions involved: *Basic types of middlemen.* Exchange and market intermediaries: *Exchange without intermediaries. The wholesaler and exchange. Number of transactions and marketing costs.* The discrepancy of assortments: *Heterogeneity of supply and demand. Total assortments ver-*

sus acquisition assortments. Aspects of sorting. Summary. Channels of distribution: *Major channels—consumer goods. Major channels—industrial goods. Use of higher cost channels. Use of multiple channels.*

Determination of basic promotional strategy: *Promotion involves communication. How communication works. Determining the promotional mix. Promotional methods. Choice of promotional methods.* Advertising: *Appraising the opportunity to make profitable use of consumer advertising. When should advertising receive main emphasis in the promotional mix? Other problems of advertising management.* Personal selling: *Factors influencing the use of personal selling. When should personal selling receive main emphasis? Other problems of sales force management.* Dealer promotion: *When should dealer promotion carry the main burden? When advertising is emphasized, how necessary is dealer promotion? When retail personal selling is emphasized, how necessary is dealer promotion? Methods of encouraging dealer promotion.* Consumer promotions. Determining the promotional mix: *Adaptive Planning and Control Sequence (APACS).*

marketing strategy

The marketing function in the business enterprise embodies many diverse activities, but the heart of marketing is the development of marketing strategy. The marketing manager, in planning his strategy, works with those marketing variables over which he has a significant measure of control, such as the product, distribution, price, advertising, and personal selling. He attempts to design and implement a marketing strategy that will most efficiently achieve the goals of the company. He must do this with full awareness of the many constraints which limit his freedom of action. Above all, he must design his strategy so that it is consistent with buyer behavior in the market he intends to serve.

Part One of this text introduces the student to marketing management and to the planning of marketing strategy. Part Two focuses on demand analysis. It takes an intensive look at buyer behavior, approaches to understanding buyer behavior, and the problems of demand forecasting. Parts Three through Six deal with the major decision areas of marketing—product strategy, distribution strategy, promotion strategy, and price strategy. Part Seven attempts to integrate strategies discussed in each of these decision areas into an overall marketing program for the firm.

chapter 1

development of marketing strategy

This chapter presents an overview of marketing and of the planning of marketing strategy. It attempts to answer such questions as: (1) What is marketing? (2) What is marketing strategy? (3) What variables are involved in development of a marketing strategy? (4) How and why does marketing strategy vary among products? Answers to these and other questions will provide a broad conceptual framework for the consideration of major decision areas in the field of marketing.

what is marketing?

Marketing is not easy to define. No one has yet been able to formulate a clear, concise definition that finds universal acceptance. To the extent that a common view of marketing does exist, that view is

Figure 1–1

usually based on the assumption that economic activity can be broadly divided into three primary categories—production, marketing, and consumption. Goods and services must first be created—on the farm, in the factory, or in the shop. Before consumption can take place, these goods must be made available to consumers. Making the goods available is assumed to be the role of marketing. If the role of marketing is so perceived, marketing can be defined as "those activities involved in getting goods and services from producers to consumers."

This definition sees marketing as essentially a bridge between two other, perhaps more basic, economic functions. Its only purpose is to make it possible for the utilities created by the production process to meet the ultimate economic purpose of serving the consumption process.

This is a limited view of the economic role of marketing. It does recognize the need for such marketing functions as personal selling and advertising, necessary to persuade potential buyers to purchase, and

Figure 1–2

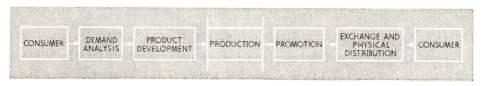

physical distribution to get products into the hands of consumers. However, it implicitly assumes the existence of a product before the role of marketing gets underway. It also takes it for granted that a demand for things which are produced exists in the marketplace and that marketing effort can successfully convert this demand into sales. This is a most unrealistic view of what marketing is all about.

In the progressive business firm, marketing is a broad and pervasive function, affecting all aspects of the business operation. It both begins and ends with the consumer. Because the basic purpose of business is to serve the welfare of consumers, it is essential that business operations be geared to this end. Relating business activities to consumer wants is accomplished through marketing. It is the role of marketing to identify consumers, to determine their wants and the manner in which they prefer these wants to be satisfied. Through demand analysis the consumer's wants are studied, measured, and understood. His behavior as a buyer is observed so that a marketing program may be devised which is consistent with that behavior. Such demand analysis is the function of marketing research activities.

Once consumer requirements and preferences are known, marketing plays a role in guiding the development of a product or service along lines consistent with consumer demand. The basic objective of the product development process is to translate consumer requirements into a physical product or a useful service. Other business functions also play a role in product development. However, it is the particular role of marketing to assure adaptation of the product or service to consumer needs and preferences.

In the case of a product, production is the next step after product development. Again, marketing has an influence. Through the information gathered about demand, product specifications are set, production schedules are determined, and inventory levels are planned. Once a product exists, consumers must be informed of its availability and its ability to serve their needs. It is through promotional activities (advertising, personal selling, etc.) that this communications function is accomplished. Informing consumers, of course, is the most commonly recognized marketing activity. It should be remembered, however, that it is only part, albeit an important part, of the total marketing process.

At some point, an exchange of the product for (usually) money must occur. The product, furthermore, must be made available where the consumer requires it. It is the role of marketing to perform these functions of exchange and physical distribution. Marketing does not end when the consumer receives the product, but it continues until his satisfaction with the product is assured. Common tools used in assuring such satisfaction are warranties, service facilities, and service contracts. These, too, are a part of the marketing process.

The broad scope of marketing poses a difficult problem of definition. In order to be sufficiently comprehensive to include all marketing activities, a definition of the marketing function must be either broadly worded or long and detailed. Perhaps the best definition of marketing that has been formulated is the following:

Marketing is the process in a society by which the demand structure for economic goods and services is anticipated or enlarged and satisfied through the conception, promotion, exchange, and physical distribution of such goods and services.[1]

A typical reaction to so broad a definition of marketing is likely to be, "But what else is there to business management? Doesn't this definition encompass all business functions?" No, not really. The underlying problem is that marketing *pervades* all other business func-

---

[1] Statement of the Philosophy of Marketing of the Marketing Faculty, The Ohio State University, College of Commerce and Administration (Columbus, 1964), p. 2.

tions and is intermingled with them. It has not proven possible, in framing a definition, to make this distinction fully clear.

In recent years there has been a trend among business firms to adopt what is known as "The Marketing Concept." Although this term has been loosely used and means somewhat different things to different people, it generally implies customer orientation of the total business firm. The implication of this concept is that the fundamental purpose of business activity is the satisfaction of consumer wants. It follows from this that a prerequisite to rational business activity is knowledge and understanding of consumer behavior. The function of marketing is to study and interpret consumer needs and behavior and to guide all business activities toward the end of consumer satisfaction. In doing this, marketing gets involved in all business functions. Successful implementation of the marketing concept is possible only if management perceives of marketing as an all-pervasive business activity.

marketing strategy

In the planning of marketing strategy, the marketing manager must make decisions about how he will employ the marketing tools he has at his disposal to achieve a predetermined goal. The variables the marketing manager works with in planning strategy are of two types: controllable and uncontrollable. He can decide, for example, whether he will or will not use advertising, how much, and what kind. He must make similar decisions about the product line, distribution, pricing, and the use of personal selling. He can weave these together into an overall marketing program in an infinite number of ways.

In planning his strategy, the marketing manager faces certain constraints which are inherent in the environment within which his strategy must be employed. For example, he is faced with certain characteristics of demand as they exist in the marketplace. His strategy must be appropriate to these demand characteristics or it cannot be successful. Competition is a fact of life that has a heavy influence on what he can and cannot do. Many legal considerations constrain his efforts. He must adapt his strategy to the needs and operations of the distributors and dealers through which his product will be sold. Production capabilities of his company may either limit his sales opportunities or suggest the desirability of changing his strategy to achieve greater volume.

In essence, marketing strategy consists of manipulating those variables the marketing manager can control and adapting optimally to those variables he cannot control, to most effectively attain his objective. Those variables he can control are, for his purposes, the relevant marketing strategy variables. The uncontrollable are environmental variables. They, in a sense, limit the strategy choices available to him in trying to achieve a favorable purchase decision by the consumer. Figure 1–3 attempts to portray this approach to achievement of an integrated marketing effort.

Figure 1–3. Controllable and uncontrollable variables in marketing.

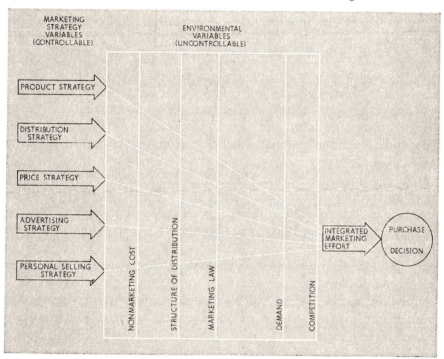

environmental (uncontrollable) variables

There are many uncontrollable variables that condition marketing strategy. Only the most basic, and each rather broadly defined, are discussed here.

Demand. A demand for goods and services is not created, in a basic sense, by marketing activities employed by sellers. Demand is a resultant of consumer needs and goals. It is colored by established consumer buying patterns. It is constrained by such basic forces as income, norms of acceptable behavior, and time pressures under which consumers operate. Demand may be latent and its existence unknown. Marketing strategy can be employed to convert it into effective demand by offering a product or service in a manner consistent with underlying demand forces.

Many social critics assign great powers to marketing, particularly to advertising, to influence consumer behavior.[2] It is claimed that sellers are able, through modern marketing methods, to induce consumers to buy products they neither need nor want. This would seem to be something of an exaggeration. The Ford Motor Company had little success in building demand for the Edsel, and campaigns to get people to stop smoking have not had the hoped-for effect on the demand for cigarettes. The marketing of goods and services would be a far easier task if a significant control over demand were possible.

Marketing actions can modify and channel demand. However, the cost inputs required to produce basic changes in demand can be very high. It is usually more efficient, in planning marketing strategy, to adapt to demand as one finds it. If a firm's objective is to maximize profits, demand can best be considered as an essentially uncontrollable variable.

Competition. The present state of competition, the expected future state of competition, and anticipated retaliatory moves of competitors necessarily affect the planning of marketing strategy. A competitor may so dominate a market that gaining a satisfactory market share is impossible, or is possible only at too high a cost. There may be so many competitors that market-share opportunities are limited. If a competitor is employing a particular marketing strategy, this may suggest that it is wise to vary one's own strategy to avoid direct confrontation in the market.

The formulation of marketing strategy requires prediction of retaliatory moves of competitors. If our firm does this, how will competitors respond? How long a time period before this response becomes effective? How can we alter our strategy to minimize our competitor's ability to respond? Expected profitability to the Ford Motor Company of varying its product offering by introducing the Mustang would very likely have been less if General Motors could have been expected to introduce a comparable car within six months instead of two years. In some instances, the mere threat of retaliation is sufficient to cause a particular marketing strategy not to be employed. The uncertainty

---

[2] See Vance Packard, *The Hidden Persuaders* (New York: David McKay Co., Inc., 1957), and John Kenneth Galbraith, *The New Industrial State* (Boston: Houghton Mifflin Co., 1967).

surrounding competitors' possible responses greatly complicates strategy planning. In short, marketing strategy planning must take into account the nature and extent of competition, both present and future, in determining the optimal course of action to be followed.

The distribution structure. Most sellers must reach the market with their products through the existing distribution structure. The distribution structure in the United States is described in Chapter 7. There are certain types and numbers of agent middlemen, wholesalers, and retailers, and they interrelate in certain ways. To distribute some products, automobiles, for example, a firm may set up its own dealership network; but this is a very costly, and often totally inappropriate, move for other sellers. Even automobile companies sell replacement parts through independent automotive wholesalers and repair shops.

Marketing strategy plans must take into account such matters as: (1) the existence or nonexistence of appropriate distribution channels; (2) a firm's ability to gain access to those channels; (3) ability of the demand for the product to support the cost of distribution through the chosen channels; (4) the intra- and interchannel competition that the product will face; (5) trends in institutions in the channels that may affect the marketing of the product; and (6) requirements placed by the channel on such other marketing functions as advertising and personal selling.

The problem of gaining acceptance of a product by channel institutions is a very real one. Most such institutions are swamped with offers of new products by manufacturers. Profitable operation for the channel institution depends on choosing from this total offering those products which will contribute most to profits within the confines of limited capacity of the channel. Products whose demand is uncertain or limited are avoided. Products that will merely divert demand from existing products and not increase total sales are likewise avoided unless a demand for choice among consumers requires that they be carried.

Marketing law. Legal constraints have been imposed upon sellers in order to protect the public interest. For example, a seller may decide that he can best maximize profit by selling to each of several segments of the market at the maximum price that market segment is willing to pay. This enables him to capture more revenue from those who are willing to pay an above "average" price and to earn still additional profit from those willing to pay a minimum price that is "below average" so long as that price covers incremental costs. However, the Robinson-Patman Act (discussed in Chapter 14) prohibits discrimination in price among buyers whenever such discrimination may serve substantially to lessen competition. This constraint upon the seller's freedom of action forces him to find alternative means of maximizing profits. One possibility is to offer different models of his product, each with features intended to appeal to a different market segment, and to follow a different pricing policy with each model.

A seller may wish to improve the quality of the selling effort devoted to his product by distributors and dealers. He may decide to accomplish this objective by getting these middlemen to agree not to carry competing products but to devote all their selling efforts to his products. This constitutes what is known as an "exclusive dealing" contract. Section 3 of the Clayton Antitrust Act (discussed in Chapter 8) prohibits such contracts if they might tend substantially to lessen competition. The so-called Truth-in-Packaging bill (discussed in Chapter 6) placed certain constraints upon package design and information included on the package. The Food, Drug, and Cosmetic Act (also discussed in Chapter 6) places many restraints upon marketing practices for foods, drugs, and cosmetics. Recent automotive safety legislation has forced automobile manufacturers to modify automobile design and to add additional safety features.

Nonmarketing cost. In planning marketing strategy, such non-marketing costs as production and overhead costs place limits on the strategy that can be contemplated. For example, if per unit production costs for a product are $100, to which overhead and marketing costs must be added, pricing strategy must involve a per unit price sufficiently above $100 to cover these several types of cost. An increase in production or overhead costs for a product through time may force a change in marketing strategy, perhaps in the direction of reduced emphasis on price and more emphasis on other variables in the marketing mix.

marketing strategy (controllable) variables

In formulating his marketing strategy, the seller manipulates the variables over which he does have control so as to arrive at the optimum strategic approach to his market goal. These controllable variables we have broadly classified as: (1) the product, (2) distribution, (3) price, (4) advertising, and (5) personal selling. Before attempting to compose these variables into a general marketing strategy for several different types of products, a brief word of explanation about each is in order.

Product. If one accepts the narrow and unrealistic view of marketing mentioned early in this chapter, namely, that marketing consists only of those activities involved in getting goods and services from the producer to the consumer, the product involved would have to be considered an uncontrollable variable in the planning of marketing strategy. In reality, the product is one of the major controllable variables the marketing manager has to work with and, in many cases, his most effective. The product can be modified in many ways better to achieve a marketing goal. It can be changed in quality, size, shape, color, variety, and in other ways.

A company is in business to serve the needs of consumers; it is not in business to sell any specific product. If consumer needs can be better served by dropping a product from the group offered by a particular firm, it can be dropped. If a new product would contribute favorably to the firm's achievement of its objective, it can be added.

Distribution. The planner of marketing strategy has many choices to make with respect to distribution policy. He must choose the geographical area in which he will market his product, and those areas he will not enter. He must decide the types of retail outlets in which he wants his product carried and the number of such outlets needed in each portion of the market. He must determine whether it is better to sell directly to retail outlets or to work through wholesalers. If he elects to sell through wholesalers, he must decide what type of wholesalers and how many. How shall he work with the institutions through which he has chosen to sell to assure their effectiveness? How much control over the efforts of middlemen should he try to exercise? These and many other decisions must be made with regard to the distribution variable.

Price. The price at which a product is offered is controllable within limits. A seller may elect to compete on a price basis and set his price low in relation to the prices of competitors. Conversely, he may strive for a high-quality image and foster this image with a high-price policy. Discounts may be utilized to vary price with quantities purchased or to achieve different prices for different classes of trade.

A seller's control over price is by no means absolute. The range of price options available in planning marketing strategy is constrained by cost considerations. Demand factors and competition determine what the market will accept. Further constraints are to be found in marketing law and trade custom.

Advertising. Marketing managers may elect to utilize advertising in various amounts and in various ways. They may choose to use it as a major method of communication with consumers, or they may use it only as a supplement to other forms of communication. They may choose from among various types of media (for example, television, radio, newspapers, and magazines), and they have many specific choices available within each of these media categories. The opportunities for choice extend to appeals to use in the advertising, amount and type of copy, layout and artwork, and so on.

Personal selling. As with advertising, the marketing manager may elect to utilize more or less personal selling, to direct it at different market targets, to use it in various ways, to employ various appeals. In some cases he has an open choice between the use of advertising and personal selling in his planning of strategy; in other cases circumstances force him in the direction of the use of one or the other.

comparative marketing strategies

Formulation of marketing strategies is more an art than a science, and creativity is an important ingredient in success. Still, because marketing strategy is molded in large measure by uncontrollable forces in the environment surrounding the marketing of a product, certain strategy patterns tend to be associated with certain types of products. Marketing strategies generally employed with some products, say, consumer durables, are substantially different from those generally used for other products such as, for example, food products. Within a given product class there are often differences in the strategies followed by different companies, but it is still possible to talk of a particular overall marketing strategy as being generally typical of a certain type of product. For example, a strategy of intensive distribution (selling through as many retail outlets as possible) is typical of food products, whereas consumer durables usually are sold through a smaller number of selected retail outlets.

The remaining chapters of this book are concerned with the many concepts and problems involved in the planning of marketing strategy. At this point we are in a position to deal only with broad profiles of marketing strategy. A comparison, however, of the general marketing strategies appropriate to different kinds of products will provide an overview of what is to follow and will serve as a framework on which to hang the discussion of individual strategy variables in marketing.

Chosen for comparison of typical marketing strategies are four different products: automobiles, automotive parts, life insurance, and

Figure 1-4. Marketing strategy planning matrix.

Marketing Strategy Variables	Automobiles	Automotive Parts	Life Insurance	Bread
Product				
Distribution				
Price				
Advertising				
Personal selling				

bread. One of these is a high-priced consumer durable, one is a replacement component, one is an intangible product, and one is a basic staple.

Figure 1-4 is a very simple decision matrix for planning a marketing strategy profile for each of these products. Our objective, a very limited one, is to indicate the relative importance of each of the marketing strategy variables in the overall marketing plan. Another way of stating it is: How can we best allocate our resources of time, effort, and money among these five variables for each product in order to achieve the best possible marketing strategy for that product? Our purpose in doing this is not to derive the only feasible strategies, or necessarily even the best ones, but rather to highlight the differences in marketing strategies for different products. In the process of doing this, we shall also focus on the factors which cause these differences.

Using a rating scale of 0 to 5, let us assign "importance values" to each variable. The most important variable for each product will automatically be given a rating of 5, and then the others can be rated in relation thereto. For each product a marketing strategy profile will be suggested, and then the rationale for the suggested profile will be offered.

strategy profile: automobiles

Figure 1-5. Marketing strategy profile: Automobiles.

Controllable Variables	Importance Value
Product	5
Distribution	2
Price	2
Advertising	3
Personal selling	1

This profile suggests that the most important strategy variable for automobiles is the product. To be more accurate, it is the image of the product among consumers that is the key to success, not the physical attributes of the product itself. The automobile is an important and a high-cost purchase. The typical consumer will spend considerable time comparing various makes and models. Unless the product fully meets his needs as he sees them, he probably will make an alternative choice. Another way of putting it is: If the product is unsatisfactory to the consumer, manipulation of the other variables cannot be expected to overcome this defect. When Ford Motor Company was unable to overcome the bad product image of the Edsel, they dropped this product from their product line. Chrysler Corporation did the same for the DeSoto. Pontiac Motors Division, on the other hand, drastically restyled its product during the 1950's and substantially increased its market share. The success of the Mustang in 1964 was undoubtedly due primarily to the strong appeal of its unique design.

The 2 rating for distribution is subject to challenge. The rating reflects what would seem to be a reasonable answer to this question: If a company already has distribution of its products in all areas (the near normal state for automobiles), can it expect substantially to increase its market share by adding more dealers? Because of the importance of the purchase of an automobile, consumers will normally go to great effort to view those they consider to have favorable product images. No one buys a Ford rather than a Chevrolet because the Ford dealer is several blocks closer. If it is a choice between spending a limited sum of money either on improving the product or on increasing the number of dealers by a small percentage, usually the product improvement would promise the greatest return. Consumer concern for postpurchase service may be the best grounds on which to challenge this view. Easy access to a dealer is more important for service than it is for initial purchase.

The 2 rating for price is based on what is thought to be a realistic situation, namely, that it is a small price difference only, say, $25, that can usually be considered in planning marketing strategy. Ford could surely outsell Chevrolet if it could sell its cars at 50 percent of the Chevrolet price, but cost considerations prohibit this. The decision is more likely to be of the sort suggested by this question: Should we forego product changes this year and drop our price by $25? A well-conceived product change would normally be expected to have a greater effect on sales than would a small price reduction. As a matter of fact, keeping prices down by foregoing product change is what Henry Ford did in the days of the Model T. This enabled Chevrolet to emphasize product refinements, at higher prices, and become the leading seller of automobiles.

Advertising is rated at 3 because of its importance in establishing a desirable product image. It is doubtful that even extensive and highly skilled advertising could compensate for an unsatisfactory product. However, given an attractive product, advertising can do much to mold the consumer's image of that product. The status value of the Cadillac owes much to skillful advertising.

The low rating of 1 for personal selling will be hard for many to accept. Personal selling comes into play at the retail level for automobiles, and the low quality of this selling effort has long been of concern to both automobile buyers and manufacturers. One might take the view that if this selling effort has been so bad, and car sales have continued to rise dramatically over the years, it cannot be a very important factor. Surely it is unlikely to offset the depressing effect on sales of a poor product. On the other hand, we have little real evidence of what personal selling can do, because it has so rarely been used effectively in the sale of automobiles.

strategy profile: automotive parts

Figure 1–6. Marketing strategy profile: Automotive parts.

Controllable Variables	Importance Value
Product	1
Distribution	5
Price	1
Advertising	1
Personal selling	3

For automotive parts, distribution is the most important variable. The purchase of such parts by the ultimate consumer is tied to his purchase of a repair service. He really has no demand for automotive parts as such. His demand is for a properly functioning vehicle, and he purchases a repair service to achieve this goal. In seeking out a repair service, he is governed by such things as past experience with the repair outlet, the outlet's reputation for quality service, convenience of location, etc. With these things governing his choice, he almost implicitly agrees to accept whatever brand of replacement parts the repair outlet chooses to install. If the repair outlet carries Brand A parts in stock, he accepts Brand A. If the outlet carries Brand B, that is the brand he receives and accepts.

The moral to be drawn from this pattern of buyer behavior for automotive parts is this: Sales can best be maximized by assuring that a manufacturer's brand of parts is stocked by as many repair outlets as possible. Where his brand is not stocked, there is no chance of a sale. Where it is stocked, his probability of a sale is determined by the number of substitute brands also carried. However, because of usually insignificant brand preference for automotive parts among car owners, the repair outlet has little incentive to stock multiple brands.[3]

The low rating of 1 on the product variable reflects the fact that there is little opportunity for product differentiation. The design of the part is largely determined by its function, and aesthetics is usually unimportant because the part is hidden from view. Quality, of course, must be adequate to gain and maintain acceptance in the repair trade.

Price competition is not strong for automotive parts except within the do-it-yourself market served by such outlets as Sears, Roebuck, Montgomery Ward, and Western Auto. The product is usually a small part of the total repair cost; hence, price differences to the ultimate consumer are small even if differences in parts prices are large percentagewise. Because a high margin to the repair outlet, even if it means a higher list price for the part, is important in inducing the outlet to stock a particular brand, there is little incentive for manufacturers to compete on a price basis.

There is some, but not heavy, advertising of replacement parts to the ultimate consumer. Advertising cannot develop a brand preference of significance for such a product or change the consumer's willingness to accept what the repair outlet offers. Therefore, it is much better to utilize funds to expand distribution rather than to advertise. What advertising to the consumer is done is usually done to help achieve distribution. The repair outlet would rather carry a known than an unknown brand, other things being equal.

Personal selling is rated as high as 3 for one reason only: It is an important tool in gaining and holding distribution. The various services provided by personal selling are important to the repair outlet in choosing which brands to stock.

---

[3] Because of greater brand preference among so-called TBA items (tires, batteries, accessories), the above comments do not apply to this group of products.

strategy profile: life insurance

Figure 1–7. Marketing strategy
profile: Life insurance.

Controllable Variables	Importance Value
Product	2
Distribution	4
Price	2
Advertising	3
Personal selling	5

Life insurance is an "intangible" product—one cannot see, feel, or taste it. The need for it, although real, is elusive. It is not likely to be within the awareness span of the average consumer. Rather, this need must be pointed out, explained, and demonstrated. Because this can be done most effectively by personal selling, a value of 5 is assigned to this variable.

Product variation is possible for intangible products. In the case of life insurance, variations are possible in coverage, terms, service, and so on. However, because the product is intangible, it is somewhat difficult to communicate these differences to consumers. Here again there is dependence on personal selling. In fact, the differences in the quality of personal selling are likely to be far more important than the differences in the product offered.

Distribution (in the case of life insurance, the number of agents) is very important to success in the marketing of life insurance. Dealing with the right agent is more important to most people than having the name of a particular insurance company on the policy. Although unknown companies might be rejected, the typical consumer has no strong preference among larger, better known companies. Rather, if he has confidence in the agent he will accept the insurance company the agent represents. Hence, it becomes very important in planning marketing strategy for life insurance to devise means to secure an adequate number of qualified agents.

For most life insurance companies, price is not heavily emphasized in marketing strategy. Competition tends to be more on a nonprice basis. It is difficult for the consumer to compare prices because of the intangible nature of life insurance. Lower priced life insurance, such as that sometimes sold by mail, has not been overly successful.

Advertising of life insurance is not an effective substitute for personal selling but can be an important supplement to it. Advertising conditions consumers to the approach of the agent and makes them more willing to accept his statements. It is likely that personal selling would be less effective if advertising did not pave the way for it. Also, advertising can be very helpful in lining up agents, thus gaining better distribution.

strategy profile: bread

Figure 1–8. Marketing strategy profile: Bread.

Controllable Variables	Importance Value
Product	1
Distribution	5
Price	4
Advertising	2
Personal selling	1

Bread is a product in the basic staple category. It is purchased frequently, without much planning or forethought, and usually in connection with the purchase of other food items. If we focus on plain white bread and disregard specialty breads, or the quality bread offered by small bakeries, there is only limited brand preference. The typical consumer will choose from the brands offered in the outlet she has entered for food shopping. She will not make a special effort to go to another outlet to acquire a particular brand. Consequently, breadth of distribution is essential to achieving maximum sales of this product.

Plain white bread is a relatively homogeneous type of product. There is little opportunity for product differentiation. Probably the most desired product characteristic is freshness, and this is likely to vary among brands over time. Product appeal can be enhanced more effectively by rapid stockturn than by varying the physical attributes of the product.

Because ordinary white bread is a largely homogeneous product class, even small price differences can have a drastic effect on demand. Therefore, price competition is severe among brands carried within a particular retail outlet. Although distribution is the most important variable in overall bread marketing, price becomes the dominant variable once adequate distribution is gained. The average housewife is well aware that small price differences "add up" on basic staples.

For the adult bread market, advertising is of limited value. It ranks far below distribution in importance. For the market influenced by children, advertising can be, and has been, effectively used to mold a differentiated product image. Perhaps childrens' requests for a particular brand of bread result in a fairly long-run family habit of buying a particular brand. It surely will not do so, however, if distribution is inadequate or price is out of line.

Personal selling, in the case of bread, serves mainly two major objectives. First, to gain distribution. Second, to gain more or preferred shelf space. As these two purposes are already reflected in the high rating for the distribution variable, personal selling is rated a lowly 1 in our strategy profile.

variation in strategy profiles

The objective in discussing the broad marketing strategy for each of these four products *has not been to establish agreement* as to the best marketing strategies to utilize. The planning of marketing strategy is too much of an art for such agreement to be expected or achieved. Rather, the objective has been to point out how marketing strategies vary for different types of products and to indicate the sorts of things that produce these variations. The differences in "importance values" we have assigned can be seen in Figure 1–9. The variables

Figure 1–9.   Variations in marketing strategy profiles.

Marketing Strategy Variables	Importance Values			
	Autos	Auto Parts	Life Insurance	Bread
Product.....................	[5]	1	2	1
Distribution..................	2	[5]	[4]	[5]
Price........................	2	1	2	[4]
Advertising..................	3	1	3	2
Personal selling..............	1	3	[5]	1

assigned high values (either a 4 or a 5) are marked so as to call attention to the differences which have been highlighted in the discussion above.

Variations in the constructed profiles are depicted in yet another way in Figure 1–10. Although these profiles are not necessarily those others might devise, it is unlikely the marked differences among them would be much diminished if any or all of them were redesigned. It is not likely that bread will ever be marketed in a manner similar to automobiles, nor can the marketing plan developed for automotive parts be used as a guide to the marketing of life insurance.

Figure 1-10.   Variations in marketing strategy profiles.

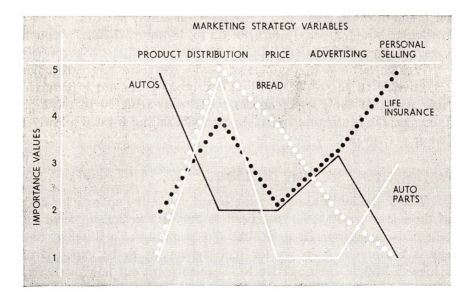

basic cause of variation

All five of the environmental (uncontrollable) variables influence the planning of marketing strategy. In a specific situation, any one of them can have the dominant influence on a firm's marketing program. As a generalization, however, it is correct to say that the demand variable is the most basic factor influencing what is done in marketing. The other environmental variables (competition, the distribution structure, marketing law, and nonmarketing cost) have somewhat less across-the-board significance. In fact, they themselves are much influenced by the demand variable.

Demand has several other characteristics that make it a special case among the environmental variables. The present state of demand cannot be known as can the state of other variables. The present distribution structure exists and can be observed. Marketing law, although often ambiguous, is known in general outline. Nonmarketing costs are often observable and can be calculated. The present state of competition is relatively well known, although future competitive moves may be highly uncertain. On the other hand, we still know very little about underlying demand factors that influence purchase. In spite of much valuable research related to buyer behavior in recent years, the consumer is still an enigma, a "black box" into which we cannot see.

The demand factor is even less predictable than the other variables, due largely to our limited knowledge of it. The competition factor may be almost as hard to predict. The other environmental variables, however, tend to change more slowly and therefore, at least the near future, can be more clearly seen. Distribution structures evolve slowly, and new legislation affecting marketing is usually years in the making. In the long run, nonmarketing costs are closely tied to labor costs. Although not easy to predict, a certain pattern of advance has been established over time. Consumer behavior, however, remains highly unpredictable, and if it is the most basic influence upon marketing strategy, a most unfortunate situation for the marketing planner is created. The fundamental influence of demand on marketing strategy can be seen in the above comparison of marketing strategy profiles.

Because of the important role automobiles play in their lives, consumers respond more strongly to the product variable than to the other variables. It is important to them to choose an automobile whose product image is consistent with their own self-images. Hence, they will seek out the product and are not easily swayed to switch brands. This means that restricted distribution will not greatly hamper sales if the product itself has high appeal. It also means that emphasis on other variables cannot overcome a weak product. Thus, it is basically the characteristic of buyer behavior with respect to automobiles that determines the pattern of their distribution.

The same statement can be made regarding the marketing of automotive parts. Outlets are chosen on the basis of service and convenience. Brand preference is low. These characteristics of buyer behavior make breadth of distribution of prime importance in marketing strategy.

Because life insurance is an intangible, and because the consumer's need for it is often not clearly or fully perceived, personal selling is the dominant strategy variable. Should people perceive their life insurance needs as clearly as their automobile needs, and possess the same strong brand preferences, the appropriate strategy pattern would change substantially.

The strategy profile for bread derives primarily from the fact that consumers perceive bread as a largely homogeneous product. Hence, they will not go out of their way nor pay a price premium for a particular brand.

What is true of marketing strategies for these four products is true of marketing strategy generally. *Appropriate marketing strategy is primarily a function of buyer behavior.* It will, as a matter of fact, become increasingly evident to the student as he proceeds through this text that almost everything done in marketing is based fundamentally on facts or assumptions about buyer behavior.

Because of this singular importance of demand in the planning of marketing strategy, it is singled out in this text for first and more intensive treatment than the other environmental variables. The next three chapters focus upon it. Attention is given to the nature of the demand for goods and services, causal factors that produce changes in demand, as well as approaches to the measurement and prediction of demand. Subsequent chapters will then incorporate this knowledge of demand into the decision-making process in planning marketing strategy.

conclusion

It is the role of marketing, more than of any other business function, to assure that economic resources are allocated effectively to serve consumer needs and wants. If marketing does not perform this role well, the business firm will not attain its objective of maximizing profits. Consumers, too, will lose. Economic resources will have been consumed, yet consumer needs and wants will not have been fully met. Thus, society has a high stake in the skill with which marketing executives perform the marketing task. The heart of this task is the planning of marketing strategy. This is the focal point of the chapters which follow.

questions

1. Construct a marketing strategy profile for each of the following products, indicating the relative importance of the five controllable marketing variables. Explain your reasoning.
   a) Electronic computers.
   b) Encyclopedias.
   c) Chewing gum.
   d) Men's suits.
   e) Deodorants.
2. Generally speaking, marketing strategy for intangible products places more emphasis on personal selling than does marketing strategy for tangible products. Why?
3. Buyer behavior in the purchase of television sets has changed substantially over the last ten years. How has this affected marketing strategy for this product?

4. People in different age groups have different buyer behavior patterns. In the case of life insurance how should marketing strategy for the over-35 age group differ from the strategy used for the 20–25 year age group?
5. In what ways is marketing different from selling?
6. Should the development of new products be considered a marketing function or should responsibility for this function be assigned elsewhere in a business firm?
7. Some critics of marketing argue that marketing strategy, because it is based on buyer behavior, takes advantage of consumer weaknesses. They suggest that marketing strategy should be based on what is best for people. For example, automobile advertising should stress safety, durability, and economy rather than styling and horsepower. Do you agree?
8. Why should demand be considered as an uncontrollable rather than a controllable variable in planning marketing strategy?
9. Why do different companies in the same industry, selling comparable products, often use different marketing strategies?
10. The marketing concept implies orientation of the business firm's total operation to the needs, wants, and desires of the consumer. What are the implications of this concept for consumer welfare?

cases for part one

Case 1–1

POP-TENT (A)

marketing program for a new product *

Some years ago, Henry Stribley and William Moss, of Ann Arbor, Michigan, were considering the question of how they should market a new type of tent which they had designed and were producing. The tent was called "Pop-Tent" and was based on a new conception of tent design which enabled the tent to be packed in a compact, light, and easily portable package and which made it possible for the tent to be erected in 90 seconds without the use of a center pole or ropes.

The idea for "Pop-Tent" had been developed three years earlier by these two men. Mr. Stribley, a retired garage owner, conceived the basic idea and designed the mechanical parts with the assistance of Mr. Moss, then an artist on the *Ford Times,* a publication of the Ford Motor Company. Originally, the purpose had been to design a portable duck blind for hunting. The first design was based on the principle of an umbrella and employed a center pole. However, after building a prototype, it was decided that the design was impractical. The blind weighed too much, was too difficult to erect, and was too bulky. From this original design, it was decided that fiber glass rods could be sewn into the cloth itself instead of the ribs, struts, and center pole of the umbrella design, these glass rods being under tension and thus holding the tent in shape. A locking hinge was also designed and perfected so that the rods could be folded into a compact package.

On the basis of their new design, another prototype was built, and it met their fullest expectations. The inventors soon realized they "had something." Going beyond the duck blind, they now designed a large size for tenting and camping purposes and applied for patent and trademark protection. (The name "Pop-Tent" was adopted because it was descriptive of how the tent erected—it just "popped-up.")

In the final design, the camping size was sufficiently large so that it could sleep two adults on the floor in sleeping bags and perhaps a child on either side of each adult. While the height in the center of the tent was only 58 inches, this was not felt by the designers to be a serious disadvantage.

---

* Written by Ross J. Wilhelm, Associate Professor of Business Economics, Graduate School of Business Administration, The University of Michigan.

The inventors then arranged for several prototypes of the new size to be built, and instead of having them made in the usual khaki color, they had them made in various attractive colors.

There probably has been no new product in recent history which received as much free publicity as did Pop-Tent. Its new igloo or dome shape, plus its attractive colors and inherent product appeals, made it a natural for inclusion in articles and features in magazines and other media on new items in the tenting-camping field. At the same time, the Ford Motor Company, as part of its promotion of station wagons, was emphasizing outdoor camping and vacation trips in station wagons, and the company included illustrations of Pop-Tents in its promotional literature.

By the spring of the year, when the final design of Pop-Tent was completed, the promoters had received a two-page color spread in the *Ford Times,* which then had a circulation of 3 million customers of the Ford Motor Company; had been on the front cover of *Popular Mechanics* with a full story with pictures inside; had a three fourths of a page picture story in *Life;* and Pop-Tent had been shown on numerous TV shows in the Detroit area in addition to mentions in other news stories and features. In most of the stories, the names and address of the inventors were mentioned, along with the fact that they were intending to market their product in the near future at a retail price of about $125 for the tent and $87.50 for the duck blind. On the basis of these stories, about 100 inquiries and actual orders had been received from prospective customers. While such publicity could not be bought outright it was "guesstimated" that comparable advertising would have cost over $100,000 to obtain.

By the fall of the same year, the investors had felt that it was necessary for them to start producing so as to be able to capitalize on the free publicity which had been received. A second feature article which had been promised in the *Ford Times* precipitated the decision to go into actual production. The inventors felt, and the *Ford Times* made it known, that this second feature depended on the inventors having the product available for sale.

As a result, a decision was made to produce 500 sleeping tents and 500 duck blinds, with Mr. Stribley putting up the money. Since these men did not have any production experience in the tenting field, they jobbed out the production. They contacted a major tent producer in St. Louis, who agreed to produce the tent, and they obtained the glass rods and hinges from Michigan manufacturers. The final cost of the Pop-Tent was $48 delivered to Ann Arbor, and the duck blinds cost $34 each. In specifying how the tent and blind were to be made, the inventors placed great emphasis on top quality, and the final product was made out of expensive, long-staple Egyptian cotton and had a sewn-in vinyl floor. It was because of this emphasis on quality and the inherent appeals of the product that the inventors felt they could get the prices they had originally set. They did not feel they could go much beyond these retail prices, however. They also knew that in the sporting goods trade, and on items of this type, retailers were accustomed to receive a 40 percent markup, wholesalers 16⅔ percent and manufacturers' agents 10 percent. As a result, they were considering the possibility of marketing their products by mail order, selling directly to consumers rather than going through the regular channels which took such a large proportion of the final selling price. Further, neither of the principals wanted to invest much more money or time in the product if they could avoid it. It just was not available.

At this time, the highest price tent being sold by Sears, Roebuck mail-order department was a four-wall tent which could hold four cots, enabled a person to stand up at full height anywhere in the tent, had screens built into all of the walls, had a canvas cover for a porch, a canvas floor, and sold for about $120. Other tents could be obtained at prices ranging from just below $20, the actual price depending on the size, screens, presence or absence of canvas flooring, height of the walls, and other such features. There were no other tents on the market which were as easy to erect or transport as was the Pop-Tent.

QUESTION

What steps should Messrs. Moss and Stribley take to market their new products?

Case 1–2

TELECTRONICS, INC.

developing a new marketing strategy

Telectronics, Inc., a Chicago-based electronics company, specialized in the manufacture and sale of a narrow line of television receivers for home and industrial use. Although the company had pioneered certain industrial applications of television, the consumer line was its major source of revenue.

During the mid-1960's, Telectronics began to face increased price competition from television sets imported from Japan. These sets were of good quality and were sold through discount houses and cut-price outlets at prices which were 10 to 20 percent below those charged by dealers for the Telectronic line. Company management was faced with the problem of developing a new marketing strategy to meet this threat.

product line

The consumer television line was composed of three medium priced console models and three lower priced portables. Retail list prices for the consoles were $399, $299, and $199. The portables sold for $149.50 for the 21-inch size, $129.95 for the 19-inch model, and $99.95 for the 14-inch personal portable. Both the console models and the portables were important sources of revenue, but the portables were most important. It was estimated by impartial trade sources that Telectronics sold more portable television sets than any other manufacturer in the country.

Telectronic television sets were styled to resemble the more expensive brands on the market. Their performance was satisfactory to most users, and the company had, on occasion, received the "best buy" rating from Consumer's Union. Although Telectronic television sets were the most popular on the market and were considered an important line by most television dealers, they had little appeal for those persons seeking the prestige and performance of a Zenith or Magnavox product. The Telectronic line competed more directly with such national brands as Admiral and Emerson, and the private brands of Sears and Montgomery Ward.

distribution channels

As was common in the television industry, Telectronic television sets were sold by various types of retailers. Radio and television stores were the backbone of the distribution system, especially for the console models. Over the years, however, the company had developed distribution through credit jewelers, furniture stores, variety stores such as K-Mart, department stores, and two mail-order chains.

Telectronics used both direct and indirect channels of distribution. The company sales force called on 5,000 factory franchised dealers directly. These direct accounts were located in metropolitan areas and larger towns and were considered to be the backbone of Telectronics' market coverage by company executives. Wholesalers were used to reach an additional 1,700 dealers. In the highly competitive New York City market, the company used an exclusive distributor. The company also used a distributor to reach the many geographically dispersed customers in the Rocky Mountain states.

Certain types of outlets were especially effective in handling different parts of the line. For example, furniture stores and department stores did well with the console models, while jewelry stores, variety stores, and the mail-order chains sold mostly the portable models. Telectronics was engaged in seeking distribution for the $99.95 portable through hardware stores and was aggressively developing a program for franchising hardware wholesalers. At the time this case was prepared, arrangements had been made to distribute the line through the National Hardware Cooperatives, which consisted of 75 hardware wholesalers and reached more than 25,000 hardware retailers.

market coverage and promotion

The use of 5,000 dealers, together with the new policy of distributing through hardware wholesalers, indicated that the company desired to follow a policy of broad outlet coverage. However, all dealers were franchised, and the management wished to avoid selling its products through retailers of questionable reputation and quality. The company's aims were to make its products available wherever quality television equipment was sold and to make its television sets available to every potential customer.

The promotional policy placed stress on (1) national advertising and (2) dealer aids. For the past several years, expenditures on television advertising and in national consumer media (such as *Life, Time, Newsweek, Look,* and selected Sunday newspaper supplements) had averaged 5 percent of total sales. The stated promotional objective was to presell Telectronic products. The advertising goal was to attract customers into the stores who would ask for Telectronic television sets. An additional 2½ percent of sales was expended for direct sales promotion activities, including counter cards, displays, and leaflets describing Telectronic products. The company also furnished dealers with prepared advertisements and with various materials which made it easy for dealers to design their own ads.

price-cutting problem

In the mid-1960's, Telectronic executives encountered an increase in price cutting. The Telectronic line was running into strong competition from Japanese imports. Companies such as Sony and Panasonic were making sets of design and quality equal to the Telectronic line yet priced from 15 to 20 percent below Telectronic recommended retail prices. Those dealers who sold on the basis of price began to cut Telectronic prices in order to remain competitive with other dealers who were handling the Japanese lines.

Telectronic was faced with a dilemma. If an attempt were made to stop price cutting on the line, then the "price" channels would drop the line in favor of the Japanese imports. Yet, if price cutting by some dealers were not stopped, the "regular" channels would shelve the line and fail to promote and display it effectively. The problem was further compounded by the fact that trade-ins served as the basis for a form of price cutting. Regular dealers often gave a generous allowance on the customer's used television set and thus bid for customer patronage on a price basis. It was estimated that between 10 to 15 percent of Telectronic television set sales involved trade-ins. In the metropolitan areas, as high as 25 percent of the sales involved trade-ins.

QUESTION

Evaluate the marketing strategy of Telectronics, Inc. How can it be improved?

demand analysis

Building an effective marketing strategy requires an understanding of both the qualitative and quantitative aspects of demand. This section begins with a qualitative approach to demand analysis with attention first focused upon a study of the purchase of consumer goods. A simple model of the consumer buying process is employed to help identify key factors influencing the purchase decision. Buying behavior results from the interplay of the consumer's personality and the environment in which he lives. What are the key elements in the consumer's personality which are relevant in making purchasing decisions? How do environmental factors influence the choice? These are the questions which are analyzed in depth in Chapter 2.

Although the initial explanation of the buying process is relatively simple, it is recognized that consumer purchasing behavior is actually very complex. In Chapter 3, therefore, additional models of buyer behavior are examined in which the simplifying assumptions of the previous discussion are removed and a closer approximation of reality is achieved. The points in the models at which marketing strategy may influence buyer behavior are also given careful consideration.

Attention is then turned to an analysis of buyer behavior in the purchase of industrial goods. How does industrial buying differ from consumer purchasing? How is it similar? What models are available to help in understanding the decision? These are the topics covered in the last half of Chapter 3.

If clear-cut marketing goals are to be set to guide the development of marketing strategy, then knowledge about buyer behavior must be supplemented with quantitative estimates of probable demand which may result from alternative marketing programs and probable environmental conditions. Accordingly, Chapter 4 deals with basic approaches to demand forecasting and thus rounds out the discussion of demand analysis.

buyer behavior:
consumer

Appropriate marketing strategy is a function of buyer behavior. Hence, to learn why prospective buyers purchase the firm's kind of product, the marketing executive needs to undertake as much research as time and money will permit. This chapter provides essential background on this important topic.

In considering the problem of buyer behavior, it will be helpful to discuss the factors that influence the purchase of consumer goods separately from those resulting in the purchase of industrial goods. Consumer goods are those destined for use by ultimate consumers or households, and these goods are in such form that they can be used without commercial processing. Industrial goods are products destined to be sold primarily for use in producing other goods or rendering services, as contrasted with goods destined to be sold primarily to the ultimate consumer.[1] Since executives responsible for purchasing industrial goods are professionals who make their decisions in the context of a complex organization, the factors that influence their buying actions tend to differ considerably from those that influence the buying behavior of the ultimate consumer. Accordingly, we shall deal with consumer buyer behavior in this chapter and discuss the behavior of the industrial buyer in the chapter that follows.

As a means of organizing our discussion, it will be helpful to conceive of consumer buyer behavior essentially as a decision-making process, although it will be recognized that experience leads the consumer to make many purchases by habit as a means of conserving time

---

[1] Reprinted by permission from *Marketing Definitions,* compiled by the Committee on Definitions, American Marketing Association, Ralph S. Alexander, Chairman (published by American Marketing Association, 1960), pp. 11, 14.

and energy. We shall then discuss some of the key concepts which help the marketer to understand buyer behavior and which are useful in guiding research designed to assist executives in deciding how best to influence purchase through product changes, price changes, and promotional effort. Finally, we shall consider the use of models of consumer buying behavior as an aid to executive decision making and will describe several different models developed to facilitate the understanding of how people buy.

consumer behavior as a decision process

In analyzing consumer buying behavior we can distinguish two broad types of approaches: (1) problem-solving behavior involved in the purchase of major items, such as a color television set, or innovations, such as Kellogg's Pop Tarts (a product introduced in 1964 consisting of a tender pastry crust with a flavorful fruit preserve filling); and (2) habitual brand choice which is characteristic of repeat purchases of well-known low-priced products such as cigarettes or coffee. While it is recognized that a considerable portion of buying is done on the basis of habit, we shall give emphasis to the problem-solving (or decision-making) type of behavior which is involved in the buying of innovations or of infrequent, major purchases. The factors influencing choice in such situations are more complex and merit careful analysis. Behavior involved in the first purchase of a new type of product, moreover, provides helpful background in understanding the formation of habits which predominate as consumers gain experience with a product such as Pop Tarts and the item appears regularly on the housewife's shopping list.

In the purchase of an innovation or a major item such as a color television set, accordingly, we can distinguish the following stages in the decision-making process: (1) recognition of a problem (felt need); (2) the search for alternative solutions to the desire; (3) evaluation of alternatives (brands); (4) purchase decision; (5) postpurchase feelings and evaluation. With this decision-making process in mind, let us consider certain key concepts which will help us to understand the behavior of the prospective buyer.

relation between the individual and his environment

The problem with which we are concerned is why some consumers buy a particular brand, why others do not, and how nonusers can be led to switch to it. It will help us to understand such behavior if we start with the following simplified equation:

$$B = f(P,E) .$$

That is, any given type of behavior, (such as the purchase of an RCA color television set) is a function of the interplay between the consumer's personal makeup, P (personality) and his perception of the environmental situation (E). Thus, any given brand is one possible choice which the consumer might make among other brands in the same category, and even among other kinds of products. Allowing for external situational influences which might have a bearing on buying behavior, we can understand the consumer's decision if we can assess the hold the brand has on its current consumers as well as the appeal it might offer to its most likely prospects. We can do this by relating the consumer's perception of the brand to his "needs."

In our analysis, therefore, we shall deal first with the individual consumer and his "needs" and "attitudes." We shall then consider the influence of the consumer's perception of the environment upon his buying behavior.

the individual consumer

basic needs or motives

The starting point in the purchase decision-making process is the recognition of a need (or a buying motive). Motives are "all those inner striving conditions variously described as wishes, desires, needs, drives, and the like. . . . Formally, then, a motive is an inner state that energizes, activates, or moves (hence 'motivation'), and that directs or channels behavior toward goals. . . . Hunger, the quest for power or status, the desire to land on the moon or to own a new car—all these are motives according to this definition." Goals, in turn, may be thought of as "the object, condition, or activity toward which the motive is directed, in short, that which will satisfy or reduce the striving."[2]

Motivational theory received its greatest impetus from Freud. Nearly all theorists who have worked with clinical data have accepted part of the Freudian scheme but have rejected other portions.[3] One of

---

[2] Reprinted by permission from Bernard Berelson and Gary A. Steiner, *Human Behavior* (New York: Harcourt, Brace & World, Inc., 1964), pp. 239–40.

[3] See D. C. McClelland, *Personality* (New York: Dryden Press, 1951), pp. 388–410, for a brief summary of Freud's motivational system, an evaluation of his conceptual scheme, as well as contributions of other scholars to motivational theory.

the more recent theories is that developed by Maslow, who has integrated most of the leading approaches to motivation into an overall scheme designed to conform to the known facts, clinical and observational as well as experimental. He refers to his synthesis as a "holistic-dynamic theory." It is especially interesting to marketing people, since it is based primarily upon a study of normal people rather than the abnormal subjects who have been the concern of most other theorists.

Maslow classifies motivational life in terms of fundamental needs or goals, rather than in terms of any listing of drives in the ordinary sense of instigation (the "pulls" rather than the "pushes.") He lists the following five levels of needs, arranged in order of their basic importance to the individual:[4]

1. The physiological needs—for example, to satisfy hunger and thirst.
2. The safety needs—for example, security, order, and stability.
3. The belongingness and love needs—such as affection and identification.
4. The esteem needs—such as prestige, success, and self-respect.
5. The need for self-actualization—to do what one is best fitted for, for example.

Also identified are two classes of cognitive needs, which are not definitely located in the need hierarchy but which are believed to exist perhaps as a function of intelligence and of gratification fairly high up the scale of lower order needs:

6. The desire to know and understand (an essential precondition to the satisfaction of basic needs).
7. The aesthetic needs, for example, the craving for beauty.

Maslow believes that the five basic needs develop in such a way that the most important, that is, the physiological needs, must be satisfied before the safety needs, which are next in importance, can fully emerge in a person's development. And so on up the ladder from the lower needs (most important) to the higher needs (least important) in the hierarcy.

For example, he explains that the physiological needs are the most prepotent of all needs.[5]

What this means specifically is that in the human being who is missing

---

[4] Adaptation of "The Basic Needs," pp. 80–101 in *Motivation and Personality* by A. H. Maslow. Copyright 1954 by Harper & Row, Publishers, Inc. Reprinted by permission of the publishers.

[5] *Ibid.*

everything in life in an extreme fashion, it is most likely that the major motivation would be the physiological needs rather than any others. A person who is lacking food, safety, love, and esteem would most probably hunger for food more strongly than for anything else. . . .

It is quite true that man lives by bread alone—when there is no bread. But what happens to man's desires when there is plenty of bread and when his belly is chronically filled? *At once other and (higher) needs emerge* and these, rather than physiological hungers, dominate the organism. And when these in turn are satisfied, again new (and still higher) needs emerge, and so on. This is what we mean by saying that the basic human needs are organized into a hierarchy of relative prepotency.

Maslow explains that the need hierarchy is not as rigid as may be implied by the above explanation. While most people feel the needs in about the order indicated, there may be exceptions in individual cases. Also, it would be a mistake to conclude that each need must be satisfied 100 percent before the next need emerges. Instead, most members of our society who are normal are partially satisfied in all their basic needs and partially unsatisfied in all their basic needs at the same time. A more realistic description of the hierarchy would be in terms of decreasing percentages of satisfaction as we go up the hierarchy of prepotency. To illustrate, it is as if the average citizen is satisfied perhaps 85 percent in his physiological needs, 70 percent in his safety needs, 50 percent in his love needs, 40 percent in his self-esteem needs, and 10 percent in his self-actualization needs.

According to Maslow, these basic needs are neither necessarily conscious nor unconscious. In the average person, however, they are more often unconscious than conscious. Moreover, these needs must be understood not to be *exclusive* or single determiners of certain kinds of behavior. For example, one may make love not only for pure sexual release but also to convince oneself of one's masculinity, to make a conquest, to feel powerful, or to win more basic affection.

One of the problems encountered in the use of the above list of motives is that we can all think of other needs that do not fit neatly into the seven classifications listed above.[6] For example, what about the desire for maturity among young people? Where does simple hedonism (seeking pleasure, avoiding pain) fit? Also, what about instrumental needs—the desire for goal objectives which help us perform various tasks such as mowing a lawn, washing dishes, or getting to work on time?

---

[6] This discussion is based upon James H. Myers and William H. Reynolds, *Consumer Behavior and Marketing Management* (Boston: Houghton Mifflin Co., 1967), pp. 89–91.

Another difficulty is to fit the purchase of each product neatly into a single motive category. Consider the following examples:

1. A man buys an expensive Omega wristwatch for a combination of instrumental and esteem needs.
2. A couple joins a country club to satisfy both belongingness and personal interest (tennis, golf, swimming).
3. A girl joins a "Great Books" discussion group both to satisfy the desire to know and to belong (her friends have joined).

Then too, different motives can lead to identical buying behavior and, conversely, entirely different buying decisions can be traced back to identical motivations. Three neighbors might satisfy their safety needs in three different ways, as follows: one might install seat belts in his automobile, another might buy accident insurance, and a third might commute to work by train rather than drive his own car.

The purchase of a color television set, however, might be made by one family primarily to satisfy the desire for entertainment of the husband and wife; by a second family mainly as a means of keeping three small children entertained and quiet during the preparation of dinner or while the father is relaxing after the evening meal; by a third family because others in their social group have purchased color television sets and they feel a need to take similar action to maintain their status (desire to maintain prestige in eyes of others).

It is evident that the marketing executive cannot infer motivation directly from behavior. Also that behavior cannot be predicted in a simple way from motivation. Realization of these complexities has led to the use of research as an aid to gaining an understanding of this important influence upon buying behavior. The task of finding out why people buy, however, is not an easy one. Often people will not, or cannot, explain their actions. Let us examine this problem briefly and indicate some of the approaches which may be taken to deal with it.

Motivation research. In discussing the basic needs that motivate human behavior in all phases of living, Maslow made the point that these motives are more often unconscious than conscious. While this may not be equally true when we restrict our analysis to buying behavior, the problem of getting behind the superficial reasons people give in response to direct questions about their buying motives has long been recognized. Smith clarified the problem by discussing three levels of awareness in the range from consciousness to unconsciousness.[7]

---

[7] From G. H. Smith, *Motivation Research in Advertising and Marketing,* an Advertising Research Foundation Publication (Copyright 1954 by McGraw-Hill Book Co.), pp. 19–21. Used with permission of McGraw-Hill Book Company.

The first level deals with conscious and public material which consumers are willing to discuss with an interviewer. A man's desire for a shirt with a collar that won't wrinkle and buttons that won't come off is a typical example.

The second level includes material rarely discussed—that is, motives only slightly outside awareness (preconscious level). Examples would be the desire to impress one's neighbors with an expensive color television set, moving to a better neighborhood as a means of social climbing, driving a high-powered car at high speed in order to let off aggressive impulses, drinking a Coke as a reward after frustrating circumstances, and smoking cigars to feel more masculine. People tend to conceal these motives behind a mask of rationalizations, intellectual discussions and half-truths. They insist that they buy the new television set because the old one had a flicker, move into the high-toned neighborhood because a home in that location represents a better investment, drive fast in order to save time, drink the Coke because it "tastes good," and smoke the cigar because it has a pleasant aroma.

The third level deals with material which is unanalyzed by the individual and not discussed with other people (unconscious level). It includes motives which are not consciously recognized by the consumer and which often would create anxiety if they came into consciousness. Examples of material at this level are the origin of some "common colds" in the need for attention and the loss of security; bargain hunting as the need to outsmart others and to express aggression toward a substitute for the bad, refusing mother; chronic psychogenic constipation as a symbol of withholding from the world ("not giving"); homosexual and Oedipus tendencies; and numerous personal experiences, sexual and otherwise.

It was to gain access to material in the preconscious and unconscious levels of awareness that marketers turned to the research methods of the behavioral scientists. The methods most commonly used are the informal, qualitative interview, and projective techniques.

The informal, qualitative interview ("depth interview") is described as casual, conversational, and free-flowing. The respondent is encouraged to talk at length in the subject area of interest and to express whatever thoughts or feelings come to mind.[8] Generally, there is no list of questions which must be asked in a prescribed way. The emphasis is

---

[8] Adapted by permission from Joseph W. Newman, *Motivation Research and Marketing Management* (Boston: Division of Research, Graduate School of Business Administration, Harvard University, 1957), p. 406.

on letting the respondent lead the way in order to find out what is important to him and why and to allow opportunity for unanticipated responses to be made. Interviews may run for one or two hours.

From this description it is clear, of course, that the qualitative interview is *not* psychoanalysis. If such interviews are properly conducted and skillfully interpreted, they offer a potentially rewarding source of hypotheses based upon material from the preconscious level of awareness. Forgotten experiences which have been deliberately submerged are not likely to be tapped. Because of the relatively high cost per interview, and the fact that neither questions nor interpretation are standardized, the qualitative approach is most useful during the exploratory stage of a research project.

Projective techniques have two principal characteristics: (1) Their specific purpose is not apparent. (2) The projective device is ambiguous—i.e., it contains no specific meaning; it can be interpreted in different ways. The object is to find out what meanings the respondent will read into it. The underlying assumption is that in responding promptly, the consumer will reveal something of himself—his thoughts, feelings, values, and needs. The main principle which is assumed to be at work is that of *projection,* or the unconscious imputation to others of the characteristics of oneself. Free association may also come into play, so that the resulting chain of thoughts is related in meaning and revealing about the respondent.

Projective devices may serve two main objectives: (1) to learn of the important ideas and feelings people have toward the product or brand under investigation; (2) to learn something about the personality characteristics of the consumer.

The kinds of projective techniques commonly used in motivation research are word association, incomplete sentences, narrative projection, cartoons, requests for descriptions of others, and picture responses (adaptations of the Thematic Apperception Test) .[9]

Skillfully designed projectives, properly administered, are helpful in approaching difficult topics and may secure motivational material of considerable depth. Even where material desired is at the conscious level, they are more likely than direct questions to produce full and valid responses. Where unstructured stimuli are used, the problem of interpretation will require about the same degree of skill as does the qualitative interview. This type of projective is most useful at the

---

[9] For a discussion of projective techniques, including examples, see *ibid.,* pp. 424–40.

exploratory stage of research. Where more structured types of projectives are used, they are suitable for testing hypotheses during the second phase of the project, since they lend themselves to sampling on a nationwide scale.

As soon as promising hypotheses are developed, direct questions may also be devised to help test these ideas during the second phase of research. Indeed, there is no point in using a projective device to test a motivational hypothesis where a direct question can be devised which would do the job equally well. The direct question is usually less costly to administer and the resulting findings easier to interpret.

Then, too, the very open research approaches (such as the qualitative interview) tend to be strongest where those which restrict response (the direct question) are weakest, and vice versa. Benefits may therefore be realized by combining these various approaches in a motivation research project and from using other techniques of a more intermediate character as well.

One of the criticisms of motivation studies employing behavioral science techniques relates to the size and composition of the sample of consumers interviewed in such research. Clearly, this is an important matter which must be handled on a sound, scientific basis. During the exploratory stage of research, when hypotheses are being sought, much benefit may be derived from a relatively small number of interviews using the informal qualitative approach or carefully designed projective techniques. If the findings are labeled "hypotheses" and are treated as such, the requirements of sound research are met.

In the second stage of the research project, however, these hypotheses should be subjected to careful testing by appropriate procedures. Well-designed direct questions or carefully prepared projective techniques, or both, may be used at this stage. At this point, however, the sample should be representative of the consumers who make up the market for the brand and should be large enough to yield a satisfactory degree of accuracy. This is essential so that the findings may be projected to that consumer population with which the seller is concerned.

Where the nature of the product and the nature of the marketing mix permit, it is good practice to incorporate the findings of a motivation research study in an actual selling or advertising campaign and conduct a test to determine the relative effectiveness of the new appeal as compared with that previously used. Validation tests of this sort, if properly conducted under favorable circumstances, may provide a much needed measure of the value of motivational studies.

attitudes

While it is true that the consumer's motives tend to activate behavior which results eventually in a purchase, the previous discussion indicates that behavior cannot be predicted in a simple way from motivations. Other intervening factors internal to the individual also come into play, factors that tend to influence the consumer's perception of the various goal objects (products, brands) which may be utilized to satisfy his desires. These intervening variables include the consumer's attitudes, self-image, and traits (habits). Let us turn to a consideration of the consumer's values or attitudes.

As mentioned earlier, the consumer purchase decision process begins with the identification of a need to be satisfied. After the desire has been aroused, the next step is to evaluate different products or services as ways of satisfying this need. The decision to buy a particular product or service is then followed by the choice of the brand or the selection of the supplier of the service. Consumer attitudes play an important part in the process of evaluation of both (1) alternative products or services as means of satisfying the desire, and (2) the choice of the brand to be purchased or the supplier to be patronized. Thus, attitudes directly affect purchase decisions.

"Attitude is the predisposition of the individual to evaluate some symbol or object or aspect of his world in a favorable or unfavorable manner. Opinion is the verbal expression of an attitude, but attitudes can also be expressed in nonverbal behavior." Attitudes have two important dimensions: (1) an "affective, or feeling, core of liking or disliking"; (2) "cognitive, or belief, elements which describe the object of the attitude, its characteristics, and its relations to other objects." Included in the latter would be evaluative beliefs which attribute to the object good or bad, desirable or undesirable, qualities. "All attitudes thus include beliefs, but not all beliefs are attitudes."[10]

Attitudes also have a third dimension which is important for marketing—an implied readiness for some kind of action toward the object of the attitude. For example, if a consumer has a favorable attitude toward Coca-Cola, there is an implication that this individual is more likely to buy this brand than alternative competing brands. This action tendency suggests a relationship with the motivational factors discussed previously and is an important consideration in understanding the buying process.

---

[10] Adapted by permission from D. Katz, "The Functional Approach to the Study of Attitudes," *Public Opinion Quarterly,* Vol. 24 (Summer, 1960) , pp. 163–204. For a broader *concept of* "attitudes" see McClelland, *op. cit.,* chap. viii.

How are attitudes formed? To a very considerable extent they are learned in the process of interaction with other people. Factors which tend to develop and change attitudes may include the following: (1) In the satisfaction of his basic desires, the individual will develop favorable attitudes toward people and objects which satisfy his needs and unfavorable attitudes toward those which block attainment. (2) Attitudes are based in part upon the kind and amount of information which the individual receives and upon the nature of the source of this information. (3) Many attitudes held by individuals come either directly or indirectly from the groups of which he is a member—for example, family, work, and social. (4) Personality factors (such as intelligence, appearance, activity levels, withdrawal tendencies, and dominance) have some effect upon attitudes. (5) Actual experience with the object—favorable or unfavorable—will have a profound effect upon attitudes toward it.[11]

Evidence on the relationship between consumer attitudes and their buying decisions comes from the work of the Survey Research Center of The University of Michigan. The Center has been making surveys of consumer finances since 1946. The information is secured through annual personal interviews with the head of each spending unit in a national sample of dwelling units selected by area probability sampling to represent the population of the United States. Through these surveys, data are gathered on consumer attitudes; income; ownership, purchases, and purchase plans of automobiles, durable goods, and houses; assets; debt; and personal characteristics. Our special interest is in the Center's studies dealing with the measurement of consumer attitudes and their relationship to spending.

Two measures of attitudes toward spending are used by the Center. The primary measure is an index of consumer attitudes based upon answers to six attitudinal questions: (1) whether the family is better or worse off than a year earlier; (2) its personal financial expectations for the coming year; (3) its one-year expectations regarding business conditions; (4) its longer range economic outlook; (5) its appraisal of buying conditions for household goods and clothing; and (6) price expectations. The six components of the index have equal weight.

A second measure of attitudes toward spending is an index of buying intentions. Data have been collected on expressed intentions to buy houses, cars, and durable household goods; to make home im-

---

[11] Adapted from D. Krech, R. S. Crutchfield and E. L. Ballachey, *Individual and Society* (Copyright 1962 by McGraw-Hill Book Co.), chap. vi. Used with permission of McGraw-Hill Book Company.

provements or repairs; and to make major nondurable goods expenditures. Only plans which respondents rated as having at least a fair chance of fulfillment were considered.

To what extent do consumer attitudes influence spending? According to Katona, a graphical comparison of disposable consumer income, consumer attitudes and durable goods sales over an 8-year period leads to the following conclusions:[12]

Sometimes attitudes change autonomously and indicate changes in demand for consumer durables which cannot be explained by changes in income or other traditional financial data; sometimes attitudes are influenced by past developments in incomes, production, sales, and the like, and do not contribute significant new information. It seems probable that the former is the case when the impending changes in economic trends are substantial.

It is always possible to translate a graphical presentation of correspondence between sets of data . . . into an algebraic equation. Thereby a measure of the degree of correspondence is obtained. . . . It may be reported that a substantial proportion of the fluctuations in expenditures on durables is explained by the fluctuations in the index of consumer attitudes. The contribution of changes in the income level to the explanation of fluctuations in sales is very much smaller.

Thus, on the basis of six years of study of changes in consumer attitudes this conclusion emerges: Changes in consumer attitudes are advance indications of changes in consumer spending on durable goods and make a net contribution to the prediction of such spending after the influence of income has been taken into account.

The work of the Survey Research Center deals with the relation of consumer attitudes to primary demand—i.e. to the purchase of *alternative* types of products such as automobiles, durable goods, and houses. Let us now consider the relationship between attitudes and the purchases of individual brands. A study by Seymour Banks provides interesting evidence on this point. Banks collected data from a representative panel of 465 housewives in Chicago during the period April-June. Each respondent was interviewed twice, the second interview coming three weeks after the first. During this three-week period, respondents reported purchases weekly by mail. The first interview was used to obtain information on brands on hand, preference statements for brands, and a statement of purchase intentions for seven classes of household products. The products used were scouring cleanser, coffee, ice cream, peanut butter, potato chips, mayonnaise and salad dressing, and catsup.

---

[12] From George Katona, *The Powerful Consumer* (Copyright 1960 by McGraw-Hill Book Co.), pp. 52–53. Used with permission of McGraw-Hill Book Company.

During the second interview, preference statements were collected again for brands of scouring cleanser and coffee. In addition, the respondents were asked to give preference scores on the product attributes of these brands. Also, if the housewife had failed to buy according to her stated intentions, she was asked why.

A brief summary of the results is as follows:[13]

1. It was found that brand preference was almost identical with purchase intention; about 96 percent of the panel included their most preferred brands in their purchase intentions.

2. Preference for brands was a good predictor of purchases; the average coefficient of correlation between preference for a brand and the relative share of purchases obtained by that brand was 0.918 for the seven product classes. Last purchase made and statements of purchase intentions were even better predictors of relative brand purchase by the panel.

3. Preference was a fairly good predictor of purchase for the individual panel member as well as for the entire group. Only 15 percent of the group who stated brand purchase intentions bought brands entirely different from those mentioned. However, another 15 percent performed only partially on their brand purchase intentions. There was much greater variance quantitatively between predicted and actual purchases.

4. As predictors of the number of units to be purchased, the panel fared poorly. Overall, they bought 61.4 percent more units of the seven product classes than they expected. The biggest error was for ice cream; the panel's members bought 2.6 times the predicted amount; the best job of quantitative prediction was for peanut butter, in which they exceeded their predictions by only 12.4 percent.

Based upon the findings of the above research, we can conclude that brand preference is a good predictor of actual buying behavior for products of the type studied—i.e., convenience goods of low unit price which are purchased frequently. Failure to make intended purchases was explained by price reductions on competing brands, item out of stock, and desire for change. Variations in the actual amounts purchased as compared to expectations are probably explained, in part, by the impulsive nature of the purchasing of certain products, such as ice cream.

While brand preference is a good predictor of purchasing behavior for certain types of products, there is evidence that attitudes toward alternative brands change more than does actual purchasing behavior. In a study by the National Broadcasting Company, for example, atti-

[13] Reprinted by permission from Seymour Banks, "The Relationships of Brand Preference to Brand Purchase," *Journal of Marketing*, Vol. 15 (October, 1950), pp. 145–57, published by the American Marketing Association.

tudes toward Scotties tissue improved from 16 percent to 42 percent under the influence of television, but consumption increased only from 15 percent to 35 percent.[14] A possible explanation of the difference is that changes in purchasing behavior tend to lag behind changes in attitudes. Quite aside from this possibility, however, is the fact that buying is subject to constraints—such as lack of money, brand out of stock—which do not limit attitude changes.

Attitude change. The previous discussion has indicated that consumer attitudes have an important influence on the purchase decision. If this is the case, the question then arises as to how the firm can lead prospective buyers to adopt more favorable attitudes toward the type of product he manufactures (for example, air conditioners) as well as to his own brand as opposed to competing brands (for example, Frigidaire versus General Electric).[15]

There are two basic approaches to this problem. One is to undertake research by which to determine current desires and attitudes of prospective buyers toward the product and the brand. Once this information is known, the firm may redesign its product so that it more adequately conforms to these desires and preferences. The firm may also modify its promotional approach in the light of this information.

A second method is to attempt to change the consumer's desires and attitudes toward the product and the brand. This is a more difficult task than the first, but it is necessary where the product represents an innovation, as was true with television when it was first introduced commercially after World War II. Such would also be the case where a product used primarily by women, such as hair coloring, is first marketed for use by men.

If the marketer wishes to change attitudes toward his brand, his approach should be chosen only after consideration of the factors which influence the formation of attitudes: biological needs, information, group affiliations, personality, and experience. Analysis indicates that certain of these attitude-forming factors cannot be changed by the marketer. Certainly this is true of basic needs, personality characteristics, and group affiliations. Under certain circumstances, experience of consumers with the brand may be changed. For example, people who have never used it may be given free samples for trial—provided the item is a consumable product of low unit price subject to repeat purchase (for example, toothpaste). If the product is superior, and its

---

[14] J. A. Howard, *Marketing Management: Analysis and Planning* (rev. ed.; Homewood, Ill.: Richard D. Irwin, Inc., 1963), p. 51.

[15] Based upon Myers and Reynolds, *op. cit.,* pp. 165–66.

want-satisfying qualities may be evaluated through usage, experience with a free sample may indeed modify consumer attitudes toward the brand. Distribution of free samples, however, is not suitable for all types of products.

Of the various attitude-forming factors, therefore, the possibility of changing the information which the consumer has about the brand is often the most effective approach. The effective use of communication through personal selling, promotion and publicity, therefore, is worthy of careful study. While space does not permit a discussion of this topic here, we shall deal with the subject of building an effective promotional mix by which to influence consumer desires and attitudes in Chapter 10. Crane summarizes a discussion of this topic, however, as follows:[16]

Attitudes are not easy to change. First, because there seems to be a tendency to restore balance when it is upset and, second, because there is a tendency to avoid an upset by avoiding exposures to messages inconsistent with the existing attitude structure. Accidental exposure does occur, however. A communicator who knows existing attitude structures and the ways in which people react to their upset, can choose the method and point of attack most likely to produce, in the end, the new attitude structure most favorable to his objectives.

Attitude measurement.[17]   A wide variety of methods is available for the measurement of attitudes. Here we shall limit our discussion to identifying certain of the more important approaches. Those interested in more background should consult the reference listed in footnote 17 below.

Projective techniques and qualitative interviews, discussed earlier, are useful in the determination of attitudes as well as motives. In addition, attitude scaling can be used to determine the position of an individual with respect to a topic, event, retail store, or brand. It can also be used to chart the entire population, or some subgroup, to determine distribution of spread of opinion about some topic. For example, what percentage of teen-age boys are hi-fi enthusiasts?

The following are some of the more useful attitude scaling techniques:

---

[16] Reprinted by permission from E. Crane, *Marketing Communications* (New York: John Wiley & Sons, Inc., 1965), p. 66. See this source for a discussion of ways to change attitudes through communications.

[17] This discussion based on Myers and Reynolds, *op. cit.,* pp. 150–57. See also, J. P. Guilford, *Psychometric Methods* (New York: McGraw-Hill Book Co., 1954), and C. E. Osgood, G. J. Suci, and P. N. Tannenbaum, *The Measurement of Meaning* (Urbana, Ill.: University of Illinois Press, 1957).

1. Continuum of feeling (for example, from "extremely important" in steps to "of no importance"; from "extremely good" to "extremely bad"; from "extremely sure" to "not sure at all").

2. Paired comparisons—items, colors, products, brands may be presented in pairs to consumers for comparison.

3. Rank order—the investigator may present all items to be compared (for example, alternative advertisements) at once and ask respondents to rank them in the order of their preference.

4. Statement selection or sorting—attitudes may be measured by having individuals respond to verbal expressions about a given topic, for example, "Almost every advertisement is honest." When a large number of such statements have been developed for a given topic, as, for example, government regulation of advertising, attitudes may be measured through several alternative approaches: (*a*) Thurstone scaling—statements are sorted into piles ranging from "most favorable" to "most unfavorable"; each statement is then assigned a point value; consumers are then asked to select statements with which they agree; attitude scores for each individual are then calculated. (*b*) Likert scaling—a scale indicating strength of agreement ("agree very strongly," "agree fairly strongly," etc.) is presented. Each respondent rates each statement according to how strongly he agrees or disagrees; the score for each is determined from both the direction and strength of the respondent's feelings toward the various statements.

5. Osgood Semantic Differential—pairs of words, or statements of opposite meaning which might describe a product are presented to respondents (for example, ball-point pens might be rated as slow-fast, loose-tight, faddish-conservative, simple-complex). The respondent rates each of several products on each dimension by placing a check at the place on a line which indicates his feelings. The average of the checks is plotted as a profile for each product.

According to Myers and Reynolds, attitude scaling techniques constitute a very powerful means of acquiring insights into the minds of consumers, and they are widely used in marketing studies today.

cognitive dissonance[18]

We have previously noted that attitudes (brand preference) directly affect purchases. Once a purchase decision has been made, how-

[18] This section is based upon H. H. Kassarjian and Joel B. Cohen, "Cognitive Dissonance and Consumer Behavior," reprinted by permission from *California Management Review*, Vol. 8, No. 1 (Fall, 1965), pp. 55–64. Copyright 1965 by the Regents of the University of California.

ever, there is evidence which suggests that this action may itself also influence preference for the brand purchased and hence subsequent buying behavior. This idea is suggested by the theory of cognitive dissonance.

The theory holds that the individual—the consumer—strives toward consistency within himself. His attitudes, values, and beliefs are ordered into clusters that are internally consistent, and consistent with his behavior. Prior to making any major decision, such as the purchase of a new color television set, the consumer is faced with the necessity of choosing between two or more alternatives—for example, Zenith or RCA—both of which have attractive features. Unfortunately, after making the decision the consumer is often faced with uncertainty as to the wisdom of his choice. He may wonder if he shouldn't have purchased an RCA television set instead of a Zenith.

These doubts that remain after purchase are identified as states of "cognitive dissonance" by Festinger. Even the worst of alternatives has some positive features, and the moment a decision is made, the positive features of the rejected alternative and the negative features of the selected alternative are dissonant with the individual's action. The feeling of inconsistency or dissonance is uncomfortable and demands reduction. According to Festinger, therefore, when there is cognitive dissonance (i.e., perceived incongruity) between the person's own attitudes and his behavior, the person may tend to reduce the dissonance by appropriate changes in attitudes. In addition, the person will actively avoid situations and information which would be likely to increase dissonance.[19]

An interesting survey testing the reactions of smokers and non-smokers to the U.S. Surgeon General's report linking cigarette smoking to various illnesses, including cancer, illustrates the behavior of consumers when cognitive dissonance exists. The survey was made by Kassarjian and Cohen three months after the release of the Surgeon General's Report. Personal interviews were conducted with a probability sample of residents of Santa Monica, California. Since there had been wide dissemination given to the Surgeon General's findings in mass media of communication, cigarette smokers were in a state of dissonance. Smoking behavior is clearly dissonant with the need to survive or stay healthy. Accordingly, respondents were asked questions to test hypotheses concerning their reactions in reducing dissonance.

---

[19] For additional background, see L. Festinger, *A Theory of Cognitive Dissonance* (Stanford, Calif.: Stanford University Press, 1957), chap. i, pp. 1–31.

The results were as follows: (1) Among respondents who were smoking at the time of the study, 75 percent stated that they had made no serious attempt in the previous year to stop smoking, while about 25 percent had made one or more serious attempts at dissonance reduction in this manner during the same period. (2) The confirmed smoker appears to be behaving consistently with his belief system by continuing to smoke. He has justified his rationality either (a) by disassociating his responsibility over the decision; (b) by denying, distorting, misperceiving, or minimizing the degree of health hazard involved; (c) and/or by selectively drawing out new cognitions and new information that will reduce the inconsistency of his behavior and achieve consonance in his own cognitive world.[20]

Note that one method of reducing dissonance is selective exposure to new information that tends to support the individual's behavior. In another study, 125 male residents of Minneapolis were interviewed to determine the extent to which they selectively exposed themselves to information about the cars they owned. Sixty-five were new-car owners, and the rest owned cars three or more years old. Results of the experiment indicated, as dissonance theory would predict, that new-car owners recalled reading significantly more advertisements of their own car than did old-car owners. When offered information about different makes of cars, a few more new-car owners than old-car owners elected to read about their own make. The difference was not statistically reliable, but it was in the expected direction.[21]

In contrast, Engel interviewed two groups of consumers in Ann Arbor, Michigan, to test the hypothesis that more recent purchasers of Chevrolets read advertisements featuring this brand than those who have not bought new Chevrolets.[22] On the basis of unaided recall 42 percent of new owners mentioned they had seen the Chevrolet dealer's advertisements while only 23 percent of the nonowners had. When the "recognition" approach was used in checking readership, however, no significant difference was found as between new owners and nonowners. Checks to determine whether new Chevrolet owners were dissonant, however, were negative. There was little indication of anxiety by Chevrolet owners following a purchase decision. This raises a question as to whether dissonance may be expected to occur following

---

[20] Kassarjian and Cohen, op. cit., pp. 55–64.

[21] D. Erlich, I. Guttman, and P. Schonbach, "Postdecision Exposure to Relevant Information," Journal of Abnormal and Social Psychology, Vol. 54, 1957, pp. 98–102.

[22] Reprinted by permission from James F. Engel, "Are Automobile Purchasers Dissonant Consumers?" Journal of Marketing, Vol. 27, No. 2, April, 1963, pp. 55–58, published by the American Marketing Association.

a consumer's free choice among alternative brands which may appear to the individual to be almost equally attractive.

There is also a problem of research methodology involved in this type of study. Did the buyer notice more ads for his chosen brand *after* the purchase than before he was faced with the necessity for making the decision? Such a research design would appear to be needed to discover the existence of dissonance. A single cross-sectional study design does not adequately demonstrate the existence of dissonance.

Judging from the evidence presented above, we cannot be sure that cognitive dissonance occurs in every buying situation. Better methods of measuring the occurrence of this phenomenon are needed to resolve the question. In the meantime the study on cigarette smoking, and other experiments, tend to support the theory of cognitive dissonance in other areas. There is enough evidence from such studies to suggest that cognitive dissonance may occur in certain types of buying situations, if only we could measure it. Where it does exist, the consumer's efforts to reduce dissonance may tend to strengthen preference for the brand purchased.

learning

After a need is recognized, alternative products and brands are evaluated, and a purchase has been made, the consumer arrives at one of the most significant aspects of the entire sequence. It is with the use of the brand that some degree of satisfaction of the initial need will be experienced. If the consumption of the brand leads to gratification of the initiating needs, then "reinforcement" will occur. If the same need is aroused at some later date, the consumer will tend to repeat the purchase of the same product and brand. We have described here the process of "learning," which is defined as any change in behavior which results from experience or practice in similar situations (as opposed to changes due to physiological variations such as growth, deterioration, hunger, fatigue, effects of alcohol, or sleep) .[23]

We are especially interested in the influence of the learning process upon attitudes toward both alternative types of products and brands, i.e., upon brand preference. If Brand A is purchased and yields a high degree of gratification upon usage, then when the same need arises at a later time, the consumer will have an increased tendency to purchase Brand A once again. Each succeeding time that Brand A is purchased and gives satisfaction, additional reinforcement occurs, thus further

---

[23] Berelson and Steiner, *op. cit.*, p. 135.

increasing the probability that Brand A will be selected in the future when the same need arises again. The increasing likelihood that the purchase of Brand A will be repeated is *learning*. Reinforcement is necessary for learning to take place.

Note that the increase in the probability that Brand A will be purchased is related to the number of times the brand has been purchased, has gratified the need, and hence has provided reinforcement. Accordingly, the opportunity for experience, or learning, to influence brand preference tends to be greater for products which are purchased frequently than for those purchased only occasionally, or those purchased once in a lifetime.

It is also important to note that reinforcement depends upon the degree to which the felt need of the consumer is gratified. This underscores the importance of product development and product improvement activities in planning the marketing mix. If the firm decides to produce a product capable of satisfying an important consumer need, and individualizes its brand in ways important to the user, then gratification of desire and reinforcement should follow purchase of the brand.

It is clear from the above discussion that learning theory helps us understand consumer buying behavior. Indeed, theories of stimulus-response learning are an important element in the Howard model of consumer behavior, which is discussed in the next chapter. Still another approach views learning as a probabilistic process, under the assumption that the best predictor of future buying behavior is the sequence, rhythm, and frequency of past purchasing behavior. As an example, Kuehn has developed a mathematical model describing brand-shifting behavior as a probabilistic process and incorporating the effects of past purchases and time elapsed between purchases. This model was tested through empirical research using sequential purchase data from 600 Chicago families over a three-year period. Although space does not permit a discussion of this approach here, it is worthy of careful study.[24]

Influence of environment upon consumer behavior

In our discussion of buying behavior up to this point, we have focused attention upon the individual consumer. Drawing upon psychology and social psychology, we have traced the influence of motives,

---

[24] See Alfred A. Kuehn, "Consumer Brand Choice as a Learning Process," *Journal of Advertising Research*, Vol. 2 (December, 1962), pp. 10–17.

attitudes, cognitive dissonance, and learning upon buying decisions. But the individual consumer lives in an environment which exerts important cultural and social influences upon his behavior. Indeed, both motives and attitudes of the consumer are patterned by the culture and the social institutions in which he lives. Accordingly, to assist in explaining certain uniformities in motives and attitudes of consumers which influence their buying behavior, we shall now draw on the fields of anthropology and sociology for a number of helpful concepts relating to the cultural and social influences. We shall consider, first, the concept of *culture.*

cultural influences

According to Kroeber, "the mass of learned and transmitted motor reactions, habits, techniques, ideas, and values—and the behavior they induce—is what constitutes *culture.*" It is all those things about man that are more than just biological or organic and that are also more than merely psychological.[25] It is the man-made part of the environment; the total way of life of a people; the social legacy the individual acquires from his group.[26]

The culture into which a consumer is born, accordingly, provides a good many ready-made solutions to problems growing out of the geographical, biological, and social environment in which he lives. These ready-made solutions are provided in the form of cultural patterns relating to the ideology, role definitions, and socialization procedures of the society in which he lives. These cultural patterns are transmitted to individuals through social institutions, such as the family, school, church, and social class, by means of language, parent's attitudes and behavior, reading, and public-school instruction, among others. The end results of this learning process are found in the individual's organization of ideas and values, role perceptions and performance, and maintenance and development conceptions (i.e., need patterns and associated goal objects). Stated differently, the cultural patterns which consumers learn influence their ideas and values, the nature of the roles they play, and the way in which they carry them out, as well as the manner in which their needs and desires are handled.

The influence of culture upon attitudes is illustrated by studies of the correlation between the attitudes a man holds and the religious, ethical, political, and economic institutions under which he lives. For

---

[25] A. L. Kroeber, *Anthropology* (New York: Harcourt, Brace & Co., 1948), p. 8.
[26] Clyde Kluckhohn, *Mirror for Man* (New York: Premier Books, 1957), p. 20.

example, it has been found that Jewish college students hold the most liberal attitudes toward the concept of a personal God, toward war, and toward birth; Protestants are intermediate; and Catholics are the most conservative.[27]

An example of the influence of our Early American heritage upon beliefs and attitudes, and hence upon buying behavior, is found in the motivation study dealing with coffee.[28] In the findings it was pointed out that strong remnants of puritanical attitudes are still alive in the American consumer, and they influence his feelings toward coffee. He enjoys coffee but is at the same time convinced that coffee has many drawbacks. Thus, he is caught in a coffee conflict. Contributing to this conflict is a punishing attitude toward pleasure, especially sensory pleasure. Any feeling of "sinning" usually is followed by an expectation and fear of "punishment," although the "sinner" may not always be aware of this. According to the consultant, therefore, one of the major tasks of the coffee industry is to help in changing the image of coffee from that of a sinful and escapist beverage to that of a positive and life accepting one.

The same motivation study also provides an illustration of a situation in which the image of the product has lagged behind cultural changes. Since World War II, according to the report, people have become aware of several cultural changes with which coffee has not kept pace: (1) A desire for more gracious living. (2) Americans are moving away from earlier restrictions imposed on enjoying sensory pleasures. (3) A new kind of individualism which has as its goal the expression of one's personality by more individualized consumption and appreciation and enjoyment of differences and variety. Attitudes toward coffee have lagged behind these trends. The image has become too utilitarian; coffee is related more to nutritional than emotional health; and coffee drinking has become routinized. Hence, there is a need to emphasize the pleasure rather than the utility to be derived from coffee, to stress its sensory pleasures and make it more of a beverage for emotional health.

Culture provides patterns that guide individuals in the satisfaction of their biological needs. Thus, the child learns the diet pattern of his culture, modesty and hygiene of elimination, proper conduct in sexual affairs, patterns of propriety in dress. The requirement for food, for example, is met in every society. But the specific foods which an individual regards as acceptable are determined by his culture. The

---

[27] Adapted by permission from D. Krech and R. S. Crutchfield, *Elements of Psychology* (Copyright 1958 by Alfred A. Knopf, Inc.) , p. 674.

[28] Newman, *op. cit.,* pp. 214–18.

Chinese, for instance, dislike milk and milk products, while dairy products make up an important part of the American diet.

Culture not only patterns the ways in which people satisfy their needs but also creates desires which exert a strong influence upon their buying behavior. The learned desires of certain consumers for cigarettes or alcohol, for example, may be just as compelling as their requirements for food. So too, the desires for a late-model automobile or television set, which are learned from the American culture, may occupy a position high in the list of products wanted by a newly married couple—perhaps even ahead of the need they may feel for a home of their own.

influence of social class

In addition to being molded by culture, the attitudes and needs of the consumer are patterned by the *social class* to which he belongs. Even though American political ideology is based on the concept that "All men are created equal," studies of many communities in all the regions of the United States clearly demonstrate the presence of a well-defined class structure. This structure is not an abstraction invented by the social scientist, but it is regarded as real by the people in each community and is referred to by them in explaining different ways of thinking and acting among their neighbors and acquaintances.

Pioneering research dealing with the existence of social class in America and how it may be measured was done during the early 1940's by Warner and his associates. This work was done in small communities located in New England ("Yankee City"), the midwest ("Johnson City"), and the Deep South, among others. Warner conceived of social class as "two or more orders of people who are believed to be, and are accordingly ranked by the members of the community, in socially superior and inferior positions."[29] Associated with this definition are the ideas that the individual must participate in the social interaction of the class and must be accepted as a peer by its members. After considerable investigation, Warner and his associates came to the conclusion that a family's position in the social structure of a community is determined by the following criteria: occupation, amount of income, source of income, house type, neighborhood, and education.[30] Further analysis indicated that the accuracy of prediction of social class would

---

[29] Reprinted by permission from W. Lloyd Warner and Paul S. Lunt, *The Social Life of a Modern Community* (New Haven, Conn.: Yale University Press, 1959), pp. 81–91.

[30] Adapted from W. Lloyd Warner, Marchia Meeker, and Kenneth Eells, *Social Class in America* (Torchbook edition), pp. 11–15, 31, 35, 174, 181. Copyright 1949 by Science Research Associates, Inc., Chicago. Copyright © 1960 by Harper & Row, Publishers, Inc. By permission of Harper & Row.

not be seriously affected by eliminating amount of income and education from the list of criteria but that some adjustment was desirable to reflect the influence of ethnic and religious factors. Under Warner's approach, individuals are classified as to social class by other people who know them.

Using this research design, Warner identifies six social classes as follows:

Upper-upper (1.4 percent): Members of "old families," the aristocracy of birth and inherited wealth, born into their positions of prestige, with enough wealth to maintain a large house in the best neighborhood.

Lower-upper (1.6 percent): Similar to the upper-upper in costly homes in the best neighborhood and in design for living, but lacking in distinguished ancestry. While their incomes average somewhat larger than families in the upper-upper class, their wealth is newer and it is not inherited.

Upper-middle (10.2 percent): Respectable, achieving, solid citizens of high moral principles and personal integrity; moderately successful business and professional men and their families. Their incomes average somewhat less than the lower-upper class, and these incomes are derived predominantly from salary rather than from invested wealth. Some education and polish is necessary, but lineage is unimportant.

Lower-middle (28.1 percent): Clerks, white-collar workers, small businessmen, schoolteachers, foremen in industry; people who live in small homes on side streets; frequently homeowners.

Upper-lower (32.6 percent): "Poor but honest" workers, usually in semiskilled occupations, who participate less in the educational and other advantages of our society and who spend a large percentage of their income on food and shelter. This class and the lower-middle class are closely related in tastes, problems, and beliefs. Together, these two classes are regarded as "the common man."

Lower-lower (25.2 percent): Semiskilled and unskilled workers; families who live in the worst homes in poor neighborhoods, people who are often on relief, who have low incomes, and who are lacking in ambition or opportunity to improve their lot. Believed by classes above them to be lazy, shiftless, and irresponsible, while research indicates that many of them are guilty of no more than being poor and lacking in the desire to get ahead.

Warner's work on social class is regarded as a substantial contribution in the field of sociology, but certain aspects of his research approach have been criticized—notably the use of the "reputational" approach in determining an individual's social class and the subjective judgments involved in evaluating two of the index factors: house type and quality of neighborhood. Then, too, other scholars have claimed that studies made in cities of from 10,000 to 20,000 population cannot be justifiably regarded as representative of the United States as a whole.[31]

Hollingshead has developed an objective system of classification of individuals into five major social classes. Individuals and families are placed in classes through the use of his Index of Social Position. This Index is based upon three assumptions: (1) that social stratification exists in the community, (2) that status positions are determined mainly by a few commonly accepted cultural characteristics, and (3) that items symbolic of status may be scaled and combined by the use of statistical procedures, so that the researcher can quickly, reliably, and meaningfully stratify the population.

The three indications of status utilized by the Index of Social Position to determine class position are: (1) the residential address of a household, (2) the occupational position of its head, and (3) the years of school the head has completed.[32]

The social class hierarchy which results from Hollingshead's system of classification is shown in Figure 2–1.

While Hollingshead's system is simpler and more objective than that of Warner, we do not know whether it provides a better representation of the social class structure in the United States. It was developed 17 years later than that of Warner, however, and it does provide a somewhat more explicit basis for classifying certain families and individuals, notably top business management as opposed to middle management.

Our interest, of course, is in the value of social class stratification to the marketing executive. Because Warner's research had been done in smaller communities, there was concern that the same social class system might not exist in more complex metropolitan centers. If some such system did exist, would the Warner research approach uncover it? Then, too, many marketers did not see the relevance of social class to consumer buying behavior, since previous research in this area had been concerned with broad differences in patterns of living, moral codes, and mental illness, as well as other behavioral science goals.

With this in mind, the *Chicago Tribune* undertook several extensive studies during the mid 1950's exploring social class in a metropolitan city and the relevance of this factor to the individual family's buying behavior. The studies were carried out under the direction of

---

[31] For an evaluation of the work of the Warner School, see Milton M. Gordon, *Social Class in American Sociology* (Durham, N.C.: Duke University Press, 1958) , chap. iv.

[32] Reprinted by permission from A. B. Hollingshead and F. C. Redlich, *Social Class and Mental Illness* (New York: John Wiley & Sons, Inc., 1958) , p. 66.

Pierre Martineau, Research Director of the *Chicago Tribune,* and W. Lloyd Warner. In this study, interviewing was done in metropolitan Chicago and involved 3,880 households. In carrying out the research, problems were encountered in relating the occupations of Chicago workers to different social classes, in securing house typings, and in

Figure 2–1. Social class hierarchy.

Class	Description	Percentage
I	"Old families," top business management and professional occupations, high incomes, highly educated, expensive homes, the social elite.	3.4
II	Business managers (but not policy formulators), lesser professionals, (engineers, etc.), often college graduates, socially sensitive, "on the way up."	9.0
III	Employees in various salaried administrative pursuits, small business owners, average incomes, high school graduates, modest homes in "good" areas.	21.4
IV	Semiskilled and skilled manual employees, below average incomes, many are homeowners but live in multiple units, many have some high school but did not graduate, often members of minority ethnic group (Italian, Irish, etc.).	48.5
V	Unskilled and semiskilled, low incomes, no savings, live in old tenement areas, most did not finish grade school, "live today, let tomorrow take care of itself."	17.7
	Total	100.0

Source: A. B. Hollingshead and F. C. Redlich, *Social Class and Mental Illness* (New York: John Wiley & Sons, Inc., 1958), pp. *passim,* chap. 10, Appendix 2. Reprinted by permission.

working out a suitable scoring system appropriate for a complex metropolitan society. The data finally used to calculate the "Index of Status Characteristics" were: (1) occupation (weighted by 5), sources of income (weighted by 4), and housing type (weighted by 3). Martineau reported the following conclusions:[33]

1. There is a social-class system operative in metropolitan markets, which can be isolated and described.
2. It is important to realize that there are far-reaching psychological differences between the various classes.

---

[33] Reprinted by permission from Pierre Martineau, "Social Classes and Spending Behavior," *Journal of Marketing,* Vol. 23 (October, 1958), p. 130, published by the American Marketing Association.

3. Consumption patterns operate as prestige symbols to define class membership, which is a more significant determinant of economic behavior than mere income. Income has always been the marketer's handiest index to family consumption standards. But it is a far from accurate index. For instance, the bulk of the population in a metropolitan market today will fall in the middle-income ranges. This will comprise not only the traditional white-collar worker, but the unionized craftsman and the semiskilled worker with their tremendous income gains of the past decade. Income-wise, they may be in the same category. But their buying behavior, their tastes, their spending-saving aspirations can be poles apart. Social-class position and mobility-stability dimensions will reflect in much greater depth each individual's style of life.

It is apparent from the descriptions of social class outlined above that there are significant differences in the standard of living, the ideas and values, the roles (occupational and other), and in the amount and character of the education of the individuals in the different social classes. It follows, therefore, that a child born into an upper-class family would be subjected to training of a different pattern than that given to a child born into a lower-lower-class family. Because of the difference in the scale of living (i.e., the amount and quality of goods and services consumed), the needs and desires of the upper-class child would be patterned differently from those of the lower-class child. Differences in social status, prestige, education, and moral values of the upper-class family as opposed to the lower-lower class might likewise be expected to produce different patterns of attitudes, beliefs, and values of the two children.

Because important differences in the attitudes and needs of consumers result from the training which they receive as members of the various social classes, the concept of social class is recognized as an important influence upon consumer buying behavior.

In discussing this influence, Levy describes social class variations as variations in life style. He then identifies broad differences between social classes in the four areas of values, interpersonal relations, self-perceptions, and daily life. He adds that these groups "do different kinds of work, have different types and amounts of financial reward, are evaluated differently along various dimensions of social esteem and importance in the community. As consequences, they think of themselves differently, behave differently, and want differently."[34]

---

[34] Adapted by permission from Sidney J. Levy, "Social Class and Consumer Behavior," in Joseph W. Newman (ed.), *On Knowing the Consumer* (New York: John Wiley & Sons, Inc., 1966), 146–160.

Levy notes that social status appears to affect how people feel about where they should shop. Lower-status people tend to prefer local, face-to-face places where they feel they will get a friendly reception, and easy credit if needed. As a result, the same products may be purchased in different channels of distribution by members of different social classes. In the purchase of cosmetics, for example, upper-middle-class women are more apt to shop in department stores than are lower-status women, who are, in turn, more likely to shop in variety stores. Drugstores seem equally suitable to all. Studies of department stores also show that among the stores available, there are sharp differences in status reputation, and that consumers tend to sort themselves out in terms of where it is appropriate for them to shop.

Interesting background on the importance of social class, as opposed to income as an influence on consumer behavior is provided by Coleman.[35] He notes that three families, all earning around $8,000 a year, but each from a different social class, exhibit a radical difference in their ways of spending money. An upper-middle-class family in this income bracket (for example, a young lawyer and his wife) is apt to be found spending a relatively large share of its resources on housing in a prestige neighborhood, on rather expensive pieces of furniture, on clothing from quality stores, and on cultural amusements or club memberships.

Meanwhile, the lower-middle-class family (headed by an insurance salesman or a fairly successful grocery store owner), probably has a better house, but in not so fancy a neighborhood. The family is apt to have as full a wardrobe though not so expensive, and probably more furniture though none by name designers. These people almost certainly have a much bigger savings account in the bank.

Finally, the working-class family (with a cross-country truck driver or a highly paid welder as its chief wage earner) is apt to have less house and less neighborhood than the lower-middle or upper-middle family of the same income. But this family will have a bigger, later model car, plus more expensive appliances in its kitchen and a bigger TV set in its living room. This family will spend less on clothing and furniture, but more on food if the number of children is greater. The man of the house also probably spends much more on sports, attending baseball games, going hunting and bowling, and perhaps owing a boat of some description.

---

[35] Adapted by permission from Richard P. Coleman, "The Significance of Social Stratification in Selling," in Martin L. Bell (ed.), *Proceedings of the 43rd National Conference of the American Marketing Association*, December 28–30, 1960 (published by the American Marketing Association, 1961), pp. 171–184.

social group

Another way in which the environment exerts an influence upon the individual consumer is through the social groups to which he or she belongs. A *social group* is "a number of persons who communicate with one another often over a span of time, and who are few enough so that each person is able to communicate with all the others, not at second-hand, through other people, but face-to-face."[36] Groups which have an important influence upon the housewife, for example, are her family, circle of friends, neighbors, and clubs, among others. These are known as *primary groups* and are characterized by intimate, face-to-face association over a long period of time. Sociologists have found that such groups tend to develop *norms* as to what the members of the group should do, ought to do, are expected to do, under given circumstances. These norms are in the nature of shared attitudes and opinions, and as such, influence the behavior of group members. Recognition of this tendency has led behavioral scientists to use the concept of the *primary group* in studies of consumer buying motivation and behavior.

Influence of primary group. The concept of the primary group is recognized as an important intervening variable in a study by Katz and Lazarsfeld dealing with personal influence in the purchase of household goods such as breakfast cereals, coffee, and soap flakes or chips.[37] They asked women who had recently changed from one type of household product to another or from one brand of food to the next, what had made them change. Specific questions were asked which were designed to assess the relative impact of personal contact, and of the mass media like newspapers, radio, TV, and magazines. The source of the personal contact was also determined.

Among the various possible influences which might lead to a change in product or brand, the impact of informal personal advice was found to be greater than the impact of mass media advertisements. And, for products of all kinds, friends and neighbors were named influentials most often, with adult female kin ranking next. The influence of primary groups on buying behavior is thus clearly demonstrated.

Another interesting finding of this study was that the flow of marketing information is horizontal—i.e., within a given status level —rather than vertical. Both advisee and "opinion leader" tended to

---

[36] G. C. Homans, *The Human Group* (New York: Harcourt, Brace & Co., 1950), pp. 1, 123. Reprinted by permission of the publisher.

[37] E. Katz and P. F. Lazarsfeld, *Personal Influence* (New York: Free Press, 1955), pp. 178, 246.

share the same status position. This finding is contrary to the previous common belief that acceptance of new products tends to move in a vertical direction—i.e., from high to low status levels.[38] It serves to underscore the influence of the primary group upon individual buying behavior.

It is noteworthy that the human group influences the individual in two ways. .(1) It is through the primary groups that the culture is transmitted and the personality of the individual is shaped. As a result, continuing influence is exercised over the individual's behavior throughout his life. (2) Personal interactions with members of primary groups influence the individual in his day-to-day decisions. And after the decisions are made, the approval or disapproval of primary-group members tends to reinforce certain kinds of behavior and discourage other kinds.

Reference groups. Individuals belong to a variety of groups of various kinds, both formal and informal—the family, a fraternity or sorority, a small dinner club meeting once a month, a teen-age gang, a bridge club, and a professional club, among others. Not all of the groups to which the individual belongs exert the same influence over him. Indeed, some groups of which he is not even a member may have a considerable effect upon his attitudes and behavior. As a means of helping to clarify which groups have the greatest influence over the individual, the concept of *reference groups* was developed. Herbert Hyman coined the term "reference groups" to designate the kind of group that an individual uses as a point of reference in determining his own judgments, beliefs, and behavior. Since the concept was originally developed, according to Shibutani, it has been applied in three different types of usage: (1) to designate that group which serves as a point of reference in making comparisons or contrasts; (2) to identify that group in which the actor aspires to gain or maintain acceptance; (3) to specify that group whose perspective constitutes the frame of reference of the actor. Shibutani believes the third usage is the most meaningful one, and thus defines a reference group as . . . "that group whose outlook is used by the actor as the frame of reference in the organization of his perceptual field."[39]

---

[38] Katz and Lazarsfeld also asked women who had made a recent change in their hairdo, clothes, or cosmetics to tell what brought about this turn in their fashion habits. As with the marketing of products, noncommercial personal influences had greater impact than did salespersons, while magazines had least of all (p. 180). In 6 out of 10 instances, the flow of influence was within the same status group. When influence did cross the status lines, there was evidence of a slight downward flow, predominantly from women of middle status to women of lower status. (*Ibid.*, pp. 180, 330.)

[39] Reprinted from Tamotsu Shibutani, "Reference Groups as Perspectives," *American*

Note that the individual may not be a member of a group which serves as a frame of reference for his judgments, beliefs, and behavior. It may be a group to which he aspires; by adopting its dress, habits, and attitudes he may hope to be invited into membership.

Our interest is in the influence which reference groups may have upon buying behavior. Whether or not reference-group influence is likely to come into play depends upon two key factors: (1) the feeling of security or insecurity which the individual consumer feels with respect to potential reference groups; and (2) the nature of the product or brand involved. Individuals enjoying the greatest amount of security by virtue of their prestige and status within a group will generally conform (both publicly and privately) to the standards of that group, but they are also freest to deviate from these standards on occasions when particular circumstances seem to justify such deviations. On the other hand, those with the weakest feelings of security and least status in a group are most likely publicly to conform to its standards on all occasions, even though harboring private opposition and resentment.

Reference-group influence is particularly potent in an informational vacuum. Where the individual has little or no knowledge about the attributes of a product, reference-group influence is at its strongest. In contrast, when the individual has personal knowledge and experience with the product, the reference-group influence is likely to be less relevant.

Then, too, there is evidence that reference group influence on purchasing varies widely from product to product. On this point, Bourne cites evidence from research conducted by the Bureau of Applied Social Research, Columbia University.[40] This research indicates that buying may be a completely individualistic activity or very much socially conditioned. Consumers are often influenced by what others buy, especially those persons with whom they compare themselves or use as reference groups.

The conspicuousness of the product is perhaps the most general attribute bearing on its susceptibility to reference-group influence. Two aspects to conspicuousness help to determine reference-group influence: (1) the item must be one that can be seen and identified by others; (2) it must be conspicuous in the sense of standing out and

Journal of Sociology, Vol. 60, No. 6 (May, 1955) , pp. 562, 563, and 565 by permission of The University of Chicago Press. Copyright 1955 by The University of Chicago.

[40] Adapted from Francis S. Bourne, "Group Influence in Marketing," in Rensis Likert and Samuel P. Hayes, Jr. (eds.) *Some Applications of Behavior Research* (UNESCO, 1957) , chap. vi.

being noticed—i.e., no matter how visible the product is, if everyone owns one it is not conspicuous in the second sense. Also, we should keep in mind that reference groups may influence either (1) the purchase of a product, (2) the choice of a particular brand or type, or (3) both.

The susceptibility of various products and brands to reference-group influence is summarized in Figure 2–2. According to the system of classification used in this research, an item might be susceptible to reference-group influence in three different ways, corresponding to three of the four different cells in Figure 2–2.

Figure 2–2. Reference-group influence (relatively weak [−]; relatively strong [+].)

	Weak − [−]	Product	Strong + [+]	
[+] Brand or Type [+]	Clothing Furniture Magazines Refrigerator (type) Toilet soap		Cars* Cigarettes* Beer (premium versus regular)* Drugs*	[+] Brand or Type [−]
[−] Brand or Type [+]	Soap Canned peaches Laundry soap Refrigerator (brand) Radios		Air conditioners* Instant coffee* TV (black and white)	
	[−]	Product	[+]	

Products and brands of consumer goods may be classified by the extent to which reference groups influence their purchase. (The classification of all products marked with an asterisk (*) is based on actual experimental evidence. Other products in this table are classified speculatively on the basis of generalizations derived from the sum of research in this area and confirmed by the judgment of seminar participants.)

Source: Bureau of Applied Social Research, Columbia University.

1. Reference-group influence may operate with respect to both product and brand (product+, brand+) as in the upper right cell of Figure 2–2. With respect to cars, both the product and the brand are socially conspicuous. Whether or not a person buys a car, and also what brand he buys, is likely to be influenced by what others do. This is also true for cigarettes and drugs (decisions made by M.D.'s as to what to prescribe) and for beer with respect to type (premium versus regular) as opposed to brand.

2. Reference-group influence may operate with respect to product, but not brand (product +, brand −) as in the case of air conditioners,

instant coffee, and TV (black and white). Instant coffee is a good example of this type of reference-group influence. Whether it is served in a household depends upon whether the housewife, in view of her own reference groups and the image she has of their attitudes toward this product, considers it appropriate to serve it. The brand, itself, is not conspicuous or socially important and is a matter largely for individual choice. In the case of air conditioners, it was found that little prestige is attached to the particular brand used, and reference-group influence related largely to the idea of purchasing the product itself. Black-and-white TV, with its antenna often visible from outside the house, also falls in this class. As the saturation point approaches, this product may shift to the "product minus-brand minus" class, and be replaced by color TV with "color" rather than brand as the element strongly related to reference groups. This transition has now taken place.

3. Where a type of product is owned by virtually all people, reference groups may influence the selection of the brand, but not the product (product −, brand +). In this cell are classified clothing, furniture, magazines, refrigerators (type), and toilet soap. Clothing is a leading example of this type of product. It is socially visible, but the fact that everyone wears clothing takes it out of the area of reference-group influence. The type of clothing purchased is, however, very heavily influenced by reference groups, with each subculture in the population (teen-agers, Ivy league collegians, workers, bankers, advertising men, etc.) setting its own standards. Similarly, such articles as furniture, magazines, refrigerators, and hand soap are seen in almost all homes, causing their purchase in general to fall outside reference-group influence. The visibility of these items, however, makes the selection of particular kinds highly susceptible to reference-group influence.

4. Purchasing behavior for "product minus, brand minus" items is governed by product attributes rather than by the nature of the presumed users. Examples are laundry soap, canned peaches, refrigerators (brand), and radios. In this group, neither the product nor the brands tend to be socially conspicuous. Reference groups, accordingly, exert very little influence over purchasing behavior.

Assuming that a product or brand has been correctly placed with respect to the part played by reference groups in influencing its purchase, how can this help in marketing the product in question? Bourne makes the following suggestions: (1) Where neither product nor brand appear to be associated strongly with reference group influences, advertising should emphasize the product's attributes, intrinsic qualities, price, and advantages over competing products. (2) Where reference-group influence is operative, the advertiser should stress the kinds of people who buy the product, reinforcing and broadening where possible the existing stereotypes of users. This involves learning what the stereotypes are and what specific reference groups enter into the picture, so that appeals can be "tailored" to each main group reached by the different media employed.

Buying decisions within the family. We have already noted the influence of primary groups upon consumer behavior. The family, of course, is an especially important primary group. Accordingly, let us examine the framework in which buying decisions are made within the family and some of the factors that influence brand choice in this setting. According to Coulson, there are three sources of influence on brand and product choices: the purchaser, the user, and the authority.[41] General areas of prerogative and responsibility relative to the brand decision exist within the family. Some areas are seen as the wife's domain, some as the husband's domain, and some as the child's domain. Usually one person in the family (generally the housewife), but occasionally more than one member, has the assigned job of "purchasing agent" for a particular product class. These roles vary from one product class to another, but they can be determined and described.

Another influencer of product and brand selection is the authority or adviser. He may be the buyer and/or the user, and his role may be more important for some product classes than for others.

In this context, it is clear that the purchasing agent has the strategic role in the brand decision, since she acts as the "gatekeeper" controlling the channel through which products flow from the stores to consumption within the family. In this context, Coulson developed some tentative propositions about how the household "purchasing agent" accommodates the user and the authority in making her brand decisions. These propositions were based on the results of previous research and also upon a pilot study among 100 housewives in Chicago. The study covered 10 product classes that have a high percentage of their sales in food stores. These were: beer, cake mix, candy bars, canned peas, canned spaghetti, chewing gum, cigarettes, cold cereals, deodorants, and margarine. A selection of Coulson's propositions follow:

---

[41] Adapted by permission from John S. Coulson, "Buying Decisions within the Family and the Consumer-Brand Relationship," from Joseph W. Newman (ed.), *On Knowing the Consumer, op. cit.,* pp. 59–66.

1. Other members of the family exert considerable influence on the housewife in making brand decisions.
2. In the role of purchasing agent, the housewife knows the family's brand preferences for some product classes better than she does for others.
   a) The housewife is most aware of the brand preferences of her family for products in which the brand name is clearly visible in use (e.g., deodorants, cold cereals), less aware for products in which the brand is not visible in use (e.g., canned peas), and least aware for products in which a substantial change is made in the product (e.g., cake mix).
3. In the role of purchasing agent, the housewife takes into account the family's brand preferences for some product classes more than she does for others.
   a) On products with the brand name clearly visible in use, she is more receptive to the brand preferences of her husband than she is of her children. (If she thinks a brand is not good for a child, she may veto the request.)
   b) The housewife is most receptive to the brand preferences of her family for products in which the brand is clearly visible, and least receptive for products in which there is a substantial change in the product before use. (If the family cannot identify the brand during consumption, the housewife is free to select the brand she desires.)

This study calls our attention to the different roles played in the buying process, distinguishing between users, influencers and buyers. We shall examine the actual process of working out a household buying decision in the discussion of models of consumer buying behavior which will be presented in the following chapter. Let us now turn to the concept of the "family life cycle" and examine the ways in which life cycle position influences consumer behavior.

The family life cycle. The family life cycle describes the orderly progression of stages through which households tend to pass in the United States today.[42] The concept of the family life cycle, which had its origins in sociology, has been studied intensively by the Survey Research Center of The University of Michigan. The Center classifies the life cycle into the following stages: (1) The bachelor stage: young, single people. (2) Newly married couples: young, no children. (3) The full nest I and II: young married couples with dependent children, (a) youngest child under six, (b) youngest child six or over. (4)

[42] Reprinted by permission from William D. Wells and George Gubar, "Life Cycle Concept in Marketing Research," *Journal of Marketing Research,* Vol. 3 (November, 1966), pp. 355–63, published by the American Marketing Association.

The full nest III: older married couples with dependent children. (5) The empty nest: older married couples with no children living with them, (a) head in labor force, (b) head retired. (6) The solitary survivors: older single people, (a) in labor force, (b) retired.

Our interest is in the influence of position in the life cycle upon buying behavior. A considerable amount of research has been done on this question, and the results are summarized briefly in Figure 2–3, which presents an overview of the life cycle and the changes in income, financial burdens, and purchasing behavior associated with the various stages. As a means of illustrating the influence of the life cycle on buying, let us compare three widely separated stages:

Full nest I, youngest child under six: House purchasing at peak; buy washers, dryers, TV, baby food, chest rubs and cough medicine, vitamins, dolls, wagons, sleds, skates.

Full nest III, older married couples with dependent children: High average purchase of durables; buy new more tasteful furniture, auto travel, nonnecessary appliances, boats, dental services, magazines.

Empty nest II, older married couples, no children at home, retired: Buy medical care, products which aid health, sleep, and digestion.

It is clear from Figure 2–3 that the products purchased by households are influenced significantly by the life cycle stage achieved. As an indication of the significance of such information to an individual firm, let us examine data gathered for the Kroehler Manufacturing Company by Social Research, Inc., concerning furniture buying and the life stages.[43]

This study indicates that interest in furniture buying is highest during two separate life cycle stages and that the type of furniture bought is different from one stage to the other. The first high-interest stage is during the early years of marriage, when the couple must acquire enough furniture to satisfy its basic living needs. Here the young family places relatively greater emphasis on sensibility and practicality than on style and beauty.

The second stage occurs, for middle-class parents, when their children (especially their daughters) have started to party and date. At that stage attractiveness, reflection of good taste, and compatibility with existing decor becomes more important than sturdiness and low cost. With the peers coming in, the family needs to put up a good front.

Information of this kind is helpful to the manufacturer in designing his line to meet consumer desires and in planning his advertising and promotional approaches.

---

[43] Adapted by permission from Social Research, Inc., *The Kroehler Report* (Naperville, Ill.: Kroehler Manufacturing Co., 1958), pp. 37–42.

Figure 2–3. An overview of the life cycle.

Bachelor Stage; Young Single People Not Living at Home	Newly Married Couples; Young, No Children	Full Nest I; Youngest Child under Six	Full Nest II; Youngest Child Six or over Six	Full Nest III; Older Married Couples with Dependent Children	Empty Nest I; Older Married Couples, No Children Living with Them, Head in Labor Force	Empty Nest II; Older Married Couples, No Children Living at Home, Head Retired	Solitary Survivor, in Labor Force	Solitary Survivor, Retired
Few financial burdens. Fashion opinion leaders. Recreation oriented. Buy: Basic kitchen equipment, basic furniture, cars, equipment for the mating game, vacations.	Better off financially than they will be in near future. Highest purchase rate and highest average purchase of durables. Buy: Cars, refrigerators, stoves, sensible and durable furniture, vacations.	Home purchasing at peak. Liquid assets low. Dissatisfied with financial position and amount of money saved. Interested in new products. Like advertised products. Buy: Washers, dryers, TV, baby food, chest rubs and cough medicine, vitamins, dolls, wagons, sleds, skates.	Financial position better. Some wives work. Less influenced by advertising. Buy larger sized packages, multiple-unit deals. Buy: Many foods, cleaning materials, bicycles, music lessons, pianos.	Financial position still better. More wives work. Some children get jobs. Hard to influence with advertising. High average purchase of durables. Buy: New, more tasteful furniture, auto travel, non-necessary appliances, boats, dental services, magazines.	Home ownership at peak. Most satisfied with financial position and money saved. Interested in travel, recreation, self-education. Make gifts and contributions. Not interested in new products. Buy: Vacations, luxuries, home improvements.	Drastic cut in income. Keep home. Buy: Medical appliances, medical care, products which aid health, sleep, and digestion.	Income still good but likely to sell home.	Same medical and product needs as other retired group; drastic cut in income. Special need for attention, affection, and security.

Source: William D. Wells and George Gubar, "Life Cycle Concept in Marketing Research," *Journal of Marketing Research*, Vol. 3 (November, 1966), p. 362. Reprinted by permission.

relevance for the marketing decision maker

It is well established that if marketing strategy is to be effective it must be based upon an understanding of buyer behavior. Success depends upon offering a product, appropriately priced, which meets important consumer desires and has characteristics which individualize it in ways important to the prospective buyer. This product must be made available in retail outlets where consumers would expect to find it. The desires which trigger the decision to buy must be understood if promotional effort is to be planned which will arouse such action. Effective promotional messages designed to create brand preference and to stimulate brand choice must be determined with a full understanding of the role of attitudes in evaluation of alternative brands. Forces determining attitudes, such as culture, social class, reference groups, and the family, must be understood if communication strategy is to be fashioned which will be effective in shaping favorable attitudes toward the firm's brand.

Factors influencing consumer behavior and variables determining responsive market segments for the product are significant considerations in executive decision making on the character of the promotional mix. Identification of types of buyers likely to be good prospects and the classification of consumers into segments expected to be responsive to the firm's selling effort are also necessary if appropriate channels of communication are to be chosen for the selling message (i.e., personal contact, media through which advertising messages may be disseminated). Understanding of the family life cycle and whether it is relevant for the firm's product may also be helpful in identifying market segments likely to be most responsive to the firm's marketing efforts.

Finally, understanding of the factors which influence buyer behavior is an essential preliminary step in taking an inventory of the facts available to aid in marketing decision making and thus assists in identifying gaps where research is necessary to furnish essential data required for sound planning.

conclusion

Since appropriate marketing strategy must be based upon an understanding of buyer behavior, we have provided such a foundation in this chapter. In seeking to understand those aspects of the individual consumer's personality which are relevant for the buying decision, we discussed the concepts of needs, attitudes, cognitive dissonance, and learning. We recognized, of course, that the purchase decision is also influenced by forces in the prospective buyer's environment. The consumer's desires, attitudes, and habits are patterned by the culture which he is taught, the social class to which he belongs, and the social groups of which he is a member.

In addition to these influences, we should note that the consumer is also affected by certain factors in the external situation, such as his income, the proximity of stores to his home, the time of day he shops, the availability of parking space near different stores, the brands carried in the stores of his choice, the exposure of goods through display, and so on. Finally, knowledge of the interplay of these factors was shown to be important to the marketing executive. How an understanding of buying behavior should influence such decisions will be dealt with more extensively in the following chapter, which discusses models of both consumer and industrial buying and identifies the points at which marketing activity may influence buying decisions.

questions

1. Distinguish between consumer goods and industrial goods. Into which classification would you place the following products?
   a) A computer manufactured by General Electric.
   b) Smith-Corona typewriter ribbons for portable typewriters.
   c) IBM typewriter ribbons used primarily on office typewriters.
   d) Champion spark plugs (1) sold as original equipment to automobile manufacturers and (2) sold through service stations for replacements.
   e) Bayer aspirin (1) distributed through drug stores and (2) sold to hospitals for patients under treatment there.
2. What needs might the following products or services satisfy? (Use Maslow's list in responding.)
   a) Simba—a new soft drink by Coca-Cola.
   b) *Book of Knowledge* encyclopedia.
   c) Sidewinder General tire (patented puncture sealing).
   d) State Farm Life Insurance.
   e) Panasonic complete stereo system (phonograph and twin speakers).
   f) Dale Carnegie course.
3. Do the needs satisfied by the following products fit into Maslow's seven categories? If not, what new classifications would you suggest?
   a) Ski-Doo Snowmobile ("Makes fun no problem").
   b) Goodyear Polyglas winter tire ("wide, deep tread; is built to keep its grip longer").
   c) Hormel chili ("It's not exactly tame!").

d) Polaroid color camera ("under $50"), ("the 60-second excitement"), (grandfather taking pictures of grandchildren during family outing).

e) Right Guard anti-perspirant ("When underarm wetness shows up, do you cover up? Check wetness with new Right Guard anti-perspirant").

4. *a)* Give examples of purchases (other than those mentioned in the text) that may satisfy more than one need.

b) Illustrate how a given need (for example, belongingness) may be satisfied by purchasing several different products or services.

5. *a)* In motivation research, what consumer research techniques may be used to get information at the preconscious level of awareness?

b) Through what stages should motivation research be carried before substantial sums of money are invested in advertising and promotional efforts? Why?

6. Distinguish between motives and attitudes. How do attitudes affect the purchase decision?

7. To what extent do consumers' attitudes influence purchase decisions:

a) Of alternative types of products (for example, color television versus outboard motor boats).

b) Of alternative brands (for example, Maxwell House, Chase & Sanborn, or Hills Bros. coffee).

8. *a)* What approaches may be taken in attempting to change consumers' attitudes toward a manufacturer's brand?

b) What factors should be considered in deciding which of the approaches identified in *a* should be used in a specific instance? Apply these factors to the following situations:

(1) At one time, Kroehler furniture was purchased primarily by the "common man"—the upper-lower and lower-middle-class families. After having consumer research done by a consultant, the firm wished to modify the brand image so that its line would also appeal to the upper-middle and upper classes.

(2) Clairol had long sold hair coloring to women successfully. In a recent year the firm introduced Great Day hair coloring for men. Clearly the firm faced a problem in overcoming long-standing attitudes of men believed to be unfavorable to such a product.

9. *a)* Explain the concept of cognitive dissonance. Give an example to illustrate your explanation.

b) In what types of buying situations is cognitive dissonance likely to be of significance?

c) What may a manufacturer do to help consumers reduce cognitive dissonance involved in the purchase of his brand?

10. *a)* What is the definition of learning?

    b) How does this concept help us to understand consumer buying behavior?

11. *a)* What criteria did Warner use to identify a family's position in the social structure of the community in which it lives? What social classes did he identify?

    b) Warner used the reputational approach in classifying families. How did Hollingshead's method differ? What indications of status did Hollingshead use to determine social position?

12. *a)* What criteria were used to determine the Index of Status Characteristics in Chicago by Warner and Martineau?

    b) What conclusions did Martineau reach concerning the value of social class stratification to the marketing executive?

    c) Would segmentation of markets along social class lines be equally significant for the marketing of automobiles, gasoline, beer, coffee, and dietary foods?

13. *a)* Explain briefly the concept of reference groups.

    b) How susceptible are the following products and brands to reference group influence? (Use the following classification system: product+, brand+; product−, brand+; product+, brand−; product−, brand−.)

      (1) automobiles.

      (2) beer (premium versus regular).

      (3) air conditioners.

      (4) radios.

      (5) color television sets.

14. For which of the products listed below does the housewife tend to take into account the preferences of other members of the family in making purchases?

    a) Kellogg's Sugar Pops (preferred by four-year old son).

    b) My Sin perfume (wanted by 13-year old daughter).

    c) Marlboro cigarettes (preferred by husband; wife likes Kents).

    d) Maybelline eye shadow (requested by 17-year old daughter).

    e) Rival dog food (preferred by Fido).

    f) Betty Crocker cake mix (preferred by 17-year old daughter; mother likes Pillsbury cake mix).

    g) Idahoan instant potatoes (liked by wife; husband likes Maine potatoes boiled and then mashed by hand).

    h) Eckrich frankfurters (preferred by seven-year old son, nearest supermarket stocks Oscar Mayer brand).

    i) Dubble Bubble gum (requested by seven-year son).

    j) Crest Mint toothpaste (preferred by 17-year old daughter; mother likes Crest Regular which is wintergreen flavored).

15. Research suggests that the position of a family in the life cycle is likely to have an influence upon its purchasing behavior. Which of the products listed would the families listed be most likely to purchase?

Products	Life Cycle Stages
Sleeping pills	Bachelor
Boats	Newly married
Ski equipment	Full nest I
Round-the-world tour	Full nest II
Piano	Full nest III
Automatic washer and dryer	Empty nest I
Bicycle	Empty nest II

chapter 3

buyer behavior: consumer and industrial

In the previous chapter, we focused attention upon problem-solving behavior involved in the purchase of major items and innovations. The purchase decision-making process was conceptualized as involving five stages: (1) recognition of a problem (felt need); (2) the search for alternative solutions to the desire; (3) evaluation of alternatives; (4) purchase decision; and (5) postpurchase feelings and evaluation. This way of thinking about buyer behavior may be regarded as a simple model of a very complex process. In the present chapter, we shall turn to a consideration of more complex models of the purchase decision-making process as a means of becoming familiar with other approaches to the problem. Such models are helpful to the marketing executive. They assist him in organizing his thinking about buyer behavior. They help by identifying the various factors which influence the decision-making process of the buyer. They show the relationships of these various influences. With such background, the executive is then in a better position to take inventory of what essential information he already has concerning consumer purchase of his own product and what additional information should be secured through research if data are to be available upon which to base sound decisions concerning marketing strategy.

Accordingly, we shall discuss three different models of the consumer purchasing process and call attention to other complex formulations which cannot be included in this discussion. We shall then turn to a consideration of the behavior of the industry buyer in order to round out our discussion.

models of consumer buying behavior

Morgan's model of family decision making

A promising approach to the understanding of important buying decisions is provided by Morgan's theory of family decision making.[1] The theory is an eclectic one that attempts to make use of variables at several different levels of abstraction, including some from personality psychology. Its major innovation is an attempt to separate the forces affecting an individual into two parts—those relevant to the decision as such (a bachelor theory) and those relevant to the individual's relationships with the rest of the family.

Morgan limits the scope of his theory in the following ways: (1) Only decisions that are salient and important to more than one member of the family are to be considered. (2) Patterns of decision making that are unusual and infrequent in society as a whole are to be neglected. (3) Situations where the individual really has no freedom of action (because of laws, social regulation, or his own previous decisions) are to be omitted. (4) Attention is to be concentrated on family decision making in the present-day United States.

In developing his theory, Morgan begins with the economist's concept that any decision to act is a choice between alternative courses of action and that there may be more than two alternatives. In buying, for example, the problem may be to decide between buying an automobile as opposed to installing wall-to-wall carpeting or taking a vacation trip to Europe. The first step in the development of the theory is to explain the factors which influence an individual's assessment of a single course of action (such as buying an automobile), remembering that the same assessment must be made of its alternatives. The second step consists of combining individual preferences for alternative lines of action into a family decision.

Factors determining individual preference. According to Morgan, an individual's preference for alternative A (for example, purchase of an automobile) tends to be determined by (1) his physical and social needs, (2) the incentive values of the possible outcome of alternative A (buying an automobile) for each need, and (3) expectation as to outcome. (See Figure 3–1 for a diagram of these various factors.)

A. *Needs.* The individual is seen as having stable, basic, physical and social needs that result from his physiological makeup and his

---

[1] Adapted by permission from J. M. Morgan, "Household Decision-Making," in N. N. Foote (ed.), *Household Decision-Making* (New York: New York University Press, 1961), pp. 81–99.

early childhood experiences and training. At the physical level we can think of an individual needing and enjoying food, shelter, sex, and entertainment. At the social level we may list, among others, curiosity and the desires for achievement, affiliation, and power.

Figure 3–1. Individual preference for alternative A—per se.

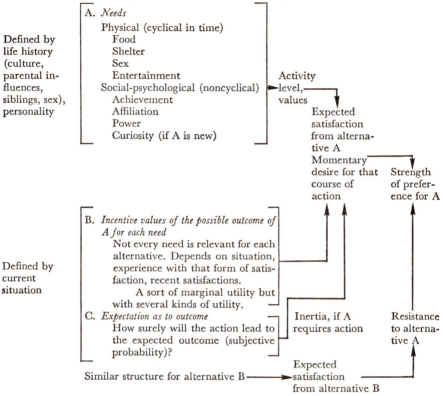

Source: J. M. Morgan, "Household Decision-Making," in N. N. Foote (ed.), *Household Decision-Making* (New York: New York University Press, 1961), p. 88. Reprinted by permission.

B. Incentive values of the outcome. "At any point in time," according to Morgan, "these needs become relevant only as they are perceived to be involved in the outcome of a path of action being considered."

How much any act will be seen as contributing to the satisfaction of some basic need will depend on the situation at the moment. Atkinson calls this the "incentive value" of the outcome. One's experience tells him that a certain outcome gives him a sense of achievement or affiliation or power or physical well-being, or he may infer it from the actions or reports of others. In the physical area, the distinction between a basic need and the incentive value of a particular outcome is analogous to the distinction between the position of food in a preference function (marginal utility curve) and the expected marginal utility (added satisfaction) from eating one more piece of apple pie just now. The latter clearly depends on how one ranks apple pie as a food and how many pieces of apple pie one has had recently. One achievement depreciates the future incentive value of that particular success and induces one to want to succeed in the future at harder tasks. We can think then, of basic personality characteristics combining with the facts of the present situation to produce expected subjective utilities of the outcome expected from some action or decision.[2]

C. *Expectation as to outcome.* Morgan says, "In this world, we must always add the element of uncertainty. Of many decisions we are not quite sure just what the outcome will be or that the expected satisfactions will really result from it. We have subjective probabilities but no certainty." He continues:

In practice, these expectations will be affected by information, particularly information that leads one to expect certain outcomes. Generalization from previous experience or from decisions made in similar situations in the past will affect the strength of these expectations or subjective probabilities. . . .

Our model, which we have really taken from personality theory, then says that an individual confronts a particular decision as it contributes in various measure to his basic needs, the contribution depending on the current situation and its uncertainties as well as the relative importance of the stable needs. Given the constraints of the situation, and perhaps certain decision-making characteristics of the individual, the evaluation of a course of action and of its closest rivals should lead to some decision or choice or, in the family, to a pattern of negotiation and discussion with others in the family. . . . One should not neglect the importance of experience and of habit as factors influencing preferences among alternatives. Recent experience affects the incentives and the subjective probabilities, whereas habit and inertia may well operate to produce resistance to an alternative if it requires an active decision. One might argue, however, that curiosity and habit-inertia are two ends of the same personality scale.

In some situations, at least, these forces may well result in expected satisfactions and even felt desires that can be elicited directly by questioning individuals. However, if our major purpose is to examine the process of decision-making in the family, reliance on such expressions may prove quite dangerous, as we shall see. We turn now to consideration of the way in which individual preferences related to individual satisfactions expected from the course of action combine with other considerations when the family must make a decision.[3]

---

[2] *Ibid.*, p. 87.

[3] *Ibid.*, pp. 87–89.

Combining individual preferences into a family decision. Morgan pictures in Figure 3–2 the way in which the individual preference for a course of action A is combined with other motivation stemming from his relationships with others in his family, to produce whatever actions or expressions he makes during the decision-making process. Morgan argues that:

. . . each individual has a strength of preference for a particular alternative (i.e., buying an automobile) depending on his own needs, including his desire to exert power and his desire to give and receive affection by doing what others desire, and that this is weighted by some index of his "power" in the family. The alternative with the most "weighted preference" would then win.[4]

The various factors incorporated in Morgan's model are explained more fully in the paragraphs which follow.

A. *Needs.* As indicated in Figure 3–2, the individual X has a strength of preference for alternative A (i.e., buying an automobile) depending not only on the strength of his own preference for A per se but also upon the expected satisfaction from attempting to dominate others in the family as opposed to the expected satisfaction from doing what others desire.

1. *Expected satisfaction from attempting to dominate* depends upon the strength of the *need* for power (a basic personality disposition), the *incentive value* of power in the form of influence on family decisions (greater if others oppose alternative A), and the *expected outcome* of the attempt to dominate in this particular family decision.

2. The expected satisfaction of doing what others desire is determined by the *need* for affiliation, the *incentive value* of A as expressing affection for others, because they prefer it, and the *expectancy* that voting for A will lead to a warm response. This expectancy, of course, will be conditioned by how sure X is that he knows what others in the family really want (i.e., do they really want alternative A or do they prefer some other alternative).

B. *Ability to exert power in the family.* The strength of attempts by individual X to influence his family toward alternative A depend not only on his strength of preference for this alternative but also upon his *ability to exert power in the family.* Five different sources of power over another person may be distinguished as follows:

1. Cultural roles, values, legitimate power.
2. Contribution of X to the family (reward power, economic and social).

---

[4] *Ibid.*, p. 91.

3. X's competence in the area of decision—expertise.
4. Desires of others for affiliation, keeping the family together, rather than exerting their power.
5. Ability to punish or coerce.

Figure 3–2. The individual X contributes to a family decision about alternative A

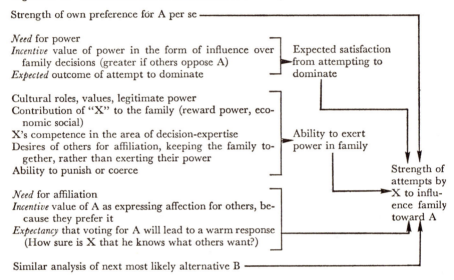

Strength of own preference for A per se

Need for power
Incentive value of power in the form of influence over family decisions (greater if others oppose A)
Expected outcome of attempt to dominate
— Expected satisfaction from attempting to dominate

Cultural roles, values, legitimate power
Contribution of "X" to the family (reward power, economic social)
X's competence in the area of decision-expertise
Desires of others for affiliation, keeping the family together, rather than exerting their power
Ability to punish or coerce
— Ability to exert power in family

Need for affiliation
Incentive value of A as expressing affection for others, because they prefer it
Expectancy that voting for A will lead to a warm response (How sure is X that he knows what others want?)

Strength of attempts by X to influence family toward A

Similar analysis of next most likely alternative B

Source: J. M. Morgan, "Household Decision-Making," in N. N. Foote (ed.), *Household Decision-Making* (New York: New York University Press, 1961), p. 92. Reprinted by permission.

As the model indicates, the strength of X's preference for alternative A is weighted by some index of his "power" in the family. A similar analysis of B, the next most likely alternative (for example, wall-to-wall carpeting), would then result in a weighted preference for this alternative. The alternative with the most weighted preference would then be the choice which individual X would attempt to urge upon the family.

According to Morgan:

Even more than in Figure [3]–1 we appear to be dealing with a situation in which it may be easier to measure more variables at more basic levels rather than the somewhat fewer intermediate resultant variables. In other words, while one might be able to measure whether or not an individual knew what others in the family preferred and whether he had a high need for affiliation and a perception that paying attention to the needs of others in the family would lead to an affectionate return from them, it would be most difficult to measure by direct questions the degree to which an individual "voted" for one course in family discussions because he felt it was what the others preferred. It would appear to be even more difficult to get individuals to report a desire to exert power over other members of the family by dominating a decision, without regard to the specific content of the decision. Finally . . . power and influence are not the same thing. Power is only potential influence.[5]

Comments on Morgan's model.[6] One criticism of Morgan's model relates to the manner in which motives, incentive values, and expected satisfactions should be combined in affecting an individual's preferences for alternative major purchases which the family has under consideration. Should amounts representing each of these variables be added or multiplied in predicting expected satisfactions from the purchase of a given alternative (such as a sports car)? If they are to be multiplied, as Morgan suggests, should each of the three variables be given equal weight or are some more predictive than others and thus deserving of heavier weights? Morgan recognizes this problem and indicates that additional research would be required to resolve it.

Even if this problem is solved, a serious question has been raised as to how individual preferences of different family members are combined in a purchase decision. Thomas argues that group decision making cannot be predicted with Morgan's model because group influences have not been taken into consideration. Research on decision making in small groups suggests that the individual's preferences, attitudes, or opinions may be greatly modified by the group in which he finds himself. The individual may change his preferences after entering into a family discussion of alternative purchases as a result of taking the role of others in the group and reacting in terms of what he knows the group norms are. Then, too, if an individual's preferences differ widely from those of other family members, the others may exert considerable pressure to get him to conform with their preferences.

Small-group studies also suggest that the contributions of the individual members of the family do not combine in any simple manner to produce a group decision. The type of task, the norms, the division of labor, the cohesiveness of the family group, and the group's size are among the potential influences upon how final decisions are reached. There are few situations where a group decision may be predicted from knowledge merely of the individual contributions. Accordingly, it is argued that decision making on major purchases may be predicted

---

[5] *Ibid.,* pp. 92–93.

[6] *Ibid.,* Edwin J. Thomas, "Discussion," pp. 106–8.

more effectively by group variables than by individual preferences and contributions to the group.

In responding to this criticism, Morgan notes that there is a problem of whether these group influences should be pushed into the structure of the model, or whether still more elaboration and other levels of variables must be added to it. He expresses the hope that such group influences might be brought to bear on the model without adding complexities. More research would be required to resolve the problem of how this might be done.

Summary and evaluation. At this point it is appropriate to summarize the salient points in the foregoing discussion, and add a few concluding comments.

1. Morgan has provided us with a useful general theory (or model) of household decision making. This theory deals only with important purchases and thus excludes a substantial portion of day-to-day purchase decisions.

2. Morgan's model relates to family decisions as to whether to buy alternative types of products or services, such as an automobile, wall-to-wall carpeting, or a vacation trip to Europe. It also includes the alternative of not buying any of these, but instead saving an equivalent amount of money. We should note that the model does not attempt to explain how the family group makes a decision between different brands of a given product—i.e., whether to purchase a Ford, Chevrolet, or Plymouth automobile. Since most manufacturers are especially concerned with the sale of their particular brand, rather than with the stimulation of primary demand for the generic type of product, Morgan's model is of limited practical value for them. After more is learned about factors influencing the family's choice among alternative types of products, however, it should be possible to adapt Morgan's model to the explanation of brand choice.

3. Even though Morgan's model is restricted to the explanation of important decisions among alternative types of products, it has been criticized as being relatively complex. Morgan recognizes this and indicates that a great deal of research needs to be done in testing his theory to determine which variables may safely be neglected and how crucial variables remaining may be expected to operate.

4. As Thomas correctly points out, group decision making cannot yet be predicted with the model, since group influences have not been taken into consideration. The problem, of course, is how to include group influences in the model without adding complexities. Further work is clearly needed on this question.

5. In spite of the criticisms mentioned above, Morgan's model of household decision making is believed to have considerable merit. Even though the theory is complex, Morgan has suggested a workable research approach by which it may be tested. As he recognizes, a great deal of research needs to be done if we are to understand decision making in the family.

Du Pont model of consumer behavior

In the process of developing a theory of how advertising might work in the sale of a consumer product manufactured by Du Pont, staff executives constructed a model of customer behavior. This model is simpler than that developed by Morgan, and it carries the decision process beyond the primary demand level to the steps involved in making a decision upon the brand to be purchased. Accordingly, this practical use of a model merits our attention.[7]

The product involved in this study was a consumer item and was associated by consumers with Du Pont. It was distributed nationally, was sold during a relatively short season, and was classified as "mature" and fairly stable. The same major competing brands had been sold in essentially the same manner for several years.

To gain an understanding of how advertising worked in the marketing mix for this product, the analysts talked to several executives responsible for the product's sales and advertising. These discussions were summarized as follows:

1. Consumers were aware of the names of competing brands, but generally were unable to judge differences in product performance. Frequently the selection of the brand was left to the retail salesperson. Moreover, because the product was bought infrequently, consumers did not develop habitual brand "loyalties."

2. Many retailers handled only one or two brands of the product, and few if any stocked all major brands. Some large retail chains distributed their own brands and gave manufacturers' brands little or no support.

3. Some prospective consumers did not buy the product every year, since purchase was not required by circumstances. The vast majority of U.S. households were, however, at least prospective buyers about once a year.

As a means of summarizing their understanding of the marketing system for the product, the staff analysts constructed a model of cus-

---

[7] Adapted by permission from Robert D. Buzzell, *Mathematical Models and Marketing Management* (Boston: Division of Research, Graduate School of Business Administration, Harvard University, 1964), pp. 163–64.

Figure 3–3. E. I. du Pont de Nemours & Co., schematic diagram of customer behavior model.

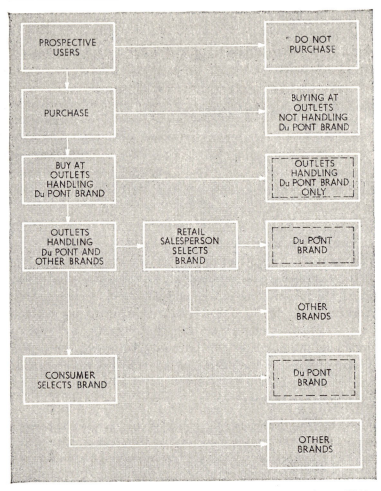

Source: Robert D. Buzzell, *Mathematical Models and Marketing Management* (Boston: Division of Research, Graduate School of Business Administration, Harvard University, 1964), p. 177. Reproduced by permission.

tomer behavior. The model, which is shown in Figure 3–3, was simply an explicit statement of the elements involved in the purchasing behavior of prospective users and the logical relationships among those elements. The various steps in the decision process may be identified as follows: (1) Initially, the prospective user makes a decision to buy the product or not during a given year. (2) If he does decide to buy, he next chooses a retail outlet at which to make the purchase. The outlet chosen may handle *only* the Du Pont brand, *only* other brands, or both

Du Pont and other brands. (3) In the latter case, the customer may specify his brand or may leave the choice to the salesperson. (4) Whoever specifies the brand, it may be the Du Pont brand or it may be a competing brand.

The share of market attained by the Du Pont brand depended, in this model, on all the decisions depicted in Figure 3–3. Out of each 100 purchasers, the number following the "decision paths" ending in the boxes with double lines around them would represent Du Pont's share. The quantity purchased per customer did not vary significantly enough to call for any separate treatment in the model.

The model shown in Figure 3–3 served two purposes. First, it reflected the understanding of the research team as to the steps involved in consumer purchasing decisions and the *sequence* of these steps. Second, discussion of the model suggested the ways in which advertising *might* affect consumer behavior.

As a result of this analysis, the five possible effects of advertising on consumer decisions were identified as follows:

1. It might influence the number of people buying the product in a given year (primary demand).
2. It might increase the number of outlets handling the Du Pont brand and/or the number of people going to existing Du Pont outlets.
3. It might influence more customers to specify a brand as opposed to letting the salesperson specify it.
4. It might increase the fraction of customers who specify the Du Pont brand (brand preference).
5. It might persuade more retail salespersons to select Du Pont when the choice is left to them.

Du Pont executives described this model as "our theory of how advertising might work." The model was designed to serve as a basis for the experimental measurement of advertising results. In the field experiments that followed, an attempt was made to measure each of the five possible effects listed above.

While the Du Pont model served the purpose of the executives who were responsible for planning research to measure the effectiveness of advertising, it deals with the *steps* involved in the decision process and not with the variables which explain *why* people chose Du Pont or some other brand. Let us turn briefly, therefore, to other models which are designed to tell us not only what steps are involved in a purchase decision but which attempt to explain the variables that determine why people buy as they do. Space limitations restrict our discussion to a description of key aspects of each model. Those interested should consult the references cited.

the Howard-Sheth model

The Howard-Sheth model is a comprehensive theory of buying behavior designed to apply to most people buying most products.[8] It attempts to explain brand choice behavior of the buyer over time. It postulates that buying behavior is caused by a stimulus either in the buyer or in the buyer's environment. This stimulus is the input to the system, and purchase behavior is the output. Accordingly, buying is explained in the context of stimulus-response theory. The model integrates ideas from learning theory, cognitive theory, and the theory of exploratory behavior, among others. (See Figure 3–4 for a diagram of this model.)

The central rectangular box isolates the various internal variables and processes ("endogenous variables") which taken together, show the state of the buyer. The inputs are stimuli from the marketing and social environments. The outputs are a variety of responses which the buyer is likely to manifest, based upon the interaction between stimuli and his internal state.

Beside the inputs and outputs, there is a set of seven "exogenous variables" which affect the internal state of the buyer: importance of purchase, personality, social class, culture, time pressure, financial status, and organization.

According to this model, the elements of the buyer's brand choice decision are (1) motives, (2) several alternative brands called to mind by the arousal of the need ("evoked set"), and (3) "decision mediators," or mental rules for matching alternative brands with motives and ranking them in terms of their want-satisfying capacity. These decision rules are developed through the process of learning either from actual experience with various brands and from information (advertising, personal selling, advice of friends). As a result of these influences, the buyer develops attitudes toward the various brands under consideration (brand preferences) which are labeled "predispositions." The effect of "inhibitors" (price, availability, time pressure, buyer's financial status) in disrupting intentions to purchase is

---

[8] From John A. Howard and Jagdish N. Sheth, "A Theory of Buyer Behavior," in *Perspectives in Consumer Behavior*, edited by Harold H. Kassarjian and Thomas S. Robertson. Copyright © 1968 by Scott, Foresman and Company. Used by permission.

Figure 3–4. A theory of buyer behavior.

INPUTS

BRANDS   A   B   C
SIGNIFICATIVE
1. QUALITY
2. PRICE
3. DISTINCTIVENESS
4. AVAILABILITY
5. SERVICE
SYMBOLIC
1. QUALITY
2. PRICE
3. DISTINCTIVENESS
4. AVAILABILITY
5. SERVICE
SOCIAL ENVIRONMENT

IMPORTANCE OF PURCHASE | PERSONALITY VARIABLES | SOCIAL CLASS | CULTURE | ORGANIZATION | TIME PRESSURE | FINANCIAL STATUS

SEARCH FOR INFORMATION

INHIBITORS

PREDISPOSITION

NONSPECIFIC MOTIVES | SPECIFIC MOTIVES | DECISION MEDIATORS | EVOKED SET

SENSITIVITY TO INFORMATION

PERCEPTUAL BIAS

SATISFACTION

INPUT–OUTPUT FLOW OF INFORMATION AND EFFECT
FEEDBACK EFFECTS
INFLUENCE OF EXOGENOUS VARIABLES

OUTPUTS

PURCHASE BEHAVIOR

INTENTION

ATTITUDES

COMPREHENSION

ATTENTION

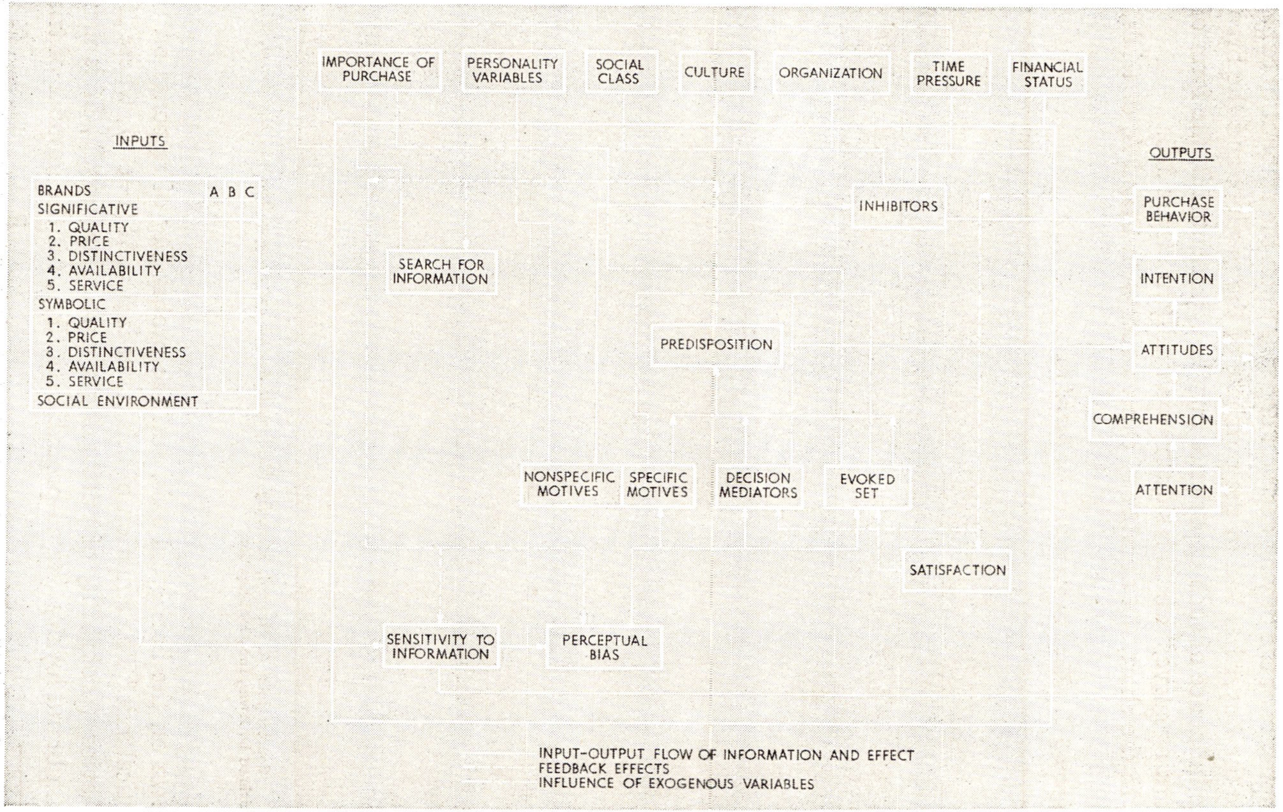

Source: From John A. Howard and Jagdish N. Sheth, "A Theory of Buyer Behavior," in *Perspectives in Consumer Behavior*, edited by Harold H. Kassarjian and Thomas S. Robertson. Copyright © 1968 by Scott, Foresman and Company. Used by permission.

recognized. Finally, "satisfaction" with the brand is identified as an important learning influence affecting future brand preference.

An important feature of the model is its recognition that the complexity of the buying decision depends upon the amount of experience the buyer has had in the purchase of the product and the brand. The influence of such experience may be represented in the form of a "learning curve," which is shown graphically in Figure 3–5.

In the chart, the number of experiences with Brand A, or trials, is

Figure 3–5. The learning curve for Brand A.

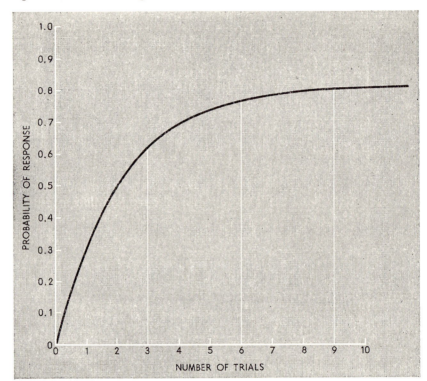

Source: John A. Howard, *Marketing Management: Analysis and Planning* (rev. ed., Homewood, Ill.: Richard D. Irwin, Inc., 1963), p. 36.

shown on the horizontal axis, and the probability of response on the vertical axis.[9] The equation of this curve is $B = M(1-e^{-kt})$, where B is behavior (probability of purchasing a particular brand), M is maximum brand loyalty (stated probabilistically), t is the number of trials

___
[9] John A. Howard, *Marketing Management: Analysis and Planning* (rev. ed.; Homewood, Ill.: Richard D. Irwin, Inc., 1963), pp. 35–37.

under given stable conditions, k is a constant expressing the learning rate, and e is the base of natural logarithms. If M is 0.8 and k is 0.5 as in Figure 3–5, after three trials the probability of repeating the purchase of Brand A is 0.62, other things being equal.

Learning is measured by the increase in the probability of making a particular response, for example, buying a particular brand. The curve indicates that the amount a person learns from each trial is less than he learned from the previous trial.

As a means of providing insight into the buyer's decision process, the learning curve is divided into three phases or levels of experience, depending upon the strength of predisposition toward brands: (1) "extensive problem solving," trials 1 to 3 in Figure 3–5; (2) "limited problem solving," trials 4 to 6; and (3) "routine response behavior," trials 7 to 9. When a buyer is just beginning to purchase a product class, he lacks experience, and buying involves "extensive problem solving." If the brand chosen proves satisfactory, the potential of that brand to satisfy his motives for subsequent purchases is increased (predisposition grows). With repeated satisfactory purchases of one or more brands, the buyer is likely to manifest a routine decision process in which the sequential steps in buying are so well structured that an event which triggers the process may also complete it (for example, an attractive display in a retail store). Routine purchasing implies that decision mediators (rules) are well established and that the buyer has strong brand preferences.

Note that this model will provide a satisfactory explanation for behavior in buying frequently purchased products (such as cigarettes) as well as those which are bought at widely spaced intervals (automobiles) or very seldom (pianos). Observe, also, that the model is dynamic in the sense that it explains buying behavior over time, thus giving emphasis to the learning theory.

Relevance for marketing management. At this point it is helpful to inquire, "What is the relevance of the Howard-Sheth model for marketing management?" The model has several uses.

1. It provides a useful service in identifying stimuli acting upon the consumer as coming from the environment (noncontrollable variables) and from the marketing plan (controllable influences). In developing marketing strategy, management should identify which of the following noncontrollable (exogenous) variables are especially significant in their influence upon the consumer: importance of purchase, personality variables, social class, culture, time pressure, financial status, and others. The executive might then ask whether adequate

information is available upon the impact of significant uncontrollable variables upon consumer response. Where data are inadequate, then research might be planned to provide missing information useful in executive decision making.

2. The model also helps to identify the points at which the marketing plan applies stimuli influencing the prospective buyer's choice process. The model indicates that the prospect's choice process is influenced by his perception of the characteristics of the firm's brand as compared with competing brands—any one of which might satisfy his desires. Management decisions which change the firm's product, its price, the service available, and its availability may, therefore, influence the consumer's evaluation of alternative brands and hence his buying decision.

3. The evoked set of brands considered by the consumer when a desire is aroused may be influenced by advertising, personal selling, and information provided through personal contact with the buyer's social groups. Recognition of this important point may be taken into account by management in working out promotional strategy.

4. The model also indicates that advertising, point-of-purchase promotion, or personal selling may serve as a triggering cue which results in a decision to buy by the consumer. This understanding may be used to identify communication objectives and to decide upon the proper promotional methods to be used to gain the maximum results.

5. The model also explains that the effects of advertising or personal selling may be transmitted to prospective buyers through interaction with members of their social groups. Such knowledge may suggest research to identify which groups influence the prospective buyer and, with such information in hand, may provide a basis for developing a promotional program aimed, in part, at groups which may serve as a channel through which information may flow by personal interaction.

6. The model calls attention to the point that advertising and personal selling may also influence the way in which prospective buyers perceive the firm's brand as compared with alternative brands. Such effort may serve to create not only favorable attitudes toward the firm's brand but also an intent to buy. This identifies another task which may be assigned to advertising and/or personal selling in developing the promotional strategy.

7. The model suggests the wisdom of adapting the marketing strategy to the amount of experience which the typical consumer has had with the brand and hence the complexity of the buying decision. The theory suggests that different strategy is appropriate for products where "Extensive Problem Solving" is involved in the purchase decision as

compared to those where "Limited Problem Solving" or "Routine Response Behavior" are followed.

8. With knowledge of points in the model at which stimuli from marketing programs may be applied, management may find it useful to undertake research or controlled experiments to develop consumer response curves which describe how prospective buyers respond to changes in product, price, advertising, and personal selling efforts. Such response curves may be helpful in arriving at management decisions as to what strategy moves to make, and in what sequence, in order to maximize sales and profits.

9. One merit of the model is its comprehensiveness. It provides a useful reminder to the executive of the various factors which need to be considered in working out marketing plans to influence consumer behavior. It also helps the executive to understand why consumers behave as they do in the process of buying.

Concluding comments. This model appears to be a powerful tool for explaining consumer behavior, especially for frequently purchased items where past experience is likely to influence future attitudes. The complexity of the model makes it difficult to explain briefly and, indeed, this characteristic is one of its chief limitations. Yet it is apparent from our previous discussion that the buying process itself is complex. Executives wishing to apply the model in research are likely to encounter a problem because of the extremely brief description of the model in published form. Certain key variables, such as "Predisposition," are defined in such an abstract manner as to make their application in a firm's research relatively difficult. Moreover, the validity of the theory which lies behind this model has not yet been established by published research.[10] It is noteworthy, however, that at this writing the validity of the model is being tested in an extensive three-year research program. We shall await the results of this research with anticipation. Those interested in learning more about buyer behavior will find it rewarding to read a more complete explanation of the model available in Howard and Sheth's writings.

the Nicosia model

Nicosia has also developed a comprehensive model of the consumer decision-making process.[11] He bases his scheme on the situation where a firm is introducing a new product. According to Nicosia:

---

[10] James F. Engel, David T. Kollat, and Roger D. Blackwell, *Consumer Behavior* (New York: Holt, Rinehart & Winston, Inc., 1968), p. 38.

[11] Francesco M. Nicosia, *Consumer Decision Processes: Marketing and Advertising Implications*, © 1966, p. 154. Reprinted by permission of Prentice-Hall, Inc., Englewood Cliffs, New Jersey.

. . . a first approximation of the scheme would consist of the flow: the firm, its advertisement, the consumer's possible exposure to it, the interaction between the advertisement and the consumer's predispositions operating or evoked at the time of exposure, the possible formation of an attitude toward the advertised brand, the possible transformation of this attitude into a motivation, the possible conversion of this motivation into an act of purchase, and then back to the consumer's predispositions and to the firm.

Nicosia's approach is to diagram consumer behavior in a flow chart as a decision-making sequence similar to a complex computer program with feedback loops. His model is designed so that it can be used experimentally either with mathematical structures or with computer simulation. Accordingly, it opens up promising avenues for further research. Nicosia's work is worth examining in greater detail by those interested in learning more about consumer decision-making models.[12]

buyer behavior in the industrial market

The first part of this chapter has dealt with buyer behavior in the consumer market. Attention has been directed to four models which have proven useful in explaining the various ways in which individuals act when faced with a purchase decision involving the satisfaction of their own needs or those of their immediate families.

Buying decisions in industry are made by people who are paid to solve buying problems and who usually function as part of an organized group. To gain insight into the nature of the industrial buying process, accordingly, requires both an understanding of individual buying behavior and a knowledge of how this behavior is influenced by the structure and goals of the organization of which the individual is a part.

individual and organizational goals

The idealized picture of those engaged in the industrial purchasing process is that of a group of men dedicated to the advancement of the profit position of their company. They seek to achieve this corporate goal by purchasing goods and services in such a way that the combination of product quality, price, and service received is an optimal one.

A less idealized picture is that which portrays the industrial buyer

---

[12] Other comprehensive models of interest have been developed by Alan R. Andreasen and Joseph Clawson. For articles describing these models, see Kassarjian and Robertson, *op. cit.*, pp. 498–510 and 511–25.

as a self-seeking individual who is not above accepting gifts or other considerations in exchange for favoring certain suppliers with orders for goods which may, or may not, best meet the needs of the firm. In actuality, the average industrial buyer is neither a calculating machine whose rationality is above question nor is he a totally selfish person always willing to subordinate the needs of the organization to his own. A more honest description is that of a human being who is trying to do a good job for the company but who is also interested in advancing his own career. Thus, the industrial buyer has two goals: to further the interests of his company and to further his own position within the organization.

Sometimes these goals overlap, while other times they may be in conflict. It has been suggested that the organizational-factors model developed in a political context by Thomas Hobbes offers a useful interpretation of the relationship between organizational goals and individual goals.[13] The Hobbesian view is that although each man is

Figure 3–6. Individual goals (*I*), group or organizational goals (*O*), and areas of goal mutuality (*M*) in three situations.

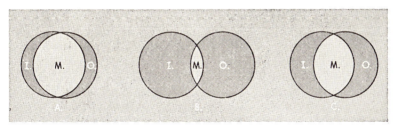

"instinctively" oriented toward preserving and enhancing his own well-being, fear of a "war of every man against every man" leads men to unite in a corporate body.[14]

Perhaps if the various blendings of goals were illustrated by a Venn diagram, the marketing implications of these goal relationships might become clearer. Such an attempt is made in Figure 3–6, which illustrates three situations. Situation A is one in which there is a high degree of overlap between individual goals and organizational goals. In situation B there is very little overlap. In situation C there is considerable overlap but still some areas where individual and group goals do not coincide.

---

[13] Philip Kotler, "Behavioral Models for Analyzing Buyers," *Journal of Marketing*, Vol. 29, No. 4 (October, 1965), pp. 44–45.

[14] Thomas Hobbes, *Leviathan*, 1651 (London: G. Routledge & Sons, Ltd., 1887).

In situation A there is a great deal of overlap between individual goals and organizational goals. In such a situation the use of rational appeals illustrating how the product will help in organizational goal achievement should receive a great deal of acceptance from purchasing personnel. Such is the case when individuals responsible for the buying decision perceive that the best way to achieve their personal ends is to seek attainment of organizational goals. Thus, promotional efforts which emphasize the congruence of goals should be most effective here. The seller's slogan in situation A might be, to paraphrase a rather famous quotation, "What is good for General Wickets Corporation is also good for its buyers."

In situation B there is very little goal overlap. This is not a desirable state of affairs from the standpoint of the buying organization. If the true nature of the goal relationship is perceived by sellers, then their promotional activity will be directed to stimulation of efforts by individuals to achieve their personal goals even at the expense of corporate well-being.

Situation C is a more normal one. There is a better balance between individual and organizational goals. The area of goal mutuality (M) is larger than the area of either segment I or O. Given this type of situation, the perceptive seller will depend heavily on rational product arguments but will supplement these appeals with others of a more emotional nature, aimed at the egos of the individuals involved in the buying process.

It must be recognized that goal overlap is a matter of degree. The type of product being purchased, the type of organization being considered, and the relative strength of individual drives to achieve specific goals influence the blend, in a given situation, of individual and organizational goals. Ability on the part of the seller to sense the blend correctly will enable him to develop a more effective promotional strategy. An appraisal of the relative importance to the individuals involved in the purchase process of attaining the two goals will indicate whether the promotional appeals should be based on rational product advantages or whether there is some opportunity to utilize some appeals to the self-interest of the individuals concerned.

stages in the buying process

The specific buying processes of individual firms or institutions vary widely. For example, no two companies seem to follow the same purchasing procedures. Indeed, within a given firm the purchasing processes appear to vary according to the kind of need being filled or the type of product being sought. In spite of this seeming diversity, investigation of the industrial buying process has indicated that it is, in reality, an orderly one consisting of several clearly defined steps or phases.[15]

A recent study has termed these steps in the industrial buying process "buyphases" and has suggested that for analytic purposes the buying process might be broken down into eight distinct stages which, although generally sequential, may occur concurrently one with the other. These "buyphases" are:

1. The anticipation or recognition of a problem (need) and the awareness that such a problem may be solved by a purchase.
2. The determination of the characteristics and quantity of the needed item.
3. The description of the characteristics and the quantity of the needed item.
4. The search for and qualification of potential sources.
5. The acquisition and analysis of proposals.
6. The evaluation of proposals and selection of suppliers.
7. The selection of an order routine.
8. Performance feedback and evaluation.[16]

Time element. The stages or "buyphases" in the procurement process may take a considerable length of time for their completion. In Figure 3–7 a period of almost four months elapses between recognition of need and delivery of the order. This rather long time was required, although the purchase was for a standard type of item which had been purchased many times in the past.

The term "straight rebuy" used in the caption for Figure 3–7 refers to a type of buying situation in which there is a recurring or continuing requirement which is handled on a routine basis. Other types of situations may be termed "modified rebuys" or "new tasks," and we shall talk about these a little later in this chapter.

multiple influence groups

Each buyphase of the industrial purchase process is the responsibility of several individuals performing different functions within the

---

[15] John H. Platten, Jr., *Scientific American* research study, *How Industry Buys.* Copyright © 1950, 1955, by Scientific American, Inc.

[16] Patrick J. Robinson, Charles W. Faris, and Yoram Wind, *Industrial Buying and Creative Marketing* (Boston: Allyn & Bacon, Inc., 1967), p. 19.

Figure 3-7. A decision network diagram of the procurement process (a straight rebuy: drills).

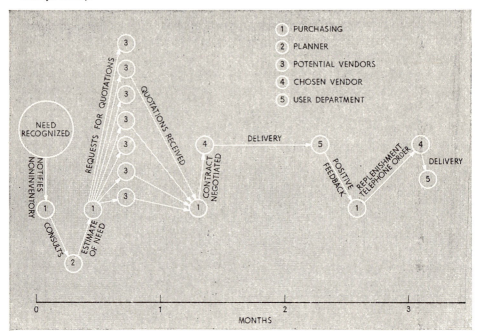

organization. Top management has routinely delegated authority to these persons to make the necessary decisions based on their evaluation of the pertinent factors.[17] Three aspects of the process which have been verified by the research findings of Platten are: (1) that top management rarely takes a direct hand in the buying process, (2) that few decisions are made by individuals and most decisions are group decisions, and (3) the composition of these groups characteristically changes from phase to phase.[18]

These groups of individuals involved in the purchase process are called "multiple-purchase influence groups." They are for the most part composed of middle-management people.[19] The major task of industrial marketers is to find out the composition of the multiple-in-

---

[17] Platten, *op. cit.*

[18] *Ibid.*

[19] "Who Makes the Purchasing Decision?" *Marketing Insights*, October 31, 1966), p. 16.

fluence group in a given company and at a specific point in time so that the correct type of promotional effort can be directed to the group members.

Platten's research, although done several years ago, is classic in that it shows clearly the changes which take place in the composition of the multiple-influence group in different phases of the buying process. His research, reported in Figure 3–8, also indicates that the composition of the group changes with respect to origin of need as well as with the type of product being sought.

The first table of Figure 3–8 shows the extent of participation by individuals representing specific functional areas at different stages in the purchase process for plant equipment. In most cases, top or operating management people are involved most heavily in the early buy-phases, especially that one which is involved with problem recognition. The engineers play a greater role in later buyphases, when it is necessary to specify the type of equipment which is most likely to fill the company's need. The purchasing people become most heavily involved in the latter stages of the purchase process, when it is necessary to make decisions pertaining to source qualification and selection.

Note, however, that in the initial buyphase for plant equipment the composition of the group may differ in a given company according to the origin of need. For example, as seen in column 1 of the first table of Figure 3–8, the participation of top management is heaviest when the purchase motive is to expand capacity. Operating management, on the other hand, is most heavily involved when the purchase motive is to replace old equipment. Given a motive involving a change in production process, it appears that the engineers take on a more important role.

The second table of Figure 3–8 illustrates how industry buys component parts. These are industrial goods which go to make up another product but which retain their physical identity. Note the lesser involvement of top and/or operating management in the earlier buyphases as compared with the extent of their involvement in the earlier phases of the purchase process for plant equipment.

It is generally easier to draw up specifications for component parts and to compare the performance of parts from various sources with respect to these specifications than to perform these tasks with plant equipment. Thus, the multiple-influence groups are composed of a greater proportion of engineering and purchasing personnel in the earlier buyphases than was true with major installations of plant equipment.

Figure 3–8. How industry buys plant equipment and component parts.

How industry buys plant equipment

In manufacturing industries personnel with these functions → participate in the percentages indicated at these steps in the development of a purchase.*	Top Manage-ment	Operating Manage-ment	Produc-tion Engineer-ing	Design and Develop-ment Engineer-ing	Main-tenance Engineer-ing	Research	Purchas-ing	Finance	Sales, Advertis-ing	Others in Com-pany	Others Outside Com-pany
Motive 1. Who is most likely to initiate project leading to new equipment purchase for:											
a) Replacement of old equipment?	16.7%	59.8%	22.1%	14.1%	34.2%	8.6%	4.8%	1.1%	0.5%	1.2%	0.8%
b) Expansion of capacity?	64.5	43.9	18.1	17.3	5.0	7.9	3.5	2.4	4.6	1.8	1.3
c) Change in process?	17.9	37.5	33.5	40.1	4.5	31.8	3.2	0.9	1.4	1.7	1.2
d) Production of new product?	41.8	25.8	20.2	40.5	2.6	40.0	3.1	2.0	11.5	1.4	1.3
Kind of Equipment 2. Who surveys alternatives and determines kind (not make) of equipment to be used?	10.1	37.1	38.5	45.8	14.9	17.9	6.6	0.5	0.2	2.1	0.8
3. Who specifies as to size, capacity, etc., of the equipment?	10.5	39.8	40.9	38.9	10.9	11.3	2.0	0.5	0.8	2.1	0.8
Make or Supplier† 4. Who surveys available makes or suppliers of the specified kind of equipment and chooses suppliers from whom to invite bids?	6.8	23.0	24.5	30.4	11.7	8.0	57.4	1.2	0.1	2.0	0.5
5. Who evaluates equipment offered by suppliers for their accord with specifications?	6.9	30.5	36.2	42.4	16.1	11.9	18.3	0.6	0.1	3.0	0.6
6. Who decides which supplier gets the order?	23.7	38.7	17.1	23.5	8.6	6.2	50.9	1.2	0.7	1.5	1.0

* Example: In industry generally, when it comes to specifying size and capacity of plant equipment, design and development engineers in 38.9% of the plants play more than an occasional role.
† Choice of make or supplier limited (due to company preferences or policy in setting up the specifications and characteristics required) to: one make, 11.4%; two makes, 11.8%; unlimited, 76.8%.

Source: From the *Scientific American* research study, *How Industry Buys*. Copyright © 1950, 1955 by Scientific American, Inc. All rights reserved.

How industry buys component parts

In manufacturing industries personnel with these functions → participate in the percentages indicated at these steps in the development of a purchase.*	Top Management	Operating Management	Production Engineering	Design and Development Engineering	Maintenance Engineering	Research	Purchasing	Finance	Sales, Advertising	Others in Company	Others Outside Company
Motive 1. Who is most likely to originate project leading to purchase of a component part:											
a) To take advantage of a price differential?	10.2%	24.6%	19.0%	25.0%	7.2%	9.8%	56.6%	2.0%	1.6%	2.3%	0.9%
b) As a result of change in design of an established product?	6.4	21.4	30.8	50.4	8.1	16.0	14.9	0.4	3.1	1.9	0.9
c) As a result of a change in production process?	5.5	30.1	48.6	35.4	5.7	15.6	9.0	—	0.5	2.0	1.0
d) For production of a new product?	15.0	23.6	26.2	52.5	4.0	31.3	7.8	0.2	4.3	1.8	1.3
Kind of Component Part 2. Who surveys alternatives and determines kind (not make) of component parts to be used?	5.3	17.7	29.8	60.9	7.7	22.6	10.2	0.2	0.9	2.0	0.8
3. Who specifies design and characteristics of the parts?	3.7	12.4	27.4	68.2	8.4	20.8	3.5	—	1.3	2.1	1.6
Make or Supplier† 4. Who surveys available makes or suppliers of the specified kind of component parts and chooses suppliers from whom to invite bids?	4.7	12.2	18.0	36.1	6.0	12.0	68.3	1.0	0.6	2.1	0.9
5. Who evaluates component parts submitted by suppliers for accord with specifications?	3.7	14.7	29.1	56.0	8.4	21.3	17.3	0.1	0.2	5.4	0.8
6. Who decides which supplier gets the order?	16.5	26.7	14.7	29.8	5.0	9.9	63.5	1.3	1.0	1.8	1.2

* Example: In manufacturing industries generally, projects leading to purchases of component parts to take advantage of a price differential are frequently initiated by design and development engineers in 25% of the plants.

† Choice of make or supplier limited (due to company preferences or policy in setting up the specifications and characteristics required) to: one make, 13.2%; two makes, 11.9%; unlimited, 74.9%.

Source: From the *Scientific American* research study, *How Industry Buys*. Copyright © 1950, 1955 by Scientific American, Inc. All rights reserved.

types of buying situations

Members of a multiple-purchase influence group at a given "buy-phase" may find that their decision-making process is a function of the type of buying situation with which they are involved. The degree of newness of the problem, the amount of information required before an acceptable solution can be found, and the extent to which alternative ways of solving the problem are considered, all go to make up or define a specific type of buying situation.

The terms "new task," "modified rebuy," and "straight rebuy" have been suggested as describing three distinct types of buying situations or "buyclasses."[20] The "new task," for example, describes a buying situation in which the problem encountered is a new one, information requirements are high, and the consideration of alternatives is very important.

Those situations characterized by an essentially recurring problem which has certain new aspects, by moderately high information requirements, and by limited importance of considering alternatives may be called "modified rebuys."

Finally, if the problem faced is not a new one, if information requirements are minimal, and if there is no consideration of alternatives, then the situation may be termed a "straight rebuy."

the search process

Having considered the impact of the buyphase, the origin of need, and the type of good being sought upon the composition of the multiple-purchase influence group and having noted briefly that the decision process may differ with respect to the nature of the buying situation, we now turn our attention to that part of the buying process known as the search procedure. The search which is conducted by those persons involved at a given buyphase may be for a specific type of good, for selection criteria, or for qualified sources of supply.[21] Figure 3–9 is a schematic representation of one buyer's search for the latter.

An examination of the figure reveals that once a stimulus is received, the buyer may search as many as six different areas in order to gain sufficient information to enable him to solve the problem of where to buy. The marketing implications of understanding the nature of the

---

[20] See Robinson, Faris, and Wind, *op. cit.* p. 25.

[21] See Frederick E. Webster, Jr. "Modeling the Industrial Buying Process," *Journal of Marketing Research,* Vol. 2, No. 4 (November, 1965) , p. 371.

Figure 3-9.　The process of a buyer's search for a source of supply.

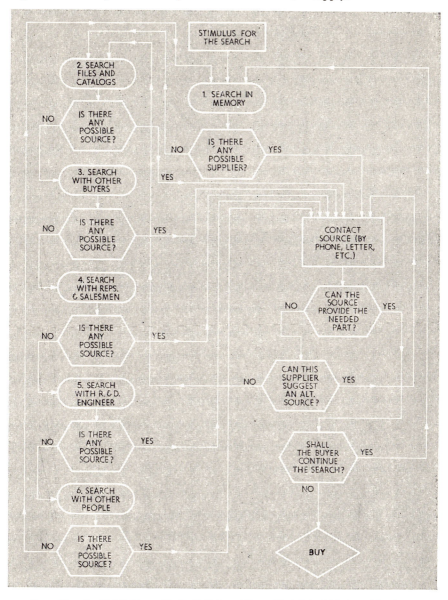

Source: From Patrick J. Robinson, Charles W. Faris, and Yoram Wind, *Industrial Buying and Creative Marketing*, p. 107. Copyright © 1967 by Allyn and Bacon, Inc., Boston. Reprinted by permission of the publisher and the Marketing Science institute.

search process are quite evident. Information input by a prospective seller in any of the six areas can direct the searcher to a specific answer. As there is no way of predicting the sequence of the buyer's search, the seller's best strategy is to make certain that information about his qualifications as a source is well dispersed among the areas most likely to be searched by the prospective buyer. The fact that not all of these areas can be reached by salesmen means that the promotional mix must include advertising, direct mail, and other methods of nonpersonal sales promotion including the use of catalogs.

Search with learning. Given a sequence of searches by the same buyer (or group of buyers) for a source to supply goods to fill a recurring need, one would expect that with time the search process would become more efficient. Memory would lead the prospective buyer to a source which had performed well in the past. If prior experience with a source had been less than satisfactory, then memory would enable the buyer to start the search process with the most effective route used last time. Figure 3–10 illustrates such a search when learning from past experience is involved.

The Howard model of consumer behavior mentioned earlier in this chapter is a stimulus-response model involving learning. By substituting the concept of source for that of product, the Howard model becomes readily applicable to an industrial buying situation. One value of looking at the industrial buying process in terms of a learning model is that the implications of the various buyclasses are readily seen.

For example, the straight rebuy which generally represents the bulk of a firm's buying transactions is characterized by behavior which is closely akin to what Howard has termed routine response behavior (RRB). In this type of buying situation a great deal of learning has occurred, very little if any searching is required, and the buyer's response to a need stimulus is largely automatic. The purchasing department has a "list" of approved suppliers and orders are routinely placed with these firms when needs arise. In many cases straight buys are made by computers which track stock levels or reorder points.

The modified rebuy situation is one in which changes have taken place with respect to the buyer's requirements and/or some aspect of the nature of supply. Instead of a recurring problem with a "learned" solution, the buyer is faced with the need to have more information, to consider alternative solutions to his problem, and to conduct a search in order to find the best way of solving the problem at hand. Again we

Figure 3–10.   A buyer's search process when learning is involved.

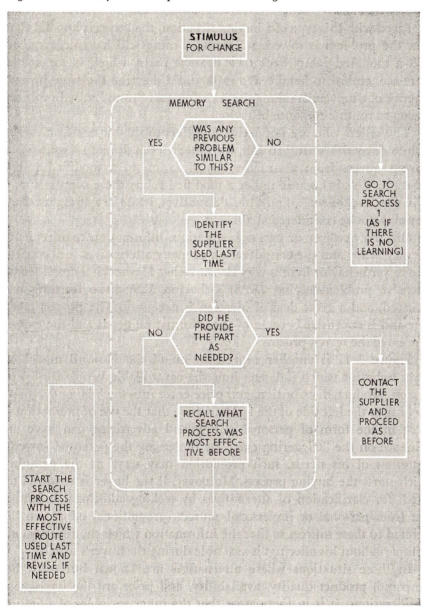

Source: From Patrick J. Robinson, Charles W. Faris, and Yoram Wind, *Industrial Buying and Creative Marketing*, p. 107. Copyright © 1967 by Allyn and Bacon, Inc., Boston. Reprinted by permission of the publisher and the Marketing Science Institute.

see a parallel with what Howard has termed limited problem-solving (LPS) behavior.

Faced with this type of a buying situation, the buyer is hopeful that once the problem is solved, sufficient learning will have occurred to shift a modified rebuy back to a straight rebuy which is easier and more economical to handle. Howard would describe the same process in terms of a movement along the learning curve from limited problem solving to routine response behavior.

The sellers who are not active suppliers to the buyer's firm might wish to delay this shift.[22] In fact, they might even develop a strategy of moving buyers from a straight buy situation to a modified rebuy situation. This is because under a modified rebuy these suppliers may be in the "evoked set" of possible alternatives, while in a straight rebuy they may not be considered at all.

Given a new-buy or new-task situation, information requirements are very heavy and the consideration of many alternatives is necessary. The buyer behavior here is very close to what Howard has described as extensive problem-solving (EPS) behavior. Very little learning has occurred, and a great deal of ideation is necessary. The process takes time and is expensive because of the information needs and the extensiveness of the search process.

Figure 3–11 is another representation of the Howard model of buyer behavior which indicates how the controllable variables of promotion, product, distribution, and price enter into the buying decision. Looking at the left side of the figure, we see that the use of promotional effort in the form of personal selling and advertising can have an influence on the "triggering cue." By increasing the potential buyer's awareness of his needs, such promotion may serve as the stimulus which starts the buying process. Moreover, if the buyer is required to search for clarification of alternatives by seeking additional information from personal or impersonal sources, promotional effort can be directed to these sources so that the information which the seller wants to impart about his offerings is available during the buyer's search.

In those situations where alternatives are known but must be compared, product quality, availability, and price are the important considerations. It is in these areas that the other variables of product design, distribution strategy, and pricing play their roles, as is seen at the bottom of Figure 3–11.

<hr>

[22] *Ibid.* p. 28.

Figure 3–11. Points of impact of marketing plan (Howard model).

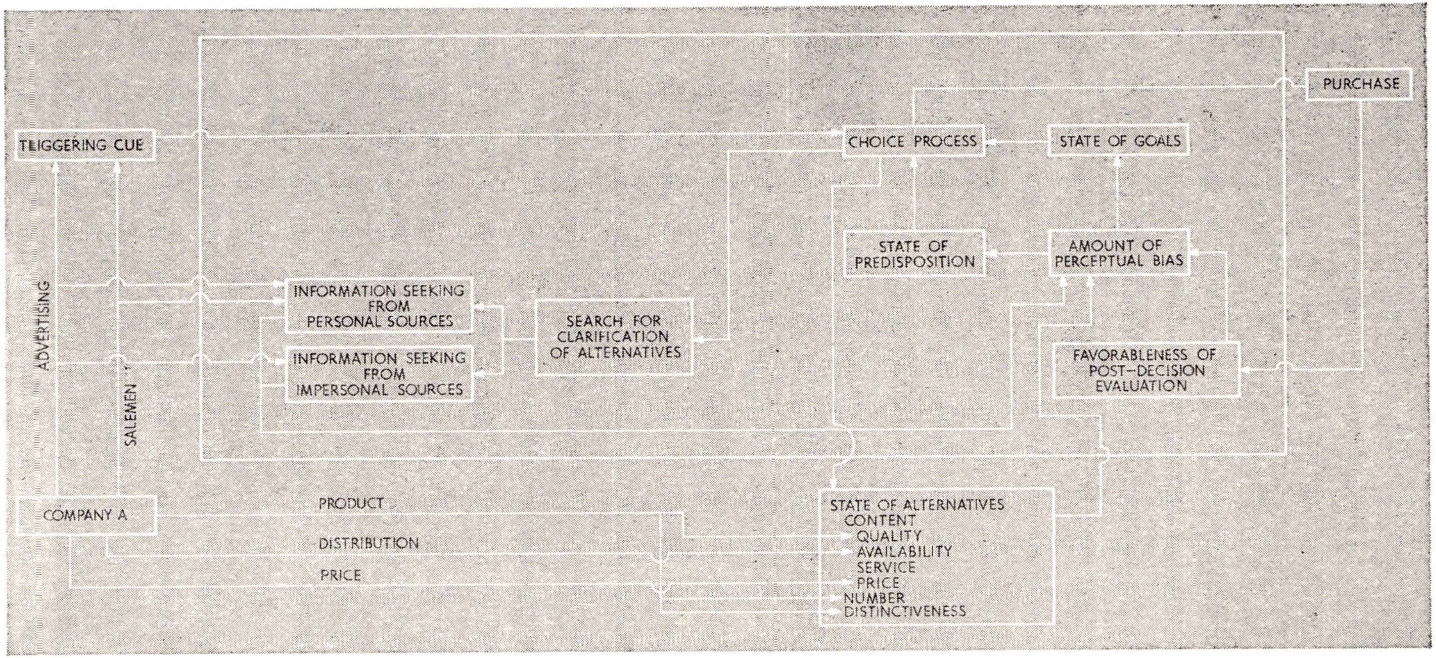

Source: John A. Howard, *Marketing Management: Analysis and Planning* (rev. ed.; Homewood, Ill.: Richard D. Irwin, Inc., 1963), p. 104.

conclusion

Knowledge of the buying process provides insight as to where promotional effort should be directed with respect to different *phases* of the buying process. The recognition that decision making is carried on by groups of changing composition is a prerequisite to the design of an effective promotional strategy.

Buying decisions also differ with respect to the *kind* of buying situation faced. The amount of information needed by a buyer, the number of alternatives to be considered, and the extent of the search process all influence whether the buyer's behavior will be oriented toward a routine response or toward what has been termed limited or extensive problem-solving behavior.

Finally, an understanding of the nature of the buying process, be it in the industrial or consumer market, is essential to the development of an effective marketing strategy. The controllable variables of product, distribution, advertising, personal selling, and price, which were mentioned in Chapter 1, must be blended together in such a way that the product attributes, including quality, availability, and price, place it in competition with other alternatives. In addition, the promotional strategy must be designed to inform potential buyers of the product's existence and to persuade them to buy.

questions

1. Let us assume that an upper-middle class family is considering the purchase of either a color television set (a three-year old black and white set is already in use) or a motorboat of approximately the same price. Suppose that you are the college-age son of this family.

   a) Following Morgan's model, work out your relative preference for both the color TV set and the motorboat. Consider (1) needs which would be satisfied by each, (2) incentive values of the alternative purchases, (3) expectations as to the outcome for each one. Which one would you prefer?

   b) In addition to the college-age son, the family includes a 16-year-old daughter, the wife (age 39), and the husband (age 43). You are aware that the daughter and the mother prefer the color TV set, while the father prefers the boat. Assume that the family has gathered to talk over the alternatives in the hope of reaching a buying decision. Taking the role of the son again, (1) what factors would influence the strength of your attempts to get the others to accept the product you prefer? (2) Would such a discussion be likely to modify your own preferences and attitudes? (3) What influences would probably lead to the final decision? (4) Would a marketing executive be able to predict the family's decision using Morgan's model? Why or why not?

2. Refer to the DuPont model of consumer behavior.

    a) What possible effects might advertising have upon a decision to buy the DuPont brand (of Lucite paint, let us assume).

    b) Suggest briefly how each of these possible effects might be measured in field experiments.

    c) Does this model explain why people choose DuPont Lucite paint? If not, what kind of research might be needed to get such information?

3. *a)* According to Howard, how is learning measured?

    b) Why is the learning curve shown in Figure 3–5 divided into three phases?

4. How does buying behavior vary as between extensive problem solving, limited problem solving, and routine response behavior?

5. What is the effect of a change in one of the exogenous variables upon the internal state of the buyer, and thus upon his buying decisions, in these examples:

    a) An increase in salary from $10,000 to $15,000 received by a man in his late 20's, married for two years, with no children.

    b) The introduction of a new product such as a Mustang automobile into the market, other exogenous factors remaining the same.

6. At what point in the Howard model (Figure 3–4) may executives apply stimuli through the marketing plan used? In what ways might such stimuli influence the consumer's buying behavior?

7. Why should the marketing plan be adapted to the amount of experience which the consumer has had with the brand? In answering, relate your response to (*a*) users of Kent cigarettes and (*b*) prospective buyers of the Polaroid color camera.

8. Of what value, if any, is a knowledge of the goals of industrial buyers in the formulation of marketing strategy for a line of industrial goods?

9. What is meant by a multiple purchase influence group? Under what circumstances may the composition of such a group change? Why is the ability to identify the membership of the relevant group so important to an industrial marketer?

10. What assumptions might be made about the composition of multiple-purchase influence groups concerned with buying major plant equipment as contrasted with groups concerned with the purchase of component parts?

11. How might different types of buying situations be contrasted in terms of the search process required? Explain the implications of search with learning for a seller of a "new" type of industrial product.

12. What is meant by the terms: new task, modified rebuy, and straight rebuy? Relate these concepts to Howard's model of buyer behavior.
13. Of what help is a model of buyer behavior in developing a marketing strategy for selling to the industrial market? What is required to adapt a consumer market model to an industrial market model?

chapter 4

demand
forecasting

Development of an effective marketing program requires (1) a clear recognition of market opportunities, (2) establishment of specific goals based on those opportunities, and (3) development of a marketing strategy to achieve these goals. Chapters 2 and 3 were concerned with buyer behavior. Such knowledge is essential to both the recognition of market opportunities and to the formulation of marketing strategy. A study of buyer behavior is not sufficient, however, to the task of setting clear-cut, specific marketing goals. These should be in quantitative terms, and performance in relation to them should be measurable. Demand forecasting is the process of gathering quantitative information about the market for use in setting marketing goals.

Demand as seen from the vantage point of the firm has been defined as "a schedule showing the various amounts of any product which customers are willing and able to purchase at different prices during some stated period of time."[1] Influences on quantity demanded at a given price are varied and include certain factors beyond the control of management (see Figure 1–3, page 7). The marketing strategy variables relating to product, distribution, promotion, and price are demand-influencing factors under the control of management. These are the elements which are blended to achieve the goals which management has agreed upon.

Because the influences on demand, especially the uncontrollable ones, change over time, demand is a highly dynamic variable. Any marketing strategy that looks beyond the immediate moment must be

---

[1] Robert J. Holloway and Robert S. Hancock, *Marketing in a Changing Environment* (New York: John Wiley & Sons, Inc., 1968), p. 102.

based on a prediction of future demand. A marketing manager has no choice but to forecast demand, regardless of how clouded the future and difficult the task. Every move he makes in planning and executing marketing strategy involves an implicit assumption about the quantitative aspects of demand. For example, a decision to launch a new product assumes that future demand will be adequate to support profitable operations; a decision to enlarge a sales force implicitly assumes a demand adequate to support the increased level of expenditure. If demand is assumed to be lower than it really is, insufficient resources will be utilized to cultivate it, and profit opportunities will be lost. Thus, demand forecasting is an essential prerequisite to effective planning of marketing operations.

Companies plan for both the short and the long run. However, the planning process is quite a different thing when the time period is 3, 6, or 12 months forward as compared to when it is 3, 5, or 10 years into the future. So it is with the forecasting task. Short-term plans require short-term forecasts, and these are generally concerned with estimates of market potential and with development of specific sales forecasts for the industry and the firm. Long-term plans include a more general statement of goals. These are usually based on marketing opportunities which are expected to derive from basic changes in the market and from the way these changes will affect industry demand in the longer run.

Because the marketing plan embodies statements of general marketing strategy as well as specific assignments of tasks to individual departments and to single individuals, many goals must be specified in the plan. Included must be a statement of overall goals for the company, marketing goals for guidance of the total marketing effort, subgoals for different departments and functions within the total marketing operation, and goals which can be assigned to specific persons to guide their individual efforts. Marketing goals must be set by products, by geographical or other marketing segments, and for each salesman representing the company in the market. Demand forecasting provides the information needed to set this myriad of goals. The most basic types of information it provides for this purpose are three in number: (1) a statement of total industry demand in units and/or in dollars; (2) a statement of demand available to the individual company in units and/or in dollars; and (3) a statement of the distribution of this demand over the market.

basic approaches to demand forecasting

There are two basic approaches to demand forecasting, the "top-down" method and the "buildup" method.[2] The top-down method is a deductive approach to forecasting, proceeding from general demand estimates to demand estimates for small market segments. It begins with a forecast of business conditions, derives therefrom a forecast of industry demand, and then breaks this forecast down to arrive at an estimate of demand for the individual company and for each segment of its total market.

In contrast, the buildup method is an inductive approach to forecasting, beginning with demand estimates for small segments of the market and ending with demand estimates for the total market served by a company or an industry. Individual market segments are studied separately, demand estimates are made for each, and then total demand is arrived at by the process of addition. An overall comparison of

Figure 4–1. Steps in demand forecasting.

Top-down Method

1. Forecast of business conditions.
2. Determination of market potential.
3. Determination of sales potential.
4. Determination of preliminary sales forecast.
5. Measurement of geographical distribution of demand.
6. Determination of sales quotas.
7. Determination of final sales forecast.

Buildup Method

1. Division of total market into market segments.
2. Measurement of demand in individual market segments.
3. Summing of demand by market segments to arrive at total demand.

the two approaches is shown in Figure 4–1. The terminology used in the listing of steps for the top-down approach will be foreign to most students at this point, but will be explained as this method is described.

top-down method of demand forecasting

Variation in the specific steps involved in the top-down approach are common. There is no one set of steps that is right, with all others being wrong. Nevertheless, the top-down approach will generally fol-

---

[2] Demand forecasting terminology is very loose. The top-down method is also known as the "overall forecast approach," the "index method," and the "breakdown method." The buildup method is also known as the "individual unit approach," the "direct evaluation method," and the "bottom-up" method.

low somewhat along the lines of Figure 4–1. These steps will now be discussed in order.

Forecast of business conditions. What can be expected in terms of sales for most products is a function of the general state of the economy. When general levels of employment and income rise, people buy and consume more goods and services. The purchase of luxury products may fluctuate widely with swings in business conditions; the fluctuations for basic staples may be very little. The assumption implicit in beginning the top-down method with an economic forecast is that there exists a known relationship between changes in business conditions and changes in demand for a given type of product. Regression analysis can be used to determine the degree of correlation that existed in the past between, say, fluctuations in levels of income and the demand for automobiles. If this relationship between levels of income and automobile purchases is expected to continue, then a forecast of future income levels has a high relevance to the expected demand for automobiles.

The character of the economic forecast that is made will depend on the product under consideration. Levels of employment and income may be most significant for automotive demand, but expected new home construction and number of family formations may be more relevant to expected demand for appliances. Expected demand for agricultural equipment will depend more on the outlook for agriculture than on the outlook for business conditions generally. A general economic forecast will include these and other components of total economic activity. However, a forecast of the peculiarly relevant components is most useful in demand forecasting.

Economists employ many different approaches to economic forecasting. Some are highly sophisticated but none, unfortunately, is fully reliable. The most common methods used for this purpose will be discussed later in this chapter.

Market potential. Market potential is "the capacity of a market to absorb a product or a group of products of an industry in a specified period of time."[3] It is, for example, the capacity of the market to absorb the output of the automotive industry during a given model year. It is an *industry-market* concept in contrast to the term "sales potential," which relates to the capacity of a market to absorb the output of a given firm. Sales potential will be discussed separately.

If a forecast of business conditions which includes those factors causally related to past sales of a given industry has been made, derivation of the market potential figure is, in theory, a simple task.

---

[3] K. R. Davis and F. E. Webster, Jr., *Sales Force Management* (New York: Ronald Press Co., 1968), p. 258.

For example, if observation of past relationships reveals that each 10 percent increase in disposable income has consistently produced a 10 percent increase in the demand for automobiles, then it is reasonable to conclude that a forecasted 5 percent change in disposable income would have a 5 percent effect on the demand for automobiles. Unfortunately, in the real world things are not this simple. Usually there are many economic factors which influence demand for a given industry and multiple-correlation analysis must be used to discover and weight them. Past relationships often do not extend into the future. Subjective factors, such as the appeal or lack thereof of new car styles muddy the waters. Hence, deriving market potential from a forecast of economic conditions is not a simple mechanical process, but one involving much expert judgment. The high order of judgment needed is all too scarce among demand forecasters.

Sales potential. Sales potential is the capacity of a market to absorb the output of a given firm. It is its share of the market potential. A good starting point in determining sales potential is a firm's past share of total industry sales. If over an extended period of years it has consistently sold 25 percent of total industry sales, it would be reasonable to conclude, in the absence of additional information, that its most probable sales potential for the year ahead is 25 percent of market potential. If there is an increasing or decreasing trend in its market share, this should be taken into account. Having started with the bench mark of past market share, all available information which might cause that share to change should be analyzed. If a firm's competitors are expected to introduce new models of their products but they themselves have no such plans, this may suggest that a decline in market share be anticipated. Conversely, if a company plans to increase advertising in relation to the rest of the industry, an increase in market share may be expected. Forecasting the effect on a company's sales of the firm's own planned actions and of the actions of other firms again involves much subjective judgment.

Preliminary sales forecast. It is not uncommon for demand forecasters to speak of sales potential and the sales forecast as if they were synonymous. In practice, they sometimes are equal quantitatively, but conceptually they are very different things. Sales potential refers to the capacity of a market to purchase a product, while the sales forecast is the sales goal decided upon. If we set as our sales target all potential sales available to us, the two values will be equal. However, there are reasons why in many cases the sales forecast may be set below potential demand. It may be considered too costly to strive for all potential sales. Profits may actually be enhanced if the sales target is set at a lower level if some potential sales can only be achieved at a marginal cost in excess of marginal revenue. An anticipated labor strike may cause an expectation of a limitation on production which makes it prudent to set a sales forecast figure below the sales potential. Limitations of other resources, such as sales manpower, promotional funds, and so on, may have the same effect.

A sales forecast is a function of more things than sales potential. It is a resultant of the opportunity for sales, the amount and kind of resources committed to exploit this sales opportunity, and the effectiveness with which these resources are employed. If there are no significant forces constraining the last two of these factors, then the sales forecast can be equal to sales potential. If such constraints do exist, it might well be less than potential.

The determination of what is called a preliminary sales forecast in Figure 4–1 is as far as some companies go in use of the top-down approach to sales forecasting. This is acceptable for some purposes. For example, it is sufficient for setting total production volume and determining overall expenditures on personal selling, advertising, and other major components of marketing strategy. It is not sufficient to the allocation problems of marketing, however. The sales forecast must be broken down by market segments to permit the optimal allocation of resources over the total market.

Use of the term "preliminary market forecast" while at the same time suggesting that some firms accept this forecast as their "final" marketing goal is undoubtedly confusing. The explanation lies in the fact that if a company goes no further than this in the demand forecasting process, this is the best sales goal they have. However, if they go on to the subsequent steps in Figure 4–1, breaking down the total demand by market segments and then converting these demand figures to sales quotas, they are almost inevitably forced to revise (and improve) their sales forecast. This will become clear as these next steps in the top-down method of forecasting are described.

Geographical distribution of sales. Demand for a company's product is rarely uniform throughout the total market. Generally, it is distributed very unevenly, depending on how the demand-causing forces for the product are distributed over the market. If automobile demand is in part a function of disposable income, the distribution of automobile demand over the market will be at least partially correlated with the distribution of disposable income. If demand varies with age, the distribution of demand will vary with the age makeup of the population by geographical areas.

A company must know how demand is spatially distributed in order to allocate its salesmen to different territories, to direct its advertising and sales promotion, and to locate its inventories. It must select wholesalers and retailers in accordance with the amount of demand in the areas served by these institutions. In order to gain this needed information, the demand forecaster must employ some means to break down the total sales forecast by geographical areas.

In the top-down approach the sales forecast (or possibly the sales potential or market potential) is broken down geographically by application of an index. There is an infinite number of indexes which might be used for this purpose, ranging from very simple single-factor indexes to highly involved multiple-factor indexes. The index chosen should reflect the demand-causing factors for the product under consideration. Regression analysis should be used to determine what these factors are. No attempt will be made here to describe all the indexes available, but attention will be focused on several major types of indexes. These will be classified, for our purposes only, into two categories: (1) market factors indexes, and (2) past sales indexes.

Market factors indexes. These are indexes in which the variables are factors in the market which produce demand for goods and services. A very simple market factors index, for example, might be composed of population data. The total population in the United States would be broken down into population of each county as a percentage of the total population. If a given county had a population of 2 million and the total U.S. population is 200 million, the index factor for that county would be 1 percent. Such an index would be useful in determining the distribution of demand for a product like table salt. If salt consumption per capita is relatively constant, then the demand for table salt could be expected to be distributed over the market in accordance with the distribution of the population. Other single-factor indexes of this sort might be such things as age, income, urban population, and rural population. Each of these can be expressed in an index as a percentage of a total universe accounted for by a particular market segment.

The most widely used market factors indexes are those published by *Sales Management* magazine (see Figure 4–2). The *Sales Management Survey of Buying Power*, published annually, includes a population index, an income index, a retail sales index, and a "buying power" index. The latter index is a composite of the first three, with income rated 5, retail sales 3, and population 2. The buying power index is included as a convenience because of its applicability to a

Figure 4–2

MICHIGAN		POPULATION ESTIMATES, 12/31/67			EFFECTIVE BUYING INCOME, ESTIMATES, 1967			% Hslds. by Cash Income Groups: (A) $0–2,999; (B) $3,000–4,999; (C) $5,000–7,999; (D) $8,000–9,999; (E) $10,000 and Over					RETAIL SALES—ESTIMATES, 1967							
COUNTIES CITIES (continued)	Met. Area Code	Total (thousands)	% of U.S.A.	Households (thousands)	Net Dollars (000)	% of U.S.A.	Per Hsld.	A	B	C	D	E	Total Retail Sales ($000)	% of U.S.A.	Food ($000)	General Mdse. ($000)	Furn.-House.-Appl. ($000)	Automotive ($000)	Drug ($000)	Buying Power
Pontiac		86.1	.0432	24.7	248,382	.0462	10,056	12.7	10.2	29.1	17.7	30.3	202,597	.0651	37,919	38,455	10,415	59,467	6,836	.0513
Rochester		6.2	.0031	2.0	24,518	.0046	12,259	10.0	7.3	21.3	18.5	42.9	27,394	.0088	6,441	990	880	10,528	967	.0056
Royal Oak		95.1	.0477	27.3	359,086	.0668	13,153	6.0	5.0	17.7	18.7	52.6	175,766	0564	31,016	18,279	14,894	53,934	8,658	.0599
Southfield		47.2	.0237	13.4	203,064	.0378	15,154	5.1	5.4	17.9	16.2	55.4	268,932	.0864	20,462	175,811	5,928	6,398	4,943	.0496
Oceana		16.2	.0081	4.7	38,894	.0073	8,275	23.7	13.2	23.0	15.7	24.4	24,018	.0077	7,086	841	366	4,975	649	.0076
Ogemaw		9.1	.0046	2.8	19,069	.0035	6,810	31.8	18.5	23.8	10.6	15.3	17,423	.0056	4,889	1,325	257	3,949	707	.0043
Ontonagon		10.7	.0054	3.1	19,958	.0037	6,438	27.6	16.3	33.1	13.4	9.6	11,329	.0036	3,727	216	494	1,917	253	.0040
Osceola		14.3	.0071	4.2	30,652	.0058	7,298	27.4	15.9	29.2	12.2	15.3	18,630	.0060	5,309	1,050	474	2,542	675	.0061
Oscoda		3.8	.0019	1.2	8,057	.0015	6,714	31.5	14.3	25.3	11.6	17.3	5,853	.0019	1,554	83	35	785	152	.0017
Otsego		9.0	.0046	2.6	19,754	.0036	7,598	21.7	15.3	31.8	14.3	16.9	23,425	.0075	5,193	772	666	3,160	385	.0050
Ottawa	103	113.3	.0569	31.9	300,441	.0560	9,418	13.6	10.3	31.7	18.6	25.8	144,261	.0463	34,250	12,536	7,433	33,769	4,582	.0533
Holland		26.2	.0132	7.8	74,589	.0139	9,563	14.7	10.9	29.7	18.3	26.4	74,230	.0239	17,517	7,949	4,256	21,543	2,362	.0168
Presque Isle		12.6	.0063	3.5	29,766	.0055	8,505	22.2	13.9	25.7	15.7	22.5	14,610	.0047	4,716	319	369	3,359	489	.0054
Roscommon		7.6	.0038	2.5	18,118	.0034	7,247	29.6	15.2	23.2	12.7	19.3	20,416	.0066	6,078	980	399	2,477	1,010	.0044
Saginaw	230	213.8	.1073	59.9	569,880	.1060	9,514	15.5	10.0	29.4	17.5	27.6	344,137	.1104	77,287	55,107	19,918	68,567	13,040	.1076
Saginaw		103.6	.0520	30.5	276,761	.0515	9,074	17.8	10.4	29.3	16.3	26.2	196,957	.0632	36,464	31,950	12,254	45,089	7,963	.0551
St. Clair	208	113.2	.0568	33.6	298,650	.0556	8,888	20.4	11.8	24.0	16.9	26.9	172,653	.0554	41,155	31,395	7,656	33,481	4,916	.0558
Port Huron		36.9	.0185	11.8	107,176	.0199	9,083	21.1	11.2	22.7	16.4	28.6	88,482	.0284	18,269	19,652	5,527	18,422	2,516	.0222
St. Joseph		43.8	.0220	13.8	119,976	.0224	8,694	19.8	13.0	26.7	15.1	25.4	73,863	.0237	18,886	6,075	3,600	15,955	2,149	.0227
Sanilac		33.5	.0168	9.9	73,926	.0137	7,467	26.0	17.9	27.0	11.9	17.2	45,072	.0145	10,577	1,783	1,974	9,552	1,489	.0146
Schoolcraft		7.8	.0039	2.3	13,482	.0025	5,862	29.9	19.0	32.8	10.3	8.0	11,389	.0037	2,994	450	363	1,270	542	.0031
Shiawassee		59.0	.0296	17.4	158,801	.0296	9,126	17.5	11.1	27.8	16.3	27.3	87,213	.0280	18,916	10,938	4,281	21,285	2,789	.0291
Owosso		18.1	.0091	5.7	53,799	.0100	9,438	19.1	9.4	25.2	17.0	29.3	46,829	.0150	10,718	8,405	2,969	10,868	1,811	.0113
Tuscola		45.9	.0231	12.8	109,175	.0203	8,529	21.3	14.9	30.1	13.1	20.6	56,020	.0179	14,774	2,831	1,602	12,474	1,685	.0202
Van Buren		53.2	.0267	16.6	129,206	.0241	7,783	24.6	14.0	27.2	14.3	19.9	68,880	.0222	20,415	2,605	2,503	15,315	2,538	.0240
Washtenaw	14	204.0	.1024	57.0	723,430	.1346	12,692	14.4	9.3	19.5	15.6	41.2	374,037	.1200	80,717	42,760	23,679	77,850	16,149	.1238
Ann Arbor		89.5	.0449	26.6	362,036	.0674	13,610	17.1	9.8	18.1	13.0	42.0	218,197	.0700	42,633	31,558	14,217	36,156	11,058	.0637
Ypsilanti		24.0	.0120	6.9	75,574	.0141	10,953	17.1	11.8	21.2	15.0	34.9	70,873	.0227	15,153	6,913	5,604	20,558	2,648	.0163
Wayne	75	2,713.8	1.3623	799.5	8,729,367	1.6249	10,919	12.1	9.5	24.2	17.5	36.7	4,667,484	1.4982	1,006,407	934,236	199,350	1,018,452	213,032	1.5344
Allen Park		43.2	.0217	11.1	103,796	.0193	9,351	19.6	11.8	25.2	14.6	28.8	50,793	.0163	24,492	9,542	2,014	331	2,990	.0189
Dearborn		117.2	.0588	36.1	485,723	.0904	13,455	7.2	6.6	18.2	16.4	51.6	280,445	.0900	52,063	52.565	20,212	63,819	11,466	.0840

Source: © 1968, *Sales Management Survey of Buying Power;* further reproduction is forbidden.

broad range of popularly priced goods. The demand forecaster can use any one of these indexes that regression analysis reveals is appropriate. He can combine them, using suitable weights, to form new indexes. If none of these indexes fits his needs, there are many others to choose from.

Past sales indexes. The distribution of past sales of a firm or an industry over the market are sometimes used as indicators of the distribution of demand that can be expected in the future. In theory, this approach is unsound. Past sales indicate what has been achieved, but not necessarily the opportunities of the future. Used without judgment, ludicrous conclusions can be drawn. For example, zero sales of television sets in an area because no television station served that area in the past is not indicative of sales opportunities once a station has been established. Also, the sales of a single firm may be very poorly correlated with true sales opportunities. They reflect how the company distributed its marketing efforts in the past, and if they were poorly distributed in relation to potential, past sales may not have reflected the actual distribution of potential demand.

Past industry sales also may not have been distributed in direct proportion to the distribution of potential demand, but maldistribution is less likely than for a single firm's sales. In the case of basic staples, such as bread and toothpaste, it is likely that past sales opportunities have been reasonably fully exploited over the many years such products have been on the market. Hence, past industry sales for such products are widely used as an index of potential demand. This is probably a sufficiently close approximation in such cases, and better data are hard to find.

Past sales of a given type of product, appliances for example, do indicate the opportunity for replacement demand. As a product matures and sales are more and more for replacement, past sales become an increasingly valuable index. If brand loyalty is strong, past sales of a single company are useful in estimating the market share it can expect. Past sales of *another* product may be indicative of sales opportunities for a given firm's product. A most obvious case is that past sales of automobiles indicate sales opportunities for automotive parts. Past sales of cameras create opportunities for the sale of film. Such relationships make past sale data very useful in estimating the geographical distribution of demand, but they should always be used with caution. In a dynamic market the past can never fully foretell the future.

Sales quotas. A sales quota is a sales goal for a segment of the total market. It is not necessarily identical with the sales potential for that market segment as revealed by application of an index of relative potential demand. The sales quota may be set below 100 percent of potential for a variety of reasons. Perhaps a firm has lost its salesman in a given territory and substantial time is required to train a replacement. Perhaps wholesale and retail dealers have gone over to a competitor. Both these events might cause a quota to be set below full potential. Each territorial potential figure must be carefully evaluated, and realistic goals, reflecting not only potential demand but the commitment of a firm's resources, must be established.

Quotas, once set, are widely used as standards for measurement of performance. Salesmen are commonly judged on the basis of performance against assigned quotas, and often their compensation is tied to such performance. Quotas are the basis for all allocation decisions in the marketing planning process and can be used as standards of performance for many marketing activities.

Revision of sales forecast. The whole must equal the sum of its parts; the sales forecast must equal the sum of territorial quotas. If quotas deviate from territorial potential figures derived by application of an index, the company's total sales forecast must be revised to reflect this fact. In a very real sense, this is a way of saying that an accurate forecast of sales depends on an objective and painstaking evaluation of each segment of a firm's total market.

Top-down method—hypothetical illustration. As both a summary of the top-down method of sales forecasting and for the purpose of further clarification, the following hypothetical illustration is presented.

I. *Basic assumptions:* Existence of an observed and high correlation between demand for product X and the level of gross national product.

Year	GNP (Billions of $)	Percent Increase
1958	447.3	
1959	483.7	8.1
1960	503.8	4.2
1961	520.1	3.2
1962	560.3	7.7
1963	590.5	5.4
1964	632.4	7.1
1965	683.9	8.1
1966	743.3	8.7
1967	785.0	5.6
1968	832.0*	6.0
1969	882.0†	6.0

* Estimated.
† Forecast.

II. *Market potential*
A. 1968 sales are $800 million.
B. Assumption: Historical relationship between sales and GNP such that sales increase for product X at two thirds of the rate of GNP. Expected that this relationship will hold for coming year.
C. Increase in GNP for 1969 forecasted at 6 percent.
D. Increase in sales of product X for 1969 forecasted at 4 percent.
E. Market potential, 1969 = $832 million.

III. *Sales potential*
A. Company A accounted for 39 percent of sales of product X in 1968.
B. Company A's share of market for product X has been increasing at average rate of 1 percent per year in recent years. Expect rise to 40 percent in 1969.
C. Sales potential for Company A, 1969 = $332.8 million.

IV. *Preliminary sales forecast*
A. Company A foresees no limitation on devoting resources necessary to achieve sales equal to full potential at this point in the demand forecasting process.
B. Sales forecast for Company A, 1969 = $332.8 million.

V. *Geographical distribution of demand* (illustrated for County B).
A. Company A's sales break down geographically in accordance with distribution of population, income, and urbanization.
B. Relative importance of these three factors (as determined by multiple correlation) are:

> Population 0.50
> Income 0.30
> Urbanization 0.20

C. County B has, as a percentage of Company A's total market:

> 1 percent of population
> 2 percent of income
> 2.5 percent of urban population

D. Then:

> Population   = 0.01 × .50 = 0.005
> Income   = 0.02 × .30 = 0.006
> Urbanization = 0.025 × .20 = 0.005
> Index value, County B = 0.016

E. Territorial potential demand, County B:

> 0.016 × $332.8 = $5,324,800

VI. *Sales quota*
   A. Unemployment rate rises in County B because of strike in major local industry. Expected to reduce demand for product X by 10 percent.
   B. Sales quota for County B:

$$0.90 \times \$5,324,800 = \$4,792,320$$

VII. *Revised sales forecast*
   A. Assume full potential sales can be realized in all markets except County B.
   B. Revised sales forecast = $332,267,520

buildup method of demand forecasting

The top-down method of demand forecasting is the most widely used method of setting marketing goals. However, it has several basic limitations which restrict its application. In order for it to be an effective forecasting tool, three conditions must be met.

1. There must be an observed correlation between forecastable economic variables and the quantity demanded of a given product.
2. This observed past relationship must be expected to continue into the future.
3. There must be a means available to break down total expected sales to expected sales for segments of the total market.

The first of these conditions is not present when forecasting demand for new products. Because the product has not before been on the market, no correlation can be observed between its sales and economic conditions. Intuition may suggest that certain relationships will hold, but there can be no empirical evidence in support of such a view.

There is always the chance that observed past relationships between economic variables and product demand will not hold into the future. Consumers continually change their patterns of behavior and come under the influence of different forces. When products change greatly in styling or other features, the assumption that past relationships will continue is particularly risky.

If a forecast of total sales cannot be broken down to reveal relative potential demand by market segments, there is no good basis for allocating marketing effort. As we have seen, this is usually done by application of some sort of an index. The distribution of demand for some products, specialized capital equipment, for example, is not reflected in any existing index. Furthermore, there is no source of information readily available from which such an index can be built. For this reason, industrial marketers often resort to the buildup method.

New consumer products. The Go–No Go decision in the process of considering new products is a particularly difficult and critical one for management. It is difficult because it involves assessment of the future with no past experience to serve as guide. It is critical because the very survival of the firm depends on a successful program of innovation. Management's decision must involve some sort of estimate of expected demand because this is the most critical variable affecting their decision. Therefore, demand forecasting for new consumer products must be tackled with the tools at hand even if those tools are not nearly as useful as one would like.

The buildup method, outlined in Figure 4–1, requires as a first step the selection of some segment of the total market to study. The market segment chosen will, in the case of new consumer products, usually be some very small portion of the total market. It may be a scientifically chosen sample of consumers who are interviewed about their reaction to a new product. On the basis of their response an attempt is made to determine their probability of purchase. The sample, because of convenience and cost considerations, is often opportunistically selected. It may be composed of all people attending an event such as a builders' show or auto show who can be induced to fill out a questionnaire. It may consist of women's clubs, church groups, and the like whose members can be interviewed at one time and in one place. It may, however, also be a representative sample of all consumers in a market segment, who are scientifically selected and interviewed in their homes. Again, usually because of cost, such samples are usually representative of only a small portion of the market.

Demand estimates based on test marketing (as described in Chapter 6) are a use of the buildup method. Sales in the test market are audited. If the test market is representative of the total market, sales in the test market will provide the basis for at least a rough estimate of total demand. The audit procedure in the test market should consist of more than just measuring unit or dollar sales. Studies should be made to relate sales results to basic market factors. For example, information may be gathered about purchasers (age, income, etc.) and compared with like data about nonpurchasers. If a profile of probable purchasers can be constructed in terms of basic demand-causing characteristics, then the distribution of demand over the total market can be estimated. This is done by use of a basic market factors index, such as the *Sales Management Survey of Buying Power,* which reveals the relative presence of these causal demand factors by geographic area.

Demand forecasts based on consumer surveys and test marketing data are not models of precision. Ford Motor Company's sales forecast for the Mustang was for only about one half of the volume actually realized, and sales could have been higher if production capacity had not been limited. In spite of this, its forecast did give reasonable assurance that demand was adequate to go ahead with introduction of the new product.

New industrial products. The top-down approach is no more applicable to new industrial products than it is to new consumer products. Fortunately, the buildup method can be employed with more precision for industrial products. There are several reasons for this. First, potential industrial buyers can be more readily identified than potential consumer buyers. Many industrial goods are specialized products with specific applications. This means there is usually a much smaller universe for which demand must be estimated, thus simplifying the forecasting task. Second, demand for industrial goods depends on more easily identified and measured factors. Consumer purchase often depends on unknown subjective considerations, whereas industrial buying depends more on tangible cost and profit considerations. Third, there is a greater geographical concentration of demand for industrial than consumer goods. This, too, simplifies the use of the buildup method and keeps cost at a reasonable level.

Assume that a manufacturer develops a new special-purpose machine tool. The steps in development of a sales forecast might be as follows:

1. Determine the industries in which this machine tool might be used. A list of such industries can usually be developed on the basis of knowledge of what the machine will do and knowledge of production processes in different industries.
2. Select a sample of companies in each industry for engineering studies related to the potential uses of this new machine.
3. Calculate the cost savings to the buyer from use of the new equipment.
4. On the basis of projected cost savings, estimate the number of machines that will be demanded by the companies included in the sample of each industry studied.

5. Expand estimated demand for the companies included in each industry sample to demand for the total industry. For example, if companies in the sample account for 10 percent of industry output, a factor of 10 may be applied to obtain a demand estimate for the entire industry.
6. Sum the demand estimates for all industries included in the sample to obtain an estimate of total demand.

In the buildup process just described, a breakdown of the total sales forecast by industries is an inherent part of the buildup process itself. Demand estimates were made by industries and then totaled. Hence, no index need be applied for this purpose. However, if it is desired to break down demand on some other basis than that used in the buildup process, further steps must be taken. An index of relative potential demand might be developed from such information as value added data, value of shipments data, and so on. Usually, however, potential industrial users are few, relatively well known to the seller, and a breakdown can be made simply from a total listing of prospective buyers. No index of other market factors need be used.

Established industrial goods. For industrial goods which have been on the market for some time, the top-down approach is often applicable. Observable correlations between forecastable economic factors and product demand may well be present. Demand for office equipment, for example, is very likely to be correlated with general business activity. Indexes for determining the geographical distribution of demand can be composed from available sources. For office equipment, Social Security data on office employment by geographical regions and type of industry is readily available.

Unfortunately, demand forecasts for all established industrial goods cannot be made with the top-down approach. This is particularly true of specialized capital equipment. Total demand, as well as the geographical distribution of demand, depends on specific investment decisions of individual potential buyers. General business conditions do not indicate that a certain company will build a new plant this year to produce a new product. No available index will indicate that the potential buyer in County X is likely to go ahead with his expansion plans but that the potential buyer in County Y is not. Under these circumstances the "sales force composite method" of demand forecasting, which is a special form of the buildup method, is widely used.

Conceptually, the sales force composite method is very simple.

Each company salesman is asked to evaluate each present and potential customer and estimate his purchases for a specified time period, usually one year. These estimates are then totaled, reviewed, and adjusted, and become the sales forecast. This approach is possible because buyers are likely to be few, they plan their own future activities and are likely to know their needs, and buying decisions are made on objective grounds. The method makes use of the special knowledge of the salesman, the man closest to the market and, indeed, often the only person who has the knowledge necessary to predict the actions of particular buyers. Sampling error is avoided because the entire market is surveyed. Salesmen, who will probably be judged by performance against quota, will have more confidence in sales goals they have participated in formulating. The method lends itself to easy development of product, territory, customer, and salesman breakdowns.

The sales force composite method is often criticized on the grounds that salesmen are often poor estimators, being either too optimistic or pessimistic depending on how their sales are going at the moment. Of course, they have an incentive to keep quotas low if their performance is to be judged against them. This method requires a lot of time on the part of the sales force and may detract from their sales efforts. However, often no other method will provide the information needed for demand forecasting.

techniques for forecasting business conditions

It has been stressed above that a forecast of business conditions is the foundation upon which the top-down method of demand forecasting is built. This step is especially important when the market demand for the output of a specific industry is strongly affected by changes in the performance of the national economy. These changes may take place over different periods of time, and thus an analysis of the overall economy is generally divided into: (1) projections of the secular or long-term trends of economic activity, (2) projections of cyclical fluctuations which occur periodically and last for four or five years, and (3) forecasts of near-term performance of from 12 to 18 months in the future.

In projecting long-term trends of general economic performance, the measurement unit is the gross national product (GNP) or the dollar value of all of the goods and services produced by the economy during a specified period of time. The tools that the forecaster might employ include econometric models, gross methods of forecasting

GNP, and statistical methods of forecasting GNP. Only a brief survey of these methods is offered here.

econometric models

The econometric approach to forecasting GNP requires that economic relationships among various components of the economy be determined and stated in mathematical terms. These statements are then combined into a "model" which can be used to simulate the performance of the economy. Thus, changes in economic output as measured in dollars of GNP can be predicted for a sequence of years into the future, given projected changes in certain input variables such as size of the labor force, percent of labor force employed, average weekly hours worked, business and government investment, and net exports. In addition, the impact of predicted changes in man-hour productivity as well as of government monetary and fiscal policy on growth of GNP can be forecast.

While not foolproof, econometric models do provide insight as to where the economy is headed, given the behavior of certain of its parts. The econometric approach also serves as a check on forecasts made by other means.

The model user makes no attempt at *precise* forecasting; instead, the result is that a description is given of what is *expected* to happen under the *assumptions* of the model. Projections are not intended to apply to a given year but to an average year around the years designated. This result is considered satisfactory and even necessary, because the ability to forecast GNP for a given future year implies more knowledge of the short (or long) business cycle than seems to be generally available.[4]

gross methods of forecasting GNP

Two projection procedures for forecasting GNP on a long-term basis are recommended as being effective as well as easy to learn.[5] These are the 4 percent method and the labor productivity method.

The 4 percent method. This method is based on the assumption that the economy is growing over the long run at an average annual rate at constant prices. Although the rate of 4 percent is derived from the assumption that productivity is increasing at an annual average

---

[4] Harry Deane Wolfe, *Business Forecasting Methods* (New York: Holt, Rinehart & Winston, Inc., 1966), p. 112.

[5] *Ibid.*, pp. 112 10.

rate of 2½ percent and that population is growing at an average annual rate of 1½ percent, the forecaster is not tied to the 4 percent figure. Most forecasters of GNP using this approach base their predictions on several assumed predictions of rates of population and productivity growth. The final figure used is what they term "the most likely" rate of growth of GNP over the longer term.

The 4 percent method may also be used to forecast long-term growth in market potential for the absorption of output of a specific industry. It is important here, however, that the forecaster find an annual growth rate that best describes the industry under consideration. The approach works best when industry growth has been occurring at a fairly constant rate in the past and where there appears to be little on the horizon to cause an important deviation from the historical rate of growth.

Labor productivity method. This approach to forecasting GNP in the longer run is based on the theory that GNP is equal to the product of the total number of man-hours worked multiplied by the dollar productivity of each man-hour.[6] The method can also be used to forecast industry production whenever industry data are available. If realistic assumptions can be made about percent of industry output which will be sold, then the method can be used to forecast industry sales. This is tricky business, especially when industries gain economies from long production runs sufficient to allow them to hold considerable inventory to cushion against fluctuations in demand.

Data input for this method include estimates of the size of the labor force and percent of labor force likely to be employed during the forecast period, average hours worked per week, and current and projected rates of man-hour productivity. These data are available from several published sources, but the *Statistical Abstract of the United States* will provide a great deal of needed information.[7]

statistical methods

There are three widely used statistical methods for forecasting business conditions. The first is projection, the second is regression and multiple-correlation analysis, and the third is time series analysis.

Projection. Projection is the procedure of identification of past trends and their extension into the future. These trends may be identified by simple graphic methods. For example, a scatter diagram may be

---

[6] *Ibid.,* p. 114.

[7] *Ibid.,* p. 115.

made by plotting on a piece of graph paper the values of GNP components for the past 10 years. Time in years can be measured along the horizontal axis, while billions of dollars can be measured along the vertical axis. A straight line can then be fitted visually to each of these scatter diagrams and extended into future periods. By summing the extrapolated values of these components of GNP for 1, 3, 5, and 10 years into the future, a fair idea of the behavior of GNP over the forecast period could be gained, assuming that the assumptions about growth of GNP components held true.

A more sophisticated approach to fitting a line to a scatter diagram is by means of the method of least squares. This is a statistical technique which minimizes the sum of the square of the vertical distances between the points in the scatter diagram and the line.

Regardless of how exact the fitting procedure, the method of straight-line projection of past trends provides rough forecasts at best. Projection as a technique can be made more sophisticated by fitting curves to the scatter of points, but the method is only as good as the assumption underlying its use, that is, that the forces which have produced change in the past will continue to operate in the same manner in the periods ahead.

Regression analysis. This is a statistical procedure for estimating the relationship among two or more variables. The analysis produces an equation of the form:

$$Y = a + b_1X_1 + b_2X_2 + \ldots + b_nX_n$$

where Y is the dependent variable (GNP) and the X_i's are the independent variables such as population, man-hours worked, and man-hour productivity. The b_i's are called regression coefficients and measure the influence of the independent variables upon the dependent variable. Thus, if an historical series of data for the dependent and independent variables can be accumulated, values of the b_i's can be determined mathematically and an estimate of Y (Y') can be made given current or estimated future values for the independent variables. When only one independent variable is considered, the procedure is known as simple regression; this was illustrated previously by the least squares method of finding a linear relationship between GNP and one of its components. Multiple regression is the technique whereby the effect of two or more independent variables upon the dependent variable is considered in one process.

Closely related to multiple regression is correlation analysis. While the former seeks to develop an estimating equation, the latter is used to measure the degree of relationship between the dependent and independent variables. Multiple-correlation analysis is thus very important in determining the factors which appear to influence sales for a given product, and it can be used as an index in the overall forecast approach.

It should be quite clear that successful use of regression analysis depends upon accurate historical data and the ability to find independent variables which have a true and meaningful influence on the dependent variable. Scatter diagrams are very useful in determining the extent of the relationship. If the points on the scatter diagram do not appear to form around a line or a curve, then the potential independent variable may be passed over in favor of those which show closer relationships with the dependent variable.

In addition, the use of regression analysis requires that values of the independent variables be known for the current period and be estimable for the future periods under consideration. To obtain such data might again require a forecast, and unless the forecasts of the values of the independent variables are easier to obtain than forecasts of the dependent variable, very little has been gained by the use of the statistical techniques.

Time series analysis. Business activity is generally a function of long-term or secular growth trends in the economy, of cyclical changes which occur periodically and last for four or five years, of seasonal variations in demand, and of random or erratic movements in economic activity. Time series analysis is an approach to forecasting based on the decomposition of an historical series (such as GNP) into the four elements just noted in an attempt to evaluate the impact of each element on the behavior of the series itself. The most commonly used model of time series analysis is:

$$Y = T \times C \times S \times I$$

where Y represents the overall series (for example, GNP) and T is the trend measured in terms of dollars or units. C is the measure of the influence of the business cycle, S is the value of the seasonal influence, and I is the value of the irregular influence. C, S, and I are stated as percent deviations from T with average values of 100 percent. Thus, GNP for the fourth quarter might be $780 billions $\times$ 0.99 (C) $\times$ 0.95 (S) $\times$ 1.01 (I) or $740.9 billions.

Time series analysis has the advantage of requiring the forecaster to consider the impact of each of the four influences on aggregate demand as well as on the demand for the output of the industry and the firm. The disadvantages of time series analysis are much the same as were seen for the methods of projection; they include the dependence on historical data to make predictions about the future and the inability to make meaningful forecasts if the irregular (I) elements are very large. Unlike projection, however, time series analysis does allow for the separation of long- and short-term factors and the consideration of each group of factors independently. The approach is especially valuable in forecasting demand which varies on a seasonal basis. Thus, demand for clothing, for electric power, or for automobiles may be forecast by month or season. The demand for airline service may even be forecast on a day-of-the-week basis.

Time series analysis requires skilled personnel, dependable forecasts of general business conditions, and the ability to develop measures of seasonal influence. Given these inputs, a great deal of the busywork can be performed by computers.[8] Time series analysis is not equally effective for all firms, however; but it does enjoy wide use by firms in those industries where sales trends have been fairly predictable in the past and where irregular influences on demand have been of small magnitude.

conclusion

This chapter brings to an end the section of this text dealing with demand analysis. The chapters on buyer behavior dealt primarily with qualitative aspects of demand. This chapter on demand forecasting dealt with quantitative aspects of demand. A thorough knowledge of both is essential to formulation of the optimum marketing strategy. Although each of these topics has been dealt with in a general way, the development of a marketing plan for a specific product requires that, as a first step, management study both of these aspects of demand in substantially greater depth.

questions

1. Because demand forecasting is an imperfect art and many forecasts prove to be not fully accurate, some companies fail to make demand forecasts. Is their position sound?
2. Is it possible that a demand forecast that is inaccurate because it understates actual market demand may serve as a factor that holds down a company's sales? Explain.
3. Define and contrast (a) market potential, (b) sales potential, and (c) sales forecast.

---

[8] See R. L. McLaughlin, *Time Series Forecasting* (Chicago: American Marketing Association, 1962).

4. Indicate whether the top-down or the buildup forecasting approach is most likely to be appropriate to each of the following products. Give a brief explanation for each choice.
   a) Office supplies.
   b) A newly developed, specialized machine tool.
   c) A newly developed breakfast cereal.
   d) Automobiles.
5. Contrast market factors indexes and past sales indexes. Under what circumstances is it reasonable to use a past sales index to determine the geographical distribution of demand?
6. Review the hypothetical illustration of the top-down method of forecasting presented on pages 120–22. What are the implicit assumptions included in this approach?
7. Why is it necessary, considering the difficulties involved, to break down a company sales forecast of the total market into demand by geographical segments?
8. The Y Company, a producer of office equipment, had for several years established sales quotas on the basis of estimates of indivudal customer demand made by salesmen. The newly appointed marketing manager of the Y Company noted that there was wide divergence between actual sales for past years and the quotas thus established. He suggested to the sales manager that perhaps these quotas were unrealistic because of the way they were established. The sales manager argued that the method of setting quotas they had been using should be retained because the salesmen had more knowledge of demand in their territories than did anyone else, the salesmen would have greater confidence in quotas they themselves had helped set, and because such quotas lent themselves readily to breakdown by territories, customers, or salesmen.

   In order to convince the sales manager that a top-down forecast approach to getting sales quotas is both feasible and preferable in the office equipment field, the marketing manager would like to present a practical plan which could be followed. Because he is not an expert in this field, he has called on you to advise him. Outline the plan you recommend and explain why you think it will work.
9. What is the difference between an econometric approach to forecasting gross national product and a projection procedure such as the labor productivity method?
10. What are the important assumptions underlying the use of statistical methods to estimate future demand? Define what is meant by simple-regression, multiple-regression, and multiple-correlation analyses.
11. Explain the difference between time series analysis and projection. Under what circumstances would it be advisable to use time series analysis to forecast future demand?

cases for part two

MICHIGAN BELL TELEPHONE CO.*

motivation research on social long-distance calls

In a continuing effort to improve the effectiveness of its long-distance sales promotion, the Michigan Bell Telephone Company retained the Survey Research Center of The University of Michigan to make a study of the motivation behind placing social long-distance telephone calls.

When the study was completed, a report was submitted to Michigan Bell by the Survey Research Center. After studying the report, the executives of Michigan Bell considered the question of whether the appeals used in the company's advertising should be changed to conform with the findings of the study.

reason for the study

Executives of Michigan Bell felt that a necessary prerequisite for expanding the potential market for long-distance telephone calls was a better understanding of why people placed these calls. With the idea of discovering new knowledge and examining old concepts, Michigan Bell commissioned the Survey Research Center to conduct a survey. The study was limited to social long-distance calls in the residence market. In this market the motives for placing calls were not as clear as in the business field, where the company had considerable background experience by virtue of the continuing analysis of long-distance needs of business customers which are made by its sales force.

past promotional devices

Prior to World War II, Michigan Bell placed primary emphasis on the speed, convenience, and low cost of long-distance calls in its advertising, with occasional reference to social calling.

During the war years, it was necessary to reverse the advertising appeal to a restrictive one to insure that circuits would be available for the large volume of calls generated by the national defense effort. The public was asked to limit the length of its calls and often to those of emergency nature.

* Written by Gary Takata, Student, Graduate School of Business Administration, The University of Michigan.

Following the war, no significant long-distance advertising was done for several years. Due to continued shortages of equipment of all kinds, it was still difficult to meet the pent-up demands for all types of telephone service.

Several years preceding the survey, it again became possible to resume promotion of long distance. However, the primary appeals of speed, convenience, and low cost of long-distance service were now combined with, or even subordinated to, the appeals that recognized the value of social calling.

This appeal had been woven into the company's advertising at the time the survey was started. But more information was needed about the specific nature of social calls and the motives behind them. Because of the desire of Michigan Bell to confirm the soundness of this as well as other past appeals, and to learn more about social calling in general, the study on the motivations of social long-distance calls was made. On the following pages the objectives, design, theory, sample, and research methods used in the study will be introduced.

objectives of the survey

The purpose of the study was to answer the following three general questions: [1]

1. What social and economic factors influence the number of social long distance calls a person will make?
2. What feelings and attitudes about the telephone influence social long distance calling?
3. What personality characteristics influence social long distance calling?

The study directors realized that ". . . it was not possible to assess the influence on long distance calling of all possible socio-economic factors or all attitudes or personality characteristics." On the basis of past studies (among them a pilot study) and the knowledge and experience of the executives of Bell Telephone and investigators of the Center, an attempt was made to select those factors which seemed most likely to show some relationship to calling behavior. The next section describes a working theory that the Center originated to explain the relationship between the factors selected and calling behavior.

working theory

The theoretical scheme can be illustrated as follows:

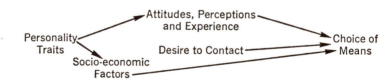

---

[1] The following material on the objectives, design, theory, sample, and research instruments of the survey is adapted from the Survey Research Center's Report, *Motives, Attitudes and Long Distance Calls* (Ann Arbor: The University of Michigan), pp. 1–10, pp. A–1 to A–2.

This diagram, obviously oversimplified, can be translated into language as follows: Whether a person habitually phones depends on the presence of some factors which make him desire to contact others frequently. How often this desire is present depends on his personality characteristics and upon socio-economic factors. The desire to contact is undoubtedly influenced by external conditions, such as emergencies or the sudden need for more information. The emphasis in this study, however, is upon those more or less permanent personality characteristics which might influence the strength of the desire to be in contact with friends and relatives. Once the desire to contact is present, whether a person uses the telephone or not depends on other socio-economic factors, as well as certain of his attitudes, his perceptions and his previous experience with phoning.

Once the theoretical model was clear in the minds of the investigators, they then searched for a suitable study design that would adequately test the model. The following two sections summarize both the study design and sample they decided to use.

design of the study

The sample consisted of 400 interviews divided equally between two distinct groups: households that made a large number of long distance calls and households that made almost no calls at all.

This design had the advantage of maximizing the likelihood of detecting those factors which differentiated high from low callers. This feature is particularly desirable when the behavior under study is influenced by many factors so that it is often difficult to detect the impact of a single one. On the other hand, with this kind of design it is not possible to tell how frequently a particular event is likely to occur in the general population.

selection of sample

The area covered in this study consisted of the southern half of the lower peninsula of the state of Michigan. The northern boundary of the area studied was the northern boundary of the following counties: Muskegon, Kent, Montcalm, Isabella, Midland, and Bay.

The universe sampled consisted of the residential subscribers of the Michigan Bell Telephone Company in this area.

Of the 400 interviews about half were taken with "heavy" long distance users and half with "zero" long distance users. A heavy user was defined to be one who made six or more long distance calls in the last period of three months for which data were available at the time the sample was selected. A "zero" was defined as a subscriber who made no long distance calls in the same period. For the purpose of this study a long distance call was defined as a call to a point over 50 miles from the point of origin.

The first stage in the selection of a sample was the selection of a sample of counties. The next stage was to select telephone exchanges. Actual telephone numbers were then selected from the exchanges. These numbers were then returned to Michigan Bell for information on long distance calls.

With the selection of the sample completed, the Center turned its attention toward deciding what type of research instruments they would employ. Their final decision is explained below.

the research instrument

Four kinds of devices were used during the interview period. The first, most frequently used, consisted of questions. Some of the questions were of the indirect type; the respondent was asked to describe a third party, or to predict how another person would respond.

The second device consisted of modifications of projective tests like the ones used in social science research. The respondents were asked to tell a story, in response to pictures which the interviewer showed them. By these means the need of affiliation and underlying orientation toward money were measured.

The third device consisted of attitude scales. The respondent was given a series of statements and was asked to indicate whether he agreed or disagreed with each statement. From his response it was possible to determine how favorable or unfavorable he felt toward an object. In this study scales were used to measure respondents' concern about ease of phoning and the extent to which phoning satisfied affiliative needs. A modified form of this kind of device was the measure of security-insecurity.

Finally, the interview session permitted an opportunity for observation of actual long distance calling behavior. Each household was given the opportunity to make a free call to any part of the country. When the offer was accepted, the interviewer was usually able to note whether a discussion preceded the call, whether the call was placed easily, how long the conversation took, and so on.

summary of the findings [2]

The main findings of the study may be summarized as follows:

SOCIOECONOMIC FACTORS

1. *Friends or relatives living away.* People who have friends or relatives living away are much more likely to be frequent users of long distance than those who do not.
2. *The "life cycle."* Young married couples who have not yet had children and older married couples whose children have left home are likely to be frequent users of long distance. The latter group is particularly important.
3. *Income.* The higher people's income, the more long-distance calls they

---

[2] The Summary is adapted from the Survey Research Center's Report.

tend to make. As people move from lower into higher income brackets they will not automatically take on the calling behavior now typical of higher income groups.

4. *Who in the family places calls.* Women are more likely than men to place long-distance calls. Among the families who are most frequent callers, however, there is a tendency for the differentiation between husband and wife in this respect to disappear.

ATTITUDES TOWARD THE PHONE

5. *Users of the phone.* People who make local calls frequently are also more likely to make long-distance calls.

6. *Other forms of communication.* People who make many long-distance calls also tend to write many letters and make many visits to friends and relatives living away. There are a few people, however, who use the phone in preference to other modes of communication.

7. *Placing the call.* Few people say that placing a call is difficult for them. Direct observation of people placing calls indicates, however, that there is an appreciable group of people for whom the mechanics of placing the call may be a barrier to making calls.

8. *Feelings while calling.* Making long-distance calls is not pure pleasure to most people. People differ in the extent to which they enjoy calling. Those who report that calling is pleasant are more likely to be frequent callers.

9. *Reluctance to call.* A few people report that they have refrained from placing a call at some time for fear of alarming the recipient.

10. *Motives for social calling.* The most important motive for social calling is to maintain family ties.

11. *Trouble hearing.* Difficulty in hearing on the phone comes primarily from poor conditions rather than from deafness.

PERSONALITY FACTORS

12. *Security-insecurity.* The most secure respondents, as measured by the test, are more likely to be in the high-caller group than persons who are less secure. More elaborate analysis suggests that this relationship is due in part to the effect of income and other factors.

13. *Need affiliations.* Respondents who have high need affiliation scores are more likely to report pleasant feelings while calling than those who have low scores, and to report enjoyment in making long-distance calls.

   Persons with high need for affiliation, as measured by the test, indicate a more positive attitude toward a high caller. They are also somewhat more likely to use the phone for social purposes than are the persons with low need for affiliation.

   Persons with high affiliation scores show a higher rate of contacting friends and relatives by means of letter than do low scorers. High need affiliation respondents are also more likely to report more use of the local phone than are low need affiliation persons.

There is no simple and direct relationship between need affiliation scores and long-distance calling, but a more complex relationship may exist.

14. *Underlying attitudes toward money.* Respondents classified as Free Spenders are more frequently in the group of extremely frequent callers. Persons classified as Conservative Spenders appear more frequently in the group of very infrequent callers.

15. *Overall status of the personality variables.* All three measures of personality characteristics show significant relationships to one or another aspect of phoning behavior. In no case, however, is there a simple relationship between a personality characteristic and frequency of use of the long distance phone.

ATTITUDES TOWARD RATES

16. *Are rates high?* High users of long distance are more likely than low users to feel that rates for long distance are high. They may have in mind the total charges they actually pay rather than the actual rates. Low users often have no opinion as to whether rates are high.

17. *Reasons why rates are high.* Of those who feel rates are high, many are thinking in terms of the company and the service it provides. Those who feel rates are not high also may have in mind the company and its service, but many of them are thinking in terms of the satisfaction they receive from calls.

THE THREE-MINUTE LIMIT

18. *Length of free calls.* When given an opportunity to place a free long-distance call of "reasonable length," almost all respondents talked more than 6 minutes and most talked 10 minutes or longer.

19. *Belief that the company wants people to limit calls.* There is still a group of people who believes the company wants them to limit the length of their calls. A smaller group of people do try to limit calls for this reason.

20. *What happens after the three minutes?* People are poorly informed about what happens to rates after the first three minutes.

NUMBER AND LOCATION OF PHONES

21. *Number of phones.* Of the high users of long distance, one out of four have more than one phone. Of the low users, 1 in 10 have more than one phone. Of all subscribers, about 1 in 10 has more than one phone.

22. *Location of the phone.* The three favorite locations for the phone are dining room, kitchen, and living room. High-income people are much more likely to have a telephone in the kitchen than low-income people.

23. *Toll charges for six months.* Of all residential customers of Michigan Bell in southern Michigan, 18 percent had no toll charges over a six-months' period. Sixty-two percent had charges of $1 per month or less on an average. Eight percent, however, averaged over $5 per month.

consideration of what action to recommend

The foregoing report by the Survey Research Center of The University of Michigan was presented to Michigan Bell management. After studying these findings, the executives of Michigan Bell gave consideration to the question of whether the appeals used in Bell Telephone advertising should be changed to conform to the findings of the study.

QUESTION

What action should Michigan Bell executives take, if any, in view of the findings of the report?

case 2–2

ROBERT JOHNSTON*

consumer behavior: purchase of ammunition loading equipment

For Christmas Mr. Robert Johnston's wife gave him a high-powered rifle for hunting and target shooting. The rifle was a former military weapon which had been used by the British Army during World War II. The weapon was in excellent condition, shot well, cost about $25 and was in the .303 British caliber.

In purchasing ammunition for the weapon, Mr. Johnston learned that surplus British Army ammunition would cost him $7.50 per 100 rounds and was available in almost unlimited quantities. Hunting ammunition loaded by American manufacturers cost $4.55 per box of 20 rounds. While for some purposes there were important differences between the two types, Mr. Johnston felt that for his needs they were the same. He shot the weapon at targets

---

* Written by Ross J. Wilhelm, Associate Professor of Business Economics, Graduate School of Business Administration, The University of Michigan.

at a rate of about 15 times a year, shooting about 20 rounds each time, and once a year while hunting for deer in Northern Michigan.

The cost of the ammunition did, however, seem high to him, so he investigated the possibility of purchasing equipment to load and reload his own ammunition.

He knew that a cartridge consisted of four major components. The first was the brass case which held the other components together. The second was the bullet or projectile which was actually shot from the gun and was held in the front end of the case. The third was the powder, which when ignited caused the explosion which propelled the bullet and was contained in the case. The fourth was the primer, which was the element which ignited the powder and was itself ignited by being struck by the firing pin of the rifle. The primer was fitted in the rear end of the case.

To reload ammunition, he learned that it was necessary to obtain a reloading tool, with the necessary dies for the particular caliber ammunition, a means of measuring the powder, and the components of the ammunition.

The steps of reloading are simple and in general terms involve (a) fitting the primer in the case, (b) weighing or measuring the powder charge and putting this in the case, and (c) properly inserting the bullet into the case.

From articles in a current issue of the American Rifleman, a publication of the National Rifle Association, he concluded that for his purposes and the general weight of the bullet he planned to use, 35.0 grains[1] of Du Pont HiVel #2 powder would be required for each cartridge he loaded. He also learned that he could either purchase the bullets at retail for $5.10 per 100[2] or he could purchase moulds, metal, and other components and equipment and make his own bullets. If he made his own bullets the variable cost would be about 2 cents[3] each.

He further learned from available publications that Du Pont HiVel #2 powder cost $2.50 per pound, and that primers cost $10.00 per 1,000. Empty cases could also be bought separately for about $3.00 per 100 cases, however, unlike the other components the cases could be reused and reloaded almost indefinitely.

On investigating the cost of the reloading tool, dies, and measuring equipment he found that he could purchase an excellent set (and yet economical) for $33.00 and that this would probably last him for a lifetime. The moulding equipment, etc. necessary for moulding his own bullets would cost $30.00 and would last almost indefinitely as well.

---

[1] This may be a little high for bullets cast in lead but is satisfactory for estimating purposes.

[2] All prices of equipment and components are estimated from The Shooter's Bible, published by the Stoeger Arms Corporation of New York City; other prices are from advertisements in various shooting magazines.

[3] Includes costs of: Bullet metal $0.50 per pound—each bullet estimated to weigh 210 grains; (Mould No. 311299) bullet lubricant $0.75 per 500 pounds; gas checks—$3.20 per 1,000.

questions

State the conditions, in quantitative terms, under which it would be "economical" for Mr. Johnston to purchase the components and equipment necessary to reload his own ammunition. What qualitative provisos would you make to this conclusion? What, if any, added information must be known to forecast Mr. Johnston's behavior?

part three

product strategy

Modern marketing management views the product as a controllable variable in the planning of marketing strategy. Products can be improved to make them more acceptable to the market, new products can be added to a product line, and weak products can be dropped. In a sense, product decisions are more basic than decisions about other marketing variables. A product that effectively meets consumer needs reduces problems associated with decisions on distribution, pricing, advertising, and personal selling. A poorly conceived product, on the other hand, creates many problems for other decision areas in marketing.

Demand is increasingly dynamic, and product life cycles are getting shorter. A company that hopes to grow and prosper over the long run must have a capability for product innovation. Marketing management, facing today's market situation, is repeatedly required to answer a very basic question: "What new product should we offer?" A company's survival depends on its ability to answer this question correctly. An approach to providing this answer is the subject of Chapter 5.

Sellers face a dilemma with regard to product policy. New products are essential to survival, yet most new products fail in the marketplace. Thus, another requirement for today's business firm is a product development process that maximizes the probability of success. This is the topic considered in Chapter 6.

product choice
decisions

Product decisions are concerned with changes in a firm's product or product line. For our purposes the term "product" will be thought of in the inclusive sense as being all that the consumer receives when making a purchase. It is not only a physical entity but also a complex of tangible and intangible attributes, including such things as warranties, service policies, packaging, color, design, and even psychic stimulation. Product policy involves the adjustment of this complex of product variables to the needs and requirements of the market on one hand, and to the capabilities of the firm on the other, along with the attendant activities of procedure and control.

Product decisions may relate to changes in existing products or their use, or to the offering of products new to the firm. These decisions are not fundamentally different, for in either case a "new" product emerges. The difference is only in the degree of newness involved. However, the greater the degree of newness, the more uncertain the outcome of the product decision. The focus of this chapter is on decisions concerning essentially new products, but the decision-making process is basically the same, albeit somewhat easier, for modifications of existing products.

Formulation and execution of a product policy requires the making of a great many decisions. Many of these are subsidiary to, or variants of, three very basic decisions. These most basic product decisions are: (1) Should a firm offer a new product? (2) What new product should be offered? (3) Should the new product be developed internally or acquired by merger?

decision to offer a new product

Not all firms engage in product development. In the array of product policy choices available to a firm, one is the null choice; that is, to stick with existing products in their present form and to forego product innovation. Company management, having observed the high rate of failure among new products, may decide this is the prudent course to follow. Most new products are failures. The record shows that in recent years in the United States, of every three products emerging from research and development departments as technical successes, there is an average of only one commercial success. Nearly half of the new products actually introduced into the market, in most cases only after careful product and market tests, are failures.[1] When this high failure rate is considered along with the often high cost of developing and launching a new product, the risks associated with product development appear formidable indeed.

On the other hand, there is risk and potentially high cost associated with not offering new products. All products have a life cycle, although there is substantial variation in life cycles by type and class of products. Products are like people: They are born, they grow (some more than others), and eventually they die (some sooner than others). In contrast with that of people, the average life cycle of products is constantly being shortened. The time scale on most products is being compressed by accelerated research and technology, rapidly changing markets, mass media, and mass distribution.

The basic life cycle of new products is illustrated in Figure 5–1. Sales of a successful new product go through a period of growth, reach a peak, and eventually decline. Also significant from the standpoint of product policy is the behavior of product margins over the product life cycle. Profits tend to peak and usually begin to decline earlier than sales volume. Maximum sales volume is often reached only after competitors have entered the field, price rivalry has become severe, and profit margins have been compressed. To sustain profits new products may be needed long before sales of established products have begun to fall.

The critical underlying causes of product life cycles are two: (1) instability of demand, and (2) instability of competitive position.[2]

---

[1] Booz, Allen & Hamilton, Inc., *Management of New Products* (New York, 1968), p. 2.

[2] For a more extensive discussion of the effect of these factors on product life cycles, see D. M. Phelps and J. H. Westing, *Marketing Management* (3d ed.; Homewood, Ill.: Richard D. Irwin, Inc., 1968), pp. 57–63.

Figure 5–1. The basic life cycle of new products.

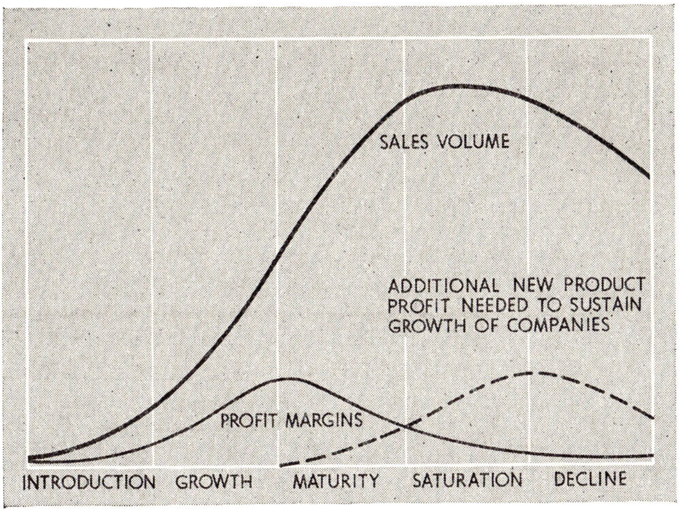

SALES VOLUME

ADDITIONAL NEW PRODUCT PROFIT NEEDED TO SUSTAIN GROWTH OF COMPANIES

PROFIT MARGINS

INTRODUCTION   GROWTH   MATURITY   SATURATION   DECLINE

Source: Booz, Allen & Hamilton, Inc., *Management of New Products* (New York, 1968), p. 4.

Consumer demand is unstable because factors which influence it are continually changing. Changes in the geographical and age distribution of the population, in income, in education, in mobility, in taste, and in other factors produce changes in consumer preferences. Competitors change and improve their products, and the company whose product does not change is likely to find its market share declining, even if basic demand conditions remain stable. It, too, must innovate to hold its competitive position.

Does a firm have a real choice insofar as product innovation is concerned? *In the short run,* the answer is yes. Given the substantial costs and high risks associated with product change, plus uncertainty about the present phase and future course of the life cycle of existing products, short-run profits may well be maximized by a decision not to offer new products. On the other hand, *long-run survival of a firm precludes choice* about product innovation. Eventual decline in the market acceptability of virtually all products is certain. "Innovate, or die" is a slogan containing a large measure of truth.

Even if survival over an extended period were possible without product innovation, most firms are not content with mere survival. They want to grow and to prosper. New products are customarily a major factor in company growth. Figure 5–2 shows expected sales increases in 11 industries for the period 1963 through 1967 and the

Figure 5–2. Contribution of new products to expected sales growth, 1963–67.

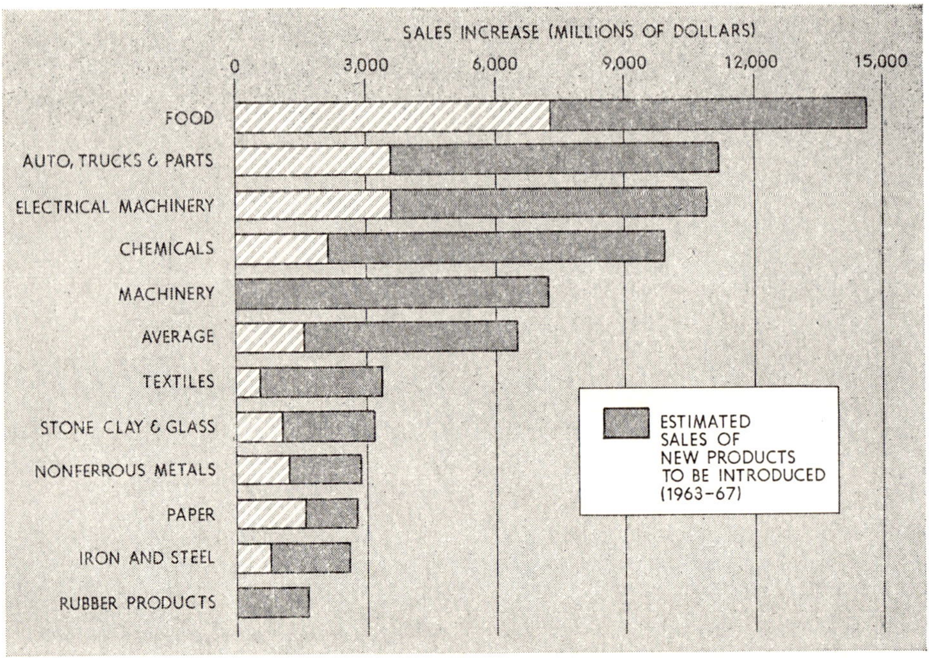

Source: Booz, Allen & Hamilton, Inc., *Management of New Products* (New York, 1968), p. 5.

portion of this increase accounted for by products first produced during this same five-year time span. Therefore, if a firm desires both survival and growth, its fundamental choices concerning product innovation narrow to two: (1) what (not whether) new products should be offered; (2) whether these new products should be gained through internal development or by external acquisition.

what new products to offer [3]

New products are "new" in varying degrees. They may be minor or major modifications of a firm's existing products. They may be new to the particular firm but not new to the market. If new to the firm, they may be closely related, loosely related, or totally unrelated to the firm's existing products. Or the product may be new to the market, something not previously available in any form to consumers. If a product is

_____

[3] Assumed in this chapter is complete freedom of choice among a large number of alternative products. This assumption permits consideration of all variables affecting selection of a new product. The choices facing a particular company would usually be more limited. Thus, fewer variables would be involved.

both new to the market, so that there is nothing by way of guidance to be found in the experience of others, and also unrelated to a firm's existing products, so that there is little carry-over of experience from these, then the risks of product innovation are great indeed. In order to minimize these risks, yet keep alive the opportunity for survival and growth that accompanies product innovation, a well-formulated "add-and-drop" policy is necessary.[4]

objective of profit maximization

The goal of business in a free enterprise society is the maximization of long-term profit. Therefore, the basic test to be applied in deciding which new product should be added is contribution to the overall profit position of the firm. Unfortunately, such a test is not easily applied. Profit is a function of many things, such as the nature and extent of demand, the activities of competitors, and costs of production and distribution. Furthermore, when deciding whether to add a new product, it is the future, not the present, condition of such variables which counts. Profit calculations relating to new products must be based on forecasting, an art which mankind has not yet mastered.

In spite of the difficulty of applying a profit test in product choice decisions, a profit calculation cannot be avoided. Any decision to add a new product *implicitly* involves an assumption concerning profitability. Other standards, if used, are at best only substitute ones which are assumed to be correlated with long-term profitability. If initial profit calculations are necessarily very crude, there is opportunity to refine them as the product development process evolves. At this stage, however, we are concerned only with the initial decision of which new product should be selected for development. Refinements of some of the calculations discussed below will be made in the next chapter.

profitability formula

The total profit directly (but not indirectly) attributable to a new product addition is expressed by the formula: [5]

$$R = D \times (P - C) \times L ,$$

in which:

R = Total long-term net profit in dollars.

D = Average total unit sales per year.

---

[4] Although emphasis here is on the adding of new products, decisions to drop existing products are governed by the same factors.

[5] Indirect contributions to a firm's total profits by a new product are discussed later.

P = Average sales price per unit.

C = Average cost per unit.

L = Expected life (in years).

estimate of demand

The existence of an adequate demand for a potential new product is basic to profit opportunity. An attempt must be made to measure the extent of demand, its strength and location, the segmentation which may be present, and other demand variables. For example, a plan to produce a new sports car which is expected to appeal to young people might involve studies of the number of people in the appropriate (for example, 18–30) age group, their geographic dispersion, segmentation by income groups, variations in tastes in car styling, mechanical features, and so on.

Estimates of future demand for established products are difficult to make because of the many factors, both tangible and intangible, which affect sales opportunities. Demand estimates for a projected new product, at the time a decision must be made whether or not to undertake its development, are far more difficult. Just how difficult depends on the nature of the demand determinants (for example, automotive replacement parts versus a new style of clothing). Still, such a decision is implicit in the choice process and, therefore, cannot be avoided.

Basic approaches to demand forecasting were discussed in Chapter 4. Management must estimate future market potential for the type of product it expects to add, as well as the share of the market it expects to serve. Because of the uncertainty associated with sales forecasts at this early stage in the product development process, several forecasts, involving various degrees of optimism and pessimism, might be made. Figure 5–3 shows three sales forecasts for a proposed new product—one highly pessimistic, one optimistic, and one considered most likely to occur. This process might be refined by assigning probabilities to the several estimates, thus making possible the derivation of expected values of unit sales for each product under consideration.

Sales of most new products can be expected to grow for a time, gradually achieve more stability, and eventually decline. If the respective sales of several products are to be compared, it is useful to convert sales data to average sales per year over the expected life cycle of the product. Such a figure can be readily calculated and easily fitted into the profitability formula above. The value of this figure, of course, depends on the expected life of the proposed new product as well as on the trend of sales during its time on the market. Expected life is discussed separately below.

price estimates

Management must have some idea of the price to be obtained for a new product throughout its life cycle in order to estimate a product's profit contribution. Valuable price information can usually be gained from demand studies, for price is basically a demand-determined variable. Needless to say, uncertainties of demand cause uncertainties also in the price estimating process. Price is quite likely to vary through

Figure 5–3. Estimates of alternative sales volumes, proposed new product.

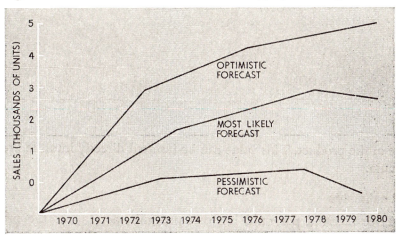

time, by size and type of customer, by markets, and so on. As was suggested for estimates of sales volume, it might be useful for price estimates also to range from optimistic to pessimistic and to attempt to derive the "most likely" behavior of price over the life cycle of the projected product. This approach is illustrated in Figure 5–4.

Price received for the new product and its behavior over the product life cycle is a function not only of demand but also of price strategies followed, activities of competitors, changes in the cost structure, and so on. Obviously, the expected price can only be a "best guess." Again, however, it can be pointed out that such a decision is inherent in the product choice process and must be made regardless of its difficulty. As was suggested for sales volume estimates, it is useful to convert price estimates into an average unit price throughout the life

Figure 5-4. Alternative price expectations, proposed new product.

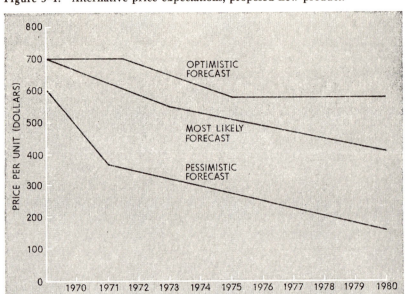

cycle of the product. This value can be inserted directly into the profit formula.

cost estimates

Price received per unit, less cost per unit, determines the profit contribution of each unit sold. Cost per unit includes both variable and fixed costs, so the sales forecast must precede any estimate of unit costs. It is in the area of production and marketing costs per unit that a firm adding a new product has a major opportunity to influence the volume of profits that a new product will generate. If it chooses a new product that "fits" production- and marketing-wise with its present products, it can obtain more efficient utilization of resources in two ways. First, fixed costs are spread over a larger volume of operations, thus reducing costs per unit. Second, proper fit may have a favorable effect on demand for both the new product and for existing products, thus increasing the total scale of operations on which profits depend.

life cycle estimates

The life cycle of a proposed product may well be the most difficult variable in the profit formula to estimate. The anticipated time period may be long and the factors which might affect it (change in consumer taste, actions of competitors, changes in technology, for example) almost impossible to predict. Nonetheless, such an estimate is highly relevant to the decision at hand. Generally speaking, management would want to avoid products whose life cycles are expected to be short and favor those whose life cycles are expected to be long, other things being equal.

The difficulty of estimating life cycles varies greatly by type of product. In some fields (such as automobiles and women's clothing,) fairly uniform cycles may be observable in past sales. These may then be used as a guide to the expected life cycle of the proposed product. In other fields, no such uniformity in life cycles may be observed. Here, perhaps, some arbitrary time period may be chosen for purposes of the profit calculation. For example, 10 years may be established as the maximum time period to be considered. All new products will be judged only on the profits generated in that time span. If the life cycle is expected to be shorter than this, the values of other variables in the formula will have to be higher in order to compensate.

net revenue

The total long-term net profit in dollars to be expected over the life cycle of the projected product can now be calculated. Because both the length and shape of life cycle curves vary greatly among products, the total profit figure should be converted to "present value" for purposes of comparison. A quick return not only has a higher present value but also a higher probability of being realized because of the greater uncertainty of longer term forecasts.

compound profitability formula

If a firm is starting operations from scratch with a new product and has no existing products, the above analysis may be sufficient for the product choice decision. Such, however, is rarely the case. Most new products are introduced to the market by going concerns which are already producing and selling one or more products. In this circumstance, it is axiomatic that it is the effect of adding the new product on overall profitability of the firm that counts. If new product sales are entirely at the expense of continued sales of existing products of equal profitability, there is no net gain.[6] When Ford Motor Company introduced the Falcon in 1960, its sales were in part at the expense of sales

---

[6] This assumes that the present-product sales would continue if the new product were not added. If it is likely a competitor will offer a new product which will cut into sales of the existing product (s) , this assumption is not valid.

of the standard Ford, whose sales declined. Introduction of the Princess telephone by American Telephone and Telegraph Company had an adverse effect on the installation of standard telephones. Conversely, the new product, because it in some way complements existing products, may favorably affect their profitability. A manufacturer of automatic washers who did not also produce dryers might find it difficult to sell his washers because of the demand among consumers for matched pairs of these products. A manufacturer of a car wax who did not offer a car cleaner might find sales difficult because consumers believe such products "go together" better if made by one company.

Because of such considerations as these, the profitability formula should be expanded as follows:

$$R = [D \times (P - C) \times L] \pm [d \times (p - c) \times l]_1 \pm [d \times (p - c) \times l]_2 \ldots \pm [d \times (p - c) \times l]_n.$$

This formula recognizes that the proposed product may either increase or reduce the profitability of every other product in a firm's product line, ranging from the product designated as 1 up to product n. The effect on profits may be a result of the influence of the new product on any of the variables involved. The new product may either increase or reduce the demand (d) for an existing product. It may make possible receipt of a higher price (p) or cause a need to lower price. If the new product is wisely chosen, it may well serve to reduce the average cost per unit (c) of producing and marketing present products. The life cycle of existing products (l) may be affected favorably or unfavorably. Any one or more of these effects would cause variation in anticipated overall profits.

resource utilization: its relationship to product planning

A business firm employs various resources (inputs) in order to produce revenues (outputs). In the short run, many of these inputs are relatively fixed in amount (for example, plant capacity, size of sales force, and advertising expenditures) and do not vary proportionately with the scale of operations. Profits will be maximized at that point where the marginal cost of the total of inputs is equal to the marginal revenue of the total output. For any *given* scale of operations, profit will be maximized when the ratio of the total output to the total input is greatest. Therefore, if profit maximization is assumed to be a firm's objective, new products should be chosen so as to optimize resource utilization. It should be borne in mind that this concept emphasizes optimum utilization of all resources, employed in combination, rather than the optimum use of each resource.

A great variety of resources is utilized in the average business firm. For purposes of simplicity, these are here divided into production resources and marketing resources. On the production side are such resources as plant, equipment, and technical know-how. On the marketing side are such resources as distribution facilities, the sales force, and established relationships with middlemen. If a proposed product and established products "converge" in production in the sense that they can share use of production resources, then production costs per unit can be expected to decline. Shared use of marketing resources (for example, sale of a new product through an established sales force) will produce the same result. In addition, a good fit marketing-wise among products may have a favorable influence on demand.

Production and marketing "fit" is one of the more controllable factors in product planning. An individual firm's influence on demand, price, and the product life cycle is likely to be slight. By assuring that new products have good production and marketing fit, input cost can be minimized and output may also be expanded. Not only does this serve to maximize profits in the short run but it also affects the probability of a firm's survival and growth. The efficient firm has all the advantages in a competitive environment.

utilization of production resources

Many production resources are employed in the production of revenues, and these vary greatly by industry classification. Among the more important resources employed in production are the following: (1) physical capacity, (2) labor skills, (3) technical know-how, (4) raw materials, and (5) by-products. Some of these are relatively tangible and fairly easy to measure, while others are less tangible and more difficult to measure. Other things being equal, that new product is best which, when added to existing products, provides optimum utilization of these production resources.

Physical capacity. Every manufacturing firm has a certain physical capacity for production in the form of plant and equipment. If this capacity is not fully utilized and sales of present products cannot be increased because of demand limitations, new products which can be manufactured with the same plant and equipment will spread fixed costs and reduce production cost per unit. Even when new production facilities must be created, it may often be desirable, because of the indivisibility of factors of production or in order to obtain other economies of scale, to plan to produce additional products so as to achieve competitive production costs on each product manufactured.

Labor skills. The skills of a labor force are as real an asset as buildings or machinery and often far more difficult to expand or modify. A firm that employs highly paid, and perhaps underutilized, fashion designers adding a new product for which style is not a critical factor would not be optimizing the use of styling resources. Many technical skills are in short supply and perhaps unavailable to a firm seeking them for the first time. Use of existing skills avoids this problem.

Technical know-how. If technical knowledge built up over many years is transferable to a newly added product, a firm has an advantage not possessed by others. Past production of military electronics gear may aid a firm in turning out civilian electronics ware. Technical knowledge derived from manufacturing stainless steel cutlery may be an asset to a firm which elects to produce stainless steel razor blades. Sometimes technical know-how has been "solidified" by the acquisition of patents on certain processes. Although intangible and difficult to assign a value, technical know-how can be a very real asset. Many companies moving into a new product field have failed because lack of experience in that field caused costly errors to be made.

Common raw materials. If new products can be added which make use of the same raw materials as existing products, several advantages may accrue. First, this may make possible a lower cost for raw materials because acquisition cost tends to be a function of volume purchased. Second, there tends to be a relationship between the use of the same raw materials and common production facilities and distinctive know-how.

By-product factor. The most obvious case of underutilization of resources occurs when potentially valuable by-products of present production activities are not used. The chemical, petroleum-refining, and meat-packing industries are excellent illustrations of the opportunity to improve the total output-input ratio by finding profitable uses for by-products.

decision matrix: utilization of production resources [7]

Isolation of a firm's tangible and intangible resources and the exposure of each new product idea to the light of these criteria is essential to a sound product policy. However, the decision of which new product to choose is complicated by the almost infinite number of

---

[7] The use of decision matrices for evaluating product choice decisions was suggested by the Van Wart Chemicals, Inc. case in Harry L. Hansen, *Marketing: Text, Techniques, and Cases* (3d ed.; Homewood, Ill.: Richard D. Irwin, Inc., 1967), pp. 517–31.

product alternatives sometimes available. Management may be in the position of having to select the product that best utilizes company resources out of hundreds or even thousands of possible alternatives. Also, in practice, the number of criteria used in making a judgment may be far in excess of the number employed here. For this decision-making process to be manageable, a practical basis for weighting the several criteria employed, and for assigning an evaluation score to each product considered, is necessary. Then the various alternative choices can be compared. In order to do these things, a reasonably objective evaluation scheme is desirable. This is the purpose of using a decision matrix.

Product-choice decisions are made under conditions of uncertainty. Even for such tangible criteria as, for example, the ability of a proposed new product to use existing plant and equipment, there may be a significant degree of uncertainty. Perhaps the product can be physically produced with these facilities, but there is doubt whether costs will be competitive. Perhaps certain desirable design features cannot be produced if present equipment is used, and modifications in the product will have to be made which may adversely affect demand. On such intangible factors as the application of technical knowledge gained from producing existing products, there may be even less certainty. Thus, there is need to consider the *probability* that a new product will, or will not, produce the benefits expected. A decision matrix facilitates such consideration.

If a proposed product is rated on conformance to each of the suggested criteria, and a probability estimate is assigned each of these ratings, then the "estimated value" of the proposed product for each criterion can be calculated. If these are totaled, an "estimated value" for each new product for total production resource utilization is obtained. The values so obtained for each of the products being considered can then be compared.

example: proposed new product "X"

Assume a hypothetical new product "X" is under consideration and a decision matrix is used to evaluate its contribution to optimum use of the firm's production resources (Figure 5–5). In constructing the matrix, weights have been assigned to the several relevant criteria discussed above. These weights are based on management's best judgment of the relative importance of conformance to each standard for the particular company. Arbitrary values have been assigned to the

Figure 5–5. Decision matrix: Utilization of production resources (proposed new product "X").

Decision Criterion	Criterion Weight	Very Good (10)		Good (8)		Average (6)		Poor (4)		Very Poor (2)		Total	Criterion Evaluation (Total EV × Wt.)
		P	EV	P	EV	P	EV	P	EV	P	EV		
Physical capacity.........	0.20	0.2	2.0	0.6	4.8	0.2	1.2	0	0	0	0	8.0	1.60
Labor skills.............	0.30	0.2	2.0	0.7	5.6	0.1	0.6	0	0	0	0	8.2	2.46
Technical know-how.....	0.30	0	0	0.2	1.6	0.2	1.2	0.6	2.4	0	0	5.2	1.56
Common raw materials.....	0.10	0	0	0	0	0.7	4.2	0.3	1.2	0	0	5.4	0.54
By-product.............	0.10	0	0	0	0	0.1	0.6	0.6	2.4	0.3	0.6	3.6	0.36

Total Production Resources Value...........6.52

possible ratings, ranging from 10 for "very good" down to 2 for "very poor." [8]

Management must now estimate the probability that the proposed new product will qualify for each of the possible ratings on each of the five criteria used in the evaluation. Note that achievement of any particular rating is not a certainty. For example, the illustrative figures included in the matrix (Figure 5–5) for utilization of physical capacity assume a 20 percent chance of a "very good" fit, a 60 percent chance of a "good" fit, and a 20 percent chance of a fit of only "average" quality. This range of possibilities is possible because of uncertainty which exists at this early stage of the product development process. For the second criterion (labor skills) the stated probabilities may reflect uncertainty about the adaptability of the labor force to production requirements of the new product. It is estimated there is a 20 percent chance that the labor force will adapt with no difficulty. If so, a "very good" rating would be achieved. However, it is more likely (probability .7) that the labor force will require some, but not expensive retraining (rating: good). It is possible (probability .1) that extensive, and expensive, training will be required (rating: average).

The probabilities decided upon for ratings on each criterion are similarly recorded in the decision matrix. Each probability is multiplied by the respective rating value (ranging from 2 for "very poor" to 10 for "very good") to arrive at the "expected value" (*EV*) for each rating. By adding across, the total expected value of each criterion is obtained. The difference in importance of the several criteria are now taken into account by multiplying the total *EV*'s by the criteria weights. The resulting evaluation scores are recorded in the right hand column. The separate criteria evaluation scores are in turn totaled to obtain the "total production resources" value. The illustration in Figure 5–5 shows a final value of 6.52 out of a possible 10. This is an index number which can now be compared with values similarly derived for other products under consideration. In general, the higher the score for utilization of production resources, the lower production costs per unit can be expected to be.

utilization of marketing resources

A going concern has marketing resources which, though often less tangible, are no less real than its production resources. These, too, can be underutilized by present products, thus again providing an opportu-

---

[8] In addition, precise definitions should be framed for each possible rating on each of the several criteria. As these must differ greatly by industry, they are omitted here.

nity for a new product to optimize a firm's input-output ratio. Marketing resources of firms are many and varied. Discussed here are four basic resources which are important in a wide array of product choice decisions. These are: (1) goodwill, (2) marketing know-how, (3) physical facilities, and (4) distribution channels.

Goodwill. In many cases the most valuable asset a firm possesses is the goodwill it has built up among consumers over the years through its present products. If this goodwill could be tapped for the support of a new product without undermining the sale of existing products, it is an underutilized resource just as much as is physical plant operated at less than capacity. General Mills, when it undertook the sale of small household appliances some years ago, did so in part because it felt the goodwill attaching to the General Mills name would help support the sale of appliances. A new Heinz food product probably finds a measure of market acceptance just because of its association in name with products already favored by consumers. A favorable association in the minds of consumers between a new product and existing products can influence the input-output ratio for the entire product line.

This relationship between new and present products can work both ways. The new product may sell better because of its association with present products. On the other hand, and at the same time, existing products may sell better because the new product helps to "round out" the line, sheds prestige on present products (for example, addition of the Continental Mark III to the Ford-Mercury-Lincoln line), or in some other way makes present products more acceptable to consumers. Unfortunately, a negative association between the new and present products in a line will produce opposite, and potentially disastrous, effects. For this reason such product relationships must be carefully considered in product choice decisions.

Marketing know-how. The knowledge management has gained through experience in the marketing of certain types and classes of products is often a very important asset. Knowledge of promotional strategies, pricing, dealer buying practices, consumer purchasing patterns, etc., can be the critical factor determining success or failure of a new product. New products similar in marketing requirements to established products trade on this knowledge, thus greatly increasing chances of success. It is far less risky for Procter & Gamble to introduce a new detergent than, for example, Monsanto Chemical Company to move into this field. Monsanto did introduce a new detergent, "All," which later it sold to Lever Brothers because of the difficulties it experienced in marketing a product with which it was unfamiliar. The rate of failure among new products introduced by firms unfamiliar with their marketing requirements is high.

The fuller utilization of marketing knowledge lowers marketing costs per unit just as does the use of a more tangible asset. Marketing knowledge is often gained only at the very high cost of trial and error. Such knowledge, of course, reduces the chance of future mistakes and, at the same time, helps assure that fuller advantage will be taken of all demand opportunities.

Physical facilities. Perhaps the most obvious opportunity for spreading marketing costs over a greater volume occurs when a new product can utilize physical distribution facilities which may contain excess capacity. Such facilities may be warehouses, truck fleets, retail outlets owned by the manufacturer, and so on. When Standard Brands, Inc., decided to distribute camera film to grocery stores along with its yeast, coffee, puddings, and other products, the dominant motivating factor was excess capacity in the direct distribution facilities which it maintained.

Distribution channels. If the new product can be sold through the same channel of distribution as existing products, it probably can be handled by the same sales force. This will increase average order size and reduce costs as a percentage of sales. If a new channel is required, then possibly an entirely new sales organization will be necessary. Because the cost of this sales force will have to be born entirely by the new product, distribution costs as a percentage of sales will tend to be high. Also, it is difficult for a firm to break into new channels with a new product. Middlemen are naturally reluctant to add products without an established demand. Normally they already are carrying competitive brands, and they are not eager to assume the risks involved in replacing established products with new and untried brands. Of course, the same factors may apply even to the channels now used for existing products, but at least the innovating firm has an established relationship with its channels which helps in getting its new product accepted.

A strong force favoring new products which can use existing channels is the natural desire of middlemen, other things being equal, to minimize their sources of supply. When the same assortment of products can be acquired from one source as from several, acquisition costs are reduced. If in addition these products are favorably associated with each other in the minds of consumers, perhaps linked by use of a common brand name, the middleman's selling costs may also be reduced. Thus, new products which can use the same channels as existing

Figure 5–6. Decision matrix: Utilization of marketing resources (proposed new product "X").

Decision Criterion	Criterion Weight	Very Good (10)		Good (8)		Average (6)		Poor (4)		Very Poor (2)		Total	Criterion Evaluation (Total EV × Wt.)
		P	EV	P	EV	P	EV	P	EV	P	EV		
Goodwill..........	0.20	0	0	0.2	1.6	0.5	3.0	0.2	0.8	0.1	0.2	5.6	1.12
Marketing knowledge......	0.20	0.1	1.0	0.5	4.0	0.3	1.8	0.1	0.4	0	0	7.2	1.44
Distribution facilities........	0.30	0.3	3.0	0.5	4.0	0.2	1.2	0	0	0	0	8.2	2.46
Distribution channels.......	0.30	0	0	0.2	1.6	0.6	3.6	0.2	0.8	0	0	6.0	1.80

Total Marketing Resource Utilization Value.................................6.82

products are preferred over products which must utilize new channels of distribution.

decision matrix: utilization of marketing resources

A decision matrix of the same type used for utilization of production resources is now employed to evaluate the use of marketing resources. Weights are assigned to the four decision criteria, probabilities of various ratings for each are estimated, the estimated values are calculated, adjusted for criterion weight, and summed to determine the total marketing resources utilization value of the proposed new product (Figure 5–6). There is now an objective basis for comparison with other proposed new products.

summary: resource utilization

With the aid of a decision matrix, two values relating to the efficiency with which a new product would use the resources of a firm have been arrived at—one for production resources and one for marketing resources. At this point, two pertinent questions arise: (1) What do these values mean? and (2) What does one do with them?

Probably the major value of these figures lies in the analysis that has been necessary in order to derive them. In this process, the potential effects of adding a new product on all operations of the firm have been carefully considered. Problem areas which might have been overlooked have been thought about by company management. Much of this analysis has been subjective, but often no other approach is possible in the real world.

The value for utilization of production resources and the one arrived at for use of marketing resources are not necessarily equal in significance. Which is more important in influencing the product-choice decision depends on the area in which potential benefits from proper "fit" between new and old products is greatest. A steel company, for example, has high fixed costs of production and, because of fluctuations in the demand for steel, is often faced with excess production capacity. Marketing costs, on the other hand, tend to be more variable. Hence, optimizing the use of production resources through the addition of new products offers the greatest opportunity to reduce average unit costs. A manufacturer of soaps or toiletries would usually have low production costs and high marketing costs. Consequently, a proper marketing fit among its products is of most importance.

A value for the utilization of total company resources can be obtained by combining these two figures. In the process, greater weight can be given to optimizing use of resources in the area with greatest potential benefits. For example, if it is desired to give 50 percent greater weight to the use of production resources than to utilization of marketing resources, then a value for efficiency of use of total company resources can be derived as shown in the accompanying table.

Utilization of company resources

	Value	Weight	Weighted Value
Production resource utilization	6.52	0.60	3.91
Marketing resource utilization	6.82	0.40	2.72
Company resource utilization			6.63

If one new product under consideration utilizes company resources more efficiently than others, this fact has an important bearing on the anticipated profitability of adding this product to the company's line. A good marketing fit, if it produces a carry-over of goodwill from one product to another, may influence demand or price.

The major impact of efficient utilization of production and marketing resources is on cost. Both manufacturing and marketing costs may be reduced because of the spreading of fixed costs which this fit brings about. This cost advantage, in turn, may result either in higher profit margins per unit or in an opportunity to charge a lower price and thus increase the number of units sold. Which of these courses is followed depends on management's decisions on pricing strategy.

A final word of caution is now in order about the interpretation and use of these numbers. The appearance of objectivity such numbers give can be misleading. Underlying them is a great deal of subjective analysis, much of it based on inadequate information. Small differences in derived values are therefore of little significance. Even larger differences should be looked at as only rough approximations. On the other hand, the calculated values constitute a useful tool. Alternative product choices can be ranked in order and sorted and classified as desired. However, their main value continues to be in the analysis required to derive them.

internal development or external acquisition

If a decision is made to offer a new product, a firm may, under certain circumstances, have a choice of developing the new product on its own or of acquiring it by taking over a company already marketing such a product. This choice is available, of course, only if the product is one new to the firm but already available in the market. Because relatively few products are truly new to the market, this choice of pathways is a prevalent one. It is a course which has been followed with increasing frequency in recent years. The desire for adding new products has become one of the dominant causes of the so-called merger movement. What is it that causes firms to acquire new products by merger rather than through their own development efforts? Is such an approach to product line diversification good or bad? If good for the firm, is this approach also good for the economy as a whole?

advantages of acquiring new products by merger

Reduction of uncertainty. Internal development of new products is fraught with uncertainty. Most new products are failures. Costs of development are high as well as difficult to estimate. The employment of sound product development procedures can reduce the risk involved, but even the best such programs do not reduce risk as much as a cautious management might desire. Merger also involves risk, but the sought-after product and its market position are relatively known quantities. The degree of uncertainty is less when a firm acquires a product whose commercial success has already been demonstrated.

Early profitability. The road to commercial success for new products developed internally may be a long one. Technical research and development may take years of effort, and this may then be followed by an extended period of market development. Market growth may be slow in coming, and costly to achieve. Substantial sums may be invested before any return is realized. Acquisition of new products by merger, on the other hand, may mean profitability beginning with the moment of acquisition if due care is exercised to assure that the purchase price is in line with profit opportunity.

Knowledge and experience. When a company by the process of product innovation moves into a new field, it assumes many risks which are associated with lack of experience. Knowledge of markets, particularly of consumer behavior, and the best means to cultivate those markets, comes in large part from marketing experience. Firms lacking such experience operate with a handicap. When new products are acquired by merger, the benefits of experience may also be acquired if knowledgeable personnel come to the new company as a result of the merger. In some cases this knowledge may take the form of patent rights or of research and development experience.

Removal of competitor. When an existing company is purchased to obtain a new product, at least one potential competitor is removed from the market. This can be an important advantage indeed, perhaps one which spells the difference between success and failure. If a firm contemplated adding tomato soup to its product line, acquisition of the Campbell Soup Company would virtually assure market success. When the Gillette Company decided to enter the home permanent field, its acquisition of the Toni Company not only removed the major competitor it would have faced, but immediately made Gillette the major competitive force in the home permanent field. Its later acquisition of the Paper Mate Company did the same thing for ball-point pens.

Market access. An obstacle to the success of new products is the difficulty such products often have in gaining access to the market. If the product is of a type new to the market, there will usually be an understandable reluctance among middlemen to handle it because a new product is an unknown quantity in terms of market acceptance and profitability. New products are risky to middlemen as well as to manufacturers. If the new product is similar to products already carried by middlemen, they may still be reluctant to stock it, but for different reasons. To add a product for which products already carried are reasonable substitutes may increase inventory and handling costs but add little to revenues. Receipts will be increased only if there is a significant brand preference or if there is a demand for variety in the market. In this case it is necessary to weigh the anticipated increase in revenues against the increase in costs. If the comparison is not favorable, the new brand will not be added.

An excellent illustration of the difficulty even a major firm may have in gaining market access is the attempt of Ford Motor Company to gain distribution for the Motorcraft line of replacement automotive parts. All automotive wholesalers already carried comparable parts, under other brands, which would fit all known applications. Brand preference in the repair trade was not strong, being outweighed by patronage considerations. Thus, there was no incentive for middlemen to add the new line either as a supplement or as a substitute for lines already carried. After an extended period of failure to gain acceptance of its new line, Ford solved the problem by acquiring the Electric Auto-Lite Company, which already had a strong distribution network.

Capitalization of development costs. Current accounting practice, because of the risky nature of new product development, is to treat development expenditures as a current expense rather than as an investment to be amortized over the market life of the new product.[9] When a product is acquired by merger, the purchase price is treated as an investment. The difference in effect on short-run profits of this difference in accounting treatment serves to discourage internal development.

advantages of internal development

Greater profit potential. Although most new products are failures, some new products are very successful indeed. In the long run, profit opportunity tends to be commensurate with risk. In particular, those products which are new to the market have the potential of a high return. On the other hand, if a new product is acquired by merger, acquisition cost can be expected to be commensurate with demonstrated profit potential. A safe return tends to be a smaller return. Few companies that acquired their new products by merger can match the rate of return achieved by such companies as Xerox, IBM, and 3M.

Progressive image. Although an intangible and hard-to-measure factor, the overall image a company projects can be very important to its long-term success. Successful product innovation marks a company as progressive and as a leader in its field. This stimulates interest and confidence in its products. Again, companies like IBM and the 3M Company are good cases in point.

Better resource utilization. Either acquisition by merger or internal development of new products may lead to better utilization of resources. On the average, however, internal development is likely to achieve this objective most effectively. It permits a larger measure of "custom tailoring" of new products so as to optimize resource utilization. When the merger route is followed, often little is contributed to the more efficient use of present assets (plant, equipment, distribution facilities, etc.) . Duplicate facilities may be acquired. Often, unwanted products must be accepted in order to get the ones which are wanted. By proceeding carefully in selecting companies for acquisition, these problems can be minimized, but in practice it is rare for them to be avoided altogether.

Clayton Antitrust Act, Section 7. A substantial disadvantage of product line diversification via merger is the danger of violation of Section 7 of the Clayton Act. This act prohibits mergers whose effect might be "substantially to lessen competition." Until 1950, Section 7 of

---

[9] John A. Howard, *Marketing Management: Analysis and Planning* (rev. ed.; Homewood, Ill.: Richard D. Irwin, Inc., 1963) , p. 318.

the Clayton Act was relatively ineffective because it prohibited only those mergers which were consummated by stock purchase. A company could expand by purchase of another company's assets unless this violated the Sherman Antitrust Act. However, in 1950, Congress made three major changes in Section 7 (the Celler Antimerger Act). First, it broadened the section's reach to cover corporations acquiring the "whole or any part" not only of the stock but also "of the assets" of another company. Second, it eliminated from the statute the illegality test of whether the acquisition's effect may be substantially to lessen competition between the *acquiring* and the *acquired* company. Finally, Congress struck the prior test of whether the acquisition might restrain commerce "in any community," and substituted as the measure whether "in any line of commerce in any section of the country" the acquisition may substantially lessen competition or tend to create a monopoly.[10] As a result of these changes, mergers are much more suspect than formerly and, consequently, a more risky approach to broadening a firm's product line.[11]

In recent years many companies have been ordered by the courts to divest themselves of merger acquisitions. Procter & Gamble Company was ordered to dispose of Clorox Company, General Foods Corporation of its S.O.S. Division, Continental Oil Company of Malco Refineries, Inc., and Ford Motor Company of Electric Autolite Company. Several of these diverstitures are now being appealed.[12] The most important test of whether a merger is illegal is the effect of the merger on the share of market controlled by the surviving company. In the *Brown Shoe Company* case the court stated, "The market share which companies may control by merging is one of the most important factors to be considered when determining the probable effects of the combination on effective competition in the relevant market."[13] In ruling against Pillsbury Mills, Inc., the Federal Trade Commission looked at Pillsbury's market position for prepared mixes before and after two

---

[10] *Report of the Attorney General's National Committee to Study the Anti-Trust Laws* (Washington D.C.: U.S. Government Printing Office, 1955), p. 117.

[11] Section 7, in relevant part, now reads: "No corporation engaged in commerce shall acquire directly or indirectly, the whole or any part of the stock or other share capital and no corporation subject to the jurisdiction of the Federal Trade Commission shall acquire the whole or any part of the assets of another corporation engaged also in commerce, where in any line of commerce in any section of the country, the effect of such acquisition may be substantially to lessen competition, or to tend to create a monopoly" (64 Stat. 1125).

[12] *Business Week*, July 20, 1968, p. 72.

[13] 82 S. Ct. 1502 (1962), p. 1534.

challenged acquisitions. Pillsbury increased its share in the Southeast market from 22.7 to 44.9 percent and moved ahead nationally from second to first place, increasing its share from 16 to approximately 23 percent.[14] This fact alone was deemed sufficient to establish a substantial lessening of competition.

Firmer base for long-term growth. Gaining new products via merger is inevitably a somewhat opportunistic approach to product line diversification. Whether or not this route can profitably be followed depends on the availability of firms with desired products whose owners are willing to sell at a particular time, on the ability to succeed against others who might be bidding for these same companies, and on ability to avoid subsequent diverstiture under Section 7 of the Clayton Act. Internal development of new products is less opportunistic. Properly executed, it contemplates product development as a continuing and permanent function of the firm. Surely this provides a firmer basis for rational long-term growth. It might be said that one of the important benefits of internal development of new products is that a firm exercises and develops its product innovation capability. Over the long term this might be the greatest competitive advantage it could possess.

product development and public policy

The government has attempted to discourage firms from acquiring new products by merger when the effect might be to lessen competition. Many have felt that the government and the courts have been overzealous in applying Section 7 of the Clayton Act, ruling out many mergers that would not have affected competition adversely and at the same time denying to business many of the advantages of product line diversification. The effect of mergers on competition is of relevant concern, but there is another possible effect which should also be considered. This is the effect of mergers on product innovation. Unfortunately, the effect of mergers on the pace of product innovation is unclear.

Assume for the moment that *all* firms acquire *all* their new products *only* by the merger route. In this case the market would gain nothing new. Already available products would merely be reassigned among various firms. There would be, in effect, no true innovation. Even the *possibility* of obtaining new products by this means may have some deleterious effects. It reduces the pressure upon management for new ideas and for the development of new processes and techniques. It

---

[14] FTC Dkt. 6000 (1953).

offers "a way out" to the lethargic, to the company that sat idly by and did not attempt to innovate.

This extreme picture is highly unrealistic. In addition, the circumstances of the individual situation have much to do with the effect of acquisition by merger on product innovation. When Gillette Company acquired the Toni Company and Paper Mate, nothing new became available in the marketplace. On the other hand, innovation may be spurred when a large, well-financed company acquires a small company, rich in ideas perhaps, but unable to afford the high costs and risks of product development. The acquisition of Philco by Ford Motor Company probably increased Philco's innovation capability. Funds received by small firms when they are bought out by larger ones may be devoted to research and development of additional new products, while the larger acquiring firm fully develops the market for the small firm's past innovations.

conclusion

Because all products have a life cycle, survival of the business firm depends on the infusion of new products into the market. In a broader sense, the economic welfare of society is based on this same economic function. Long-term growth in man-hour productivity is due primarily to development of new machines and processes, not to people working harder. The affluent society owes its present comfort more to the new products developed by this and preceding generations than it does to attempts to lower production costs. One automatic washing machine is worth, in terms of its effect on our way of living, an infinite number of old-fashioned washboards.

questions

1. Profit margins usually reach a peak and decline at an earlier point in the product life cycle than does sales volume. Why is this so?
2. A manufacturer of central home heating equipment is considering the possibility of adding a line of electric space heaters selling at $9.95, $14.95, and $19.95. The company's present line is sold through heating contractors and is used both in new home construction and in renovation of older homes. The electric space heaters are portable, and it is thought a large market for them exists among homeowners for supplemental heating, in cottages and resorts, and as a major heat source in parts of the country where central heating is not required.

What factors should be considered by the firm before committing itself to the manufacture and marketing of these electric space heaters?

3. The National Safety Razor Company is a major producer of safety razors, razor blades, shaving creams, and men's toiletries. Management is now considering a proposal to add a line of electric razors. One executive doubts the wisdom of this move. He points out that the Gillette Safety Razor Company failed in its attempt to introduce an electric razor. The reason for this failure, he says, is that electric razors do not fit well with the rest of the Gillette line. Is this executive's reasoning sound?

4. This chapter emphasized the importance of a good production and marketing fit between a company's present products and a new addition. Yet many companies, particularly the so-called "conglomerates," have in recent years entered businesses completely unrelated to their present businesses. Is a decision to do this necessarily unsound?

5. When deciding to add a new product is it more important that there be a good production fit or a good marketing fit between present products and the proposed addition? Explain.

6. Business firms have a substantial degree of choice in the amount of emphasis they place on product innovations in planning their long-term marketing strategy. What arguments can you offer in favor of relatively heavy stress on this strategy variable?

7. The rate at which new products are introduced into the market has increased greatly in the last decade. Some observers of this fact view this as evidence of economic progress; others view it as no more than an increase in planned obsolescence, which is wasteful. What is your view? Explain.

8. "When a company produces a wide line of products, management should take care to determine that each product covers its full costs and yields a satisfactory rate of profit." Appraise this statement.

9. "Trolley cars and newsreels. Milk bottles and Mason jars. Argyle socks and blue-suede shoes. Where are they now?

   "They're with shaving mugs, soap flakes, Burma-Shave signs, automobile seat covers and 78 rpm records—vanishing from the American scene.

   "It's all due to technology and taste. Both are changing more rapidly than ever, causing a fast turnover in the artifacts of everyday life. Change is so fast that yesterday's dream is today's necessity—and tomorrow's fond memory" (*The Wall Street Journal,* February 6, 1968) .

   The above quotation suggests the importance of an innovation capability to the business firm. By what criteria do you judge whether a firm does or does not possess such a capability? Explain.

10. Discuss the proposition that acquisition of new products by merger, although this course might best serve the interests of the firm, is not necessarily beneficial to the total economy.

chapter 6

product
development
decisions

The process of developing a new product is broad in scope. Directly or indirectly the process must involve all operations of the business firm—marketing, production, research and development, finance, and even the legal department. Because of its inherent risk feature, top management is usually intimately involved in it. In order for so complex a task to be carried out effectively, it is imperative that a sound program for product development be formulated and then followed.

The most basic and critical decision involved in the product development process is the one discussed in the preceding chapter—selection of the product which, for the particular firm in question, provides the best profit opportunity. If this decision has been made wisely, with due consideration given all variables involved, the remaining steps in the process are made much easier, and chances of success are greatly enhanced. Still, much remains to be done and many opportunities for error remain after this choice has been made.

Product development is, in essence, the process of fitting the proposed product to the requirements and opportunities of the market. The decision to produce, say, a sports car still leaves unanswered questions about styling and configuration, size, color, convenience options, the image to be projected, and so on. An almost infinite number of specific decisions must be made to provide this market adaptation. If they are made wisely, the profit opportunity visualized will be realized. If not, the profit opportunity will be lost.

Selection of the best product for development is, as previously explained, a procedure fraught with uncertainty—uncertainty concerning demand, price, cost, and the product life cycle. In a very real sense, the product development process is a procedure for gradually reducing this uncertainty by increasing the information available to the decision maker.

the product development process

The product development process is not, and cannot be made, uniform for all companies. Each company is unique, and this uniqueness finds expression in differences in goals, requirements, and procedures. Figure 6–1 shows how the product development process might be carried through in a hypothetical firm. Although not necessarily applicable to situations faced by all companies, it will serve as a useful frame of reference for discussion of the types of decisions involved in product development.

characteristics of product development

An overview of the product development process as depicted in Figure 6–1 reveals certain important characteristics.

Process span. Product development begins with the conception of an idea for a new product and does not end until an established sales position for the new product has been achieved in the market. In a very real sense, a product has not been "developed," nor has a true innovation been accomplished, until that product has been accepted in the market. This achievement marks the adaptation of the new product to the market in an overt, profit-making, sense. It is the point at which the basic objective of new product development, maximization of profits, begins to be realized. In fact, it can be argued that product development doesn't end even here, that it is necessary to continue to change and improve products throughout the total life cycle if profits are to be maximized. However, this process is more commonly referred to as product improvement.

Concurrent marketing and production development. As discussed above, product development involves all operations of a business. Figure 6–1 stresses the concurrency of marketing and production development. Production must be geared to marketing requirements as closely as possible. It must provide the product the market wants, in the right quantities, at the right time. Marketing strategy, on the other hand, must reflect certain realities of the production process. For example, offering many varieties of size, color, and style may maximize sales, but only at prohibitive production costs. Profit is a function of efficiency of the total firm, not maximum efficiency in one part or another.

Concurrent development of a new product marketing-wise and production-wise offers certain economies. Test marketing, for example, provides an opportunity to experiment with production processes so as to eliminate bugs before full-scale production is required.

Figure 6–1. Steps in conversion of new product idea into new business.

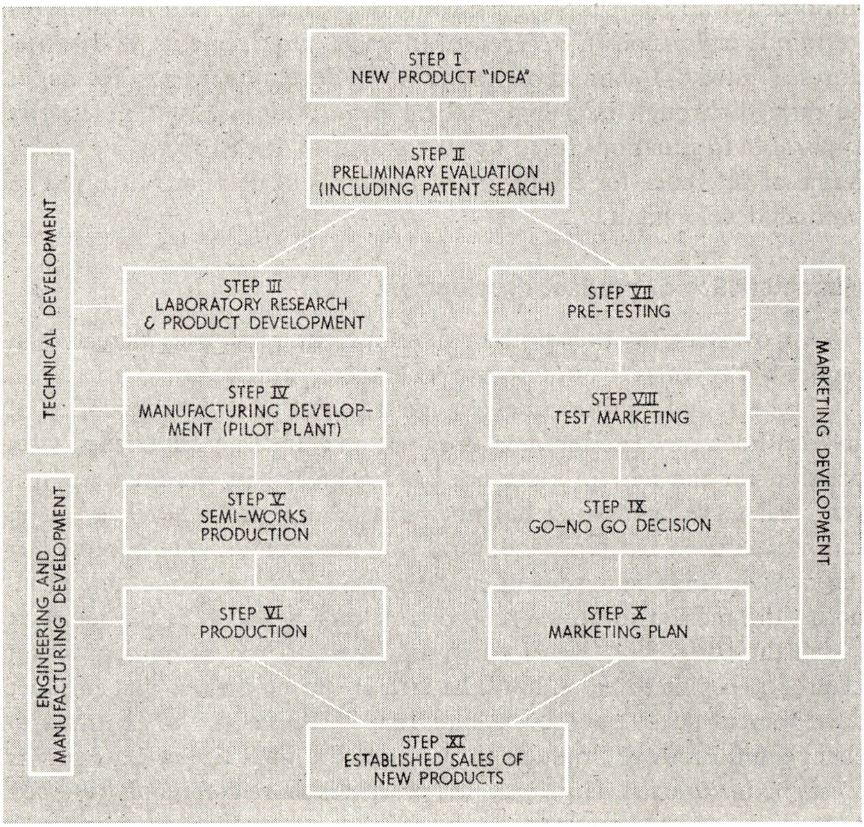

TECHNICAL DEVELOPMENT

ENGINEERING AND MANUFACTURING DEVELOPMENT

MARKETING DEVELOPMENT

STEP I
NEW PRODUCT "IDEA"

STEP II
PRELIMINARY EVALUATION
(INCLUDING PATENT SEARCH)

STEP III
LABORATORY RESEARCH
& PRODUCT DEVELOPMENT

STEP VII
PRE-TESTING

STEP IV
MANUFACTURING DEVELOP-
MENT (PILOT PLANT)

STEP VIII
TEST MARKETING

STEP V
SEMI-WORKS
PRODUCTION

STEP IX
GO–NO GO DECISION

STEP VI
PRODUCTION

STEP X
MARKETING PLAN

STEP XI
ESTABLISHED SALES OF
NEW PRODUCTS

Interdependence of marketing and production development. Each of the steps in product development on the production side (steps III through VI in Figure 6–1) is related to the corresponding step (VII through X) on the marketing side in the sense that each depends on the other. Perhaps this interdependence is most clearly seen in the case of laboratory research and marketing research. Laboratory research without accompanying marketing research can easily be misdirected and sterile. In a market-directed economy, the standards employed in laboratory research should reflect what people want from the product. High quality reflected, say, in durability is not a reasonable standard if consumers prefer low price and are willing to sacrifice quality in order to get it.

Before laboratory testing can be meaningfully undertaken, marketing research is usually necessary. The extent to which this is true, however, varies by products and by the type of standards involved. In many cases, important market standards for a product are already well known (for example, safety and durability of tires, efficacy of drugs, purity of food). Some laboratory testing is often possible without market testing; *complete* laboratory testing usually is not.

The same type of interdependence exists between the other steps in production and marketing development. Essentially, the market testing activities provide feedback which allows production development accurately to reflect marketing requirements.

Product development is a cautious process. It is a step-by-step feeling out of the market as the process evolves. Each step taken is intended to reduce further the uncertainty inherent in the product development process by increasing the information available about marketing requirements for the new product. Implicit in the taking of each step, therefore, is the need to decide how much additional market information is worth—in research expenditures, in time, and in relation to the cost of assuming more risk. The cost of reducing risk to zero, if this were possible, would usually be prohibitive. In carrying through this cautious approach, another objective is to retain as long as possible the option of *not* introducing the new product, with a minimal investment loss should this decision be made.

Product development involves the "total" product. There is equal need for development of such things as distribution strategy, promotional appeals, service policy, and warranty policy, as for development of the physical product. Because of the difficulty of depicting the product development process in a fully accurate fashion, Figure 6–1 may err in conveying the impression that development of these aspects of the new product is separate and apart from development of the physical product. In reality, they too are a part of each of the steps. Marketing research, for example, done on the new product is equally relevant to such matters as service, warranty, and so on. In fact, the physical product may even be changed to adapt to such things as distribution strategy and promotional appeals.

The previous section considered some characteristics of product development as a total process. This section will take a closer look at what is involved in carrying out the specific steps in product development.

new product ideas

Ideas for new products come from many sources—from the market, from production, from home office and research personnel, from salesmen, from other companies, and even from independent inventors. No one knows just where a good idea for a profitable new product might come from. Some sources are more likely to be productive than are others, but no company wants to close off any of them.

Most firms claim to be receptive to new product ideas, but few make an overt attempt to stimulate them or to ferret them out. Rather, this important process is left more or less to chance. This is a mistake. Some sort of organization for seeking out and handling new ideas is required; what form this organization takes is of secondary importance. Unless responsibility is centered somewhere, both the search and the processing will be neglected. Both line and staff personnel are usually fully busy with current operations, and added burdens are neither welcomed nor pursued.

The search for new product ideas can go on in many ways, the most appropriate approach depending on the industry involved. Primarily for industrial goods, but to some extent for consumer goods, call reports of salesmen may be so constructed and analyzed that they reveal consumer problems with present products, comparisons with competing products, unmet needs, and so on. Basic research may turn up many ideas which can profitably be followed up. Even brainstorming sessions may be worthwhile. What is most important is that ideas be actively sought, whatever the methods used.

preliminary evaluation

The next step in Figure 6–1, preliminary evaluation of new product ideas, is in essence the product-choice decision discussed in the preceding chapter. However, it is usually not feasible to subject every new idea to complete and rigorous analysis. Most ideas are not worthy of extensive consideration. Therefore, some sort of preliminary screening method is usually employed. It is quite customary to have a screening committee, made up of representatives from different functional areas of the business (marketing, production, research and development, finance, and so on) to look over and discuss new product ideas. On the basis of the breadth and background of experience of committee members, these ideas are reviewed. Usually, most are rejected. Those that look most promising are turned over to some sort of new product task force for detailed study. This study might well follow the procedures outlined in the preceding chapter. This group then reports back to the preliminary screening committee, which reports, in turn, to top management.

pretesting

The fundamental purpose of pretesting is the acquisition of knowledge useful in assuring that the new product properly reflects demand factors. The "pre-" in pretesting can mean preproduct, preproduction, premarketing program, and so on. Of necessity, it is a step that must come early in order to provide proper guidance. Because it must come early, it also usually means testing under circumstances which are somewhat artificial and in other ways difficult.

Methods used in pretesting of products are almost infinite in number. It is an area with much room for ingenuity. A few of the more common are: (1) Consumer panels and juries: Groups of various sorts and sizes (women's clubs, company visitors, etc.) are asked their opinion of various proposed product features (styling, color, etc.). (2) Consumer surveys: Representative samples of consumers may be selected, asked to view and comment on proposed new products. (3) Field tests: Tentative versions of new products may be presented to consumers for use in the home and their reactions ascertained. Pillsbury Mills asked housewives to bake two different formulas of cake mix, serve them to their families, and then record their preferences. Chrysler Corporation gave consumers new turbine cars to drive for several weeks and then interviewed them to learn their reactions. (4) Trade shows: American Telephone and Telegraph displayed the Princess telephone at the International Home Builders' Show. Five thousand visitors filled out cards giving their impressions of the new phone.[1]

Many other methods of pretesting are in use. All of them involve certain dangers. It is both difficult and costly to choose representative samples. The consumer's ability to indicate a true preference under artificial conditions is always a source of doubt in the results. Even if

---

[1] *American Telephone and Telegraph Company* case, in M. P. Brown, W. B. England, and J. B. Matthews, Jr., *Problems in Marketing* (3d ed.; New York: McGraw-Hill Book Co., 1961), p. 79.

consumers have true preferences, it is difficult to conclude what this means in terms of actual sales in the real marketplace. Still, admittedly inadequate information is better than no information and usually well worth its cost.

test marketing

Test marketing involves the sale of a proposed new product under conditions as near normal as possible in a test market which is as representative as possible of the target market. Sales performance of the product in test markets is observed and measured in order to ascertain what can be expected to be future sales performance in the total market.

The need for preliminary market testing of new products stems from the inherent limitations of pretesting. Pretesting is, as mentioned above, artificial in varying degrees as far as market conditions are concerned. Also, pretesting usually involves only some, and not all, aspects of the new product. A pretesting of Pillsbury Cake Mix, for example, was limited to taste preference between two alternative formulas. It revealed no information on such matters as package design, price, promotional appeals, comparisons with competing products, and so on. Consequently, it left a large measure of uncertainty about future market performance.

Test marketing, too, has limitations. The basic problem of sampling error is an important one. Cost limitations usually prevent use of a truly representative sample of the total market. Usually only one or a few cities are chosen. Also, the cost of arranging for the gathering of maximum information in the test market is high. Expensive store audits and consumer surveys may be necessary to do this. Some companies set up their own test markets and do their own data collection. Others use the test markets of such market research organizations as the A. C. Nielsen Company, which have elaborate facilities for data gathering.

Because of cost as well as for other reasons, the time that can be devoted to test marketing is usually limited. It is questionable whether sales in a short time period are representative of longer term sales experience. The difference between initial sales and repeat sales is particularly critical. Initial sales may indicate a high consumer interest in a new product, but only repeat sales indicate presence of the sort of consumer satisfaction on which long-term success must be built.

Preliminary market testing runs the risk of loss of secrecy for a firm's new product plans. This may take away the promotional advantage associated with a dramatic, nationwide introduction. Also, it divulges a company's plans to competitors and may lessen the time it takes for them to retaliate. For such products as automobiles, these two limitations are deemed highly important.

Test marketing of new products provides an opportunity for experimentation on the production side (step IV in Figure 6–1). The manufacture of limited quantities allows development of production processes and techniques so as to minimize production cost.

the go–no go decision

The process of product development up to this point has been one of gradual and continuous improvement in information available for product decisions. Information seeking can vary greatly in its extent, time consumed, and cost incurred. Throughout this process, management would normally attempt to retain as long as possible the option of going ahead with introduction of the new product or not. At some point it becomes uneconomic to continue to seek information, and a decision must be made to "go" or "not go" with the product in question. Success of the new product at this point is always still uncertain, sometimes highly so. It is a question of weighing carefully the probability of success and deciding whether or not to proceed.

The go or no go decision is a difficult one. Information is never complete. Furthermore, the decision makers have a vested interest in a favorable decision in order to justify the substantial investment that has been made bringing the product to this point. A no go decision is, in a sense, tacit admission that previous expenditures should not have been made. This is a difficult psychological barrier to overcome. An objective approach to this decision would, of course, ignore costs already incurred. These are "sunk" costs. The only relevant decision variables are future revenues in relation to future costs. This relationship determines the expected controllable profit associated with the new product.

The go–no go decision involves, in essence, a careful review and correction of the several variables in the profitability formula developed in the previous chapter.[2] Hopefully, as a result of pretesting and preliminary market testing, demand can now be more accurately defined both qualitatively and quantitatively. Expectations of price behavior, likewise, can now be refined. A recalculation of production and marketing fit, based on expanded knowledge of marketing and produc-

---

[2] $R = [D \times (P - C) \times L] \pm [d \times (p - c) \times l]_1 \pm [d \times (p - c) \times l]_2, \ldots\ldots\ldots\ldots$
$\pm [d \times (p - c) \times l]_n.$

tion requirements, should allow a refinement of earlier cost calculations. Expected life usually will still be a major uncertainty, but perhaps some estimating improvement is possible here. Effects on these same variables for existing products should now also be better known.

These refinements of the component variables in the profitability formula will now permit a more precise estimate of expected profits associated with adding the new product. A comparison with alternatives available for investment will then allow the go–no go decision to be made.

the marketing plan

The final step in this process, before actual introduction of the new product into the market, is the formulation of a detailed marketing plan. The purpose of such a plan is to give form, direction, and control to the market introduction process. The new product marketing plan must, of course, be integrated with, and fully consistent with, the overall marketing plan of the company.

Actually, development of a marketing plan doesn't start from scratch at this point. Previous steps in the development process are as relevant to this activity as they are to the go–no go decision. Evolution of the marketing plan began with the new product idea and grew with each succeeding step. What remains is to give concrete form and structure to this plan and to fill in the still-missing details.

The essential parts of a marketing plan for new product introduction are the same as for the company's overall marketing plan: a situation analysis—facts about demand, competition, marketing law, the available distribution structure, and nonmarketing costs—can be based on information gathered in the earlier steps in production and marketing development. If these steps were well handled, the requisite information will be available. The problems and opportunities this situation provides should also now be known.

What remains is the planning of marketing strategy and tactics. The essence of marketing strategy is the setting of objectives and the determination of methods to be employed to accomplish them. Objectives can be stated in terms of the market (s) to be served—geographical area, income, and age groups, etc.—as well as sales volume in units and/or dollars. A specific profit goal is the most important objective to be decided upon.

The methods to be utilized in marketing strategy fall into such categories as product strategy—models, sizes, package design, etc.; distribution strategy—direct versus indirect channels, types of outlets, degrees of selectivity, etc.; price strategy—skimming versus penetration pricing, trade discounts, etc.; advertising strategy—media, appeals, etc.; and personal selling strategy—size and distribution of the sales force, selling methods, and so on. These objectives and methods, when the necessary detailed decisions concerning each have been made, constitute the heart of the marketing plan for the new product.

Before this plan can be implemented, this strategy must be converted into specific marketing tactics—who will do what, when, how, where, and so on. We are now ready to proceed to the final step of actual introduction of the new product into the market. Only when this step is successfully accomplished can we consider the product development task completed.

ancillary product decisions

The term "product" is used in this text to refer to everything the consumer receives when making a purchase. Consequently, product decisions cover a wide spectrum. This has been recognized in the discussion up to this point, but emphasis has been on the physical product and little has been said about some of the special problems associated with such functions as packaging, branding, warranty policy, and service policy. A closer look at these areas is now in order.

packaging

A package has two major functions: containment and promotion. Containment is essential to efficiency in physical distribution, while the promotional aspects of packaging operate to influence demand. Problems of containment tend to be technical and reasonably objective, such as requirements as to strength and size and resistance to moisture and other chemical elements. Promotional requirements concern such things as the package's ability to attract attention, its comparison with competing packages, its adaptability to advertising and point-of-sale promotion, its reflection on product quality, and so on. Development of a package to serve these functions well is a more subjective process. Although technical problems of containment are very difficult ones for some products, for most products the promotional aspects of packaging pose the most difficult decision requirements.

The role played by the package in the marketing mix, and hence the importance of the package development function, depends on many things. Packaging is usually a more critical element for convenience goods than for shopping or specialty goods. Within the convenience goods category, its importance varies with differences in buying behavior of consumers; for example, fresh vegetables, which consumers wish to see and touch, and detergents, which they will buy sight unseen. Self-service enhances the role of the package. Product-use requirements of consumers (for example, frequent reseal and reuse) may make the package a major sales-influencing factor. For some products (for example, cosmetics, table salt) package differences among brands may be more important than anything else. In some cases promotional requirements (use of television, for example) may strongly influence package decisions.

Diverse effects of package decisions. Package decisions are complicated by the fact that they may have many indirect, and often unanticipated, effects on both the production and marketing functions. Such "side effects" are often difficult to foresee and even more difficult to evaluate. Take, for example, the decision of many soft-drink manufacturers to package their products in cans as well as in returnable bottles.[3]

In the 1950's, soft-drink companies began experimenting with the sale of soft drinks in cans. Cans were thought to have several distinct advantages: (1) They did not need to be returned and thus relieved consumers of an inconvenience and removed a major problem for supermarkets, who objected to handling bottle returns. (2) They substantially reduced product weight. A case of 24 6-ounce bottles weighs 50 pounds, while a case of 48 6-ounce cans weighs about 25 pounds and takes one third less space. (3) Bottles are hard to stack and take a great deal of room in storage. Cans could be stacked in displays and on shelves just as any other canned goods.

Among the side effects associated with this product change are the following: (1) Taste. It was feared consumers might object to the slight metallic flavor picked up by carbonated beverages in cans. (2) Price. Although cans cost less per unit than bottles, the average returnable bottle made about 25 round trips. Thus, canned drinks would have to sell for $3\frac{1}{2}$ to $4\frac{1}{2}$ cents more per unit. (3) Channels of distribution. Present distribution was through bottlers who purchased syrup from soft-drink firms. These bottlers were not equipped for canning of soft drinks. (4) In-store promotion. Present promotion strategy relied heavily on bottlers, who made frequent deliveries to retail stores, set up displays, and so on. The soft-drink manufacturer was not equipped to do this. (5) Present distribution through bottlers.

---

[3] The following illustration is based on *Orange Crush Company* (Michigan Business Cases, Marketing Series, No. 21).

If canned soft-drink distribution bypassed bottlers, yet cut into their sale of bottled beverages, their profit position might be endangered. This might lead them to dilute their sales efforts by adding other soft drinks or, in extreme cases, to relinquish their franchise. As bottled soft drinks were expected to continue to account for at least 90 percent of sales, this would seriously hurt the soft-drink firms.

In the 1960's, canned soft drinks grew from 2 percent to 10 percent of total soft-drink sales. This, along with other package changes in the industry, has changed the entire distribution structure. Only high-volume bottling plants can justify the expense of installing canning lines. This has probably had no small part to play in the reduction in the number of bottling plants in the United States from 4,300 in 1962 to 3,600 in 1968.[4] Parent companies have taken on the job of supplying smaller bottlers with canned soft drinks. What started as a "simple" package change has revolutionized the whole industry.

Package development *is* product development; hence, the steps in package development are the same as those already discussed but with some change in emphasis. There is the same need to elicit ideas and for screening these ideas, for pretesting, and for test marketing.

Legal constraints on packaging. The principal legal constraints upon packaging decisions are those contained in the Food, Drug, and Cosmetic Act of 1938. The provisions of this act relating to packaging have two basic purposes: (1) to protect health, and (2) to prevent deception. Health protection is the purpose of provisions prohibiting packaging under unsanitary conditions, the use of packaging materials which may cause the contents to be injurious to health, or enclosing such potentially dangerous items as children's favors in the package along with its contents. Prevention of deception is the objective of provisions outlawing any food, drug, or cosmetic container which is "so made, formed, or filled as to be misleading." For food containers, minimum standards of fill are prescribed.

Information to appear on or within the package is controlled by the Food, Drug, and Cosmetic Act as well as by the Wool Products Labeling Act of 1939, the Fur Products Labeling Act of 1951, and the Textile Fibers Products Identification Act of 1958. For foods, Section 401 of the Food, Drug, and Cosmetic Act requires the establishment of definitions and standards for foods whenever such action will "promote honesty and fair dealing in the interest of consumers." The provisions for the labeling of drug products have long been very exacting and in

---

[4] *Marketing Insights,* March 4, 1968, p. 15.

1964 were further strengthened by an amendment to the act. The other three acts mentioned above are primarily designed to prevent deception by requiring on the label an accurate and clear description of the product's composition.

Government-imposed standards for packaging and labeling have long been a subject of controversy. Some consumer groups and government agencies recommend more rigid controls. Extensive hearings were held by the antitrust subcommittee of the U.S. Senate, chaired by Senator Phillip A. Hart, in 1961. Witnesses contended that the use of odd weights and sizes by competing brands made price comparison difficult, that net contents were often obscurely stated in small print, that illustrations, descriptions, and terms such as "giant half-pound" and "jumbo quart" were misleading. Many other charges of consumer abuse through packaging were also strongly pressed.

The outgrowth of these and subsequent hearings and congressional debate, spread over five years, was the passage in 1966 of the so-called Truth-in-Packaging law.[5] When finally passed, the act was a substantially watered-down version of the one originally introduced. The only mandatory provisions remaining concerned certain information to be included on the label; all other provisions are discretionary. A brief summary of the act follows:

Mandatory labeling provisions. A primary objective of the act is to promote uniformity and simplification of labeling. The bill provides that:

1. The identity of the commodity shall be specified on the label.
2. The net quantity of contents shall be stated in a uniform and prominent location on the package.
3. The net quantity of contents shall be clearly expressed in ounces (only) and, if applicable, pounds (only) or in the case of liquid measures in the largest whole unit of quarts or pints.
4. The net quantity of a "serving" must be stated if the package bears a representation concerning servings.

Discretionary labeling provisions. The act authorizes the administering agencies to promulgate regulations when necessary to prevent consumer deception or to facilitate value comparisons:

1. To determine what size packages may be represented by such descriptions as small, medium, and large.
2. To regulate the use of such promotions as "cents off" or "economy size" on any package.

---

[5] Public Law 89–755, 89th Cong., S. 985 (November, 1966).

3. To require the listing of ingredients in the order of decreasing predominance.
4. To prevent nonfunctional slack fill.

Packaging provisions. The act provides for the *voluntary* adoption of packaging standards. It authorizes the Secretary of Commerce to call upon manufacturers, packers, and distributors to develop voluntary standards whenever he finds that undue proliferation of weights, measures, or quantities impairs the ability of consumers to make value comparisons. If voluntary standards are not adopted, the Secretary of Commerce shall report this fact to Congress together with his legislative recommendation.

Enforcement. Responsibility for enforcing the provisions of the act is divided between the Food and Drug Administration (FDA), which has jurisdiction over food and cosmetics, and the Federal Trade Commission (FTC), which is supposed to regulate the labeling of all other consumer commodities. The Truth-in-Packaging law does not provide for criminal penalties.

branding

Another integral part of almost every product is a brand. Products which traditionally have been sold unbranded (such as fresh fruits and vegetables) are increasingly making use of product branding. For some products (such as cosmetics, some watches) the brand and its implicit connotations may be the most important value received by the consumer when he makes a purchase. Selection of an appropriate product brand, one which produces maximum acceptability of a product, is an important part of the product development process.

A brand is any letter, word, name, symbol, or device or any combination thereof which is adopted and used by a manufacturer or merchant to identify his goods and services, and to distinguish them from those manufactured, sold, or, in the case of services, performed, by others.[6] The term "brand" is a business term; the term "trademark" is its legal counterpart. A brand name is that part of the brand that can be vocalized. It should be remembered, however, that "brand" refers to *anything* which serves to distinguish one product from another.

There are many types of brands. In addition to those which identify products, there are "service marks" (for example, name of motel, laundry, or car-rental agency), "certification marks" (for example, the Good Housekeeping Seal of Approval) and "collective marks" (for example, seals of labor unions and trade associations). Brands owned by manu-

---

[6] For definitions of brands and trademarks and other terms related to them, see the Lanham Act, Public Law 489, Title 10, "Constructions and Definitions"; also, "Report of Definitions Committee," *Journal of Marketing*, Vol. 13, No. 2 (October, 1948), pp. 202–17.

facturers are known either as "manufacturers' brands" or as "national brands," regardless of the scope of the area served. Brands controlled by wholesalers or retailers are known either as "distributors' brands" or as "private brands."

Basic objective of branding. The basic objective of branding is market control. A brand is essential to promotional activities of the firm. Through promotion, acceptance or preference for a product can be established among consumers. If the product bears a manufacturer's brand and is available through many retail outlets, the goodwill of consumers is directed toward the manufacturer. Retailers will find it difficult to substitute other products for the branded one consumers prefer. On the other hand, if the wholesaler or retailer places his brand on a product, the goodwill of consumers attaches to the wholesaler or retailer, and the manufacturer loses much of his control over the market for his product.

The degree of market control which can be established through branding varies greatly. It depends very much on the distinctiveness of the product in the eyes of consumers, on whether this distinctiveness is based on hidden or apparent product qualities, and on the extent of consumer knowledge about a product. The industrial buyer who is a trained engineer, for example, will rely on his own judgment of a product's quality rather than on the reputation of a brand. In addition, the effectiveness of a company's brand strategy affects the degree of market control which is achieved.

Brand selection. Selection of a brand for a new product is an extremely important, and often treacherous, operation. New product names such as Chrysler's Valiant, Du Pont's Corfam, and Cities Service's Citgo grow out of meticulously planned campaigns involving computers, psychological tests, opinion surveys, and other scientific procedures. Too much is at stake to leave the choice to flashes of inspiration.

A good brand must meet two important requirements: (1) maximum promotability, and (2) minimum risk of loss of ownership rights. Promotability is a result of a combination of factors, and no absolute criteria can safely be established. Normally, however, those brands are considered best which are short; easily pronounced, spelled, and remembered; distinctive; appealing; and adaptable to various promotional media. A hidden nuance in a name can do a lot of damage, undermining the consumer's image of the product. For this reason, some companies insist on "nonsense" words for brand names, and rely on computers to find them. Among these is Du Pont, who reasons that a nonsense word is likely to have fewer connotations than a word familiar to consumers.[7]

Ownership rights to a brand can be lost in many ways, the two most common being infringement of another brand and by becoming a generic term. The danger of inadvertent infringement is great. There are more than 300,000 brands registered with the U.S. Patent Office and at least that many more registered with state bureaus; and according to the U.S. Trademark Association, there are probably a million more that aren't registered but could lead to lawsuits if copied.

A brand name becomes generic when the public adopts it as a word to describe a general class of products. The courts may then rule that it is a part of the American language and cannot be appropriated for the exclusive use of one firm. Until 1921, "Aspirin" was a brand name of the Bayer Company. Then it became a generic name. In the same way, Du Pont lost "Cellophane," the Haughton Elevator Company lost "Escalator," and American Thermos Product Company lost "Thermos."[8]

Unfortunately, there is a conflict between the twin objectives of promotability and protection for brands. The factors which make a brand promotable are also the ones which might tend to cause it to be infringed by others or to become generic. There is need in brand administration to reconcile these two objectives, to achieve the optimum level of each without jeopardizing the other. Registration of a brand under the Lanham Act (Trade Mark Law of 1946) is a partial aid in accomplishing this goal.

Registration of brands. Under common law, ownership rights in a brand are based on priority of use; whoever first used a particular brand in commerce is the "owner" of that brand. Registration of a brand is not essential to the protection of fundamental rights in that brand, but registration under the Lanham Act modifies and extends basic ownership rights.

The Lanham Act is administered by the U.S. Patent Office. It provides for registration of brands on either the Principal or Supplemental Register. Full benefits of registration are accorded only to marks placed upon the Principal Register; the Supplemental Register provides more limited protection to marks which, for one reason or another, do not qualify for the Principal Register. The major purpose served by registration on the Supplemental Register is protection of a

---

[7] Max Gunther, "We've Got to Call It Something," *The Saturday Evening Post,* September 11, 1965, pp. 60–61.

[8] *Ibid.,* p. 61.

brand used in sales to foreign countries. In many countries, rights to a brand derive from registration rather than from priority of use. Registration in these countries often can be made only for marks already registered in the seller's own country. Hence, the Supplemental Register was created to provide U.S. firms selling abroad the sort of protection for their brands they have at home under the common law.

Among the more important benefits which are gained by registering a brand on the Principal Register under the Lanham Act are the following:

1. *Registration is prima facie evidence of ownership.* This means that in case of conflict over ownership rights in a brand, the burden of proof is on the owner of the unregistered brand. Because use of a particular brand by both parties may have begun many years ago, and evidence of the exact date of use is often skimpy, this can be a very important advantage.

2. *Registration is constructive notice of registrant's ownership claim.* Under the common law an infringer can often gain ownership rights to a brand if the infringement was innocent, made without knowledge of the existence of the infringed brand. If a brand is registered, all parties are *presumed* to know of its existence, whether they do in fact or not, and cannot claim innocent infringement.

3. *Registration permits cases of infringement to be tried in federal courts.* This is important to protection of a brand because federal courts will interpret cases in light of provisions of the Lanham Act, with its relatively clear provisions, rather than under the common law, which is far from clear, as will the state courts.

4. *Possible collection of triple damanges.* In cases of brand infringement, courts normally award damanges to the owner of the infringed brand. Under the Lanham Act, federal courts are authorized to assess up to three times the actual damages. This serves as an obvious deterent to infringement.

5. *Protection against imports which infringe registered brands.* Brands recorded on the Principal Register are filed in the U.S. Treasury Department and are checked against brands on imported goods to discover and halt cases of possible infringement.

6. *Achievement of incontestability.* After five years of registration on the Principal Register, a brand becomes "incontestable." As defined in the Lanham Act, this means that ownership rights cannot be lost to someone else on the grounds of priority of use. This limits to five years a risk which under common law is eternal.

Other lesser benefits are also derived from registration. Of those listed above, although all of them are important, incontestability is probably the most significant. Before passage of the Lanham Act, registration was no more than a claim to priority of use, which could be set aside if someone else could prove he was the first user of a particular brand. Now, after five years of continuous use, even though someone else proves prior use, the owner of the registered mark is assured he can continue to use the brand in which he may have invested large sums. It is possible that the first user may gain the right of concurrent use, either on a different product or in a different market area.

warranty policy

Decisions on warranty policies are also a part of the product development process. The assurance provided by a warranty to the consumer that he will actually receive the utility he anticipated is a part of the value of his purchase. A warranty is an obligation to the buyer assumed by a seller. It provides that the seller shall be answerable to the buyer for various matters relating to the product.

Warranties may be either express or implied. An *express* warranty is one that is stated by the seller in either written or spoken words. A warranty is *implied* if, from the nature of the sale and the circumstances of the parties, the law believes it reasonable that a warranty was intended, although none was actually mentioned. Implied warranties have been codified and incorporated in the Uniform Commercial Code, which has been adopted by the legislatures of most states. Among the principal implied warranties are: (1) warranty of title, (2) warranty that goods sold by description are as described, (3) warranty that goods sold by sample conform to the sample, and (4) warranty that goods intended for consumption are fit for consumption. With regard to product quality, (5) there is no implied warranty as to quality or fitness for any particular purpose except where the buyer makes known to the seller the particular purpose for which the goods are required and relies on the seller's skill or judgment. Also, an implied warranty as to quality or fitness for a particular purpose may be annexed by the usage of trade.

Objectives of warranty policy. Specific objectives of warranty policy might be any in a long list of possibilities. Most of these can be classified as part of one of two general objectives: promotional advantage or protection of the seller. When a product is offered on a "satisfaction or your money back" basis, the purpose is usually to induce trial of a product by removing risk to the purchaser. On the other hand, an express warranty which restricts the buyer's redress to claims approved by the seller, and at the same time disclaims all other liabilities, expressed or implied, has as a major purpose protection of the seller against buyer claims.[9] The situations noted here represent the two extremes in warranty terms. If these are thought of as the extrema of a continuum, the terms of any particular warranty can fall at any point in between.

These two general purposes of warranties are not necessarily mutually exclusive. Surprisingly, perhaps, it is possible to serve both of these objectives at the same time. This is a result of the role of warranties in consumer purchase behavior. Consumers rarely subject written warranties to careful scrutiny and are thus uninformed of the extent to which their rights are assured or restricted. They seem primarily concerned with whether or not a written warranty accompanies the product, not in its terms. Any written warranty, no matter how restrictive, is assumed to be better than no written warranty. Actually, a highly restrictive warranty may offer less protection than no warranty at all because it disclaims liability under implied warranties.

The ability of manufacturers to limit their liability by use of disclaimers is increasingly being restricted by the courts. It has long been held that a manufacturer cannot disclaim responsibility for his own negligence. Several recent decisions have held manufacturers strictly accountable for damages suffered by consumers, even though negligence cannot be proved.[10] Courts are beginning to move away from the principle that warranties do not "run with the product." For example, automobile warranties have long been held to be part of the contractual relation between manuffacturer and dealer. The dealer, in turn, warrants the product to the car purchaser. The consumer's only claim is against the dealer. The only exceptions to this principle recognized were for products taken internally (foods, drugs, beverages, etc.) or where negligence on the part of the manufacturer could be proved. Increasingly courts are taking the view that restriction of warranties to privity of contract is unrealistic in these days of mass distribution and are extending the responsibility of manufacturers to consumers even though no contractual relationship between these parties exists.

---

[9] For example, the New Vehicle Warranty used by Oldsmobile Division of General Motors on 1965 models states: "There are no warranties, expressed or implied, made by either the Dealer or the Manufacturer on new Oldsmobile motor vehicles except the Manufacturer's Warranty against defects in material and workmanship set out below." In addition, repair or replacement of defective parts is restricted to those "which examination shall disclose to Manufacturer's satisfaction to have been thus defective." (*1965 Oldsmobile Owner Protection Plan*, pp. 28–29.)

[10] Arthur Southwick, "Mass Marketing and Warranty Liability," *Journal of Marketing*, April, 1963, pp. 6 ff.

Warranty terms versus warranty administration. A warranty may be administered either strictly or liberally with respect to the terms it contains. For many years prior to 1961, the standard automobile warranty specified terms of 90 days or 4,000 miles, whichever came first. During this same period, however, it was customary for dealers, backed up by the manufacturer, to provide free service under the warranty for one full year. The change in 1961 to a 12-month, 12,000-mile warranty did not necessarily represent a change in the service the consumer actually received, but merely modified the written warranty to bring it into conformance with what was already practiced. In 1963, vehicle manufacturers adopted a 24-month, 24,000-mile warranty as standard for the industry. At the same time, Chrysler adopted a five-year, 50,000-mile warranty on power-train components. In 1967, the rest of the industry followed suit. Just how much this liberalized the granting of redress under warranty is uncertain. However, high costs of warranty administration presumably account for reducing warranty terms for automobiles to 12 months with the introduction of the 1969 models.

Whether a restrictive warranty, liberally administered, or a more generous warranty, restrictively administered, is the better strategy depends on the objectives to be attained. Liberal administration of a restrictive warranty probably has a favorable psychological effect on a firm's customers; they are receiving more by way of service than they have a right to expect. If a company's objective is to build loyalty among its present customers, this might well be a good policy to follow. On the other hand, a warranty with more generous terms can be very useful as a promotional weapon, underscoring a company's confidence in the quality of its products. In 1961, Ford Motor Company was the first to adopt the 12-month, 12,000-mile warranty for automobiles. It promoted this more generous warranty heavily at that time in conjunction with its promotional theme of "The Car that Cares for Itself." This is probably a better approach for a company whose primary goal is to expand its market share than it is for the company that wants to hold its present customers. A more liberal warranty also may serve as a means of promoting service business for dealers—it tends to tie consumers to the dealers for service for a longer period of time.

product service

The term "service" is used loosely in marketing; it is employed in reference to promptness of delivery, returned goods privileges, treatment of customers by retail salesclerks, and so on. By "product service" we have reference to service work intimately associated with the physical product itself—its adjustment, maintenance, and repair so as to assure the consumer the utility he can reasonably expect as a consequence of his purchase. Such service is sometimes referred to as "technical service," although the amount of technical expertise involved varies widely. In the industrial market the adaptation of products to the individualized needs of the buyers may call for a high order of engineering knowledge, whereas repair of some consumer durables may be essentially a task of exchanging a new part for one which has proven defective.

Product service is today a major problem area for manufacturers of many products.[11] The increased complexity of products and the rapid growth of markets have outstripped the development of service facilities. As a consequence there is widespread dissatisfaction among consumers with the general quality of product service, and widespread concern among manufacturers because of their inability to cope satisfactorily with the situation.

Manufacturers are uncertain of the role product service should play in marketing strategy. For example, should a manufacturer stress his service program in his promotion, or will this have a negative effect on the consumer's purchase decision because it brings to mind service problems he has previously experienced? Evidence exists that consumers pay little attention to future service requirements when making a purchase. One study shows future service needs to have been overtly considered by only 2 percent of buyers.[12] Product service, to the consumer, is something like a toothache; he does not look forward to it, wants immediate attention when his need arises, and wishes to forget about the matter as quickly as possible. Perhaps the greatest need for a manufacturer concerning service is to develop a rationale concerning the role of service in his total operation—what should be its objectives and how should it "fit in" with other elements in his marketing program.

Product service strategies.[13] Manufacturers follow many different strategies with regard to product service. Their strategies are in part an

---

[11] See "The American Repairman: A Vanishing Breed?" *U.S. News and World Report*, September 13, 1965, pp. 88–90.

[12] George Katona and Eva Mueller, "A Study of Purchase Decisions," in Lincoln H. Clark (ed.), *Consumer Behavior* (New York: New York University Press, 1955), p. 49.

[13] The following discussion of product service strategies is based on E. A. Anthony, "Product Service: The Fourth Dimension of Marketing," in Stewart H. Rewoldt (ed.), *Conference of Sales Management: Contributed Papers* (Ann Arbor: Bureau of Business Research, The University of Michigan, 1957), pp. 11–26.

outgrowth of the ways in which they view product service—the philosophies and attitudes concerning it which shape their thinking about its role in marketing strategy. Among the more common approaches to product service among companies are the following.[14]

The negative view. This view holds that product failures are clearly mistakes and that product service is a kind of fire-fighting operation; the cost of performing it is a penalty paid for shortcomings in engineering and manufacturing performance. Product service is not seen as an activity providing added value to a product, but as an unfortunate expense which should be kept at an absolute minimum until the deficiencies which causes it can be removed.

The quality-policeman view. This view of product service is an extension of the negative view and places primary emphasis upon the information-gathering role. Product defects are clues to needed product improvements. Careful records must be kept of the nature and incidence of defects so that the extent of the problem, as well as the need for corrective action, can be assessed. Primary allocation of product service resources should be to such information gathering, and only secondary consideration should be given to correction of defects in products now in the hands of consumers. Product service is basically an adjunct of technical research rather than a means of building consumer goodwill in the short run.

The service-is-a-business view. Service can be looked at as a business in itself, as a profit-making opportunity which should be exploited. When service is inevitable and the out-of-warranty product population is large, the opportunity profitably to employ this approach is present. Automobile manufacturers, among others, cultivate service business at a profit through the manufacturer and sale of replacement parts and the provision, through their dealers, of service facilities. A basic problem associated with this approach is the possibility of conflict between the service end and the manufacturing end of the business; product improvement can cut directly into service profits by reducing the incidence of repair. An attempt to compromise these two profit goals may lead to confusion of purpose.

The natural agent view. This view holds that the dealer, rather than the manufacturer, has primary responsibility for product service. Because he is nearest to the customer, he has a higher capacity to act quickly and economically. Also, he is the one to whom the customer will naturally turn when he has a service problem. Acceptance of this

---

[14] The views of product service presented here are not necessarily mutually exclusive. Approaches to product service often reflect a combination of these views.

view by the manufacturer limits his obligation to seeing that the dealer is properly supplied with the parts, service manuals, and so on, that he needs to perform his service function. The dealer becomes the prime service factor, with the manufacturer assuming a facilitating role.

The factory service view. Diametrically opposed to the natural agent view is the factory service view. It is argued that the manufacturer has most at stake, that his brand appears on the product, and hence that it is he the consumer will blame if the product is faulty. It is also pointed out that dealers have defaulted on the service function, that the manufacturer is more competent, and that consumers have more confidence in service provided by the manufacturer. In recent years automobile manufacturers have experimented with factory service centers in metropolitan areas. Appliance manufacturers have moved heavily in this direction.

The limited obligation view. This view holds that the manufacturer's product service responsibility is limited to the length of the warranty, that this is all he promised when the consumer made his purchase. After expiration of the warranty, service is the function of independent repair shops, which can and do provide such service at a profit on a wide array of products. It can be argued that the reduction in the manufacturer's service cost which might be associated with this approach may lead to reduced product prices, thereby compensating the consumer for any increase in the cost of out-of-warranty service.

The competitive weapon view. Product service is, of course, an effective marketing tool which can be used to influence product value, acceptance, and brand reputation to a significant degree. To achieve this objective, the service organization and its policies and functions should be designed around a concept of customer needs and wants in relation to product service. The promotion of Zippo lighters is a good case in point. This company has long advertised that "no one has ever had to pay for repairs on a Zippo lighter." The effect of such promotion on sales is, of course, difficult to measure.

The competitive weapon approach is not limited to small and inexpensive products, although the risks inherent in such a policy are least for such products. In the case of automobiles, many foreign makes have had disappointing sales in the United States because of consumers' concern about adequacy of service. Volkswagon has placed heavy stress on the quality and availability of its service, perhaps thus gaining a competitive advantage over other imports.

The optimum quality view. This view of product service holds that service can be useful in permitting an optimum level of quality to be attained. Product failure patterns are studied carefully and continuously to discover areas where too much money is spent on quality as well as those where quality improvement is needed. Cost dollars can then be shifted away from areas which indicate little complaint activity to areas having high complaint ratios and service costs, thus achieving the optimum relationship between product quality and service requirements.

The socioeconomic view. Product service presents excellent opportunities to influence a firm's public image. Service provides opportunity for the "personal touch," the chance to demonstrate that the large, impersonal corporation is concerned about the individual consumer and his personal problems. Conversely, the failure to provide competent and responsible service may be considered the manifestation of a "public be damned" attitude. Some public utilities seem to have learned this lesson well. Through extensive services reflected in their rate structures, they have gained widespread support among consumers. Others, often with lower rates but fewer services, have very unenviable reputations. Organizations whose activities are extensively controlled by public boards, who in turn are responsive to public opinion, can ill afford such adverse public reactions.

Quality-service interrelationships. The complementarity of product quality and product service, and the trade-offs possible between the two, are not always clearly recognized. Critics of business are fond of pointing out that the quality of many products is below the quality level possible. Vance Packard, in *The Wastemakers,* makes much of this charge. What such critics often fail to recognize is that the highest quality is not necessarily the "right" quality in terms of demand and cost considerations. Sellers must offer consumers what they want, and they often prefer lower quality to higher prices.

This suggests that there is an optimum relationship between product quality and product service, although that point might be hard to locate. The optimum relationship depends on many things, among them such factors as: (1) consumer attitudes toward the inconveniences associated with product service; (2) consumer purchase behavior—for example, do consumers weigh service requirements heavily or lightly in purchase decisions? (3) the capabilities of a company's service organization; and (4) a company's ability to control quality.

Some of the criticism of business that is embodied in charges of "planned obsolescence" seems to involve a lack of recognition of the relationship between product quality and service cost. In a competitive economy, it is unlikely that business does not build products of as good quality as they are able to build, given the price at which these products must be offered. They do, however, control quality, and accept certain product service costs, in order to provide consumers something that best meets their needs and buying patterns.

Service versus exchange. A basic trend affecting the service task has recently emerged and already seems rather well established. Increasingly, exchange of products and parts is replacing field service. In 1951, General Electric Company began a policy of exchange rather than repair of electric blankets during the warranty period.[15] This practice has now spread to many other small appliances. Automotive repair increasingly consists of installing new or rebuilt parts rather than attempting field repair of defective units.

There are several reasons for this trend. Foremost among them is rapidly rising field repair costs because of increasing wage rates. The cost of repairing is rising much faster than the per unit manufacturing costs of new or rebuilt parts, the production of which can benefit from economies of scale. Compounding this problem is the growing technical complexity of many products, which complicates the repair function. In addition, there is the failure of service personnel and facilities to grow apace with the expanding economy. Increasingly, young people shun such employment.

Special service problems for industrial goods. Service often plays an even larger role for industrial goods than for consumer goods because of the specialized nature of the products and the need for continuous operations of the industrial user. It is not unknown for the cost of service to exceed the cost of the physical product itself.

One simple classification of industrial service is based on the time at which the service is performed: presale, time-of-sale, or postsale. In each of these cases the amount of service rendered may greatly exceed what is normal for consumer goods. For time-of-sale and postsale service the problems differ from those associated with consumer goods primarily in degree, not in kind; presale service causes the greatest perplexities.

Presale service may consist of extensive and expensive engineering studies necessary to adapt a seller's offering to the specific requirements of the potential buyer. It may be composed of detailed cost studies essential to the buyer's purchase decision. These studies, or others like them, may utilize high-priced talent and consume much time.

The purpose of such presale service is, in large part, to convince

---

[15] Harry R. Tosdal, General Electric Company (A) case in *Introduction to Sales Management* (4th ed.; New York: McGraw-Hill Book Co., 1957), p. 93.

the buyer he should purchase. It is a particularly expensive form of promotion. If the service is rendered and no sale is made, a substantial loss may be suffered. If an attempt is made to charge separately for presale service, its promotional value is reduced. If the seller attempts to recoup his loss in higher prices to those who do purchase, his competitive position is threatened. The seller faces a real dilemma from which there is no easy escape.

Approaches to the solution of this problem vary widely. In most cases they involve an uncomfortable effort to reconcile these various considerations to arrive at a viable approach to the market. Firm policies are hard to establish, and a normal result is to "play it by ear," compromising as necessary with regard to each potential sale.

organization for product development

Effective organization for product development poses many problems, and companies have adopted various approaches to their solution. Most basically, there is the problem of overcoming the still-too-widespread belief that formal organization for new product development is unnecessary. Often, this function is thought to be a part of everyone's job, and therefore it is the responsibility of no one. Because product development is a complex function, involving nearly all aspects of a business operation, there is a difficult problem of coordination. The skills of many people in many departments (technical research, engineering, production, market research, finance, etc.) must be brought together to compose an effective overall effort. In addition, top management must be intimately involved in the product development process because often the very future of the business enterprise is at stake. In less extreme cases, profits may still be greatly influenced, now and in the future, by product development decisions.

The organization for new product development presented in Figure 6–2 is that of a large, widely diversified company with a strong success record in product innovation. Obviously, this particular organizational approach is not suitable for all companies, but it contains many specific ideas and procedures which have wide applicability.

In this company, each product (operating) division is responsible for research and development of new products associated with its present activities. The New Product Division is responsible for research and development of products not associated with present product divisions. The product divisions, however, may call on the New Products Division for advice and assistance and may "employ" them to carry out certain functions. The New Products Division is charged with coordinating product development activities throughout the company.

The New Products Screening Committee reports directly to top management. Ideas for new products which are received by top management are referred to the committee for evaluation. Members of the committee come from major functional areas which are affected by the product decision. This group may reject a proposal on the basis of initial review or, very rarely, give immediate approval to proceed. Most commonly the proposal is referred to the New Products Division

Figure 6–2

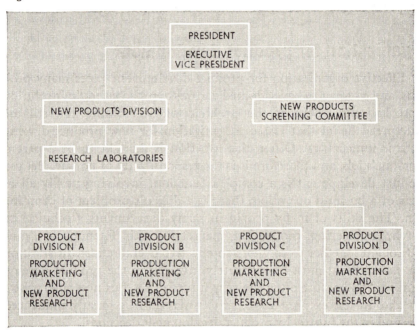

for careful analysis of technical, market, financial and legal matters, and a report is returned to the Screening Committee. If it approves, the New Products Division is then authorized to proceed further with development.

Within the New Products Division each "unrelated" new product is organized as a small business unit with personnel responsible for market research, advanced product development, experimental manufacturing, and test marketing. Each such new business unit is headed by a project manager who is fully responsible for all phases of the new business development program. Its basic goal is to put itself out of business as soon as possible. It achieves this goal when it completes the following tasks to the satisfaction of the top management. The "new business" is then turned over to an operating group, either one already in existence or a new one formed for this purpose. The tasks are:

1. Determine market potential for the new product.
2. Establish goals for research and development people.
3. Supervise technical and market research.
4. Design and develop the package.
5. Investigate competitive products.
6. Determine if present productive capacity can be used or if new facilities are needed.
7. Evaluate extent to which the new product is patentable.
8. "Test sell" the new product.
9. Evaluate market acceptance of the new product.
10. Work out a profit target for the new product.
11. Obtain a "go" decision from top management.

Not evident in this description of one company's approach to product development is the normally heavy use of the committee system in organizing for new product development. The facts that successful product development involves all parts of the business firm and that successful integration of their efforts is a major key to success makes the committee system appropriate.

conclusion

The approach of many companies to new product development has in the past been casual. It has often been thought of as a one-shot activity to be engaged in when necessary and then forgotten until the need for additional new products can no longer be ignored. Such an approach is not adequate to today's dynamic market. One of the strongest assets a company can have in a world of rapidly changing consumer wants is an effective product development capability.

questions

1. The introduction of a new product into the market is a treacherous business, with the chance of failure greater than the chance of success. In the light of this situation is it ever desirable for a firm to undertake the sale of a new product without extensive market testing?
2. The Tosca Company, manufacturers of automotive electrical equip-

ment, recently introduced a new automotive battery into the market. Sales have been very disappointing to date. This puzzles the company's executives because they are convinced this is a very superior battery. It is carefully made, and its quality has been carefully checked in the laboratory. Although it is higher priced than other batteries on the market, it carries a five-year warranty in contrast to the typical two- or three-year warranty. Thus, its cost per year of use to the consumer is less.

The president of the company believes that the fault may lie in the standards used in the laboratory to check quality. He has, therefore, called on you, a management consultant, to advise him on: (1) how laboratory standards should be determined, and (2) once determined, how much reliance can be placed on conformance to these standards as an indicator of market success. What do you advise?

3. P. Lorillard Company originally offered its king-size and filter Old Gold cigarettes in packages virtually identical with the package containing its regular-size Old Gold cigarettes. Both the king-size and filter cigarettes failed to sell in the volume anticipated. In order to improve their sales performance, the company undertook to differentiate the packages of both its king-size and filter cigarettes.
   1. How might this package similarity be at least in part responsible for the unsatisfactory sales of the king-size and filter cigarettes?
   2. What steps should P. Lorillard have taken in developing new packages for its Old Gold King Size and Old Gold Filter cigarettes?

4. In an article entitled "Packagers Rap Hart Bill" (*Business Week*, May 8, 1965), Lee S. Bickmore, president of National Biscuit Company, was quoted as calling the proposed packaging bill "stupid." Albert N. Halverstadt, a Procter & Gamble vice president, reportedly said it would "grant federal officials extraordinary powers to impose their preferences on the marketplace." On the other hand, the Department of Commerce saw the bill as a boon to consumers.

Evaluate the gains and losses to consumers and to business likely to result from passage of the Hart bill.

5. A brand, to be of value to its owner, must have some meaning and significance to consumers. Under what circumstances is a brand most likely to possess such meaning and significance?

6. How might it be argued that there is a basic conflict between the promotional requirements of a brand name and the protection of ownership rights in a brand name?

7. Contrast the warranty policies you consider appropriate to (1) a manufacturer of cigarette lighters and (2) a manufacturer of air conditioners.

8. Discuss the role of warranties in marketing strategy for small appliances. What are the implications of this role for a decision on whether or not to liberalize warranties on small appliances?

9. Some manufacturers of consumer durables argue that the retail dealer is

the "natural agent" to provide product service to consumers; others endorse the view that the manufacturer has prime responsibility for service. (1) What is the rationale behind each of these positions? (2) To what extent are these views in conflict? (3) What major problems would you expect to be associated with each of these two policies?

10. Many service problems now faced by consumer goods manufacturers would partially disappear if manufacturers built into their products the higher quality of which they are capable. Are they shortsighted not to do so?

cases for part three

HOLMES MANUFACTURING COMPANY*

decision to offer a new product

In December of a recent year, the sales executives of the Holmes Manufacturing Company were faced with the problem of devising a comprehensive marketing program for the Wheel-Burner, a combination wastepaper and leaf incinerator, outdoor grill, and garden wheelbarrow which had recently been added to the company's line of products.

The Wheel-Burner had been conceived by Mr. Carter, the company's sales manager, as a result of his personal experience with the problem of household wastepaper disposal. Mr. Carter had observed that modern automatic home heating systems had one rather significant drawback—they could not be used as incinerators for wastepaper and other combustible material which families formerly could dispose of in coal-fired furnaces. This meant that many households which had gas or oil heating systems had to acquire outdoor paper burners.

The ordinary burner, however, was deficient in several respects. Many of them were unsafe. They were frequently made of steel wire· in an open mesh construction, through 'which hot ashes and sparks could be blown about. This constituted a significant fire hazard which could be overcome satisfactorily only by having most of the incinerator enclosed. Added to the danger of the conventional burner was its unattractiveness and the damage that it usually caused by scorching the lawn area where it was used. Moreover, ash disposal was generally a dusty and unpleasant chore when the ordinary burner had to be emptied.

In recognizing these limitations of existing incinerators, Mr. Carter realized that the utility of a burner designed to be safer and cleaner than those then on the market would be enhanced considerably if it could be used for purposes other than burning household wastepaper and leaves. He had noticed that many families were purchasing outdoor picnic grills. He also felt that, in line with a general trend to more informal, outdoor activities, they were spending more time gardening than formerly.

* Written by William J. Watkins, Research Associate, Bureau of Business Research, Graduate School of Business Administration, The University of Michigan.

These observations suggested to him that in designing a superior waste-paper burner, he might with slight additional effort devise a product that could also be used as an outdoor grill and as a wheelbarrow for gardening tasks. His reasoning was that to overcome the problem of burning the lawn area where the conventional trash burner was placed, it would be desirable to have the burner on a *raised* platform. To overcome the problem of ash removal, it would be desirable to have the burner on a *portable* platform. A low, flat wheelbarrow onto which the burner might be fastened seemed to be the answer to these requirements. Moreover, if the incinerator were designed properly, this portability would enable it to be stored in a garage or shed out of sight. As a leaf burner, portability was a desirable characteristic because the burner could easily be wheeled to piles of leaves and loaded. These leaves could then be burned as the user raked other piles together.

An additional requirement had to be met if Mr. Carter's burner was to be superior to the type then on the market. The burning chamber had to be enclosed within a box or cylinder made of some nonflammable material such as sheet metal. This would prevent sparks or embers from being blown about when paper or other waste was being burned. When this was accomplished, Mr. Carter observed that the box constituted a rigid enclosure which would easily support an insert which, in turn, could be used to hold a charcoal fire. Since the top of the Wheel-Burner was about waist-high for adults when the insert was in place, the owner had a portable outdoor grill at a convenient level for outdoor cooking.

The Holmes Manufacturing Company was a producer of gas-fired water heaters and of burners for installation in conventional furnaces to convert them to the use of natural or artificial gas. The company normally employed about 130 workers and had specialized in the production of gas appliances since its organization in 1936. All of its manufacturing operations were conducted in the company's home city of Oakdale, Michigan.

The sales organization of the company consisted of Mr. Carter and his two assistants. The company's field selling activities for its established products were in the hands of 20 manufacturers' representatives throughout the nation. They sold to wholesale distributors in the heating and plumbing industry who, in turn, sold to local dealers. The Holmes Company had several accounts with public utilities; these were handled by direct sale. Sales promotion of waterheaters and conversion burners was limited to trade paper advertising directed toward dealers and distributors.

Fabrication of the Wheel-Burner was essentially a metalworking task. The component parts were either stamped to shape or cut to the proper length and then assembled. The company's labor force was well acquainted with the necessary processes as a result of the firm's long experience in the production of its major lines.

Although the company's engineers had never developed a product similar to the Wheel-Burner, they were able to embody most of Mr. Carter's ideas in

Exhibit 1. Wheel-Burner—Grill

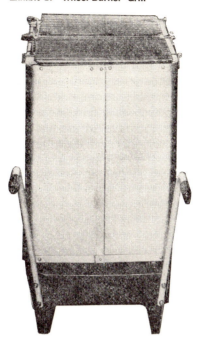

a light, compact, and well-made piece of outdoor household equipment. The finished product had many construction features that added to its serviceability. Several concealed expansion joints, for example, had been provided to avoid the warping that might develop in the sides of the burner without them. The grill insert was so designed that it provided complete temperature

Exhibit 2. Charcoal grill insert

control by allowing the user to elevate or lower the fire to any desired position. A partition was included with the grill insert so that if only a small charcoal fire was desired, it could be built in one end of the grill. Consideration had even been given to the width of the tread of the semipneumatic tire used on the wheelbarrow. It had been decided to use one relatively broad wheel rather than two of a narrower tread to avoid the formation of ruts or lines on the owner's lawn. In addition, one-wheel construction allowed lower production costs and permitted easier handling and dumping of ashes.

Although no quantitative estimates of the market for the Wheel-Burner had been made by Mr. Carter or his staff, it was felt that the product met the

Exhibit 3. Wheel-Burner for use as leafburner.

needs of a sufficiently large number of homeowners to warrant its introduction to several furniture, hardware, and appliance dealers within a radius of about 80 miles from the company's home city. This resulted in arrangements with 29 dealers in 11 cities, all of which were within broadcasting range of the television station in the city of Harperville, 40 miles to the north of Oakdale.

In selling these retailers, Holmes did not follow the practice of giving exclusive agencies. Instead, two or three outlets were usually sold in each of the communities where initial distribution had been achieved.

This pattern of distribution had been selected as an initial measure because the company had undertaken a limited amount of television advertising of the Wheel-Burner. Oakdale had no television station; the nearest was at

Harperville. The program which carried announcements of the product dealt primarily with new cooking and homemaking topics. The only promotion of the Wheel-Burner directly to dealers consisted of a small brochure which outlined the product's uses and construction features. No trade paper advertising had been attempted, although the Wheel-Burner had been exhibited at garden merchandise shows in New York and Chicago.

The television program which the company had sponsored appeared on Monday, Wednesday, and Friday for one half hour during the early afternoon of each day. The Holmes Manufacturing Company sponsored the program for a six-week period during October and November of the introductory year. During this time, there were two sales messages devoted to the Wheel-Burner on each program. In addition to the television program, the company offered to share with any dealers who would participate the cost of one one-quarter-page newspaper advertisement announcing the television program and describing the Wheel-Burner. The total cost for the program and the cooperative newspaper advertising during this period was approximately $2,500.

The results of this preliminary promotional activity were not discouraging (55 units were sold by the 29 dealers), but Mr. Carter felt that there was a strong seasonal factor involved in the purchase of outdoor household equipment, even though it might be designed to be used on a year-round basis. He felt that the grill and the garden wheelbarrow aspects of the Wheel-Burner would heighten its salability in the coming spring season and provide much more customer appeal than the leaf and paper burner improvements alone had during the period of recent promotion.

Despite the Wheel-Burner's novel combination of several basic products and its distinct improvement over them in many respects, the sales executives realized that the device faced substantial competition. For example, there were other *portable* incinerators making their appearances on the market. They consisted, usually, of wire basket-like containers which were mounted on a pair of wheels. There were other *enclosed* burners on the market, but they were typically designed to be used in one part of the owner's yard as a permanent installation, and thus lacked the portability of the Wheel-Burner.

The executives were well aware of the fact that outdoor cooking grills had been available for many years. In this area, there was a much broader range of product types than in the case of incinerators. There were modest picnic grills that could be quickly disassembled and stored in the luggage compartment of the family automobile. There were elaborate and expensive grills that had motor-driven spits and ceramic condiment containers. Between these two extremes, there were grills at many different price levels which provided varying degrees of outdoor cooking convenience and luxury.

In the case of wheelbarrows, there was much less diversity in product types than was true of outdoor grills. Even here, however, there had been developments which had made them more useful to householders. The use of light metals and the design of two-wheeled "garden carts" were some of the improvements that had recently been embodied in products intended to serve the function for which conventional wheelbarrows had been used.

The strength of this kind of competition was not underestimated by Mr. Carter and his staff. At the same time, they felt that the Wheel-Burner's combination of products, together with the actual improvements which it contained in the component elements (burner, grill, and wheelbarrow), gave it a sales appeal not matched by any of the three product types individually.

The sales executives had devised a price schedule for the Wheel-Burner and for the grill which was sold as an attachment available at extra cost. The prices were based upon cost and profit estimates for production volumes of between 5,000 and 10,000 units per month. Terms and prices decided upon were as follows:

Model	Suggested List Price	Dealer's Net Price	Distributor's Net Price
Wheel-Burner.................$36.95		$24.76	$18.47
Wheel-Burner grill.............. 11.95		8.01	5.97
Terms: Net 30 days from date of invoice, f.o.b. Oakdale, Michigan.			

In early discussions with representatives of one of the large mail-order chains, it was pointed out to the executives of the Holmes Manufacturing Company that the Wheel-Burner was considered to be too expensive for the market which that retail organization attempted to serve. Mr. Carter and his staff were inclined to agree with this observation, but felt that in view of the materials, workmanship, and design of the Wheel-Burner, it was actually not overpriced. They were of the opinion that the product provided a great deal of utility and could fill a real need for a large number of families in the middle and upper-middle income levels. In support of this view, they had the experience of several reorders by some of the merchants to whom Wheel-Burners had originally been sold. One of these retailers, a hardware store owner, had canceled his account, but the others had continued to handle the product and looked forward to a greater rate of sales in the spring.

The field saleswork for the Wheel-Burner had been entirely in the hands of one of the assistant sales managers, a Mr. Webster. Mr. Webster had handled the exhibits of the product at the garden merchandise shows and had obtained all the accounts which the company had with retail outlets. So far, no wholesale distributor had indicated any significant interest in the Wheel-Burner. Mr. Webster was assigned to the sales development of the Wheel-Burner on a full-time basis and had been traveling extensively about the state to solicit new retail accounts. He also felt that consumer acceptance for the product would increase with the warmer weather and was attempting to place the Wheel-Burner with as many retail outlets as possible before the advent of the spring merchandising season.

Mr. Webster and Mr. Carter had discussed the possibility of attempting direct distribution of the Wheel-Burner to dealers and of changing the price structure for the Wheel-Burner to the levels shown below:

Model	Suggested List Price	Dealer's Net Price
Wheel-Burner............	$29.95	$20.07
Wheel-Burner grill........	9.95	6.67

At this time, however, no decision had been reached concerning the contemplated price adjustment and change in distribution from the use of distributors.

QUESTION

Should the Holmes Manufacturing Company have added the Wheel-Burner and grill to its line of products?

case 3–2

WEDEMEYER ELECTRONIC SUPPLY COMPANY*

reduction in number of brands stocked

The president of Wedemeyer Electronic Supply Company was considering the possibility of reducing the amount of inventory carried in receiving tubes and transformers. While certain considerations suggested that it would be advantageous simply to carry fewer brands, the anticipated reactions of competitors and suppliers led the president to make a careful review of these product lines in the light of established criteria for dropping products from the firm's line.

The Wedemeyer Company was a large wholesaler of electronic parts,

* Written by A. R. Krackenberg, Professor of Marketing, Dearborn Campus, The University of Michigan.

equipment, and supplies in the south central Michigan area. Its main office and warehouse was located in Ann Arbor, with branches located in Lansing, Adrian, and Ypsilanti. Its sales were directed both to retailers (including both those selling electrical equipment and those operating repair outlets), and to industrial users such as manufacturers, public utilities, radio and T.V. stations, and research laboratories both public and private.

Major product groups distributed by Wedemeyer included: radio and TV receiver tubes; TV picture tubes; electronic parts of all kinds—i.e., capacitors, coils, condensers, etc.—used in a variety of consumer durables and industrial equipment; dry cell batteries of all types; antennas and their accessory hardware; testing and measuring equipment; and a line of phonographs and tape recorders. Phonographs were not truly within the scope of an electronics parts and equipment wholesaler's operation being rather the type of item carried by a music or TV set wholesaler. However, Wedemeyer started carrying them by accident and found it desirable to retain them to supplement sales volume.

No competitors of any importance existed in the immediate Ann Arbor area; in fact, there were no electronics wholesalers as such in that area. Competition was extremely keen, however, from wholesalers comparable to Wedemeyer in product offering and size, who were located in Jackson, Battle Creek, Lansing, and Detroit. In addition to direct wholesaler competition, there was also competition from mail-order wholesalers, and manufacturers who sold direct or through their own branches.

During the years following World War II, the company had been faced with an increasingly serious problem regarding the adding and dropping of product lines from its stock, plus the maintenance of an adequate inventory both with regard to quantity and variety of items carried. The increasing seriousness of the problem was traceable directly to the dynamic nature of, and the fantastic postwar growth of, the electronics industry as a whole.

The extent of Wedemeyer's problem of maintaining an adequate assortment of parts and equipment was readily illustrated by the fact that for anything that existed before the war, by the 1960's there existed twice as many parts and varieties. For example, regarding radio receiving tubes there were over twice the number of varieties that had to be stocked by a wholesale distributor to meet normal customer demands in the 1960's than in 1940.

In addition, there were many items that had not existed before the war but which now were items of major importance. For example, TV picture tubes accounted for a substantial part of most electronic wholesalers' business. (They accounted for approximately 8 percent of Wedemeyer's dollar volume.) They came in approximately 150 varieties and sizes, over 100 of which the average wholesaler had to carry if he were to give adequate service to his customers.

Moreover, most current items were generally of a higher unit price than earlier counterparts (even discounting the inflation factor). Accordingly, it required a substantially higher dollar investment to establish and maintain a suitable stock on hand. When the Wedemeyer Company decided to add a line of transitors to its stock, for example, it was required to make a minimum investment of $10,000.

With more than 30,000 different items actually on hand and well over 50,000 items being offered by the sum total of all manufacturers from which it bought, stock control and product line decisions were a continuing and pressing problem to the Wedemeyer Company. On the one hand, if a part was not available when needed, a sale was frequently lost. On the other hand, there was the problem of limited funds and the need to maintain an adequate return on investment.

Wedemeyer's president annually evaluated the firm's entire inventory-sales picture for the preceding calendar year by product groups and by major items within each group. On the basis of industry experience, as well as on the basis of minimum profit standards established by the president of the company, an annual inventory turnover of 4 had been set as the minimum desired rate for all lines of products. In making his annual survey, then, the first thing noted by the president for each product line was its inventory turnover rate. When a new product line addition was being considered, a rough estimate was first made regarding both average inventory requirements for the year and average first-year sales. Thus demand and inventory requirements furnished the starting point from which Wedemeyer analyzed all additions to and deletions from the line.

Beyond this consideration there were three or four other basic criteria which usually entered into every decision. One criterion consisted of an evaluation of the supplier of the line and, more specifically, his policies on a variety of items. Among the most important considerations were such points as assistance to wholesalers through dealer aids and sales meetings; completeness of the line being offered, both as to variety of items within a given product line and total variety of product lines offered; policy on industrial referrals, i.e., whether he sold direct or referred all inquiries to the local wholesaler; the flow of technical information between the manufacturer and wholesaler; promptness of filling new orders and back orders; transportation charge policy on filling back orders; reasonableness in handling adjustments and complaints; policy on return of obsolete items; and finally, the importance of the manufacturer's brand name to the retailers and consumers.

Regarding brand importance, it may be noted that while in some items, such as TV picture tubes, the brand was most important to the consumer and to the retailer, on other items, such as parts, the brand was of minor importance to the consumer.

Interestingly enough, price and sale terms were not too important so far as the evaluation of an individual manufacturer was concerned because the industry was so competitive that prices and terms were reasonably consistent between all manufacturers of comparable products.

A second element bearing on the product line decision was the character and capabilities of the manufacturers' and/or the manufacturers' agents' salesmen. So far as large manufacturers were concerned, their salesmen were generally of extremely high caliber. With smaller manufacturers and manufacturers' agents, however, salesmen's capabilities varied widely; and consideration was often given to a salesman's ability, knowledge, and character before selecting a given product line.

A third factor considered when making a product line decision was the potential impact of the proposed action on Wedemeyer's competitive position in the area. This refered both to the possible retaliatory measures of a manufacturer if a product deletion decision was under consideration, and to the actions of other wholesale competitors, and competing manufacturers to a lesser extent, if the action involved a product line addition.

Electronics manufacturers on the whole did not practice a policy of exclusive territory distribution. Rather, they were interested in fairly intensive coverage of the market and there was a fair amount of overlapping of territories covered by individual wholesalers representing the same manufacturer. There was no emphasis by a manufacturer on exclusive product representation; the wholesaler was free to handle as many competing brands of the same product or product-line as he desired. In fact, since there was in general a shortage of top-quality electronics wholesalers, most wholesalers carried more than one brand and were constantly being beseiged by manufacturers whose lines they did not carry to "give their line a try."

With the extreme competition in the industry at the manufacturer level, every manufacturer made maximum efforts to be represented in every location. When a manufacturer found his line dropped by a given wholesaler, or for some reason found himself not represented in an area, he made every effort to find or develop alternative means of distributing in that area. These alternatives involved everything from direct selling to trying to induce large retailers to perform a wholesaling function. If the later approach was followed, it tended to upset the competitive status quo in the area, and in extreme cases might mean a price war until the upgraded retailer secured a place for himself in the market.

The final factor which Wedemeyer evaluated when making a decision had to do with the completion-of-the-line concept. Every product carried had to satisfy the general needs of the customers to which Wedemeyer was selling. Every product had to fit the firm's present line; that is, complement the salability of the other products carried, or in some way better meet customers' desires.

During the annual inventory turnover analysis for the preceding year's activity, the president of Wedemeyer noticed that for the past several years inventory turnover of transformers and transformer products had been slowly declining and had dropped well below the minimum desired turnover rate of 4. Further analysis uncovered the fact that since the advent of TV, transformers and their component parts had been increasing in varieties and types by leaps and bounds. Wedemeyer was now buying from four sources— Stancor, Thorason, Merritt, and United. All four manufacturers were equally reputable and reliable. All four brands, moreover, were equally acceptable to the trade and a substantial degree of interchangability existed between the four lines.

Mr. Wedemeyer felt that this was definitely a product line where some overt action should be taken to reduce the level of investment.

Inventory turnover analysis also pointed up the fact that although the turnover for TV picture tubes and receiving type tubes was reasonably satisfactory, the amount invested in this line was extremely high and rising. Wedemeyer had four sources of supply for these tubes: RCA, GE, Sylvania, and Tung-Sol. In this case, however, all four were extremely well known and were specifically demanded by the retail dealer. Several were specifically requested by the consumer market as well.

Shortly after these observations were noted, a major change in price policy took place on the receiving tube product line. GE was the first to announce this change in terms and GE's action was immediately met by every other tube manufacturer. The new terms were in the form of a quantity discount which offered a maximum of 6 percent on annual distributor purchases of $100,000 and over. Wedemeyer's annual total purchases of the four brands averaged a little over $200,000 and this amount had customarily been split among the four suppliers noted above. Thus by concentrating its purchases the company could readily take advantage of this change in terms. Moreover, since receiving tubes accounted for approximately 18% of Wedemeyer's business, this change in terms could have a major impact upon the firm's profit picture.

The potential impact of this change is illustrated by the following price and cost data for the receiving tube line. The competitive wholesale resale price of receiving tubes was 50–10 percent off suggested retail prices, which ranged from $1.50 to $6.75 each and averaged $2.50. Assuming the retail price to be $1, for illustrative purposes, the net resale price would be equivalent to $0.45. Prior to the new price terms, the merchandise cost to Wedemeyer was equivalent to $0.36 on $1 of purchases, hence the markup would be $0.09 or 20% ($0.45 − 0.36 = 0.09). This 20 percent markup may be compared to the average cost of doing business for Wedemeyer of approximately 21–22 percent of sales.

QUESTIONS

1. What recommendations would you make to the Wedemeyer Company regarding. (a) transformers, (b) receiving tubes?
2. Did Wedemeyer use sound criteria for product addition and deletion decisions? Are there other criteria that might profitably be considered?

case 3–3

YARD-MAN, INC. (A)*

adding new products to line as means of utilizing excess capacity

Yard-Man, Inc., of Jackson, Michigan, was one of the nation's largest manufacturers of hand- and power-operated lawn mowers. For over a decade the firm had sold its entire output to Sears, Roebuck and Company for distribution under the Sears "Craftsman" label. Early in 1957, the management of Yard-Man, Inc., was considering the problem of how to utilize excess plant capacity. When this problem had first arisen in 1953, the advisability of marketing power mowers under the Yard-Man brand outside the Sears channel had been considered and rejected. In 1957, the firm was investigating the possibility of adding new products to the line as a means of utilizing excess plant facilities.

historical background

The Yard-Man Company had been incorporated in 1933 to produce a new type of lawn mower. Its unusual design was based on the use of hardened steel blades which did not touch the cutter bar. This new concept resulted in a mower that was efficient, long-lasting, and almost silent in operation.

In the years that followed, the company grew slowly, building up distribution through hardware jobbers, who in turn sold to hardware retailers. In 1938, Sears, Roebuck, having been impressed by Yard-Man's evident skill in low-cost production of quality merchandise, requested that the company design and produce a power-operated lawn mower for exclusive distribution under the Sears Craftsman brand. Yard-Man agreed to do so, and 1938 marked the production and distribution of 5,000 such mowers.

The year following, Sears requested that Yard-Man develop a hand-mower line for similar distribution. This also was done, but not until after a pricing agreement had been reached in which Sears was to give price protection to Yard-Man's dealers by selling the Craftsman mower at a retail price $1 higher than the comparative model that Yard-Man distributed through orthodox jobber-retailer channels.

---

* Written by Martin R. Warshaw, Professor of Marketing, Graduate School of Business Administration, The University of Michigan.

This policy of dual distribution continued until World War II curtailed civilian production, but as early as 1943, Sears was negotiating with Yard-Man to become an exclusive supplier of Sears in the postwar era. The management decision to produce solely for distribution through the Sears organization was made that year. However, Yard-Man did reserve the right to maintain its brand name and to use it in conjunction with the Sears Craftsman label. It was felt that this arrangement would prevent the trade name from becoming void through nonuse, and would provide brand identification in case Yard-Man wanted to return to its former type of distribution in the future. Accordingly, all jobbers were informed that their relationships with the company were being terminated well in advance of the resumption of peacetime business.

Some measure of the results of this decision may be seen in Exhibit 1,[1] which dramatically shows the increasing success of the Sears Yard-Man team in the postwar decade. During the period between 1947 and 1956, sales increased from approximately $2,509,000 to $12,257,000 (532 percent) while net profit increased from $198,225 to $722,476 (365 percent).

composition of product line

Yard-Man had concentrated on the top-quality mowers in the Sears line. Other sources furnished mowers for Sears selection of over 30 different models available to the Sears stores. The only deviation from this policy of producing high-priced units occurred in 1956, when Sears requested that a stripped-down mower be produced that could compete on a price basis with the many off-brand mowers that were appearing on the market and being sold by many nontraditional outlets such as low-price variety stores, furniture stores, and department stores. The result was the production of a model that was marketed under the Sears economy brand "Dunlap."

cost estimation

At the beginning of each fiscal year, Sears would estimate their needs for mowers during the coming period. Yard-Man formulated cost estimates based on the Sears volume forecasts. To these would be added an increment that would provide a flat rate of return to Yard-Man. This total would be the price that Sears would pay for the volume specified. A Yard-Man executive emphasized the fact that Sears' concept of merchandising was to allow their suppliers to realize a fair profit on sales. He further noted that this arrangement was not entered into lightly, but rather after the two companies realized the partnership nature of their relationships. The president of Sears commented on this situation when he stated:

. . .The buyer must be certain that the manufacturer believes in good engineering and product development; that he is a capable, low-cost

---

[1] Exhibits appear at the end of the case.

producer. The manufacturer must be certain that Sears will assure continuous production over a long period of time, and buy at a fair and equitable price.[2]

engineering and design

Product design was carried on in Yard-Man's own engineering department. The firm owned all patent rights on unique patentable features. The designs originated in the company, but conferences held with Sears representatives resulted in an integration of both Sears' specifications and Yard-Man's design developments to produce the best results from both performance and cost standpoints.

The chief engineer of Yard-Man stated that the pressure for product improvement was constantly coming from management, who emphasized the fact that competition was always pressing from two sources: from other manufacturers distributing through outlets other than Sears and from the other models in the Sears line itself.

It was further noted that only through good design and efficient production and management could Yard-Man hope to compete in the marketplace.

nature of the selling task

The vice-president in charge of sales explained that rather than selling to one large buyer, Yard-Man was in actuality supplying the needs of over 700 independently managed Sears stores in addition to the Sears mail-order division. He further explained that the Sears setup gave each manager considerable autonomy in choosing the items to be carried in his store. Sears was made up of five regional divisions, and each divisional headquarters sent a list of suitable products to store managers. Each manager could choose from the wide assortment offered and could price the merchandise to suit local competitive conditions.

Yard-Man's vice-president in charge of sales and his staff of three men performed continuous missionary saleswork by personal visits to the Sears retail outlets. Yard-Man was one of the few companies which had Sears' permission to make retail contacts with their stores. The purpose of these visits was to inform sales personnel of product features and selling points; the men were also trained to help with service, display, and other technical problems, and to assist in setting up service facilities in the Sears stores.

The continuing nature of the task was made necessary by the high rate of turnover of Sears retail sales forces due to shifts within or from the Sears organization. The task of making these contacts had been eased by an innovation developed jointly by Sears and Yard-Man, in which mower demonstration clinics were held in each of the Sears districts in the spring. The clinics were generally held at a golf course or other grassy spot, and representatives

---

[2] F. B. McConnell, president of Sears, Roebuck and Company, in an address before the New York Security Analysts on February 2, 1956.

from all the Sears stores and from all Sears mower and engine sources were present for product demonstration and general discussion of new features and service procedures. It was felt that by means of these clinics a great part of the retail selling force of Sears could be contacted either directly or indirectly just prior to the beginning of the major selling season.

Until 1956, Yard-Man had printed and distributed full-line folders to Sears. In 1957, Sears was introducing a complete garden equipment catalog, and Yard-Man was charged pro rata for space devoted to their products.

the service function

Until 1954, Yard-Man had provided the major part of the service required by Sears through its own repair shop facilities. Warranty service was done free of charge, while other service was charged to the Sears' store at current rates. In 1954, Sears' policy of servicing what they sold, plus the rising cost of freight, caused the shifting of the service function from Yard-Man to the Sears organization. The factory service shop was still kept open for special jobs and for training. Yard-Man still maintained an extensive parts inventory and sent out periodic service and operational bulletins to the Sears service shops.

financing inventory

Although Yard-Man sales showed a very strong seasonal bias in favor of the second six months of the fiscal year, January through June, production was scheduled to take place throughout the calendar year. July through December was primarily devoted to building up a balanced inventory.

Inasmuch as the annual requirements of Sears were fairly well estimated in advance of production, this task was performed with greater assurance of accuracy, although changes in demand due to market or weather variables could cause serious problems. Leveled-out production permitted more even use of plant and labor. This made possible savings which more than compensated for the risk of carrying excess inventory. It was not unusual in recent years for inventory buildups in anticipation of the selling season to reach as much as $3 million.

The financial pressure of assuming the inventory storage function was somewhat relieved by arrangements with banking sources in Jackson, Detroit, and Chicago which accepted either commitments from Sears or inventory produced for Sears at 100 percent collateral for loans up to $4 million.

production

The Yard-Man plant was modern and well equipped. It covered an area of over 5½ acres and had five production lines. In the annual cycle of manufacturing operations, hand mowers were produced first. They had fewer components and required less storage space when completed. After estimated inventory levels for hand mowers had been reached, production shifted to the lines producing power-operated machines. The work force was stabilized at about 200 people in 1957 and was noted for its low turnover and high morale. Labor flexibility was very great in that workers could be shifted from place to place depending upon the need at the time. This flexibility gave Yard-Man a high degree of labor productivity and made the workers proficient in many areas of mower production.

Shipments to Sears stores were made directly from the Yard-Man factory either by rail or motor freight depending on time and cost variables. All shipments were f.o.b. Jackson, Michigan.

development of the problem of excess capacity

The first president of Yard-Man, Inc., one of the company's original founders, retired early in 1952. He was replaced by a man who had had considerable experience in the production of lawn mowers for sale through orthodox jobber-retailer channels. In attempting to orient himself, the new president reviewed the situation which had developed since civilian production has been resumed in 1946. In this postwar period, demand had been so great that deliveries were made to Sears as soon as the mowers came off the production line. There was no seasonal fluctuation, no inventory problem, and no need for storage and warehousing facilities other than had existed before the war. In 1947 and 1948, the demand continued in excess of ability to produce, although assuming a more normal seasonal pattern.

However, the new president was concerned with the estimated 30 percent excess of plant capacity which appeared to have been caused in prior years by the inability of motor suppliers to furnish sufficient numbers of components to allow Yard-Man to produce all the units it could have produced and sold. In the early 1950's, he found the excess capacity problem further complicated by a slackening off in sales volume caused by the changing of consumer preference in favor of the rotary type mower over the reel type, in which Yard-Man had specialized.

By 1952, this preference for rotary power mowers had had a serious effect on Yard-Man's sales figures, and management realized that this could be overcome only if Yard-Man produced rotary mowers of its own design. Such mowers were in late stages of planning and were scheduled to be introduced in 1953.

the president's proposal

As of 1952, the president felt that sales could be increased in the future if Yard-Man would return to its prewar policy of dual distribution. In its agreement with Sears in 1943 which heralded the beginning of a period of exclusive production for distribution through the Sears organization, Yard-Man had retained the right to keep its brand name and to have it incorporated with that of Sears Craftsman brand. The president felt that by utilizing the prestige of the Yard-Man brand, a line of mowers entirely different in appearance could be produced and distributed to independent retailers. He envisioned a gradual policy of covering the market, with an eventual goal of doubling the company's sales volume.

The task of evaluating the president's proposal was given to the management committee, which consisted of the senior executives of the firm. In discussing the proposal, the committee gave careful consideration to the following factors:

a) Costs of tooling and design necessary to develop a new line sufficiently different from that being sold to Sears.
b) The time and expense necessary to build and train a sales force.
c) The promotional costs necessary to achieve distribution and to gain brand recognition.
d) The financial ability of the company to undertake such a venture.
e) The length of time necessary to reach breakeven.

committee recommendations

After considerable study the committee discovered, first, that to obtain the degree of product difference required, tooling and design costs would be extremely high. They estimated that a minimum volume of 40,000 units would be needed to break even on these costs alone.

Second, time and financial limitations would allow only a small selling and promotional program to be developed the first year, and an orderly penetration of the market would probably result in the sale of 5,000 units.

Third, on the basis of sales projections and consideration of variable as well as fixed costs, it was felt that a minimum of five years would be needed before the new venture would assume profitable proportions.

Thus, on the basis of the difficulties involved, the long period to break even, and the risk of disturbing what had hitherto been an excellent relationship with Sears, the management committee suggested to the president that he table his proposal. These deliberations continued until fiscal 1954, and although the management committee had pointed out the difficulties involved in dual distribution, Sears was asked to release Yard-Man from its agreement to produce solely for distribution through Sears' outlets. This release was granted by Sears in the fall of 1954.

Early in 1955, however, a vigorous resurgence of sales took place (see Exhibit 1). As in the past, the supply of engines for power mowers became the only factor limiting output. Under these circumstances, there was no longer any problem as to the utilization of excess plant capacity. This fact, plus a change in the top management of Yard-Man, led company officials to abandon the idea of developing a new line of power mowers and of distributing them under the Yard-Man brand through independent wholesale-retail channels.

recurrence of the excess capacity problem

During the remainder of 1955, production continued at a rate limited only by the availability of power-mower engines. As long as this condition continued, Yard-Man operated on only a one-shift basis. Yet management felt that the best utilization of plant would require the operation of two 40-hour shifts per week. By 1956, accordingly, when an adequate supply of engines became available, Yard-Man was in the position to be able to double its output without requiring additional capital expenditures.

In an effort to reduce unit costs, moreover, certain improvements in plant and equipment had been made which served greatly to increase productivity. Thus, the number of production lines had been increased from two to five as a means of gaining flexibility in production scheduling. An elaborate overhead conveyor system had also been installed. Automatic electrostatic paint booths had likewise been added.

Then, too, the greater emphasis on rotary power mowers in the product mix resulted in a striking increase in ability to produce. The simplified work processes required in the production of rotary mowers as compared with reel mowers had reduced direct labor requirements by two thirds. With the same labor force, therefore, Yard-Man production lines were able to produce rotary mowers almost three times as fast as when reel-type models were being made.

As a result of these developments, Yard-Man entered 1956 with the ability to make a substantial increase in output of power mowers over and beyond 1955 accomplishments. However, while Sears' requirements served to increase total sales from about $11 million in 1955 to $12 million in 1956, an unseasonably cool spring and summer limited Sears' sales to an amount considerably less than Yard-Man facilities could have produced. Indeed, Yard-Man officials felt that unused productive capacity was exceeding tolerable limits by the end of 1956. Early in 1957, accordingly, top management again faced the problem of finding ways to increase sales to the point where the firm's substantially greater capacity to produce could be fully utilized.

A review of possible lines of action indicated that there were two major alternatives open to the firm. One possibility would be to reconsider the proposal of 1952 that the company produce power mowers under the Yard-Man brand for distribution outside of Sears channels. This alternative was not given serious consideration, however. Since 1952, the relationship with Sears had developed so well and had been so profitable that Yard-Man officials did not wish to reopen the question.

A second alternative was to seek new products to add to the Yard-Man line. If suitable new products could be developed and marketed, such action would serve not only to utilize excess production capacity but also to diversify the firm's manufacturing activities. Careful consideration of all aspects of the problem led Yard-Man executives to decide upon the second line of action. The steps taken to implement this decision are outlined in a report dated February, 1957, as follows:

> Yard-Man is widening its search for appropriate products to help diversify its manufacturing activities. Particular consideration is being given to product lines which offer the possibility of fitting into the seasonal pattern of its mower business, of using present plant facilities, and of being consistent with Yard-Man's long-established relationship with Sears, Roebuck and company, as distributor of its lawnmowing equipment. . . . Emphasis in being placed on expanding the corporation's engineering staff to develop such products and to examine such lines for their sales and earnings potential.[3]

QUESTIONS

1. Would Yard-Man have been wise to follow the president's proposal of 1952 to return to its pre-war policy of dual distribution?
2. As of 1957, should Yard-Man reconsider dual distribution or should it seek new products to add to its product line?

Exhibit 1. Ten years summary of sales and earnings.

Year Ended June 30	Net Sales (*)	Profit before Federal Income Taxes	Percent of Net Sales (Pretax)	Net Profit	Earnings per Share (†)	Cash Dividends per Share (†)
1947............	$ 2,509,223	$ 319,502	12.7	$198,225	$0.41	$0.09
1948............	3,444,064	729,619	21.1	452,354	0.94	.375
1949............	4,250,015	848,090	19.9	523,090	1.09	.375
1950............	4,826,863	931,851	19.3	576,569	1.20	.375
1951............	6,433,711	1,339,785	20.8	538,085	1.12	.375
1952............	5,820,798	936,936	16.0	419,936	0.87	.375
1953............	6,816,574	1,000,112	14.6	440,112	0.92	.375
1954............	9,404,942	1,211,278	12.8	531,278	1.11	.375
1955............	10,991,454	1,547,696	14.0	729,498	1.52	.375
1956............	12,256,601	1,424,185	11.6	722,476	1.50	.50

*Practically all sales have been to Sears, Roebuck and Company.
†In terms of the 480,000 shares of common stock outstanding June 30, 1956.

Exhibit 2. Recent changes in relative demand for different classes of product.

Fiscal Year	1952	1953	1954	1955	1956
Hand mowers.................	34%	31%	20%	11%	9%
Power mowers					
Reel type.....................	63	50	33	22	14
Rotary type..................	0	15	44	63	74
Parts and attachments..........	3	4	3	4	3

[3] S. D. Loring Co., Yard-Man Report, February, 1957

FORD MOTOR COMPANY, SPECIAL PRODUCTS DIVISION

naming a new car

In the fall of 1955 the Special Products Division of the Ford Motor Company was faced with the problem of selecting a brand name for an important new series of cars being developed for introduction late in 1957. In this connection, the following exchange of correspondence took place between an official of the Special Products Division and Miss Marianne Moore, Brooklyn's celebrated poet.*

October 19, 1955

Miss Marianne Moore
Cumberland Street
Brooklyn 5, New York
Dear Miss Moore:

This is a morning we find ourselves with a problem which, strangely enough, is more in the field of words and the fragile meaning of words than in car-making. And we just wonder whether you might be intrigued with it sufficiently to lend us a hand.

Our dilemma is a name for a rather important new series of cars.

We should like this name to be more than a label. Specifically, we should like it to have a compelling quality in itself and by itself. To convey, through association or other conjuration, some visceral feeling of elegance, fleetness, advanced features and design. A name, in short, that flashes a dramatically desirable picture in people's minds. (Another "Thunderbird" would be fine).

Over the past few weeks this office has confected a list of three hundred-odd candidates which, it pains me to relate, are characterized by an embarrassing pedestrianism. We are miles short of our ambition. And so we are seeking the help of one who knows more about this sort of magic than we.

As to how we might go about this matter, I have no idea. But, in any event, all would depend on whether you find this overture of some challenge and interest.

---

* Reprinted by permission of the authors from *The New Yorker*, April 13, 1957, pp. 130–36.

Should we be so fortunate as to have piqued your fancy, we will be pleased to write more fully. And, of course, it is expected that our relations will be on a fee basis of an impeccably dignified kind.

Respectfully,
David Wallace
Special Products Division

October 21, 1955

Dear Mr. Wallace:

Let me take it under advisement, Mr. Wallace. I am complimented to be recruited in this high matter.

I have seen and admired "Thunderbird" as a Ford designation. It would be hard to match; but let me, the coming week, talk with my brother, who would bring ardor and imagination to bear on the quest.

Sincerely yours,
Marianne Moore

October 27, 1955

Dear Mr. Wallace:

My brother thought most of the names I had considered suggesting to you for your new series too learned or too labored, but thinks I might ask if any of the following approximate the requirements:

THE FORD SILVER SWORD

This plant, of which the flower is a silver sword, I believe grows only on the Hawaiian Island Maui, on Mount Haleakala (House of the Sun); found at an altitude of from 9,500 to 10,000 feet. (The leaves—silver-white—surrounding the individual blossoms—have a pebbled texture that feels like Italian-twist backstitch allover embroidery.)

My first thought was of a bird series—the swallow species—Hirundo, or, phonetically, Aerundo. Malvina Hoffman is designing a device for the radiator of a made-to-order Cadillac, and said in her opinion the only term surpassing Thunderbird would be hurricane; and I then thought Hurricane Hirundo might be the first of a series such as Hurricane Aquila (eagle), Hurricane Accipiter (hawk), and so on. A species that takes its dinner on the wing ("swifts").

If these suggestions are not in character with the car, perhaps you could give me a sketch of its general appearance, or hint as to some of its exciting potentialities—though my brother reminds me that such information is highly confidential.

Sincerely yours,
Marianne Moore

November 4, 1955

Dear Miss Moore:

I'm delighted that your note implies that you are interested in helping us in our naming problem.

This being so, procedures in this rigorous business world dictate that we on this end at least document a formal arrangement with provision for a suitable fee or honorarium before pursuing the problem further.

One way might be for you to suggest a figure which could be considered for mutual acceptance. Once this is squared away, we will look forward to having you join us in the continuation of our fascinating search.

Sincerely,
David Wallace
Special Products Division

November 7, 1955

Dear Mr. Wallace:

It is handsome of you to consider remuneration for service merely enlisted. My fancy would be inhibited, however, by acknowledgment in advance of performance. If I could be of specific assistance, we could no doubt agree on some kind of honorarium for the service rendered.

I seem to exact participation; but if you could tell me how the suggestions submitted strayed—if obviously—from the ideal, I could then perhaps proceed more nearly in keeping with the Company's objective.

Sincerely yours,
Marianne Moore

November 11, 1955

Dear Miss Moore:

Our office philodendron has just benefitted from an extra measure of water as, pacing about, I have sought words to respond to your recent generous note. Let me state my quandary thus. It is unspeakably contrary to procedure to accept counsel—even needed counsel—without a firm prior agreement of conditions (and, indeed, to follow the letter of things, without a Purchase Notice in quadruplicate and three Competitive Bids). But then, seldom has the auto business had occasion to indulge in so ethereal a matter as this. So, if you will risk a mutually satisfactory outcome with us, we should like to honor your wish for a fancy unencumbered.

As to wherein your earlier suggestions may have "strayed," as you put it—they did not at all. Shipment No. 1 was fine, and we would like to luxuriate in more of same—even those your brother regarded as overlearned or labored. For us to impose an ideal on your efforts would, I fear, merely defeat our purpose. We have sought your help to get an approach quite different from our own. In short, we should like suggestions that we ourselves would not have arrived at. And, in sober fact, have not.

Now we on this end must help you by sending some tangible representation of what we are talking about. Perhaps the enclosed sketches will serve the purpose. They are not IT, but they convey the feeling. At the very least, they may give you a sense of participation should your friend Malvina Hoffman break into brisk conversation on radiator caps.

Sincerely yours,
David Wallace
Special Products Division

November 13, 1955

Dear Mr. Wallace:

The sketches. They are indeed exciting; they have quality, and the toucan tones lend tremendous allure—confirmed by the wheels. Half the magic—sustaining effects of this kind. Looked at upside down, furthermore, there is a sense of fish buoyancy. Immediately your word "impeccable" sprang to mind. Might it be a possibility? The Impeccable. In any case, the baguette lapidary glamour you have achieved certainly spurs the imagination. Car-innovation is like launching a ship—"drama."

I am by no means sure that I can help you to the right thing, but performance with elegance casts a spell. Let me do some thinking in the direction of impeccable, symmechromatic, thunderblender. . . . (The exotics, if I can shape them a little.) Dearborn might come into one.

If the sketches should be returned at once, let me know. Otherwise, let me dwell on them for a time. I am, may I say, a trusty confidante.

I thank you for realizing that under contract espirit could not flower. You owe me nothing, specific or moral.

Sincerely,
Marianne Moore

November 19, 1955

Dear Mr. Wallace:

Some other suggestions, Mr. Wallace, for the phenomenon:

THE RESILIENT BULLET

or Intelligent Bullet

or Bullet Cloisonné or Bullet Lavolta

(I have always had a fancy for THE INTELLIGENT WHALE—the little first Navy submarine, shaped like a sweet potato; on view in our Brooklyn Yard.)

THE FORD FABERGÉ

(That there is also a perfume Fabergé seems to me to do no harm, for here allusion is to the original silversmith.)

THE ARC-en-CIEL (the rainbow)

ARCENCIEL?

Please do not feel that memoranda from me need acknowledgment. I am not working day and night for you; I feel that etymological hits are partially accidental.

The bullet idea has possibilities, it seems to me, in connection with Mercury (with Hermes and Hermes Trismegistus) and magic (white magic).

Sincerely,
Marianne Moore

November 28, 1955

Dear Mr. Wallace:
MONGOOSE CIVIQUE
ANTICIPATOR
REGNA RACER (couronne à couronne) sovereign to sovereign
AEROTERRE
Fée Rapide (Aérofée, Aéro Faire, Fée Aiglette, Magi-faire) Comme Il Faire
Tonnerre Alifère (winged thunder)
Aliforme Alifère (wing-slender, a-wing)
TURBOTORC (used as an adjective by Plymouth)
THUNDERBIRD Allié (Cousin Thunderbird)
THUNDER CRESTER
DEARBORN Diamante
MAGIGRAVURE
PASTELOGRAM
I shall be returning the sketches very soon.

M. M.

December 6, 1955

Dear Mr. Wallace:
Regina-rex
Taper Racer   Taper Acer
Varsity Stroke
Angelastro
Astranaut
Chaparral
Tir à l'arc (bull's eye)
Cresta Lark
Triskelion (three legs running)
Pluma Piluma (hairfine, featherfoot)
Andante con Moto (description of a good motor?)

My findings then, so I terminate them and am returning the sketches. Two principles I have not been able to capture: 1, the topknot of the peacock and topnotcher of speed. 2, the swivelaxis (emphasized elsewhere), like the Captain's bed on the whaleship, Charles Morgan—balanced so that it leveled whatever the slant of the ship.

If I stumble on a hit, you shall have it. Anything so far has been pasttime. Do not ponder appreciation, Mr. Wallace. That was embodied in the sketches.

M. M.

I cannot resist the temptation to disobey my brother and submit TURCOTINGA (turquoise cotinga—the cotinga being a South-American finch or sparrow) solid indigo. (I have a three-volume treatise on flowers that might produce something but the impression given should certainly be un-labored.)

December 8, 1955

Mr. Wallace:

May I submit UTOPIAN TURTLETOP? Do not trouble to answer unless you like it.

Marianne Moore

December 23, 1955

MERRY CHRISTMAS TO OUR FAVORITE TURTLETOPPER.

David Wallace

December 26, 1955

Dear Mr. Wallace:

An aspiring turtle is certain to glory in spiral eucalyptus, white pine straight from the forest, and innumerable scarlet roses almost too tall for close inspection. Of a temperament susceptible to shock though one may be, to be treated like royalty could not but induce sensations unprecedented august.

Please know that a carfancyer's allegiance to the Ford automotive turtle—extending from the Model T Dynasty to the Wallace Utopian Dynasty—can never waver; impersonal gratitude surely becoming infinite when made personal. Gratitude to unmiserly Mr. Wallace and his idealistic associates.

Marianne Moore

November 8, 1956

Dear Miss Moore:

Because you were so kind to us in our early days of looking for a suitable name, I feel a deep obligation to report on events that have ensued.

And I feel I must do so before the public announcement of same come Monday, November 19.

We have chosen a name out of the more than six thousand-odd candidates that we gathered. It fails somewhat of the resonance, gaiety, and zest we were seeking. But it has a personal dignity and meaning to many of us here. Our name, dear Miss Moore, is—Edsel.

I hope you will understand.

Cordially,
David Wallace
Special Products Division

case 3–5

LINCOLN-MERCURY DIVISION*

use of marketing research to aid in making brand-name and styling decisions for a new car

The sales success of imported automobiles during the middle and late 1950's exercised a profound effect on marketing policies of domestic automobile companies. Within a period of several years, virtually every established make of automobile below the high-priced class appeared in a "compact" version. Consistent with this trend, the Lincoln-Mercury Division of the Ford Motor Company marketed the Comet in 1960. Prior to the date of introduction, however, the division was faced with the problem of designing and promoting a compact automobile which differed distinctively from its sister make, the Falcon, while retaining basically the same body shell.

background

As the imported economy car became established in the American market, domestic firms found it necessary to assess the values which attracted buyers to foreign makes. Accordingly, 16 marketing research studies were undertaken by the Ford Motor Company. Market research results disclosed that foreign-car buyers tended to represent a distinct segment of the market, composed mainly of young professional people with high education and high income. "Economy" and "efficiency" appeared to be dominant purchase motives. It was decided upon review of research findings that any smaller automobiles to be developed by the company would be aimed toward the mass market, not the relatively confined market served by imported makes.

The products offered by the two divisions of the company in 1958 were as follows:

Ford Division	*Lincoln-Mercury Division*
Ford	English Ford
Thunderbird	Taunus (German)
Ford Truck	Edsel
	Mercury
	Lincoln

*Written by James F. Engel, Professor of Business Organization, College of Administrative Science, The Ohio State University.

It was discovered further through marketing research that the average potential buyer of smaller cars would prefer a vehicle which is bigger and more comfortable than foreign makes, while retaining the economy features. A proposal for a new automobile meeting these specifications was presented to the board of directors of the company. In April, 1958, the board approved a proposal to develop a vehicle designated as the XK Thunderbird. This automobile was later to be marketed as the Falcon by the Ford Division.

The Lincoln-Mercury Division initiated studies in May, 1958, to determine the feasibility of also marketing a compact automobile. These early studies centered around the issue of how much the division would have to spend in order to offer a compact car, as opposed to the amount of financial return which could be expected. A preliminary presentation was made to the Product Planning Committee in the middle of June, and instruction was given to proceed with the development work. At this point, the code name "Australian 'B' Car" was assigned to the program.

Development on this preliminary program continued throughout the summer, and status reports were made periodically. A second major presentation was made to the Product Planning Committee in September, 1958. Approval was requested and granted for the division to proceed with the "B" program. The decision was made to expend whatever funds were necessary to differentiate the Mercury offering from the Falcon by changing front and rear fenders, hood and rear deck, and by including a unique Thunderbird-type roof. Mechanical interchangeabililty was to be maintained wherever possible in order to minimize total cost.

the role of marketing research in the "B" program

Perhaps automobile firms are among the most "research minded" of all companies manufacturing consumer goods. At Lincoln-Mercury, the director of marketing research reports directly to top management. While research programs are outlined and developed within the department, the actual field-work is delegated to independent marketing research agencies.

Considerable attention was directed toward marketing research as the "B" program progressed. Research was utilized extensively in testing possible product names, in ascertaining consumer acceptance of styling features prior to introduction, and in determining market potential following introduction. Each of these areas of research will be described more fully in the following pages.

Before discussing the specific surveys undertaken, however, it should be noted that most of the research undertaken by the division in the "B" program involved random samples of new car buyers owning makes which were not more than four years old. Interviews were usually conducted simultaneously in as many as 20 representative markets. The pressure to produce results within a short time period virtually precluded interviewing large samples in one market only. Sample sizes usually totaled 400 1,000 car owners.

name research

A significant amount of discussion was carried on within the Lincoln-Mercury Division concerning the final name to be assigned to the automobile. The alternatives were to designate the vehicle as a Mercury, as an Edsel, or as a completely different car with a name not heretofore used by the company. Three major marketing research studies were undertaken to provide information to aid in this decision.

Name research survey number one. The first major survey of possible names was run in April, 1959. A sample of 300 automobile owners was interviewed. A number of alternatives were tested, many of which intentionally were chosen to enhance the "celestial" connotations of the Mercury name. The three basic questions from this survey are reproduced in Exhibit 1.[1]

The first question reproduced involved the '"word association" method, whereby the respondent was requested to state his initial reaction when a name was mentioned. Question number two involved a slight variation on the word association procedure; the person interviewed was asked to state which "product" comes to mind as each name is read. The last question appearing in Exhibit 1 comprehended a rating scale for sports car names. The respondent was requested to circle the number which best described his opinion on the appropriateness of each name for a sports car. The identical procedure was utilitized also for small economy cars.

In general, it was felt that the Comet name stood out from all others as the best potential candidate for the "B" car.[2] Those interviewed stated that Comet was an especially good name for a sports car, but the name was not associated strongly with a small economy car. One interesting problem disclosed by the research, however, was that many consumers linked the name Comet with a brand of household cleansers.

Name research survey number two. The second major name research project was conducted during May, 1959, and involved 200 consumer interviews. While the general questionnaire design was very similar to that used in the first study, a different list of names was tested. The rating scale used for a small economy car lists the names and is included in Exhibit 2. Survey results directly corroborated those discussed above. Again, it was felt that the Comet name fared quite well; as before, Comet was deemed most appropriate for a sports car but was associated weakly with a small economy car.

Name research survey number three. The final phase of the name research series was undertaken during August, 1959. The survey covered 1,200 interviews. The general intent of this study was to measure the association of the name Comet with Mercury. Examination of Exhibit 3 will disclose that a

---

[1] Exhibits appear at the end of the case.

[2] Specific research results are confidential, so findings can be disclosed only in general terms.

rating scale once again was used as the central question in the survey. The respondent was presented a picture of the "B" car which was clearly designated as the "1960 Mercury Comet, a Compact Car: Product of the Ford Motor Co., Sold at Mercury Dealers." He was then asked to indicate strength of agreement or disagreement with a number of statements concerning the automobile. An identical procedure was followed for the Chevrolet Corvair, Ford Falcon, and Plymouth Valiant.

Research findings indicated that Comet, when associated with Mercury, gave a distinct high-priced connotation. In addition, the Comet styling, as depicted in the picture, produced a highly favorable response from the consumers who were interviewed.

A final decision on the name designation of the "B" car was made in late summer of 1959. At this point, it was decided to name the car the Comet and avoid any association in the name itself with vehicles presently produced by the Lincoln-Mercury Division. The major reason for this decision was a desire to avoid drawing sales from existing Mercury models. Furthermore, it was decided as a minor consideration that the high-priced image produced when the vehicle is called the Mercury Comet was incompatible with the desired Comet appeal.

styling research

A second major stage of the marketing research conducted during development of the Comet was concerned with assessing consumer reaction to various style features. Several phases were also undertaken in connection with this research effort.

The major study of style acceptance was conducted during May-June, 1959. A random sample of car owners was shown artists' drawings of several makes of compact cars, including Comet. The pictures were not labeled as to brand name. On the basis of these pictures, respondents were asked to rate many attributes of each car in terms of the degree of "like" or "dislike." Following this question the consumers were requested to indicate which of four cars represented pictorially best fit a number of statements, such as "most comfortable riding," "costs least to buy," and "is best looking." A final major question involved the assessment of the "personality" of two of the cars, one of which was the Comet. The respondent was expected to indicate which of the two makes best agreed with such statements as "for a banker," "has a racy look," and "heavy." These three questions appear in Exhibit 4.

The results of this styling study were most gratifying to management. As was pointed out earlier, a conscious attempt had been made to differentiate the Comet from the Falcon, and findings verified that a successful job had been done. Of all the compacts on the market at the time of the survey (Falcon, Corvair, and Valiant), the Comet connoted the greatest degree of luxury. Related to the strong luxury image was the widespread feeling that the Comet was a higher priced car than other compacts. Furthermore, consumers voiced the opinion that the Comet gave a "sporty" image.

It is interesting that many consumers viewed the Comet as being a "large" compact. The car intentionally was designed to create this impression. The wheelbase was 7 inches longer than its nearest competitor's, and the styling was "straight line" in nature. "Soft-line" styling, featuring a streamlined appearance, tends to understate overall dimensions of the vehicle. On the other hand, the abrupt Thunderbird-type roof and tail fins all contributed to the "straight-line" boxey Comet appearance and served to enhance its overall size.

Finally, the research findings suggested that the appeal of the Comet was by no means limited to any one class of consumers. The favorable reaction to Comet styling was uniform throughout owners of automobiles in all price classes.

Several other studies were designed to follow up the picture research survey. In one such study, 400 consumers were actually brought to a dealer's showroom where they viewed the Comet at their leisure and were later interrogated concerning their opinions. A similar effort was undertaken at the Detroit Auto Show in 1960, where those consumers viewing the new Comet were asked to state their reactions. It is said that the Comet was the "hit of the show." Finally, interviewers were actually placed outside showrooms in Chicago, Los Angeles, Detroit, New York, and Atlanta on the day of introduction, March 17, 1960. A number of people were interviewed upon leaving the showrooms. Results of these studies corroborated the highly favorable reactions observed in the earlier project. Therefore, the potential success of the Comet seemed to be great.

promotion undertaken in introduction of the Comet

All advertising for the Comet was directed by the Detroit office of Kenyon and Eckhardt Advertising Agency. A broad scale promotional program was designed to capitalize upon the mass market appeal of the new car, and the promotional program comprised five main types of effort:

1. The Lincoln-Mercury Division sponsored three network television shows at the time of introduction—Startime on NBC, Wagon Train on NBC, and Leonard Bernstein's New York Philharmonic broadcasts on CBS. Commercials for the Comet, of course, appeared on these programs. In addition, network spot announcements were run on other shows.
2. Magazine advertisements were run in *Life* and *Look.* The introductory advertisements were full-page four-color appeals featuring the Comet itself prominently. (See Exhibit 5 for the introductory and follow-up magazine ads.)
3. Newspaper advertisements were run simultaneously in every market where Lincoln-Mercury dealers were located. Therefore, all types of newspapers

were included, running from small-town weeklies to metropolitan dailies. The introductory newspaper announcement is in Exhibit 6.

4. Extensive use was made of radio announcements. Local spot advertisements of one minute in length were inserted in disk jockey shows and related programs.

5. The Comet was "put on the road," so to speak, through nationwide billboard advertisements.

Careful analysis of the magazine and newspaper advertisements reproduced in Exhibits 5 and 6 will indicate clearly how the dominant themes discovered in preintroduction research were turned into major selling points:

1. Style was stressed prominently. In the first magazine advertisement, for example, a major copy point was "First of the compact cars with the fine-car styling," "No sawed-off, cut-down look here."

2. The image of greater length was turned into an important selling point. Notice how the factor of length was emphasized as giving "Comet a ride far smoother than any other compact car."

3. It will be recalled that research findings indicated a definite high-priced image, so the low-price appeal of the Comet was stressed heavily. In much the same sense, the proven economy of performance was capitalized upon as a selling point.

4. The general theme of a "better compact" was enhanced through emphasis on features included in the base price. The reader was asked to "Check the features. Comet gives you dual headlights, fine interior fabrics and appointments. There's no extra charge for arm rests, foam rubber seats, door-operated dome lights. Some compacts even charge extra for cigarette lighters—but not the Comet."

5. A general unfamiliarity with the name, a phenomenon often encountered when introducing a new product, was softened substantially by subtly linking the new Comet with established names through inclusion of the Ford, Lincoln, and Mercury emblems.

6. Finally, it should be pointed out that the newspaper announcements placed heavy emphasis on the local dealer, even to the point of instituting a Comet Sweepstakes. The emphasis was especially necessary at the time of introduction, because many consumers did not know where the car could be purchased.

market success of the Comet

A sales target of 125,000 units was established for the 10-month period remaining in 1960 after introduction. The Comet was such a smash success, however, that actual volume exceeded 190,000 units. Early production schedules called for 300 units per day. A month after introduction, this volume was raised to 600 units. By the end of April, the daily rate had climbed to 870 units, but still demand had not been satisfied.

Because upward revisions definitely were needed in productive capacity, it was necessary to determine market potential with more exactitude. Three markets were given an unlimited supply of automobiles, while promotion was held constant. The major market utilized in this test was Cleveland, and it was found that the Comet could attain a 10 percent market penetration in the Cleveland area with unlimited supply. Sales throughout the rest of the country totaled approximately 3 percent of the total automobile market. The future of the Comet indeed appeared bright. To satisfy unmet demand new assembly plants were added in Kansas City, Missouri, and San Jose, California.

Analysis of figures provided by the R. L. Polk organization emphasizes further the startling impact of the Comet. Of those sales where trade-ins were involved, roughly 50 percent were made to former owners of General Motors cars. Only 12 percent of sales were made to former Mercury owners, thus reflecting the extent to which new buyers were attracted. Moreover, about 10 percent of sales came from previous owners of imports and domestic compacts, one half from the traditional low-price field, and about a third from previous owners of medium- and luxury-priced cars.

Following introduction of the Comet, several new makes of compact cars appeared on the market, including the Buick Special, Oldsmobile F–85, and the Pontiac Tempest. Even in the face of enhanced competition, Comet maintained a 3 percent market share as of Summer, 1961. Sales expectations for the 1961 model year were 190,000 units.

QUESTIONS

1. Evaluate the research program outlined above from its inception in idea form to the culmination in finished advertisements. Were the research objectives fulfilled? Were findings utilized properly?
2. What, if any, additional information would have been helpful in solving the problems facing Mercury management?

Exhibit 1. The three basic questions used in styling survey number one.

I'm going to show you several words. As I show you each word, please tell me the *first* word that comes into your mind. For instance, if I showed you the word "long," the first word that comes to your mind might be "short," so you would say "short."

There are no right or wrong answers. I'm just interested in the first word that comes to mind. Just tell me the first word you think of as quickly as possible. Now let's try one (SHOW CARDS, ONE AT A TIME, AND RECORD RESPONSE BELOW).

Name	Response
Comet	_____
Falcon	_____
Cadet	_____
Star	_____
Firefly	_____
Pacer	_____
Scamp	_____
Meteor	_____

Exhibit 1—Continued

Now I would like to show some brand names which could be used for different products. Would you tell me what kind of product each name calls to mind. I know the names are unfamiliar to you, but I just want to know what kinds of products they make you think of. For example, if I said "Shaeffer" you might say "fountain pen"—all right? (SHOW CARDS AGAIN, ONE AT A TIME).

Name	Response
Comet	_____
Falcon	_____
Cadet	_____
Star	_____
Firefly	_____
Pacer	_____
Scamp	_____
Meteor	_____

Now here are some names for a new Sport Car which one of the big automobile companies is thinking about making (HAND SPORT CAR SHEET AND PENCIL TO RESPONDENT).

Each of these names is on a rating scale numbered from −3 to +3. I'd like your opinion on how good you think each of these names is for a Sport Car. The better you think the name is, the higher the number you would circle. For example, if you thought a name was very good you would circle +3 on the far right. If you thought a name was very poor you would circle the −3 on the far left. Please rate each name on this sheet.

Rating Scale for Sport Car

Comet
Very poor	−3	−2	−1		+1	+2	+3	Very good

Falcon
Very poor	−3	−2	−1		+1	+2	+3	Very good

Cadet
Very poor	−3	−2	−1		+1	+2	+3	Very good

Star
Very poor	−3	−2	−1		+1	+2	+3	Very good

Firefly
Very poor	−3	−2	−1		+1	+2	+3	Very good

Pacer
Very poor	−3	−2	−1		+1	+2	+3	Very good

Scamp
Very poor	−3	−2	−1		+1	+2	+3	Very good

Meteor
Very poor	−3	−2	−1		+1	+2	+3	Very good

Exhibit 2. The basic question from name survey number two.

Each of these names is on a rating scale numbered from 1 to 6. I'd like your opinion on how good you think each of these names is for a new small economy car. The better you think the name is, the higher the number you would check. For example, if you thought a name was very good you would place an X in the 6 box. If you thought a name was very poor you would place an X in 1 box. Please rate each name on this sheet.

Small Economy Car

(Rating Scale)

FUTURA

VERY POOR	1	2	3	4	5	6	VERY GOOD

COMET

VERY POOR	1	2	3	4	5	6	VERY GOOD

COUGAR

VERY POOR	1	2	3	4	5	6	VERY GOOD

APOLIO

VERY POOR	1	2	3	4	5	6	VERY GOOD

COMANCHE

VERY POOR	1	2	3	4	5	6	VERY GOOD

ATMOS

VERY POOR	1	2	3	4	5	6	VERY GOOD

DOLPHIN

VERY POOR	1	2	3	4	5	6	VERY GOOD

ENVOY

VERY POOR	1	2	3	4	5	6	VERY GOOD

CHEROKEE

VERY POOR	1	2	3	4	5	6	VERY GOOD

JAVELIN

VERY POOR	1	2	3	4	5	6	VERY GOOD

Exhibit 3. The major question from name survey number three.

Present Comet Exhibit

3. Would you tell me what your thoughts are as you look at this car?

_____
_____
_____
_____

Exhibit 3—Continued

1960 Mercury Comet

A Compact Car:
Product of
the Ford Motor Co.

Sold at Mercury Dealers

Exhibit 3—Continued

Present Exhibit F

4. Now I would like you to use the rating scale just as before to tell me how much you agree or disagree with each of the following statements. The more you agree with a statement, the bigger the plus number you should give; the more you disagree with a statement, the bigger the minus number you should give it.

Now what number would you give the statement—

Mercury Comet is a beautiful car... ———
Mercury Comet is a well-built car.. ———
Mercury Comet is easy to get in and out of................................. ———
Mercury Comet is an inexpensive car.. ———
Mercury Comet is a car for people who want to be different................ ———
Mercury Comet is a comfortable car.. ———
Mercury Comet has advanced styling... ———
Mercury Comet is economical to operate..................................... ———
Mercury Comet is a good buy for the money.................................. ———
Mercury Comet is a car for people with good taste.......................... ———

Exhibit 4.   The major questions in the first styling survey.

(Show Respondent Picture of Car #J)

The first thing I would like you to do is rate this car's appearance on the scale which is shown on this page.

You notice that on this page there are 10 boxes and that next to each box there is a number. The PLUS numbers are for styles that you like. The *more* you like a style, the larger the PLUS number you would choose.

For example, if you like a style very much, you would rate it +4 or +5; while if you like it just a bit you would rate it +1 or +2. The MINUS numbers are for styles you do not like. The *less* you like a style, the larger the MINUS numbers you would choose. For example, if you dislike a style very much, you would rate it −4 or −5.

a) How far up or down the scale would you rate . . .

The overall appearance of this styling?	+5	+4	+3	+2	+1	−1	−2	−3	−4	−5	DK
The front view, as a whole?	+5	+4	+3	+2	+1	−1	−2	−3	−4	−5	DK
The headlights?	+5	+4	+3	+2	+1	−1	−2	−3	−4	−5	DK
The grille?	+5	+4	+3	+2	+1	−1	−2	−3	−4	−5	DK
The side view of the roof?	+5	+4	+3	+2	+1	−1	−2	−3	−4	−5	DK
The side view as a whole?	+5	+4	+3	+2	+1	−1	−2	−3	−4	−5	DK
The tail lights?	+5	+4	+3	+2	+1	−1	−2	−3	−4	−5	DK
The rear window styling?	+5	+4	+3	+2	+1	−1	−2	−3	−4	−5	DK
The rear view, as a whole?	+5	+4	+3	+2	+1	−1	−2	−3	−4	−5	DK

b) Considering just the appearance of this car, what would you say is the *most* attractive feature?

c) Considering just the appearance of this car, what would you say is the *least* attractive feature?

(This method was used for all compact cars.)

(Lay Out Pictures of Cars J, P, M, W)

Now I would like your opinions about four of these cars in another way. I am going to read you a list of statements about cars. As I read each one, please tell me which of these four stylings fits best with that statement.

Exhibit 4—Continued

	J	P	M	W
Most comfortable riding	—	—	—	—
Has best built body	—	—	—	—
Costs least to buy	—	—	—	—
Appeals most to young people	—	—	—	—
Has the best pickup and getaway	—	—	—	—
Appeals most to adventurous people	—	—	—	—
Has the most advanced styling	—	—	—	—
Appeals most to business executives	—	—	—	—
Is best looking	—	—	—	—

Here is another list of words and phrases I would like to read to you. They describe how a car styling might appear to you—or what kind of "personality" you think a styling has. As I read each one, please tell me if you think this word or phrase fits with car____. (*Repeat List for All Cars, One at a Time, in Sequence Printed.*)

	P	J
For a banker	—	—
For a traveling salesman	—	—
For a farmer	—	—
For college kids	—	—
For a movie star	—	—
For an explorer	—	—
For a scientist	—	—
For a jet pilot	—	—
For a hick town showoff	—	—
For a big time gambler	—	—
For a man moving up	—	—
For a man going nowhere	—	—
For a man on the skids	—	—
Deer	—	—
Panther	—	—
Lion	—	—
Bear	—	—
Elephant	—	—
Seems poised to move	—	—
Looks expensive	—	—
Looks cheap	—	—
Looks European	—	—
Looks tinny	—	—
Looks solid	—	—
Safe to drive	—	—
Best mechanically	—	—
Invites you to enter	—	—
Man's car	—	—
Woman's car	—	—
Kids would like it best	—	—
Seems styled for people like myself	—	—
Light	—	—
Heavy	—	—
Massive	—	—
Fleet	—	—
Smooth lines	—	—
Broken up lines	—	—
Looks like a Thunderbird	—	—
Looks like a Cadillac	—	—
Looks like an Imperial	—	—
Looks like a Continental	—	—
Has a classic look	—	—
Has a racy look	—	—

Ford Motor Company Announces

The Debut of the Comet

First of the compact cars with fine-car styling and priced with or below other compact cars. Now at Mercury-Comet dealers.

It's here—the new standard of value in compact cars—Comet. Come see, conquer Comet with all other compacts.

NOTE FIRST, THE STYLING. No sawed-off, cut-down look here. Comet is perfectly proportioned. Though it's two feet shorter than standard cars, the lines have a fine-car flair and beauty.

CHECK THE FEATURES. The Comet gives you dual headlights, fine interior fabrics and appointments. There's no extra charge for arm rests, foam rubber seats, door-operated dome lights. Some compacts even charge extra for cigarette lighters—but not the Comet.

LOOK IN THE TRUNK. No skimping here. There are 26 cubic feet of luggage space. Enough for the whole family on a long trip.

LIFT THE HOOD. Comet's new simplified six is a miracle of power and economy. There are 122 less parts than in standard car engines. Repairs and maintenance costs are cut to a minimum. While it has 90 horsepower, twice that of many foreign makes, the Comet engine delivers up to 26 miles per gallon of regular gas.

TAKE A RIDE. Comet gives you a quiet secure feeling. The longer wheelbase (114" compared to only 109" in the average compact) and superior springing give Comet a ride far smoother than any other compact car.

NOW COMPARE THE PRICE. It's hard to believe that with all this beauty and downright value, the Comet is priced with or below other compact cars like the Rambler, Corvair, Valiant, Lark and Falcon!

SEE THE COMET. It's the value-packed compact. Study it carefully. Add up all the extras you get. Then—look at the low price tag. The Comet is unquestionably the new standard of value in compact cars.

COMPARE all the compacts and you'll come away with a Comet. Now at your Mercury-Comet dealer's.

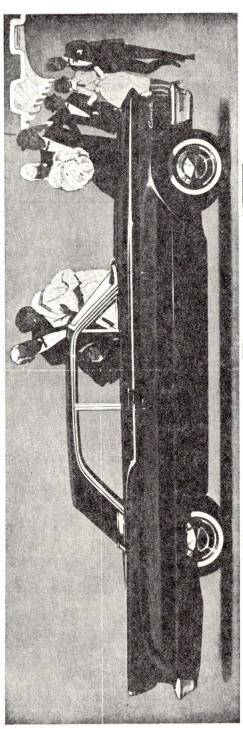

LINCOLN-MERCURY DIVISION Ford Motor Company
Builders of finer cars of every size for every purpose

LINCOLN AND LINCOLN CONTINENTAL—the ultimate in motor cars.

MERCURY—the best built—best buy in its field.

COMET—first of the compact cars with fine-car styling.

Exhibit 5—Continued

Now available at Mercury-Comet dealers'

The Comet

—first of the compact cars with fine-car styling, and it's priced with or below other compacts.

FULL LINE INCLUDES 2 BEAUTIFUL WAGONS. Along with the Comet two- and four-door sedans, there are two- and four-door station wagons. Each wagon gives you 76 cubic feet of storage space (as much as there is in some standard size station wagons). There is a retractable rear window to replace the usual clumsy liftgate.

Compare it for style, features and price. Compare all the compact cars—and you'll come away with a Comet.

Today, come in and see the new standard of value in compact cars.

COMPARE THE STYLING, FIRST. Note the beautifully balanced proportions. There's no sawed-off, cut-down look here. The Comet has an unmistakable fine-car flair.

NOW, COMPARE THE FEATURES. There are dual headlights, classic exterior trim, and fine, completely finished interior fabrics and appointments. No extra charge for arm rests, foam padded front seats, door-operated dome lights. Some compacts even charge extra for a cigarette lighter—not the Comet.

COMPARE THE TRUNK. No bulging on space here. It's 26 cubic feet big. You can take everything you need for the whole family.

COMPARE THE ENGINE FOR ECONOMY. Comet delivers up to 28 miles per gallon of regular gas. With 122 less parts than many standard car engines, repairs and maintenance are cut to a minimum.

COMPARE THE SMOOTHNESS OF THE RIDE. The longer wheelbase (114" instead of the average of 107" for other compacts) gives you a secure and solid feel of the road, yet Comet turns on a dime.

FINALLY, COMPARE THE PRICE. With all of its beauty and downright value, Comet is priced with or below other compact cars like Rambler, Corvair, Valiant, Lark and Falcon.

ADD UP THE EXTRAS YOU GET. Look at the low price tag. Compare all the compacts...and you'll come away with a Comet.

LINCOLN-MERCURY DIVISION

Ford Motor Company,
Builders of finer cars of every size for every purpose

LINCOLN AND
LINCOLN CONTINENTAL
—the ultimate in motor cars

MERCURY
—the best buy in its field

COMET
—first of the compact cars
with fine-car styling

Exhibit 6. The initial newspaper advertisement for the 1960 Comet.

Ford Motor Company announces the

Debut of the Comet

Today, at your Mercury-Comet dealer's, first compact car with fine-car styling —priced with or below other compacts.

You're looking at the exciting new value-packed compact—Comet.

NOTE ITS BEAUTIFUL STYLING. No sawed-off, cut-down look, here. The Comet is proportioned like a fine car—long flowing lines, outstanding good looks.

LOOK CLOSELY AT THE EXTRA FEATURES. You pay nothing more for dual headlights, front and rear arm rests, door-operated dome light, foam padded front seat. And the trunk holds enough for the whole family on a long trip.

YOU'LL MARVEL AT THE ECONOMY. Comet's new simplified "six" engine delivers up to 28 miles per gallon of regular gasoline.

YOU'LL REVEL IN THE RIDE. No choppy steering, no bumpy travelling in Comet. The longer wheelbase (114″ instead of the 107″ in average compacts) and superior springing give Comet a smoother ride, yet it turns on a dime.

NOW, CHECK THE PRICE. With all its beauty and downright value, Comet is priced with or below other compacts like Rambler, Corvair, Lark, Valiant and Falcon.

COMPARE ALL THE COMPACT CARS—and you'll come away with a Comet. See it now at your Mercury-Comet dealer's.

FINEST COMPACT WAGONS ON THE MARKET. The new Comet wagons go far beyond what you might expect in a compact station wagon. There is over 76 cubic feet for storage—as much room as in some wagons costing hundreds of dollars more; a retractable rear window takes the place of the old-fashioned liftgate. And, there is ample room for six adults with plenty of space left over for baggage. Along with the Comet two- and four-door sedans, there are two- and four-door wagons as well.

LINCOLN-MERCURY DIVISION
Ford Motor Company.

WIN A NEW COMET! 50 COMETS GIVEN AWAY FREE!

ENTER THE COMET SWEEPSTAKES—**MARCH 17 THROUGH 31.** NOTHING TO DO! NOTHING TO WRITE! **JUST SEE YOUR MERCURY-COMET DEALER.**

Subject to state and local regulations.

(DEALER'S NAME)

distribution strategy

Distribution strategy is concerned with making goods available to potential customers. It involves the selection of paths or channels through the maze of marketing middlemen which composes the distribution structure. In this first phase of distribution strategy, the producer attempts to identify those channels of distribution which will most effectively reach the markets he wishes to serve. He then tries to gain the support of those intermediaries in the desired channels so that they will take on the line and move it to market.

Another distribution strategy decision area deals with the number of middlemen to use at each level in the channel. Here the producer must weigh the benefits of intensive coverage of the market gained by using large numbers of middlemen versus the benefits derived from using fewer middlemen each of whom can give the line more concentrated promotional support.

Finally, decisions have to be made as to how the goods are to be distributed physically once the channel or ownership paths have been decided. A level of customer service must be specified which is consistent with the overall marketing strategy of the firm. Then different physical distribution systems can be analyzed to find the one which meets the required service level most efficiently.

chapter 7

the distribution
structure

Few products are sold by producers directly to consumers. More commonly, products pass through one, several, or many market intermediaries—institutions which exist for the distribution, rather than the manufacture, of goods. In contrast to manufacturers, who provide products with form utility, these institutions create time, place, and possession utility. It is not sufficient that products capable of satisfying human wants exist. They do not truly serve a purpose unless consumers are able to obtain them when and where they are needed. Marketing institutions help in the storage of goods from time of production until time of consumption, and they see to it that these goods are available at the particular place the consumer needs them. Performance of these activities is as essential to consumer well-being as is the creation of form utility at the factory. It is the sum total of the marketing institutions which perform these functions—agent middlemen, wholesalers, and retailers—which constitutes the *distribution structure* through which manufacturers must work in marketing their products.

The course through this structure which a manufacturer chooses for his product to follow on its way to the consumer is referred to as a "channel of distribution." Any manufacturer, in selecting a channel of distribution, would usually choose to sell through only a very small percentage of the institutions which make up the distribution structure. If he chooses his channel of distribution wisely, he will be in a position to obtain adequate market coverage and sales volume for his product. If he chooses unwisely, he will deal a crushing blow to his chances for marketing success.

This structure of market intermediaries can be thought of as the "anatomy" of distribution. It is the framework within which and around which the marketing man must work in formulating his entire marketing program. And, just as the surgeon must have a sound knowledge of human anatomy to proceed with confidence and skill when performing an operation, so the marketing manager requires a thorough knowledge of the anatomy of distribution in order to bring his product to market successfully. He must understand the function, the strengths, and the weaknesses of each of the institutions available to serve as links in his distribution channel. Otherwise, he cannot make effective use of them.

the institutions involved

Before we can consider how the distribution structure works, a brief overview of the institutional makeup of this structure is necessary as background. This is not an easy task because of the number and variety of marketing institutions. In 1963, there were 1,708,000 retail institutions in the United States, and 308,000 wholesalers.[1] Among the marketing institutions of today, variety in organization, functions, and methods of operation is almost infinite. In at least small degree, each and every institution is unique. For this reason generalization is hazardous, yet it is also useful and necessary. Effective decision making concerning channels of distribution cannot take place unless marketing institutions and their operations can be categorized so as to reduce to a manageable level the number of variables involved in the decision-making process.

basic types of middlemen

All middlemen can be divided into three broad categories: agent middlemen, who do not take legal title to the goods they buy or sell, but rather perform these functions on behalf of others; wholesalers, who do take title and sell primarily to retailers and industrial buyers; retailers, who take title and sell to consumers. Within each of these general classes there are many variations, each variation reflecting some specialization of function. Also, some marketing institutions cut across the boundary lines of these classes. Combination wholesaler-retailers, for example, are common in the marketing of some products.

Agent middlemen. Agent middlemen are paid commissions for their services. They can be roughly divided into five classes: brokers,

---

[1] *Statistical Abstract of the United States, 1967,* pp. 786 and 795.

commission merchants, resident buyers, manufacturer's agents, and sales agents. The *broker* may represent either buyer or seller, and his basic function is to bring the party he represents into contact with the other. He seeks out potential buyers for sellers, and potential sources of supply for buyers. He then negotiates the transfer of title. The broker cannot bind his principal, which means that each transaction must be approved by the broker's client before it is binding. He does not physically handle the goods he buys or sells. He usually represents many clients, and not necessarily on a continuing basis. Brokers offer a low-cost method of distribution because they represent many parties, provide minimum services, may be used only when and as needed, and are compensated only if they produce results.

A *commission merchant* is in many ways similar to a broker, but differs in two essential respects. He can bind his principal and usually takes physical possession of the goods. For these reasons sale through a commission merchant is less time consuming then sale through a broker. Commission merchants are common in the marketing of fresh fruits and vegetables because of the high degree of perishability of these products. They are also used in the marketing of many other products.

Resident buyers are of importance primarily in the marketing of style goods. They are located in various style and production centers and represent retailers throughout the country. They provide their clients with information on style and sales trends and buy merchandise for the account of their principals. They are particularly significant in the purchase of "fill-in" orders.

The *manufacturers' agent* (or manufacturers' representative) is one of the more ubiquitous of agent middlemen. He serves, in effect, as the salesman for several manufacturers who, for a variety of reasons, do not find it desirable to have their own salesmen in the market. The manufacturers' agent handles complementary rather than competing products. He usually is limited by the manufacturer to a certain geographical area and is quite carefully controlled in other ways as well. Narrow-line manufacturers may use manufacturers' agents in all markets in which they sell. Broader line manufacturers may use them in sparse markets, and employ their own salesmen in more concentrated areas.

The *sales agent* performs many more functions than does the manufacturers' agent. He offers the manufacturer, in effect, a marketing department—often providing design services, marketing research, advertising and sales promotion, and so on, as well as field representation.

He may take a manufacturer's entire output and handle its distribution in all markets. Because he represents a number of manufacturers, he can perform the marketing operation more cheaply than manufacturers can provide it for themselves. This is particularly true in the case of manufacturers who have limited sales in a widely dispersed market.

Wholesalers. In contrast to agent middlemen, wholesalers take title to the goods they sell and, therefore, assume the risks associated with product ownership. There are many types of wholesalers and to attempt a complete classification of them at this point is not possible. One of the more basic distinctions is between *full-service* and *limited-function* wholesalers. Full-service wholesalers provide a wide range of traditional wholesaling services, such as carrying stocks, making delivery, extending credit, maintaining a sales force, and so on. Limited-function wholesalers, in contrast, restrict in one way or another the functions they perform. Cash-and-carry wholesalers, as their name suggests, neither grant credit nor make delivery. Drop shippers do not physically handle the products they own and sell; hence they perform none of the functions associated with physical handling. Wagon (or truck) jobbers limit the inventory-carrying function. Other limited-function wholesalers restrict functions in other ways.

The typical wholesaler, whether full-service or limited-function, restricts himself to all or a portion of the product line carried by a particular type of retailer. Thus, we have grocery wholesalers, drug wholesalers, auto parts wholesalers, and so on. A special terminology applies to wholesalers in some fields. Petroleum wholesalers are known as "bulk tank stations" because of the type of facilities required by the products they handle. Wholesalers of consumer durables are generally known as "distributors." In the industrial goods field, wholesalers are referred to as "industrial supply houses." If they sell to the mining industry, they are "mine supply houses"; if they serve machine shops, they are "mill supply houses."

Some wholesalers are more important in the assembly than in the distribution of goods. Agricultural products must be brought together from many relatively small producers into lots sufficiently large for economic handling. Local grain elevators, for example, buy the grain of local area farmers. They ship this in carload lots to terminal elevators, which bring together the grain of many local elevators. At this point begins the job of distributing the grain to the many and varied users.

Oftentimes wholesaling functions are integrated into the operations of manufacturers and retailers. Manufacturers may operate wholesale establishments, known as *manufacturer's branches*. Large retailers, such as grocery chains, operate district and regional warehouses which perform for their retail units many of the same functions independent wholesalers perform for independent retailers.

Retailers. Institutions at the retail level are more numerous, and even more varied, than those at the wholesale level. Because of personal contact and experience, students already possess a general familiarity with most retail institutions. The complexity of the retail structure is suggested by the many bases commonly used for classifying retail institutions. We classify retail institutions on the basis of size, ownership, lines carried, method of organization, and method of operation. The size distinction is obvious. Regarding ownership, we distinguish between "independent" (each establishment is separately owned) and "chain" (several retail establishments under one ownership). Outlets are designated as grocery stores, drugstores, hardware stores, and so forth, on the basis of the major types of products carried. Because of a trend toward scrambled merchandising, this basis of classification is losing its usefulness. Grocery supermarkets, for example, have added broad assortments of products formerly sold primarily in drugstores. They have also added many houseware and hardware items, certain apparel items, and in a few cases, major appliances. The "discount house" and "mail-order house" are classifications that reflect methods of operation. The term "department store" refers to a type of organization—separation of merchandise lines into separate and distinct departments, each under a "buyer" who is responsible for that department's operation.

Retailing has been undergoing continuous evolution, with constantly changing methods of operation and organization. One result of this is that as practices change, but terminology doesn't, commonly employed terms tend to lose their meaning. For example, many discount houses of today are hard to distinguish, on the basis of methods of operation, from many other retail institutions that bear higher prestige labels.

exchange and market intermediaries

The existence of the complex of marketing institutions which form our distribution structure, and which results in products often passing through many hands on the way to consumers, causes much criticism of marketing and distribution costs. One of the suggestions commonly made for reducing the cost of distribution is to "cut out the middleman." It is a popular belief that costs are least when producers sell directly to consumers as, for example, in the case of door-to-door sales of vacuum cleaners and cosmetics. Quite the contrary is true. This is a very high-cost channel of distribution. Sometimes manufacturers who use such a direct channel attempt to capitalize on this misunderstanding by claiming an ability to charge lower prices because they have circumvented the middlemen who make up the distribution structure. This helps to perpetuate this misunderstanding. To overcome this misconception, a better understanding of the nature of the exchange process and the role played therein by marketing institutions is necessary.

exchange without intermediaries

Why have so many market intermediaries arisen to carry out the exchange process? Why do producers and consumers not deal directly with each other to a greater extent than they do? To illustrate the basic, and perhaps obvious, but still ignored, principle underlying the existence of market intermediaries, let us assume a primitive society consisting, for the sake of simplicity, of but five families. Initially these families were self-sufficient, each producing all things needed for its own existence. Soon it was discovered, however, that each family produced some things better than others. It would be to the advantage of all if a family concentrated on producing the product it could produce best, and then the families exchanged products with each other. Because of the commonly recognized advantages of division of labor, this

Figure 7–1. Exchange without market intermediary.

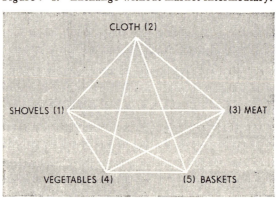

Source: Adapted from Wroe Alderson, "Factors Governing the Development of Marketing Channels," in Richard M. Clewett (ed.), *Marketing Channels for Manufactured Products* (Homewood, Ill.: Richard D. Irwin, Inc., 1954), p. 7.

would give a larger total product. As illustrated in Figure 7–1, one family concentrated on the production of shovels, one on cloth, one on meat, one on vegetables, and one on baskets. By trading among themselves, each then acquired a supply of the other items.

Let us now focus on the exchange process involved in Figure 7–1. In order for each family to acquire all 5 products requires that 10 exchanges take place. The number of exchanges required can be expressed by the formula $\dfrac{n(n-1)}{2}$, where n is the number of consuming units involved.[2] The number of exchanges (10) in relation to the number of products (5) is high. Each exchange, of course, involves a cost in time and effort. If the families are located close together, this cost may be low. If the distances involved are great, the cost will be high.

Figure 7–2. Exchange with market intermediary.

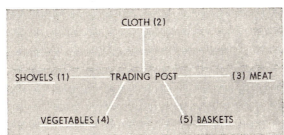

Source: Wroe Alderson, "Factors Governing the Development of Marketing Channels," in Richard M. Clewett (ed.), *Marketing Channels for Manufactured Products* (Homewood, Ill.: Richard D. Irwin, Inc., 1954), p. 7.

In Figure 7–2 we assume that some sort of market intermediary, say a trading post, is established to facilitate the exchange process. Each family now brings the amount of the product it has produced in excess of its own needs to the trading post and there exchanges it for the other four items that it requires. In this case only 5 transactions are necessary in contrast to the 10 required when no market intermediary was present. The time and effort (cost) involved in the exchange process has been greatly reduced. If our trading post is just an unmanned meeting place, no cost may attach to its existence. When a structure and manpower become necessary to carry out the market intermediary functions, there will be a cost. However, if the resultant

_____

[2] Each family (n) must contact all other families ($n-1$) and, when such contact is made, two (2) products change hands.

saving in time and effort is great, this cost may be small by comparison.

The ratio of advantage from use of a market intermediary in our illustration is small (2:1) because the number of consuming units is small.[3] In the real world, the number of producing and/or consuming units would be far larger. If there were 25 such units, the ratio of advantage would be 12 to 1. If there were 100, it would be 49.5 to 1; if 500, the ratio would be 249.5 to 1; and if 1,000, the ratio of advantage would be 499.5 to 1. These are not large numbers in the real world of exchange. It is apparent, therefore, that use of market intermediaries greatly expedites the exchange process.

the wholesaler and exchange

To make more realistic the role played by middlemen in our real-world distribution structure, let us apply the above reasoning to the presence of a wholesaler who distributes the products of several manufacturers to a number of retailers. Figure 7–3, which is grossly

Figure 7–3. Role of the wholesaler.

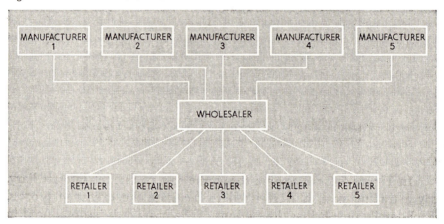

oversimplified, contains five manufacturers and five retailers. Each manufacturer produces one of many products carried by each of the five retailers. If each manufacturer sold directly to each of the five retailers, a total of 25 transactions would be involved.[4] However, if

---

[3] The ratio of advantage is $\dfrac{n(n-1)}{2}/n$.

[4] Because we are now assuming that the manufacturers in our illustration sell only to retailers, and not to each other, the formula for calculating the number of transactions used in our previous illustrations must be modified to:

$$\frac{n(n-1)}{2} - \frac{n}{2}\left(\frac{n}{2}-1\right).$$

each manufacturer sold only to the wholesaler, and then the wholesaler combined these five products and sold them to the retailers, a total of only 10 transactions would be required. In even this simple illustration, involving a mere handful of manufacturers and retailers, the use of a wholesaler reduces the number of transactions by 60 percent. If our illustration were more realistic, containing hundreds of manufacturers and perhaps thousands of retailers, the ratio of advantage from use of a wholesaler would be far greater. The ability of the wholesaler to reduce transactions in this manner is the fundamental explanation for his existence.

number of transactions and marketing costs

By now it should be clear that the existence of a distribution structure made up of various types of middlemen serves to reduce the number of transactions involved in getting goods from producer to consumer. It has been implied that this increases the efficiency of distribution and thus reduces marketing costs. But we have really not explained why this is so. The answer lies in the fact that distribution costs tend to be *relatively fixed per transaction.*

Consider some of the activities involved in the sale of goods to a retailer, regardless of whether this sale is made by a manufacturer or a wholesaler. Some sort of contact must be made with the retailer, probably by a salesman. This involves travel and the costs associated therewith, plus the time spent in talking with the retailer. If this is a new account, a credit investigation should be made. Assuming an order is received, it must be processed. The goods must be delivered, and, finally, the retailer must be billed for the price of the order.

The cost of a sales call on a retailer will be approximately the same whether the salesman is selling one product or many products. The many costs of getting the salesman to the account do not vary on this basis. The time spent on the sales call itself may vary somewhat with the number of products, but not proportionately. The cost of a credit check will be the same in either case. Order processing costs will not increase proportionately with the number of products, nor will delivery costs. Billing costs, surely, will be the same. The wholesaler, because he represents many manufacturers, has a far broader line of products than a typical manufacturer. Thus, his cost of distribution *per product, or per dollar of sales* (assuming equal sales effectiveness) tends to be less.

To restate concisely: (1) The use of middlemen reduces the number of transactions involved in the distribution of goods (2) Distribution costs tend to be relatively fixed per transaction. (3) Therefore, a reduction in the number of transactions reduces distribution costs. This is sometimes known as the "principle of minimum total transactions."

the discrepancy of assortments[5]

Up to this point we have been concerned with exchange and the contribution of marketing intermediaries to the exchange process. The basic economic benefit of exchange per se lies in the increase in production it makes possible by facilitating the division of labor. The contribution of marketing intermediaries to the exchange process is a reduction in the number of transactions required to accomplish the exchange. An explanation of this reduction is not to be found, however, in the nature of exchange. Rather, a reduction in transactions because of the presence of marketing institutions is a function of the discrepancy in the assortment of goods at various levels of distribution. That is to say, goods are associated in different ways and for different reasons at the manufacturing, wholesaling, retailing, and consumer levels.

heterogeneity of supply and demand

Goods are associated at the manufacturing level in a way which, in most cases, has little to do with the particular assortment the consumer is seeking. What products are associated in production is governed in large part by manufacturing considerations. Can they be made in the same plant? Do they utilize the same raw materials? Is there a carry-over of manufacturing know-how from one product to another? These and other pertinent questions bear on the manufacturer's decision on what products to associate together. Although he will also surely consider marketing questions in reaching his decision on product assortment, the extent to which he can do so is limited by production considerations. In general, manufacturers tend to produce a large volume (compared to the needs of any one consumer) of a limited assortment (compared to the needs of any one consumer) of goods.

Consumer demand is for a very different, far broader, assortment of goods than that made available by any one manufacturer. Generally speaking, the consumer wants an assortment of goods made up of a small quantity of each of many different things. On a given day he may

---

[5] The concept of discrepancy of assortments and its significance in marketing was first suggested by Wroe Alderson. For a fuller discussion of the ideas expressed in this section, see Wroe Alderson, *Marketing Behavior and Executive Action* (Homewood, Ill.: Richard D. Irwin, Inc., 1957), chap. vii.

wish to purchase a shirt, a book, a garden hoe, and a package of cigarettes. The assortment he demands is determined by the requirements of living and has nothing whatsoever to do with the manufacturing or distribution requirements of the products. Thus, supply assortments and demand assortments are entirely different things. It is through market intermediaries that assortments of goods are built up which more nearly match those wanted by consumers. In performing this function, a reduction in transactions is a natural by-product.

To illustrate this point, assume for the moment a situation contrary to fact: namely, that one producer turns out all varieties of grocery products that would make up the total grocery assortment wanted by any and all consumers. This, then, would be the assortment that grocery stores would want to carry. It would also comprise the total inventory of all grocery wholesalers. The product assortment would be the same at all levels of distribution. Under these circumstances, the wholesaler would be selling to retailers the same product line as would the manufacturer if he bypassed the wholesaler. The use of a wholesaler, instead of reducing the number of transactions involved, would instead increase them. If there were 10 retailers to be reached, transactions would rise from 10 to 11 when the wholesaler entered the picture. Now, on the other hand, if production of this same assortment of goods were dispersed among 10 manufacturers, the number of transactions involved in selling to 10 retailers would decline from 100 to 20 when a wholesaler was employed. Because of the heterogeneity of assortments that exists in the real world at different levels of distribution, the latter situation is the realistic one.

total assortments versus acquisition assortments

It is useful to distinguish between the total assortment of goods *possessed* by a consumer, and the assortment *he is seeking* in the marketplace at a given time. The total assortment will change slowly over time with changes in income, age, taste, and so on. It is not, however, a highly volatile thing. Rather, it is evolutionary in nature. This is in sharp contrast to the situation regarding the acquisition assortment. The latter is highly volatile and, at least in the case of the individual consumer, highly unpredictable. It is necessary that the distribution structure be prepared to cope effectively with this uncertain situation. Fortunately, it is able to do so to a remarkable degree.

Perhaps a person has been having some difficulties with his car and one morning decides to stop at the automobile repair shop on his way to work to have it checked. After an examination, the repairman informs him that the car requires two new spark plugs, a replacement for a defective headlamp, and a new shock absorber. In addition, he points out that a change of oil filter is long overdue and one of the tires is worn and no longer safe. This then—two spark plugs, one headlamp, one oil filter, one tire, one shock absorber—is the assortment of goods he requires. Because he needs his car later in the day, he would like to have the repairs completed by noon.

The parts required to repair the car are not all made by one manufacturer. Rather, in this particular case, each is made by a different manufacturer, and these manufacturers are located at different places around the United States. In order to achieve reasonable production costs, the volume of output of these manufacturers is large. The spark plug manufacturer may produce a hundred million or more spark plugs per year, and this customer's requirements are for only two. A similar relationship between production quantities and consumer needs exists for the other items. Somehow, these concentrated, massive stocks of repair parts must be dispersed over the market in accord with the incidence of automotive repair. In this industry, each manufacturer is likely to sell to a relatively small number of large

Figure 7–4. Movement of several automotive parts from manufacturer to consumer.

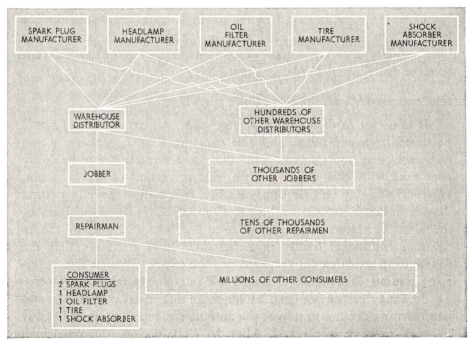

wholesalers, known as warehouse distributors. They sell, in turn, to thousands of small wholesalers, known as jobbers. There are tens of thousands of repairmen, and each has a jobber located relatively nearby. The repairman need not carry on hand the parts necessary to repair any car that drives into his shop. This would be an impossible task. Rather, he will go to his local jobber and acquire the items he needs. He will be able to obtain these parts, install them, and have the car ready by noon as requested. This demand for a unique assortment of products, perhaps not duplicated by one other consumer out of a million, can be met satisfactorily and at low cost. The same parts assortment could have been provided by any other repair shop the customer might have selected. This is possible because of the distribution structure which exists and through which the sorting process is carried out. An oversimplified picture of a portion of the structure used for automotive parts is shown in Figure 7–4.

aspects of sorting

The purpose of the sorting process is to convert a heterogeneous, conglomerate supply of goods into appropriate demand assortments readily available to consumers. To accomplish this, four different kinds of sorting activity must take place. These have been labeled: (1) sorting out, (2) accumulation, (3) allocation, and (4) assorting.[6] Although some of these aspects of sorting occur more at one level in the distribution structure than at other levels, all of them pervade the distribution structure and take place to some degree at each and every level.

Sorting out. This is the process of dividing a heterogeneous supply into a larger number of smaller, more homogeneous groups. It is essentially a grading process and is most prevalent and clearly recognized in the case of agricultural products. Eggs are sorted out into grade categories on the basis of color, size, and so on. Apples are sorted by size, color, and freedom from blemishes. The retailer might sort out today's shipment of head lettuce into that which he will sell at 25 cents per head and that which he will offer at 15 cents. Perhaps his criterion will be size, perhaps something else.

Sorting out is not a process limited to agricultural products. It is also prevalent in manufacturing. In fact, some industrial processes are essentially a "sorting-out" activity in and of themselves, such as the smelting of ore and petroleum refining. When goods come off the

---

[6] *Ibid.*, pp. 199–211.

assembly line, the defectives are usually sorted out from the nondefectives. In the case of smoking pipes, those with minor flaws are sold as "seconds" at reduced prices and find a wide market. The sorting-out process is less prevalent for manufactured goods than for agricultural products because of the greater ability to control production.

Accumulation. This is the bringing together into larger quantities of the scattered (over either space or time) homogeneous supplies that result from the sorting-out process. The local grain elevator assembles the grain produced by local farmers so as to obtain a quantity sufficient for economical shipment. The manufacturer accumulates units of output until he has enough for economical shipment or storage. He may also accumulate raw materials so as to have a reserve supply in case they should cease to be readily available for any reason. The principle motivation for the accumulation process is economical handling, either in storage or in transit.

Allocation. This is the opposite of accumulation. It consists of breaking down homogeneous supplies into smaller quantities. The manufacturer may have an accumulation of hundreds of tons of output, whereas the individual consumer may want to buy approximately one pound. The allocation process would begin with the manufacturer who would allocate smaller quantities, perhaps carload lots, of his product to wholesalers. The wholesalers would allocate still smaller, perhaps one-case lots, to retailers. The retailer would break open the case and sell the product, probably one package at a time, to consumers.

Assorting. This is the combining of unlike commodities in order to obtain an assortment of goods suited to use requirements. The housewife builds an assortment of many different food products in order to offer well-balanced and attractive meals to her family. She builds assortments of items of clothing to meet varied use requirements. She builds assortments of cleaning supplies, etc., to meet the needs of cleaning and maintaining a home, and so on. This process of building assortments that fit consumer requirements is seen most clearly in the case of the housewife doing her shopping, but actually the process begins far back in the distribution structure.

The manufacturer brings together different raw materials in order to make a product he thinks will be attractive to consumers. A product, in a sense, is an assortment of the things that go into its manufacture. The manufacturer may go further, and add products to his line in order to gain a product assortment that comes a few steps closer to matching the product assortment wanted by consumers. If he has been producing bread, he may add dinner rolls, breakfast rolls, and cookies.

The wholesaler attempts to build an assortment that will have maximum appeal to retailers. To do so, he will acquire goods from many different manufacturers. He will constantly juggle this assortment to keep pace with the changing requirements of retailers. The retailer, in turn, will try to build an assortment that will be attractive to consumers. To do this, he will probably buy from at least several wholesalers. There is a strong tendency at present for retailers to broaden the assortments they offer so as to come a bit closer to matching the assortments required by consumers. This appeals to consumers because it reduces their "friction cost" in obtaining the assortment of goods that best meets their needs.

summary

Our complex distribution structure, then, is not just a group of middlemen, each "taking his cut" and driving up the cost of distribution. To the contrary, this structure is essential to marketing efficiency. Although exchange could theoretically take place directly between producers and consumers, and in some cases does, it is far more efficient for the exchange process to be carried out through market intermediaries. By carrying out the sorting process that is necessary in order to match heterogeneous supply with heterogeneous demand, they succeed in bringing about a substantial reduction in the number of transactions that would be required to do the same thing by direct exchange between producers and consumers. And, because marketing costs are relatively fixed per transaction, a reduction in transactions serves to reduce marketing costs. A complex distribution structure is essential to efficient distribution. How efficient this proves to be for the particular manufacturer's product depends on how skillful he is in choosing the proper channel of distribution from among the countless number that the distribution structure makes available to him. Next we take a look at some of the more common channels employed by producers of manufactured goods.

channels of distribution

The number of specific channels of distribution utilized by manufacturers is so large that all channel alternatives cannot possibly be described. It is possible, however, to point out certain basic types of channels and compare them with each other. In doing so, we shall speak in general terms and not distinguish between types of institutions at either the wholesale or retail level. Rather, emphasis is placed on whether a particular *institutional level* in the available distribution structure is or is not included in the channel appropriate to certain types of goods.

major channels—consumer goods

The major basic types of channels used for manufactured consumer goods are the following:

Manufacturer......Consumer
Manufacturer......Retailer...Consumer
Manufacturer......Wholesaler...Retailer...Consumer
Manufacturer......Agent...Wholesaler...Retailer...Consumer

Although there are many examples of the sale of consumer goods by manufacturers directly to consumers, this is a relatively unimportant channel from the standpoint of both number of products and sales volume. It is most significant for perishables and specialty products. Eggs, fresh fruits and vegetables, and other perishables are sometimes sold in this manner. The appeal of freshness is strong and will compensate for other inefficiencies attached to the use of this channel. Such specialty products as encyclopedias, cooking ware, and high-priced vacuum cleaners employ this channel because it permits use of highly aggressive selling. Usually these are products for which consumers do not feel a great need until they are demonstrated. Under such circumstances, aggressive and high-cost selling can have a substantial "payout." The greater sales volume realized may well offset the high costs that use of this channel involves. Because this is true for relatively few products, this channel is quite unimportant.

Sales by manufacturers directly to retailers is a more important channel of distribution. Its use is, however, almost always associated with restricted retail distribution. Products which need to be sold through only a limited number of retail outlets can be distributed directly to retailers at reasonable cost if retail outlets buy in sufficiently large quantities. Although the number of transactions is larger than if a wholesaler were employed, the ratio of advantage from use of a wholesaler is limited because of the restricted number of retail accounts. One of the major products sold through this type of channel is clothing, for which style considerations are important. This places a premium on close contact with the consumer market, in order to keep abreast of style trends, as well as on speed of delivery so the product will be available at the particular time it is in demand. The fact that a direct channel is more effective on these two counts is a significant offset to the higher costs stemming from the larger number of transactions.

Sales by manufacturers to wholesalers, who in turn sell the retail trade, is the channel commonly employed for products requiring widespread distribution, such as groceries, drugs, hardware, and automotive parts. Because of the large number of retailers involved, each accounting for but a very small fraction of total sales, direct contact between manufacturer and retailer would be prohibitively expensive. The number of transactions would be very high in relation to sales, and there would be insufficient offsetting benefits derived from the direct contact. Of course, where sales are to large retail units, such as grocery chains and large department stores, this same reasoning does not apply, and a direct channel is normally employed.

When the manufacturer is very small, has a narrow product line, and sells to a widely dispersed or sparse market, it is common to interpose an agent middleman between the manufacturer and wholesaler. This reduces the number of transactions that would otherwise be involved in sales to a large number of wholesalers. Canned vegetables are a good case in point. The typical food canner is small and has a narrow line because he usually processes only those products native to the region in which he is located. Yet the market served is widespread and reached by a very large number of wholesale and retail accounts. Another complicating factor is the seasonality of his production. For all these reasons, canned foods are normally sold through food brokers. This is more economical than if the canner dealt directly with the wholesalers.

major channels—industrial goods

The major channels of distribution employed for manufactured industrial goods are:

Manufacturer......Industrial User
Manufacturer......Manufacturer's Agent......Industrial User
Manufacturer......Industrial Supply House.....Industrial User

In contrast to the situation for consumer goods, the most important channel of distribution for industrial goods is a direct one, involving no middlemen between manufacturer and the industrial user. In light of our previous discussion of exchange and the role of middlemen in the exchange process, this should not be surprising. Unlike the consumer market, the industrial market is made up of a smaller number of relatively large buyers. In addition, these buyers often are concentrated geographically. Thus, the ratio of advantage stemming from the use of middlemen tends to be far lower than for consumer goods. Also, industrial goods are often technically complex and require skilled selling. The gain in sales from more skillful selling can more than offset the higher costs brought about by the larger number of transactions because of not using middlemen. Where conditions such as those mentioned are not present, and the industrial market is more like the consumer market, indirect channels again tend to predominate.

Manufacturers' agents are used in the marketing of some industrial goods for the same reasons that agent middlemen are used for consumer goods—the manufacturer is small, has a narrow line, and sells in a dispersed market. The use of a manufacturer's agent reduces transactions and provides for a reasonable cost level, but not to the same degree as would the use of a wholesaler. This limitation is offset, however, by the more aggressive selling effort the agent provides compared to the wholesaler. The employment of a manufacturer's agent is sort of an "in-between" choice between direct sale and going through wholesalers. He provides some of the advantages of direct sale to a greater degree than does the wholesaler, while at the same time providing some reduction in the number of transactions.

The industrial supply house—the wholesaler of industrial goods—is used primarily for supply and maintenance items and for low-cost, fairly standardized industrial equipment. These are products which have highly dispersed markets, yet the products must be readily available when needed. Also, such products require no high degree of selling ability. They could be described as the "convenience goods" of the industrial market. Like convenience goods in the consumer goods category, the reduction in number of transactions, and therefore distribution costs, by use of a wholesaler is very great.

use of higher cost channels

Two seemingly contradictory facts have now been established: (1) Indirect channels tend to be lower in cost as a percentage of sales than are direct channels. This is due, of course, to the reduction in the required number of transactions that the use of market intermediaries makes possible. (2) In spite of the fact that more direct channels tend to be higher cost channels, they are extensively used in the distribution of goods. This situation suggests an obvious question: *Why does a manufacturer choose to use a higher cost channel when lower cost ones are available?*

The answer to this seeming paradox is, in general terms, quite simple. Low distribution cost as a percentage of sales is not necessarily a reasonable objective for a manufacturer to pursue. His objective, rather, is to maximize profit on investment. Frequently this goal can be better achieved by the use of higher cost channels rather than lower. This is true because these higher cost channels may produce sales that would not otherwise be realized. If sales are increased more than costs, profits will be greater. A 10 percent return on sales of $1 million for example, may provide a far better return on investment than a 20 percent return on sales of $100,000. It is the favorable effect on sales that explains the use of shorter channels.

With few exceptions middlemen handle the products of more than one manufacturer. Sometimes they represent thousands of manufacturers. As a result, their sales efforts for any one product are diluted because such efforts are spread over many products. The salesmen of a grocery or hardware wholesaler are often mere order takers rather than salesmen. Because they handle so many products they are not well informed about any one. Usually they do not even have time to mention most of the products in their line to potential customers. Consequently, products which require substantial sales push cannot use this channel. Low distribution costs, in the absence of sales, provide little consolation and little profit.

Encyclopedia publishers rely heavily on direct sale to consumers through their own sales forces. Why do they not restrict themselves to distribution through bookstores? Their direct contact with consumers is very costly indeed, and the relative cost of going through bookstores would be substantially less. So too, probably, would be their sales and their profits. An encyclopedia is a high-priced product. The average consumer will not purchase it unless he is fully convinced the expenditure is justified by the benefits he or his family will receive. These benefits are somewhat intangible and not readily apparent to someone browsing in a bookstore. They must be pointed out to him, and this must be done forcefully and well. The bookstore clerk has neither the time nor the knowledge to do this. The publisher's own salesman, in contrast, concentrates entirely on this one product, and he is trained to sell it effectively. Oftentimes such salesmen are too "high pressure," and consumers are antagonized and refuse to purchase. In many cases, however, this aggressive selling results in sales—sales that would never have been made if a more indirect channel had been used.

The marketing of encyclopedias may be an extreme case, but it illustrates well the basic point that the use of high-cost channels may be essential to sales success. Manufacturers who choose to sell directly to retailers rather than employ wholesalers usually do so for the same reason—increased sales. The effect on sales is the reason for use of higher cost channels, but it is also the crucial factor that determines when such a practice is sound. The effect on sales and profits must be sufficient to compensate for the higher costs involved. For many products, this is not the case.

Cake mixes, in contrast to encyclopedias, could not be sold by manufacturers directly to consumers. The need for aggressive selling is not there. The housewife planning to bake a cake is well aware of her need for cake mix and does not have to be convinced of this fact. The price is low. The housewife will buy this product in the grocery store when she shops for other items. The major factor affecting sales will be availability, and this can best be achieved by getting the product into as many grocery stores as possible. To do this at reasonable cost, wholesalers must be used.

Cake mixes are at one extreme, encyclopedias at the other as far as channel requirements are concerned. The majority of products would be somewhere in between. Thus, various degrees of directness in channels will be found. In all cases the relationship between distribution cost and sales effectiveness should have been carefully considered when the channel was chosen. In general, the more a product requires aggressive selling, the more direct the channel should be. The more important availability compared to aggressive selling, the more appropriate is the indirect channel.

The appropriateness of a particular channel for a particular product is not constant through time. Often products which are new to the market require aggressive selling. Gradually, as they become commonplace items, the need for aggressive selling declines and market availability becomes more important. Thus, at one time radios were sold directly to consumers, but today such a channel would be absurd. Vacuum cleaners have long been sold directly, and they still are. But, many manufacturers have changed over to indirect channels as the need for aggressive selling of this product has declined. As products lose distinctiveness, price becomes a more important factor in sales success. Because an indirect channel is usually lower in cost, it becomes more desirable as price competition intensifies.

use of multiple channels

Some manufacturers choose to follow but one path through the distribution structure, while others elect to use multiple channels of distribution. There is a basic difference on this score between manufacturers of different types of products, and frequently different manufacturers of the same product choose to follow different policies. Higher priced consumer specialty products often move to market through a single channel, while most convenience goods, such as food products, move through several channels. For a given product, such as appliances, one manufacturer will choose to sell only to franchised retail outlets, while another will sell to any retailer wishing to buy—including discount houses.

For certain products a single channel of distribution may be capable of reaching a substantial part of the available market. This tends to be true of specialty products for which there exists a strong brand preference. Automobiles are a case in point. Although a given make of automobile can normally be acquired by the consumer through one channel only, sales are not unduly handicapped, because the consumer will make substantial effort to acquire this particular product. The market for many other products, however, is such that restricting distribution to any one channel means a severe reduction in market coverage. A grocery manufacturer, for example, who elects to sell only through independent wholesalers is cutting himself off from the market represented by retail grocery chains. If he elects to sell only directly to chains, he loses the market made up of independent grocery retailers who normally buy from independent wholesalers. In the case of products for which, because of consumer buying patterns, broad availability is important, use of only one channel can restrict sales unduly. Because most products are in this category, the use of multiple distribution channels is common.

One product for which broad availability is extremely important is oil filter cartridges for automobiles. Every car owner must change oil filter cartridges at intervals, and he wishes to have this done along with other normal maintenance services. He has little brand preference and will normally accept any cartridge the serviceman chooses to install. Under these circumstances, broad market availability is essential to maximizing sales and profits. Figure 7–5 illustrates how this broad availability is achieved through the use of multiple channels of distribution. The filter manufacturer sells his product through vehicle manufacturers to car dealers. Car dealers, however, account for a very small part of the filter cartridge replacement business, so the manufacturer also sells to mail-order houses and chains in order to reach the self-repair market, through direct jobbers and warehouse distributors to reach the general repair trade, and through the parts programs of oil and rubber companies in order to gain access to the retail trade they control. The net result of use of these several channels is achievement of a higher probability that the car owner will find a particular brand of oil filter cartridge in whatever type of outlet he chooses for maintenance services.

The use of multiple channels of distribution helps to create many marketing problems. Those involving promotional strategy and pric-

Figure 7–5. Major channels of distribution—oil filter cartridges.

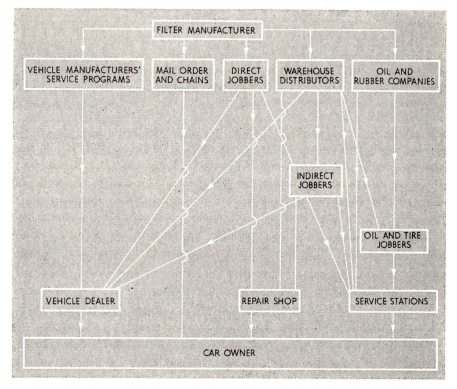

Source: C. N. Davisson, *The Marketing of Automotive Parts* (Michigan Business Studies, Vol. 12, No. 1 [Ann Arbor, Bureau of Business Research, The University of Michigan]), p. 652.

ing we shall ignore until later chapters. The most basic and important problem is the creation of interchannel rivalry. Note in Figure 7–5 that four different types of middlemen compete for the oil filter cartridge business of the vehicle dealer, three compete in sales to the repair shop, and five sell to service stations. All of these retail service shops, in turn, compete with mail-order houses and chains in sales to consumers. Such overlap in the markets served by different distribution channels is commonplace, but it can cause ill will and difficulties for the manufacturer. Middlemen tend to resent the competition that such a channel policy creates. As a result, they are less willing to push the manufacturer's product, and sales effort is low in aggressiveness. This pushes back onto the manufacturer the job of doing whatever demand creation is necessary.

When a manufacturer elects to use multiple channels of distribution, he is usually sacrificing "sales push" in order to gain availability. For many products this choice must necessarily be made, because sales push cannot possibly compensate for not having the product readily available in the market. The problems, therefore, which go with use of multiple channels are very often unavoidable.

conclusion

If consumers are to have readily available the vast variety of products required in order for them to complete their demand assortments with reasonable effort and at reasonable cost, a complex distribution structure is a necessity, not a sign of waste in distribution. But it cannot be denied that this situation complicates the problem of channel choice for the manufacturer, who must choose the right path through this intricate maze of marketing institutions. In making this choice, many variables must be considered. We have mentioned in this chapter only the most basic of these. The following chapter, which considers at greater length the problem of channel selection, will focus attention on other things.

The most fundamental consideration, however, in making decisions about the channel of distribution to be used is the one stressed in this discussion of the distribution structure—the relative importance of sales effort on one hand and market availability on the other. If aggressive sales effort is required within the channel, then shorter, higher cost channels may be the correct choice. To gain better selling effort, one must usually expect to pay the price of restricted distribution, because such channels can provide widespread market coverage only at prohibitive cost. If market availability is more important than sales push, then a longer, more indirect channel is better because it can provide such availability at reasonable cost. The greater the need for widespread availability, the more likely also is the decision to use multiple channels. Other considerations will always be present to modify and becloud this basic choice, but they will not remove the necessity for making it.

questions

1. What is the basic difference between agent middlemen and merchant middlemen?
2. Compare and contrast (1) a manufacturer's agent with (2) a sales agent.
3. In general, the costs of distribution (as a percent of sales) are less when an indirect channel rather than a direct channel is used. Why is this so?
4. If indirect channels are less costly than direct channels, why do so many sellers choose to sell (at a higher cost as a percentage of sales) through a direct channel?
5. A few years ago a major publisher of encyclopedias failed in an attempt to sell encyclopedias through department stores. An attempt by Sears, Roebuck to sell encyclopedias by mail also failed. What do you think caused these failures?
6. The X Company produces baking powder, baking soda, and other staple grocery products, with total sales of roughly $100 million per year. The company has long been dissatisfied with the lack of aggressive selling of its products by wholesalers and is considering distribution directly to retail stores. Would you recommend that this change be made? Justify your answer in terms of (1) the relative costs of the two channels, and (2) the difference in attainable sales volumes for the two channels.
7. A reduction in transactions that is a result of using indirect channels of distribution is a function of the discrepancy in the assortment of goods at various levels of distribution. Explain.
8. How might it be argued that the choice of a channel of distribution depends largely on the nature of buyer behavior?
9. Refer to Figure 7–5. Explain why manufacturers of oil filter cartridges use multiple channels of distribution. Discuss the problems this causes.
10. How might a manufacturer adjust his marketing strategy so as to minimize the problems inherent in the use of multiple distribution channels?

chapter 8

distribution
policy decisions

The distribution structure described in Chapter 7 is the sum total of all channels of distribution used by all sellers. An overview of this distribution structure has been presented, and some of the major channels of distribution have been described. With this background we now turn to a consideration of the kinds of distribution policy problems which confront the marketing managers of individual manufacturing firms in developing and executing a plan which will achieve a profitable flow of their products to the ultimate consumer or industrial user. The problems faced by the firm introducing a new product are especially complex and challenging. Among the more important distribution policy decisions which must be made are the following:

1. Should the manufacturer sell direct to the final buyer or should middlemen be used?
2. If middlemen are to be utilized, what specific types (both wholesale and retail) are most appropriate?
3. What degree of selectivity is desirable at the several levels of the distribution structure?
4. How much control should be sought over the institutions in the channel and how does this affect the channel problem?

The executive's task is complicated by the fact that these several decisions are not mutually exclusive. For example, a decision concerning the appropriate degree of selectivity bears on the decision concerning the degree of directness in the channel which should be employed. A policy of restricted retail distribution tends to reduce the costs of direct sale. If other factors are favorable, therefore, restricted distribution might make it profitable for the manufacturer to eliminate wholesalers from his channel and sell directly to selected retail outlets. In contrast, a decision to seek widespread distribution would tend to make it costly for the manufacturer to sell directly to the retailer and thus would favor a policy of using wholesalers instead.

A decision as to the amount of control a manufacturer wishes to exercise over his middlemen also has a bearing on the choice of a channel. The less direct the channel of distribution, the more difficult it is to exercise control over channel institutions. The manufacturer might willingly give up some of the cost savings typically associated with an indirect channel in order to gain a larger measure of control over retailers.

Space is not available to discuss all decisions concerning distribution policy which the marketing manager of a manufacturing company might be called upon to make. Instead, we shall concentrate attention on the more basic channel policy decisions. Specifically, we shall discuss the issues of directness and selectivity as outlined above. We shall also bring in issues of selection of specific types of middlemen and determination of the appropriate degree of control. These various issues are interrelated, but for clarity of presentation they will be treated separately.

degree of directness

The degree of directness which can appropriately be used in a channel of distribution is influenced by many specific factors. For purposes of simplicity we shall organize these specific considerations under the major headings of (1) nature of the product or product line, (2) characteristics of the market, (3) nature and availability of middlemen, and (4) characteristics of the manufacturer. Where possible the relationship of these major considerations to sales volume, costs of distribution, and profit contribution will be traced. Obviously, the aim of the executive is to select the degree of directness of distribution which will produce the maximum contribution to profits for the firm. In our thinking we should also avoid the temptation to identify the "ideal" channel for a particular product. Instead, we should focus our attention upon the realities of the environment in which the manufacturer operates and recognize the importance of working out a decision which it will be feasible for the firm to execute.

nature of the product

The selling effort required to maximize sales volume depends upon the nature of the product and the needs of the prospective buyer.

Technical complexity in a product, for example, increases the amount of skill and knowledge necessary on the part of the salesman as compared to what would be required in the sale of a simple, standardized item. Likewise, prospects are likely to devote more time and attention to the purchase of an item of high unit value than would be true where the product is not regarded as an important purchase. Executives considering the purchase of an electronic computer, for example, might be expected to devote considerable attention to this matter. Considerable knowledge and skill would also be required on the part of the salesman to explain the benefits of owning such equipment and to point out the merits of his own particular brand as compared with alternative makes. Both the importance of the purchase and the technical complexity of the computer would require a considerable amount of high-caliber selling effort on the part of the salesman.

In resolving the issue of directness under such circumstances, it is pertinent for the executive to inquire whether the available middlemen have the requisite order of skill and knowledge to sell the product effectively. If it appears that available middlemen would not be likely to furnish the desired selling effort, this factor would then favor direct sale by the manufacturer's own sales force.

The average industrial distributor handles a large number of items and represents a considerable number of manufacturers. His salesmen, accordingly, are not in a position to devote much selling time to the product of an individual firm. Instead, their approach is to take orders for whatever products the industrial user needs. For the same reason, it is likely to be difficult to get industrial distributors to undertake promotional work for a firm's product on their own initiative. If the manufacturer's product needs aggressive sales support to achieve satisfactory sales volume, industrial distributors are not likely to provide it. These considerations help to account for the fact that many complex products tend to be sold directly to the industrial users by the manufacturer's own sales force.

The service requirements associated with the product should also be considered in deciding whether to sell directly to the final buyer or distribute through middlemen. Where the buyer requires highly technical service, this requirement tends to favor the use of direct distribution. Middlemen are not likely to have the interest, the training, and the equipment to provide such high-quality service. Such would tend to be the case, for example, for electronic data processing systems. On the other hand, the need for relatively simple but readily available service may favor the use of middlemen. Where ready availability of service close to the user is important, and available middlemen are able and willing to maintain service facilities of the desired quality, then there is an advantage in distributing through them. An example of these conditions is found in the case of manufacturers of relatively simple standardized industrial machine tools. One of the factors which might lead such a firm to favor distribution through industrial supply houses is that these middlemen maintain service departments which are available to provide repair service when needed.

Another product characteristic which should be considered in analyzing the issue of directness is the bulk of the item. Handling, transportation, and storage costs tend to be relatively high for bulky products as compared with nonbulky items. The distribution costs which must be covered by the price paid by the ultimate user tends, therefore, to be less if the product is sold directly to the final buyer as compared to the expenses which have to be covered when middlemen are used. Producers of sand and gravel, for example, would find the loading and unloading costs associated with the indirect channel prohibitively high. Consequently, sand and gravel are typically sold by the producer directly to the ultimate buyer. The same reasoning would apply to bulky manufactured products where high storage costs are involved. There is a tendency to use a direct channel to minimize such costs, even though there may be some sacrifice in product availability in the market.

Still other products are perishable in either a style or a physical sense. Style perishability, growing out of fashion changes, places a premium upon the producer maintaining close contact with the ever changing market. Speed in distribution is also essential. Both of these factors tend to favor direct sale from the manufacturer to the retail middleman as opposed to the use of wholesalers. Products which are physically perishable, such as milk, eggs, and bakery products, require speed in distribution, although refrigeration and cold storage facilities may lengthen the time which may elapse before freshness is lost and spoilage takes place. As a consequence, such products tend to be either distributed directly to the consumer or through specialized middlemen who are geared to the tasks of providing the necessary refrigeration, storage, and rapid transportation facilities.

In analyzing the issue of whether to use middlemen or sell directly to the buyer, it is helpful to consider the unit value and/or the unit sale of the product. Contrast, for example, how this factor might influence the analysis in deciding upon the degree of directness desirable in the distribution of $100 watches and table salt priced at 10 cents per package. In either case it may be assumed that direct sale to retailers would be more costly than distribution through wholesalers. Let us also assume that the sale of fine watches directly to retailers would add $1 to the distribution costs of each watch. This would have a relatively minor effect on the demand for such watches, since an increase of $1 in costs of distribution would add only 1 percent to the final retail price paid by consumers. In contrast, if $1 were added to the distribution costs of each package of table salt, thus raising the price from 10 cents to $1.10, the effect upon demand would be catastrophic.

In addition to unit value of the product, it is necessary to consider the average size of order which may be expected. If the typical order were for 10 case lots of table salt, then the dollar value of the order (price times quantity) might be large enough to absorb the higher costs of direct sale. For some low-unit-value products this is the case. The significance of the unit value of the product in the analysis, therefore, is to provide a floor below which the dollar value of the order cannot fall.

Products have other characteristics which affect the channel selection problem. Those mentioned, however, are sufficient to suggest the importance of product characteristics in resolving the issue of directness in distribution channels. They are the more important characteristics which need to be taken into account in the analysis.

characteristics of the market

In analyzing the wisdom of direct sale versus the use of middlemen, it is logical to move from a consideration of the product to questions dealing with the influence upon our decision of the size and characteristics of the market. Helpful orientation is achieved by asking what types of prospects might purchase the product, where they are located, how many good prospects exist, and what their buying habits are? If possible, market research should be used to provide answers to these questions. Research may help determine the size of the potential demand and serve to define market characteristics which will tend to influence the cost of alternative distribution approaches.

Extent of demand. The size of the market for the product is a key factor in determining whether or not it is feasible to sell directly either to retailers or final buyers. If the total demand for the product in each market area is large enough, it may be more profitable to use a direct channel and gain the benefits of more aggressive representation and better control. Since the distribution costs involved in a direct channel tend to be relatively fixed in total, there is a minimum sales volume below which sales should not fall if direct sale is to be advantageous.

Assume, for example, that a manufacturer of complex technical equipment is currently selling to industrial distributors, who receive a discount of 16 percent of the final price to compensate them for their services, and that their total sales amount to $48,125,000. Since the manufacturer believes that his product would benefit from the increased aggressiveness of direct sale, he has worked out some cost estimates for setting up a sales force which would give him approximately equal market coverage, together with cost estimates for establishing the necessary branch warehouses and sales offices required by the new arrangement. Let us also assume that he plans to pay his salesmen on a salary basis and that the total additional costs of the necessary sales force, supervisors, warehouse and office space, order-handling clerks, warehousemen, and shippers would amount to $7,700,000. A large portion of these costs would tend to be fixed in total, regardless of sales volume.

Under these circumstances, the elimination of the industrial distributors would provide the manufacturer with additional income equal to the 16 percent gross margin on the combined sales, or $7,700,000, which these firms now receive. If the proposed plan of selling direct to users is to add to the firm's profits, the market for the product must be large enough so that the sales can be increased to substantially more than the distributors' current sales volume of $48,125,000. At this figure, the industrial distributors' margin of 16 percent, or $7,700,000, is just equal to the additional costs involved in performing the distributors' functions as estimated above. If the market is large enough so that direct sale will increase sales volume to $75 million, the new plan will clearly increase profits. Now the distributors' margins saved would amount to $12 million while the additional costs of direct sale would only be $7,700,000—a gain of $4,300,000. If there is no possibility of expanding sales above their current level, there would be no profit advantage of switching to the more direct method of distribution. Once the costs of direct sale have been estimated, then, analysis of the size of the demand which may be created for the product is an important consideration influencing the line of action to be taken.

Anticipated fluctuations in the demand for the product in the future also have a bearing on the wisdom of direct distribution. In the above case, assume that a recession sets in after three years and that sales of only $25 million are achieved. Since the costs of direct distribution tend to be fixed, they would remain at approximately $7,700,000. Had industrial distributors been handling the product, their discounts would have only amounted to 16 percent of $25 million or $4 million. Accordingly, the firm's profits would suffer to the extent of $3,700,000 as a result of the decision to adopt direct distribution (additional costs $7,700,000 − margin saved of $4,000,000 = deficit of $3,700,000) .

Concentration or dispersion of demand. An important factor influencing the cost of distribution is the extent of geographic concentration or dispersion of demand. In the sale of industrial goods, localization of industry tends to produce geographic concentration of prospective buyers for many products. This favors direct sale to the user, since the cost of maintaining a sales force tends to be low in relation to realized sales. If prospects are dispersed widely throughout the entire United States, salesmen will have to travel more extensively to reach them and achieve a similar sales volume. Fewer calls per working day and higher travel expenses would tend to make direct sale less attractive than the use of middlemen even if the size of the average order were the same.

If there is only a limited number of prospects and they may be expected to place large orders, as may be the case with certain industrial goods, this type of concentration of demand would also tend to favor direct sale. Tire manufacturers selling to automobile firms for original installation provide an example of such a situation. In contrast, the demand for replacement tires by ultimate consumers generally involves relatively small purchases (one to four tires) by buyers located throughout the entire United States. Where the average purchase is small and there are large numbers of prospects scattered throughout a large area, direct sale to consumers is clearly out of the question, and the use of retail middlemen is commonplace. In selling to retailers, the concentration or dispersion of demand is still an important consideration. Because tires should be available in each community where motorists live, sale through a relatively large number of retail outlets is desirable. Costs of direct sale to independent retailers tend to be high under these conditions, and if the average size of order is small, circumstances favor the use of wholesalers. Petroleum companies maintaining their own service station outlets, however, are in a position to place relatively large orders. The possibility of securing large orders from the operators of service station chains, together with the limited number of sales calls involved in securing such business, tends to favor direct sale to such customers.

Buying patterns. Not only are the total yearly requirements of the final buyer or the retailer middleman important in determining direct-ness but also the frequency of purchase, the regularity with which orders are placed, and thus the average size of order which may be anticipated. If buyers anticipate their needs for a product, buy in substantial quantities, and carry an inventory from which their recur-ring needs can be met, such behavior may result in an average size of order large enough to favor direct distribution. (In effect, demand is concentrated.) On the other hand if they prefer to follow a hand-to-mouth buying policy, maintain small inventories, and expect quick deliveries, then the average size of order will be substantially smaller and the costs of distribution higher, thus making direct distribution less feasible.

To take an extreme illustration, if consumers anticipated their requirements for cigarettes for 10 years in advance and, being heavy smokers, purchased a carload quantity of cigarettes at one time, it would be economically feasible for the manufacturer to sell directly to consumers. If, instead, consumers wished to purchase one package of cigarettes per day throughout the 10-year period, the costs of selling directly to them would be prohibitive as compared to the small average size of purchase. When consumers purchase in this latter manner, market availability of the product becomes of prime importance. It is then necessary to have small stocks of the product available in many retail outlets scattered widely over the market so that consumers can follow their established purchase patterns with the minimum of incon-venience and effort.

The extent to which purchase of a product can be postponed determines the need for stocks located near to consumers and thus has an important bearing on the costs of direct distribution. Consumers can postpone the purchase of a new automobile for a period of time, but they cannot defer the purchase of gasoline if they use their car to commute back and forth to work each day. Automobiles would thus require a lower degree of availability in each market area than gaso-line, and fewer retail outlets would be required to serve consumer needs for cars than for motor fuel. A smaller number of automobile dealers per market area than service stations tends to make it less costly to reach them through direct sale than to distribute to gasoline dealers in this way. The need for availability, therefore, is an important consideration in determining the number of retail outlets required to service a market adequately and thus influences the cost of direct distribution as opposed to the use of middlemen.

Other aspects of consumer buying behavior may also influence the directness which is appropriate in distributing a particular product. In the sale of industrial goods, for example, prospective buyers may prefer to purchase directly from the manufacturer rather than through middlemen. If the costs of serving them are reasonable when compared with the size of orders they may be expected to place, their preferences might well be controlling. Again, if consumers place heavy emphasis on price and are willing to accept less service in order to achieve such savings, an indirect channel tends to have an advantage. Consider, for example, the distribution of milk. Household delivery is convenient, involves a minimum of effort on the part of the housewife, and offers the advantage of weekly or monthly payment of bills. Distribution of milk through supermarkets tends to be lower in cost, however, because it is sold under conditions of self-service, cash and carry. If the housewife's family consumes enough milk each week so that she is anxious to buy as economically as possible, she may tend to buy her dairy supplies in the supermarket. Where a milk producer believes that a substantial segment of his potential market is price conscious, therefore, he may wish to reach these prospects through retail supermarket channels.

characteristics of the manufacturer

Two companies with similar products appealing to the same market may reach different decisions as to the use of a direct versus an indirect channel of distribution. This does not mean that if one firm is correct in its decision, the other must necessarily be wrong. Instead, manufacturers themselves may differ in important respects which have a bearing on the channel selection problem.

Size and resources. One of these differences is the size and financial resources of the manufacturer. Assume, for example, that a firm has developed an improved food product which requires widespread availability in grocery outlets throughout the United States if sales are to be maximized. While the product is superior, it needs to be promoted aggressively to consumers through advertising and to grocery stores through personal selling in order to get them to add it to their stocks. Under these circumstances, direct sale to chain stores, supermarkets, and independent stores would achieve the desired exposure to purchase. A new firm, with limited financial resources, however, would find it prohibitive to organize and train the necessary sales force for direct sale to retailers, set up branch warehouses, purchase a fleet of trucks for delivery of merchandise, undertake necessary advertising and promotion to create consumer demand, and do the other things required to achieve a profitable level of sales. Instead, such an organization might find it necessary to rely primarily upon wholesalers to sell its new product to retailers because of the smaller financial resources required in using this channel. It might restrict its introductory effort to one market initially because of its limited budget, utilize local advertising to stimulate consumer demand for the product, and offer free-deal inducements to wholesalers and retailers to get them to stock the product. Later the same method might be applied in other areas, opening up only as many markets at any one time as resources permit. Such an approach might well require several years before national distribution could be secured.

In contrast, a large, well-financed manufacturer distributing an established line through wholesalers would have been in a position to provide the sales force necessary to sell the product directly to retail stores throughout the entire market area during the introductory period, undertake extensive consumer advertising, and perform other tasks essential to securing national distribution of the new product within the desired time period. Even though two or three years of effort might be required before a breakeven volume was achieved, the large firm could afford to make the necessary investment, but the limited finances of the small firm would probably make it impossible for it to wait that long for the ultimate payoff.

Width of product line. The choice between a direct and indirect channel is influenced by the width of the product line which the manufacturer is already marketing to the target market. The broader the line of products a manufacturer is selling to a given market, the higher the average order which salesmen can secure, and therefore, the more feasible the use of a direct distribution channel. As the manufacturer broadens his line of products, he takes on more and more the characteristics of a wholesaler in that he can spread distribution costs over a greater array of products and thus lower distribution costs per unit. In contrast, manufacturers of narrow product lines may find it difficult to secure an average size of order which will cover the costs of direct sale. For them, indirect distribution channels may be more feasible.

Stage of development. It is also clear that the stage of a company's development is a factor which has a bearing on the issue of directness. An unknown company introducing a new product may have to be very aggressive in order to establish a foothold in the market. Direct sale to final buyers in the industrial field, or to retail middlemen in the consumer market, offers greater aggressiveness in the introduction of the new product than the use of less direct channels. Whether the firm can utilize the direct channel depends, of course, upon the anticipated sales volume which might be achieved in relation to the estimated costs of the more direct approach. The character of the product, whether the market is concentrated or dispersed, and the size of the potential average order, among other factors mentioned above, must be weighed along with the need for aggressiveness. A firm with a line of well-established products is in a position to accept the lower level of aggressiveness of indirect channels in the sale of its line. In this case the new product will benefit from the reputation of the remainder of the line, especially if a family brand is used.

Experience of executives. A direct channel is, in a sense, a "do-it-yourself" project. Successful use of this approach requires that company executives have the know-how and experience to deal with the various problems that may be encountered. Executives lacking such background may regard this as a good reason for selling through middlemen. In this manner they may be able to take advantage of the marketing experience and customer contacts which the middlemen possess.

nature and availability of middlemen

In analyzing the issue of directness, it is clear from earlier discussion that an important consideration is the nature of the middlemen who are available to perform the necessary distribution functions. In this analysis one side of the coin is the definition of the distribution tasks which must be performed and this we approached through an analysis of the characteristics of the product, the market and the manufacturer. The opposite side of the coin is to ask what types of middlemen might the firm seek to perform these tasks and whether these types of organizations are likely to function as effectively as the manufacturer's own direct selling organization might be able to do. How aggressively is the selling function likely to be performed by the middleman and would this degree of support make a substantial amount of difference in the sales volume which might result? Where do prospective buyers customarily purchase the product and are middlemen likely to conform better to these buying habits than our own direct sales organization? How important is widespread availability of our product and can we achieve the desired coverage more economically through middlemen than through direct sale? Is the contribution to profits likely to be larger if the firm distributes through middlemen than through its own marketing organization? Answers to such questions involve a thorough understanding of the nature of the middlemen who serve the industry.[1]

Although the foregoing analysis may indicate that indirect channels including certain types of middlemen should ideally be used, it may not be possible to get these firms to order the product. This difficulty is commonly faced by the manufacturers of new products and may force a more direct channel than theoretically desirable. The producer of a new type of deodorant, for example, did not attempt to get distribution through drug wholesalers and retailers originally, although this would have been a desirable channel. Instead, the sales manager of this company decided to try to get initial distribution by selling directly to Chicago department stores. Although he offered to pay for advertisements over the retailers' names if they would place an initial order for a specified quantity, he was rebuffed by several cosmetic buyers before he finally secured initial orders from three department stores. When advertising produced an unusual sales response, the sales manager was able to use this experience to help him get distribution through department stores in other cities. Only after the product had proved to be profitable in department stores was the firm able to get distribution through drug wholesalers and retailers.[2]

Another situation is illustrated by a small manufacturer of industrial casters located in Michigan who had built up a sales volume of about $300,000 through direct sale to automobile companies. As a means of trying to increase sales throughout all industrial areas in the United States, the president of the company explored the possibility of distributing through materials-handling equipment distributors. He found, however, that most of the good distributors in the areas he wished to reach had long since been retained by the firm's older competitors. He was of the opinion that it would be difficult to get distributors through advertising, and his firm lacked the resources to finance the hiring of a sales force adequate to do the job. The possibil-

---

[1] Brief mention of the characteristics of different types of middlemen has been made in the previous chapter. Further background may be secured in references such as C. F. Phillips and D. J. Duncan, *Marketing: Principles and Methods* (6th ed.; Homewood, Ill.: Richard D. Irwin, Inc., 1968), Parts III and IV; R. S. Alexander, J. S. Cross, and R. M. Hill, *Industrial Marketing* (3d ed.; Homewood, Ill.: Richard D. Irwin, Inc., 1967), chap. vii.

[2] Adapted from N. H. Borden and M. V. Marshall, *Advertising Management*, (rev. ed.; Homewood, Ill.: Richard D. Irwin, Inc., 1959), pp. 498–519.

ity of developing a channel through distributors was therefore limited.[3]

These examples indicate that the new company, or the firm considering new channels, will generally find that preferred types of outlets are already handling competing products. Such middlemen tend to be reluctant to add another brand to the variety they now offer unless the prospective dollar gross margin is sufficient to outweigh increased inventory and other costs of adding the line. The problem of overcoming the reluctance of middlemen to stock new brands may be solved if the firm has developed an attractive product and has the resources to work out an effective strategy for getting distribution. The difficulty of getting middlemen to accept a new brand should not be underestimated, however, in the process of arriving at a decision on whether to use direct or indirect channels.

selectivity in channel selection

A basic policy decision concerns the number of outlets at each of the several levels in the distribution structure that the manufacturer will strive to obtain in the marketing of his product. A sound decision on this issue is important, since both cost and effectiveness in distribution can be vitally affected by the action taken. A policy of attempting to gain distribution through any and all outlets of good credit risk willing to carry a product is referred to as intensive distribution. When a firm follows the policy of limiting the sale of the product to chosen middlemen who meet certain criteria, it is using selected distribution. If this policy of restricting distribution is carried to the extreme of selling the product through only one reseller in a given geographic area, the policy is commonly referred to as exclusive agency distribution. This section is concerned with the number of resellers through which the firm distributes: wholesale distributors, if they are used, and retail dealers.

illustrations of the above policies

Intensive distribution. While the goal of intensive distribution is sale through all of the chosen types of middlemen with good credit standing who will stock and sell the product, actually the density of

---

[3] Adapted from *Midwest Precision Co.*, Michigan Business Case No. 32, written by L. B. Milliken and Peter Repenning, Research Assistants, Bureau of Business Research, The University of Michigan.

distribution attained will vary among companies and products. One study indicated, for example, that 12 firms producing toothpaste secured retail coverage of from 71 to 98 percent of the drugstores, while 7 firms producing tooth powder had retail coverage of from 51 to 97 percent of the stores surveyed.[4] While these firms aimed at intensive distribution, they had achieved varying degrees of success in executing their policy.

Selected distribution. At the point where a firm decides that it is advisable to restrict distribution to chosen retailers according to specified criteria, then a selected distribution policy is being followed. The degree of restriction will tend to be a compromise between the desire to have the product on sale wherever prospective buyers might expect to look for it and the desirability of limiting the number of middlemen in each market area as a means of encouraging desired reseller sales support, adequate inventories, and suitable service facilities (if needed), among others. The number of outlets per market area resulting from a policy of selected distribution commonly varies depending upon the size of the area, the total number of outlets serving it, and the share of market the firm has in mind as a goal. One manufacturer of automobile tires, for example, reported that on the average the firm had 5 retailers in cities of 100,000; 12 retailers in cities of 1 million; 25 in Chicago; and 35 in New York City. Likewise, on the average a manufacturer of shoes had 2 retailers in cities of 10,000; 25 retailers in cities of 100,000; 150 retailers in cities of 1 million; 300 in Chicago; and 700 in New York City. The extent to which representative firms restricted distribution is indicated by dividing the number of dealers used in New York City by the number commonly selling the product as reported in the census. The percentage of possible outlets used by companies varied as follows: automobile tires 0.7 percent, mechanical refrigerators 3.9 percent, men's suits 5.5 percent, shoes 6.4 percent, radios 10.4 percent, and ladies' silk hosiery 14.2 percent.[5]

Theoretically, the percentage of outlets used could be much larger, and still constitute selected distribution, as long as the firm selects less than the total potential number which might be available. Competition among sellers for distribution, together with the desire of resellers to limit the number of competing brands carried, tends to reduce the percentage of outlets which will sell a given brand in a particular

---

[4] J. D. Scott, *Advertising Programs for Products with Selected Distribution* (Business Research Studies No. 26 [Boston, Bureau of Business Research, Graduate School of Business Administration, Harvard University]), p. 5.

[5] *Ibid.*, p. 13.

market to a figure considerably less than the total number of outlets in that area stocking the type of product under consideration. It is conceivable, however, that a policy involving only a limited degree of restriction on the part of one manufacturer might approximate the degree of coverage secured by another who aims at intensive distribution but experiences difficulty in getting retailers to stock his product.

Exclusive agency. Although exclusive agency distribution might be regarded as simply an extreme policy of selectivity, common practice is to distinguish between them. An exclusive agency restricts the sale of the manufacturer's brand to one reseller within a specified market area. When more than one reseller is used per geographic area, but the number of outlets is restricted as a matter of policy, then selective distribution is being practiced.

Even under an exclusive agency policy there is some opportunity for variations in the extent to which distribution is restricted. One source of difference is the size of the geographic area within which the reseller has exclusive sales rights. The area may be relatively small, such as a community of 5,000 population, or it may include a market as large as the metropolitan New York City trading area. An illustration of a highly restrictive policy of exclusive agency distribution is a manufacturer of high-grade pianos which appointed only one retail outlet within a community and its trading area. Even in markets the size of Chicago and New York City, the brand was sold through only one retailer. In international trade, also, the exclusive territory of a reseller sometimes consists of an entire country, or possibly even a group of countries.

An important feature of the exclusive agency agreement is the designation of the brand to which exclusive selling rights apply. Some manufacturers may find that an exclusive agency policy tends to limit sales unduly in large-city markets but may be reluctant to modify the arrangement because of the strong preference of dealers for it. One way of achieving a more satisfactory share of market in a large city is to add a second or a third brand to the line and appoint a different exclusive outlet for each new brand.

Although the policies of selective and exclusive agency distribution have been discussed separately, they are commonly combined in actual practice as a means of adjusting the degree of product exposure to potential market areas of different sizes. A manufacturer of women's shoes, for example, had only one outlet, on the average, in communities of 10,000 population—an exclusive agency. In cities of 100,000 population two dealers were usually selected, while in cities of 1 million population the number of outlets averaged four or five. In Chicago the firm had 20 dealers and in New York City 30 sold the brand.[6] Thus, the policies of exclusive agency and selected distribution were combined as a means of achieving desired coverage of markets of different sizes.

wisdom of restricting distribution

Obviously, policies which restrict distribution limit the market availability of a product. For some products such a limitation may be offset by benefits which justify the policy in terms of contribution to profits. For other items the opposite may be true. Clearly policies of selected and exclusive agency distribution should, therefore, be adopted only after discriminating analysis. Let us turn, therefore, to a consideration of the merits and limitations of restricted distribution with the goal of coming to a better understanding of the considerations which should be taken into account in making policy decisions.[7]

Benefits of restricted distribution. The more restricted the distribution of a particular product, the more the interest of the middleman comes to parallel the interest of the manufacturer. Restriction of distribution makes the product more valuable to retail and wholesale outlets which sell it. They must share the market with fewer competitors; hence they have greater market opportunity. A policy of restricted distribution, therefore, tends to stimulate resellers to be more aggressive in their selling and promotional efforts than they would be under a policy of intensive distribution. To a varying degree, depending upon the extent to which distribution is restricted, the individual reseller is in a position to reap the benefits of his own aggressive selling effort without benefiting his competitors. In consequence, he is willing to put forth more aggressive efforts than otherwise would be the case.

For what types of products is aggressive selling and promotion by resellers important? Clearly, aggressive sales effort is especially beneficial for mechanical or technical products which require explanation and demonstration. New-model automobiles and household appliances would certainly fall in this category. Where sales resistance must be overcome because the product is an important purchase (high unit price) and is purchased infrequently, aggressiveness by the reseller is

---

[6] *Ibid.,* p. 11.

[7] Portions of the discussion which follows are adapted from *ibid.,* pp. 14 and 15.

required to offset the natural tendency of prospects to procrastinate in making a purchase decision. The task of getting retail dealers to stock and push a new product also requires aggressiveness on the part of the middlemen charged with such an assignment. A beverage company secured aggressive sales support for a new chocolate drink, for example, by granting exclusive agencies to retail milk distributors.

Then, too, for products such as shoes and paint, retailers are required to make a large investment in order to provide an adequate stock of the manufacturer's product. If the retailer's competitors are selling the same brand, the available sales volume may be too small to justify the investment necessary to provide an adequate inventory of the item. The retailer may then carry an inadequate stock with the result that sales will suffer. On the other hand, even though a large investment is required, he will tend to carry an adequate stock of the brand provided distribution is restricted sufficiently to give an adequate return on investment.

For products such as household appliances, where manufacturers often produce a complete line of items, the market protection they receive through restricted distribution would also tend to encourage resellers to carry the full line of products, including the less desirable along with the more desirable items.

There are other products, usually mechanical in nature, that require repair and maintenance service if they are to operate satisfactorily. Color television sets, automatic washers and dryers, and automobiles are good examples. To maintain a properly equipped service department with adequately trained personnel, however, involves the reseller in considerable expense. If the manufacturer sells his products through as many dealers in a given community as will stock the item, and still expects them to provide the necessary service facilities, the result is almost certain to be an inferior grade of service or no service at all. By restricting distribution, the manufacturer makes it worthwhile for the dealer to provide the desired quality of service.

Consideration must be given to the size of the market area required to provide resellers with a profitable sales volume. The characteristics of expensiveness, high unit price, incidence of the need (or desire) for the product among consumers, and infrequent purchase tend to limit the potential sales volume for certain products to a relatively small amount per 1,000 population. Such products as high-grade silk hosiery and pianos are good examples. Where the potential market is thin per 1,000 population, the policy of intensive distribution tends to make the line unprofitable for the dealer. In contrast, properly administered policies of selected or exclusive agency distribution tend to make the line profitable and serve to develop a more enthusiastic, successful and cooperative dealer organization than would otherwise be possible.

For this reason, retailers selling high-grade men's suits and high-grade men's hats prefer exclusive agencies if they are to handle a given manufacturer's line. Because of this a policy of restricted distribution helps a firm build up a strong dealer organization.

A number of the products cited above might be classified as either specialty goods or shopping goods. The benefits of restricted distribution are not necessarily limited to these classes of merchandise, however. This is illustrated by the example of a manufacturer who was following a policy of intensive distribution and was selling to about 90 percent of all the retail stores in the country handling his type of merchandise.[8] Many of the customers were small stores, and many of the orders were ridiculously small. Yet the firm's salesmen called upon these stores on an average of once a week. A study was made of the cost of serving customers in two of the firm's branches. It was found that two thirds of the company's orders and almost half of its accounts were costing more in marketing expense than they were worth in terms of gross profit. As a result the firm increased the size of the minimum order sixfold and drastically reduced the number of contacts the salesmen had to make. Unprofitable customers were dropped. Sales increased 82 percent, marketing expenses were reduced from 31.8 to 18.2 percent, and operating profit rose from 4.7 to 14.8 percent. Wherever the potential volume of business to be secured from resellers during a given time period varies widely, it is desirable to analyze the contribution to profits made by customers of different sizes and then ask whether a policy of selective selling (restricted distribution) might not be desirable.

A policy of restricted distribution may help a manufacturer deal with the problem of predatory price cutting at the retail level. When the aim is intensive distribution, competition between a number of retailers in the same community may tend to result in price cutting which makes the brand unprofitable for the retailers who handle it, with the result that desirable types of retailers refuse to stock the item. The manufacturer may also feel that price cutting damages the reputation of his brand. The policy of exclusive agency distribution eliminates competition between retailers in the same community and tends to prevent price cutting. A manufacturer of textiles, for example,

---

[8] C. H. Sevin, *How Manufacturers Reduce Their Distribution Costs* (Washington, D.C., U.S. Government Printing Office, 1948) , p. 17.

reported that it was not uncommon for several retailers in a single shopping area to carry the same brand of sheets. In several instances this fact had caused price cutting; a few mills therefore adopted an exclusive agency plan of distribution in order to overcome price cutting.

The above discussion serves to call attention to the fact that the control which a manufacturer exercises over the members of his channel of distribution is based primarily upon achieving cooperation through policies which recognize the reseller's point of view and which appeal to his self-interest. The degree of "control" (or cooperation) which can be exercised by the manufacturer depends upon the value of the franchise to sell his product. If it is a valuable right highly regarded by resellers, the manufacturer is in a favorable position to gain cooperation from them (or exert control over them). Automobile manufacturers, for example, exert a large measure of control over the marketing policies of their retail dealers. This they are able to do because the right to sell a particular brand of automobile can be a very valuable right to the dealer. In contrast, the manufacturer of chewing gum or cigarettes is able to exercise virtually no control over retail outlets handling his product. The policies of intensive distribution which such firms follow mean that the right (or the franchise) to sell an individual brand of such products tends to be of very limited value to the individual retailer. Restricted distribution, if it is consistent with consumer buying habits, is a means of increasing the value to middlemen of the right to sell a given product. The manufacturer provides this benefit to resellers in his channel of distribution as a means of gaining for himself some or all of the advantages mentioned in the preceding paragraphs.

Limitations of restricted distribution. In considering the wisdom of restricting the distribution of his product, the manufacturer should count not only the potential benefits he may receive but also the limitations (or "costs") which may result. A key question is: In the light of consumer buying habits, what will be the effect of restricted distribution upon sales? If the firm produces convenience goods, the sacrifices involved in gaining the benefits of restricted distribution will be too great. Consumers insist on buying these items with a minimum amount of effort. Consequently, ready availability throughout the market is the single most important factor influencing sales volume. Examples of products in this category are cigarettes, razor blades, staple food products, and candy bars. They tend to be purchased frequently and usually have relatively low unit value. To the extent that restricted distribution reduces market availability, it would make serious inroads on sales. While such products may benefit from favorable point-of-purchase promotion, they generally do not require explanation or demonstration. (An exception might be a distinctive, new product being introduced to consumers for the first time.) Usually the inventory investment required to support satisfactory sales volume is small as compared, say, with women's shoes or men's clothing. Service is generally not required. Except for reducing the distribution costs of reaching dealers, restricted distribution of such products has only limited benefits to offer as a counterbalance to the serious sacrifice involved in limiting exposure to sale.

By way of contrast, the manufacturer of specialty goods is likely to find the benefits of restricted distribution substantial indeed. Such products characteristically have achieved brand preference among consumers, who are willing to make considerable effort to seek out the retail outlet (or outlets) which stock them. Accordingly, the limitation in exposure to sale involved in restricted distribution is of little consequence when compared with the benefits which such a policy can bring in terms of dealer cooperation and support.

Where a substantial proportion of the prospective buyers shop around in the purchase of a product, restricted distribution may likewise offer benefits which considerably outweigh limitations on exposure to sale resulting from the policy. Consumers are willing to make considerable effort to inspect and compare different brands of high-grade women's dresses and furniture, for example, in making their selection. Adequate inventories and aggressive sales promotion encouraged by restricted distribution would be important advantages to be gained.

In addition to buying habits, the preferences of resellers also should be taken into account in reaching a decision on the wisdom of a restricted distribution policy. A strong preference for the exclusive agency arrangement among retailers is an important reason why certain manufacturers of high-grade men's clothing have adopted this policy. Yet some of these firms find that this policy limits product availability so much that large-city markets are not adequately developed.

A policy of restricted distribution creates another difficulty which is not encountered under intensive distribution arrangements. Because the number of outlets appointed per community is limited under a policy of restricted distribution, it is necessary for the manufacturer to make certain that the local source of supply is identified through signs, window displays, and advertising over the retailer's name. Unless this identification is made, the demand created by the manufacturer's general advertising may be dissipated because of the consumers' lack of knowledge of where to go in order to buy the product. Failure to recognize the importance of this problem may result in ineffective advertising. If the difficulty is recognized, of course, appropriate promotional policies and procedures may be developed to correct the deficiency.

Finally, restricted distribution may tend to promote substitution. Dealers who cannot get the agency for a given brand may double their efforts to take business away from that brand by offering substitutes. The seriousness of this problem will depend upon the strength of the brand preference which the manufacturer can create. If information is secured through market research on the degree of brand discrimination which has been created for the product, this knowledge can be taken into account in deciding whether restricted distribution is desirable, and if so, the extent to which the firm should go in limiting the number of outlets per market.

Both the benefits and the sacrifices involved in a policy of restricted distribution are illustrated by the experience of the Consumer Products Division of the Magnavox Corporation.[9] This firm markets through a franchised dealer network of 3,000 outlets, which facilitates the maintenance of list prices, service, and advertising standards. An executive of the company, however, admitted that Magnavox is losing "tens of millions of dollars" by making it too difficult for consumers to buy the product. "We've got to find other ways of getting product exposure," he said. One way, he said, was the company's current agreement with Singer retail centers to sell Magnavox products. This move secures the patronage of people who don't normally go into the firm's franchised stores. So far, Magnavox dealers are not "up in arms" about this development, he reported.

Still another way to reduce the "cost" of gaining the benefits of restricted distribution is illustrated by an example from the paint business. In order to provide consumers with an adequate range of choice among different types and colors of paint, it is essential that retailers carry a large inventory of the brands they sell. Yet they are reluctant to make the necessary investment unless they are granted the protection from sharing their markets with competitors which restricted distribution provides. Accordingly, exclusive agency distribu-

---

9 *Advertising Age,* May 6, 1969, p. 26.

tion is typically used in marketing paints, except in large metropolitan markets, in order to encourage the maintenance of adequate stocks. The buying patterns for paint are such, however, that restricted distribution often involves a substantial sacrifice of sales volume. Although the prospective buyer will make considerable effort in the purchase of paint when he is buying large quantities for a special purpose, he will not do this when he is picking up a very small amount for use in routine household maintenance. Consequently, restricted distribution means reduced availability and lost sales in this segment of the market. In recognition of this problem, certain paint manufacturers sell paint under a number of different brand names and grant "exclusive" distribution rights on each of these brands. In this way each of the retailers is provided with protection from direct competition on the particular brand for which he has a franchise. At the same time, the manufacturer is assured of an adequate number of outlets for his paints and thus is more likely to achieve a desired share of market. While this practice probably limits the value of the franchise on a particular brand to the retailer, some benefits still remain, since consumers may not be aware of the fact that the same firm produces competing brands. Undoubtedly the manufacturer is able to achieve greater dealer cooperation in marketing each of the brands (and thus greater "control") than if he followed a policy of intensive retail distribution.

legal aspects of restricted distribution

At the present time, there are no legal restraints on the practice of restricted distribution *as such*. The courts have long upheld the right of a seller to choose his customers even when this extends to the practice of choosing to sell to only one customer in a certain market. From time to time, so-called "right-to-buy" laws have been proposed, but they have not been enacted, and there is at present no great prospect that they will be. The intent of these laws is to force a seller to make his product available to any one who wishes to purchase. This would, of course, make impossible the practice of effective restricted distribution.

Certain practices often associated with restricted distribution, particularly with exclusive distribution, are of doubtful legality. The most important and most controversial of these are: (1) exclusive dealing, and (2) territorial protection. Exclusive dealing is the practice of not allowing the dealer to carry competing products. Not all exclusive agency contracts involve exclusive dealing. The manufacturer may agree to sell through no competing dealers in a particular market but still allow the dealer to carry competing products. On the other hand, many manufacturers have sought to restrict the dealers to their own products under exclusive agency contracts.

The major reason why a manufacturer might wish to practice exclusive dealing is to encourage more aggressive selling and promotion on the part of his dealers. The retailer who handles only one brand of a particular type of product has no alternative items to push in competition with it. He must succeed in the sale of this one brand, or he will find his sales of the generic product unsatisfactory. For this reason he is likely to be a more aggressive dealer than if he carried competing brands. He is also likely to be more cooperative in maintaining necessary inventories of the line, in providing repair service of satisfactory quality where necessary, and in maintaining resale prices if the manufacturer requests such action.

Territorial protection clauses in exclusive agency agreements were common practice prior to the late 1940's. The essence of such agreements is that the manufacturer will attempt to prevent the sale of his product by any other party in a territory assigned to an exclusive outlet. The request for such clauses in exclusive agency agreements is likely to come from the dealer rather than from the manufacturer. The dealer wishes to protect himself against direct competition from other retailers who are handling the same brand. Various ways of enforcing such clauses have been utilized. These may involve penalty payments from the dealer who has made a forbidden sale to the dealer whose territory has been invaded. If such violations are continued, they may, of course, lead to cancellation of the franchise of the invading dealer.

legal status of exclusive dealing

Section 3 of the Clayton Act prohibits exclusive dealing contracts where the effect of such agreement "may be to substantially lessen competition or tend to create a monopoly in any line of commerce." Note that exclusive dealing contracts are not illegal as such, but rather their legality depends upon the effect that they have upon competition.

The bench mark court case involving exclusive dealing was that involving the Standard Oil Company of California, decided in 1949. In this case the Department of Justice had charged that the company in its exclusive agency contracts had violated both Section 1 of the Sherman Act and Section 3 of the Clayton Act. The specific complaint was that the company's practice of entering into agreements with its 6,000 plus dealers for exclusive handling of its petroleum products and automotive accessories substantially lessened competition and tended to create a monopoly. At that time this kind of contract was common in the petroleum industry as well as in many other industries. The Standard Oil Company of California then accounted for 23 percent of gasoline sales in the Pacific area; its products were sold through 10 percent of the available independent retail outlets. The stations with which it had exclusive dealing contracts pumped only 6.7 percent of the gasoline in this area. An additional 6.8 percent of gasoline sales in this area was made through stations owned and operated by Standard. The firm attempted to demonstrate that its exclusive dealing contracts did not substantially lessen competition. It cited its small share of the total market, the still smaller share of gasoline sales through outlets with which such contracts had been arranged, and the fact that its share of the market had not increased during the time these contracts were in force.

In spite of this defense, the district court ruled against the Standard Oil Company of California, and its decision was upheld by the U.S. Supreme Court in 1949.[10] The Court made two main points. First, it held that these exclusive dealing contracts violated Section 3 of the Clayton Act because they covered a substantial number of outlets and a substantial volume of sales. When this is true, said the Court, a substantial lessening of competition is a natural result and an actual reduction in competition need not be proved. This is the per se or "quantitative substantiality" doctrine. Second, the Court called attention to the fact that there had been widespread adoption of exclusive dealing contracts by other major competitors in the area with the result that independent producers were foreclosed from distributing through the outlets serving a substantial share of the market in the area. When the exclusive dealing contracts of a particular firm involve a substantial volume of trade and when there is widespread use of such contracts by the firm's competitors, therefore, there is serious danger that such arrangements will be regarded by the courts as a violation of Section 3 of the Clayton Act.

Under different conditions, however, a manufacturer may make use of exclusive dealing contracts without violating Section 3 of the Clayton Act. The J. I. Case Company, for example, followed a policy of exclusive dealing in the distribution of its farm implements. The firm made a serious effort to get dealers who would carry the full line

---

[10] *Standard Oil Co. of California* v. *U.S.*, 337 U.S. 293 (1949).

and devote the major part of their activity to Case implements where the market in the area justified it. The handling of two full lines (Case plus a competing brand) was consistently discouraged. Dealers handling competitive lines to the detriment of Case were dropped. These practices led the firm to be charged with a violation of Section 3 of the Clayton Act. In a 1951 ruling, however, the district court found the evidence insufficient to establish an adverse effect upon competition.[11] During the trial no evidence was presented from any farm implement manufacturer that his outlets had been restricted by Case's policy and, further, there was no indication that available outlets had been narrowed in any way thereby. Because of the nature of the market, strategic location for dealers in farm machinery was not essential. Apparently, competitors had found no difficulty in obtaining dealers. There was an adequate number of full-line and short-line manufacturers represented in most markets in agricultural areas.

As pointed out in a 1961 Supreme Court decision, Section 3 of the Clayton Act was not intended to reach every remote lessening of competition—only those that were substantial—but earlier Court decisions had not drawn a line to indicate where "remote" ends and "substantial" begins. The case involved was that of the Tampa Electric Company, where the district court had ruled that an exclusive contract violated Section 3 of the Clayton Act, but where the Supreme Court reversed the judgment.[12] In reviewing this case, the Court indicated that an exclusive dealing arrangement does not violate Section 3 unless the Court believes it probable that execution of the policy will foreclose competition to a substantial extent. In determining the probable effect upon competition, the Court outlined the following considerations which must be taken into account: (1) the line of commerce—i.e. type of goods; (2) the geographic area of affected competition; and (3) whether the competition foreclosed constitutes a substantial share of the affected market (relative strength of the competing firms and the percentage of the total volume of business involved). Applying these guidelines, the Court reasoned that the exclusive dealing contract in this instance did not foreclose competitors from a substantial share of the business in the relevant market area. In effect this approach applies the "rule of reason" in evaluating the effects of exclusive dealing contracts. The central issue is the ease with which rival suppliers can secure access to customers in alternative ways.

It should be borne in mind, however, that Section 5 of the Federal Trade Commission Act has also been used by the Commission in

[11] *U.S.* v. *J. I. Case Company,* 101 F. Supp. 856 (1951).

[12] *Tampa Electric Co.* v. *Nashville Coal Co.,* 365 U.S. 320, 327–29 (1961).

attacking exclusive dealing contracts. Here the approach has been to charge that such contracts may constitute an unfair method of competition which may substantially lessen competition. In the *Brown Shoe Company* case, for example, retailers who promised not to sell shoes made by competitors received a combination of benefits ranging from architectural plans and display materials to sales training and group rate insurance. The FTC issued a complaint against this exclusive dealing arrangement on the grounds that it denied Brown's competitors the opportunity of selling to a substantial number of dealers. Brown argued that dealers were not coerced to join the plan, the FTC hadn't shown any harmful effect upon competition, only 650 out of 6,000 dealers participated, and these outlets bought only 75 percent of their shoe stocks from Brown. The Appeals Court set aside the FTC decision on the grounds that the Commission had failed to prove the system an "unfair method of competition."

In 1966, however, the Supreme Court reversed this ruling in an opinion written by Justice Black.[13] If the attack had been brought under the Sherman or Clayton Acts, Justice Black said, such injury to competitors would have had to be proved. But, he added, the purpose of the FTC Act was to stop unfair competitive practices before they become monopolistic. This case shows beyond doubt, he wrote, that Brown, the country's second largest manufacturer of shoes, has a program which requires shoe retailers substantially to limit their trade with Brown's competitors. This obviously conflicts with the central policy of both the Sherman Act and the Clayton Act. In rejecting the argument that the Commission need prove injury to competition, Justice Black said that the Commission has power under (the FTC Act) to arrest trade restraints "in their incipiency" without proof they amount to an outright violation of the other provisions of the antitrust laws.

While the decision does not mean that all exclusive dealing systems are illegal, it does suggest that large companies are especially susceptible to attack if the plan is used to help the firm gain a more dominant position in the industry. The ability to challenge potential restraints of trade in their incipiency tends to make such plans more vulnerable to attack than in the past.

legal status of territorial protection

In addition to the questions raised concerning exclusive dealing, the legality of other aspects of exclusive agency arrangements are very

---

[13] *Wall Street Journal,* June 7, 1966.

much in doubt. In granting an exclusive agency to a dealer, the manufacturer agrees to limit his distribution in a specified geographic area to this outlet. In effect, this protects the dealer against neighboring retailers who might otherwise be competitors. In return for this protection, the manufacturer hopes to gain better cooperation from the dealer in maintaining inventories, giving service, and providing aggressive promotional support for his brand. The granting of exclusive distributorships in a specified territory is not covered by Section 3 of the Clayton Act as long as there is absence of restrictions on the sale of competitive products. Indeed, certain consent decrees have permitted such firms as the Wurlitzer Company and Philco to designate geographic areas as areas of primary responsibility for specific distributors.[14]

The manufacturer may, however, go one step farther and require his dealers to confine their sales activities to a described geographic territory—that is, prohibit them from invading the territories of other exclusive agents handling the firm's brand. While such territorial security clauses have never specifically been ruled illegal in a higher court of law, much has occurred to raise serious doubt as to their legality. In 1949, for example, General Motors consented to the entry of a judgment which restrained the firm from incorporating in any contract a provision excluding dealers from any designated territory.[15] Later, all automobile manufacturers dropped the so called "territorial security and antibootlegging" clauses from their dealer contracts. Philco Corporation also signed a cease and desist order of the FTC which prohibited such clauses in dealer contracts.[16]

Even though the territorial security provisions tend to be suspect, in a 1963 decision on the *White Motor Company* case the Supreme Court refused to support a district court decision declaring vertical territorial limitations illegal per se.[17] The White Motor Company allocated exclusive territories to distributors but reserved government, fleet, and large national accounts to itself—a vertical territorial limitation. In presenting the case in the district court, the Justice Department had merely presented evidence establishing the company's use of exclusive territories and the accompanying vertical territorial limitations, without attempting to prove that these practices unlawfully restrict competition. Accordingly, the district court handed down a summary judgment without full trial. The Supreme Court held that

14 *U.S.* v. *Wurlitzer Co.*, D.C., New York (1958) ; *U.S.* v. *Philco*, D.C., Penn. (1956) .

15 "G.M. Precaution," *Business Week*, Oct. 1, 1949, p. 52.

16 *U.S.* v. *Philco Corp.*, D.C., Penn. (1956) .

17 *The White Motor Co.* v. *U.S.*, 83 Sup. Ct. 696 (1963) .

whether vertical territorial limitations violated antitrust laws could not be determined on motion by summary judgment in the absence of evidence which would enable the Court to determine whether the arrangement had the effect of stifling competition or had some redeeming virtue. The Court explained it was reluctant to declare vertical territorial arrangements illegal per se because this was the first case involving such a restriction in vertical arrangements and too little was known about the "economic and business stuff" out of which such an arrangement emerged.

The Justice Department is reported to have interpreted this decision as a mandate to bring up more cases and to try them more exhaustively. Federal judges, on the other hand, have accepted the companies' argument that competition is sometimes best served by letting companies contain the struggle for business among their own distributors in order to concentrate on "the real enemy"—i.e. their competitors.[18]

One of these cases involved a charge by the Justice Department that the General Motors Corporation and three associations of automobile dealers violated the Sherman Act by participating in an alleged conspiracy to discourage dealers from selling to auto discounters. This case grew out of the action of some Los Angeles Chevrolet dealers who, in the late 1950's, began to sell cars through discount houses and "referral services" at bargain prices.[19] Of the 100,000 Chevrolets sold in the Los Angeles area in 1960, about 2,000 were sold through discounters. About a dozen of the 85 dealers in Los Angeles were furnishing cars to discounters in that year. As the volume of discount sales grew, nonparticipating dealers began to feel the pinch. The problem was discussed at a meeting of one of the dealer associations; then General Motors took action to deal with the matter. GM notified the offending dealers that sales to discounters violated the provision in their franchise contracts fixing dealership's locations and got them to promise not to do business with discounters in the future. Later, a private investigator was hired to police this agreement. By the spring of 1961, the campaign to eliminate discounters from the sale of Chevrolets was a success. In mid-1962, the Justice Department brought a civil antitrust suit in the U.S. District Court for the Southern District of California to enjoin GM and its dealers from conspiring to prevent discount selling of Chevrolets. The district court ruled in favor of General Motors, but

---

[18] "Is the Franchise System Legal?" *Business Week*, April 3, 1965, p. 66.

[19] *U.S.* v. *General Motors Corp. et al.*, No. 46, *Supreme Court Reporter*, Vol. 86, No. 14 (May 15, 1966), pp. 1321–32 (St. Paul, Minn., West Publishing Co.).

the case was appealed directly to the Supreme Court, where the decision was reversed on April 28, 1966.

The defendants had argued that dealers who sold through discounters were violating the "location clause" in their franchise agreements which prohibits them from moving to, or establishing a new or different location, branch sales office, branch service station, or place of business without the prior written approval of Chevrolet. The defendants contended that the described arrangements with discounters constituted the establishment of additional sales outlets in violation of the clause. They also claimed that the location clause was lawful and that GM acted lawfully to prevent its dealers from violating this clause.

In the Supreme Court decision, Mr. Justice Fortas said that it was not necessary to rule on the meaning, effect, or validity of the "location clause." He said:

"We have here a classic conspiracy in restraint of trade: joint, collaborative action by dealers, the defendant associations, and General Motors to eliminate a class of competitors by terminating business dealings between them and a minority of Chevrolet dealers and to deprive franchised dealers of their freedom to deal through discounters if they so choose. Against this fact of unlawful combination, the "location clause" is of no avail.

There can be no doubt that the effect of the combination or conspiracy here was to restrain trade and commerce within the meaning of the Sherman Act. Elimination, by joint collaborative action, of discounters from access to the market is a *per se* violation of the Act. . . . Where businessmen concert their actions in order to deprive others of access to merchandise which the latter wish to sell to the public, we need not inquire into the economic motivation underlying their conduct.

He also pointed out that the effect of this combination was a substantial restraint upon price competition—a goal unlawful per se when sought to be effected by combination or conspiracy. He explained that there was evidence that one of the purposes behind the concerted effort to eliminate sales of new Chevrolet cars by discounters was to protect franchised dealers from real or apparent price competition. On the basis of these findings, therefore, the Supreme Court reversed the decision of the district court and remanded the case to this court for the fashioning of appropriate equitable relief.

This case illustrates the importance of the choice of methods used by a manufacturer in attempting to prevent his dealers from selling through discount houses. The Court did not rule on the validity of the "location clause" or whether it may be used to prohibit a dealer from selling through discount houses. Nor did the Court express an opinion as to whether GM could, by unilateral action, enforce the clause without violating the antitrust laws. Had GM acted alone in this matter without involving either dealer associations or individual dealers in its approach, then the decision might possibly have been different. It was the evidence of the existence of a "classic conspiracy" which led directly to the Supreme Court's decision.

It is noteworthy, also, that discount selling of automobiles has thrived only when regular retail car sales were sagging. The impact of the Supreme Court ruling in the GM case may be nominal, therefore, as long as new auto sales through franchised dealers hold at a prosperous level. If sales slack off, however, and inventories begin to pile up, the problem may become acute. Better sales forecasting in periods of changing demand coupled with quick intelligence identifying areas where inventories are beginning to pile up, might enable an alert management to take steps to minimize the problem out of which sales to discount houses tend to grow.

justification of legal restraints

Any restraints on distribution policies imposed either by legislation or by court interpretation are likely to cause substantial controversy among those parties who have a stake in the distribution of goods. The legislation and court rulings concerning territorial security, the franchise system, and exclusive dealing are no exception. Are such restraints on distribution policies warranted?

Business is, in a sense, like an athletic contest. Various parties compete with each other and vie for attainment of a specified goal. Everyone would agree that ground rules are necessary in an athletic contest. The same is true of business. Rules are necessary and desirable in order to channel the competitive efforts of business along lines which best serve the interest of the entire economy. The real question is not whether rules and regulations are necessary, but rather whether these rules are sound and also whether they are properly administered.

It would seem that the prohibition of territorial security clauses in exclusive franchise agreements is sound and serves a major social purpose, namely, the enhancing of competition. To permit such clauses would give dealers a degree of monopoly in territories in which they are located. This, by serving to remove them from various competitive pressures, might reduce the quality of service which they render to consumers and conceivably could be a factor causing higher prices for consumers. Manufacturers, however, must be realistic if they hope to gain the benefit of aggressive selling by their dealers. To accomplish this objective they must offer the dealer a franchise which has value to him. Appointing too many "exclusive dealers" would be tantamount to a policy of nonexclusive distribution, would give minimum benefits to dealers, and would deny to the manufacturer the benefits he sought when he initially embarked on a policy of exclusive distribution. Recognition of this point should prevent harm to dealers by the absence of territorial security clauses.

Whether it is socially desirable to limit the action a manufacturer may take to prevent his dealers from selling through unauthorized discount outlets is a debatable question. An automobile manufacturer may claim that his dealers are already in vigorous competition with each other in view of the limitations on territorial protection which now exist. Also, they are certainly competing aggressively with dealers handling other makes of automobiles in the same territory. In addition, legal limitations on action which may be taken to prevent dealers from selling through discount outlets may serve to erode the franchise system, which depends upon the strategic location of dealerships to make sales and service facilities and parts suppliers conveniently available to consumers. To permit dealers to sell through discount outlets might negate the manufacturer's attempts to build strong dealers through the use of the exclusive agency system. Moreover, the manufacturer would have no control over the amount and quality of service offered by discounters, who in practice provide little or no service.

On the other hand, we should bear in mind that the prevention of sales through discounters may serve to protect dealers from the keen price competition of outlets capable of operating on a low markup. The spur of meeting such competition might stimulate innovation in the character and methods of operation of automobile dealers which would tend to benefit consumers in the long run. Also, prohibition on sales through discount outlets prevents dealers from exercising their freedom to dispose of surplus inventory at a low markup when they find themselves overstocked because of sudden changes in the rate of consumer buying, miscalculation, or the establishment of unrealistic sales quotas. Finally, choking off automobile sales through discount outlets denies consumers the benefits of low markup discount selling which have been available in the purchase of household appliances, jewelry, and many other types of goods.

On balance, it is probably not wise to impose such strict legal restrictions as to prevent a manufacturer from taking any action to limit sales by his dealers through discount outlets. Both consumers and dealers benefit from the maintenance of a franchise system which makes sales, parts, and service readily available through reputable firms. It might be wise, however, for automobile manufacturers to encourage certain of their dealers to experiment with types of operations which permit low costs of distribution and hence low markups and prices. It may be that certain dealers in large metropolitan areas could specialize on low-cost sales operations at the same time that others in the same area provide necessary parts and service facilities. It is also evident, however, that better market intelligence, sales forecasting by dealer areas, and closer control over physical distribution need to be practiced as a means of preventing the accumulation of excess inventories which tend to encourage dealers to turn to discount outlets for relief.

The legislative and court rulings concerning exclusive dealing have the same laudable objective as those applying to territorial security, i.e. the maintenance of competition. However, a good case can be made for the fact that they have not served this objective very well. The per se doctrine does not clearly recognize the effect upon competition of exclusive dealing practices. The mere fact that a substantial volume of trade is involved is not the equivalent of a substantial lessening of competition by any stretch of the imagination. Indeed, exclusive dealing contracts could serve to enhance the degree of rivalry practiced by the dealer who must devote all his effort to the sale of one brand of a particular product because he has no others to distract his attention. This gives him the same stake in the sale of the manufacturer's product within his territory as the manufacturer himself has.

Yet when the firm practicing exclusive dealing is a large manufacturer, and other leading competitors also follow the same policy, the result may be to foreclose a substantial segment of the retail outlets from use by smaller firms seeking distribution for their products in that market. Under these circumstances, such potential competitors might be injured by the exclusive dealing policies of dominant firms in the industry. Whether competition within the industry suffers, however, depends upon how vigorous the established firms are in vying with each other for market position and whether smaller firms can develop a strategy which will enable them to develop a profitable business in spite of the limitations imposed by exclusive dealing practices of leading companies.

If conditions prevail which are similar to the situation in the farm implement industry, where competing manufacturers were not foreclosed from reasonable access to retail outlets in markets where they wished to distribute, then it would seem that exclusive dealing might be as likely to increase competition as to reduce it. The difficulty faced by the courts, of course, is to draw the line between situations where exclusive dealing may tend to produce a substantial lessening of competition and those where a reduction in competition is relatively remote. Certainly, it is socially desirable that the Justice Department and the courts exercise discrimination in analyzing the exclusive dealing arrangements as practiced by different companies in different industries. It is to be hoped that the "rule of reason" will be applied to the end that the policy may be used where it is likely to bring about a favorable effect upon competition and discouraged where it may tend to have a substantially unfavorable influence upon competitive activity.

conclusion

Distribution policy decisions are among the most basic and important decisions the marketing executive must make in planning his marketing strategy. He must decide whether to sell direct to the final buyer or through middlemen. If an indirect channel is decided upon, he must select the types of middlemen to use, determine the desirable degree of selectivity to employ, and establish methods of control over channel institutions. These decisions in turn, will profoundly affect physical distribution requirements, promotional strategy, and pricing strategy. The influence of distribution policy decisions on other aspects of marketing strategy will be seen in subsequent chapters.

questions

1. Under some circumstances, after-sale service requirements cause a manufacturer to employ a direct channel of distribution; under other circumstances, service requirements cause an indirect channel to be employed. What circumstances surrounding service push a manufacturer in each of these directions?
2. Approximately 37 percent of machine tools are sold directly to industrial users, while 45 percent are sold to the industrial market through manufacturers agents. The remainder is sold through industrial supply houses. *Why* are some machine tools sold directly to users, while others go through manufacturers agents and industrial supply houses?
3. The H. J. Heinz Company and Standard Brands, Inc., both broad-line manufacturers of grocery products, previously sold direct to small inde-

pendent grocery store. In the past 10 years both have switched to selling through grocery wholesalers. What sort of changes in the situation surrounding the sale of grocery products probably explain this change in distribution channels?

4. Some manufacturers in an industry may utilize an indirect channel of distribution, whereas other companies in the same industry may elect to sell through a direct channel. What might explain this difference in choice?

5. Distinguish between intensive, selected, and exclusive agency distribution.

6. Manufacturers of major brands of household appliances usually follow a policy of selected retail distribution. What is the explanation for this choice?

7. As products move through their life cycles from the innovation stage to maturity, their distribution often becomes less selective. What explains this?

8. The Ahso Radio Corporation of Japan has made a decision to export its line of transistor-operated portable color television sets to the United States. The company enjoys an excellent reputation in Japan but is largely unknown elsewhere. The product line includes three models, and each contains the basic feature of remarkably clear reception on an 8-inch screen, with power coming solely from a rechargeable battery. Under most conditions a built-in "rabbit ears" antenna is sufficient for effective operation. Model A, featuring the basic set in a simple metal case, will sell at $199.95. Models B and C contain certain additional features, such as deluxe cases, with more convenient controls and will sell for $229.95 and $269.95 respectively. Each set weighs 23 pounds and can be carried easily. Competition is confined to the newly introduced Fuji portable set, also a Japanese import, and several models made by American firms. The American products were judged by management to be less convenient to use and poorer in reception, with the result that sales success has been disappointing.

   The firm is undecided concerning the distribution scheme to be used in the American market; but management feels that exclusive retailers should be employed. Evaluate the tentative plan for exclusive distribution. What recommendation would you make to management?

9. A large manufacturer of low-priced ($9.95–$29.95) transistorized radios secured his distribution through approximately 100 wholesalers and 20,000 nonexclusive retail outlets. Most retail dealers sold radio lines of a number of well-known competitors whose radios were in the same price range. The question arose as to whether the company should continue the present distribution policy or adopt a selected-dealer distribution in which a limited number of dealers in each community would be given franchises and special consideration and help. For example, in the

city of Chicago the company proposed to reduce the number of retail outlets from 450 to 100 selective, semiexclusive accounts. It was asserted that franchises would thus become more valuable immediately and cause dealers to exert greater willingness to promote the line through an extensive use of displays and campaigns. The distribution would be placed in the hands of larger, well-known dealers and removed from the weaker, smaller outlets. Some executives contended that the proposed reduction in number of outlets might seriously jeopardize the company's competitive position, since it was difficult to forecast the probable effect on sales volume.

What should be done? Why?

10. Distinguish between exclusive agency distribution and the practice of exclusive dealing. Is one ever found without the other?

11. Discuss the effect of exclusive dealing on competition. Under what circumstances might it reduce competition? Might it sometimes serve to increase competition?

12. Do territorial protection clauses in franchise agreements tend to reduce competition? Explain.

chapter 9

physical
distribution

The preceding chapters have discussed the structure of distribution as well as those policy decisions made by management in developing paths through the structure to reach the market. These decisions dealt with the type and number of resellers to be used, the extent of promotional effort to be expended by these intermediaries, and whether or not some portion of the output of the firm was to be sold directly to end users.

After channel-of-distribution strategy has been determined and policies established for its implementation, management must consider a closely related set of questions dealing with the physical distribution of goods. Such questions include, among others, the location of fixed facilities, the size of inventories to be held in these facilities, and the modes of transportation to be used to move stock from factories to warehouses and thence to resellers or to direct-buying customers.

Answers to the above and similar questions must be found and incorporated into policies which govern the performance of the physical distribution function. Effective management here is doubly important because not only does physical distribution account for a considerable portion of a firm's outlay for marketing but it also provides a level of service for customers which increasingly is becoming a prime weapon in the firm's struggle for competitive advantage.

The purpose of this chapter will be, therefore, to provide a brief overview of the physical distribution function in terms of what it encompasses, how it is related to the other functions of the firm (both marketing and nonmarketing), and why effective management of the physical distribution function is so important, given the nature of the present business environment.

Physical distribution has been called, "the other half of marketing" because it accounts for approximately one half of the total outlay for marketing effort by American business firms.[1] While the promotional processes of seeking out buyers and persuading them to buy are relatively well known by businessmen and consumers alike, that portion of the marketing task which is responsible for the distribution of goods after they have been produced has been shrouded in mystery. Indeed, only during the past decade or so has a real effort been made to reexamine that portion of the marketing task which provides time and place utilities in goods by moving them and storing them. The reasons for this revived interest in physical distribution (or PD as we shall sometimes refer to it) are varied. Three basic reasons are noted below.

rising costs

The costs of performing the functions of physical distribution have been rising steadily since the close of World War II. These costs have been incurred for labor, equipment, storage facilities, inventory holding, and transportation. Although cost behavior in this area has not been appreciably different from that in other sectors of business activity, the increased outlays needed for physical distribution have attracted the attention of management. Costs of physical distribution have also increased rapidly because of changes in overall product line strategy. Lines have been expanded in both depth and breadth, and this activity has resulted in a sizable increase in the costs of handling and holding inventory. Figure 9–1 illustrates how inventories increase 60 percent when three items are used to gain the same volume that had previously been brought in by one item. If volume with three items increases 50 percent, inventory must be at a level 25 percent greater than held previously.

cost-saving potential

A second reason for the increased attention being paid to the area of physical distribution is that although costs have been rising throughout all segments of business, there appears to be a greater opportunity to achieve cost reductions in the logistics area than elsewhere. For

---

[1] Paul D. Converse, "The Other Half of Marketing," in *Twenty-Sixth Boston Conference on Distribution* (Boston: Boston Trade Board, 1954), pp. 22–25.

example, physical distribution activities offer opportunities for organization and systematization which are not available in the promotional area. Further, these opportunities have not been fully exploited over

Figure 9–1. Inventory behavior as the product line is broadened and sales volume increases.

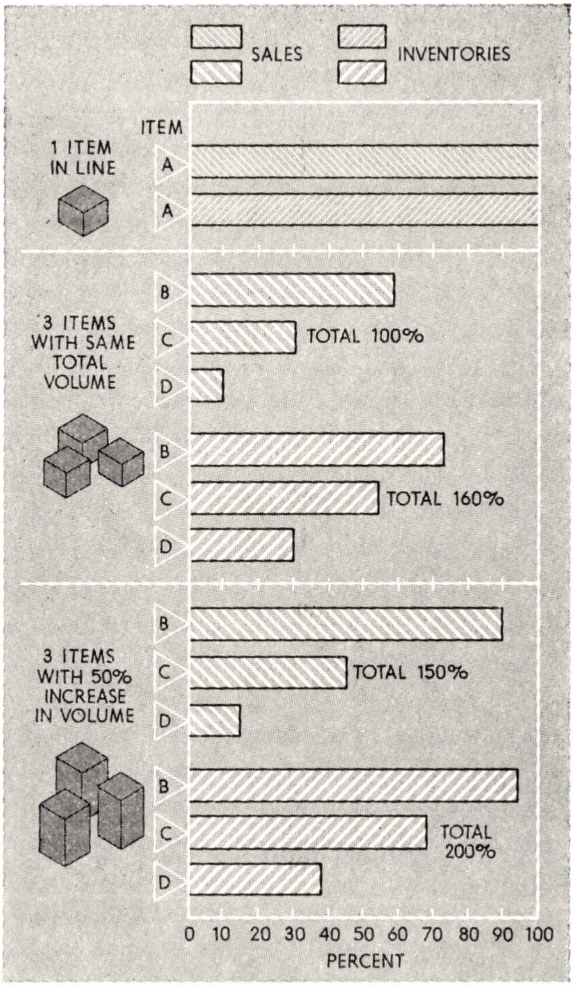

Source: From John F. Magee, "The Logistics of Distribution," *Harvard Business Review*, Vol. 38, No. 4 (July-August, 1960), pp. 89–101.

the years as has been the case with similar opportunities in the area of production.

promotional potential

Last, but far from least, management has discovered that effective physical distribution is a potent promotional weapon. Prompt deliveries, a minimum of back orders, infrequent customer need to file damage claims, etc., can provide the seller a considerable advantage over rivals who do not provide equivalent levels of service. Of special interest to management is the fact that the cost of providing a given level of service to customers can be calculated and compared with the costs of other promotional alternatives of both a price and nonprice variety.

implications

Because of the reasons stated above, many firms have ceased to view physical distribution as a peripheral area supporting their production and promotional activities. Instead, managers in these firms are treating physical distribution as a major functional area responsible for the movement of goods to customers and for the coordination of supply with demand as stimulated by the firm's promotional activities. By bringing the two halves of marketing—promotion and physical distribution—closer together, by coordinating efforts in both areas, and by giving physical distribution more attention than it has received in the past, these managers hope to achieve a synergistic effect. Their goal is a more desirable combination of cost savings and competitive advantage than would be achieved if promotion and physical distribution were treated as separate and unrelated functions.

Increasing costs are the prime motivating force behind a managerial review of how the firm is performing its physical distribution job. These costs may be the outlays required to sustain a given level of functional performance or they may be profits foregone because of lost sales due to ineffective logistics. Regardless of specific causation, management action is usually aimed at reducing both outlay and opportunity costs from present levels. After such reductions have been achieved, then attention can be given to increasing the extent of customer service provided by a given expenditure.

Firms vary widely in how far they go in attempting to tackle their physical distribution problems. A recent analysis of 26 companies indicated that their efforts fall into three categories:

1. The narrowest of these can appropriately be labeled the *traffic department* concept. Here, the principal role of the distribution function is to secure the most advantageous rates and routes, usually with a strong bias toward a single mode of transportation.
2. Less narrow is the *transportation* concept, which concentrates on minimizing total transportation and warehousing costs. Companies which are governed by this distribution philosophy often show con-

siderable skill and imagination in ferreting out the lowest cost ways to transport their products.

3. The most sophisticated of the three approaches can be termed the *total logistics* concept. Companies committed to this approach, by thoughtfully balancing the economics of transportation against other key factors such as customer service, manufacturing, and warehousing, are able to get markedly more from their distribution dollars than the other companies in the sample.[2]

Of the 26 companies surveyed, 5 appeared to be doing an outstanding job of managing the distribution function. These companies applied the total logistics concept, with consistent regard for the total economics of getting the product to the customer being manifested in three ways: (1) by dealing with distribution activities on a corporate rather than a functional basis, (2) by having transportation personnel free from functional parochialism, and (3) by stressing adequate and timely cost information to enable them to identify and price out alternatives as a basis for making trade-offs.[3]

The "total logistics" concept is, essentially, a systems approach to the management of the physical distribution function. Our attention in this chapter will, therefore, be oriented to a brief discussion of systems analysis in general. This will be followed by a more detailed coverage of a physical distribution system in terms of its design and operation.

In conclusion, some attention will be paid to the management organization problems of systems implementation in the firm.

systems analysis[4]

During World War II, scientists and engineers who were faced with the problem of developing advanced weapon systems often found that although parts of the system worked within acceptable tolerances, the system as a whole would not perform well. Adjustment of the interactions or linkages among components was necessary before the master system would operate as required. This focusing of attention on system performance rather than on component performance, and the

---

[2] Robert P. Neuschel, "Physical Distribution—Forgotten Frontier," *Harvard Business Review*, Vol. 45, No. 2 (March-April, 1967), pp. 125–34.

[3] *Ibid.* p. 133.

[4] See Donald J. Bowersox, "Research Procedure in Distribution System Design," in Edward W. Smykay (ed.), *Essays on Physical Distribution Management* (Washington, D.C.: The Traffic Service Corporation, 1961), pp. 17–26.

subsequent experimentation with alternate system designs to improve efficiency, marked the birth of modern systems analysis.

In the years following the close of the war, systems analysis came into prominence in many fields of human endeavor. Our interest here is, of course, in the application of systems analysis to the area of physical distribution. A brief review of some systems terminology and logic will be helpful before we move to a discussion of the physical distribution system.

systems terminology and logic

A system is composed of three basic elements: input, components, and output. It is designed to operate in a given environment, which is usually constraining, and to achieve certain goals or levels of output.

A system is stimulated into action by the receipt of an input signal. The exact nature of this signal depends upon the system, but among other things it may be a specific type of data or condition. The components accept the input and perform a single or series of functions as directed. The output of a system consists of some result or variable which, hopefully, is measurable.

Systems may be classified as open or closed. In an open system there is no connection between input and output. When output controls the extent of input by means of a feedback channel, then the system is said to be closed. A common example of a closed system is a home heating system. The fuel is the input, and heat measurable in British thermal units is the output. The thermostat is the feedback mechanism that regulates the input to the system by measuring the output of the system. If the home heating system had no thermostat, it would be an open system, and fuel would not be provided automatically to the furnace when needed in order to maintain a desired temperature.

Systems may be structured or semistructured. In a structured system outputs are statistically predictable, given standard inputs. For example, a furnace will provide so many BTU's per cubic foot of natural gas input. A semistructured system is one in which outputs vary widely, given standard inputs, and prediction of results with any degree of accuracy is most difficult.

A function in systems terminology refers to an activity of a component. It is important to recognize that a component itself is a system of functions. When a component is part of a larger system it is said to be a subsystem. Thus, a furnace is a subsystem of the heating system.

Trade-off is the process by which subsystems (components) are integrated into the master system. The trade-off concept is vital to systems analysis. It is by "managing trade-offs" that system designers and operators balance benefits against costs and thus improve system performance and efficiency.

The performance of a system may be measured in terms of how well the system output measures up to what the system was designed to do. The term "figure of merit" is sometimes used as the basis against which actual or simulated output is measured when system configuration or input is changed. System efficiency is quite another measure and, quite simply, is the ratio of system output to system input.

a physical distribution system

Now that we have some terminology let us look at a simple distribution system. In the Figure 9–2 we see a typical simple distribution system in which the order is the input, transport is the component

Figure 9–2. A simple distribution system.

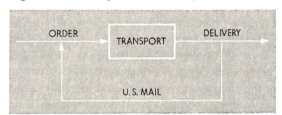

providing for the delivery function, and an actual delivery of an order is the output. It is a closed system in that delivery of the order in a satisfactory manner or an unsatisfactory manner might provide feedback that in turn would trigger either a new or replacement order as the case might be. Because people are involved in most physical distribution systems, these systems are semistructured. Thus, output per given input is not as predictable as would be the case if the system were structured.

As additional components are added to a simple physical distribution system, the interaction among these components becomes more complex. The more complicated the system, the more difficult system analysis, operation, or alteration becomes. Before we discuss the nature of the components, however, it is necessary to make a few generalized statements about the inputs and outputs associated with a physical distribution system.

System output. The level of service provided to customers is generally the measurement variable for the output of a PD system. Called CSL (customer service level) in the trade, this variable is a complex combination of several factors. The length of the order cycle (time between submission of an order and receipt of goods), the percentage of orders received in which some goods are back ordered because the supplier was out of stock, and the physical condition of goods when received are three of the more important factors which go to make up a CSL.

System input. The most widely used input variable for a PD system is the cost, measured in dollars, of men and materials utilized in the operation of the system. The determination of costs associated with the performance of the physical distribution function is very difficult because traditional accounting practices do not usually identify the cost elements of a firm in terms of whether or not they have been expended to create time and place utilities.[5] In fact, the commonly used methods of accounting may distort the cost consequences of a PD decision. Figures 9–3 and 9–4 illustrate such a situation.

Figure 9–3 compares the costs per hundred pounds (cwt.) of shipping goods rail direct with shipping by a rail-barge combination. By reducing the costs of preparing and storing goods for shipment within the plant, by reducing transportation costs, and by assuming increased terminal expense, total costs are lowered from $3.15 to $2.50 per cwt. Annual savings accrue to $130,000, on a volume of 20 million pounds.

Figure 9–4 illustrates the change in accounts resulting from the change in distribution methods. In-plant physical distribution cost reductions show up as lowered production costs, while decreases in transportation costs appear as increases in net sales. The terminal expenses which are assumed to make the other cost savings possible resulted in an accounting effect which indicates a substantial increase in field warehousing costs.

Unless care is taken to dig behind the traditional accounts or, preferably, until accounting procedures are changed to reflect better the true costs of physical distribution, the calculation of input cost to a PD system will be a difficult undertaking.

System linkages. We will touch upon the problem illustrated above in greater detail when the total cost approach to PD systems management is discussed. But even at this point, when the PD system is being

---

[5] George G. Smith, "Know Your P.D. Costs," *Distribution Age*, January, 1966, pp. 21–27.

Figure 9–3. Comparison of direct rail and barge-rail.

	Cost per Cwt.	
	Rail Direct	Barge-Rail
Production plant cost		
Packaging	$1.00	$0.00
Storage and handling	0.30	.10
Financial costs inventory	0.10	.25
Administrative	0.15	.05
Subtotal	$1.55	$0.40
Transportation cost		
To customer	1.60	0.20
To terminal	..	.30
Subtotal	$1.60	$0.50
Terminal expense		
Packaging	0.00	1.00
Storage and handling	.00	0.30
Financial costs inventory	.00	0.15
Administrative	.00	0.15
Subtotal	$0.00	$1.60
Total Cost per Cwt.	$3.15	$2.50
Total Cost 20,000,000 #/Year	$630,000	$500,000

Figure 9–4. Change in accounts resulting from change in distribution method.

	Cost per Cwt.	
	Rail Direct	Barge-Rail
Production costs (plant)		
All costs except PD	$10.00	$10.00
Physical distribution	1.55	0.40
Total Production Cost	$11.55	$10.40
Accounting effect—apparent reduction in plant production cost		
Transportation cost		
Gross sales price	$15.00	$15.00
Net freight cost	1.60	0.50
Net Sales	$13.40	$14.50
Accounting effect—net sales dollars increase		
Warehousing and storage	$ 0.00	$ 1.60
Accounting effect—field warehousing cost substantially increased		

Source: Figures 9–3 and 9–4 are taken from H. G. Miller, "Accounting for Physical Distribution," *Transportation and Distribution Management*, December, 1961, p. 10.

viewed in terms of its elements, it becomes apparent that decisions in the area of physical distribution impinge upon production as well as the non-PD portion of the marketing function. Thus, PD, itself a system, must be viewed as a subsystem of the master system which is the firm. As such the PD system is linked to the other subsystems within the firm. In addition, the PD system is linked to other systems which are external to the firm.

Figure 9–5 illustrates a PD system which has been defined to include the storage and handling of raw materials and parts prior to assembly. Our definition of PD in this chapter is a narrower one in which PD is concerned with the distribution of finished goods. Nevertheless, the figure illustrates the connections which exist among subsystems within the firm prior to its shipment of finished goods. In addition, the figure shows how the PD system of the firm must be interlinked with those PD systems of resellers.

System components and their interrelationships. A physical distribution system may be thought of as being composed of three principal components: (1) a set of fixed facilities at which goods are produced or inventories are stored; (2) a set of inventories of goods; and (3) a transportation network connecting the fixed facilities one with another as well as with customer receiving points. It is over this network that goods flow from producing points to intermediate holding points and thence to resellers or end users.

These components are linked together in a functional sense and are highly time dependent. Stewart's concept of the PD system being made up of various activity cogs is useful in seeing the true nature of these linkages.

Stewart holds that the inventory component is the key to total system management. Inventory is viewed as the buffer between customers' orders and manufacturing activities. The filling of orders reduces the level of inventory held by the firm, while production activity increases the level. As the manufacturing process uses up raw materials, the flow of such materials into the firm must be increased. Finished goods leaving the assembly line require the multiple activities illustrated in the figure. The completion of each activity takes time, and the activities are linked sequentially in that certain of them cannot be started until others are completed.

Components of a PD system are also linked spatially. It is evident that no facility should be considered fixed in the sense that it would not be moved if cost or demand conditions so warranted. Indeed, a major option open to distribution system planners is to change the location of facilities. Such changes, however, cannot be considered in isolation but must be examined also in terms of their effect on inventory holding costs, transport costs, and the level of service provided to customers.

Figure 9–5. A physical distribution system for a consumer appliance manufacturer.

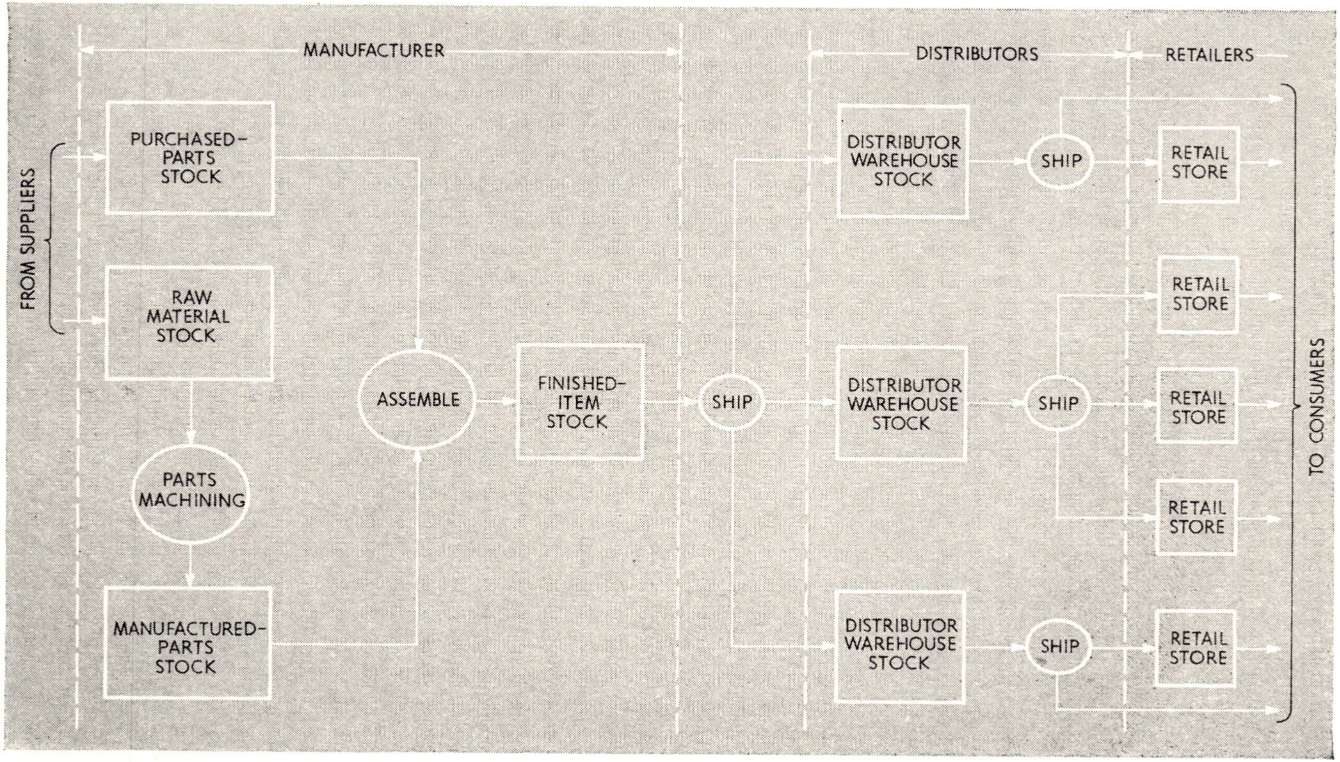

Source: John F. Magee, *Physical Distribution Systems*, p. 11. Copyright 1967, McGraw-Hill Book Company. Used with permission of McGraw-Hill Book Company.

implications

Physical distribution systems are made up of complex assortments of components that accept inputs of men and physical resources. They perform the functions necessary to store and move goods in order to provide a level of service to customers. Such systems are linked to other systems both within and without the firm and operate subject to various environmental constraints including, among others, law, competition, financial resources of the firm, and the structure of transportation.

Figure 9–6. Activity cogs in a physical distribution system.

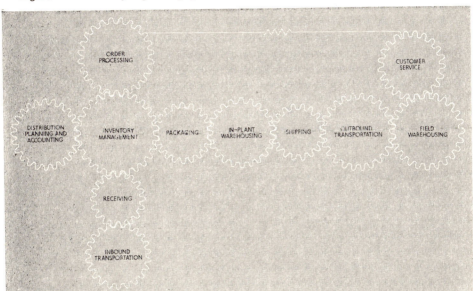

Source: Wendell M. Stewart, "Physical Distribution: Key to Improved Volume and Profits." Reprinted from *Journal of Marketing*, Vol. 29 (January, 1965), p. 66. Published by the American Marketing Association.

Our purpose in the following section is to discuss the design of a PD system and the testing of system alternatives. Because of the nature of a PD system, it is quite clear that decisions pertaining to components must be made in the context of the effect on the total system.

Each unique system has its own associated total costs and customer service level. The objectives of PD system design may be to (1) improve CSL at the present level of expenditure, (2) reduce cost while maintaining the present CSL, or (3) to provide a higher or lower level of service with concomitant increases or decreases in total system costs.

designing a physical distribution system

The design of a physical distribution system must begin with a clear statement of system objectives. Certainly, management wants a system which provides a given level of service at least cost, but not everyone has the same definition of what CSL really means. For example, how important is the prevention of stock-outs? How great is the need to improve market coverage or to avoid loss to competitors of

Figure 9–7. A systems approach to designing a physical distribution system.

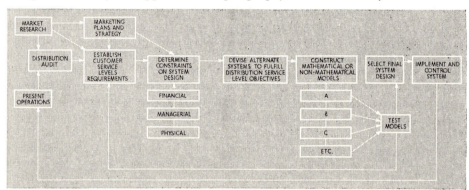

Source: From William B. Saunders, "Designing a Distribution System." Reprinted from *Distribution Age*, January, 1965, pp. 32–36.

customers located on the market periphery? How much freedom must be allowed the marketing people in their efforts to create demand? These and many other similar questions must be considered before system design can begin.

The definition of system goals and the development of an orderly approach to system design to achieve these goals can be facilitated by use of a systems approach as illustrated below.

Figure 9–7 illustrates that a key part of system design is the establishment of CSL requirements. These requirements are a function of the present and future marketing plans and strategies of the firm as well as of the competitive environment which presently exists and is predicted for the future. Meeting these requirements as efficiently as possible is, of course, the immediate purpose of the analysis of the

Figure 9–8. Cost components of a physical distribution system.

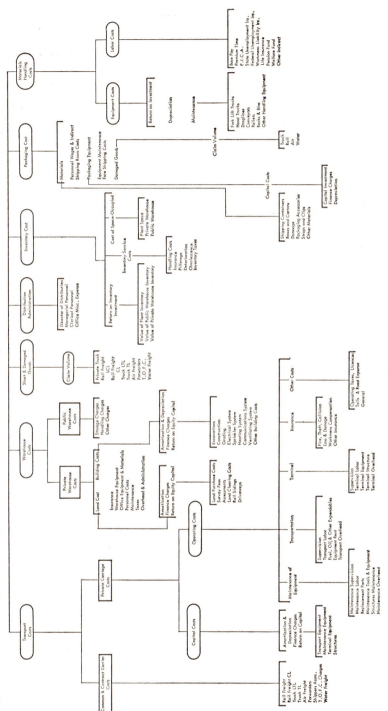

Source: William B. Saunders, "Designing a Distribution System." Reprinted from *Distribution Age*, January, 1965, pp. 32–36.

system. A subsequent, and perhaps more important, objective is the design and testing of alternate systems to find a new system which will provide higher levels of service at cost levels which make these service improvements economic.

How does one go about reaching these objectives? One authority states that "the first principle to bear in mind is that you have to start where you are."[6] Finding out where you are, however, is not an easy task and requires an approach which is called a distribution audit. After the audit has defined the present cost/service relationship then attention may be directed at improving this relationship or in developing a new system which will have a cost/service relationship superior to any that can be obtained by changing the present system.

the distribution audit

A traffic analysis is the first component of a distribution audit. Determination should be made of "what shipments are made from where to where, in what frequency, under what conditions, by what modes, with what degree of reliability, etc."[7] Obviously, the cooperation of people in traffic, warehousing, order processing, and marketing will be required here.

The second part of the distribution audit is concerned with a buildup of the costs associated with the present performance of the PD function. This is a time-consuming task because PD costs are dispersed throughout the firm and are often difficult to identify or to quantify. The step is vital to the analysis, however, because determining the cost of providing the present CSL is a prerequisite to justifying investments of time and money in system improvement or alteration.

The utilization of a graphic representation of the distribution organization in terms of its cost components, as illustrated in figure 9–8, is most helpful in performing the cost analysis. Bowersox notes with reference to system costing that:

During the audit stage of systems analysis, it is desirable to obtain management agreement concerning standards to be used in system costing. Since very few firms carry on detailed distribution cost accounting, establishing standards can be an essential first step. While developing standards at this

---

[6] William B. Saunders, "Designing a Distribution System," *Distribution Age*, January, 1965, pp. 32–36.

[7] *Ibid.*

point may appear to be putting the cart before the horse, it may also take considerable time to arrive at final agreement on appropriate distribution costing. A typical problem concerns interest on capital invested in inventory. Interest rates currently in use vary from 5 to 35 per cent of inventory capital value. To a large extent, the final rate selected will depend on top management's evaluation of a great many factors. A highly liquid firm's attitude is normally very different than that of one involved in a capitalization program.[8]

Regardless of the methods used and the assumptions made, the essential requirement of an audit is that it provide dependable background information to facilitate the development of the system study.

Marketing requirements and the distribution audit.[9] The final portion of the distribution audit is aimed at finding out what level of customer service is realistically required in light of the firm's current marketing programs and longer run marketing strategies. Because marketing activities impose loads on the PD system which materially affect its costs of operation and because many marketing requirements are system constraints, a substantial responsibility for system design and operation must be assumed by marketing management. Product line policy, channel policy, and promotional policy are all intimately related to PD system design in that they determine to a large extent what the system has to do. Conversely, PD system performance can influence the effectiveness of the marketing mix.

In discussing the relationship of marketing and PD in the context of a distribution audit, Magee suggests that the following steps be taken:

1. Data on the company's markets and customers should be gathered, organized, and analyzed. The system study starts with study of customers, not so much by field interview as by organizing market data that are available. Occasionally a moderate amount of skilled—not routine—interview work may help obtain customers' estimates of service requirements and their comparisons of the company's distribution skills and policies with those of competitors.

Analysis of sales data should be directed at such questions as these: Are there several different markets, served by different channels? Are these located differently? Do they buy in different patterns, in different quantities, and with different service and stock availability requirements? How are sales

---

[8] Bowersox, *op. cit.* p. 23.

[9] See John F. Magee, *Physical Distribution Systems* (New York: McGraw-Hill Book Co., 1967), pp. 25–26, 96–97.

distributed among customers? Do they follow [recognizable] patterns . . . ?

Do the same customers tend to buy high-volume items as buy low-volume items? The answer to this question has an important bearing on how slow-moving items, for which distribution costs are often relatively high, should be handled. While opinions on this question usually can be readily found, few companies seem to have really analyzed the question.

2. Statistical analysis of demand characteristics of products should be made, with special attention to the nature of sales fluctuations. Data on the product line . . . must be gathered, and in addition the variability of demand for item sales must be measured. Some variation, such as seasonal patterns, may be reasonably predictable. In most cases, item demand will exhibit short-term (day-to-day or week-to-week) unpredictable variations, and the magnitude of these unpredictable variations will significantly affect the design of an economical system.

3. In analyzing demand variation, the analyst must pay special attention to variations in relation to volume of item demand, time period covered, and geographic or market area covered. The degree of correlation in demand variations from one time to the next or from place to place will affect requirements for safety stock in relation to the replenishment lead time or to the geographic area served, and thus will affect the economy of steps taken to shorten lead time or the desirability of greater centralization of warehousing.[10]

When the traffic, distribution cost, and marketing requirements analyses have been completed, the nature of the present cost/service level parameter should be known. It is now possible to suggest changes in the present system or to devise alternate systems which will provide a more desirable cost/service level combination.

alternate systems design

Perhaps the most effective way to illustrate how changes made in present systems or the adoption of new systems can change cost and service levels is by means of a specific illustration. The Hypo Company history as developed by W. Clayton Hill of Clayton Hill Associates for the General Electric Company is an excellent vehicle for demonstrating how systems analysis can work in the area of PD management. The Hypo Company is not an actual firm, but the material is based on data collected from 65 real distribution points handling a wide variety of products.[11]

---

[10] Magee, *op. cit.* pp. 96–97.

[11] W. Clayton Hill, "Distribution Systems Management: Key to Profits in the Sixties." Reprinted from Charles H. Hindersman (ed.), *Marketing Precision and Executive Action*, pp. 121–28. Published by American Marketing Association, 1962.

Hypo Company

The Hypo Company with headquarters in Indianapolis, Indiana, has an annual sales volume of $50 million dollars. It ships 500,000 units of merchandise a year at an average price of $100 per unit and at an average value of $1 per pound. The Hypo product line consists of 1,000 stock items and is distributed to 10,000 dealers by means of a 100-point distribution system.

The company operates with a warehouse replenishment time of 25 days, and it attempts to provide a CSL of 90 percent, defined by the company as having 90 percent of products on hand for shipment the day that the order is received from a customer.

The company undertook a systems analysis to determine the effects of making changes in the present system or of selecting a new system from among several alternates. The first decision faced by Hypo was whether or not to reduce the number of distribution points from the present level of 100.

decision I: number of distribution points

To make a decision as to the optimal number of distribution points to employ, it was necessary for Hypo to analyze the impact of such a decision on system distribution costs and delivery times. The major considerations are illustrated in Figure 9–9.

Delivery service/transportation costs. Figure 9–10 indicates that the ability of Hypo to provide first-day delivery service to its customers is markedly reduced as distribution points are decreased in number. The ability to provide second-day delivery is also impaired but not as much as with first-day service.

Transportation costs increase as the number of distribution points is decreased. This is because with fewer distribution points more tonnage travels longer distances at less-than-carload (LCL) or metropolitan rates which are often 50 percent higher than are carload (CL) rates.

It is clear that if a decision were to be made only on the basis of delivery service and transportation cost criteria, it would be in favor of maintaining the present 100-point system. There is, however, more evidence to be considered.

Warehouse handling costs. Figure 9–11 indicates that as the number of distribution points decreases, there is a rather marked decline in the costs of receiving, retrieving, locating, and loading stock.

Figure 9–9. Distribution cost/delivery service comparison of five alternate distribution systems.

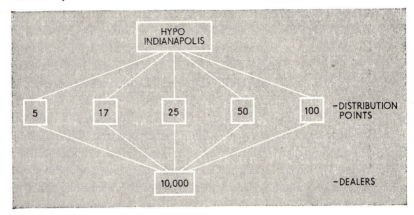

Major Considerations

Transportation costs   Data processing costs
Inventory costs   Delivery times
Warehousing costs

This is due to the smaller total inventory required to sustain a system of fewer distribution points. This smaller inventory, in turn, reduces total handling costs.

The analysis of warehouse handling costs indicates that a reduction in the number of distribution points would reduce costs. This conclusion is in opposition to that which would be reached if delivery service and transportation costs were the only items under consideration. The next step is to look at an analysis of data processing costs.

Figure 9–10. Behavior of delivery service and transportation costs as number of distribution points is decreased.

	Delivery Service		*Transportation Costs†*	
Number of Distribution Points	*% Hypo Customers* Delivered on 1st Day*	*% Hypo Customers* Delivered by 2nd Day*	*Annual Costs (000)*	*Cost Index*
100	89%	90%	$1,847	100%
50	87	90	1,934	105–110
25	81	90	2,082	110–120
17	73	87	2,211	120–130
5	30	78	2,632	135–145

* Slightly changed from original version.
† CL rate—Indianapolis to distribution point.
  LTL and metro rates—distribution point to customer.

Figure 9–11. Hypo Company warehouse handling costs (present methods).

Number of Distribution Points	Hypo Cost (In Thousands)	Warehousing Cost Index
100	$514	100%
50	368	65–75
25	265	45–55
17	235	40–50
5	190	35–45

Receiving—Retrieving
Locating—Loading

Data processing costs. These costs associated with the provision of order service, inventory control, and billing are illustrated in Figure 9–12.

In this example it can be seen that data processing costs behave in much the same way as did warehouse handling costs. As the number of distribution points decrease, the various transactions which require data processing decrease in number and increase in size. Thus, once more costs go down as the number of points in the system decreases.

Inventory investment and maintenance costs. The final area to be considered before arriving at a decision with respect to the number of points to include in the PD system deals with the investment and maintenance costs of inventory. As can be seen in Figure 9–13, the investment in inventory needed to sustain sales of $50 million annually for this company is very great and varies widely as a function of the number of distribution points in the system. An estimated annual maintenance cost of 22 percent of average investment in inventory has been used. Because the need to duplicate inventory assortments in diverse locations is diminished with fewer distribution points, the amount of inventory needed to sustain a system and to provide a given

Figure 9–12. Hypo data processing costs under present methods.

Number of Distribution Points	Hypo Cost (In Thousands)	Data Processing Cost Index
100	$777	100%
50	585	70–80
25	496	60–70
17	486	60–70
5	448	55–65

Figure 9–13. Investment in inventory and inventory maintenance costs.

Number of Distribution Points	Investment		Maintenance Costs	
	Hypo Inventory (In Thousands)	Inventory Investment Index	Hypo Cost @ 22%	Inventory Maintenance Cost Index
100............	$14,418	100%	$3,172	100%
50............	11,423	75–85	2,513	75–85
25............	9,079	60–70	1,997	60–70
17............	8,004	50–60	1,761	50–60
5............	5,475	35–45	1,205	35–45
	25-day replenishment time 90% customer service level		Capital charge, insurance, taxes, depreciation and obsolescence, storage space..............22%	

level of service goes down drastically with a reduction in the number of points at which stock is held. Figure 9–13 illustrates the behavior of investment in inventory and maintenance costs with a 90 percent CSL and a 25-day replenishment time.

optimizing number of distribution points

Now that the various elements of the decision have been examined individually, it is time to put them together in order to arrive at an optimum solution to the problem of how many distribution points to utilize. Figure 9–14 is an attempt to portray graphically the total cost-service characteristics of each of the five proposals for system design. The 100-point system gives maximum service but at maximum cost. The 5-point system is very economical, but the service level is extremely low. On the basis of this analysis, it appears that a change to a 25-point system is merited.

Moving from a 100-point system to a 25-point system will allow a 35 to 40 percent reduction in inventory, a total cost reduction of between 20 and 25 percent, and a 9 percent reduction in first-day service. Hypo executives felt that the small reduction in first-day service would not have harmful competitive consequences and that the $1.4 million in cost savings made the move to 25 points a desirable one.

decision II: customer service level (CSL)

After finding that a substantial cost saving could be realized by changing from a 100-point system to a 25-point system with very little

Figure 9–14. Total distribution costs and delivery service levels associated with five system alternatives: 5, 17, 25, 50, and 100 distribution points.

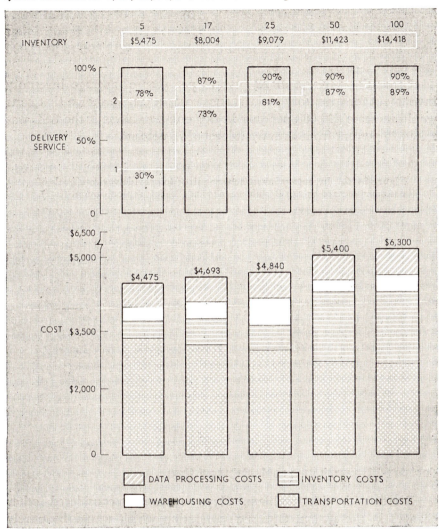

deterioration in *delivery* service levels, the attention of Hypo executives shifted to the problem of *customer* service level. They felt that CSL was extremely important because of its impact on customer patronage motives and thus upon the success of Hypo's marketing efforts.

As noted earlier, Hypo defined CSL as the percentage of products available for shipment to customers on the day an order was received. Hypo's CSL goal was 90 percent and this applied to each of the 1,000 items in the line. An analysis of selected warehouses in the system indicated that CSL's offered by many of them fell short of the level that Hypo considered necessary in the face of competitive levels. In Boston, for example, the CSL was 75 percent. An analysis of the Boston warehouse indicated that to achieve a 90 percent CSL would require that investment in inventory be almost doubled from $211,000 to $402,000 (see figure 9–15).

Using the estimate of 22 percent per year of average inventory investment for inventory maintenance costs, it can be shown that costs would increase $42,600 per year in this one area alone if the CSL was raised 20 percent from its current level of 75 percent.

Figure 9–15. Inventory investment required to provide various levels of customer service at the Boston warehouse (25-day replenishment time).

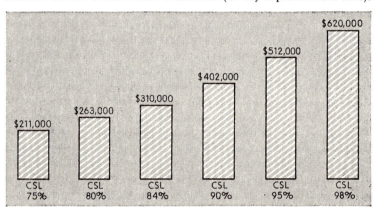

decision III: warehouse replenishment time

Faced with this problem, Hypo executives considered other changes in the system. One such alteration which would be purely internal and thus have no effect on customers was the reduction of warehouse replenishment time from 25 to 10 days. This would be accomplished by daily reporting of requirements to Indianapolis by means of teletype. This policy would replace the present one under which orders for replenishment were made up each two weeks and mailed to Indianapolis.

If such a change could be accomplished, a smaller inventory would be needed in each warehouse to sustain a given volume of sales and a given CSL. Figure 9–16 shows that with a 10-day lead time the Boston warehouse could provide a 90 percent CSL with about the same amount of inventory ($208,000) as was needed currently to provide a 75 percent CSL. Of course, associated with the reduction in lead time are increased costs of daily ordering and of using more expensive communication methods.

Once the analysis of Boston was completed, an attempt was made to see what the impact of lead-time reduction would be on the operations of the 25-point system.

Lead-time reduction for 25-point system. The analysis of the 25-point system indicated to Hypo executives that the levels of customer service provided by the various warehouses in the system varied between 70 and 90 percent with an average of 80 percent. To move from

Figure 9–16. Effect of replenishment time reduction on Boston warehouse inventory requirements to provide 90% CSL.

	Replenishment Time	
Order frequency	14	1
Communications	3	1
Factory processing transit	8	8
Total	25	10

	Units	Amount
25-day lead time	4,020	$402,000
10-day lead time	2,080	208,000
Net reduction	1,940	$194,000

this level to an average level of 90 percent with a minimum of variability would require a 50 percent increase in inventory investment under current policy. A system-wide change from a 25-day to a 10-day replenishment lead time, however, would allow the provision of a system-wide 90 percent CSL with a *reduction* in inventory investment of $773,500. Applying the 0.22 factor to this amount gives an inventory maintenance cost saving of $170,000. Hypo management felt that the changes needed to reduce lead time from 25 to 10 days could be made without expenditures exceeding the inventory maintenance cost savings. They also felt that a 95 percent CSL was not required to maintain a competitive advantage and, therefore, did not warrant the investment in inventories which would have been required. Figure 9–17 gives some idea of inventory investment required in a 25-point system as lead times and service levels change.

decision IV: selective stocking

To see if further improvements in system operation were possible, Hypo executives returned to the analysis of the Boston warehouse, which they considered as being fairly representative of other distribution points. A breakdown of sales at Boston indicated that the 1,000 items in the Hypo line fell into four distinct categories. Fifty items accounted for almost three quarters of the sales volume and almost half of the inventory. The other 950 items were slower movers and could be categorized as B, C, or D items depending upon their sales-to-inventory ratio. Figure 9–18 shows the relationship among the four classes of items in the line.

The next step in the analysis was to propose that groups of items be handled differently and to estimate the cost consequences of these

Figure 9–17. Investment in inventory needed to sustain different CSL's with 25- and 10-day replenishment times—25-point system.

	Customer Service Level		
	80%	90%	95%
25-day replenishment time			
Total....................	$6,165,800	$9,079,000	$11,318,000
10-day replenishment time			
Total....................	$3,790,050	$5,392,300	$ 6,623,750
Difference...............	$2,375,750	$3,686,700	$ 4,694,250

alternatives. It was decided that A and B items would have to be kept at Boston, but the really slow movers in groups C and D could be held in reserve at the factory or at the distribution point located in New York. The cost/service consequences of stocking C and D items at the factory and using either LTL truck shipments or airfreight to supply them to Boston, as well as stocking C and D items at New York and using LTL truck shipments to supply Boston, are illustrated in Figure 9–19. It is clear that alternative (1) offers the lowest cost while alternative (3) provides the best service.

An extension of the selective stocking proposals to the full 25-point system was analyzed. Three alternative proposals were evaluated on the basis of cost and service criteria. The first was to keep the present policy of stocking each of the 1,000 items at each distribution point. The second was to keep A and B items on hand locally while C and D

Figure 9–18. Breakdown of sales by item at Boston warehouse.

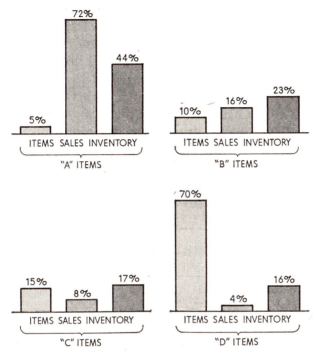

A Items—Small Inventory
B, C, and D Items—Large Inventory

Figure 9–19. Selective stocking alternatives (A and B items at Boston; C and D stocking alternatives).

	(1) At Factory Using LTL	(2) At Factory Using Air-freight	(3) At New York Using LTL
Inventory at Boston			
Reduction in inventory.......$112,540	$112,540	$112,540
Cost			
Net cost reduction...........$ 19,071	$ 2,311	$ 15,116
Delivery service (days)			
A and B Items (88% Total Sales) 90% CSL	Same	Same	Same
C and D Items (12% Total Sales) 90% CSL...............	6–7	4–5	3–4

items were held at five dual warehouses located across the country. The third alternative was to stock A and B items locally while C and D items were held at the factory. All transportation would be by LTL truck shipments. Figure 9–20 illustrates the cost/service parameters of the three alternatives.

Alternative A, keeping current policy and stocking 1,000 items at each point, provides the highest level of delivery service but also requires the largest investment in inventory. Alternative C is the lowest cost, but as C and D items are kept at the factory the service level for one- to three-day delivery falls to 79 percent from a former level of 90 percent. Alternative B, in which five dual warehouses are used for stocking C and D items, offers a $146,000 cost saving over alternative A

Figure 9–20. **Cost/service parameters of three alternatives for selective stocking in a 25-point system (90% CSL, 10-day replenishment time).**

	Inventory Investment	Inventory Maintenance Costs @ 22%	Delivery Service, Days	
			1–3	4–10
A. Stocking 1,000 items each point.......................$9,079,000		$1,997,000	90%	100%
B. A and B items local; C and D items 5 dual warehouses, New York, Indiana, San Francisco, Atlanta, Dallas......$8,182,000		$1,851,000	88%	100%
C. A and B items local, C and D items factory..............$5,118,000		$1,323,000	79%	100%

while only dropping 2 percentage points in one- to three-day delivery service. Hypo executives felt that this saving was sufficient to override the minor decline in delivery service and suggested that alternative B be adopted.

total system optimization

The results of the analysis of the Hypo system indicated that the following might be achieved by system redesign and optimization: (1) a net saving of $1,460,000 from reducing the number of distribution points from 100 to 25; (2) a net saving of $801,000 from shortening the warehouse replenishment time from 25 to 10 days; and (3) a net saving of $146,000 by selective stocking using five dual warehouses.

The total savings possible through system redesign and optimization total $2,417,000 or 4.8 percent of current annual sales. These savings can be obtained, however, with a concomitant increase of customer service level from a range of 75–80 percent to 90 percent. There will be only a slight (2 percent) decrease in 1- to 3-day delivery service and no change in 4- to 10-day delivery service.

Although the results of system redesign have been calculated on the assumption that sales volume will remain stable, it is very likely that the increase in CSL will markedly improve Hypo's competitive position and thus increase its sales.

inventory management

In the Hypo example, various cost components were examined as a distribution system was subjected to both design and operating policy changes. It soon became quite clear that the largest cost was that associated with maintaining inventories. Although marketing management is not solely responsible for inventory policy, the demands which its members make on the distribution system are sufficiently large so that marketing executives must be in on major inventory decisions and share responsibility for them.

Before managers can make meaningful decisions with respect to inventory policy, it is necessary for them to have some understanding of the basic function of inventory as well as of the various specific types of inventories which serve to fill special needs. With respect to basic function Magee notes:

Fundamentally, inventories serve to uncouple successive operations in the process of making a product and getting it to consumers. For example, inventories make it possible to process a product at a distance from customers or from raw material supplies, or to do two operations at a distance from one another (perhaps only across the plant). Inventories make it unnecessary to gear production directly to consumption or, alternatively, to force consumption to adapt to the necessities of production. In these and similar ways, inventories free one stage in the production-distribution process from the next, permitting each to operate more economically.[12]

There is no denying the fact that inventories provide economic benefits but they also incur costs. The big question facing managers with respect to inventory decisions is at what point do the benefits of holding inventory cease to justify the costs involved. Before tackling that question, however, it would be useful to be able to specify the type of inventory being considered.

---

[12] John F. Magee, "Guides to Inventory Policy I. Functions and Lot Size" *Harvard Business Review*, Vol. 31, No. 1 (January–February, 1956) . p. 51

Some inventories are needed because goods are in transit for a period of time and are thus unavailable for consumption. These are called "movement" or "process" inventories, and the size of such inventories is a function of the average sales rate and transit time. Thus, the size of the movement stock required to sustain a given volume of sales may be reduced by changes in the distribution system which shorten transit times. Of course, the inventory maintenance savings must be balanced against the costs of using the more expensive modes of transport which are usually required to move goods more quickly.

Movement inventories may be contrasted with what have been called organization inventories. These inventories allow different parts of a production-distribution system to operate with a minimum of coordination. If inventories of this type are already being used efficiently, they can only be reduced by assuming the expense of greater organization effort, including scheduling and expediting.[13]

There are three major kinds of organization inventories: (1) replenishment or lot-size inventories, (2) fluctuation or "safety stock" inventories, and (3) seasonal or anticipation inventories.

The replenishment or lot-size inventory is the most common type used in business. Such inventories are maintained whenever it is advantageous to produce or to purchase in quantities larger than are currently needed. The benefits gained by holding lot-size inventories may accrue from purchase discounts based on quantity, ability to provide quick delivery to customers, and so on.

Fluctuation or safety stocks cushion the shocks arising from unpredictable fluctuations in demand or in replenishment lead time. The cost of maintaining such stocks must be balanced against the costs of sales lost due to stock-outs.

Anticipation or seasonal inventories are held when the demand for goods although predictable is highly seasonal. The buildup of inventory allows a stabilization of production and employment over the year. The savings so realized must be compared with the added costs of holding stock. Such stocks may also be built up in anticipation of special selling events or some other contingencies.

Because lot-size or replenishment inventories are so important, a great deal of attention has been devoted to them. Of special interest has been the answering of the questions of when to order (order point) and how much to order (order quantity). The first of these variables, the order point (R), is a function of the lead time required between

---

13 *Ibid.* p. 52.

Figure 9–21. Characteristic pattern of lot-size stocks.

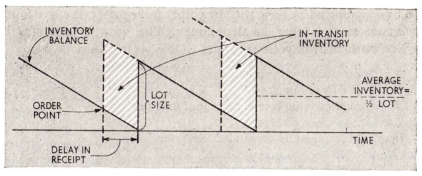

Source: John F. Magee, *Physical Distribution Systems*, p. 51. Copyright 1967, McGraw-Hill Book Company. Used with permission of McGraw-Hill Book Company.

order placement and receipt of goods. It is also a function of the rate of usage or depletion (D) of inventory, as well as the CSL requirements. The higher the degree of variability of lead time or usage rate, the higher must be the order point (R) to sustain a given CSL.

Given the sawtooth pattern which typifies the behavior of lot-size inventories, the problem of when to order is quite clearly defined. Assuming constant rates of usage and a stable lead time, the reorder point is easily found once the optimal order quantity has been determined.

The optimal-size lot to purchase is known as the economic order quantity (EOQ) or simply Q^*. It is determined by balancing the costs of placing an order against the cost of holding inventory. Figure 9–22 illustrates a graphic method of finding Q^*.

Figure 9–22. Costs of holding and ordering stock as function of order size.

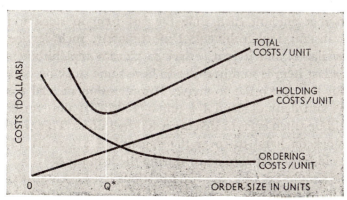

By summing the two cost functions to obtain a total cost function and by dropping a line from the low point on the total cost curve to the horizontal axis, Q^* can be determined. The quantity can also be derived mathematically. Let:

Q = Order quantity in units.
C = Unit cost per item.
I = Annual carrying cost as percent of unit cost.
S = Cost to place one order.
D = Number of units demanded per year.

The total cost function T is as follows:

$$T = CD + \frac{D}{Q}S + IC\frac{Q}{2}.$$

Finding the first derivative of T with respect to Q:

$$\frac{dT}{dQ} = -DS/Q^2 + IC/2.$$

Setting the first derivative $= 0$, and solving for Q,

$$Q^* = \sqrt{\frac{2DS}{IC}}.$$

Let us look at a simple example of formula application. Demand estimates show that about 400 items per year will be needed on a fairly steady basis. Each item has a cost of $100. Annual inventory maintenance costs will run about 0.25 of average inventory investment and the cost to place one order has been estimated at $5. The problem is to determine Q^*:

$$Q^* = \sqrt{\frac{2(400)(5)}{0.25(100)}} = \sqrt{160} \text{ or } 12.8.$$

Thus Q^* can be considered as 13 units, and an order could be placed in that amount each time the last item in stock were sold, assuming instant replenishment. Unfortunately, such service is not usually available, and it is necessary to place a replenishment order before the last item is sold in order to have some stock on hand while waiting for the new order to arrive. If replenishment lead time were three days and daily demand 1⅑ units (400/360), the reorder point (R) would be when current inventory fell to 4 units. This would keep enough stock on hand to cover the demand of 3⅓ units (3 × 1⅑) which would be expected to occur during the lead time.

In this simple example the two questions have been answered. An order is placed whenever the inventory is down to 4 units and the size of the order is 13 units. Unfortunately, many of the assumptions underlying the above example do not hold in reality. Usage rates are rarely constant, and lead times are not always dependable. What is required is a "safety stock" or additional inventory to serve as a buffer against stock-outs. The larger the safety stock, the less will be the costs incurred by lost sales. However, the larger the safety stock, the greater will be the costs of inventory maintenance.

Figure 9–23 illustrates the use of a safety stock to cushion against stock-outs caused by variations in usage. The safety stock could be used also to protect against the effects of variations in the lead time.

Figure 9–23. Safety stock used as a buffer against stock-outs caused by variations in usage.

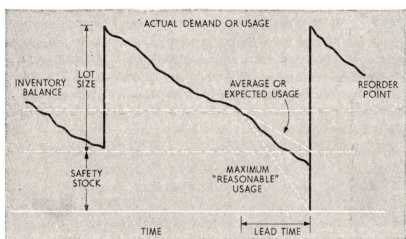

Source: John F. Magee, *Physical Distribution Systems*, p. 53. Copyright 1967, McGraw-Hill Book Company. Used with permission of McGraw-Hill Book Company.

There is an approach to finding a Q^* and R^* (optimal reorder point) combination which will balance the costs of holding stock against the costs of ordering and of being out of stock. The user of this approach must estimate the dollar cost to him of being out of stock and must also determine the probability of expected usage during the lead time period exceeding the reorder point (R). Using the same notation as in the previous example and adding (π) as the stock-out penalty, u for usage rate during lead time, $E(u > R)$ as expected usage in excess of the order point during lead time, and $\bar{u}$ as average usage during the lead time, the following total cost function may be constructed:

$$T = CD + \frac{D}{Q}\left[S + \pi E(u > R)\right] + IC\left[\frac{Q}{2} + (R - \bar{u})\right].$$

Finding the first derivative of the above function with respect to Q and setting same equal to zero:

$$Q^* = \sqrt{\frac{2D\left[S + \pi E(u > R)\right]}{IC}}.$$

Once Q^* is found R^* can be calculated. It is not our purpose to go more deeply into this approach here, but several excellent references are noted below.[14] Regardless of the complexity of the formulation and the introduction of probability into the problem, the issues are still the same: the balancing of costs and benefits.

It is also clear that effective inventory management is dependent on accurate forecasts of demand. With the advent of the computer it has been possible to develop tracking models which follow demand patterns for individual items and trigger lot-size reorders when the appropriate levels of stock on hand have been reached. Perhaps the computer will allow management to apply more widely the techniques which have been available technically but which have not until recently been economically feasible.

location decisions

Just as the decisions pertaining to the amount of inventory which is to be held in a physical distribution system are vital to efficient system performance, so are the decisions which determine *where* goods are to be produced, processed, stored, and delivered. The distribution system manager is, therefore, concerned about the location of producing points, storage and transit warehouses, transportation facilities, and customer receiving points. Because most of these locations must be assumed to be fixed, at least over the short run, they are constraints on system design and operation. In the longer run, however, fixed facilities may be relocated or new facilities can be planned. In such circumstances the logistics considerations may play an important role in the location decision.

The term logistics rather than physical distribution is used to indicate that location decisions are a function of the total flow of

---

[14] Robert B. Fetter and Winston C. Dalleck, *Decision Models for Inventory Management* (Homewood, Ill.: Richard D. Irwin, Inc., 1961) ; J. L. Heskett, Robert M. Ivie, and Nicholas A. Glaskowsky, Jr., *Business Logistics* (New York: Ronald Press Co., 1964) , chap. xi; John F. Magee, *Production Planning and Inventory Control* (New York: McGraw-Hill Book Co. 1958) .

materials through a fixed facility rather than of the flow of goods leaving a facility. For the producing plant this means that the costs associated with receiving, storing, and handling raw materials and purchased parts must be considered along with the costs of physical distribution of finished or semifinished goods. In similar manner the costs associated with the inflow of goods as well as with the outflow has an impact on the location of warehouses, transport terminals, and customer receiving points.

The impact of logistics costs on the location decision differs with respect to the firm's product line and the type of facility involved. If a company produces a line of scientific instruments which is composed of assembled items which are light in weight for their value, the costs of logistics is not an important factor in plant location. As the transportation costs of inbound raw materials and outbound finished goods increase, these costs, which are known as transfer costs, assume greater importance in the firm's locational decisions. Studies of plant location checklists have indicated that transfer costs are only one of six major cost categories to be considered and that "Of nineteen major factor categories listed, only two deal directly with matters of logistics."[15] In contrast, logistics factors can be of crucial importance in warehouse location. Decisions here can influence system service levels as well as related costs.

Unless the firm wields considerable economic power, it cannot usually influence the location of fixed transport or receiving facilities owned by others. This does not mean that a firm may not get a rail spur built to its plant or may not offer suggestions for the location of a customer's warehouse. What is implied is that such changes are not under the direct control of the management of the firm and thus cannot be considered as changes which can be accomplished in a relatively short period of time. We shall, therefore, concentrate our attention here on the locational decisions involving the relocation of a single producing plant as well as the location or relocation of storage warehouses. Although of necessity brief, this coverage will give some idea of the approaches possible in resolving some of the firm's locational problems. We shall consider single-plant relocation by the ton-mile-center approach first.

single-plant relocation

A relatively unsophisticated but useful method in considering the relocation of a producing plant is to calculate the ton-mile center of

---

[15] Heskett, Ivie, and Glaskowsky, Jr., *op. cit.* p. 181.

the geographic market area. This approach, suggested by several of the early locational economists, has been formalized and described in detail in recent literature.[16] The basic idea underlying this approach is to locate that point in the geographic area under consideration where the producing plant might be located to minimize the number of ton-miles traveled by raw materials moving from their sources to the factory and by finished goods moving from the factory to the various customer receiving points.

This process requires that a grid overlay be placed on a map of the geographic area under consideration. Then the location of raw material supply points and customer finished goods receiving points can be identified and assigned grid coordinates. The next step is to calculate the weights of materials moving between points, the distances traveled by these materials, and the costs of transport. The object of the analysis is to find a location for the producing plant that will minimize the total cost of inbound raw material transport plus outbound finished goods transport. Several assumptions must be made. One of these is that freight rates are linear with distance. This is not a valid assumption in terms of the actual tapered behavior of rates, but it can simplify the calculations and indicate a location which then can be rechecked on the basis of actual freight rates.

The Comclean Company example developed by Heskett *et al.* is useful in illustrating the ton-mile-center approach (sometimes called the least-cost transportation center approach). The Comclean Company, a manufacturer of industrial cleaning compounds located in Easthampton, Massachusetts, received its raw materials and served a group of customers located in that portion of the eastern United States shown in Figure 9–24. A grid overlay divided the geographic area into boxes approximately 80 miles square.

The Comclean Company recognized that its markets were moving westward. In considering a new location for its manufacturing facility, management came across a very attractive site near Pittsburgh, Pennsylvania. A logistics least-cost analysis was made to see where the optimal location for the company might be and also to compare the present location and the Pittsburgh location with the optimal location.

The results of the study indicated that the logistics least-cost location was situated in the box marking the intersection of row 5 and column 5. It is marked by a *Y* in Figure 9–24 and is in central Pennsylvania a considerable distance northeast of Pittsburgh. Location

---

[16] Edward W. Smykay, Donald J. Bowersox, and Frank H. Mossman, *Physical Distribution Management* (New York: Macmillan Co., 1961), pp. 176–201.

of a manufacturing plant somewhere near point Y would offer total logistics cost savings of over $316,000 per year as compared with Easthampton. A move to Pittsburgh, however, would incur additional costs of $407,000 over those expended for logistics at Easthampton.

Although the grid size used on the map is large and does not pinpoint a specific location, the analysis can indicate the approximate

Figure 9-24. Comclean Corporation: Raw material sources, manufacturing plant, and customer locations.

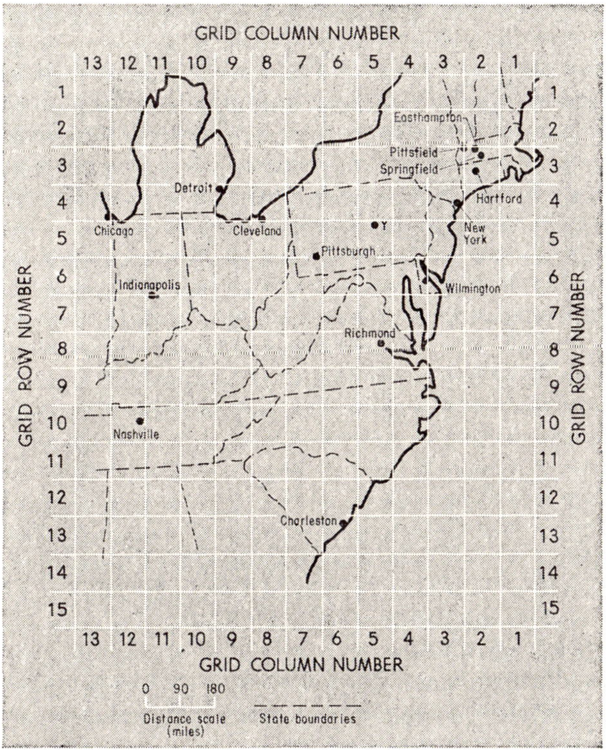

Source: J. L. Heskett, Robert M. Ivie, and Nicholas A. Glaskowsky, Jr., *Business Logistics—Management of Physical Supply and Distribution* (New York: Ronald Press Co., 1964), p. 188.

magnitude of the increase or decrease in logistics costs over current levels associated with plant relocation to different parts of the geographic area. Such information is most useful in evaluating a site in terms of logistics costs in relation to other cost factors, such as production costs, building and land costs, and power costs. Logistics cost data are also important in evaluating a site in relation to its intangible costs or benefits, such as climate, quality of surrounding territory, educational facilities, and potential for growth. Given a possible site for a new factory which offers many intangible advantages as well as nonlogistics cost savings, the logistics least-cost-center approach can indicate the size of the transportation cost penalty which must be paid to gain the other benefits offered by the site.

The location of the least-cost center is only the first step in the locational decision process. Other steps to be taken include: (1) the investigation of the actual behavior of transport rates with special attention being given to obvious non-linearities; (2) the consideration of whether or not a shift of a few miles would place the plant in another transport rate territory which would offer rate advantages; (3) the investigation of possible alternate sources of supply for raw materials; (4) the desirability of rate negotiation with present carriers under implied threat of relocation; (5) the extent and variety of transport service to and from the proposed location; and (6) the trend of directional growth of the company's markets.[17]

multiple-facility location

The decision where to locate an additional producing plant when one or more plants are already in existence can be quite a difficult one. This is because it is based on a series of other decisions, many of which are made for nonlogistics reasons. For example, if a decision is made that the new plant will produce the same product mix as is being currently produced by the one existing plant, the problem becomes one of two single-plant locations. If, on the other hand, the new plant will not produce the same array of products as the existing plant and if it has different production costs as well as logistics costs, the problem becomes so complex as to defy solution except on a trial-and-error basis. It is not our purpose here to delve into this area. What this chapter is concerned with is physical distribution, and the best way to see how locational decisions with respect to fixed facilities affect physical distribution costs and customer service levels is to reorient the multiple-facility location problem from producing plants and toward warehousing facilities.

warehouse location and relocation

The decision where to locate warehouses is more of a logistics problem than is the decision where to locate producing plants. The

---

[17] Heskett, Ivie, and Glaskowsky, Jr., *op. cit.* pp. 191–92.

location of warehouses in the PD system determines to a large extent the ability to provide a given level of service to customers and also has an important influence on overall system operating costs. The warehouse location (or relocation) decision is essentially a cost-balancing one. We have seen in the Hypo example that the greater the number of distribution points (warehouses) in a PD system, the higher are some components of cost and the lower are other components of cost.

Single-warehouse decisions can be handled very much like single-plant location decisions. The least-cost-center analysis can indicate that geographic location which will minimize the costs of inflow of goods and outflow of goods. The approach has been modified by Bowersox to enable the use of time rather than transport costs in location determination when time is the key factor in a firm's marketing strategy.[18]

In addition, consideration must be given to the size of the warehouse, as scale of operation will affect unit costs of handling throughput. With scale comes the associated problem of the service area of the warehouse. This decision will affect the level of operation of the warehouse and thus once more the unit costs of handling goods.

One very useful approach to determine the service area of a warehouse is the Bowman-Stewart formulation.[19] This mathematical approach can be used to determine the service area of a single warehouse in relation to that of the producing plant (which may have warehousing facilities) as well as to other proposed warehouses in the system. The approach is based upon the cost behavior illustrated in Figure 9–25.

The model assumes that as coverage area increases, and if volume of business per unit of area (concentration of demand) is constant, the unit warehousing cost will decrease and the unit delivery cost will increase. Although all other costs associated with warehouse operations were assumed to be equal regardless of location, the model can accommodate cost differences arising from intrafacility shipments such as from plant warehouse to field warehouse. The model further assumes that costs associated with warehousing and materials handling vary inversely with volume and that costs associated with delivery vary directly with the square root of the area served (relation of radius of a circle to its area) and that other categories of costs would not change with changes in volume handled or area served.

---

[18] Donald J. Bowersox, "An Analytical Approach to Warehouse Location," *Handling and Shipping* (February, 1962), pp. 17–20.

[19] Edward H. Bowman and John B. Stewart, "A Model for Scale of Operations," *Journal of Marketing*, Vol. 20 (January, 1956), pp. 242–47.

The following is the Bowman-Stewart expression of total costs to serve an area through a distribution warehouse:

$$C = a + \frac{b}{V} + c\sqrt{A},$$

when

$C =$ Cost (within warehouse district) per dollar's worth of goods distributed, the measure of effectiveness.

$V =$ Volume of goods, in dollars, handled by the warehouse per unit of time.

$A =$ Area in square miles served by the warehouse.

$a =$ Cost per dollar's worth of goods distributed independent of either the warehouse's volume handled or area served.

Figure 9–25. Factors influencing the total costs of supplying an area from a given location.

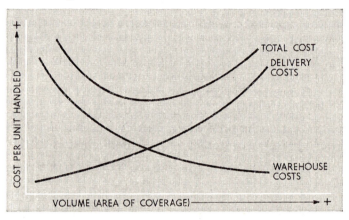

Source: Edward H. Bowman and John B. Stewart, "A Model for Scale of Operations," *Journal of Marketing*, Vol. 20 (January, 1956), pp. 242–47.

$b =$ "Fixed" costs for the warehouse per unit of time, which when divided by the volume will yield the appropriate cost per dollar's worth distributed.

$c =$ The cost of the distribution, which varies with the square root of the area; that is, costs associated with miles covered within the warehouse district, such as gasoline, truck repairs, and driver hours.

To apply the formula it is necessary to find the values of C, V, and A for each warehouse currently in the system. By using multiple regression techniques it is possible to use past experience to determine values for the parameters a, b, and c which when used in conjunction with the actual values of V, and A for each existing warehouse, will be the closest predictors of the actual C or cost per dollar's worth of goods distributed through each warehouse.

To use this approach for warehouse location or relocation, it is necessary to find a value for A which will result in a minimum cost. This step requires that density of sales per area be determined. This expression is called K with $K = V/A$ and $V = KA$. Substituting into the original formula gives:

$$C = a + b/KA + C\sqrt{A},$$

and differentiating C with respect to A and setting the derivative equal to zero,

$$dC/dA = -b/KA^2 + c/2\sqrt{A} = 0,$$

and solving for A,

$$A = (2b/cK)^{\frac{1}{3}}.$$

Once A is calculated for any site based on appropriate values for variable K and parameters b and c, then the radius (r) of the service area which will minimize cost C can be found (radius of a circle as a function of area, $r = \sqrt{A/\pi}$).

If the value of r equaled 10 miles, then a circle could be drawn on a map to scale with its center at a proposed warehouse location. The entire market area could then be viewed as being covered by circles of varying diameters, each circle representing the most economic service area for a given size warehouse. Individual warehouses either currently in operation or proposed might then be evaluated in terms of optimal combination of location and scale of operation.

The above approach is but one of several which have been suggested to improve the quality of the location decision. Another approach, for example, which shows considerable promise is computer simulation. Consultants who designed a system simulation for the H. J. Heinz Company to test costs and service levels associated with different numbers and locations of warehouses reported that the company was able to redeploy its warehouses, improve service levels, and reduce costs.[20] Other writers have described the use of heuristic programs based on certain rules of thumb for warehouse location[21] and the uses of modified linear programming techniques.[22]

[20] Harvey N. Shycon and Richard B. Maffei, "Simulation—Tool for Better Distribution," *Harvard Business Review*, Vol. 38, No. 6 (November–December, 1960), pp. 65–75.

[21] Alfred A. Kuehn and Michael J. Hamburger, "A Heuristic Program for Locating Warehouses," *Management Science*, July, 1963, pp. 643–66.

[22] William J. Baumol and Philip Wolfe, "A Warehouse Location Problem," *Operations Research*, March–April, 1958, pp. 252–63.

Regardless of the method used, the location problem must be attacked in a logical manner. The system itself must be clearly defined as well as the environmental constraints which limit its operation. Although service and cost oriented, locational decisions must provide for flexibility in system design. Fixed facilities are not easy to move once they are located, yet sources, markets, and competitors rarely stay fixed over time. It is a poor system which is designed for optimal performance today but is so inflexible that it cannot be readily and economically changed to accommodate future contingencies.

managing the physical distribution function

The discussion which has preceeded this concluding section of the chapter should by now have clearly indicated that effective management of the PD function requires coordination among the diverse activities of the business enterprise. A PD system must be tuned to receive inputs from the production process as well as to furnish output as required by the marketing department. Even within the heart of the system the problems of managing the functions of transport, warehousing, and inventory holding must be considered as interrelated issues.

Unfortunately, the typical firm is not organized to facilitate fully such coordination. Traffic seeks to route goods as economically as possible. Sales promises prompt delivery of goods. Warehouse managers try to run their show as efficiently as they can. But, in all too many instances, there is no one person or group of persons to manage the cost trade-offs available among diverse functional areas and thus to optimize the performance of the total distribution system.

Some of the nation's more progressive firms have sensed that great opportunities for gains in performance and reduction in costs could be exploited if the systems approach could be applied to PD and if the components of the PD system could be viewed as pieces of the whole. These companies have attempted to provide the management structure needed to implement the systems approach.

In certain companies, for example, committees have been formed to set service-level goals and to coordinate the activities necessary for the attainment of these goals. The authority of these committees cuts across traditional functional lines and is exercised to prevent what is called suboptimization or the seeking of higher levels of performance by components at the expense of total system performance. Other companies have gone still further by establishing a separate department for physical distribution. The status of this department may be equivalent to that granted to production and marketing. The more usual procedure, however, is to recognize the PD function and to place it under the control of an established function such as production, control, or marketing. Those firms which are cost conscious and do not have service level problems generally choose to place PD under production or control. Those firms which are concerned with the levels of customer service provided for a given input of resources generally place the function within the marketing area.

The exact location of responsibility for PD management within the firm is not the major issue. Rather, what is vitally important is the recognition by top management that wherever management responsibility is located the people involved must have the authority to effect the coordination of activities both within and without the firm which is essential if distribution efficiency is to be fully achieved.

conclusion

This chapter has provided a brief overview of the physical distribution function. Marketing managers must be familiar with the scope of the PD function as well as how it is related to the other functional areas of the firm. Of special importance is the concept of the customer service level (CSL) as an important means of nonprice competition. Effective management of the PD function, wherever located in the hierarchy of the firm, requires the coordination of those activities both within the firm and without which are necessary if the required PD services are to be provided as efficiently as possible.

questions

1. What are some of the reasons for renewed interest in the area of physical distribution?
2. Explain how the implementation of the "marketing concept" by many firms has had an impact on their performance of the functions of physical distribution.
3. Why do firms vary with respect to how far they go in attempting to implement the "total logistics" concept?
4. What is systems analysis and why is it so useful an approach for managing the functions of physical distribution?
5. What is the output of a physical distribution sytem? How is system input measured? How would one determine the efficiency of a physical distribution system?
6. What difficulties might you expect to encounter if you attempted to im-

plement the systems approach in a situation where traditional accounting methods were used?

7. "A physical distribution system encompasses elements beyond the boundaries of the firm." What is meant by the statement? What are the implications for management?

8. Why is a statement of system objectives so crucial to the design of a physical distribution system?

9. What is a distribution audit? How is it related to the firm's marketing requirements?

10. What criteria should management consider in choosing from an array of distribution system designs?

11. Why is inventory management so important a component of a physical distribution system? What is the basic compromise involved in the design of an optimal inventory policy?

12. Of what value is the "logistics least-cost" approach to facility location? What are its limitations?

13. What is the economic purpose of a warehouse?

14. The physical distribution manager has been called, "a manager of trade-offs." Explain what this means. Also, discuss where in the organizational structure of the firm the physical distribution function should be located.

cases for part four

case 4–1

THE UPJOHN COMPANY*

decision on channels of distribution for new veterinary product

The research and development division of The Upjohn Company had discovered a new product for the treatment of mastitis in dairy cattle. If established distribution and sales policies were followed in the marketing of this discovery, it was anticipated that sales would be limited to a fraction of the potential market. As a means of capitalizing to the maximum possible extent on research findings, therefore, company officials were considering the possibility of opening new distribution channels and of deviating from customary promotional policy. They did not want to act without giving the matter careful consideration, however, because of the likelihood that such innovations would meet with disfavor by veterinarians who provided the traditional outlet for such products. There was also concern over the possible reaction of physicians and laymen, either users or potential users of the company's main product line of human-use pharmaceuticals.

history

The Upjohn Company, producers of ethical drugs and pharmaceuticals was established in 1886 in Kalamazoo, Michigan, and its headquarters and manufacturing plants are still located there today. The company was founded by Dr. W. E. Upjohn, at the time a practicing physician, for the purpose of manufacturing better pills, which were the most common form of medication at that time. After pills declined in popularity, the company began to move toward its present line of ethical drugs and pharmaceuticals. A reputation for outstanding research, high-quality products, and aggressive merchandising have all contributed to making The Upjohn Company one of the largest ethical drug firms in the industry.

distribution and sales policies

Ethical pharmaceutical houses are distinguished from proprietary drug firms by the fact that their promotional efforts are aimed at the profession (physician, druggist, hospital buyers) rather than at the ultimate consumer. Over the years, The Upjohn Company has followed the basic distribution

---

* Written by Donald Mattison, Marketing Research Department, The Upjohn Company.

policy of selling directly to retail druggists. In accordance with the "ethical" formula, the Upjohn sales force has been responsible for "creating" a demand for the firm's prescription drugs by "detailing" the physician (i.e., by missionary saleswork with doctors) and by selling the retail druggist on stocking Upjohn products. Heavy sales of nonprescription items such as vitamins, however, have resulted from direct sales and promotional efforts of the retail druggists.

Physical distribution of Upjohn products was handled through 18 company-owned sales branches and warehouses located throughout the country. No account was farther than two days' delivery service from any branch warehouse. Most major trading centers received either same-day or following-day service.

While the company's main line of products was human pharmaceuticals, over the years ambitious salesmen had started calling on veterinarians to obtain additional sales on certain items of their line which also had applications in the DVM's practice. Examples of such products were antibiotics, sulfa drugs, cortisone, vitamins, antidiarrheal preparations and cough products. The basic policy of selling direct to retail professional outlets (druggists, hospitals, etc.) made it possible to open new accounts in allied fields such as the animal health market.

Company officials had recognized this segment of business by establishing a separate research unit and sales force to give specific attention to its development. Ten salesmen had been added recently to call upon DVM's at an estimated annual cost of $150,000 for salaries and travel expenses. These men did not call upon druggists, farm supply stores, cooperatives, or hatcheries. The regular Upjohn sales force did call upon druggists, however, and took orders for pharmaceuticals which the druggist dispensed for the treatment both of humans and animals.

In addition to the establishment of the separate sales force, a special line of products was being developed for veterinarians. In the year prior to the discovery of the new product, the sales of products in the animal health market amounted to approximately $250,000.

background for problem

In the animal health goods market, according to an Upjohn official, the veterinarian's role is somewhat different from that of the physician in the human health goods market. In the human field, the physician and druggist act as a team with the physician "creating" the demand by writing a prescription to be filled by the druggist. In the animal health field, prescription writing is at a minimum with the exception of a few small animal hospitals. The DVM, for the greater part, considers the druggist as a competitor. Different types of outlets, accordingly, serve the animal health goods market. These are: (1) the veterinarians, (2) drugstores, (3) farm supply stores and cooperatives, (4) hatcheries, (5) all other types (door-to-door, mail order, etc.).

As of the year of the new product discovery, the relative importance of each type of outlet in the sale of pharmaceuticals was as shown in Exhibit 1:

Among the more important pharmaceuticals included in the sales figures shown in Exhibit 1 are antibiotics, sulfa drugs, and anthelmintics.[1] The most important types of outlets for these three kinds of pharmaceuticals vary considerably, as indicated below:

Pharmaceutical	Types of Outlets Listed in Order of Importance
Antibiotics	1st—DVM's; 2d—Farm Supply; 3d—Drugstores
Sulfa drugs	1st—Drugstores; 2d—DVM's; 3d—Farm Supply
Anthelmintics	1st—Farm Supply; 2d—Drugstores; 3d—DVM's

According to a company official, the proportion of pharmaceuticals administered to animals without diagnosis by a DVM varies widely by class of

Exhibit 1. Estimated annual sales by type of outlet, all animal health pharmaceuticals (at manufacturer's level).

Type of Outlet	Estimated Sales (Add 000)	% of Total Sales
Veterinarian	$ 28,000	25%
Drugstore	31,000	28
Farm supply and cooperatives	35,000	32
Hatcheries	9,000	8
All other	8,000	7
	$111,000	100%

Source: Company studies.

livestock and poultry and by disease being treated. The farmer can administer any and all to his animals if he so desires. If he believes he knows what the nature of the illness is, he may secure and administer what he thinks is the proper drug himself. His choice of what drug to give may be based on previous treatment of the same illness by a DVM, upon his own background in veterinary medicine, upon the advice of his neighbors, or information from literature, advertising, and so on. If the animal does not readily respond, a DVM is normally called. Also, if the farmer does not have confidence in his own ability to diagnose a particular illness, he would usually call in the DVM to examine the animal and supervise the treatment. Since only 25 percent of the sales of animal health pharmaceuticals are made through veterinarians there is a strong implication that a large proportion of the drugs are administered by the farmer without the benefit of professional help.

Unless the advice of a DVM is required in the treatment of an animal, the

---

[1] Anthelmintic an agent to expel or destroy intestinal worms thereby improving growth.

buying habits of farmers do *not* differ in purchasing remedies for specific illnesses like mastitis, as opposed to vitamins, food supplements, and similar items.

statement of problem

The research and development division of The Upjohn Company developed a new product called "Corbiot" for the treatment of mastitis in dairy cattle. Mastitis is a disease of milk cattle which renders the milk useless until the disease is cured. This results in a serious economic loss to the farmer. In most cases the farmer diagnoses mastitis without the services of a DVM. If he knows of a suitable remedy, he can also administer it without the aid of a DVM. Where a case does not respond, however, a DVM is normally called.

Corbiot was proven to have definite advantages over any product on the market at that time. However, it was suspected that competitors would, in a relatively short time, have a similar product on the market. It was believed that six months to a year would be the maximum time in which Upjohn could hope to maintain this competitive advantage.

The estimated market for mastitis products at that time was in the neighborhood of $5 million at manufacturers' level or close to $10 million at retail level. While good estimates of the breakdown of this market by types of outlet were not available, it was assumed that it approximated the breakdown of all pharmaceuticals for animal health as shown in Exhibit 1.

Under the company's basic sales and distribution policies, the product, if announced, would be placed with and actively promoted to veterinarians, who accounted for 25 percent of the market. However, without active promotion to farmers it was doubtful whether Upjohn could expect active introductory sales support from druggists. If Upjohn actively promoted the new product to farmers, it was feared that serious objection would be raised by the veterinarians, possibly to the point where they would not only refuse to accept the new product but also would discontinue using other Upjohn products.

The key question facing Upjohn management, therefore, was that of determining what marketing strategy would maximize the returns from the new product discovery. The effect of such decisions upon the existing sales of other products to veterinarians, as well as its effect upon sales of human products, was also a major part of this problem.

The importance of establishing sound distribution and sales policies for this new product was underscored by the fact that two other products were nearing the end of the development period and would soon be ready for marketing. It was also anticipated that other products would be forthcoming in the future as the research and developmental work gathered impetus.

alternatives

In evaluating the problem, Upjohn management listed and considered the following alternatives:

1. Announce this product only to the veterinarian. It was realized that under this alternative the company would be competing in only 25 percent of the potential market for the product.
2. Follow the basic company policy of announcing the product both to the DVM and the drugstore with no direct consumer advertising (i.e., advertising to the farmer). Without promotion to the farmer, the druggist could be expected to provide little active support for the product, even though he accounts for 28 percent of the animal health products market.
3. Announce the new product both to the DVM and the drugstore, but also back the druggist with heavy consumer advertising (i.e., advertising directed to farmers). Here the company would be actively competing in 53 percent of the market (25 percent for DVM + 28 percent for drugstore). However, Upjohn would be taking the risk of the veterinarian's disfavor, a reaction which might possibly affect the entire line. In the past other pharmaceutical companies had tried to promote their products to farmers and sell DVM's simultaneously. In these cases the reaction of the DVM's had been negative, but the degree of buying resistance resulting had not been measured. It was the observation of this experience that led Upjohn officials to anticipate unfavorable reactions from DVM's if Corbiot were heavily promoted to farmers. Some of the drugs distributed by competitors through channels other than DVM's were advertised to farmers, others were not.
4. Follow alternative No. 3 above, reaching DVM's and drugstores by direct sale, but also add jobbers to obtain distribution in other farm outlets (i.e., farm supply stores, co-ops, hatcheries, and so on). It was thought that jobbers would have to be allowed a 20 percent margin to get them to handle the line. From the standpoint of the farmer, purchase of Corbiot through outlets other than the DVM would offer advantages of (1) convenience, (2) availability of credit, and (3) possibly a lower price. This plan would provide active competition in 100 percent of the market, but might possibly result in a stronger DVM reaction than anticipated in reaction to No. 3 above.
5. Sell under one trade name for the veterinarian market and select a second trade name for sales to all other outlets. The product having the second name would then be advertised to farmers. It was not known what the DVM's reaction would be to such a plan, but it was suspected that there would be at least some degree of objection.
6. Announce the new product to the veterinarian under the Upjohn label and, also, either sell the product to another company for distribution to other outlets under its label or have Upjohn produce for marketing under private labels for feed companies and/or distributors. By giving up the marketing of the new product to all outlets except the veterinarians, it was recognized that profits from the research discovery would be shared with others.
7. Form a subsidiary company or acquire another company with established distribution in outlets other than the DVM's. This alternative would give

distribution under a different brand name in the missing types of outlets and might possibly overcome the DVM's objections to alternatives No. 3 and No. 4. However, it brought up the serious question of whether one or two products plus future expectations which could not be fairly evaluated at the time, were enough to warrant such a drastic step.

QUESTIONS

1. Assuming no change in brand policy, which of the first four alternatives should the company choose? Why? (Disregard alternatives No. 5 through 7 in this phase of the analysis.)
2. Next, broaden your analysis to take into consideration possible changes in brand policy outlined in alternatives Nos. 5, 6 and 7. Which line of action would you now recommend? Why?

case 4–2

THE BUHR MACHINE TOOL COMPANY*

wisdom of substituting company salesmen for manufacturers' agents

The Buhr Machine Tool Company of Ann Arbor, Michigan, manufactured and sold multiple-spindle high-production machinery to the metalworking industries. The company employed 240 persons and was one of the first firms to manufacture such automation machinery.

The Buhr (rhymes with "pure") machines were sold under the brand name of "Economatics," and each machine, while constructed from standardized components, was designed to meet the specific needs of the particular customer to whom it was sold. The Buhr Economatics were characteristically designed to perform simultaneously many different metal removal operations and inspection operations on a product: operations that prior to the purchase of the Economatic were performed by many different machine tools at a number of different work stations. An Economatic was designed to accomplish such a set of operations on a single machine and at one work station. One such Economatic designed for a large automobile manufacturer

---

* Written by Ross J. Wilhelm, Associate Professor of Business Economics, Graduate School of Business Administration, The University of Michigan.

performed four milling operations, eight drilling operations, two rough taper reamings, two finish taper reamings, two spot facings, five chamferings, one tapping, one threading, one steel brushing, and three automatic probing and blow-out operations before tapping on an automotive steering knuckle. The machine's output was two pieces every 32½ seconds. Another Buhr Economatic was designed to do the complete machining on an automotive intake manifold which required 78 separate operations. This machine took the part from rough casting to finished part in 38 seconds.

Among the various types of machine tools which a single Buhr Economatic might replace were drill presses, milling machines, boring mills, heavy-duty grinders, and broaching machines, as well as various other operations, such as inspection. The Buhr machines were usually sold to perform a set of such operations on a single piece, but were so designed that they could be adapted to changes in the product and for different pieces as well.

Exhibit 1. Buhr Machine Tool Company sales by territory.

Territory*	Average Annual Sales
A	0
B	0
C	0
D	$120,000
E	0
F	480,000
G	0
H	0
J	30,000
K	596,000
L	98,000
M	0
N	220,000
P	90,000
Q	27,000
R	0

* The eastern Michigan territory is not included.

The typical situation where it might be advisable for a customer to consider the use of an Economatic was where he had a production line consisting of a set of machine tools performing repetitive metal removal, finishing, and inspection operations on one or a few parts rather than the situation found in a job order shop. In most instances the larger the number of different machines being used and the greater the number of standardized operations being performed, the larger the potential returns from an investment in a Buhr machine. The Buhr Company, over time, hoped to expand the potential uses for its machines by adding other types of operations which could be performed automatically by the Economatics, such as the assembly of components and perhaps the packaging of the assembled parts.

Over 80 percent of the firm's annual sales, which totaled $8 million to $9

Exhibit 2. Selected data on industrial equipment, machinery and supplies manufacturers' agents.

Region	Number of Firms	Dollar Sales (000)	Operating Expenses as % of Sales
New England.................134		65,663	9.4
Middle Atlantic.................560		372,763	7.5
E. N. Central...................679		439,041	8.7
W. N. Central.................131		53,608	9.2
S. Atlantic......................169		102,126	7.5
E. S. Central.................. 63		42,129	6.3
W. S. Central..................155		74,942	8.1
Mountain...................... 37		14,729	8.1
Pacific 196		191,433	6.1

Source: *Census of Business*, Vol. IV, *Wholesale Trade Area Statistics*, Table 1D.

million, were to customers located in eastern Michigan and in the automotive industry. The company also sold its line nationally to manufacturers of appliances, farm machinery, business machines, road-building equipment, and other such industries. In the eastern Michigan territory, the company employed a direct sales force; however, in other territories (see Exhibit 4) the company employed manufacturers' agents. The average annual sales for a five-year period, for the company by territory (exclusive of eastern Michigan) are shown in Exhibit 1.

Data from the U.S. *Census of Business* on the sales, operating expenses,

Exhibit 3. Other lines carried by Buhr's manufacturers' agents by territory.

Territory*	Cutting Tools	Broaching Machines	Milling Machines	Boring Mills	Drill Presses	Grinders	Lathes	Sheet Metal Presses
A			x		x	x	x	x
B					x	x	x	
C				x	x		x	x
D								
E								
F		x	x				x	x
G			x			x	x	x
H								
J								
K	x	x						
L								
M						x	x	
N	x	x						
P								
Q	x	x						
R								

* In those territories where no other lines are indicated, the firm had no manufacturers' agent.

Exhibit 4. Sales territories by states, Buhr Machine Tool Company.

Territory Code Letter	Geographical Coverage
A	Northern California, including San Francisco and Fresno
B	Southern California, including Los Angeles; southern Nevada; and Arizona
C	Texas
D	Kansas, western Missouri, and Oklahoma
E	Nebraska and western Iowa, including Sioux City
F	Eastern and central Iowa; Wisconsin; northern Illinois, including Springfield; and Indiana
G	Central and eastern Missouri, including Jefferson City, and southern Illinois
H	Tennessee, Alabama, Georgia, Florida, and central and northern Mississippi, including Jackson
J	Western Michigan, including Lansing and Jackson
K	Northern Ohio, including Lima and Mansfield and Akron but not including Youngstown nor Canton
L	Central and southern Ohio and northern Kentucky to a line running just below Louisville
M	Eastern Ohio, including Youngstown, Canton, and Parkersburg; West Virginia; western Pennsylvania, including Altoona; Western Maryland from Hagerstown westward
N	Western and northern New York, including Binghamton and Gloversville
P	Eastern and southern New York, including Albany and New York City, and all of Connecticut
Q	Eastern Pennsylvania, New Jersey, Delaware, rest of Maryland
R	Maine, New Hampshire, Vermont, Massachusetts, and Rhode Island

Areas Other than Eastern Michigan
Not Assigned to a Territory

Washington	Colorado	Southern Mississippi
Oregon	New Mexico	Upper Peninsula of Michigan
Northern Nevada	North Dakota	Central and Southern Kentucky
Idaho	South Dakota	Virginia
Utah	Minnesota	North Carolina
Montana	Arkansas	South Carolina
Wyoming	Louisiana	

and number of manufacturers' agents selling industrial machinery, equipment, and supplies, by region are shown in Exhibit 2.

The Buhr Company usually had a manufacturers' agent in each of its territories outside eastern Michigan. Such agents were paid on a sliding commission scale. The company estimated that these agents employed a total of about 150 outside salesmen, who called regularly on customers in their territories. These agents were selected on the basis of their knowledge of the metalworking industries, their size and reputation, the other lines they carried, and the customers they normally called upon. These agents sold other lines in addition to the Buhr line of Economatics, and their other lines, while varying between agents, included cutting tools, broaching machines, milling machines, boring mills, drill presses, sheet metal presses, grinders, and lathes. A breakdown of other lines carried by the manufacturers' agents, by territory, is shown in Exhibit 3.

The role which the manufacturers' agents have fulfilled in selling the Buhr line has been: a) Developing leads to customers who are in the market for this type of machinery. b) Providing the Buhr engineers with initial information on the customer's need. After this information was received, the Buhr engineers generally took over the sale and worked directly with the customer's staff. c) Introducing the Buhr representatives to the personnel in the customer firm who would be participating in the purchase decision and providing information on these individuals, how they thought, etc. d) Maintaining continuous representation for Buhr with its potential customers.

The company also believed that its manufacturers' agents through their long association and close contact with the customers were able to develop leads more readily than would direct salesmen. The leads to potential customers did not, however, come exclusively through the agents; a substantial portion came directly from the customers.

Buhr also carried on an advertising program using top trade publications which had a horizontal coverage in the metalworking industries.

QUESTIONS

1. Should the Buhr Machine Tool Company continue to use manufacturers' agents in selling its products outside of the Eastern Michigan territory?
2. What were the weaknesses of Buhr's staff of manufacturers' agents? What were the advantages of such a staff?
3. What are the alternatives to using manufacturers' agents for selling this line and how would you evaluate them?
4. Under what future conditions would you recommend that Buhr drop the manufacturers' agents and employ a direct sales force?

AMERICAN MOTORS CORPORATION*

selective distribution through dual agencies

During 1956 and 1957, the American Motors Corporation was engaged in a vigorous campaign to enlarge and strengthen its dealer organization. In the spring of 1957, a small number of dealers of competitive manufacturers were granted franchises to operate dual agencies. By fall of that year, due to a combination of circumstances, American Motors faced an ever-growing number of such requests. The marketing executives were confronted with the problem of reevaluating the role of dualing in their program for better market coverage, and of establishing criteria for the selection of dual dealerships which would best serve the company's marketing objectives.

history

The American Motors Corporation, manufacturer of both automobiles and home appliances, distributed its automotive line through over 2,000 dealer agencies in the United States. Since the company's inception in May, 1954, as a result of a merger between the Nash-Kelvinator Corporation and the Hudson Motor Car Company, its production and promotional objectives had been the development and sale of a smaller and more economical automobile than the standard American model.

As of September 30, 1957, the conclusion of its fiscal year, the company disclosed sales in excess of $400 million. Besides the output of the appliance and special products divisions this figure included the sale of over 116,000 Nash, Hudson, Rambler, and Metropolitan automobiles.

Because of the problems inherent in an attempt to integrate two separate manufacturing and distributing organizations in the midst of a severely competitive market, American Motors had not succeeded in attaining profitable levels of operation in the three years since its founding.

Management philosophy was based on the belief that it was inadvisable to buck the "Big Three," General Motors, Chrysler, and Ford, by producing a nearly identical type of product. Therefore, in an attempt to outflank them,

---

* Written by Martin R. Warshaw, Professor of Marketing, Graduate School of Business Administration, The University of Michigan.

American Motors had concentrated its efforts on the development of an auto that combined the economical operating costs and handling ease of a foreign car with the interior roominess and the road stability of an American model. The Rambler series seemed to fulfill its designer's intent in these respects and was well received by the American public, as its increasing sales volume and extremely high rate of value retention on the used car market seemed to indicate.

product line

The 1958 automotive product line introduced between November, 1957, and January, 1958, consisted of the following models:

At the lower end of the line was the "Metropolitan," a small two-passenger personal-type auto built in Great Britain to American Motors' specifications. Designed on an 85-inch wheelbase it was powered by a 52-horsepower overhead valve four-cylinder engine.

The Rambler series included the Rambler "American." The model was built on a 100-inch wheelbase with a 90-horsepower L-head six-cylinder engine. It carried five passengers and had sufficient fuel economy to attain over 30 miles per gallon of gasoline.

On the 108-inch wheelbase, AMC offered the "Rambler Six" and "Rambler V-Eight" models, while the "Ambassador" series on a 117-inch wheelbase was priced in the lower medium price range.

development of the issue

Dual agency was not an altogether new concept in auto distribution. During the depression it was not uncommon to see one agency handling the lines of two competing factories. Dualing of an independent with a "Big Three" dealer was a less general occurrence; although, within the structure of a company such as General Motors, dual agencies selling the products of two divisions were quite common. Especially in smaller towns such combinations as Chevrolet-Cadillac or Pontiac-Cadillac were not unusual. The Ford Motor Company followed a similar practice and achieved distribution of the Mercury in 1939 largely by dualing it with Lincoln dealers. Chrysler was an extreme example in that it placed Plymouth in almost every agency as a low-priced leader. It should be noted that because of the heavy number of Plymouth dealers in certain market areas as a result of this dualing, Chrysler had been attempting to split Plymouth off from some of the dualed agencies in order to obtain a dealer pattern more in line with that used by Ford and General Motors.

automobile supermarkets

During 1955, the extreme pressures to produce at the manufacturers' level forced many dealers to accept more cars than they were capable of selling. The franchise contracts then in force left little alternative but to accept the inventory burden or give up the franchise. Many of these autos forced on the dealers were sold at cost, or slightly above, to wholesale operators who either operated or supplied automobile supermarket lots.

By the end of 1955, many students of auto distributional methods felt that the trend toward such supermarket merchandising of automobiles was rapidly accelerating.

The O'Mahoney hearings of 1956 greatly lessened the restrictiveness of the franchise agreements and relieved dealers from the fear of loss of franchise for refusal to accept unwanted inventory. As a result the auto dealer gained considerable bargaining strength, and the manufacturers were constrained from taking peremptory action which would affect the dealer's welfare.

The scheduling by the manufacturers of production more closely related to the dealer's capabilities to sell took most of the impetus out of the super-market movement but did not destroy it. By 1957, several people in the industry, concerned with what they felt were adherences to archaic selling methods, once again raised the question of whether or not auto supermarkets were to be the important distributive institutions of the future.

To one man who spent more than 20 years directing auto sales efforts, auto supermarkets must come—but in a form not anticipated a few years ago when the growth of "bootlegging" hinted at the retailing of many makes of cars at one location. What this man means by an auto supermarket is a giant lot—he thinks new cars must be sold outdoors for proper display—with the cars neatly arranged by model and type: all six-cylinder, standard transmission, four-door sedans here; all eight-cylinder hardtops over there; and so on. Each car would be marked with its price, and a price subject to little if any dickering.

"A customer could walk through, just as he does in a food store," says this executive, "and pick out the car he wanted. No ordering. Dealers lose sales when they don't have a car in stock the customer wants and has to wait several weeks for the factory to build. Maybe this means we'll have to build fewer models; hardtops and station wagons in one make; two-door sedans, hardtops and wagons in another make. A dealer has to carry a complete selection and with all the various models we build today he would be able to."

"Most present-day dealers," says this man, "are 'warehousers,' not merchants." "They should study Sears," he says, "and Kroger's and the big department stores to learn how to merchandise and sell products. Dealers today sell price, nothing else."[1]

the medium-priced market

Since the resumption of auto production after the conclusion of World War II, the combined effects of a rising price level and a policy of selling-up,

[1] "Giant Questions Plague Detroit," *Business Week,* November 9, 1957, p. 82.

initiated by the low-priced division of the "Big Three," caused considerable pressure to be placed on the dealers handling the medium-priced auto lines. It was no secret that the deluxe series of the previously mentioned autos seriously overlapped the middle price range.

Beside the pressures from the low-priced "Three," the medium-priced group also anticipated the entry of a new member. Ford Motor Company had scheduled the introduction of the Edsel for the fall of 1957. This car was backed by the largest promotional program ever budgeted for a new-car introduction.

As if domestic competition was not enough, the rate of foreign car imports also stepped up during 1957. It was estimated that in excess of 200,000 units would be imported and sold in the United States during 1957.

The medium-priced cars have fluctuated sharply in the percentage of the market they have been able to take.

In the 1930's when car ownership was more sharply defined by income strata and credit terms were strict, the cars in between the Ford-Chevrolet-Plymouth and Cadillac-Packard-Lincoln categories took less than one third of the market.

After the war, with personal incomes high, medium-priced cars accounted for 40% of all sales in 1950 through 1952, dropping to 38% in 1953 and 36% in 1954 when the economy dipped.

In 1955 came the heyday of the middle-priced class. With credit exceptionally easy, this group of cars rose to 40.8%. Car prices increased in 1956 and 1957, and credit tightened. Medium-priced buyers dropped last year (1956) to only 35.6% of the total and made up only 31.4% of the total through September of this year. (1957)[2]

With these combinations of circumstances, it was understandable that many dealers selling cars in the medium-priced group were actively searching for a solution to their problems.

General Motors took an active step in providing its medium-priced dealers with an extension of their product lines. The Opel "Rekord" and the Vauxhall "Victor," both manufactured by European subsidiaries of General Motors, were being imported and assigned to selected Pontiac and Buick dealers. Ford also arranged for a stepped-up importation of its British-made Anglia. Chrysler acknowledged that the problem was being studied, but as of late 1957 had made no move in the direction of providing its dealers with another automobile.

It was not possible to provide all dealers with foreign imports, and a considerable number of "Big Three" dealers were left in what they considered to be an unhappy situation. These dealers were actively seeking a lower priced line to add to their present selection, and the Rambler, as a well-

---

[2] "The Cars in the Middle in 1958," *Business Week,* November 16, 1957. p. 200.

accepted product of a domestic manufacturer, seemed to be an exceedingly tempting possibility.

beginning of large-scale dualing

In early 1957, the sales executives of AMC received a request from a Buick dealer in northern New Jersey for permission to add the Rambler line. A decision, made at the highest echelons of AMC, granted this request, and the results of the "dualing" were carefully observed for reactions both from General Motors and the members of the AMC dealer organization. Actually nothing happened to indicate that further dualing would not be possible. Accordingly, American Motors experimented further and franchised dual agencies in various market areas until by August, 1957, it was estimated that 120 dealers, or a little over 5 percent of the dealer strength, were dual agencies. Most of these duals were in the smaller market areas of the country.

advantages and disadvantages of dualing

It appeared that the possibility of widespread dualing would open the way to market penetration of areas previously inaccessible to American Motors. These open points had insufficient market potential to support a single Rambler dealership but could provide a profitable increase in volume to established dealers who took the line on as an addition to a present line.

Besides the increased market coverage, dualing provided American Motors with new, financially strong, well-located additions to their dealer organization.

Some executives of American Motors pointed out the difficulties involved in pushing too fast and too far with the dualing program. These men noted that dualing meant divided loyalties and divided sales efforts on the parts of the dealers. They held that if the "Big Three" manufacturers felt that dualing was proving detrimental to their dealer organizations, drastic steps would be taken to pressure these dealers into dropping their Rambler franchises.

It was recognized that introduction of a new dealer into a market by dualing would have effects on the morale of the American Motors dealer organization. There was usually a dealer relation problem when a new franchise was granted in an area which an established dealer considered his own territory. American Motors executives had generally been able to resolve these problems by a clear exposition of their thinking and by convincing the established dealer that the introduction of a new dealer generally increased sales for the established person as well as for the American Motors Company. The question was whether or not this problem would be compounded by granting a franchise to a dealer of a competitive factory.

Also noted was the feeling that, especially in the lower-priced lines, dual dealers would tend to use the Rambler line as a means of selling-up to their regular lines. It was pointed out that it was just a short jump from the prices of many models in the Rambler series to their counterparts in the low-priced models in the Chevrolet, Ford, and Plymouth lines. This problem also existed at the top of the Rambler line, as the "Ambassador" approached the lower end of the Buick "Special" series in selling price.

Dualing presented additional problems to the dealer as well as to the manufacturer. First, dualing required a substantial investment in both fixed and working capital. Dualing meant added service problems and training of servicemen in new techniques and procedures. Second, it was not inconceivable that the dealer would have to keep a second set of books to satisfy the informational requirements of his franchise agreements. Even with such expedients the American Motors executives doubted if an accurate apportionment of profit or loss could ever be made between the two lines of a dualed agency.

Dualing with American Motors had great significance for the medium-priced dealer. The Rambler franchise provided an opportunity to tap a new segment of the market, a segment primarily interested in price and economy of operation. It also gave the dual dealer a product in conjunction with his medium-priced line to sell to a customer for a second car. Two franchises also protected the dealer against the results of a bad model year by providing a second line to push when the first line was meeting consumer resistance. The existence of this alternative course of action for the dealer did not please many factory men, who felt that the pressure on the single dealer to sell his line in order to survive regardless of model popularity gave a great impetus to his selling effort. To give the dealer an alternative would diminish his selling effort at the very time that the manufacturer needed it most.

The problems of franchising in general and dualing in particular became compounded in urban areas. Competition was intense in these markets, and dualing of lines could have very well touched off explosions of dealer resentment or "Big Three" retaliation. Since the spring of 1957, American Motors had dualed in three urban areas, but in each case separate facilities were required although common ownership was allowed. It was hoped that such procedure would not prove controversial, as it had been common industry practice for single families to operate more than one competing agency in a single market area.

In August, 1957, *Business Week* magazine gave nationwide publicity to the American Motors' program of dualing. An article, based on an interview with a Louisville, Kentucky Oldsmobile dealer, left little doubt in the reader's mind that "Big Three" dealers were signing up with American Motors with the tacit consent of their factories.[3]

The resultant deluge of applications for franchises which flooded American Motors' headquarters was a clear indication that the end of the experi-

---

[3] "New System for Selling Cars?" *Business Week,* August 24, 1957, p. 105.

mental stage had arrived and that a clear-cut decision on the role of dualing in the AMC program had to be forthcoming.

Generally, the executives had to reflect upon the long-run effects of dualing on the stability and efficiency of the dealer organization. The question was posed as to whether or not the current enthusiasm over dualing would diminish the role of the single-line dealer. It was agreed that dualing greatly increased American Motors' ability to attain market penetration, but the negative effects of divided loyalty and competitive frictions had still to be more closely evaluated.

Specifically, policy decisions had to be reached on the granting of franchises to dealers whose lines were priced competitively with the Rambler line. The executives also felt that a clarification of the company's attitude toward urban dualing was essential and that, perhaps, the development of a list of criteria to aid in the selection of new dualed outlets would aid them in the selection of those agencies which would best fulfill the requirements of the American Motors Corporation in its campaign to become a successful independent automobile producer.

QUESTIONS

1. To what extent should American Motors Corporation pursue the policy of dualing with "Big Three" dealers?
2. What criteria would you recommend for selecting new "dual" dealers?
3. Why did the "Big Three" manufacturers allow this "dualing" to take place?

case 4–4

YARD-MAN (B) (1958-62)*

gaining independent distribution to offset loss of major private brand account

Immediately after the end of World War II, Yard-Man, Incorporated, of Jackson, Michigan, accepted a proposal from Sears, Roebuck and Company to manufacture lawn mowers for sale exclusively under the Sears Craftsman

---

* Written by Martin R. Warshaw, Professor of Marketing, and Tom Buck, a student in the Graduate School of Business Administration, The University of Michigan.

brand name. By the end of 1946, Yard-Man sales to Sears exceeded $1 million. During the next 10-year period, sales volume rose to $12 million, and Yard-Man profits on these sales were more than $700,000. The product line at this time consisted of silent hand mowers as well as powered reel and rotary mowers. In 1958, Sears decided to manufacture their own mowers. They announced that Yard-Man would be phased out over a three-year period as their principal supplier.

The decision of Sears to sever relations with Yard-Man prompted an immediate reorganization of the latter's operating personnel. An executive with an outstanding record as sales manager at Sears, Roebuck was appointed vice president in charge of sales for Yard-Man. A short time later, a sales manager experienced in independent distribution was brought in and given responsibility for the sales program. At the same time, the vice president in charge of sales moved to the position of executive vice president. In August, 1958, these two men sat down to figure out a strategy that would create a new marketing program for the Yard-Man corporation.

The problems facing the company were numerous. They included: (1) the task of winning support from the independent wholesale distributors, who had been alienated by the selling practices of the company during its relationship with Sears; (2) the necessity to regain the public acceptance that the Yard-Man brand name had lost during the time that it was subordinated to the Sears' Craftsman label; (3) the intense competition faced by Yard-Man from manufacturers of low-priced, medium-quality mowers as well as from five manufacturers of quality products, who were firmly established in the existing trade channels; and (4) the fact that there was very little money available for retooling. In addition, plant overhead was costly, since it was based on the capacity needed to produce from $10 to $12 million worth of lawn mowers, most of which had formerly been sold to Sears. There was little surprise, therefore, at the industry's attitude that Yard-Man was in serious trouble.

The two men came to the following conclusions after considering these problems: First, they felt that the product line, although needing improvement, was of a caliber that could successfuly compete against the products of other manufacturers. Second, the jobbers' antagonism seemed sufficiently strong to preclude Yard-Man from getting their support in distributing to retailers. In addition, these jobbers (especially the hardware jobbers) were apparently not doing a good job with those products that they did carry. The two executives decided that if Yard-Man were to penetrate the market, they would have to go directly to retail dealers, although this would be a most costly method of distribution. The long-range strategy was to do such an effective job of selling directly to key dealers that jobbers would before long recognize the importance and the profitability of the Yard-Man line and welcome the chance to sell it to many smaller retail outfits.

If direct selling were decided upon, the planners for Yard-Man had two alternative courses of action: to use manufacturers' representatives or to develop their own company sales force. They calculated that although company men handling only the Yard-Man line would provide greater concentration of selling effort, the cost of maintaining a nationwide sales force would be about $160,000 per year. During the initial stages of the selling program, this cost could be spread over only a limited number of units (sales for the first year were estimated to run about $1 million). The cost of this alternative was deemed to be prohibitive, and the decision was therefore made to use manufacturers' representatives working on a commission basis. Under this plan sales costs would be variable, depending on sales volume. The comparison was as follows: 10 company salesmen averaging $16,000 a year in salary and travel expense per man would cost $160,000. These costs were contrasted with the alternative cost of paying a 5 percent commission on $1 million worth of sales to manufacturers' representatives, which would amount to $50,000.

Having decided to use manufacturers' representatives, and having estimated the cost of this type of distribution to be $50,000, the planners discussed whether distribution would be on a selective or intensive basis. Because the Yard-Man line was high in quality and priced accordingly, it was decided to use selective distribution to obtain dealers with an equally high reputation. The Yard-Man product had to be sold by retailers having good service facilities and able to engage in skillful and energetic merchandising. The executives of Yard-Man felt that circumstances might warrant offering exclusive dealerships to the better retailers handling hardware and lawn, garden, and farm implements.

In order to reestablish the Yard-Man name, to build up sales volume quickly, and to locate selected dealers, advertising was given an important role. Yard-Man decided to enter into a cooperative advertising program with dealers, covering media such as newspapers, radio, and television. In addition, $80,000 was budgeted for national consumer and trade advertising. In respect to personal selling, three company fieldmen were to be appointed to supplement the efforts of the manufacturers' representatives.

the first year's program

Within 30 days after the initial planning session of August, 1958, a nationwide organization of manufacturers' representatives was formed. In October, the Yard-Man line was formally introduced at the National Hardware Show in New York City. By the following June, sales through independent channels had risen from zero to $920,000. Yard-Man executives regarded this as a good start considering the many problems which the company faced. The product line in addition to mowers consisted of go-carts, motor scooters, and school furniture. It is interesting to note that none of these additions to the line proved profitable, and they were therefore dropped within a year or two after their introduction.

Because of the phasing-out program of Sears, Roebuck, sales to that corporation amounted to $7.5 million.

the second year

Somewhat encouraged by the first year's results, the company decided to tailor its program to the larger dealers and to feel out the effect which the initial direct-to-dealer program had had on jobbers. Therefore, a program of sliding discounts based on volume purchases was emphasized during the second year. This movement in the direction of jobber distribution had to be accomplished diplomatically so as not to disturb relations with those dealers who were buying directly. To this end, purchasing classifications were established on a "dealer" and "key-dealer" basis. The margins to "dealers" were reduced slightly, and the margins to "key-dealers" were increased to a point where they were sufficient to compensate jobbers. During the second year, independent sales reached $2,649,428. Once again Sears contributed about $7.5 million. In addition to setting up "key-dealers," Yard-Man made its first sale to a large chain organization—the retail affiliates of the Firestone Rubber and Tire Company.

the third year

After appraising the results of the second year of operations, Yard-Man executives were convinced that they should make a more definite move in the direction of jobber distribution. Feedback from the field indicated that jobbers were beginning to have more respect for the Yard-Man line. The terms "key-dealer" and "dealer" in the discount schedule were replaced with "AA" and "A" classifications. The "AA distributor" was now receiving a full jobbing discount. The idea here was that only a jobber could obtain the stipulated volume that would make the buyer eligible for this higher margin—a margin which was adequate to allow redistribution to retailers. Margin adjustment in anticipation of full jobber distribution was thus undertaken. The increasing prestige of the Yard-Man brand would, of course, make it easier to secure the proper acceptance of this program.

The "AA" classification brought in between 40 and 50 jobbers. In addition, Yard-Man started producing a special silent hand mower for the O. M. Scott and Sons Company under the Scott name. Additional sales were made to Firestone as well as to two hardware-buying cooperatives. Sales to these customers were $3,254,436. In their last year as a Yard-Man customer, Sears' purchases were $3.7 million.

The two cooperatives which purchased from Yard-Man represented a combination of 800 retail stores which engaged in a very aggressive selling program. Buying cooperatives were a new development for the hardware industry but were gaining strength so rapidly that hardware jobbers who did not keep up with modern distribution methods and promotional programs were losing out. Many of the hardware jobbing companies were old organizations that had lost their aggressiveness and had neglected to adapt to the changing needs of their retailer customers. Regular jobbers disliked cooperatives because retailers who were members of a cooperative received broader margins and could therefore charge lower prices or realize greater profits than the customers of the traditional jobber organizations. Yard-Man accepted the risk that they might alienate the newly formed jobber organization by selling to the two cooperatives. It was thought, however, that cooperatives represented the distribution methods of the future and would continue to affect sales of the hardware jobber. In any event, dual distribution was initiated, and Yard-Man attempted to adjust the program so that the two types of wholesalers could live with each other. No immediate problems occurred with respect to the jobber organization at this time.

During this year, the inefficient manufacturers' representatives were weeded out of the distribution program and replaced by company salesmen. This measure was feasible because Yard-Man sales volume had reached the point where it could economically support the salary and travel expenses of the company salesmen. Each of the salesmen was given a defined territory that may or may not have been covered by manufacturers' representatives. Each of these company salesmen was held responsible for attaining monthly quotas set by the sales manager after he had conferred with the salesman.

the fourth year

By this time Yard-Man executives felt that the way had been sufficiently prepared, by gradual reductions in dealer margins and the building of brand recognition and product reputation, to achieve full jobber distribution. Therefore, it was decided to eliminate the "A" and "AA" classifications and to use one margin to sell only to jobbers.

Yard-Man also made the decision to sell through some of the larger department stores and to accept offers from some of the trading-stamp people. Not only did this latter group represent another type of outlet, but their high standards were a complement to the excellent reputation of the Yard-Man line. The success of the sales to cooperative buyers in the previous year, achieved without greatly irritating established jobbers and dealers, indicated to Yard-Man that it would be advantageous to sell to more of these cooperative buying organizations.

During the fourth year, full jobber distribution was attained without much objection from retailers who had formerly bought directly. The Yard-Man product line was selling well, and dealers and jobbers alike readily accepted the terms of distribution set up by the company. The shock of these innovations was not severe for the retailers because the change in margins was made gradually, and jobbers were chosen who offered the retailers a great deal of support.

During this fourth year, Montgomery Ward, Sears traditional competitor, purchased Yard-Man reel mowers for sale under private label and indicated that there might be a possibility of full-line purchases in the future. Another large cooperative gave Yard-Man its business which had formerly gone to Yard-Man's top competitor, who had withdrawn from distribution through cooperatives. Dealings with this new customer proved even more lucrative later in the year when the cooperative added 300 additional highly successful stores. Yard-Man, Incorporated, also sold in considerable volume to one of the larger trading-stamp companies. The last great stride in extending distribution during the fourth year was taken when sales of the Yard-Man line were made to the J. L. Hudson Company of Detroit and other large department stores.

All of these additional accounts, although still in the initial stages of development, combined to give Yard-Man a total sales volume of $5,664,029. As mentioned previously, Sears, Roebuck made no purchases from Yard-Man during this year.

QUESTIONS

1. Comment on the company's channel policy. What problems are especially pressing for a firm changing from private brand supply to distribution through independent channels?
2. What do you think of company policy with respect to sales to buying cooperatives, stamp companies, department stores, Firestone, and Montgomery Ward?
3. Do you approve of the company's willingness to manufacture for sale under reseller brands after its experience with Sears, Roebuck?

part five

promotional strategy

This section deals with the fundamental issue of how best to sell the firm's product. Decisions on other elements of the marketing mix (product, brand policy, distribution policy, and price) influence promotional strategy. The fundamental task is to determine what message to communicate to prospective buyers and then to decide through what channels to transmit these messages. What to say will depend upon an understanding of consumer behavior gained both through research and experience. Once the message has been determined, the problem is to choose appropriate methods of communication from among available alternatives (advertising, personal selling, consumer promotions, and reseller stimulation) and to combine them into an effective promotional mix. These are the issues with which we shall be concerned in Chapter 10.

Closely intertwined with the decision on the character of the promotional mix is the question of how much to appropriate for such activity. In Chapter 11, a theoretical solution to this problem is first developed and then methods used by business firms are examined to see how closely they approximate this ideal. Problems to be resolved in reaching a sound decision include (1) how to separate long-run and short-run results of promotional effort, and (2) how to measure the contribution to gross margin which may be expected from various sized expenditures upon advertising, consumer promotions, personal selling, and reseller stimulation. Suggested research approaches for dealing with these questions will be evaluated.

Finally, Chapter 12 explores the promotional implications of brand strategy decisions. It is concerned with issues relating to family versus individual brands, brand-price-quality relationships, and the wisdom of manufacturing products to be sold under distributors' brands as opposed to the firm's own brand.

chapter 10

promotional
strategy
decisions

Business success depends upon the firm being able to sell at a profit the merchandise it produces. Earlier discussions have demonstrated that the ability to sell a product depends upon sound action by executives on questions of product policy, branding, pricing, and the selection of effective channels of distribution. Yet these activities are wasted unless consumers or users are led to buy as the result of effective selling efforts.

What is the most effective way of selling a given product? This is the central issue with which we shall be concerned in the present chapter. Later we shall deal with the important related question of how much to appropriate to support the promotional program. We shall then turn to a consideration of the promotional aspects of brand strategy. In this discussion our point of view will be that of the marketing manager of a manufacturer or producer.

The development of an effective program of sales promotion involves both effective planning and skillful execution of plans. Because of the fundamental importance of sound sales planning activities, we shall give emphasis to this phase of the problem in our discussions here. Questions of execution can best be considered in the specialized courses which customarily follow the basic marketing course.

promotion involves communication

The cutting edge of the marketing instrument is the message which is communicated to prospective buyers through the various elements in the promotional program. But the messages communicated by advertising, personal selling, and point-of-purchase promotion constitute only a portion of what the firm's marketing program tells prospective buyers. When the prospect perceives the firm's product, certain impressions are communicated—either positive or negative—and thus the product serves as a symbol of communication. Indeed, the product comes to have a "personality" or image in the prospect's mind as a result of its design, appearance, and who uses it, among other influences. So, too, the trademark and brand name are symbols which communicate messages to the prospective buyer. The package also communicates ideas which may enhance or detract from the product's image. The price communicates ideas as to quality, and the images which consumers have of the middlemen who display and sell the brand may add to or detract from the brand's image. Realization of the ways in which these aspects of the marketing program assist or detract from the image of the brand underscores the importance of recognizing the communication value of these factors and of shaping them to provide the desired impressions.

Even so, it is the promotional program which serves as the primary channel of communication to prospective buyers. It will help us in the planning of effective promotional programs if we review communication theory briefly and show its application to the development of promotional strategy.

how communication works[1]

The term *communication* comes from the Latin *communis,* common. When we communicate, therefore, we are trying to establish a "commonness" with someone. The marketer, for example, is attempting to share information about the features of a brand, the benefits it will provide users, and the desires its consumption will satisfy.

The basic elements of a communication system are the *source,* the

---

[1] This section is adapted by permission from Wilbur Schram, "How Communication Works," in Wilbur Schram (ed.), *The Process and Effects of Mass Communication* (Urbana: University of Illinois Press, 1955), pp. 3–26.

message, and the *destination.* A source may be an individual (such as a salesman) or a communication organization (such as a television broadcasting system, a newspaper, or a magazine). The *message* may be in the form of printed words (as in a direct-mail letter), a spoken radio commercial, a picture, a symbol (such as the Chrysler Pentastar), or any other "signal" capable of being interpreted meaningfully. The *destination* may be an individual consumer listening, watching, or reading; the members of a group (such as housewives invited to the home of Mrs. Consumer to watch a demonstration of Tupperware), a football crowd (seeing a helicopter towing a sign promoting frankfurters), or an individual member of a mass television audience watching Rowan and Martin in their "Laugh-In" program.

Figure 10-1. Diagram of a communication system

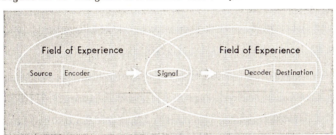

Source: Wilbur Schram, "How Communication Works," in Wilbur Schram (ed.), *The Process and Effects of Mass Communication* (Urbana: University of Illinois Press, 1955), p. 6. Reprinted by permission.

What happens when a source, say, a manufacturer of Buick automobiles, tries to build up a "commonness" with intended receivers (prospective buyers)? First, the Buick advertising manager has his advertising agency encode his message (prepare a television commercial involving words and pictures). Next, the signal (television commercial) must be transmitted via a television network. If this message is to have effect, owners of television sets must tune in the channel upon which the commercial is broadcast, remain in the room while the commercial is being presented, pay attention to the message transmitted, and decode it. That is, the meaning of the words and pictures must be interpreted by the consumer. If the full meaning of the message is to be understood, the fields of experience of the creative men who prepare the commercial and the consumers who view it must have a large area in common. (Figure 10-1 is a diagram of this communication process that illustrates what has been said.)

If the consumer who receives the message understands its meaning, he may respond in various ways. That is, he may become a sender and encode some kind of message in return. If the commercial offers an attractive premium for a box top and 25 cents, the housewife who receives the message may buy the product and send the box top plus the money to the manufacturer. If the message urges the consumer to visit the Buick dealer and see the most recent model, just put on display, he and his wife may decide to make such a visit within the next few days. If the commercial is designed to get the consumer to consider the brand the next time she is in the market, then no immediate action may result but a favorable attitude may be created which will lead to examining the brand when the need for it arises. Of course, the consumer may also simply do nothing at all.

If communication is between a salesman and a prospective buyer, we need to add the element of *feedback* in our conceptual scheme. As the prospect hears the sales message of the salesman, he will decode it, interpret its meaning, and encode a response. The element of feedback enables the salesman to determine whether his message is being understood and whether it is having the desired effect. He can then adjust subsequent messages accordingly. In mass communication such as a television broadcast, this direct type of feedback is impossible, and indirect responses must be substituted. Of course, interviews with television viewers may provide important feedback which will indicate whether the message is understood, believed, and has influenced attitudes toward the brand.

In summary, if communication is to have effect it must (1) gain attention, (2) employ signs which refer to experience common to both sender and destination to get the meaning across, (3) arouse personality needs in the destination and suggest some way to meet those needs, (4) suggest a way to satisfy needs which is appropriate to the group situation in which the destination finds himself at the time when he is moved to make the response desired by the source.

Let us now return to the point that the promotional program is the primary channel through which messages are communicated to prospective buyers. If this is to be done effectively, obviously the marketing executive must have a good understanding of who the prospective buyers of his product are, what desires may be satisfied through its use, what prospects know about his brand, what attitudes they hold toward it, and what image it holds in their minds. Research is needed to gain this information, and the planning of this research is helped by an understanding of consumer behavior and appropriate models of the buying process presented earlier in this book. Research to get feedback from prospective buyers on the impact of the messages communicated is also essential if weak links in the process are to be identified and communication improved in the next campaign.

The above discussion underscores the importance of the selling program in providing the methods by which appropriate information and persuasive messages are communicated to prospective buyers. Unless this job is done effectively the entire marketing program fails. Let us turn now to a consideration of the determination of basic promotional strategy.

determining the promotional mix

In determining how best to sell a given product, the basic decision which has to be made deals with the character of the promotional mix which is likely to be most effective. Specifically, how should advertising, personal selling, consumer promotions (contests, premiums, and combination offers), and dealer promotional activities be combined into an effective selling mix? The solution of this basic problem involves two subissues: (1) What promotional methods should be selected for use from among the alternatives available? (2) In what proportions should they be combined in order to get the best results?

In the solution of this problem, the business executive may be compared with a skilled cook who is going about the task of baking a cake. Depending upon the kind of cake to be made, the cook begins by selecting the various ingredients which will produce the desired product. These ingredients must be mixed together in proper proportions if the cake is to come up to expectations. In the same way, the development of an effective selling program involves selection of the right ingredients and mixing these ingredients together in the proper proportions in order to get the desired result. Let us now turn to a consideration of the various promotional methods from which the executive may choose the ingredients of his program.

promotional methods

Listed below are the more important promotional tools (order-getting ingredients) which may be used in building an effective selling program.

1. Advertising
2. Personal selling
3. Consumer promotions ("forcing methods")
   a) Premiums
   b) Contests
   c) Combination offers
4. Methods designed to stimulate dealer advertising & promotion
   a) Cooperative advertising
   b) "Merchandising the advertising"
   c) In-store promotions
   d) Display and advertising aids
5. Shows and exhibitions
6. Reciprocity
7. Warranty and service
8. Competitive bidding

choice of promotional methods

In view of the wide variety of promotional methods from which to choose, the question naturally arises, "How does the business executive approach the task of selecting those ingredients which will work most effectively for his particular product?" Unfortunately, there is no generally accepted mix of promotional methods which will fit the wide variation of circumstances which surround the marketing of the many different products produced and sold in our country today. Experience has demonstrated that different types of products require different mixtures of selling ingredients. This may be illustrated by contrasting the promotional strategies which might normally be used for an industrial product as opposed to a consumer good.

In the sale of diesel locomotives to railroads, for example, the Acme Corporation relies primarily upon personal selling because of the size of the investment, the technical nature of the product, the fact that the order will be placed by railroad executives, and the further fact that the number of prospective buyers is relatively limited (in number) while the size of the individual order is likely to be large. Along with personal selling, a supplementary campaign of advertising in trade journals read by railroad executives is also used.

In the sale of a patent medicine, however, the Mandell Company places the sole emphasis upon consumer advertising. This method is used because it offers the most economical way of reaching the large number of prospects who are scattered throughout the United States. The company has found that the demand created through such advertising is strong enough to pull the product through wholesale and retail channels of distribution. Since the company has no sales force, orders from wholesalers and large retailers are received by mail. Thus, it is apparent that the patent medicine, a consumer good, requires an entirely different selling strategy from that needed for the diesel engine, an industrial product.

Even within the same industry, however, it may not be wise for all firms to use the same mix of promotional methods in the sale of their various brands. Experience has shown that variations in the characteristics of competing brands, as well as differences in brand policy, distribution channels, and pricing policy, tend to require differences in the promotional mix if profitable results are to be achieved. The influence of these factors upon basic promotional strategy will be illustrated in the following paragraphs.

1. *Influence of brand policy.* A manufacturer may elect to sell under his own brand, under the private brands of middlemen, or without brand identification. The decision reached on this question will exert an important influence upon the character of the promotional mix. In considering alternative branding policies, for example, a coffee roaster may decide to supply a chain of supermarkets with coffee for sale under the chain's private brand. If this is done, then the chain will be responsible for all selling and promotional effort directed to the ultimate consumer. Personal contact between an executive of the coffee roaster and the buying offices of the chain may be the only selling effort required on the part of the firm furnishing the coffee to the supermarkets. In contrast, if the coffee roaster were to decide to market under his own brand, then the executives of this firm might well decide to make use of (1) personal selling to get middlemen to stock and promote the product at the point of sale, and (2) consumer advertising in order to create a brand preference for the item.

2. *Influence of channels of distribution.* Basic decisions on distribution policy will also influence selling strategy. One manufacturer of ladies' hosiery may distribute his brand to the ultimate consumer through house-to-house canvassing. A second firm may sell the same type of product to ultimate consumers by a mail-order plan. Where house-to-house canvassing is used, the main emphasis is placed upon personal selling. If consumer advertising is used at all, it would probably be for the supplementary purpose of paving the way for the compa-

ny's sales organization. In contrast, where ladies' silk hosiery is distributed through the mail-order method, personal selling is omitted and reliance is placed upon consumer advertising to get mail orders.

A third manufacturer of silk hosiery may follow the practice of distributing his high-grade brand direct to selected department stores and specialty shops. In this situation, the firm might well decide that the best way to sell the brand would be to get the selected dealers to push the brand aggressively at the point of sale. As a means of encouraging retailers to undertake aggressive selling efforts on behalf of the brand, the manufacturer might offer to share the cost of each retailer's advertising of the product on a 50–50 basis and to furnish advertising aids and display materials without charge. Salesmen might also be hired whose job it would be to take orders for the brand from the retailers and to assist them in the planning of point of sale display and promotion. Note the wide differences in promotional strategy followed by the firm distributing through retailers, the manufacturer distributing by mail-order methods, and the company relying upon house-to-house canvassing.

3. Influence of pricing and price policy. In the pricing of a given product, wide variations in practice may be observed. On the one hand, a manufacturer may decide to compete largely on a price basis, with the result that only a narrow margin is available for selling activities. A sugar refiner might well follow such a policy. As a result, this refiner might make use of no consumer advertising and might rely entirely upon the personal relations between his sales force and both chain supermarkets and grocery wholesalers to sell his brand.

On the other hand, a different firm may set prices which allow wide margins and at the same time make plans to compete through emphasis on "nonprice" factors such as product quality, service, or advertising. A manufacturer of patent medicine might well illustrate such an approach. This firm might price its brand so as to permit a margin of 50 percent of its price to be devoted to selling expenses. The entire promotional burden might then be placed upon an aggressive campaign of consumer advertising with no provision for sales contacts with the wholesalers and retailers who stock the brand. Here the pull of consumer advertising is relied upon to force retailers and wholesalers to handle the product. Clearly, there is a definite interrelationship between the promotional methods which a firm may use and the size of the margin available to cover the costs of these methods.

4. Suggested approach to the determination of promotional strategy. Since it has been demonstrated that no single mixture of promotional methods is suitable for all products, or even for different brands of the same product, how then should the business executive proceed in the selection and combination of selling ingredients? The most promising approach involves three steps. First, it is helpful to appraise the opportunity of making profitable use of advertising, personal selling, and other order-getting ingredients, in the light of certain basic considerations which have been found by experience to influence the success of their application. Some of the more important of these factors are:

1. The characteristics of the product and its stage in the life cycle.
2. Buying habits and buying motives of consumers or industrial users.
3. Point of view of middlemen.
4. The promotional strategy of competitors.
5. Probable size of promotional funds.

The significance of these considerations will be explained and illustrated at appropriate points in the following discussion of individual selling methods.

The preceding analysis will indicate in broad terms the relative emphasis which should be placed upon advertising, personal selling, and other order-getting ingredients in order to achieve desired promotional objectives. The second step then involves the use of this background in determining the total promotional appropriation and in working out its optimum allocation among the promotional methods to be used. In theoretical terms, the task is to set the total promotional appropriation at the point where the marginal revenue produced (output) equals or just exceeds the marginal cost of the last unit of input. Likewise, the amounts devoted to each promotional method (advertising, personal selling, dealer stimulation) should be set at levels where the marginal gain per dollar cost among all promotional methods is equal. The practical adaptation of the marginal approach to the allocation of promotional dollars among alternative methods will receive consideration later in this discussion.

Third, wherever possible, it is desirable to check the decisions reached by this analytical process through the use of research designed to measure the effectiveness of the promotional methods chosen as well as alternative combinations of promotional ingredients. Thus, if analysis indicates that there appears to be a good opportunity to make effective use of advertising, it is wise to check this decision by utilizing suitable research techniques to measure the results of using the advertising method. If possible, research should also be used to verify deci sions to include other methods in the promotional mix. Also, various combinations of advertising, personal selling, and dealer promotion should be tried out on an experimental basis as a means of identifying the most effective mix of these elements. Such research will serve to narrow the margin of error and will provide the facts needed to improve the quality of executive judgment.

At the same time, it should be recognized that the problem of measuring the results of using any given promotional method or combination of methods will often be a difficult one. Where the product has high unit value and is purchased at infrequent intervals, it may well be impossible to devise any small-scale test which will measure within a three- to six-month period the sales results of using advertising, personal selling, or other available promotional methods. Since many factors exert an influence upon sales in the marketplace, it may also prove to be very difficult for the manufacturer of such a product to isolate the influence of a single method, such as personal selling, where a given mix is subjected to appraisal by actual trial throughout the entire market. The point to keep in mind is that while under certain conditions, research may provide helpful checks on management decisions on the choice of selling methods, there are other circumstances where research has little to contribute because of the complexities of the problem. Where this is true, success depends upon the artistry and judgment of the executive as he attacks the problem of choosing the ingredients of his promotional plan. We may still conclude, however, that wherever possible it is wise to check decisions on the choice of promotional ingredients through the use of appropriate research methods.

Let us now turn to a discussion of some of the more important promotional methods available and the considerations which may guide the executive in the task of selecting the proper ingredients for the selling mix.

advertising

Advertising includes any paid form of nonpersonal presentation and promotion of ideas, goods, or services by an identified sponsor.[2] It is evident that advertising may be classified into two main types: (1) product advertising, and (2) institutional advertising. Institutional advertising is designed to create favorable attitudes toward an institu-

---

[2] *Marketing Definitions: A Glossary of Marketing Terms,* compiled by the Committee on Definitions of the American Marketing Association, Ralph S. Alexander, Chairman (Chicago: American Marketing Association, 1960), p. 9.

tion or an idea. Since our primary concern is with the use of advertising as a selling tool, the following discussion will deal with product advertising.

Product advertising may be used by manufacturers or producers to perform a variety of tasks as the following outline indicates:

1. Promote the sale of a manufacturer's or producer's brand through present retail dealers
   a) by getting new customers to buy, and
   b) by getting present customers to buy more of the product than in the past.
2. To assist in the sale of a branded product by giving consumers the names and addresses of the selected retailers who carry the item.
3. Where products are sold house-to-house, to help sell the brand
   a) by paving the way for the salesmen, and
   b) by getting leads for salesmen to follow up.
4. To help get distribution for a new product, or extend the distribution of an old product
   a) by creating a demand at retail stores through consumer advertising, and
   b) by stimulating interest of retailers in the product through advertising directed to them.
5. To encourage retailers to display, advertise, and sell the product actively
   a) by telling them through advertising of the opportunity for increasing profit through such activity, and
   b) by informing them of the manufacturer's promotional plans and encouraging them to capitalize on such effort through tie-in promotion.
6. To expand the sales of an industry, or to counteract an adverse sales trend
   a) by advertising sponsored by a group of competing manufacturers or producers.

In the performance of the foregoing tasks, you will note that advertising may be directed to (1) the ultimate consumer or industrial user and (2) to the middlemen involved in the distribution of the product. In the discussion which follows, we shall be concerned with an appraisal of the opportunity of making profitable use of advertising addressed to ultimate consumers or industrial users for the purpose of promoting the sale of the manufacturer's or producer's brand.

If advertising campaigns were analyzed to determine their objectives, we would find that they could be classified into two basic types, depending upon the nature of the appeals used. On the one hand is advertising designed to create a *primary demand,* which is a demand for a generic type of product. In order to accomplish this aim, primary appeals are used in the advertisements—appeals which may be expected to arouse a desire for a certain type of product rather than for an individual brand. Another kind of advertising is that which aims to create a *selective demand,* which is a demand for the brand of an individual manufacturer. Where such advertising is used, no attempt is made to increase the demand for the type of product. Instead, the purpose is to secure for the brand which the manufacturer sells as large a percentage as possible of this volume. The method which is generally followed is to show that the advertiser's brand will satisfy a given desire more effectively than other brands. This is done by dwelling on the superior qualities or individualizing features of this brand which make it a better solution to the desire than other brands would be. Appeals of this sort are called selective appeals, since they aim to get the consumer to purchase only the advertiser's brand.

By far the greater proportion of the advertising of individual manufacturers and producers is designed to increase the share of the market secured by the seller's individual brand—i.e., it is intended to create a selective demand. The discussion which follows, accordingly, will deal with the problem of appraising the opportunity to make profitable use of consumer advertising to stimulate a selective demand.[3]

In deciding whether to choose advertising as a sales-making ingredient, the executive must do more than arrive at a judgment on whether the use of advertising will increase sales. He must estimate the cost of an adequate campaign of consumer advertising, and then determine whether that advertising will stimulate enough additional sales —at profitable prices—to cover advertising costs and leave a margin sufficient to increase profits.

appraising the opportunity to make profitable use of consumer advertising

In estimating the opportunity profitably to stimulate selective demand through advertising to consumers or users, accordingly, the following leading considerations stand out:

------

[3] For a discussion of appraising the opportunity to stimulate primary demand, see N. H. Borden and M. V. Marshall, *Advertising Management: Text and Cases* (rev. ed.; Homewood, Ill.: Richard D. Irwin, Inc., 1959) , chap. iv.

First, advertising is likely to be more effective if a company is operating with a favorable *primary demand trend* than if it is operating with an adverse trend.

The second condition governing a concern's opportunity to influence its demand is the presence of a *large chance for product differentiation*. When products can be significantly differentiated, advertising is likely to be effective. Conversely, advertising is of smaller help when there is a marked tendency for the products of various producers to become closely similar.

A third condition is the relative importance to the consumer of the *hidden qualities of the product* as contrasted with the external qualities which can be seen and appreciated. When these hidden qualities are present, consumers tend to rely upon the brand, and advertising can be used to associate the presence of the qualities with the brand. Conversely, when the characteristics of a product which are significant to a consumer can be judged at time of purchase, brand tends to lose some of its significance, and advertising is not needful in building mental associations regarding these characteristics.

A fourth condition is the *presence of powerful emotional buying motives* which can be employed in advertising appeals to consumers. Conversely, if such strong appeals cannot be used effectively, then the advertising opportunity is not so great.

A fifth condition of importance is whether the concern's operations provide *substantial sums with which to advertise and promote* its products in the markets it seeks to reach. Advertising must be done on a scale large enough to make an effective impression upon its market. Consequently, the size of the advertising fund is an important consideration in an appraisal of advertising's opportunity. The matter of an advertising fund for any period depends upon the number of units of the product which can be sold in the period and upon the margin available for advertising. The size of the margin depends very largely upon the effectiveness of advertising in influencing consumer valuations for a product. This influence of advertising, in turn, is dependent upon the extent and significance of product differentiation and upon the strength of appeals which may be employed to present the differentiated qualities. The amount of margin available for aggressive selling work depends also upon conditions of competition within an industry, that is, whether competition is carried on in price or in nonprice forms.

Other conditions which may bear upon the opportunity of individual concerns to make effective use of advertising in influencing the demand for their brands need not be enumerated, for the five conditions mentioned above are most universal and are of first importance. It should be stressed, however, that the opportunity to use advertising effectively generally depends not so much on the presence of one of these conditions alone, but upon the combination of conditions which exists.[4]

---

[4] Adapted from *ibid.*, pp. 162–65.

when should advertising receive main emphasis in the promotional mix?

After having appraised the opportunity to make profitable use of consumer advertising, the executive is then in a position to determine its relative importance in the selling mix. While consumer advertising may be the only promotional method used in certain exceptional cases, more commonly other selling ingredients, such as personal solicitation and dealer promotional efforts, are likely to be included in the mix. The combination of several promotional methods is often likely to be more effective in producing desired sales results than the exclusive reliance upon one.

The process of determining whether the main burden of selling should be placed upon advertising, with other promotional ingredients occupying supplementary positions in the mix, begins with a careful estimate of the opportunity to make profitable use of each method which appears likely to make a useful contribution to the achievement of desired objectives. Consumer advertising is likely to receive main emphasis under the following conditions: (1) When appraisal indicates that conditions are especially favorable for affecting consumer valuations and for the creation of quick buying action through the use of consumer advertising. (2) When analysis leads to the conclusion that retail personal selling is not important in the profitable marketing of the product. (3) When dealer promotional efforts and other selling methods, if used alone, appear to offer less promise in consummating sales than consumer advertising.

Examples of situations where a firm might be wise to rely primarily upon the pull of consumer advertising to sell its products would include the following: (1) promotion of citrus fruits by the California Fruit Growers Exchange; (2) sale of proprietary medicines such as Geritol; (3) sale of highly individualized grocery specialties such as Maxim freeze dry coffee; (4) promotion of cosmetics and beauty preparations such as Miss Clairol Shampoo Formula; (5) sale of individualized dentifrices such as Mint Crest.

other problems of advertising management

If a careful appraisal indicates that there is a profitable opportunity to make effective use of advertising, the executive responsible for the management of the advertising force faces additional problems. (1) A decision must be reached on how much to spend upon advertising. (2) Media to carry the advertising message must be selected. (3) Arrangements must be made for the preparation of effective advertisements. (4) Steps should be taken to measure the effectiveness of advertising, through pretesting and posttesting, where appropriate, as a means of maximizing returns from the money spent. The task of preparing and placing effective advertisements is usually turned over to an advertising agency. The agency also assists in the selection of media, in recommending how much to spend, and in devising means of measuring the results of advertising.

Space does not permit detailed discussion of these problems of advertising management. They constitute the subject matter of courses in promotional strategy and advertising management.[5]

personal selling

Personal selling is a second important order-getting ingredient available to the executive responsible for determining the promotional mix. It involves face-to-face contact between the seller or his representative and the prospective buyer. Among others, the purpose of such personal contacts may be: (1) to get an order for the product; (2) to get retailers actively to promote and display the product at the point of purchase; (3) to get wholesalers to cooperate with the manufacturer by selling the products actively or by encouraging retailers to tie-in at the point of purchase with the seller's advertising and promotional efforts; and (4) to educate those who may influence purchase to favor the company and its product.

Personal solicitation differs from advertising in that the selling message is delivered by personal contact as opposed to presentation through nonpersonal media such as newspapers, magazines, television, or industrial papers. For this reason, the salesman may adapt his message to the needs, interests, and reactions of the prospect. The same advertising message, however, is delivered to all who see or hear the particular medium carrying the advertisement. Herein lies an important difference between advertising and personal selling.

Several different kinds of personal selling may be distinguished. Most familiar, perhaps, is retail selling as illustrated by the activities of the clothing salesman in a men's shop. While the activities of the automobile salesman also illustrate retail selling, they often involve

---

[5] For a discussion of these topics, see J. F. Engel, H. G. Wales, and M. R. Warshaw, *Promotional Strategy* (Homewood, Ill.: Richard D. Irwin, Inc., 1967), Parts III, IV, and VI.

contacts with prospects in their homes rather than in the dealer's place of business. House-to-house selling by the representatives of a manufacturer such as the Fuller Brush Company illustrate a third type of approach. A fourth would be personal contacts with industrial users by the salesmen of a firm manufacturing producers goods. The sale of electronic computers to manufacturers by the representatives of International Business Machines would illustrate this type of sales job. A fifth type would be the manufacturer's salesmen calling upon wholesalers as is illustrated by the representatives of the R. J. Reynolds Tobacco Company who take orders for Winston filter cigarettes from tobacco, drug, and grocery wholesalers. The manufacturer who has his salesmen call directly upon retailers would illustrate a sixth kind of selling. Here an example would be the salesmen of Standard Brands, Inc., selling coffee, tea, and yeast to grocery retailers. A seventh kind of selling job is that of the salesman for a wholesaler whose function is to take orders from retailers. The salesmen of wholesale distributors representing the General Electric Company in calling upon dealers who retail color television sets would illustrate this type of selling.

In each of the above examples, the main function of the salesman is to secure an order. Manufacturers distributing through wholesalers, who in turn sell to retailers, also may use missionary salesmen in carrying out their marketing plans. Missionary salesmen are sometimes used to extend distribution by getting orders from retailers and turning them over to wholesalers to be filled. Missionary salesmen may also call upon retailers for the purpose of encouraging them to promote and display the manufacturer's brand more actively. On such calls, the salesman may help the dealer plan advertising and display activities featuring the company's brand, may set up window or floor displays, may train retail salesclerks to sell more effectively, or may simply encourage the dealer to tie in more aggressively with the manufacturer's promotional program.

In the sale of prescription drugs, manufacturers customarily use "detail men" who perform missionary selling functions. In this field, however, they are generally assigned the task of calling upon physicians and pharmacists in order to inform them about new drugs being introduced or promoted. If appropriate, samples may be provided. The task of the detail man is thus basically educational; generally he is not expected to seek orders. If the pharmacist does place an order, however, it is usually turned over to a drug wholesaler for handling provided such a middleman is the customary source of supply.

The introduction of Pablum baby cereal, by Mead Johnson & Company illustrates a situation where the main burden of selling was placed upon detail men. In keeping with Mead Johnson's status as a pharmaceutical house strongly identified with ethical drug specialties, Pablum was distributed through the drug trade. The product was promoted entirely through physicians by Mead Johnson sales representatives.[6]

factors influencing the use of personal selling

Whether the manufacturer sets up a sales force to call upon ultimate consumers or industrial users is influenced by decisions on distribution policy of a type which have been previously discussed. Thus, if a decision is reached to distribute through middlemen instead of selling directly to the consumer or industrial user, then the manufacturer relies upon the dealers to furnish the kinds and amounts of personal sales contact with prospects that appears to be essential. If personal contact is essential, he may then seek types of dealers who have the necessary sales organizations to perform the desired task. To make sure that his brand is supported by effective personal selling by middlemen, he may also assist dealers to do a better job of selecting and training salesmen.

Whether a manufacturer organizes a sales force to call upon retailers is likewise determined largely by decisions on distribution policy. The seller has the alternative of selling directly to retailers or of relying upon wholesalers to provide the necessary retail sales contacts. If a decision is reached to use wholesalers, the task of maintaining sales contact with dealers rests upon their shoulders. Under some conditions, however, the manufacturer may decide to set up a missionary sales force to supplement the work of the wholesalers' sales representatives. Whether a missionary sales organization is necessary will depend in part upon the kind of support which may be expected from the salesmen of the wholesaler. If the wholesalers' lines are wide, and salesmen are little more than order takers, occasions may arise when the manufacturer feels that missionary salesmen would be desirable to provide more aggressive contact with retailers. If the company plans to introduce a new product, special effort will be needed in order to gain distribution through retail outlets. Missionary salesmen are often used

[6] L. L. Duke, *Packaging Problems in Redesigning a Product Line (American Management Association Packaging Series No. 42* [New York, American Management Association, Inc]) , pp. 31–32.

temporarily to help build distribution for the new line. Where active dealer promotion and display is desired as a tie-in with the manufacturer's advertising effort, missionary salesmen may be used to encourage the necessary retail cooperation. Of course, the use of missionary salesmen is justified only where enough additional sales result from such effort to justify the additional expense incurred.

Where wholesalers are used, most manufacturers will set up a sales organization to maintain sales contracts with them. Except where advertising is strong enough to pull the brand through channels of distribution, the manufacturer is likely to rely upon personal selling to make sure that his brand is stocked and given the customary sales support by the wholesalers' sales organizations. Where consumer advertising is especially effective, as may be the case with individual brands of patent medicines, for example, firms have been known to operate without a sales organization and to rely upon securing orders from wholesalers by mail. Such cases are rare, however.

Even where distribution is achieved through middlemen, the manufacturer is still faced with the problem of determining whether personal selling to consumers or industrial users should be included in the marketing mix. If best results appear to come through emphasis on personal contact with consumers at the point of purchase, the manufacturer will want to take active steps to influence dealers to provide the necessary personal sales effort to reap maximum returns. Experience indicates that the following considerations tend to determine the wisdom of including personal solicitation of ultimate consumers or industrial users in the selling mix.

Personal salesmanship appears to be an effective method when the size of the purchase is relatively large, when the product has features which require explanation and demonstration, when the item is purchased at infrequent intervals, and when prospects already own old models of the product upon which they will want a trade-in allowance.

When a consumer has to sacrifice a considerable amount of his surplus for discretionary spending in order to buy a television set, a mechanical refrigerator, an automobile, or a home, it takes persuasion on the part of a salesman to overcome the natural resistance to purchase which is likely to be felt. Likewise, when the installation of a textile machine involves an expenditure of $30,000, those responsible for the buying decision may need a certain amount of urging to bring themselves to the point of signing an order. Aggressive personal selling tends to be an essential method of marketing such items.

Again, there are a number of products like an automobile, a television set, a private airplane, and a broaching machine, with features which need to be explained and demonstrated in order to facilitate purchase. Catalog descriptions, direct mail, or other types of printed or oral advertisements, cannot explain a complicated product nearly so well as a salesman who, at the same time, can also show how the product operates. For this reason, personal selling to consumers or users tends to occupy a key part in the sale of such products.

If a product has a relatively long life and thus need not be repurchased for some time, the owner may tend to postpone buying a new model until absolute necessity forces the issue. Automobiles and household appliances would fall in this class. As a means of increasing sales by speeding obsolescence, many of the manufacturers of such products make it a practice to redesign their products periodically. Such action opens up the possibility of encouraging earlier replacement than might normally occur. The normal consumer tendency to procrastinate in making such a purchase still must be dealt with, however. The salesman is especially effective in helping to make the owner of an old model car realize fully how out-of-date his automobile really is. Where the life of the product is long and replacement may be delayed, therefore, personal selling coupled with the introduction of significantly improved new models may be used to stimulate replacement earlier than would normally occur.

There are a number of products like automobiles, trucks, sewing machines, vacuum cleaners, and even television sets, where it is common practice for the owner of an old model to seek a trade-in allowance on the purchase of the new product. Such allowances are generally the result of bargaining; face-to-face negotiations between prospect and salesman are required to deal most effectively with such a transaction. Personal selling tends to be common practice in the handling of such products.[7]

In the marketing of certain industrial goods a survey of the prospect's needs is an essential preliminary to the making of a sale. Heavy installation equipment may sometimes need special adaptations in order to fit into the prospect's production line. Installation service may also need to be planned. In such cases, personal contact between the manufacturer's sales force and the industrial user is an essential element in the selling plan.

when should personal selling receive main emphasis?

Consideration of the factors outlined above enables the executive to make an estimate of the opportunity to make profitable use of

---

[7] Adapted from J. D. Scott, *Advertising Principles and Problems*, © 1953, pp. 321–22. Reprinted by permission of Prentice-Hall, Inc., Englewood Cliffs, New Jersey.

personal solicitation in the selling program.[8] The question next arises as to when it is likely to be desirable to place the main burden upon personal solicitation in the selling mix. If the product is distributed through middlemen, such an approach involves getting the retailer or the industrial distributor to organize and maintain an effective personal selling organization. From what already has been said, it is clear that the policy of placing the main burden upon personal selling would tend to be desirable when two sets of conditions are present. (1) Circumstances would have to be unfavorable to the profitable use of consumer advertising to stimulate either primary or selective demand. Otherwise, a balanced program including both advertising and personal selling would seem to be indicated. (2) Conditions would have to be favorable to the profitable use of personal selling.

An example of a situation where the main burden should be placed upon personal selling would be in the marketing of electronic computers. Advertising to users would tend to occupy a relatively minor role because of the high price of such equipment and the infrequency with which such installations are made. These same factors, along with the need for explaining how the computer can be used in different situations and the necessity for adaptation of the installation to individual circumstances, would indicate the necessity for heavy reliance on personal solicitation.

other problems of sales force management

Once the decision has been made to include personal selling in the marketing mix, then a number of important problems arise for consideration by the manager of the sales force. Among the more significant are: (1) how to recruit and select salesmen of the desired caliber; (2) how to train new salesmen so that they will perform their functions effectively; (3) what methods of compensation to use; (4) how to stimulate the men to exert maximum effort on the job; (5) how to supervise the men so that they will make the most of the opportunities existing in their territories; (6) how to determine the territories in which the men are to operate; and (7) how to evaluate the salesmen's performance. Space does not permit the discussion of these problems of sales force management. Those interested will find these topics dis-

---

[8] For the results of a landmark study of the personal selling function, see P. J. Robinson and Bent Stidsen, Marketing Science Institute, *Personal Selling in a Modern Perspective* (Boston: Allyn & Bacon, Inc., 1967).

cussed in specialized sales management texts and in advanced courses in this field.[9]

dealer promotion

Dealer promotion is a third order-getting ingredient which many manufacturers may want to include in the selling mix. Dealer promotion efforts may include various kinds of advertising, window and interior displays, demonstrations of the product, use of consumer contests, use of premiums, use of combination offers, distribution of free samples, and other activities designed to promote the sale of a given brand.[10] Regardless of how limited or how extensive the promotional efforts desired of the retail dealer in the promotion of a manufacturer's brand, it should be noted that the retailer's voluntary cooperation must be enlisted if the project is to succeed. Before the dealer can be led to promote a manufacturer's brand, he must be convinced that it is to his advantage to do so. Securing retail cooperation in promotional work, therefore, requires careful planning and execution on the part of the manufacturer. In considering whether to include dealer promotion in the selling mix, accordingly, the problems involved in getting the desired cooperation should be kept in mind.

At the outset, it is obvious that only those manufacturers or producers who distribute through retail dealers or industrial distributors will be concerned with whether to include dealer promotion in the selling mix. Among those who would not use this selling method would be: (1) manufacturers selling by mail order to consumers or users; (2) firms whose salesmen call directly upon the consumer or user; and (3) producers who sell their products to chains or department stores to be marketed under the distributor's private brand.

It is also noteworthy that the need for identifying the retail middleman with the manufacturer's brand is related to the firm's distribution policy. Thus, where the policy of selected retail distribution is followed, it becomes essential for the manufacturer to take active steps to see to it that the local source of supply is identified with his brand.

Under the policy of selected distribution, a relatively small percentage of the available retail outlets will stock the manufacturer's brand; where exclusive agency representation is followed, it will be only a

---

[9] See W. J. Stanton and R. H. Buskirk, *Management of the Sales Force* (rev. ed.; Homewood, Ill.: Richard D. Irwin, Inc., 1964).

[10] This discussion adapted by permission from Scott, *op. cit.*, chap. vii.

single retailer in the community. Unless the local source of supply identifies himself with the manufacturer's brand through signs, window displays, and advertising over his own name, the demand created by the manufacturer's general advertising may be dissipated because of the consumer's lack of knowledge of where to go in order to buy the product. Failure to recognize the importance of this matter may result in ineffective general advertising.

Among those manufacturers who distribute through retail middlemen, two contrasting types of promotional strategy may be distinguished. One approach involves pulling the product through channels of distribution by placing main emphasis on a strong program of consumer advertising. Where this is the approach, dealer promotion is used in a supplementary role. A contrasting method is to rely upon dealer push to consummate sales. Here the manufacturer relies upon his dealers to promote his brand locally through retail advertising, window and interior displays, or other promotional devices. Accordingly, the manufacturer's efforts are primarily directed at the dealer in order to encourage him to promote the brand aggressively. Dealer sales and advertising helps may also be provided as a means of facilitating the dealer's promotional work. The manufacturer, however, undertakes little or no consumer advertising on behalf of his brand.

when should dealer promotion carry the main burden?

Under what conditions would it appear to be wise to place the main burden of selling upon dealer promotion? The first condition which would encourage an executive to consider this strategy would be the lack of an opportunity to stimulate a profitable demand through consumer advertising. Since a poor consumer advertising opportunity may stem from several conditions, let us comment briefly upon some of the more important possibilities. At the same time, let us consider whether these conditions would tend to interfere with the possibility of getting effective dealer push.

Where the product is relatively standardized, the opportunity to make profitable use of consumer advertising tends to be limited. A standardized item such as cheesecloth, however, may be sold profitably by retailers provided it is displayed on aisle tables where there is considerable consumer traffic. Thus, the Claybon Company persuaded a department store to carry a special display of cheesecloth in handy-sized packages for one week. During this test period, the store sold 25,000 yards, which was 50 percent of its previous yearly sales. Dealer displays would therefore appear to offer a promising method of promoting the sales of a standardized item of this sort.

Again, when the important qualities of the product may easily be judged at the point of purchase, the possibility of stimulating brand discrimination through consumer advertising is very limited. This tends to be the situation in the sale of inexpensive children's toys, where prospects tend to select the product on the basis of personal observation of the qualities of design, color, and motion represented in the individual items. Nevertheless, these surface qualities lend themselves particularly well to effective retail advertising and to attention-getting window and interior displays. Dealer push would thus be an especially fruitful method of promoting the sale of children's toys.

Likewise, products likely to be purchased on impulse lend themselves especially well to sale through displays at points where a large number of consumers pass by. Items such as candy, neckties, inexpensive costume jewelry, and perfume fall in this category. Even though such products may not provide an opportunity for profitable use of consumer advertising, they may be sold effectively by getting retailers to display them in busy locations.

In contrast to the foregoing products, there are items with few important hidden qualities, in the purchase of which consumers are willing to exert more effort. Women's dresses are a good example. Qualities such as style, color, and type of material are surface characteristics which may be appraised by the consumer in the retail store. Yet women are willing to make a special trip into town and visit several stores in the process of buying a new dress. Products in this class may also be sold very effectively not only through window and store displays but also through retail advertising. Getting retailers actively to advertise and display such products is therefore sound strategy.

There are some products in the sale of which the retailer's name is likely to be more important than the manufacturer's brand. Rayon cloth manufactured by Burlington Mills is a good example of such an item. Bedspreads, curtains, tablecloths, shower curtains, bath mats, fiber rugs, and window blinds, among others, are other examples of such products. Although the influence of fashion, the lack of hidden qualities, and the absence of individualizing features may tend to make the producer's brand unimportant, such items may be sold effectively through display. Manufacturers of such products might well aim at getting adequate dealer promotion as the key point in their selling strategy.

Finally, there are situations where the product is distinctive and has hidden qualities but will not support an adequate expenditure for consumer advertising. A limited market, price resistance, or infrequency of purchase may prevent the early response needed to cover advertising costs. Or the firm may be handicapped by limited financial resources. Under these conditions, there is much to be said in favor of adopting the inexpensive strategy of encouraging active dealer display and promotion of the firm's brand.

when advertising is emphasized, how necessary is dealer promotion?

In the preceding section, conditions were outlined under which a manufacturer would be wise to follow the strategy of placing primary emphasis upon getting retailers actively to advertise, display, and sell his brand. When the main selling burden should be placed upon consumer advertising, however, how necessary is dealer promotion? Carefully conducted sales tests demonstrate that window displays of nationally advertised brands tend to stimulate substantial sales increases in the store where the displays are located.

Similar tests of the use of interior displays appear to show conclusively that an advertised product would benefit considerably by being promoted in an appropriate manner within the retail store.

There are a number of conditions which tend to explain why window and interior displays increase the retail sales of even those brands which are most responsive to the pull of consumer advertising.

1. The effectiveness of advertising designed to create a brand discrimination is enhanced by window and store displays which reinforce the advertising message, serve as a reminder of a need, and encourage an immediate purchase.

2. Where a product is purchased infrequently, brand advertising is especially dependent upon window and store displays to recreate buying urges which have become dormant, to remind of a need, and to encourage immediate action.

3. Where a substantial portion of customers shop for the generic product in a self-service store, prominent display at the point of purchase tends to stimulate sales.

4. Since a substantial portion of those who trade in self-service stores do not arrive with a shopping list, point-of-purchase displays serve to remind them of what they need.

5. Any brand which is purchased on impulse by a portion of the buyers will tend to benefit from point-of-purchase display.

Retail advertisements tend to enhance the effectiveness of a manufacturer's brand advertising. They provide the additional stimulus which may be needed to convert a brand preference into a buying urge. They add to the penetration of the advertising message within a local market. They serve as reminders of a need.

Of course, there are some highly individualized patent remedies of a personal nature which are sold entirely on the basis of consumer advertising without the support of either display or retail personal selling. Lydia Pinkham's Vegetable Compound is such a product. In such instances very powerful buying motives, together with a lack of substitutes as far as the consumer is concerned, results in the buyer asking for the product by brand name. Because the brand satisfies a strong need on the part of the consumer, its purchase tends to be planned and not made on impulse. Under these circumstances, display at the point of purchase assumes a position of relatively small importance. Such examples are in the minority, however.

It is apparent from the foregoing discussion that with some exceptions, even where the main selling burden is placed upon consumer advertising, the addition of retail advertising, display, and promotional efforts tend to enhance the effectiveness of the promotional program. Although dealer promotion would thus appear to be an essential part of the selling mix in the majority of these instances, we should not lose sight of the fact that its position is strictly supplementary to consumer advertising.

when retail personal selling is emphasized, how necessary is dealer promotion?

In an earlier discussion, it was pointed out that retail personal selling tends to be effective when the size of purchase is large, when the items need explanation and demonstration, when purchase is infrequent, and where trade-in allowances are offered on old models. When the main emphasis is placed upon retail personal selling, how necessary is dealer advertising, display, and promotional effort?

If the manufacturer follows the policy of selected retail distribution, it is important for him to take active steps to make certain that his dealers identify themselves as the local source of supply. Otherwise, the desire to examine the brand before making a buying decision may be frustrated by lack of knowledge of where to go for a demonstration. Although a diligent search might uncover the name of a dealer, the manufacturer would be well advised to make it as easy as possible for the prospect to acquire the necessary information. Advertising over the dealer's name, store identification signs, and window displays thus serve a useful purpose in helping to bring prospects into contact with retail salespeople.

Where the price is relatively high, as in the case of a color TV set, the prospect has to sacrifice a substantial portion of the family's surplus for discretionary spending in order to make the purchase. If the product also has a relatively long life and thus is replaced infrequently, the natural resistance to the price may lead the prospect to postpone the purchase. Under these conditions, the manufacturer's brand advertising needs to be supplemented by strong direct-action stimuli designed to get prospects to visit the dealer's store and examine the new model. Since dealers tend to favor advertising designed to bring an immediate response, the manufacturer may find it wise to encourage active dealer advertising and promotion.

If a product requires aggressive personal salesmanship by the dealer's organization, this effort may be made most effective if it is supported by an active program of dealer promotion. The retail salesmen need to be assisted in making contact with likely prospects. Retail advertising, display, and promotion will tend to bring such prospects into the store or stimulate them to inquire by telephone or mail. With such assistance the salesman can make the most effective use of his time and his persuasive talents.

methods of encouraging dealer promotion

After determining the role of dealer promotion in the selling mix, the manufacturer then faces the problem of selecting suitable methods for encouraging the desired degree of dealer support. A common method is to provide retailers with dealer helps which will aid them in their display, promotional, and advertising work. Some firms offer dealer cooperative advertising allowances as a means of encouraging local advertising. Others rely upon the persuasive efforts of their salesmen to encourage dealers to tie in with the manufacturers' general advertising by using retail advertisements, window displays, counter displays, and other promotional methods. Factors to be considered in selecting proper methods include: (1) how important active dealer promotion is believed to be; (2) whether distribution is selected or nonselected; (3) competitive practice; and (4) relative cost of alternative methods.

consumer promotions

A fourth classification of order-getting ingredients includes various types of short-run consumer promotions designed to stimulate a quick buying response—contests, premiums, combination offers, coupons, and consumer price-offs, among others. Since these devices employ strong direct-action stimuli to force immediate purchasing action, they may also be termed "forcing methods." The basic appeal is to the desire for a bargain or to get something for nothing. Closely related are various types of trade promotions such as free goods, allowances, and special discounts which are designed to influence reseller cooperation. Such methods relate to the task of stimulating dealer promotion, previously discussed.

Consumer promotions are designed to achieve quick impact at the point of purchase, possibly along with one or more underlying goals. Specific objectives commonly identified include the following:[11]

1. Getting prospects to try a new product (through "forced sampling").
2. Calling attention to improvements in established products.
3. Stopping the loss of old customers resulting from vigorous competition.
4. Encouraging active point-of-purchase display and promotion.
5. Helping and stimulating the firm's sales force.

The use of consumer promotions is highly controversial. Some argue that their use is harmful, since it diverts advertising and promotional effort away from the merits of the product and toward the contest, the premium, or the bargain which is being offered. Others say consumer promotions are a useful way to stimulate "forced sampling" of a new product or to inject interest in an advertising campaign through the "change of pace" provided by a creative consumer promotion. Others adopt their use as a defensive measure in an attempt to nullify the effect of competitors' consumer promotions.

Obviously, the need for strong stimuli in the promotional program depends upon whether or not an early buying response may be expected to result from the combined impact of consumer advertising, personal selling, and dealer promotion. Quick buying action may be expected (1) where strong, dynamic appeals may be made to consumer

---

[11] From the Marketing Science Institute, *Promotional Decisions Using Mathematical Models,* p. 10. © Copyright 1967 by Allyn & Bacon, Inc., Boston.

buying motives; (2) when the price of the product is small and the potential market is relatively large; (3) if promotion appears at a time when consumers' needs for the generic product are greatest; and (4) where the product is bought frequently. If these conditions are met, there is little need for using consumer promotions to force an early response. Where such conditions do not exist, however, the use of consumer promotions may properly be considered.

Even where a strong stimulus appears to be necessary to achieve a desired degree of early buying response, the wisdom of including a consumer promotion in the mix tends to depend upon the following considerations.[12]

1. In addition to a quick buying response, what underlying objectives does management wish to achieve through the use of the proposed consumer promotion? (See common objectives listed above.) Are these goals in harmony with, or antagonistic to, the objectives established for other elements in the promotional mix?

2. In planning the introduction of new products, would a properly designed consumer promotion plus consumer advertising be likely to stimulate more prospects to sample the product than the use of consumer advertising alone? Considerable buyer resistance must usually be overcome to get prospects to switch brands and try a new product. Properly designed consumer promotions may stimulate forced sampling at a lower cost than distribution of free samples door to door, through the mail, or via space advertising. If the new brand is superior to competing products and its qualities may be appraised through usage, a properly chosen promotion would appear to be wise. This is especially true where frequent repurchase of the brand may be anticipated if it meets with consumer favor. If the product cannot be evaluated through usage and purchase is infrequent, the advantage of using a promotion may be limited, and its cost may not be justified by the incremental revenue produced.

3. Does a relatively large percentage of the prospective buyers of the generic product lack brand loyalty? That is, would they be willing to accept any one of several leading brands (including the firm's brand), or do they have no brand discrimination at all? This may be the case where the generic product has reached the stage of maturity in its life cycle and the leading brands have all been improved until they are equally satisfactory to the consumer. If the firm's brand is equally as good as competition, then a portion of the prospects who buy it

---

[12] Adapted by permission from Scott, *op. cit.*, chap. vi.

under the stimulus of a consumer promotion will tend to make repeat purchases after the promotion is withdrawn.

4. Are competitors likely to retaliate with similar strong inducements to win back lost customers and to maintain their shares of industry? If so, then gains from consumer promotions may tend to be temporary. Ultimate winners in such a tug-of-war would tend to be the firms offering the most imaginative and creative types of promotions against the background of effective promotional and marketing mixes.

5. Are prospective buyers partially sold by advertising? Some firms use consumer promotions periodically to make customers out of prospects who have been previously influenced by advertising but who may still be in the "twilight zone of indecision." Such action would appear to be helpful where primary and selective appeals used in advertising are not strong enough to lead a substantial portion of prospects to take quick buying action. The habit of buying at infrequent intervals would also tend to increase the number of partially sold prospects over what might be expected where users make repeat purchases frequently. Carefully spaced use of consumer promotions would tend to provide partially sold prospects with a reason for choosing the firm's brand.

6. Will the promotion tend to build up the audience for the firm's TV or radio programs? If so, this will tend to make its advertising more effective.

7. Will the forcing method help get valuable free publicity for the brand? If so, and this publicity is of the proper type, it may add significantly to the effectiveness of the promotional effort.

8. Will the consumer promotion assist and stimulate the company's sales force? Wisely planned promotions used at properly spaced intervals may make retailers more receptive to sales effort and may serve as a device to stimulate the sales organization.

9. Will forcing methods tend to encourage active dealer promotion? If properly planned and tested, promotions tend to bring quick action at the point of purchase. Anticipation of such results may tend to stimulate dealers to tie in with appropriate display and promotion in support of the brand.

Consumer promotions are short-run tactical devices aimed at stimulating an early response at the point of purchase. Applied under proper circumstances, along with other elements in the promotional mix, short-run gains may result from their use. Long-run benefits of using promotions are more problematical, however. Where they are used to promote forced sampling of a new product, long-run benefits may indeed result. When they are utilized in the promotion of well-known established brands, increases in share of market are usually temporary.

Under what circumstances might we expect the use of a promotion to prove an exception to the common experience and achieve long-run gains? The following questions are suggestive: (1) Will consumers like the brand when they try it? (2) Are price, distribution methods, and advertising policies favorable to the improvement of the brand's competitive position? (3) Have successive and frequent use been made of forcing methods so that smaller and smaller incremental gains may be expected?

While such considerations may help to identify circumstances where both short-run and long-run gains may be anticipated, a recent Marketing Science Institute study summarizes the limitations of our knowledge on this topic as follows:

It is plain that promotion plays an important role in marketing, but our knowledge of its effectiveness is lacking. The unfortunate facts that many promotional efforts seem to be prosaic, that no distinct goals are set, that postaudits are unimaginative, and that brand profits are jeopardized by intrinsic risks or wrong decisions may be attributed primarily from our inability to effectively tailor promotional endeavors to particular products, markets and circumstances. This problem of promotional selection is essentially the executive's responsibility, although effective research can assist in narrowing the areas for unaided judgment.[13]

As a means of improving decision making in this area, this MSI study emphasizes the following points: (1) the desirability of establishing explicit goals for consumer promotions; (2) the need of writing down such objectives so that all participants in the company's marketing effort will see what they are expected to do to achieve the desired objectives; (3) the wisdom of evaluating past performance to develop guidelines for the present and future; (4) the need of conducting scientifically designed tests or experiments to guide in decision making; and (5) the necessity of making carefully planned postaudits of both short-run and long-run results of consumer promotions used.

The primary purpose of the MSI study was to explain and demonstrate some applications of quantitative techniques, using real data, to measure and evaluate market response to promotions. While space does not permit a discussion of the quantitative methods used, those interested will find it rewarding to examine the study itself for further information.

---

[13] Marketing Science Institute, *Promotional Decisions Using Mathematical Models,* *op. cit.,* p. 17. Reprinted by permission of the publisher.

As you think back over the preceding discussion, it is apparent that the task of determining the promotional mix includes the following steps. (1) Decide which of the various available promotional methods to include in the mix. Factors to consider in appraising the opportunity to make effective use of consumer advertising, consumer promotions, personal selling, and dealer promotion have been outlined in the previous pages. (2) Determine whether it is likely to be most profitable to place the main burden of selling upon consumer advertising, personal selling, dealer promotion, or other selling methods chosen for use. Estimates of the relative suitability of these several methods will guide this decision. (3) Reach a decision on how supplementary promotional methods may be combined with the method to be emphasized in order to perform necessary selling tasks and to achieve maximum effectiveness from the total mix. Most promotional programs are a combination of several methods. This fact highlights the need for careful integration of methods chosen to comprise a well-coordinated total program. This desired coordination may be achieved through a careful definition of sales and promotional tasks and the intelligent choice of the various methods to be used in performing these necessary tasks. The use of checklists showing tasks to be performed and methods selected to achieve desired goals may be helpful in achieving proper integration of effort. Timing schedules listing jobs to be done and those responsible for their performance may also assist in bringing about the necessary coordination.

While the generalizations outlined above may be of assistance in the determination of an effective promotional mix, preliminary decisions based upon desk analyses should be checked by local area test campaigns wherever suitable and possible. Procedures should also be set up for measuring the results of the various promotional methods utilized. Such information will provide the basis for modification and improvement in subsequent campaigns in the light of previous experience.

Adaptive Planning and Control Sequence (APACS)

The foregoing discussion of the determination of the promotional mix focuses on the decision-making process and discusses the considerations to be taken into account in analyzing the various subissues involved in working out a solution to the problem of how best to sell a given product. Let us now turn briefly to a Marketing Science Institute study of the process of promotional decision making based upon procedures followed in 12 companies and involving interviews with 100 key personnel within these organizations and their advertising agencies.[14] This will serve to position our discussion within the total planning and control sequence involved in the allocation of funds among the elements of the promotional mix and will also introduce the topic of determination of the promotional budget which follows.

The MSI study was concerned with how funds for the promotional mix of advertising, personal selling, and sales promotion are allocated in the marketing of new products. It covers the process of promotional decision making from the time work is begun on planning the program to the allocation of funds for specific activities. Out of the analysis of the practices of the 12 companies, a conceptual model of the decision-making process was developed. It is called the "Adaptive Planning and Control Sequence," or "APACS." According to this conceptual model, the promotional decision-making process is a series of eight steps, each of which is listed and described briefly below.

1. *Define problem and set objectives.* Define problem associated with promotional actions to be planned, and set objectives conforming with overall corporate goals.

2. *Appraise overall situation.* Determine market potentials, manufacturing costs, pricing policies, competitive activities, channels of distribution, buying habits and motivations, and practical constraints; and review past experience.

3. *Determine tasks and identify means.* Define subgoals to be accomplished and identify appropriate means to achieve these aims.

4. *Identify alternative plans and mixes.* Delineate feasible alternative marketing strategies and promotional mixes, and identify additional information required.

5. *Estimate expected results.* Employ judgment and analogous experience, field tests, and any suitable management science techniques to forecast results in terms of accepted performance criteria (for example, market share, sales quota, profit).

6. *Review and decision by management.* Submit line and staff advice to supplement management's judgment in adopting plans and budgets and delegating authority to conduct approved program.

---

[14] From P. J. Robinson and D. J. Luck, *Promotional Decision Making* (New York: McGraw-Hill Book Co., 1964), chap. iii, and Exhibit 1 opposite p. 244. Copyright 1964 by Marketing Science Institute. Used with permission of McGraw-Hill Company.

7. *Feedback of results and postaudit.* Provide for communication of field data and market intelligence and for monitoring performance of pilot or full-scale operation.

8. *Adapt program if required.* Revise or reaffirm goals, subgoals, and expenditures as necessary.

A. If at this stage (or any other stage in the sequence) agreement cannot be obtained, or the program appears infeasible, return to previous stages and recycle as necessary.

B. Proceed with other problems if satisfactory promotional allocation plan is achieved.

It will be noted that the discussion earlier in this chapter relates especially to steps 3, 4, 5, and 7 in the APACS model.

In summing up their findings, the authors state that their study offers effective evidence that a systematic approach such as the one provided by APACS would benefit promotional decision making. The following deterrents to systematic decision making were identified, among others: failure to maintain records of performance of previous promotional programs, lack of sufficient information about overall corporate goals and objectives, and failure to define specific objectives for promotional activities. It was noted that the tasks of forecasting performance and evaluating risks were two of the decision maker's most perplexing problems. It was also pointed out that there was a need for carefully designed experiments and proper field testing if promotional decision making were to be improved. A better understanding of current techniques for measuring marketing performance was likewise identified as essential.

conclusion

We have turned, in this chapter, from the basic questions of product policy and development, branding, pricing, and selecting channels of distribution to the all-important area of selling the product. To sell one must communicate, so we have described the nature of communication. The special theme of the chapter is the importance of sound promotional strategy and of effective selection of appropriate methods of communication from those available in order to achieve the best promotional mix. The decisions the marketing manager of a manufacturer or producer makes as to emphasis on advertising, personal selling, dealer promotion, or consumer promotion will be crucial to the success of the entire marketing program and of the business. It becomes clear that different products and different marketing situations call for different mixes of selling ingredients.

We now move on, in Chapter 11, to the decisions involved in determining the promotional appropriation.

questions

1. Define "communication." Explain and illustrate the basic elements in a communication system using the following situations:
   a) A Ford Mustang salesman talking with a lower-middle-class prospective buyer who has a three-year-old Fairlane to trade in.
   b) RCA-Victor advertising color television sets in The Netherlands.
   How do these two situations differ? What implications do these differences have for marketing management?
2. What conditions must be present if communication is to be effective?
3. Give examples which illustrate how prior decisions on product, brand policy, distribution policy, and price influence the promotional mix.
4. Using the following as examples, illustrate how the position of a product in its life cycle would tend to influence the character of the promotional mix:
   a) Diet Cola.
   b) Xerox photocopying equipment.
   c) Crest toothpaste.
   d) Turtleneck sweaters for dress wear by men.
5. How might the buying habits of consumers influence the promotional mix for the following products?
   a) Hickey Freeman suits.
   b) Wrigley's Chewing Gum.
   c) Aluminum siding for houses.
6. Explain how the character of middlemen used and their point of view might tend to affect the nature of the promotional mix for the following products:
   a) A new brand of mentholated shaving cream in a aerosol can being introduced by Alberto-Culver.
   b) Cessna aircraft for pleasure and personal use.
   c) Volkswagen automobile.
   d) An imported Japanese camera offered exclusively by a large mail-order house at a special bargain price.
7. Illustrate how the possible size of promotional funds available would tend to influence the character of the promotional mix in the following situations:
   a) Introduction of a new spray deodorant by a firm which had only $50,000 of working capital at the time the marketing program began.

b) Introduction of antiperspirant in an aerosol can by a firm capable of investing $1 million in the first year's promotional effort.

8. Distinguish between (*a*) product advertising and institutional advertising; (*b*) dealer promotion and consumer promotions; (*c*) missionary salesmen and detail men.

9. Using Borden's criteria, appraise the advertisability of the following products (assuming adequate funds available to perform necessary promotional tasks) :

   a) Sugar.

   b) Patent remedy offering a sure cure for athlete's foot.

   c) Toys for three- to five-year-old children (colorful, offering movement and sound).

   d) Fine furniture in colonial styles sold nationally through 40 department stores, each with an exclusive agency for its market.

10. Other things being equal, what influence would the presence or absence of "hidden qualities" have upon the opportunity for making effective use of consumer advertising for the following products?

    a) Pillsbury Cake Mix.

    b) Velvet trousers for young men.

    c) A cold remedy containing antihistamine, decongestant, and aspirin.

11. *a*) What considerations tend to determine the wisdom of using personal selling in the promotional mix?

    b) Would you place the main burden of promotion upon personal selling in the following situations?

       (1) A line of cosmetics.

       (2) A central home air-conditioning system.

       (3) A new brand of freeze-dry coffee.

       (4) A line of apparel offering 200 different styles, including knit suits, dresses, slacks, sweaters, and blouses in casual designs aimed at the homemaker market and sold at modest prices.

12. *a*) Under what circumstances should dealer promotion carry the main burden of selling?

    b) Would you place the main emphasis upon dealer promotion in the sale of the following products?

       (1) Neckties.

       (2) Drapes for the living room.

       (3) A new soft drink with unusual thirst quenching qualities.

       (4) Women's high-grade nylon hosiery.

       (5) Necklaces for men.

13. When advertising is emphasized in the promotional mix, is dealer promotion necessary? In answering apply your analysis to the following products:

    a) Marlboro cigarettes.

b) Toni hair coloring.

c) Maxim freeze dry coffee.

14. When retail personal selling is emphasized, is dealer promotional activity necessary? Answer by applying your analysis to the following products:

a) Hickey Freeman high-grade men's suits.

b) Singer sewing machines.

c) Hi-Fi sound systems.

d) Vacuum cleaners sold through department stores.

15. In the following cases, where dealer promotion is essential, would you favor the use of dealer cooperative advertising allowances to encourage the desired effort, or would you emphasize "merchandising" the advertising to retail dealers to get their support?

a) High-grade men's shoes with selective retail distribution.

b) Medium-grade upholstered furniture.

chapter 11

determining the
promotional
appropriation

Closely related to the decision on the character of the promotional mix is the task of determining the size of the promotional appropriation. If analysis indicates that the main burden should be placed upon consumer advertising, the size of the promotional appropriation is likely to be larger than if the strategy should place primary emphasis on dealer push. Conversely, the size of the expenditure which the product will support and which the company can finance is an important consideration in determining what promotional strategy is likely to be most effective for a given product and in deciding the appropriate combination of promotional methods to include in the selling mix.

The task of determining the promotional appropriation is of key importance, since the ultimate decision will have a significant influence upon the effectiveness of the promotional program and hence upon profits. Therefore, we have singled this problem out for special consideration at this point. Our primary purpose is to provide essential background on the approaches commonly used by executives in determining the appropriation for the total promotional effort in a given year, or in the case of new products, for a period of several years. A secondary goal is to suggest some of the more important considerations to be taken into account in reaching a decision on this important problem.

theoretical analysis of the problem

The marginal approach to the determination of the promotional appropriation provides a useful theoretical framework against which we can later compare actual business practice. This approach is illustrated in Figure 11–1, which is a short-run analysis developed by Joel Dean based upon the following assumptions:[1] (1) Advertising cost is assumed to include all pure selling costs and is identified by the curve *SC*. Incremental advertising costs are the additional expenditures required to produce one additional unit of sales. (2) Incremental production costs are assumed to be constant at 20 cents per unit over the range of output covered in this example. In the short run, this tends to be true for firms whose production is mechanized. (3) Unit price is assumed to be constant at 70 cents over the range of volume under

Figure 11–1. Short-run determination of advertising outlay by marginal analysis.

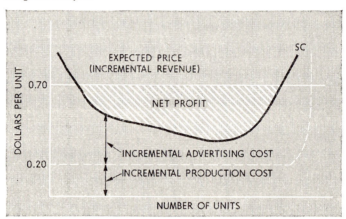

consideration and does not change as a result of changes in selling costs. (4) The relationship between incremental advertising costs (*SC*) and sales volume is assumed to approximate a "U-shaped" curve which first declines as volume increases, then is constant, and then rises at an accelerating rate. Incremental advertising costs (*SC*) may be determined from Figure 11–1 by identifying a given volume of sales and by running a vertical line to intersect curve *SC*. Then run a horizontal line from the point of intersection with *SC* to the vertical axis to read off the corresponding dollars per unit figure shown there —for example, 50 cents. From this figure subtract incremental production costs of 20 cents per unit to get selling costs of 30 cents (50 cents − 20 cents = 30 cents). In this way it may be determined that

[1] Adapted from Joel Dean, *Managerial Economics*, pp. 356–61, © 1951. Reprinted by permission of Prentice-Hall, Inc., Englewood Cliffs, New Jersey.

incremental advertising costs amount to $1 per unit at low volume, decline progressively as sales increase until a low point of 15 cents is reached, and then increase rapidly as volume increases still more until a figure of $1 is reached once again.

What is the rationale behind the U-shaped incremental advertising cost curve? The declining phase is explained in part by the economies of specialization: (1) As the appropriation increases in size, it becomes possible to make use of expert services. (2) Larger expenditures tend to make it possible to use more economical media. Even more important, however, are the economies that come from repetition of the advertising message and the learning that results. The increasing phase of the advertising cost curve results primarily because successively poorer prospects tend to be reached as the advertising expenditures are increased. Then, too, increasing advertising expenditures may progressively exhaust the most vulnerable geographic areas or the most efficient advertising media.

Based on these assumptions, then, how should the advertising appropriation be determined? Clearly it would be profitable to increase advertising expenditures step by step until the incremental costs of advertising and production (as measured by the SC line) intersect the price line (i.e. until these costs are equal to the marginal revenue produced). In terms of the chart, if incremental production cost equals 20 cents and the price amounts to 70 cents, then the gross margin is 50 cents. Accordingly, advertising costs per unit may be increased up to 50 cents per unit. Beyond this amount, the incremental revenue will be less than the incremental costs, the total profits will be reduced.

This analysis, of course, represents an ideal which most firms find difficult if not impossible to achieve. It assumes that the executive is able to make accurate estimates of the effect of advertising upon sales volume. Yet for most firms, the task of measuring the sales generated by advertising is a most challenging—if not impossible—research problem.

Part of the difficulty grows out of the fact that the sales volume achieved in any given year is the effect of both external environmental forces—such as general economic trends, changes in primary demand, competitive activity—and internal influences such as the marketing program. Within the marketing program itself, changes in sales volume may result not only from changes in the level of promotional expenditures but also from changes in the impact of other elements in the marketing mix, such as product improvements, increased effectiveness of the distribution organization, and changes in prices. Finally, there is the problem of tracing any residual changes in sales volume which might result from the total promotional program to the individual elements of which it is comprised—i.e., changes in advertising, in personal selling, or in sales promotional activities. Truly, the task of measuring the sales influence of a single factor such as advertising is a complex, challenging, and often impossible task. While a few firms have been able to devise research approaches which they claim have enabled them to measure the sales results of promotional investments of different size, such organizations are the exception rather than the rule.

Again, this theoretical analysis does not recognize the cumulative effect of past advertising upon current or future sales. Many firms find that only a portion of the results of this year's advertising occur in the form of present sales, while the remainder will tend to carry over into future years. This problem is especially acute in the promotion of products of high unit value and infrequent purchase, such as automobiles. For such firms a sizable proportion of this year's advertising expenditure is likely to pay off in terms of creating awareness, preference, or intent to buy which will tend to influence sales one, two, or more years into the future. At the same time, past advertising will have created attitudes which will lead to current purchases. Since the advertising of many firms has such carry-over effects, the short-run marginal analysis outlined above tends to have only limited value.

In spite of these limitations, this theoretical analysis makes some conceptual contributions of practical importance. If the major part of a firm's advertising is designed to stimulate an immediate response, and if conditions are favorable to such results, then the marginal approach provides a simple test of how much to spend and when to stop. It is also useful in providing management with guidelines as to the kind of information needed in making a decision on how much to spend on advertising. By the same token, it serves as a guide in designing research to evaluate the results of advertising and in gathering information which will help improve the quality of the appropriation decision.

common approaches to determining the appropriation

Now that we have outlined the theoretical approach to the determination of promotional expenditures, let us turn to a consideration of some of the more common approaches followed by business firms in actual practice. Four of the more important alternative methods will be discussed: (1) percentage of sales; (2) all available funds; (3) competitive parity; (4) research objective. While our discussion will be in terms of determining the advertising appropriation, the analysis may be applied equally well to the determination of budgets for personal selling and sales promotional activities.

In making a survey of approaches to the determination of the advertising appropriation for the Association of National Advertisers some years ago, Richard Webster recommended that advertisers use a two-way classification originally suggested by C. M. Edwards and W. H. Howard: (1) breakdown and (2) buildup methods.[2] The breakdown method is described as providing a lump sum to be disbursed by the advertising department as it sees fit, and the buildup method is characterized as an appropriation that tells in detail exactly how the funds are to be expended. Since this classification will aid us in our analysis, let us take a moment to explain the principle upon which it is based.

In the breakdown method, the lump sum granted by management is the control. After the lump sum has been determined, advertising executives work out what they believe to be the most effective division of this amount by different kinds of promotional effort and by types of advertising media. Under this approach, the primary emphasis is placed upon what the firm can afford. In the buildup method, the task to be accomplished by advertising is the control. Once the task has been defined, the budget is built up by determining the kinds and amounts of advertising and promotional efforts needed to achieve the desired goal and by estimating the cost of the necessary program.

percentage of sales[3]

A common approach falling under the breakdown classification is where a lump sum for advertising is determined by multiplying dollar sales by a more or less arbitrarily chosen percentage. In making this computation, either past sales or estimated future sales may be used. The percentage applied may be either fixed—remaining the same over

---

[2] Adapted by permission from Richard Webster, *Setting Advertising Appropriations* (New York: Assoc. of National Advertisers, Inc., 1949), pp. 3–19.

[3] For a more complete discussion of all methods commonly used in determining the advertising appropriation, see A. W. Frey, *How Many Dollars for Advertising* (New York: Ronald Press Co., 1955), pp. 48–82.

a period of years—or variable—changing from year to year. A variation of this plan is to substitute a specified number of dollars per unit for a percentage figure and multiply this figure by unit sales instead of dollar sales.

Fixed versus variable percentage. In evaluating this approach, let us begin by considering the use of a fixed percentage in determining the lump sum available for advertising. This approach is quick and easy. It has the further advantage of keeping the advertising appropriation within what the firm can afford—since expenditures are tied to revenue—indeed, this is the key consideration in such an approach. Then, too, it may lead to competitive stabilization. If all or most of the competitors in an industry used this method and applied the same percentage of sales, competitors' advertising expenditures would be roughly proportional to their market shares. This would tend to have a restraining effect upon advertising competition.

If a fixed percentage is used over a period of several years, however, it is evident that no allowance is being made for the differences in the promotional needs of a new product as compared with the requirements of the same item after it has become established. It also fails to take into account changes in the competitive situation and changes in the responsiveness of prospective buyers as they react to actual or anticipated changes in their incomes, as well as differences in the ability of a firm to finance advertising in periods of prosperity as compared with times of recession.

Of prime significance, however, is the fact that the fixed percentage-of-sales method assumes that the advertising appropriation should be a *result* of sales achieved rather than a *cause* of sales increases. It overlooks the fact that advertising, when appropriately used, has the power of *creating* the income out of which its expenditures may be covered—and that in so doing, it may add to profits.

Some of the objections to the percentage-of-sales method may be removed if the percentage allowed for advertising is changed from year to year. Within the limits of the operating budget, a larger percentage of sales may be set aside to help introduce a new product than would be provided when the new brand has achieved an established place for itself in the market. Subject to the limitations of the budget, the percentage may also be changed to reflect changes in competition, responsiveness of buyers, and business conditions. Since the size of the percentage is still controlled by what the firm can afford in a given year, however, the amount appropriated for advertising will tend to fall far short of what might be made available if management were primarily guided by the size and the nature of the promotional tasks to be accomplished. Where the advertising appropriation is governed primarily by the size of the job to be done in a given year, executives may provide a sum for promotion which results in a substantial current period loss if it is anticipated that revenue in the next year or two will counterbalance this figure and result in long-run profits.

Past sales versus future sales as a base. In the earlier years, the percentage figure was often applied to past sales to arrive at the advertising appropriation. Where this is done, the appropriation is actually made out of "money in the bank," since management has the chance to study actual sales in the previous year, as well as the resulting profits, before deciding on the percentage of past sales to set aside for advertising for the year ahead. This approach may result in appropriations which are either too small or too large, depending on how the sales prospects for the coming year compare with the year just past. This would be especially undesirable in periods which are turning points in the business cycle and where industry sales may, therefore, change more than usual. Looking backward may also lose a firm its best opportunities for maintaining or expanding its position in the industry. Clearly this approach is entirely unsuited to the task of setting the appropriation for a new product. It is apparent from these comments that the major weakness of the use of past sales as a base is the assumption implicit in the approach that advertising follows sales instead of creating them. This limitation is most serious when a fixed percentage of past sales is used. Even though the use of a varying percentage may make partial allowance for changes in the job to be done, the fact that this percentage is applied to past sales may still result in lost opportunities.

Because of these limitations, the percentage of past sales approach has been generally abandoned. Instead, estimated future sales tend to be used as the base by those favoring the percentage of sales (or breakdown) approach. If estimated future sales are taken as the base, then the advertising appropriation will be better adjusted to anticipated market conditions than when past sales are used. There will be less danger of overspending or underspending than when a percentage of past sales is applied.

Of course, the case in favor of using estimated future sales as a base depends upon the ability of executives to estimate future sales results. If experience indicates that their estimates vary widely from actual sales, then it may be unwise to base the advertising appropriation upon a percentage of estimated future sales. If sales forecasts have been reasonably accurate, however, then the practice of using a percentage of estimated future sales is to be preferred over that of applying this percentage to past sales.

We should remember, however, that the percentage-of-future-sales approach still gives primary emphasis to keeping advertising expenditures within the limits of what the firm can afford, taking into account the constraints of the operating budget for the coming year. Giving primary emphasis to what the firm can afford, instead of to the income-producing potentialities of advertising, is still a serious limitation.

Indeed, it is clear that the percentage-of-future-sales approach involves a logical inconsistency. If we agree that the size of the advertising expenditure affects the sales volume achieved, as is certainly the case where a favorable advertising opportunity exists, then how can future sales be estimated without knowing how much is to be spent upon advertising during the coming year?

It is clear from these comments that the variable percentage of estimated future sales is the most defensible variation of this breakdown method. Under what conditions can the best possible case be made for following this approach? (1) If the product is well established and has achieved a satisfactory share of market. (2) If the external environment is relatively static during the period, so that the job to be done by advertising varies little from year to year. (3) If management believes that a substantial change in advertising expenditures would be likely to stimulate strong competitive retaliation. (4) If there is considerable uncertainty as to the effectiveness of advertising and thus some merit in giving considerable emphasis to what the firm can afford in determining the appropriation.

Since this approach treats advertising as an effect rather than a cause, however, it is still, in most instances, a questionable approach for management to use. Instead we might argue that it would be preferable to use an approach which makes the job to be done the guiding principle, and then check the firm's ability to finance the resulting appropriation by expressing it as a percentage of estimated sales.

all available funds

An extreme example of the breakdown approach is where a firm allocates a share of all available liquid resources and borrowable funds to support the advertising program. This approach was followed by

Brooks-Ledford Company in determining the initial advertising appropriation for Galaxy hair dressing and conditioner. Taking into account what portion of the sales dollar was needed to pay for direct production expenses, overhead, and amortization of bank loans, the firm allocated the remainder for selling and advertising expenditures. Salesmen were used in getting distribution and point-of-purchase promotion for Galaxy, while $75,000 was made available for cooperative advertising. This promotional program started Galaxy on its way to becoming a market leader in its field.

Note, however, that the limit of the appropriation following this method is the immediate availability of funds rather than estimated future profits.

The "all-available-funds" approach is likely to come closer to supporting the performance of necessary promotional tasks than when the appropriation is limited to an agreed-upon percentage of sales which fits within the operating budget of a given year. If the advertising opportunity is good, but sales results are likely to be delayed for one or two years, then the allocation of all available funds to promotion may result in more rapid progress toward desired share of industry than when the effort is limited to a percentage of sales which is adjusted to permit current profits on the product.

Even where advertising may be expected to bring highly profitable results ultimately, financial embarrassment may occur if short-run cash and credit limits are ignored in deciding upon advertising expenditures. From the viewpoint of financial management, therefore, there is merit in limiting promotional outlays to what the firm can afford in terms of immediately available funds. If what the firm can afford is interpreted without recognizing the long run income-producing possibilities of effective advertising, however, opportunities for increasing profits through aggressive promotion may be foregone. This is a serious danger, since the controlling principle in appropriating "all available funds" is what the firm can afford to allocate to the promotion of a particular product.

This leads us to the most serious limitation of the all-available-funds approach. It is that there is no logical connection between the availability of funds and the advertising opportunity. This approach may lead a firm to limit the advertising appropriation for a new product to an amount far below the point where marginal revenue produced by advertising is just equal to the marginal cost of the promotional effort. At the other extreme, the advertising budget for a successful, established product may conceivably be pushed beyond the point where the marginal revenue produced is equal to or less than the marginal cost of the effort.

Under what circumstances, then, might this approach be defensible? (1) This method might be justified where there is an excellent opportunity to make use of consumer advertising in the introduction of a new product and where such promotional effort may be expected to produce an early, measurable sales response. Here current profits may well be sacrificed in favor of attaining a sizable market share for the brand and, accordingly, a favorable rate of long-run profits. (2) Where the firm can estimate the marginal effectiveness of advertising, it may result in reasonably satisfactory appropriations as long as the product is operating short of the point where incremental advertising costs and incremental revenue are equal. Note that the use of such knowledge involves a combination of the marginal approach with the all-available-funds method.

At best, then, the all-available-funds approach is only a temporary expedient which may appear to meet the requirements of a new, inadequately financed firm, or a company which is short of working capital because of rapid growth. Circumstances may force the firm to give primary emphasis in setting the advertising appropriation to what the firm can afford. If this is the case, management should be impatient to shift to a more defensible approach as soon as circumstances will permit. We might argue, however, that it would be preferable to approach the determination of the appropriation by estimating the advertising opportunity, by defining desired promotional tasks, and then by considering whether management can find some way to finance the necessary expenditures to implement the desired program.

competitive parity

The guiding principle of the competitive-parity approach is to base the advertising appropriation in some systematic way upon what competitors are doing. One variation is to match competitors' advertising dollars. Another is to use the same percentage of sales for advertising as key competitors use or the same ratio as is representative of the industry. A more sophisticated variation is to make the product's share of industry advertising dollars equal to its share of market.

Is it wise to use the average percentage of sales spent on advertising by the industry as the ratio to be used in setting the advertising appropriation for the firm's own product? Such an approach might be advocated on the grounds that the industry ratio represents the combined wisdom of competitors. It might appeal especially to a firm entering a new market in which it lacks experience. A medium-sized manufacturer of industrial timers, wishing to introduce a new automatic timer to consumers to control lights and appliances automatically, would be a good example. Lacking experience in consumer marketing, the executives of such a firm might be attracted by the idea of basing the advertising appropriation for the new automatic timer upon competitive parity.

Such an approach would, however, be highly questionable. The advertising ratios of individual firms in the industry might be expected to vary considerably from the industry average. In a study of the percentage invested in advertising by 22 manufacturers of small appliances, some years ago, for example, it was reported that the median was 5.12 percent, but the range was from 0.83 to 45.0 percent.[4] Clearly the industry average is of little value as a guide, since the ratios of individual firms may be expected to vary depending upon their size, objectives, share of market, promotional strategy and marketing mix.

Moreover, where industry ratios are available, the data will reflect the advertising decisions of the past year and *not* the ratios planned for the coming year. Yet it is future advertising ratios of individual competitors which would be most useful in working out promotional strategy and the appropriation required to implement such plans. Such data are generally regarded as highly confidential and are closely guarded from competitors.

In spite of these limitations, it might be argued that the competitive-parity approach will tend to safeguard against advertising wars which might result if other methods of setting the appropriation were followed. Here a parallel is being drawn between the retaliation which may result under conditions of oligopoly when one firm makes a drastic price cut. An increase in the amount spent on advertising by one firm, however, is less likely to stimulate quick retaliation from competitors than would a price cut. An increase in advertising effort is harder for competitors to identify. Information on planned appropriations is not customarily made public by the decision maker and estimates of advertising expenditures secured by research organizations through counting advertisements and applying published media rates are generally available only after considerable time lag. Moreover, the results of increased advertising by one firm are difficult for a competitor

---

[4] S. H. Sandage and S. R. Bernstein, *Advertising Expenditures per Dollar of Sales.* Copyright, 1956, University of Illinois and Advertising Publications, Inc.

to measure. These problems tend to slow down competitive retaliation to increased advertising effort.

Even if retaliation is to be expected ultimately, this should not necessarily stop a firm from increasing its advertising of a brand in an effort to expand its share of market. How else can the manufacturer of a new brand with a demonstrable individualizing feature expand sales until a profitable target share of market is achieved? Even though some of the ground gained through increased advertising may be lost later on as a result of competitive retaliation, the net result may still be an increased scale of output together with lower unit production costs which will produce higher long-run profits.

Although competitive parity does not make sense in setting the advertising appropriation for the new brand, this approach may be more defensible for the firm with an established brand which ranks in second or third place in an oligopolistic industry. If the firm is making reasonable profits on its brand, executives may hesitate to provoke retaliation from larger firms in the industry by increasing the advertising ratio substantially—especially if conditions are such that this action is likely to be noticed by competitors.

Even so, the competitive-parity approach provides no guides as to the appropriation strategy which will result in the most favorable long-run profits. The advertising outlays of competitors will, of course, influence the size of the expenditures required to achieve a desired increase in share of market. But the responsiveness of the market to the firm's brand is influenced by other factors, such as the advertising opportunity and the effectiveness of the marketing mix. Accordingly, the industry advertising ratio will be of no value in helping the executive to determine how much advertising expenditures may be increased before the point is reached where the last $1,000 spent on advertising produces just enough additional revenue to cover its cost.

A more sophisticated variation of the competitive-parity approach is to make the product's share of total industry advertising expenditures equal to the brand's desired share of market. That is, if a 35 percent share of market is desired, then the advertising appropriation would be set at a figure which would represent 35 percent of total estimated advertising expenditures for the industry. The idea for this approach grew out of studies of the relationship between percent of industry advertising by a single advertiser and that firm's market position. Preliminary studies of this sort, for example, led one researcher to state the hypothesis that to maintain or increase share of market, the percent of industry advertising for the product involved should be equal to, or exceed, the market position desired. Conversely, if advertising volume as a percent of total industry volume is less than the brand's share of market, it can be forecast that market position will decrease.[5]

This approach is an improvement over using the industry advertising ratio as the base, since consideration of the desired share of market for the brand involves an attempt to define the size of the job which must be performed by advertising during the coming year. It assumes, however, that the desired share of market, say 25 percent, may be achieved by investing 25 percent of estimated industry advertising expenditures in the promotion of the company's brand. This may or may not be true. The market position achieved by a brand tends to be influenced by how it compares with competing brands in terms of product innovation, quality of distribution organization, price-quality relationships, and effectiveness of promotional strategy, as well as the size of the expenditures allocated to personal selling, sales promotion, and finally advertising.

Significant light is thrown on this matter by General Electric's extensive analysis designed to test the hypothesis that there is a direct and measurable relationship between share-of-industry advertising and share-of-industry sales.[6] The study extended over a period of four years and covered 16 different products: 6 major appliance product lines, 5 traffic appliance lines, 1 consumer supply line, and 4 industrial component or supply lines. G. A. Bradford summarized results of this research:

> An objective summary of the study would have to state that the analysis did *not* prove the theory "that there is a direct relationship between share-of-industry advertising and share-of-industry sales." At the same time, it did not *disprove* the theory, but rather underlined the importance of other factors and influences in the selling situations.

He also commented that the tests did provide some hints as to other factors which appeared to influence the relationship under study. (1) High-saturation industries did not show the same sensitiveness to changes in share-of-industry advertising as did low-saturation industries. (2) Significant differences were noted in the advertising payoff enjoyed by the leaders of the industry versus the followers. (3) Evi-

---

[5] C. J. Coward, "A Definitive Approach to Determining the Advertising Budget," *Marketing Times* (Marketing Services, General Electric) , July, 1958, p. 3.

[6] Adapted by permission from G. A. Bradford, "What General Electric Is Doing to Evaluate the Effect on Sales of Its Industrial and Consumer Advertising," a paper presented at the Association of National Advertisers, *Advertisers Evaluation Workshop,* January 27, 1960.

dence would suggest that there is a ceiling on the share of advertising any company should attempt to run. (4) Influences other than advertising can swing the anticipated share of market completely out of the ball park. (5) Predicting the direct influence on sales of any single element in the marketing mix is an unlikely possibility. The only way correlation studies will make an ultimate contribution in the future, he concluded, is to measure and correlate the effect of several key influences on market share at one and the same time.

The approach of making the brand's share-of-industry advertising equal the brand's market share also involves the problem mentioned earlier of being forced to work with past data rather than with information on competitors' planned future advertising outlays. This version of the competitive-parity approach likewise fails to consider whether the required share-of-industry advertising expenditure will be profitable or not. While anticipated advertising activity by competitors should obviously be considered by a firm in determining the appropriation for its product, strict adherence to the competitive-parity approach would, therefore, be unwise. Instead, it may be preferable to undertake experiments in an attempt to determine what share of industry advertising expenditure is required in order to achieve a desired brand market share. The findings which result might then be considered along with other data in working out the decision on next year's advertising appropriation.

research objective

The research-objective approach (sometimes called the objective-and-task approach) is in direct contrast to the methods discussed up to this point.[7] It is a buildup method where the job to be done receives primary emphasis, whereas the all-available-funds, percentage-of-sales, and competitive-parity approaches emphasize the appropriation of a lump sum for advertising which is then broken down into specific types of promotional methods and media as advertising executives see fit.

Under the research-objective method the firm first undertakes research to serve as a guide in setting reasonable objectives for the coming year's advertising. Guided by additional research, the firm then determines how much and what kind of advertising is necessary to

---

[7] In his landmark study of advertising appropriation methods, A. W. Frey substitutes the label "research-objective method" for the traditional title, "objective-and-task approach." This change in nomenclature appears desirable, since it emphasizes the reliance upon research which would characterize the approach. See Frey, *op. cit.*, p. 51.

achieve the stated objectives. The estimated cost of such advertising is the size of the appropriation to be recommended to top management. At this point consideration is given to the question of whether the budget will permit the appropriation of the sum believed to be necessary to achieve desired goals. If the initial sum appears to be excessive, then the firm will have to proceed more slowly and scale down the objectives until the estimated cost of their achievement comes within what the advertiser can afford.

The research-objective approach, if properly applied, is clearly superior to the methods previously discussed. It encourages management to think in terms of realistic objectives for its promotional effort, to seek the most effective methods of achieving these goals, and then to recognize the necessary relationship between the costs of the resulting advertising program and the size of the job specified in the planning effort. While ability to finance the recommended advertising effort is taken into account, management is encouraged to think of advertising not as just a cost but also as an income-producing method. Imaginative and aggressive use of advertising is thus encouraged.

This approach also implies reliance upon research to provide management with facts upon which to base decisions as to appropriate goals, proper methods, and necessary amounts of promotional effort to achieve desired objectives. Intuition and guesswork in setting the appropriation should therefore be reduced and, hopefully, the quality of decision making improved.

The chief limitation of the research-objective approach, as commonly defined, is that it does not require the decision maker to determine whether his stated objectives are likely to contribute enough incremental revenue to justify the costs involved in achieving them. Instead, it assumes that agreed-upon goals are always worth the cost of achieving them. This criticism has two parts. (1) While the research-objective approach requires the identification of reasonable objectives, it does not specify that these goals should be related to desired sales increases. Indeed, because of the difficulty which many firms face in measuring the sales results of advertising, they tend to identify their promotional goals in terms of changes in awareness, preference, and intent to buy. While such goals are helpful in guiding the planning of promotional programs, they contribute little to the development of advertising appropriations. If objectives are to be helpful in this respect, they must be stated so that they are measurable in terms of incremental sales results. To relate communication goals to sales results requires ingenuity in research, which is not identified as a requirement under the common definition of the research-objective method. (2) The research-objective method does not specify that the value of achieving stated objectives be measured in terms of the incremental revenue which will result. Only when this is done is it possible to determine whether the additional costs of achieving desired goals are justified by the incremental revenue produced. Such information is required, of course, if alternative objectives are to be properly evaluated and the most appropriate goals identified.

If the research-objective approach is modified to eliminate the deficiencies noted above, it approximates the marginal approach which was identified as the theoretical ideal earlier in this discussion. Even then, executives who attempt to use this modified method face challenging research problems in (1) determining how much and what kind of advertising is required to achieve stated objectives; (2) estimating the incremental sales which may result from the achievement of specified communication goals. While the difficulties involved are challenging, the modified research-objective approach tends to direct analysis and research efforts into promising channels. While we are still a long way from solving the problems involved in developing an ideal approach to the determination of the advertising appropriation, several significant attacks have been made on various aspects of the problem. In the following section we shall review certain key developments.

advertising as an investment

In previous discussion it has been noted that advertising has two effects: (1) it stimulates sales during the current year; (2) it builds awareness, preference, and favorable attitudes toward the firm which tend to produce sales in the future. Advertising which has an immediate effect may properly be treated as a current expense, but that which brings results in the future takes on the character of an investment and may justifiably be treated as such.

Consider, for example, the situation faced by Brooks-Ledford in planning to introduce a new aersol shaving lather to the market under the brand name Jupiter. Jupiter shaving lather was a protein-based cream and thus was less irritating to the skin than the customary soap-based product. Because of this competitive edge, it was believed that the new brand could secure 7 percent of the market the first year, 10 percent the second, and 15 percent the third. To reach these objectives, the advertising agency believed that it would be necessary to outspend the market leader the first year. Advertising pressure might then be reduced somewhat during the second and third years as the new brand became established. Nevertheless, it was anticipated that it would take three years for the full effects of the introductory effort to be felt and for the brand to achieve break-even status.

Accordingly, the following payout and spending plan for the first three years was worked out to guide decision making on the advertising appropriation. These estimates were based on a $1 retail price, a 40 percent discount for wholesalers and direct buying chains, and a contribution to advertising and profits of 80 percent of the unit price the firm collected.

Note that the expenditure necessary to launch the product was expected to result in a loss of $1,600,000 the first year, no profit the second year, and a profit of $1,850,000 the third. On a cumulative

	Year 1	Year 2	Year 3
Share objective......................	7%	10%	15%
Estimated dollar sales (000)...........	3,200	4,700	7,400
Contribution available (000)...........	1,600	2,350	3,700
Advertising expense (000).............	3,200	2,350	1,850
Profit/loss (000).....................	−1,600	—	+1,850
Cumulative P/L (000)................	−1,600	−1,600	+250
Advertising/sales ratio................	100%	50%	25%

basis, therefore, it was anticipated that it would take three years for Jupiter shaving lather to reach the desired market share objective of 15 percent and to achieve a break-even status on the investment made to introduce the new brand. In a situation such as this, management would clearly have to regard advertising as an investment in order to justify the heavy expenditures of the first year and the resulting substantial loss. Only if management were willing to treat advertising as an investment and wait three years or longer for the payoff, would the proposed advertising appropriation strategy be approved and steps be taken to develop the full potential of the new brand.

In recognition of the fact that advertising often produces benefits which provide a payoff in the future, Joel Dean has suggested that such advertising be treated as a capital investment.[8] He argues that deter-

---

[8] The material in the two following paragraphs is based upon Joel Dean, *Managerial Economics, op. cit.*, pp. 368–69; and Joel Dean, "Does Advertising Belong in the Capital Budget?" *Journal of Marketing*, Vol. 30, No. 4 (October, 1966), p. 21. Published by the American Marketing Association.

mination of the advertising appropriation then becomes a problem of capital expenditure budgeting. Profitability of capital invested in advertising would then be determined by the estimated amount and timing of added investment in comparison with added earnings, the duration of advertising effects, and the risks involved. Productivity of capital invested in this way should be measured by the discounted cash flow method in preference to the payback period approach. In short, advertising which is expected to have long-run effects should be placed in the capital budget. Promotional investments should then compete for funds on the basis of profitability, that is, discounted cash flow rate of return.

The chief deficiency of the return-on-investment approach is the difficulty of estimating the rate of return to be secured on advertising investments. Problems encountered involve (1) distinguishing investment advertising from that expected to have short-run effects; (2) estimating the evaporation of the cumulative effects of advertising; and (3) measuring the effect of advertising accumulation upon long-run sales volume and eventual price premiums. These measurement difficulties tend to rule out this approach as the sole criterion for decisions on investment-type advertising appropriations. Thinking about appropriations for institutional and cumulative advertising in this manner, however, would encourage research oriented toward providing the kind of estimates that are relevant to the decision. Experimentation along these lines is, therefore, encouraged.[9]

research to determine expenditure levels

A key problem in setting the advertising appropriation is to determine how much advertising is required to achieve a specified goal. Experimentation with different levels of advertising expenditures in different test markets is one way to attack this problem. The approach used by Du Pont in deciding how much to appropriate for advertising "Teflon" coated cookware is an interesting example.[10]

Test marketing cookware coated with Du Pont Teflon. The research design used was to undertake television advertising in 13 carefully chosen test and control cities. Three levels of advertising effort

---

[9] For an explanation of capital budgeting theory, see Harold Bierman, Jr., and Seymour Smith, *The Capital Budgeting Decision* (New York: Macmillan Co., 1960).

[10] J. E. Moyer, "Teflon, an Advertising Case History" (mimeographed case published by Advertising Department, E. I. du Pont de Nemours & Co., Wilmington, Del., 1964), pp. 28–30. Reprinted by permission.

were tested in two 11-week periods—during October to December, 1962, and from January to March, 1963. By means of an experimental crossover design, it was possible to test at national levels of $1 million (10 one-minute commercials in the fall and 7 one-minute commercials in the winter), $500,000 (5 and 3) and $250,000 or a promotional campaign (5 and none).[11]

Originally it was planned to conduct an extensive audit of retail stores to measure the impact of the varying levels of expenditures in television advertising on the sales of Teflon-coated utensils. This proved to be impractical, however, because certain retailers refused to cooperate in the research venture. Thus, the research measurement of sales was based on telephone interviews with 1,000 female heads of households, randomly selected, in each of the test markets and during each of the test periods in the fall and winter.

The results of this research effort indicated:

1. Sales of cookware finished with Teflon could be increased with a proper level of advertising.
2. Test markets where advertising on TV was carried on at the lower levels showed no discernible effect on sales.
3. Promotional effort in test markets at the $1 million level resulted in the doubling of purchases of Teflon-coated cookware as compared with the lower level or no-advertising test markets.
4. There was strong evidence of a "carry-over" effect of advertising in test cities where promotion was carried on at the $1 million level of expenditures.

These and other data provided Du Pont with a solid basis for planning a national advertising effort. The advertising agency prepared a media schedule which included network television advertising to consumers at a level which cost $1,035,000 for time and $110,000 for production, or a total of $1,145,000 in 1964. Based on the evidence secured from the research in test markets, Du Pont management approved this appropriation.

In the Teflon case, research in test markets was an essential step in determining the advertising appropriation. Although it seemed advisable for Du Pont to undertake advertising on behalf of Teflon, top management originally was reluctant to make the huge budgetary commitments anticipated without having facts upon which to base

---

[11] For a detailed discussion of the experimental crossover design, see J. C. Becknell, Jr., and R. W. McIsaac, "Test Marketing Cookware Coated with 'TEFLON,'" *Journal of Advertising Research*, Vol. 3, No. 3 (September, 1963), pp. 2–8.

judgments. They wanted assurance that such advertising would in fact produce results. Also they wanted data on what level of advertising would be required to move Teflon-finished cookware. They also wondered whether the funds required to do an adequate promotional job in the consumer market would be prohibitive from Du Pont's point of view. The test-market research provided the necessary data on the level of advertising support required to accomplish the desired objectives. This research also indicated the sales results which might be expected and thus provided management with a basis upon which to decide whether the anticipated sales would justify the estimated cost.

It is noteworthy that the researchers were not able to get retail cooperation to permit the measurement of sales results through the retail-audit approach. Instead the less satisfactory approach of determining purchases through telephone interviews had to be substituted. While this change resulted in some sacrifice in accuracy in the sales estimates, the data were apparently accepted by Du Pont management as providing a rough indication of the results that widely different levels of advertising expenditure would tend to produce. This provides a good illustration of the problems researchers encounter in attempting to plan experiments which will measure the sales results of advertising. Nevertheless, it is still desirable to make the effort in a situation such as that which Du Pont management faced.

Relation of advertising outlays to market-share objectives. Firms marketing nondurable goods in food stores and drugstores can make use of syndicated research services such as those offered by A. C. Nielsen Company to measure the relationship between advertising expenditures and retail sales of their brands expressed in share-of-market terms. Here sales are determined by the retail inventory method based on audits of the operations of a scientifically selected sample of food and drug outlets. Through analysis of the actual results secured in the marketing of both new and established products, the firm may discover useful guidelines as to the amount of advertising required to achieve market-share objectives. The possibilities of this type of research are illustrated by a study of 34 new brands of consumer nondurable goods made by James O. Peckham, Executive Vice President of the A. C. Nielsen Company.[12]

The purpose of this study was to determine whether useful guide-

---

[12] Adapted by permission from James O. Peckham, Executive Vice President, A. C. Nielsen Company, "Can We Relate Advertising Dollars to Market Share Objectives?" *Proceedings, 12th Annual Conference, Advertising Research Foundation,* October 5, 1966, pp. 53–57. © Advertising Research Foundation, Inc., 1966.

lines could be developed from the analysis of past experience concerning the relationship between advertising outlays and share-of-market objectives. With this in mind, Peckham selected 34 new brands that had achieved a "respectable market position" within the first two years from the decision to launch and actively market the brand nationally. Of this number 5 were food products, 11 were household products, 6 were proprietary drug brands, and 12 were toiletries. The criteria used in choosing these products were as follows: (1) The brand selected actually had to be new—not merely an added flavor, package, form, size, or formula change of an existing brand. (2) It had to be a brand generally considered to have a demonstrable consumer-plus both recognizable by and merchandisable to the consumer—not merely a "me too" brand. (3) The new brand had to sustain a share of market position at least reasonably close to its attained two-year introductory market share in subsequent years. Almost without exception these brands were developed with the benefit of adequate consumer product studies, thoroughly market tested in the crucible of actual sales conditions at the retail store level, introduced to the trade by a skilled sales force (either manufacturer or broker), and finally subjected to whatever introductory inducements were necessary to secure adequate distribution, trade support, and consumer trial.

Once these 34 brands were selected, their performance was examined over a 24-month period to determine whether there was any meaningful relationship between advertising dollars and market-share objectives. Share-of-industry sales figures for each brand were taken directly from Nielsen Retail Index Reports. Share-of-industry advertising expenditures were based upon estimates of newspaper, magazine, newspaper supplement, network TV, and spot TV advertising expenditures derived from published sources. These two sets of data were plotted for each brand on a chart such as that presented in Figure 11–2 for new Food Brand 102.

As Figure 11–2 indicates, over the entire two-year period Brand 102's share of advertising averaged about 16 percent. Since the brand attained a 10 percent share of market by the 24th month, we see that the share of advertising devoted to the brand was about 1.6 times the share of market secured.

In the same manner the average share of advertising for the 34 brands during the 24-month introductory period was compared with the attained share of sales at the end of the period. Dividing the share of advertising percentage by the share of attained sales percentage, the following ratios were secured for each of the product groups studied:

Product Group	Ratio of Share of Advertising to Share of Sales	
	Average	Median
5 brands of food products..........1.7		1.5
11 brands of household products....1.9		1.7
6 proprietary drug brands.........1.8		1.8
12 toiletry brands................1.5		1.5

When all of these 34 new brands were considered as a whole, the relationship between average share of advertising and attained share of sales over the initial two-year period was so consistent that it was possible to derive a "marketing experience curve" showing the approximate relationship between these two variables. This experience curve, shown in Figure 11–3, was secured by plotting a given brand's share of sales to scale horizontally from left to right against the same brand's share of advertising to the same scale vertically from bottom to top. The slope of the curve or the relationship between the vertical distance representing a share of advertising and the horizontal distance representing share of sales is approximately 1.5 or 1.6.

Of course, this share of advertising—share-of-sales experience curve is only an approximation of the situation for the average brand. Note that Brand 301 attained a 29.8 percent share of market after two years

Figure 11–2. New Food Brand 102—ratio of share of advertising to share of sales.

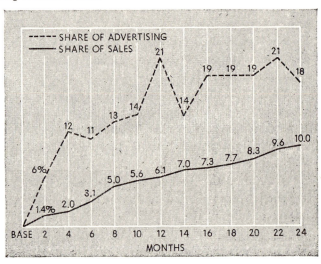

with a share of advertising expenditure of only 35 percent while the experience curve derived from studying all 34 brands indicates that a firm should normally expect to advertise at a 45 percent rate to obtain a 29.8 percent share. In contrast, Brand 210 spent an 18 percent share of advertising and only secured a 6 percent share of sales instead of the 10 percent share called for by the experience curve.

In commenting on how these findings might be used as a guide in

Figure 11–3. Attained share of sales—average share of advertising experience curve—first two years, 34 brands of consumer nondurable goods.

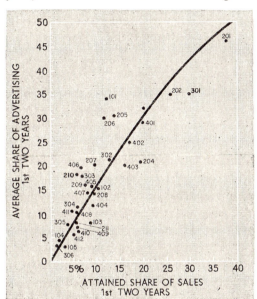

determining the advertising appropriation for a new brand, Peckham made the following suggestions: (1) Set the share-of-market goal within the practical range that marketing judgment and experience indicate can be attained—preferably aided by the result of a sales campaign in test markets conducted over a long enough period of time to establish consumer buying and repeat patterns under actual competitive conditions. (2) With this share of market as a goal for the new brand, use the experience curve to provide a basis for estimating the share of advertising that should be maintained over the brand's normal growth period—normally two years on the average. (3) Estimate *total* advertising expenditures for all brands combined over the two-year period—including the firm's own brand. (4) Multiply total advertising expenditures by the required share of advertising to get an estimate of the dollar advertising investment required to realize the share of industry established as the objective. (5) If the new brand is really unique with a strong consumer-plus, it may be possible to reduce the advertising expenditure below what would be indicated by the average share of advertising to a share-of-sales ratio of 1.5 or 1.6 to 1. Just how much of a reduction may be possible is a matter of judgment and experimentation. If the new brand is the second or third brand to exploit a particular consumer-plus characteristic, or if the product advantages are minor or difficult to develop into an effective copy story, it may be necessary to increase the advertising outlay by 50 percent or more above the average shown by the experience curve (a share of advertising—share-of-sales ratio of 2.2 plus). Here again judgment and experimentation would have to be used in reaching the final decision.

Now that we have Peckham's formula before us, it is desirable to ask whether the approach he suggests is a satisfactory way to deal with the problem of determining what level of advertising expenditure is required to achieve desired goals.

1. At the outset, it is wise to remind ourselves that the share of sales which may be achieved by a new brand will be influenced by the entire marketing mix and not just by the amount spent on advertising. In selecting his 34 case histories, Peckham implicitly recognized that market share would be influenced by uniqueness of product, introduction by a skilled sales force, and use of introductory inducements to get distribution, trade support, and consumer trial. Accordingly, he picked brands where these various mix elements had been handled wisely so that their impact on share of sales might be expected to be roughly the same. While no mention was made of the important variable of price, this sales influence might also have had approximately equal weight among the 34 brands if each were priced at approximately the competitive level. As Peckham suggests, then, the individual firm would have to utilize each of these marketing-mix elements effectively if the experience curve were to be of any value.

2. Then, too, most of the new brands chosen for study by Peckham were unique food, drug, and toiletry products with a demonstrable consumer-plus. As such they would meet the criteria for advertisability, and consumer advertising was, therefore, probably the dominant sales-producing element in the promotional mix. Influence of point-of-purchase promotion and retail personal selling probably had a much smaller impact than consumer advertising. Accordingly, application of

the findings of the experience curve would have to be limited to new products of equal superiority and where primary reliance might likewise be placed upon consumer advertising. As Peckham explains, adjustments would have to be made in the share of advertising investment to make allowance for deviations from the average quality of the 34 brands and hence the average level of the effectiveness of the advertising done on their behalf.

3. It should also be recognized that the share of sales results would be influenced not only by the amount of advertising but also by the effectiveness of the media mix and the creative approach used. Presumably, deviations of individual brands from the experience curve are explained, in part, by differences in the effectiveness of media and message. Research is recommended, therefore, to identify the most effective media mix and the best creative approach. Once this is accomplished, then these factors may be held constant and attention directed to the amount of advertising required to achieve the desired market share.

4. These comments underscore the problems involved in separating the impact of advertising dollars from other marketing-mix influences upon the brand's share of sales. They also serve as a reminder of the difficulty of using past results in making future plans. We can see that planning and executing research to measure the sales results of advertising is a difficult and challenging task. It becomes clear that Peckham's formula does not remove the need for well-planned research in determining the level of advertising needed to achieve desired market position for a new brand. It does suggest, however, the kind of research which may be useful in providing information needed by management in arriving at a judgment on how much to spend on advertising.

5. While Peckham was able to develop an experience curve by relating share of advertising and share of sales for nondurable products, it is significant to recall that General Electric failed to establish such a relationship in analyzing data covering experience with 16 product lines—in the durable goods classification—major appliances, traffic appliances, consumer electrical supplies, and industrial components and supplies. Among other factors, this may be due to the smaller influence of advertising in the selling mix for such items as well as the infrequency of purchase which characterizes them. As General Electric suggests, the only way correlation studies will make a useful contribution for such products is to measure and correlate the effects of *several key influences on share of market at one and the same time. Clearly the*

research approach must be determined in the light of the nature of the product, the frequency with which it is purchased, and the role of advertising in the promotional mix.

relation of communication objectives to sales results

As mentioned previously, manufacturers of durable goods purchased infrequently find it difficult if not impossible to measure advertising results in terms of sales. This leads them to adopt communication goals for their advertising instead of sales or share-of-industry goals. A problem then arises in deciding whether the desired objectives are worth the costs involved in their achievement. Recognition of this problem has led to research designed to study the relationship between communication objectives (such as awareness, preference, intent to buy) and actual sales results. This experimentation has led to the development of the "media-schedule" approach to setting the advertising appropriation, a method which falls within the research-objective category and involves practical applications of the ideal-incremental approach previously discussed.[13]

Of particular interest to us is the manner in which objectives are identified in following this approach. The basic idea involved is to recognize that advertising creates sales by making conscious impressions upon the minds of prospective buyers. Thus, the goal of the advertiser is to purchase an optimum number of conscious impressions with his dollars. It is recognized that the effectiveness of an advertisement scheduled a given number of times in any medium—a magazine, for example—results from a screening sequence somewhat as follows: (1) The magazine has a total circulation among people who are potential buyers or "influencers." (2) A larger number than this actually reads the magazine. (3) A smaller number of individuals than readers of the magazine is "exposed" to the page on which the advertisement appears. (4) A still smaller number actually pays attention to the advertisement. (5) A still smaller number receives a conscious impression. (6) The conscious impressions (a) make some readers *aware* of the product for the first time, (b) strengthen already present awareness in others, (c) move some people from mere awareness to a favorable *attitude,* and (d) move some people all the way to a *purchase.*

In recognition of this screening sequence, research is then under-

---

[13] Reprinted by permission from A. W. Frey, "Approaches to Determining the Advertising Appropriation," in George L. Baker, Jr. (ed.), *Effective Marketing Coordination,* pp. 326–39. Published by the American Marketing Association, 1961.

taken to establish the relationship among (1) conscious impressions, (2) awareness and favorable attitudes, and (3) purchases of the product. If such a relationship is established, then the next step is to determine the number of conscious impressions which may be secured through various combinations of media schedules. The advertiser is then in a position to determine the optimum advertising appropriation.

This approach is illustrated by C. Maxwell Ule's solution of a media problem at a 4A's convention some years ago.[14] The problem, which was assigned to three advertising experts, involved the preparation of a media schedule for a brand-new revolutionary kind of filter-tip king-size cigarette, produced by a major U.S. cigarette manufacturer. It was assumed that the product had been test marketed for 26 weeks under various conditions in various sizes of markets in different regions of the country. The test-marketing results were very satisfactory; the manufacturer planned to move the brand into national distribution as quickly as possible. Distribution was to be accomplished almost automatically, since the new brand would be sold by the company's nationwide sales force handling other tobacco products manufactured by the company.

The marketing objectives for Sputnik cigarettes, as defined by Ule, may be stated as follows: (1) The goal was to capture 8 percent of the total cigarette market, or 20 percent of the filter-tip market. (2) To achieve this sales goal, the aim was to get 10 million of the nation's 50 million smokers to try Sputnik cigarettes—from which 4 million would become regular Sputnik smokers. This was based on past general experience of the relationship between experimental buyers and regular customers. (3) To achieve this sales goal, a level of product awareness of 80 percent would have to be attained by the advertising input, figured accumulatively by the end of the fiscal year. That is, 80 percent of the prospects would have to become well enough aware of the brand by the end of the year to recall the brand unaided in a consumer survey. Based upon experience in other fields, it was estimated that this cumulative awareness by the end of the year would produce enough experimental buyers to deliver a market share equal to 8 percent of the total market, or 20 percent of the filter-tip market.

With this background, the following communication goals were then established:

---

[14] Reprinted by permission from G. Maxwell Ule, "A Media Plan for 'Sputnik' Cigarettes," *How to Plan Media Strategy*, papers from the 1957 Regional Conventions, pp. 41–52. Copyright, American Association of Advertising Agencies, 1958.

1. To achieve these marketing sales objectives, it would be necessary to reach 80 percent of the U.S. households with an average of 40 conscious advertising impressions per household reached during the introductory year. Multiplying the coverage objective (80 percent) by the number of conscious advertising impressions to be delivered (40), the communications objective for the year became 3,200 rating points of conscious advertising impressions.

2. Each conscious advertising impression had the estimated net effect of creating an unaided brand awareness of 2 percent among the households reached. Forty impressions would create 80 percent awareness among the 80 percent of U.S. households reached (40 × 2 percent).

The next step was to work out the optimum media schedule to deliver the desired number of conscious impressions (3,200 rating points). Ule's proposed media schedule for the first 13 weeks of the year would deliver 1,280 conscious advertising rating points by using 39 commercial minutes on network TV, 35 class A Spot TV announcements, six full-page color insertions in Sunday supplements, four 1,500-line color insertions in newspapers, and 50 radio spot announcements weekly for eight weeks. A more limited schedule on network TV, spot TV, and Sunday Supplements would also deliver another 1,920 conscious rating points during the remaining 39 weeks of the year, thus providing the total of 3,200 conscious advertising impressions.

Finally, the cost of this optimum schedule was estimated at $10,488,000 for the introductory year. This amount was then recommended as the advertising appropriation.

While this media-schedule approach has conceptual value, the critical question is whether the individual advertiser will be able through research to establish a useful relationship between conscious impressions, awareness, favorable attitudes, and purchases. It is reported, however, that some advertisers have been able to establish this relationship to their own satisfaction.[15] Certainly an attempt should be made to do so, if at all possible. If no satisfactory relationship can be found for certain types of products, however, the obvious answer is to disregard the goal of purchases and select a certain goal of awareness and favorable attitude as a guide. This is a better goal than is used by some advertisers in their decision making.

---

[15] For a helpful discussion of the use of marketing experiments in determining the relationship between communication and sales, see Charles K. Ramond, "Must Advertising Communicate to Sell?" *Harvard Business Review*, September–October, 1965, pp. 148–59.

conclusion

The task of determining the size of the promotional appropriation is an important, but difficult problem. The character of promotional strategy influences the size of the appropriation; simultaneously, the size of the funds available is an important consideration in deciding what type of promotional approach will be most effective. Ways of dealing with this problem which break this circularity are suggested in this chapter.

We have evaluated commonly used approaches such as basing the appropriation decision on a percentage of sales, using "all available funds," considering competitive parity, and applying the research-objective (or task) approach. It is concluded that a modified research-objective approach, if properly applied, is clearly superior to the approaches previously mentioned. We shall now proceed to a discussion of brand strategy decisions.

questions

1. a) Explain the basic essentials of the marginal approach of determining the advertising appropriation.
   b) What practical difficulties are encountered in applying this approach in actual practice?
2. What are the basic principles behind (a) the breakdown and (b) the buildup methods of determining the promotional appropriation? Which approaches discussed in this chapter fall into each classification?
3. a) Under what conditions may a case be made for the use of a variable percentage of estimated future sales in determining the promotional appropriation?
   b) Even under the best of circumstances, what criticisms may be made of this approach?
4. Under what conditions can you defend the use of the all-available-funds approach to determining the appropriation? What limitations does this method have?
5. a) Evaluate the plan of setting the advertising appropriation by making the product's share of total industry advertising expenditures equal to the brand's desired share of market.
   b) Would this be an appropriate plan to follow in determining the appropriation for a new brand just being introduced? An established brand which rates number 3 in share of market? Number 1 in share of market?
6. a) What are the basic essentials of the research-objective approach

to setting the promotional appropriation? What are its chief limitations?

b) How might the plan be modified to eliminate these criticisms?

7. a) Under what circumstances might it be desirable to treat advertising as an investment?

b) What difficulties are involved in following this approach? Does it appear likely that these problems may be overcome?

8. Does Peckham's study of the relation between advertising outlays and market-share objectives provide a helpful guide for setting the advertising appropriation:

a) For a new product like Simba, which is promoted as a means of quenching the "African thirst"?

b) For a new portable color TV set?

c) For Cessna aircraft marketed for pleasure and personal use?

9. a) Under what circumstances would it appear to be desirable to base the advertising appropriation upon communication objectives rather than upon sales goals?

b) What difficulties are encountered in following this approach (as illustrated in the media-schedule method) ?

c) What attitude should management take toward the use of this method?

brand strategy
decisions

In an earlier discussion, consideration was given to issues of brand policy related to product development decisions. We turn now to certain major questions concerning branding which arise in the process of working out the basic promotional strategy of a manufacturer. Of particular significance are the following issues: (1) What policies should be followed regarding the number and coverage of brands to be marketed by the firm? Specifically, should the manufacturer use one brand to identify many different products as opposed to marketing each product under its own individual brand name? Where different qualities of the same product are produced, should all be sold under a single brand name or should high-, medium-, and low-quality products be identified by separate trademarks? (2) Should the firm manufacture products to be sold under distributors' brands or concentrate exclusively upon marketing products under its own brands? Each of these topics has important promotional strategy implications and will be analyzed on the pages which follow.

family brands versus individual brands

A producer following a manufacturers' brand policy faces the important question of whether to market his line under a family brand or under individual brand names. A family-brand policy is where two or more products are sold under the same brand name. Avon Products, Inc., is an example of a firm which follows this approach. In a recent year, the firm sold approximately 300 items under the "Avon" brand name including fragrances, make-up articles, bath products, skin care items, hair preparations, dental care accessories, deodorants, and shaving products, among others. Although products appealing to women were emphasized, items were also marketed for children and men.[1]

What advantages might Avon gain from this family-brand policy? Since Avon products were sold house-to-house by company salesmen, a key advantage of family branding would be the possibility of gaining ready acceptance by regular customers of new products added to the company's line. The favorable brand image held by users of existing Avon products would tend to influence them to accept new items carrying the same brand more readily than if new individual brand names were used. This, in turn, would tend to reduce the amount of introductory advertising required to create a demand for the new products and would also cut down the time and effort required on the part of the salesman to get orders for these new items.

While Avon management obviously believe that family branding is desirable, Lever Brothers Company made the opposite decision when introducing a new beauty soap in test markets early in 1968. This new product, which was being tested in Albany, New York, and Columbus, Ohio, was identified by the brand name, "Caress." Rather than attempting to associate Caress with the firm's established brand, Lux Toilet Soap, Lever Brothers apparently intends to promote Caress separately as a means of more effectively exploiting this new entry into the competitive beauty soap market. While this approach may require a larger appropriation for advertising and promotion, such an investment is customarily made in the expectation that it will produce larger sales and profits than the decision to market under a family brand would yield. The contrast in brand policy illustrated by the Avon and Lever Brothers examples lead naturally to the question as to what guidelines to use in making a decision concerning family versus individual branding when a new product is being added to an established product line. In considering this issue it is helpful to approach the problem from the consumers' viewpoint. What is the psychological explanation of the tendency to develop generalized preferences for different types of products identified by a common family brand? What product characteristics tend to foster such generalization? What tend to discourage it? These questions will be considered in the following section.

---

[1] Seymour Freedgood, "Avon: The Sweet Smell of Success," *Fortune,* Vol. LXX, No. 6, December, 1964, pp. 111, 113.

generalized preferences for family brands[2]

The policy of family branding is based on the assumption that this practice leads to a "connection in consumers' minds" which generalizes consumer preferences to all product categories under a brand. A brand name linkage acts as a medium through which consumers spread or generalize preferences and loyalties from one category of products to another. The psychological theory which underlies this assumption deals with the effect of cognitive set on perception. The cognitive set influence important in this analysis is the "assimilation effect," the tendency of people to assimilate, or to shift classification of set-related stimuli in the direction of their existing set. According to Fry:

Extension of assimilation effects to family branding seems quite reasonable. A consumer's attitudes toward a family brand (his brand image) can act as a set-inducing cognitive variable. Through assimilation the consumer's perception of characteristics of individual products under the brand will be drawn in the direction of this set. In other words, his judgments of products under a family brand will tend to be consistent with his overall brand image. He will tend, for example, to ascribe to any individual product the quality he thinks is generally represented by the brand. This assimilation effect applies only to attributes which the products under consideration have in common, such as taste appeal in the case of foods or cleaning power for soaps and detergents. Except as they support (or detract from) such basic attributes, characteristics unique to particular products are of no concern.[3]

Generalized preferences for family brands are intervening variables that influence consumer brand choice. Since they are not directly observable, they are inferred from consumer buying behavior. Fry tested the hypothesis that consumers have generalized preferences by analyzing consumer purchasing behavior as reported by the *Chicago Tribune* consumer panel. Analyses were limited to frequently purchased packaged goods and covered about 600 households resident in metropolitan Chicago. Purchases of the following family brands of packaged goods were analyzed among others:

1. Canned goods—Del Monte, Libby's, Hunt's, Heinz.
2. Frozen foods—Birdseye.
3. Paper products—Scott, Kleenex.
4. Baking products—Pillsbury.

---

[2] Reprinted by permission from Joseph N. Fry, "Family Branding and Consumer Brand Choice," *Journal of Marketing Research*, Vol. 4 (August, 1967), pp. 237–47. Published by the American Marketing Association.

[3] *Ibid.*, p. 238.

The degree of generalized preference for a given family brand was measured by analyzing the behavior of consumers in purchasing two different product categories (for example, canned peaches and canned corn) under a single family brand (for example, Del Monte). What percentage of the consumers who purchased Del Monte canned peaches also purchased Del Monte canned corn? How does this compare with the percentage of the consumers who purchased *only* Del Monte canned peaches or *only* Del Monte canned corn? More precisely, this comparison was made by using a probability model, as follows: Assume a family brand is available in two product categories A and B and that a population of consumers who have made purchases in both product categories has been identified. Denote by $P(A_1, B_1)$ the joint probability that a consumer selected at random from the population will have purchased the family brand in *both* product categories. For comparison, denote by $P(A_1)$ and $P(B_1)$ the marginal probabilities that a randomly selected consumer will have purchased the family brand in product category A *only* or B *only*. A generalized preference for the family brand is said to exist if:

$$P(A_1, B_1) > P(A_1) \cdot P(B_1).$$

The degree to which the joint probability $P(A_1, B_1)$ exceeds the product of multiplying the marginal probabilities $P(A_1) \times P(B_1)$ is used as the index of the degree of generalized preference for the family brand under analysis. The results of this analysis as applied to the Del Monte family brand are illustrative. Thus, 39 comparisons were made of the behavior of consumers in purchasing two different products (such as peaches and corn) marketed under the Del Monte family brand. In 36 out of 39 comparisons the index of generalized preference was positive—i.e., a generalized preference for the family brand was demonstrated. In only 3 of the 39 comparisons were the estimates negative, indicating no generalized preference for the family brand in the purchase of these particular pairs of products. According to Fry, statistically significant indexes of generalized preference for the Del Monte family brand were found in over half of the product pairings analyzed.[4]

----

[4] Technical note: In more complete terms, it can be said that if there are two events, A_1 and B_1, and the two events are independent of each other, then the joint probability, $P(A_1, B_1)$, that is, the chance of both events occurring together, is the multiple of the individual, or marginal, probabilities.

1. For independent events: $P(A_1, B_1) = P(A_1) \cdot P(B_1)$.

If the two events are not independent, then the actual occurrence of one event increases the probability of the other's occurrence. This is the conditional probability, or

Analysis of the data for all of the family brands of frequently purchased packaged goods listed above led Fry to conclude that consumers do have generalized preferences for family brands.[5] The results were consistent with the hypothesis for a variety of brands, product categories, and purchase classifications indicating degree of brand loyalty.

Fry also inquired as to what factors contribute to the degree of generalized preference. He hypothesized that the degree of generalized preference for a family brand varies directly with (1) the degree of similarity in the competitive brand sets of two product categories identified by a family brand, and (2) the degree of price similarity of the brand in two product categories.

Analysis of the data gave tentative confirmation to these secondary hypotheses. Accordingly, the findings of this study provide support for the common and important assumption that for frequently purchased package goods the promotion of one product under a family brand has beneficial effects for other products under that brand. The study does not, however, throw any light on the relative efficacy of family and individual branding.

semantic generalization and family branding[6]

In contrast, a study of semantic generalization as applied to family brands of household appliances raises some doubt as to the use of a common brand name as a means of transferring attitudes between dissimilar products of high unit value. As in Fry's study, the starting point is the principle of generalization which holds that people have a tendency to view individual items as being similar, disregarding points of character that would differentiate them. Generalization may occur on either the physical or semantic level. Kerby is concerned about semantic generalization where a person views two or more objects as similar because they carry a *common meaning*, even though the objects themselves may have different physical characteristics. Specifically, he

---

the probability of the second event, given that the first has already occurred. Using the same notation as above, the joint probability for the two nonindependent events is the product of the conditional probability of the second event given that the first has occurred, $P(B_1/A_1)$, and the marginal probability of the occurrence of the first.

2. For nonindependent events: $P(A_1,B_1) = P(B_1/A_1) \cdot P(A_1)$.

[5] See *ibid.*, pp. 241–47, for a more complete discussion of the evidence resulting from this analysis.

[6] Reprinted by permission from J. K. Kerby, "Semantic Generalization in the Formation of Consumer Attitudes," *Journal of Marketing Research*, Vol. 4 (August, 1967), pp. 314–17. Published by the American Marketing Association.

tested the hypothesis that meaning should be transferred between two or more products that are physically dissimilar, if they share a common brand name.

Kerby had a group of 99 female homemakers in Maplewood, New Jersey, evaluate eight branded products. Four of these products had different physical characteristics but shared a common brand—i.e., vacuum cleaners, automatic washers, portable TV sets, and refrigerators made by General Electric and Westinghouse. The other four products corresponded with the first four in terms of physical characteristics, but each had an individual brand name—i.e., Sunbeam and Eureka vacuum cleaners, Philco and Maytag automatic washers, Motorola and Admiral portable TV, and Norge and RCA refrigerators.

Respondents were asked to evaluate the eight branded products listed above in terms of 47 semantic differential scales using carefully selected adjectives such as: safe-hazardous, superior-inferior, follower-pioneer, exorbitant-reasonable, adequate-inadequate, dull-colorful, unsanitary-sanitary, simple-intricate, satisfactory-disappointing.

The completed questionnaires were subjected to factor analysis to determine how similar the respondent's rating of one product (GE vacuum cleaner) was to that for another product (GE automatic washer). If a housewife saw a similar meaning between two or more products marketed under a family brand, she would mark the semantic differential scales for the two items similarly. The resulting intercorrelations between these products would then be relatively high and the resulting factor loads relatively large.

Variable	1	2	3	4
GE vacuum cleaner	0.216	0.762	0.032	−0.108
GE automatic washer	−0.017	0.785	0.149	0.033
GE portable TV	0.107	0.910	0.016	0.076
GE refrigerator	0.070	0.706	−0.240	0.002
Sunbeam vacuum cleaner	0.925	0.030	−0.129	−0.156
Maytag automatic washer	0.868	0.165	0.187	0.033
Admiral portable TV	0.931	0.156	−0.025	0.072
RCA refrigerator	0.973	0.061	−0.038	0.016

The accompanying factor matrix is one of the 99 matrixes from the study and illustrates the nature of the results of the analysis. Note that the factor loadings on the second factor are uniformly high for the GE group of products and relatively low for products in the heterogeneous-brand group. Such an arrangement indicates that this particular respondent saw a similar meaning between the four GE products and is evidence of a strong tendency toward generalization.

The above matrix illustrates the criteria used in evaluating the study's results. In general, if all four factor loadings associated with the family-branded group of products were large relative to the remaining factor loadings (a spread of about 20 or so percentage points), a respondent was classed as giving "very strong indication" of semantic generalization. If all four factor loadings were larger than the others by a spread of about 5 to 20 percentage points; if three of the four were larger than the others by about 20 or more points; or if two of the four were larger than the others by about 50 or more points, the respondent was classed as giving a "good indication."

If three of the four were larger than the others by about 5 to 20 percentage points, or if two of the four were larger by about 20 to 50 points, the respondent was classed as giving a "weak indication." If none of the patterns described above appeared in the factor matrix, the respondent was classed as giving "no indication" of semantic generalization.

Applying these criteria to each of the 99 factor matrixes produced the following results:

> Very strong indication.......... 1
> Good indication............... 5
> Weak indication..............11
> No indication................82

Of the 99 respondents in the study, therefore, only one exhibited a very strong tendency toward semantic generalization. An additional 5 respondents showed a reasonably strong tendency in that direction, but the remaining 93 had either a weak tendency or no tendency toward semantic generalization.

Why did such a large proportion of the respondents show little or no tendency toward semantic generalization in rating family brands as opposed to individual brands? Kerby suggests two possible explanations. (1) Perhaps the physical characteristics of major appliances varied too greatly to permit the occurrence of effective generalization. (2) Or perhaps semantic generalization comes in only when the products involved are relatively unimportant, requiring a minimum of intellectual and emotional effort.

factors influencing choice of family versus individual brands

The empirical evidence just cited points up the importance of careful analysis in reaching a decision on whether a new product should be marketed under a family brand or an individual brand. In making such an analysis, it is helpful to begin with considerations which may tend to foster or retard the consumers' tendency to develop generalized preferences through the process of assimilation.

1. Is the new product of the same type as the existing line? The Del Monte family brand, for example, is applied to canned fruits and vegetables. Also, the Kleenex label covers facial tissues, paper napkins, and paper towels among others. In both cases the products covered by the family brand are of the same general type, although they are still individual items. In contrast, let us consider an illustration involving the Avon Company. As explained earlier, this firm applied its family brand to cosmetics and toiletries. As a matter of policy, the firm refused to add nonrelated items, such as floor polishes, to its line under the family brand.

2. Is the new product similar in quality-price relationship to the existing line? Where this is true, the quality image which consumers associate with the established brand may be extended through assimilation to the new product. This may make them more willing to try the new product than if the innovation were introduced under a new and unfamiliar brand name. One of the highly successful products initially marketed by Brooks-Ledford Company for example, was Galaxy—a superior hair dressing for women—which achieved a position of market leadership and for which women had a substantial feeling of brand loyalty. When company research developed a superior new hair fixative six years later, it was introduced nationally under the family brand as Galaxy Hair Spray. Undoubtedly, the sale of the new product under the highly regarded Galaxy label was one factor which helped Galaxy Hair Spray to gain initial acceptance and become a top-selling brand in the hair fixative field within 11 months.

3. Is the new product similar to the established brand in terms of uses to which it is put, basic consumer desires which it may satisfy, and appeals to buying motives which may be used in its promotion? For some time, Standard Brands, Inc., has packed peanuts under its Planters label. Early in 1968, the firm introduced five snack products packed in corrugated cans with tear-open lids. The five varieties are Cheese Curls, Cheese Balls, Corn Chips, Corn Stix, and Potato Stix. Since peanuts are also used as snacks along with various types of

refreshments and satisfy the sense of taste, it was appropriate to market the five new snack products under the Planters brand.[7]

In contrast, Brooks-Ledford developed a new product which was described as "the first all-clear floor wax" and in a recent year, was testing it in Minneapolis and other markets. This new floor wax was not marketed under a family brand but instead was identified as "Saturn Floor Wax." Such action appeared wise since the product was a floor wax and not a hair preparation and accordingly differed as to uses, basic desires satisfied, and appeals to buying motives which might be used to sell it to the ultimate consumer.

4. Is the market for the new product likely to be found among the same segments of the population when classified by sex, race, age, income, and social status as currently constitute the prospective buyers of the established brand? Obviously, we are not thinking about a new product which might be a substitute for an established brand but instead a new item which is complementary or which might also be purchased by a substantial proportion of the same prospective buyers, thus increasing the total sales of the company. If the same consumers purchase both the old and the new product, then there is maximum opportunity for generalization to take place. If none of the firm's current customers is a prospect, then there is no opportunity for associating the two products in the consumers' minds. Consider, for example, Ivory toilet soap and Ivory liquid detergent—products showing a considerable degree of generalization in Fry's study of family brands. Since Ivory toilet soap is used in the bath while Ivory liquid detergent is used in the wash, these products are not substitutes. Yet they might be expected to find their potential markets among approximately the same prospective buyers and thus would offer a good opportunity for generalization to take place through family branding.

In contrast, prior to 1959 Brooks-Ledford marketed all its products to women. In that year the firm developed a new hair dressing for men which was available either in tube or aerosol can. Although the new product was a hair preparation, the firm decided against introducing this item under the Galaxy brand name. Since its potential market was among men and not among women, the firm identified the new item as "Jupiter Hair Dressing" thus avoiding an association with a brand which had a feminine image. The firm's marketing strategy was effective, and by 1962 Jupiter Hair Dressing was among the six best selling hair preparations for men in the country.

---

[7] "DFS New Product News," mimeographed publication of Dancer-Fitzgerald-Sample, Inc., New York, April, 1968, p. 12.

In addition to factors that tend to influence generalization through family brands, there are considerations which relate to the efficiency with which a new product may be introduced to the market. Let us consider these briefly.

1. Can the new product be distributed through the same types of retail outlets as the existing line? If this is possible, then the existing sales force and distribution organization may be utilized in the introductory process. If retailers are familiar with the established brand, they may be more willing to stock the new product when offered under this label than if the product were sold under an entirely new brand name. They will be influenced, of course, by their estimate of the reputation which the established brand has among consumers and consequently by whether they believe use of the family brand will help to get consumers to try the new product. If the new product must be sold through entirely new types of retail outlets, however, there will be no opportunity to use the reputation of the established brand to help sell the new item. An individual brand would then be equally acceptable as far as getting retail distribution is concerned.

2. Can the new product be promoted jointly with other established products being sold under the family brand? If joint promotion is possible, this will tend to reduce the cost of introducing the new product. Joint promotion would be favored if the products appeal to similar market segments, are similar in nature, are associated in use, are like in quality-price relationships, and appeal to similar buying motives. If these criteria are not met, however, joint promotion under a family brand may not be as effective as a separate campaign for the new product under its own individual brand name. Against the higher costs of such effort may be balanced the increased aggressiveness and effectiveness of the special introductory campaign. The introduction of new cosmetic products under the Avon family brand is a good example of a situation where the new items may be sold effectively along with existing items. While Avon's line included approximately 300 items of cosmetics and toiletries which had an established market, the firm was active in product development and added a number of new items each year—all under the Avon family brand. As a new product was added, advertising would serve to announce the availability of the new item under the Avon name and to stimulate a desire for it. Salesmen calling in the prospects' homes could also introduce the new product and attempt to take orders for it, but they would also be able to sell other items in the line during the same visit. This possibility would tend to reduce the cost of introducing the new product. Such economies would

appeal to small firms with limited financial resources and lead them to favor family branding.

The foregoing discussion emphasizes the cost efficiencies which may result from family branding under certain circumstances. Even more important, however, is the question of whether introduction of a new product under a family brand will produce a larger sales volume, profit, and return on investment than the alternative of marketing the new item under its own individual brand. It will facilitate our consideration of this question if we shift our point of view and focus attention on the considerations which may tend to favor the use of an individual brand as opposed to a family brand.

This leads us to ask, is the new product individualized in ways important to the consumer? The opportunity of making effective use of consumer advertising depends in part upon the extent to which the new product is distinctive when compared to competing brands. (Other considerations influencing advertising opportunity include a favorable primary demand trend, presence of hidden qualities, ability to use strong emotional buying motives, and ability to support an adequate advertising program.) If the new product is highly individualized in ways important to the consumer, then this factor favors the strategy of giving it its own brand name and of introducing it to the market through an aggressive campaign of advertising and promotion. Although this would probably require a larger advertising appropriation than if the new product carried a family brand, the sales results would probably be substantially greater. By associating the distinctive features of the product with its own individual brand name, a stronger and sharper brand image could be created in consumers' minds than if the new item was identified by a family brand which it shared with other products. The family brand becomes associated only with the common characteristics of the various products it identifies—such as uniform high quality—and not with all of the special features of the product which set it apart from competing brands. The process of generalization involved in creating a family brand image, therefore, involves a loss as well as a gain. For the highly distinctive product, the loss far overshadows the gain.

In our opinion, the results which may be achieved by giving a product an individual brand name and promoting it aggressively are illustrated by the experience of Bristol-Myers in the introduction of Ban deodorant.[8] Prior to the introduction of Ban, Bristol-Myers

---

[8] This case is reported in more detail in N. H. Borden and M. V. Marshall, *Advertising Management: Text and Cases* (rev. ed.; Homewood, Ill.: Richard D. Irwin, Inc., 1959), pp. 519–33.

marketed Mum—a cream deodorant which they rated as one of the two leading deodorants on the market. Stopette, a competing spray deodorant had recently been introduced to the market and had quickly achieved a market share which placed it among the top five brands then available. Undoubtedly this event spurred product research at Bristol-Myers as a means of developing an improved product which would counter the competitive threat of Stopette as well as other brands. Recognizing that both the cream and spray types of deodorants were messy to use, Bristol-Myers undertook research work which resulted in an effective liquid deodorant to be applied by a large plastic marble mounted in the end of a bottle—a "roll-on deodorant." Although the new product was tested in six leading markets as "Mum Rolette," the firm finally decided to market the new product as "Ban" lotion deodorant. The method of application made Ban highly distinctive, and introductory advertising claimed that Ban was "more effective than creams; easier to apply than sprays!" Ban was introduced to the market through a national advertising campaign, including newspapers, magazines, television, and radio, which cost $1 million during the first eight months. By the end of this period, Ban had achieved number three position in the industry and in 17 months had become the top-selling deodorant in dollar volume in drug and food outlets combined. In this case the effectiveness of the deodorant lotion and the convenience of the roll-on applicator individualized the product in ways important to the consumer. Not only was Ban individualized as compared with competing brands, it was also significantly different from Bristol-Myers' own brand—Mum. By assigning the new product its own brand name—Ban—and by supporting it with an aggressive introductory advertising campaign, the firm was able to push Ban into market leadership within a relatively short time. This strategy was probably much more effective than that of calling the new item "Mum Rolette" and of relying on the reputation of Mum plus a joint advertising campaign to help it gain acceptance among consumers.

It is clear that a policy of individual branding is favored where a product is highly individualized as compared with the competition, a condition which suggests an aggressive pull type of promotional strategy. If these distinctive features also make the new product different from the remainder of the company's line, as we might expect, then the case favoring an individual brand is strengthened. In contrast, a new product which is not distinctive but which is as good as, but no better than, competing brands, would offer only a mediocre opportunity for individual promotion through consumer advertising. If this new product does have characteristics in common with the existing line, then it would benefit by being promoted as a new addition to a reputable family brand. Here the process of generalization might well offer a substantial net gain. What the brand strategy should be when the new product falls in between these extremes—i.e., when it has minor points of difference as compared with competition and with other items in the firm's own line—would appear to be a matter which would have to be decided through executive judgment supplemented by appropriate market testing of alternatives.

In this connection, the decision of Procter & Gamble Brand Managers to introduce their new mint-flavored stannous flouride toothpaste under the established name "Crest" is interesting. The original Crest (with stannous fluoride) was flavored with wintergreen and had developed a significant market share. It faced direct competition from other fluoridated toothpastes, which were also available only in wintergreen flavor. There was no major stannous fluoride mint-flavored product. Research indicated that a segment of the market which wished the protection against tooth decay provided by a fluoridated brand, did not like the wintergreen flavor of Crest but did like mint flavor in toothpaste. In recognition of this preference, P&G undertook the difficult task of developing an acceptable mint-flavored stannous fluoride toothpaste. After considerable time and effort, the research team came up with a new product which received favorable responses in consumer taste tests. The new product, accordingly, differed from the original Crest primarily in flavor (mint instead of wintergreen). While its stannous fluoride formula may have differed from competing fluoridated brands in some respects, its chief distinction was its mint flavor. The new product might have been given an individual brand name as is generally the policy when new products are added to the P&G line. The Brand Group, however, recommended marketing the new mint-flavored fluoridated toothpaste under the name "Mint Crest." From this action it may be inferred that P&G decision makers believed that the new product would gain substantial benefit from the reputation achieved by the original Crest brand. Here the benefits from generalization were apparently believed to be greater than any promotional advantages which might result from using an individual brand name. By calling the new product "Mint Crest," however, the Brand Group obviously hoped to attract a new segment of consumers who may have tried wintergreen-flavored Crest but who turned away from it to buy a less effective mint-flavored competing brand. It is noteworthy, however, that P&G introduced new Mint Crest with a heavy campaign of advertising and promotion. While new Mint Crest was featured it was associated with but distinguished from the original Crest (wintergreen).

summary and conclusions

In summary, the following factors would tend to favor marketing a new product under its own individual brand: (1) If it is highly individualized as compared with competing brands and also meets other criteria which indicate a profitable opportunity to make use of consumer advertising. (2) If it differs in product features, benefits, and hence selective appeals from the firm's own established brand and thus requires individual promotion. (3) If it is either higher or lower in quality than other products sold under the existing brand. (4) If it offers an opportunity to expand the company's market coverage by appealing to new segments of consumers. (5) If it should be distributed through different types of retail outlets from those handling the existing brand.

In contrast, the following considerations would tend to favor selling the new product under an established family brand: (1) If the new product is of the same type as the existing line. (2) If it is similar in uses, wants satisfied, and in appeals to buying motives. (3) If it is of the same quality-price relation as the existing brand. (4) If its market is likely to be found in the same segments of the population as the present line. (5) If it can be distributed through the same types of retail outlets as now used. (6) If it can be promoted jointly with established products sold under the family brand.

In the final analysis, what must be done is to estimate the sales volume, profit, and return on investment which may be achieved if the new product is introduced under the family brand as compared to what might be expected if it is sold under its own individual brand and choose the alternative which offers significantly greater returns. Since the results of such analysis may not be clear-cut, judgment may be improved if market tests involving an introductory strategy based on an individual brand may be compared with that making use of the family-brand approach.

company name combined with individual brand

Some firms have found it desirable to establish an association between individual brands by tying them together with the company name. One example is the Kellogg Company, which consistently uses the company name along with individual brand names such as Corn Flakes, Rice Crispies, Sugar Corn Pops, and Pop-Tarts. Here the new products may be given individual promotional support and may develop individual brand images, yet they all gain from the association with the well-established Kellogg name. Another example is the Ford Motor Company, which gives strong emphasis to individual brands of automobiles such as Lincoln, Mercury, Thunderbird, Cougar, Fairlane, Falcon, and Mustang. Yet the entire line is tied together under the Ford name through such corporate advertising themes as: "The Ford Family of Fine Cars" (1955–59); "Ford Built Means Better Built" (1959–64); and "Ford Has a Better Idea" (1965 to date).

This strategy enables a firm to gain family recognition for its products at the same time that the benefits of individual branding are also achieved.

promotional implications of brand-quality-price relationships

In the foregoing discussion, quality price relationships were identified as an important consideration in deciding whether to seek generalization by using a family brand or aim at distinctiveness by using an individual brand. In those instances where the new product being introduced is of the same identical type as the existing line, for example, cameras, but is of either higher quality or lower quality than the present product, the question of whether to sell both products under the same brand assumes special importance. If the firm markets a high-quality line of men's shoes under a highly regarded brand name such as "Status," for example, adds a medium grade line under the same brand, and promotes the new line aggressively, the sales of the medium-priced line will tend to increase at the expense of the higher priced product. Consumers may tend to impute the high quality associated with the brand name, Status, to the medium-priced line and thus buy it in the belief that they are getting a bargain. This phenomenon is commonly identified as "trading down." Management should recognize the possibility of getting the trading-down effect when considering the wisdom of selling a lower quality version of the product under the brand name already associated with a higher quality level. Whether such action is wise depends upon a number of considerations.

A key factor is whether consumers are able to discriminate between the higher and lower quality versions of the same product. If the characteristics of importance to the consumer are "hidden qualities," then the prospective buyer is likely to assume that the quality of the lower priced item is the same as the higher priced item and buy it thinking she is getting a bargain. If she can appraise these qualities through usage, however, then she will be disappointed in the lower priced item, and this will damage the reputation of the firm's higher quality product. If these hidden qualities cannot be evaluated through usage, the consumer will probably be satisfied with her purchase and will continue to buy the lower priced item. Under these circumstances, the firm will be trading sales of the lower priced item for the higher priced product. If this result is being sought in the belief that it will bring greater long-run profits than to produce only the higher quality item, then addition of the lower quality item under the established brand name may be justifiable. If this shift in volume from high- to low-quality product is not desired and results in lower long-run profits, the action would be unfortunate.

If the characteristics important to the consumer are features of design, style, or appearance which can be evaluated through inspection, then the consumer will probably be able to distinguish the low-quality item from the high, and will not be confused as to what she is buying. If she really values the features which are associated with the high-quality item, she will pay the higher price for it. Those who buy the lower quality item will probably constitute a different market segment not reached by the high-quality version of the brand. By reaching a new market segment, management may expand the total market for its brand.

Another consideration is whether the new low-quality item will be sold through different retail channels from the high-quality product. High-quality men's watches, for example, might be sold through jewelry stores. The manufacturer might then add a lower quality version under the same brand name and distribute it through discount houses and mail-order firms in the hope of expanding the market for his brand to include price-conscious lower income prospective buyers. If the prospective buyers of the higher quality watch shop only the jewelry stores in making their purchase then the addition of the lower quality line in discount stores will not tend to erode the original market. If these prospective buyers do shop the discount houses, however, they may confuse the quality of the two lines and purchase the lower priced version. Research on buying habits would be necessary to resolve this question.

Still another factor to be considered is whether salesmen are present in the retail store to aid the consumer in making a selection. If the same retail store carries both the higher and lower quality versions of the brand, salesmen could justify the higher price by pointing out its higher quality. In this case there would be no confusion as to quality, and prospective buyers of both the higher and lower quality items would be reached. If salesmen are not properly trained and supervised, however, they might have a tendency to give up too easily when they run into sales resistance in trying to sell the higher quality product. Instead of pointing out the benefits of buying the higher priced item, they might switch to pushing the lower priced version on the grounds that it is almost as good, but substantially lower in price. If this danger were recognized, the firm could take steps to minimize it by giving dealers larger margins on the high-priced item than on the low, and by taking steps to make sure that salesclerks are properly trained to push the higher priced item adequately before bringing out the lower priced product. In considering whether trading down is likely to occur, therefore, management should make a careful assessment of the kind of behavior which may be expected from the retail clerks selling the line.

What has been said above relates to consumer goods. If the firm is selling industrial goods, however, there is little danger that the addition of a lower priced line under the established brand will result in a shift of volume from the higher quality to the lower quality product. Industrial buyers are likely to specify the quality of product desired and inspect the items delivered to make sure that they conform to specifications. Several persons are likely to influence the purchase. Buying is likely to be more rational. Purchasers are not likely to buy the wrong quality because the price is lower.

In summary, when a manufacturer wishes to add a lower or higher quality version of an existing product to his line and wishes to maintain sales of the original item, he would be well advised to give it a separate brand name in those cases where consumers are not likely to be able to discriminate between the two products at the point of purchase, where quality can be evaluated through usage, where consumers are likely to shop the different types of retailers who handle the different quality levels, and if salesmen are likely to switch too readily to the sale of the lower quality item when sales resistance appears. If the market for the higher quality version is shrinking to unprofitable levels, however, the firm may wish to take advantage of the trading-down effect to help build up sales volume of a lower quality line which will tap a new market segment. While we might question the ethics involved in deliberately setting out to confuse consumers, the above discussion indicates how the firm might proceed to achieve the desired result.

The reverse of the above situation occurs when a firm originally sells a low-quality product and adds a higher quality version of the same item to the line. If management wishes to reach a higher income segment of the market through this action, the brand policy to follow will depend upon the same factors mentioned above. If consumers cannot distinguish the two quality levels, are unable to judge quality through usage, and find both the higher and lower quality items in the same retail outlets, then management would be well advised to sell the higher quality line under a separate brand name. If the objective of management is to get a trading-up effect, however, then the higher quality version should be given the same brand name and should be promoted aggressively. The prestige associated with the higher quality version will tend to rub off on the lower quality item, and the sales of the lower quality product will increase. Under this strategy the potential of the higher quality item will not be fully achieved, since it is being used as a means of stimulating the sales of the original lower quality line. Again we might question the ethics of a firm which relies upon confusion of the consumer to gain its objectives. Nevertheless, it is important to understand this phenomenon so that management will make its brand policy decision with a full realization of the probable consequences.

Finally, if consumers can discriminate between the two quality levels through inspection, and the two lines are distributed through different channels not customarily shopped by the same prospective buyers, then both higher and lower quality lines may be sold under the same brand name with little risk.

Another way to distinguish between quality levels, while still identifying the different items with the family name, is to follow the practice used by automobile manufacturers. Oldsmobile, for example, combines the family name with a model designation to distinguish between products with different price-quality levels within its line as follows: Delta 88, Ninety-Eight, and Toronado. Here there is little danger of confusion between quality levels, but the different lines all benefit from association with the Oldsmobile family name.

whether to manufacture under distributors' brands[9]

This issue is of fundamental importance to manufacturers, since the decision made has an important bearing not only upon the promo-

---

[9] Summarized from Victor J. Cook and Thomas F. Schutte, Marketing Science Institute, *Brand Policy Determination,* pp. 66–97. © 1967 by Allyn and Bacon, Inc., Boston. By permission of the publisher and the Marketing Science Institute.

tional strategy followed by the firm but also upon product development, distribution policy, pricing, production, and finance. Reaching a wise decision may influence market share and profit performance for years to come. Recognition of this fact has led some of our largest corporations to set up special task forces to make a thorough study of the risks and opportunities of supplying large-scale distributors with products to be sold under their private brands.

While there has been a substantial resurgence of distributors' brands during the years since World War II, the impact of private brands upon different industries varies considerably. In a recent study of brand policy by the Marketing Science Institute, it was found that the share of industry achieved by distributors' brands varied as follows: shoes 52 percent, replacement tires 36 percent, major appliances 33 percent, gasoline 16 percent, grocery products 13 percent, and portable appliances 7 percent. It is apparent that the opportunities of profiting from distributors' brand production as well as the risk involved in following such a policy vary widely in different product classifications.

There are three basic brand policy options available to the manufacturer. A company can elect to produce only its own brands, and follow a "manufacturers' brand policy." Or a firm can follow a "distributors' brand policy" where it produces exclusively for sale under private labels and manufactures nothing under its own brand. In between these two extremes falls the "mixed-brand policy," where both private and national brands are produced. Analysis indicates that each of these policy options may be appropriate under certain conditions. Reaching a wise decision therefore calls for careful analysis and discriminating judgment.

The executive faced with such a decision may get helpful guidance from the findings of the MSI study mentioned above.[10] This study was based upon intensive interviews with 112 different manufacturing organizations. Of this number, 33 companies had a manufacturers' brand policy, 65 were committed to a mixed-brand policy, while 14 produced only private brands. Factors influencing management in following each of the alternative policies are outlined below.

distributors' brand policy

Companies following a distributors' brand policy are essentially experts in the production of a given product line. The major marketing function is shifted to distributors. They tend to have a limited sales

---

[10] *Ibid.*

force and capability in market research, restricted product development and consumer research activities, limited warehousing and distribution facilities, and undertake little promotion and advertising. Such firms tend to have low sales volume, often less than $50 million. Most of these companies share a common characteristic. At a crucial point in their histories, usually prior to World War II, they lacked the management resources or the financial backing to strengthen a dwindling market position and began producing distributors' brands as a means of increasing sales and profits. The distributors' brand policy was probably the best alternative open to these companies. Although the management of some of these companies hope eventually to go into the production, distribution, and promotion of their own brands, most of them do not have the management capabilities or financial strength necessary to compete effectively as producers of their own nationally advertised brands.

manufacturers' brand policy

In contrast are the companies which are fully committed to the manufacturing and marketing of their own brands—to a manufacturers' brand policy. These firms are often giants in their industries with broad product lines, large brand shares, and established distribution systems. Such companies consider themselves to be specialists, not just in production, but in marketing and distribution as well. Often they have the required management and capital resources to keep their complex operations going at a highly profitable level. Management of some of these firms does not view private brands as a serious threat, and in other companies, management does not even view private brands as serious competition. Accordingly, these firms do not produce distributors' brands because they feel that to do so would mean giving up more than they would gain.

mixed-brand policy

There are other manufacturers, however, with marketing capabilities and sales volumes comparable with the top manufacturers' brand concerns, who choose to enter private-brand production under a mixed-brand policy. These firms are often large, well-established, experienced in marketing, and with sufficient financial resources to stay near the top of their industry with their own brands, yet they still turn to the production of private brands. Indeed, in all the industries studied, MSI found that an increasing number of manufacturers were turning to a mixed-brand policy. Moreover, a mixed-brand policy is probably the most common brand policy in existence today in most consumer product industries, both in terms of the number of companies involved and in the proportion of industry volume they represent. What rationale explains the adoption of a mixed-brand policy? Among the more important considerations are the following.

1. *Recognition of profit opportunities in the production of private brands.* The vice president for marketing of one firm, for example, stated: "We were advised that the percent of private label merchandise was growing—it's now between 11 and 23 percent of total chain-store sales in most markets. We're losing millions in sales by refusing to produce chain brands."[11] Especially where earnings per share have been declining for a number of years, competing for substantial private-brand volume may appear to offer the quickest way to improve the picture.

2. *An interest in reducing the average collection period, and improving the working capital position.* Adoption of a mixed-brand policy enabled some firms to channel more sales into a few large-volume, quick-paying accounts (private-brand distributors) and proportionately less into many small-volume, slower paying accounts.

3. *Gains in production efficiency.* Many of the firms studied were led into private-brand business by production considerations. From a short-run viewpoint, a mixed-brand policy may be used as a stopgap measure to deal with sudden declines in sales volume, temporary excess capacity, or overproduction. The petroleum industry, for example, is characterized by continuous production and high shutdown-startup costs. As a result, refiners frequently sell excess output to independents for distribution under private brands. While the production of private brands as a stopgap maneuver may appeal to certain nondurable goods manufacturers, this approach is not as applicable to companies producing consumer durables. Here too much long-term planning is needed before entering into private-brand production, and withdrawal from such business is equally difficult.

Certain manufacturers may also enter into private-brand production as a means of achieving stability in normal production scheduling operations with attendant gains in production efficiency. Neither this consideration, nor the stopgap tactic, however, proved to be crucial elements in the large, long-term private-brand programs studied by the

---

[11] *Ibid.,* p. 89.

MSI. Instead, two other production advantages were found to be extremely important in certain situations. First, long-term contracts with large distributors may provide a basis for plant expansion resulting in a general reduction of unit costs on both national and private-brand volume through economies of scale. Second, even where private-brand volume does not justify large building programs, manufacturers may still experience a significant reduction in unit costs as a direct result of the distributors' brand business.

4. *Marketing considerations.* Gains in the marketing area are often important considerations leading to the decision to adopt a mixed-brand policy. Among the more important are the following:

a) Private-brand production provides a way of achieving rapid market information feedback. In the process of controlling their operations, the operators of large chain-store organizations collect valuable information upon changes in consumer demand as they relate to product features, price lines, and new products, among others. Regardless of whether this information is freely shared with the manufacturer, or must be inferred from the character of private-brand orders, it is valuable feedback which could not be gained cheaply or quickly in any other way.

b) A mixed-brand policy enables a firm to get detailed knowledge of the merchandising operations of a distributor (who is a major competitor) by supplying him with private-brand products.

c) The close working relationship between the manufacturer and his private-brand account may allow him to exert some influence upon the product line and merchandising programs of this distributor (who is also a competitor). One manufacturer, for example, was asked by a private-brand account to provide assistance in merchandise planning. As a result, the producer and the distributor agreed that they would both be better off if the appeal of the private brand were to be based upon value rather than price and that traditional price lines would not be departed from significantly by the private label.

d) A mixed-brand policy may also provide a manufacturer with the opportunity of spreading marketing overhead to the added output generated by the private-brand contracts. Indeed, many companies interviewed in the MSI study found this advantage to be more important than the ability to spread manufacturing overhead.

e) Some manufacturers with broad product lines may adopt a mixed-brand policy as a way to escape defensive, costly promotional competition encountered on certain of their products. Although the national brands of such firms may be market leaders in product categories accounting for most of their sales volume, they may be unable to maintain leadership in others where large advertising and sales promotion expenditures are made by competition. By manufacturing these products for private-brand distributors, they may recoup their volume at the same time that the burden of promotional competition is passed on to distributors.

f) One of the important reasons for adopting a mixed-brand policy is the high degree of pricing flexibility which may be achieved. Under the Robinson-Patman Act a seller is prohibited from discriminating in price between different purchasers of commodities of *like grade and quality* where the effect of such discrimination may be substantially to lessen competition or tend to create a monopoly. The difficulties of justifying price differences in the sale of the manufacturer's own brand tend to discourage the quoting of special discounts to large chain distributors. If a firm decides to adopt a mixed-brand policy, however, it may produce variations of its product to meet the specifications of large-scale distributors, who will then sell these items under their own private brands. Indeed, if these private brands differ enough from the manufacturer's own brand so that he may justifiably claim that they are not of "like grade and quality," this will take them out from under the restrictions of Section 2 (a) of the Robinson-Patman Act and enable the firm to charge such buyers lower prices than his own national brand customarily brings. In this manner greater pricing flexibility may indeed be gained, since the limitations imposed by the Robinson-Patman Act may be avoided.

The feasibility of following such an approach depends upon the nature of the products which a firm produces. The critical question, of course, is how much of a change must be made in the product produced under the manufacturer's brand to remove the private brand from the jurisdiction of the Robinson-Patman Act and how much these modifications are likely to cost. Unless the costs of such variations can be held to a limited amount, the ability of the manufacturer to quote an attractive price to the large distributor may be wiped out. With these points in mind, then, it is apparent that the ability of firms to make minor variations of limited cost in their private-brand products will differ considerably as between items such as household appliances and packaged food products. Minor modifications in appearance and design of a household refrigerator may be enough to meet the specifications of a chain distributor and thus permit the manufacturer to justify a special discount on the private-brand item. A packaged-food processor, in contrast, may find it difficult if not impossible to make obvious physical differences between its private-label merchandise and its national brand without incurring costs which would eliminate the profits of private-brand business. Failure to make the private brands different would open the producer to the risk of an FTC charge of violating the Robinson-Patman Act.

While it is difficult to assess the degree of risk of an FTC charge in the latter case, the court decisions in the *Borden Company* v. *Federal Trade Commission* case may provide producers with some helpful guidelines.[12] In this case the Borden Company sold physically identical evaporated milk at a lower price to distributors under private labels than it charged for the Borden brand. While the Supreme Court ruled that the products sold under both brands were of "like grade and quality," it remanded the case to the Fifth Circuit Court of Appeals for a finding on whether the sale of the private brands at a lower price injured competition. The circuit court found that the difference in price between the Borden brand and the private brands was roughly equivalent to the consumer appeal of the Borden label and that, accordingly, competition was not injured.[13] Although these decisions might encourage packaged-goods producers to consider turning to a mixed-brand position by merely changing the label on the product, there would still appear to be considerable risk in such an action. Unanswered in the circuit court decision is the question of how much of a price differential an established manufacturer of a national brand might quote in selling a private brand for the first time. How could he measure initially the value of the consumer preference for his own brand at the retail level as compared with the new private brand? The lack of some objective guideline might make it difficult to justify the differential should he be charged with illegal price discrimination by the FTC.

Then, too, it is apparent that the circuit court decision ran directly counter to the guidelines previously followed by the FTC in determining whether to charge violations where the issue of "like grade and quality" is involved. Since Borden won its case in Circuit Court of Appeals, it is entirely possible that the FTC might wish to institute another test case to attempt to get a Supreme Court ruling on the question of how much of a price differential may be permissible as a

---

[12] *Federal Trade Commission* v. *Borden Company*, No. 106, decided March 23, 1966, 86 *Supreme Court Reporter*, 383 U.S. 685, pp. 1092–1106.

[13] *Federal Trade Commission* v. *Borden Company*, U.S. Court of Appeals for the Fifth Circuit, 381 F. 2d 175, No. 20463, July 14, 1967. Commerce Clearing House, *Trade Cases*, 1967, p. 84, 171–84, 176.

measure of the "commercial value" of the manufacturer's national brand. In short, it would still appear to be risky for a packaged-goods manufacturer to offer his product without change under private brands as a means of achieving greater price flexibility than he now has in selling his national brand. As pointed out earlier, however, producers of other types of products which lend themselves more easily to distinctive minor variations tend to regard the increased flexibility in pricing achieved by moving to a mixed-brand policy as an important advantage of this approach.

5. *Risks of a mixed brand policy.*[14] It is recognized that certain risks are involved in the adoption of a mixed-brand policy. Accordingly, it is helpful to identify the risks anticipated by firms considering production under distributors' brands and to discover how serious these problems turned out to be in actual practice. Findings of the MSI study relating to these points are reviewed below.

a) Loss of trade support for the national brand. Manufacturers relying on franchise outlets for distribution of their national brand were concerned that the production of private-brand merchandise might result in a reduction of sales efforts by their dealers and even a loss in franchise outlets. For a few manufacturers these fears were realized. Others found dealers less critical than they expected, however. Still others found it possible to minimize adverse dealer reactions by offering wider margins made possible by accepting private-brand business, or by handling the private-brand business through subsidiary companies not identified directly with the parent concern.

b) Recognition by consumers that products of the same manufacturer are available under both national and private brands. This risk is especially serious where personal selling is used at the point of purchase, since the source of the private brand may be mentioned by the clerk in attempting to make a sale. Even where products are sold on a self-service basis, such identification may also take place if package designs and container shapes are the same for both national and private brands, since they are often stocked side by side on retail shelves by distributors. Manufacturers adopting a mixed-brand policy usually did all they could to minimize recognition by consumers that their products were available under both national and private labels. Some took steps to make the appearance of the private brand different from that of the national brand. Others put provisions in contracts with distributors to prevent mention of the supplier's name in promo-

---

[14] Summarized from *op. cit.,* pp. 93 96.

tion. Yet for some companies the problems of consumer recognition were well known in advance and were accepted philosophically as a part of the private brand business.

c) Loss of exclusive rights to new product developments through adoption by private-brand customers. Where distributors work closely with manufacturers on research and development work, and contribute significant amounts to R.&D. activities, they may be expected to want equal access to new product developments which may result. Before entering into such an arrangement, of course, the gains and losses may be evaluated and cooperative R.&D. activities undertaken only if the net result is beneficial. One firm saw the advantage of fast, widespread distribution and consumer acceptance in simultaneous introduction of a major innovation under both national and private labels. A disadvantage of this approach, however, was the risk of consumer recognition that the same company manufactured both the national and private label and the possibility that the manufacturer's brand might, therefore, achieve a lower share of market than otherwise possible.

d) Disclosure of costs and operating data to a major competitor (the private-brand distributor) through known cost contracts. This was recognized as an unavoidable problem of a mixed-brand policy, although few executives believed that this information would be used to their disadvantage by their private-brand customers.

e) Certain risks long associated with private-brand business were recognized by firms adopting a mixed-brand policy, but were discounted as being of less concern than the problems discussed above. One was the risk that a mixed-brand policy might result in trading volume and dollars under the manufacturers' brand for volume and fewer dollars under the private label. Only a few firms following a mixed-brand policy actually experienced a drop in sale of their own brands with private-brand production. On the contrary, the result was most often a substantial increase in total volume and at least maintenance of previous sales levels under the manufacturers' brand.

Another commonly recognized risk is that of becoming unduly dependent upon giant private-brand distributors through gradual increases over time in the proportion of output going into distributors' brands. While firms moving from complete reliance on national brands to a mixed-brand policy recognized this potential danger, many expressed a keen interest in increasing their private-brand sales—some even by 100 percent or 200 percent. Apparently they regarded this potential risk as one not of immediate concern in view of the magnitude of their current national brand volume.

6. *Relative profitability of different brand policies.* According to the MSI study, firms following a mixed-brand policy were more profitable than firms committed entirely to private-brand production, but were less profitable than producers following a manufacturers' brand policy. Even so, examples of highly profitable mixed-brand organizations were found during the course of the study. According to MSI, "It cannot be concluded that a manufacturers' brand firm is likely to suffer a loss in profits by adopting a mixed-brand policy."[15] This finding led the researchers to examine the characteristics of the more profitable mixed-brand policy manufacturers in an attempt to discover why they had been unusually successful in their approach. The results of this analysis are outlined below.

a) Such firms have formal policies which provide for the production of private brands on a continuing basis as an integral part of each company's operation, rather than for short-run, in-and-out tactics.

b) They have a full-time private-brand administrator reporting most often to the vice president of marketing.

c) Most of these firms have specific criteria used in making a careful selection of private label customers.

d) Corporate resources—such as research and development staffs, marketing research data, and merchandising and promotional planning experience—are made available to the private-brand administrator.

e) The use of "known-cost" contracts—the type of contract which provides details on the manufacturers' cost structure—is one of the characteristics shared by the more profitable mixed-brand policy companies. The known-cost contract often appeared responsible for a close management contact between supplier and customer, another distinguishing characteristic of the more profitable firms.

7. *Summary.* As indicated in the foregoing discussion, many well-established firms view private-brand production under a mixed-brand policy as a normal, profitable market opportunity. Often they see production under private labels as a means of reaching a market segment not covered by their national brand business. In considering adopting a mixed-brand policy, it is recognized that there may be serious risks involved. Such recognition indicates the wisdom of careful analysis of corporate, financial, production, and marketing considera-

---

[15] *Ibid.,* p. 83.

tions in evaluating the desirability of adopting a mixed-brand position. Judging from the MSI study, many firms believe that the advantages of a mixed-brand policy outweigh the risks associated with the production of private brands. Then, too, the mixed-brand policy is viewed as the most flexible of the three policy options. It offers the opportunity to adapt quickly to basic changes in the market structure as large-scale distributors grow and capture an increasing share of industry for their private brands. It also opens up large amounts of volume that would remain unavailable under a policy of producing only manufacturers' brands. Companies included in the MSI study that integrated private-brand production into the mainstream of corporate activity by developing well-planned, long-term policies, apparently found that this approach resulted in higher volume, greater overall market strength, and improved profits.

decision-theory approach to mixed-brand policy choice

The foregoing discussion of the problem of whether a national brand producer should seek private-brand business makes it abundantly clear that the consequences of such action are not known with certainty. This suggests that management might well consider the possibility of applying the "decision-theory" approach to the analysis of this problem—i.e., the method of *individual decision making under risk.*

The decision-theory approach may be illustrated in terms of a hypothetical problem fashioned by Buzzell and Slater to approximate actual conditions in the wholesale bakery market, which one of the authors had studied for a number of years.[16] In this model bakery market let us assume that there are three wholesale bakeries designated as A, B, and C; and two chain bakeries, those of the Blue Chain and the Red Chain. Wholesale baker Z, located in a nearby city, is a potential "outside" competitor. The customers served by these bakeries are designated as follows: Blue, Red, and Green corporate chains; retailer cooperatives I and II; voluntary chain I; independent supermarkets; small independent stores. Let us assume that the Blue Chain asks baker B, the second largest wholesale baker in the market, to produce a private brand of bread for sale in the Blue Stores. The problem is, how should baker B respond to such a request?

---

[16] The following discussion is reprinted by permission from Robert D. Buzzell and Charles C. Slater, "Decision Theory and Marketing Management," *Journal of Marketing,* Vol. 26, No. 3 (July, 1962), pp. 7–16. Published by the American Marketing Association.

The decision-theory approach to the solution of this problem may be summarized briefly as follows:

1. *Identification of alternative possibilities.* The decision maker, B, must choose among several possible "acts" or "strategies" denoted as $A_1, A_2 \ldots A_n$. The different possibilities open to baker B are as follows:

A_1—Ignore the request.

A_2—Make a counteroffer to produce a "secondary brand" bread to be sold at a lower price than the regular "B brand" Bread.

A_3—Reduce the price of the regular brand.

A_4—Accede to the request of the Blue Chain.

A_5—Institute a system of price differentials based on quantity and service rendered by baker B.

2. *Identification of possible states of nature.* Choice among the above "acts" depends upon certain *conditions* which cannot be predicted with certainty. The conditions may be termed "states of nature" and designated as $S_1, S_2 \ldots S_m$. These states of nature include all factors which determine the effects of a decision—for example, the responses of customers, and competitors' reactions. If baker B follows possibility A_1 and ignores the Blue Chain's request, there are six possible outcomes:

S_{11}—Blue is supplied by outside baker Z. Having achieved a foothold in the market, Z also supplies private-label bread to the Yellow Chain and to Coop I.

S_{12}—Blue is supplied by Z, but Z fails to get any other business.

S_{13}—Blue is supplied by local bakery A or bakery C.

S_{14}—Blue acquires its own bakery plant and decreases its purchases from B.

S_{15}—Blue decides to wait; but resentful of B's refusal, adopts minor countermeasures, including reduced display space and less careful maintenance of B's display stocks.

S_{16}—Blue decides to wait and does *not* adopt any countermeasures.

In similar fashion, the outcomes of other decision possibilities should be enumerated.

3. *Exploration of further possibilities and outcomes.* The analysis cannot stop realistically with a single "round" of actions and their outcomes. Instead it is necessary to explore the whole chain of effects and reactions that would follow a given decision by baker B. To illustrate, let us return to decision A_1 and the possible outcomes outlined above. Suppose baker B refuses (A_1) and baker Z supplies the

Blue Chain as well as the Yellow Chain and Coop I (S_{11}). Baker B is then confronted by a new set of possibilities: he can retaliate by supplying retailers in Z's own market, hoping to drive Z out of the local market; or he can meet Z's competition locally. If he retaliates in Z's market, the outcome will again depend on the "state of nature." The possible outcome, for instance, is that legal action will be taken against B for geographic price discrimination. An illustrative series of moves and outcomes is shown in a tree diagram in Figure 12–1.

4. *Estimation of payoffs.* For each alternative decision and each outcome, the "payoff" to the decision maker should be estimated through tracing the effects upon the firm's sales, costs, and profits. Baker B's computations cover profits for a five-year period, discounted to present values.

5. *Assessment of probabilities.* Since the outcome of a given decision is uncertain, a key element in the analysis is to assign probabilities to the various possible "states of nature." These probabilities represent the decision maker's "betting odds" as to the probable responses of customers, competition, and so forth. This is a difficult step, but it is an essential element in decision theory. The probabilities associated with the six possible outcomes of decision A_1 are shown in Figure 12–1.

6. *Computation of expected payoff.*[17] The expected payoff of an act is defined as the average of its net payoffs under all possible states of nature, each weighted by its probability of occurrence. With respect to decision A_1, refusal to furnish a private brand of bread for sale in the Blue Stores, the expected payoff of this action may be computed as shown in the accompanying table. With respect to each outcome, the estimated payoff is multiplied by its associated probability and the result is shown in the "expected payoff" column. The sum total of the ex-

Outcome	Estimated Payoff (000)	Probabilities	Expected Payoff (000)
S_{11}—Z supplies Blue, Yellow, Coop I	$-225.7	0.05	$-11.285
S_{12}—Z supplies Blue only	-225.7	0.05	-11.285
S_{13}—A or C supplies	-188.1	0.05	- 9.405
S_{14}—Blue acquires bakery	-370.5	0.05	-18.525
S_{15}—Blue waits, harasses B	- 75.0	0.30	-22.500
S_{16}—Blue waits, no harassment	0	0.50	0
Total Expected Payoff			$-73.000

---

[17] For a full explanation of the approach followed in estimating payoffs, in assessing probabilities, and in computing expected payoff of each alternative decision, see Buzzell and Slater, *Ibid.*, pp. 14–15.

Figure 12-1. Illustrative analysis of decision possibilities and outcomes—A_1: B refuses Blue's request (payoffs in thousands of dollars).

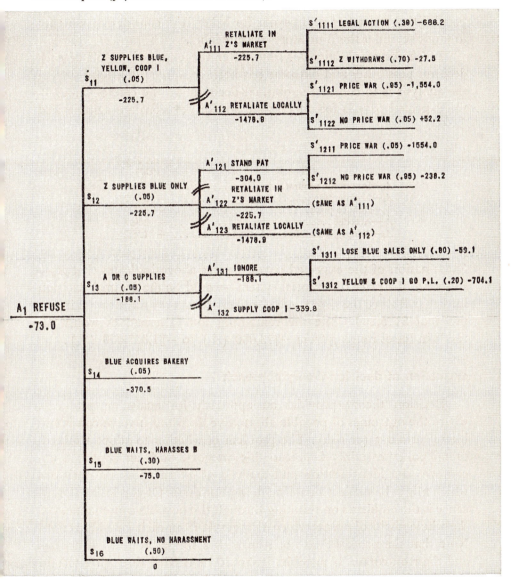

pected payoff figures for each of the six possible outcomes is the expected payoff for decision A_1, refusal to produce under Blue's private brand.

In the same manner, the expected payoffs of decisions A_2 through A_0 are computed and brought together in a summary table. The

results of such computations are shown on the tree diagram reproduced in Figure 12–2, which summarizes the first round of decision
possibilities, outcomes, and payoffs for baker B in considering whether
to produce under the Blue Stores private label.

7. *Choice of optimal decision.* After the expected payoff of each
decision possibility and outcome has been computed, the final step in
the analysis is to choose the optimal decision. In the case of baker B,
the expected payoffs for all possible acts or decisions are summarized
below.

Acts	Expected Payoff (000)
A_1—Ignore the request	$- 73.0$
A_2—Counteroffer	$- 265.2$
A_3—Reduce price	$-1,337.0$
A_4—Accede	$- 260.7$
A_5—Adopt price differential system	$+ 125.2$

Examination of the expected payoff figures above indicates that A_5—
adoption of a price differential system—would be the optimal decision
for baker B since the firm would be likely to achieve an increase in net
profit of $125,200 while the remaining four alternatives would all
result in losses ranging from −$73,000 ($A_1$) to −$1,337,000 (A_3).

evaluation of decision-theory approach

Decision theory provides an approach for analyzing problems
where the outcomes of possible alternative decisions involve considerable uncertainty (or risk). The problem of whether to adopt a mixed-
brand policy certainly falls into this category. Such an approach encourages the identification and analysis of *all* the possible decisions
which might be made (including doing nothing). Of particular significance is the emphasis on thinking through the possible consequences of
the whole chain of events which may result from each possible action.
Note that the process does not stop with a single "round" of actions
and their outcomes. If possible, it should be carried through a second
round and—if estimates of payoffs and probabilities can be made with
satisfactory confidence—through a third and possibly even a fourth
round. This aspect of the approach focuses attention on the critical
issues involved in the various possible ways of dealing with the problem.

In most cases of this sort, determination of the probabilities for the
relevant "states of nature" (reactions of consumers, competitors, and
so on) is difficult. A firm does not make a mixed-brand policy decision

A₁ IGNORE OR REFUSE -73.0

- S_{11} Z SUPPLIES BLUE AND OTHERS (.05) -225.7
- S_{12} Z SUPPLIES BLUE ONLY (.05) -225.7
- S_{13} A OR C SUPPLIES BLUE (.05) -188.1
- S_{14} BLUE ACQUIRES BAKERY (.05) -370.5
- S_{15} BLUE WAITS, HARASSES B (.30) -75.0
- S_{16} BLUE WAITS (.50) 0

A₂ COUNTER OFFER -265.2

- S_{21} Z SUPPLIES BLUE AND OTHERS (.02) -225.7
- S_{22} Z SUPPLIES BLUE ONLY (.03) -225.7
- S_{23} A OR C SUPPLIES BLUE (.01) -188.1
- S_{24} BLUE ACQUIRES BAKERY (.01) -370.5
- S_{25} BLUE WAITS, HARASSES B (.01) -75.0
- S_{26} BLUE WAITS (.02) 0
- S_{27} BLUE ACCEPTS A AND C / FOLLOW SUIT (.80) -275.1

A₃ REDUCE PRICE BY .02 -1337.0

- S_{31} Z SUPPLIES BLUE AND OTHERS (.03) -225.7
- S_{32} Z SUPPLIES BLUE ONLY (.04) -225.7
- S_{33} A OR C SUPPLIES BLUE (.02) -188.1
- S_{34} BLUE ACQUIRES BAKERY (.01) -370.5
- S_{35} BLUE ACCEPTS, A AND C DO NOT MEET (.05) -456.6
- S_{36} BLUE ACCEPTS, A AND C MEET, B RETAINS ADVAN. (.10) -1249.2
- S_{37} BLUE ACCEPTS, A AND C MEET, RETURN TO ORIGINAL SHARE (.75) -1554

- S_{41} BLUE ACCEPTS, A AND C / OFFER SECONDARY (.70) -22.2
- S_{42} BLUE ACCEPTS, A AND C / REDUCE PRICES (.10) -1442.7
- S_{43} BLUE ACCEPTS, A AND C / SUPPLY COOP I AND YELLOW (.20) -504.3

A₄ ACCEDE -260.7

A₅ PRICE DIFFERENTIAL SYSTEM +125.2

- S_{51} Z SUPPLIES BLUE AND OTHERS (.05) -225.7
- S_{52} Z SUPPLIES BLUE ONLY (.05) -225.7
- S_{53} A OR C SUPPLIES BLUE (.05) -188.1
- S_{54} BLUE ACCEPTS, A AND C FOLLOW SUIT (.60) 0
- S_{55} BLUE ACCEPTS, A AND C REDUCE PRICES (.25) +828.5

Figure 12–2. Summary of first round of decision possibilities, outcomes, and payoffs for wholesale bakery private-label decision (payoffs in thousands).

often enough to gain experience which may guide future estimates. Nevertheless, even very crude approximations of probabilities for various states affecting outcomes of a decision are better than none at all. Decision theory forces executives to recognize the subjective "betting odds" that lie behind their judgments and put them into quantitative form as probability estimates.

Likewise, the task of estimating profit payoffs for each possible line of action several years into the future tends to encourage executives to be more careful in their analyses. Estimating payoffs and determining probabilities, accordingly, tends to encourage management to examine the mixed-brand problem in concrete terms and provides a stimulus to more systematic thinking on the part of those involved. Equally important, structuring the problem in formal terms helps to indicate the direction which future research should take if such analyses are to be improved.

It should be recognized, of course, that application of decision theory to the mixed-brand policy problem will encourage estimates which may be based upon inadequate data and thus may represent only crude approximations of the information desired. It is necessary, therefore, to avoid imputing greater accuracy than they merit to the figures on estimated payoff which represent the end results of the analysis. If the limitations of the data are kept in mind, however, the decision-theory approach may aid management in the difficult task of making choices among alternative lines of action under conditions of uncertainty.

Perhaps the chief advantage of decision theory grows out of the fact that this approach requires the executive to *formalize* his thinking about a problem—to structure his judgment and write it down in black and white. It is self-evident that this is likely to improve the quality of executive judgment. Experimentation with this approach, therefore, would appear to be desirable.

conclusion

Decisions on brand strategy have important promotional implications. In this chapter, we have focused on issues relating to family versus individual brands, brand-quality-price relationships, and the wisdom of manufacturing products to be sold under distributors' brands as opposed to the firm's own brand. Evidence has been cited that for frequently purchased package goods, the promotion of one product under a family brand has beneficial effects for other products under that brand through the principle of generalization. In contrast, a study of semantic generalization as applied to family brands of household appliances raises some doubt as to the use of a common brand name as a means of transferring attitudes between dissimilar products of high unit value.

On the question of distributors' brands versus manufacturers' brands, each of the three policy options open may be appropriate under certain conditions, but a Marketing Science Institute study indicates that a mixed-brand policy is probably the most common posture in existence today in most consumer product industries. In our discussion we also noted that the outcomes of adopting any one of the three alternative policies involved considerable risk or uncertainty. Accordingly, the possibility of applying the "decision-theory" approach was examined and its merits and limitations discussed.

questions

1. Explain how the "assimilation effect" from psychological theory may be applied to family branding.
2. *a)* Did Fry's research verify the hypothesis that consumers have generalized preferences for family brands? To what product categories do his findings apply?
   b) What factors appear to contribute to the degree of generalized preference likely to exist in a given situation?
3. *a)* In studying semantic generalization, what hypothesis did Kerby test and for what types of products?
   b) Why do you suppose Kerby had consumers evaluate branded products in terms of "semantic differential scales" instead of in terms of percent of consumers purchasing one brand as compared with another?
4. Did the results of Kerby's research verify the hypothesis that "meaning should be transferred between two or more products that are physically dissimilar, if they share a common brand name"? How does Kerby explain his results?
5. The text suggest several factors which tend to foster or retard the development of generalized preference for family brands through the process of assimilation. In the light of these criteria, in which of the following situations would you recommend a policy of family branding?
   a) A new hair lightener for men to be introduced by Clairol, Inc., formerly marketing hair preparations exclusively for women.
   b) A double-edged razor designed for teen-agers by Gillette.

c) A new snow blower added to its line by Yard-Man, Inc., a manufacturer of power lawn mowers.

d) A stereo-phonograph added to its line of sewing machines by Singer Company.

e) A diaper pail spray in an aerosol can introduced by the owners of the firm producing Lustur-Seal, an automobile paint conditioner.

6. Under what conditions might it be desirable to combine an individual brand name with the corporate name in identifying a product? When might it be undersirable?

7. Until 1965, Polaroid Land Cameras capable of producing color pictures in 60 seconds were priced at about $135 and $165. In 1965, Polaroid announced the addition of Model 103 to sell at about $90 and Model 104 priced at $60. Later that same year, an economy model producing only black-and-white pictures was introduced at about $20. All of these models were sold under the Polaroid name. What is your analysis of the probability that these actions would result in trading down? If you believe that trading down would be likely to occur, would you regard this result as desirable or undesirable? Why?

8. In which of the following hypothetical situations would trading down be likely to occur?

a) If Cadillac introduced a medium-priced car under the Cadillac name.

b) If a manufacturer of high-grade women's dresses identified by the Smartset brand added a medium-grade line under the same brand name.

c) If the manufacturer of the Hamilton high-grade watches were to offer a low-priced watch available only through mail-order houses.

d) If a materials handling company making industrial fork trucks selling at $7,000 introduced an economy line priced at $1,500 under the same brand name.

e) If the Kroehler Co., emphasizing medium- and low-priced upholstered furniture, were to add a high-grade line under the Kroehler brand name and sell it through retail outlets handling the original line.

9. Under what conditions are firms likely to concentrate their production on the manufacture and sale of products under distributors' brands? What are the risks of such a policy? How may these risks be minimized (if at all)?

10. Under what circumstances are firms likely to limit themselves entirely to the manufacture and sale of their own brands? What limitations, if any, does this policy have?

11. List briefly the considerations which tend to lead a firm to adopt a mixed-brand policy.

12. Identify briefly the risks of following a mixed-brand policy.

13. In view of the risks which such a policy involves, why have many well-established firms adopted this approach in the marketing of their products?

14. *a)* What are the merits of applying the decision-theory approach to the solution of the question of whether to manufacture for sale under distributors' brands (assuming the firm now concentrates on its own brands) ?

    b) What conditions should exist if the decision-theory approach is to be applied successfully?

cases for part five

case 5–1

MIDWEST PRECISION CORPORATION*

relation of distribution policy to selling strategy

The Midwest Precision Corporation of Jackson, Michigan, was a small manufacturer of industrial casters and materials handling trucks. The products were sold direct to users within 300 miles of Jackson and through materials handling equipment distributors in other industrial areas in the United States. After reviewing the firm's progress during the previous five years, Mr. W. A. Bootes, president, was seeking ways of expanding his company's sales volume.

history

The company was founded by Mr. Bootes shortly after World War II. Its plant consisted of a large corrugated steel-sided building where from 12 to 24 men worked, and an attached two-room cinder block building where 3 men and a girl administered the business. The firm had sales of about $350,000.[1]

Midwest made a complete line of medium and heavy-duty casters for use on materials handling equipment. The casters were precision made of high-quality bearings, bushings, wheels, and other parts, to withstand heavy loads. Practically all of the casters were a standard product, i.e., they were nearly the same in design and quality as those of competing brands. They were sold to industrial firms who made their own materials handling equipment and to equipment manufacturers. The casters were used on platform trucks, dollies, bins, racks, and so on. Other applications of these casters were limited. Casters for furniture and light weight equipment were of different design, and conveyor manufacturers made their own casters. The 5,000 to 7,000 casters sold each year constituted about 40 percent of the company's dollar sales.

As time went by, many industrial firms that had formerly made their own materials handling equipment and equipped it with Midwest casters began to buy their handling equipment complete with casters, and many equipment

---

* Written by L. B. Milliken and Peter Repenning, Research Assistants, Bureau of Business Research, The University of Michigan.

[1] Sales figures have been multiplied by a constant.

manufacturers began to make their own casters. Therefore, in order to become more competitive with the caster manufacturers who also made complete equipment, and in order to maintain volume production of casters, Midwest began making complete materials handling trucks. It produced flat trucks, trucks with sides, and trucks for special racks or bins. Some were hand trucks and others were pulled in trains. About 50 percent of the cost of some trucks was in the casters. Although Midwest lost a few of its caster customers when it began competing with them in the sale of trucks, total dollar sales did not suffer. Trucks accounted for about 60 percent of the firm's sales.

The casters varied in price from $25 to $75 for a set of four, and trucks were sold for $60 to $300 including the casters.

potential market

Mr. Bootes believed the potential market for Midwest casters and trucks covered all industrial areas in the United States. His casters could be used by any maker of medium-sized or heavy-duty materials handling equipment. There was some variation in the quality of casters, but those produced by Midwest and its competitors were of uniformly high quality. There were some price cutters in the industry, but they were makers of lower quality casters and so were not really competitors. The leading manufacturers belonged to a trade association which had successfully promoted the idea of nonprice competition. Since the competitors had nearly uniform quality and prices, caster sales volume was dependent on sales ability and service. Practically all industries provided a potential market for Midwest trucks, but thus far all sales had been to auto manufacturers around Detroit. Midwest was small and a comparative newcomer in the market. It had about 1 percent of the industry sales. Among its larger competitors were the Rose Truck and Caster Company in Detroit; Albion Industries in Albion, Michigan; and the Bassick Company of Bridgeport, Connecticut.

sales methods

Midwest casters and trucks were sold in two ways. Mr. Bootes and his assistant, Mr. Carpenter, sold direct to users within an area of about 300 miles from Jackson. The main customers in this area were the auto manufacturers around Detroit, including Ford, Chevrolet, Buick, Cadillac, and Fisher Body. The company supplied casters and trucks to all Ford plants in the United States, and the business was about 50 percent of all Midwest sales. About 75 percent of total sales were made by Mr. Bootes and Mr. Carpenter in the area.

The other 25 percent of sales were in casters sold by 20 materials handling equipment distributors and 10 manufacturers' agents in major industrial centers. The distributors usually handled one or two lines of trucks, casters, conveyors, lift trucks, racks, and containers. They had warehousing facilities and did limited fabricating of special jobs for their customers. They delivered the equipment and often extended credit, which they refinanced at banks. Most of them had aggressive sales forces. Midwest often paid 50 percent of the cost of their advertising in telephone books, direct-mail pieces, and local trade papers. The manufacturers' agents usually handled the same line of products but performed none of the wholesale functions. They did no promotional work, but were considered quite aggressive salesmen. Midwest sold casters to both distributors and agents at 50 percent and 10 percent off list price. They in turn sold them at prices ranging from 30 percent to 50 percent off list, depending on the amount of business involved.

The main selling method used by Midwest and its distributors was personal contact with users of casters and trucks. In making a sale, usually the customer's industrial engineer or master mechanic was contacted first. He was shown the design features of the caster or truck. Then the purchasing agent was contacted and a price quoted or bid submitted. Since the quality of all brands of casters was about the same, the buying decision was usually made by the purchasing agent on the basis of price and service. In the Detroit area Mr. Bootes and Mr. Carpenter worked with customers' engineers in designing casters or trucks for special applications. Mr. Bootes spent about 25 percent of his time selling and the remainder at the plant. Mr. Carpenter spent about 75 percent of his time selling.

advertising and promotion

The company retained a small advertising agency, the Knickerbocker Press of Grand Rapids, to handle the promotion of its products. In regard to Midwest, the agency's objectives were to aid in:

1. Broadening and strengthening the dealer organization through advertising and personal selling by Midwest representatives.
2. Establishing brand-name recognition in industry through national trade journal and direct-mail advertising.
3. Increasing the sales volume through stimulation of inquiries which could be followed up by the distributors and agents.

Mr. Bootes and the agency agreed that advertising would not produce immediate sales increases. But since the company was a relative newcomer competing with well-established firms, they believed advertising to build recognition of the Midwest name was necessary.

To accomplish the objectives listed with the small appropriation available, the agency advocated the use of trade journal and direct-mail advertising. The theme of the space ads was that of inviting inquiries about Midwest casters. The ads contained pictures and factual information slanted toward industrial engineers. Many uses of the casters were listed. A direct-mail list was built from inquiries received and other lists purchased from trade journals. The mail pieces included a caster catalog, a card device which looked like a caster with windows cut in it so that the proper caster for any application could be "dialed" by turning the caster wheel, and several brochures describing specific casters and the trucks.

The company appropriated about $8,000 for promotion. About $3,500 was used for catalogs and direct-mail pieces. The remaining $4,500 was used for space advertising. Twelve 1/9-page ads were run in *New Equipment Digest* and also in *Equipment and Material Reporter*. The latter trade journal was circulated in 11 western states and had good circulation in the southern California industrial area. Mr. Bootes was very much interested in entering that market, but said that Midwest was not yet competitive there. The company was also listed in *Thomas' Register*.

Mr. Bootes was fairly well pleased with the results of Midwest advertising, although they were intangible. Sales had definitely increased over the past five-year period, but he did not believe much of the increase could be attributed directly to the promotion. The greatest sales increases had come from the Detroit area. The company usually received from one to five inquiries each day, and about 10 percent of the inquiries were converted to sales—some by the distributors and some directly by Midwest. Mr. Bootes was quite satisfied with the number of inquiries received but disappointed in the rate of conversion to sales. He did not have accurate information on whether these sales had covered the cost of advertising.

efforts to increase sales volume

Although the firm had made progress during the previous five years, Mr. Bootes was concerned with the problem of how to stimulate an even greater rate of increase in sales volume. He and Mr. Carpenter were making 75 percent of the firm's sales direct to customers—mostly in the Detroit area. Sales by the distributors and agents in other markets were low in dollars and as a percentage of total sales. About one half of the sales were to the Ford Motor Company, so a more diversified customer list as well as increased sales was desired. There were two basic alternatives in the solution of the major problem. The firm could concentrate on the Detroit market and raise its sales direct to users. Or it could try to raise its sales through distributors and agents in other markets.

There were several advantages in selecting the first alternative. Through his contacts with other trade association members, Mr. Bootes knew many of them were making good profits on small sales in one industrial area. The company had done well in the Detroit market, and the fact that it had always been able to raise sales there by increased sales effort indicated that there was more potential for Midwest. Mr. Bootes and Mr. Carpenter knew the Detroit market well, were close enough to serve it well, and could control the sales effort there easily. One disadvantage of concentration there was the dependence on the auto industry, Ford in particular.

There were several ways of trying to raise sales in other industrial centers. The company could hire another salesman to sell direct in some of these areas. It could use space and direct-mail advertising to get more distributors and agents in other markets. Or it could try to stimulate the existing distributors and agents by having a Midwest representative call on them periodically and by sending advertising to them.

If another salesman were hired to sell direct in other areas, he would be paid a commission on his sales and given an expense allowance. Mr. Bootes did not know what the dollar cost of this compensation and allowance would be, or how much increase in sales would be necessary to cover the cost. He did know that the expense could not be met out of their current selling prices. He believed the cost of hiring a man could be covered if all advertising and promotion were eliminated. On the basis of the current promotion appropriation, there would have been about $8,000 with which to work.

Mr. Bootes believed it would be difficult to get more distributors through advertising. Most of the good distributors and agents in most industrial areas had long since been retained by Midwest's older competitors. Occasionally a distributor's salesman started his own business and sought sources of supply. Midwest had gained some good distributors and agents by retaining them. In general, Mr. Bootes believed top-quality distributors were not attracted by advertising.

Of course, the company desired to stimulate the sales efforts of the existing distributors and agents, but how to do it was not an easy problem to solve. The advertising agency believed Midwest should have a representative visit each distributor every six months. The representative would make calls with the salesmen to contact the users and advise the salesmen. It was believed such a visit would create goodwill and give the company opportunity to evaluate the distributors regularly. Although Mr. Bootes believed this was a good idea, he knew neither he nor Mr. Carpenter had time to do the traveling, and he thought it would cost $12,000 to $15,000 a year to hire the right man and pay his expenses. The company could not afford that expense.

Midwest had attempted to stimulate its dealers by using direct-mail pieces to merchandise its promotions. In the past two years, it had sent the distributors and agents pieces using such phrases as "We're on the ball," "Watch for ads . . . ," and "More volume and profits for you. . . ." These pieces had cost $150 for 500 copies, and Mr. Bootes believed that was too expensive for the effect created. In the future he planned to produce direct-mail pieces for the distributors to send to their customers.

After giving the matter considerable thought, Mr. Bootes decided to concentrate in the Detroit area first and build up sales in other industrial markets slowly. He believed about 10 of the 30 distributors and agents were doing a good job and decided not to worry about the others' performance until he had determined the success of the Detroit experiment. If it worked well, the poor distributors would be released. Mr. Carpenter's brother became a part-time salesman in the Detroit market. If sales rose enough, he would become a full-time salesman to sell in Detroit and other areas. He was paid a commission on his sales, and the expense was covered with funds formerly used in promotion. This required a reduction in the advertising appropriation for the coming year to $3,800. The firm's sales were still largely dependent on Ford, but increased sales to other auto manufacturers had added some stability.

QUESTIONS

1. Appraise the distribution policy of Midwest. Would you recommend any changes? If so, why?
2. *a)* Would it appear to be profitable for Midwest to attempt to increase sales by concentrating on the Detroit market? Why?
   b) If this were to be done, what promotional strategy would you recommend? Why?
3. *a)* Does there appear to be a profitable opportunity to stimulate sales through giving emphasis to markets other than the Detroit area? Explain.
   b) If the firm were to follow this alternative, what promotional strategy would you propose? Why?
4. In the light of your analysis, do you agree with the president's decisions on promotional strategy to follow in order to achieve the desired sales increase? Explain.
5. How does the company's existing distribution policy influence decisions on appropriate promotional strategy?

case 5–2

MICHIGAN STATE APPLE COMMISSION*

decision on how best to utilize increased promotional budget

In January, 1968, Mr. F. G. Hasler, secretary-manager of the Michigan State Apple Commission, was reviewing his promotional budget for the 1968–69 fiscal year, which would begin July 1, 1968. This work was particularly important for the Michigan State Apple Commission and its secretary-manager, because the Michigan apple producers and processors, at the request of the

* Written by Bradley D. Lockeman, Research Fellow, Graduate School of Business Administration, The University of Michigan.

Introduction to marketing management

Michigan State Apple Commission, were to vote in March on an increase in assessments to enable the Commission to expand its advertising and promotional program. Mr. Hasler was faced with the problem of how best to utilize the increase in his promotional budget which might occur if the increased assessment passed.

history of the Apple Commission

The Michigan State Apple Commission was created by the Baldwin Apple Act in 1939 as one of many similar commissions in all apple-producing areas in the United States. Its sole purpose, like the other commissions and the national trade association, The National Apple Institute, was to promote the use of apples. Although it was a state government agency, the Commission was financially supported through assessment of Michigan apple producers. Initially the apple growers were assessed 1 cent per bushel sold, but this levy was raised to 2 cents in 1955. In 1958 it was changed to 6 cents per hundred pounds of apples sold for fresh market use and processing. Producers who sold apples for juice, cider, or vinegar (by far the least lucrative use of apples) were exempt from payment. Any other producers who did not wish to participate could claim exemption and receive a rebate of their contribution to the Commission during the fiscal year.

trends in apple consumption

Although the meaning and usefulness of statistics on per capita consumption of apples were much disputed, particularly by Mr. Hasler, it appeared evident that the apple industry had for some time been faced with a steadily declining primary demand. From 61.3 pounds per year in 1909, national per capita consumption had declined to 19.3 pounds per year in 1954 and 15.9 pounds by 1966. Michigan consumption was slightly, but not significantly, above the national average. With the increased use of refrigerated railroad cars and other modern methods of handling produce, the more perishable fruits, mainly citrus, had become available in all markets throughout the year. Fresh Michigan apples competed not only with these increasingly available citrus fruits, bananas, and pears but also with apples produced in such other regions of the United States as New York state, Appalachia, and Washington state, which had its own apple commission to advertise "Washington, the world's finest apples." Michigan apple products, which consisted primarily of applesauce, frozen slices, and various forms of juice, had become increasingly important in the market, but so had competing items: new frozen and dehydrated citrus products, as well as frozen slices and juice produced outside of Michigan.

Mr. Hasler was not particularly worried about the apparent long-range decline in consumption of apples. In the first place, he doubted the validity of the high per capita consumption figures recorded earlier in the century. Second, by the end of World War II the effect of competition from citrus fruits had been felt in all markets, and he believed that the rate of decline in apple consumption was decreasing so rapidly that per capita consumption would soon level off and stabilize. This belief seemed to be supported by a study which showed that processed apple products in 1966 were gaining in acceptance, while fresh use was remaining about the same. Since 1957, there had been only a 5 percent drop in the number of fresh apples eaten in the entire country. And although only one family in five, or 20 percent, was believed to use apples regularly, about 95 percent had purchased some fresh apples within the preceding 12 months, according to a nationwide survey of homemakers.

the market

The Michigan apple market covered the United States from eastern Ohio to the western Dakotas and from the Gulf of Mexico all the way up to and including parts of Canada. The heart of this mid-American market was the territory north of Nashville, Tennessee, west of Cleveland, Ohio, and east of Fargo, North Dakota. This market had generally absorbed nearly 100 percent of the fresh apples produced in Michigan, although apples from other apple-producing regions of the United States competed with Michigan apples in this same market. This was the territory where Michigan enjoyed the greatest transportation advantage over other apple-producing regions of the United States. East of Cleveland, the Michigan apple growers faced a transportation disadvantage compared to the situation of competing growers in the Appalachia area and New York State. As a result, Michigan apples had not usually been able to compete effectively in the eastern states.

The size and composition of the crop in each U.S. apple-producing region determined to a large degree the boundaries of the market which each producing region carved out and attempted to serve each year. If one apple-producing region had a bad crop in one year, another region was almost certain to exploit the situation and extend its own sales efforts into the other's market.

Whenever the Michigan Apple Commission's market expanded because of an abundant supply of apples, the expansion was usually into the southern states of Georgia, Alabama, and Florida—rather than westward—because there were more people immediately to the south than to the west and because any expansion to the west encountered increasingly stiff competition from the powerful Washington State Apple Commission which enjoyed almost national distribution. In years when the Michigan growers did not exploit this tri-state southern market, it was usually served by apple producers in the Appalachia region or New York State. These three southern states were thus supplied as a rule by apple producers in Washington, Michigan, Appalachia, and New York.

The state of Michigan ranked third among the states in commercial apple production in 1965, and the value of apple production in that year was nearly

$25 million. Approximately 75–80 percent of this apple production was sold outside the state. About half the fresh apples sold in the Detroit metropolitan market originated in Michigan, this proportion increasing during the fall harvest season and decreasing in late winter and early spring. In remote parts of the Michigan growers' market or places closer to other apple-producing regions of the country, the proportion of Michigan apples to those originating from other regions was apt to be somewhat less than half, dropping to one sixth or one seventh at times in a few of the markets in the South. About 60 percent on the average of all apple products sold in the heartland market were processed from Michigan apples.

Fifteen years earlier each Michigan grower had sold his apples independently to jobbers and wholesalers in the area, but by 1960 a change had occurred in the marketing structure. The producers had formed sales organizations. These were private corporations made up of perhaps 10 principal producers, with some growers as associate members who had merged their selling efforts to effect economies in operations and to obtain better quality control through centralized packaging, sorting, and handling. It was estimated that in 1968, five sales organizations made more than 50 percent of the sales of fresh Michigan apples; a large part of these sales went to chain-store buyers.

Consolidation had also taken place in the buying practices of most chain food stores. For example, at one time each of 20 Kroger divisions had bought Michigan apples directly from the growers. In 1965, a centralized purchasing department bought all of Krogers' requirements for all of their divisions, a change that eliminated most of the contact between the food chain divisions and the Michigan Apple Commission's members. Similar consolidations in the market had taken place with most of the Commission's other large chain customers, such as A&P and Safeway. Mr. Hasler felt that as a result the sales organizations had lost some rapport with consumers and some of its ability to tailor its offering to the needs of a particular supermarket division or locality, where different types of fresh apples might be desired or where some uses might be more prominent than others.

The Michigan State Apple Commission had achieved some success in developing Michigan apples into a standardized product through its efforts to establish standard grading and to reduce the number of varieties produced. In 1945, 10 major varieties were grown in Michigan, but by 1955 the number of major varieties had been reduced to 4—Jonathan, McIntosh, Delicious, and Northern Spy. Since about 85 to 90 percent of the Northern Spy apples were used for cooking or for processing, these apples were not generally sold for fresh consumption as were the other three varieties.

price

The prices that a producer obtained for one hundred pounds of apples were largely determined by the demand for a particular variety and the supply available at any given time, although prices did not invariably increase to reflect a rising demand, especially in the short run. Consequently, even if demand increased as a result of the Commission's promotional effort, the price to growers would not necessarily increase, since pricing was beyond the control of the Commission. While the Commission had suggested from time to time that the number of apples available and the rate at which they were selling would justify higher prices, the processors and growers were under no compulsion to follow the Commission's suggestions; and there were times when the quantity demanded in the market increased without any attempt by the growers to exploit the situation by charging more for their apples.

The marketing of fresh apples had been characterized in the past by an excessive supply and a concentration of sales in the months of October, November, and December, when most of the apple crop was harvested. This problem had been alleviated by controlled-atmosphere storage. By means of this modern innovation in inventory methods, fresh apples could be sold throughout the year. Apples can now be stored perfectly well for one full season—until the following November or December if necessary. Under laboratory conditions the storage period can extend to three years. Prices for apples from storage have generally been higher. While in the fall of 1967 producers received an average of approximately $3.50 per 40 pounds of fresh apples, in the spring of 1968 the apples sold from controlled-atmosphere storage brought an average of about $4.25 per 40 pounds.

the National Apple Institute

Promotion by the Michigan State Apple Commission complemented the primary promotion done by the National Apple Institute and paid for by the contributions from the members of the regional apple commissions belonging to the Institute. Beyond its political activities in representing the interests of apple growers in Congress and acting as a political watchdog for the industry, the National Apple Institute sponsored two distinctly promotional activities. It maintained the Apple Kitchen, essentially a public relations program, which for the last 15 years had produced a continual series of recipes, photos, and story material for public release through food editors across the country. A second promotional project engaging the interest of the National Apple Institute had been to teach schoolchildren to value apples for their taste, the part they can play in the care of teeth, and their importance to nutrition. Teaching aids, film strips, and other audio-visual aids had been circulated to school systems, health organizations, and other interested groups. Teaching guides on the same subject were made available to teachers, and advertisements were placed in national journals of education. Additional advertising space had also been purchased from time to time in medical and dental journals with national distribution.

The fact that the National Apple Institute performed these functions freed the Michigan Apple Commission's funds for additional promotion in the several remaining areas.

promotional strategy

Back in 1955, Mr. H. F. Patterson, a former secretary-manager of the Michigan State Apple Commission, had expressed a definite opinion about the organization's promotional efforts, and these have obtained in a general way until the present time. He felt that the Commission's function was to ensure that apple merchandising by retailers at least keep up with efforts made for other fruits, or even surpass them if possible. He believed that the dealers must be continually convinced of the profits in good apple merchandising. In the attempt to stimulate consumption of Michigan apples, the Commission had therefore emphasized point-of-purchase promotion and had developed a point-of-purchase kit from which the average store could assemble an attractive display to be set up in the produce section to stimulate the purchase of apples. This kit could be easily used even by untrained employees, and it had been well accepted in previous years. Retailers received the kits free of charge at their direct request.

In its annual promotional campaigns, the Commission had extensively promoted these kits to retailers. An added push was given by two full-time merchandising representatives which the Commission maintained in the field, as discussed later. Experience had demonstrated that grocery retailers would sell more apples if they gave them a larger-than-usual display. According to a 1966 USDA national survey of homemakers, two thirds of the respondents said that high quality and attractive displays would have the most effect in encouraging purchases of fresh fruit.

Therefore, the Commission concentrated much of its effort on persuading retailers to give Michigan apples more display space during the season, and the promotion kit was used to further this objective. In the past the kits had succeeded in gaining adequate display space and point-of-purchase promotion for Michigan apples. Many retailers had also participated actively in building displays for contests sponsored by the Commission. During periods of greatest use of displays, grocers had reported that their sales of Michigan apples rose from 25 percent to 300 percent, with an average sales increase of around 75–100 percent. The greater sales were usually maintained to some extent for about three weeks after the promotion ended.

relationship of budget to crop

Because the size of the assessment had not been increased since 1958, the funds available to the Commission to support all of its promotional activities depended on the size and composition of the apple crop each year. In general, the size of the crop had been increasing; and therefore the Commission's budget had been growing in total, even though the assessment rate in cents per hundred pounds of apples had not changed since 1958. Two notable exceptions to the consistent increase in production and in the contributions to the Commission's promotional budget occurred in 1966–67 and 1967–68. During 1966–67, many of the apples harvested were so small that they had to be used up in cider, vinegar, and juice. As a result, the Commission did not collect any revenue from the many small apples which were marketed for these uses. Although the apples harvested in 1967–68 were of normal size, they were fewer. For the second successive year the Commission's anticipated revenue did not fully materialize, and economies had to be effected, the principal source being cancellation of nearly all of the Commission's planned consumer advertising for the 1967–68 fiscal year.

merchandising representatives

To assist in its promotional activities, the Michigan State Apple Commission had hired two full-time fieldmen or merchandising representatives in the early 1960's to work with wholesalers and large retailers. These representatives were to keep customers appraised of the number and variety of apples available in the market and provide point-of-purchase materials for retail apple displays. One of their key objectives was to get the cooperation of retail stores in setting up displays and utilizing the point-of-purchase materials which the Commission supplied. Each man covered half of the Michigan apple growers and processors' market, one handling the territory to the east and the other the territory to the west of the Mississippi River. These merchandising representatives mainly promoted fresh apples, although from May through August, that is, in the four months before the new crop of apples would become available, they promoted processed frozen apple slices, apple sauce, juice, and so on. The activities of these merchandising representatives reached only as far down as the divisional level of the Commission's large retail chain customers. Consequently, one of the Commission's two representatives might have called at the divisional headquarters of a retail chain to encourage the produce manager to push fresh apples and the grocery manager to push applesauce, but he would not call on individual retail store managers.

marketing of processed apples

Over the past 10 years or more, there had been striking innovations in food processing and storage; and consumers had become more pressing in their demands for more convenient forms of food. As a result, Michigan apple growers and processors had witnessed a shift from fresh to processed apple products. Sharp increases had occurred in the quantity of apples that were being canned, frozen, used for vinegar, or processed in other ways. In the 1967–68 season, for example, 53 percent of the production was processed and 47 percent was sold fresh, whereas the percentages had been reversed only a few years before, and in the late 1950's, two thirds of the apples marketed by the Commission had been fresh. In line with this trend toward relatively greater sales of processed fruit, the Commission's point-of-purchase materials and other promotional efforts were being directed somewhat more at processed apple products rather than fresh apples, although since the processors tried to imitate the fresh product, it was felt that the promotional emphasis should still remain on the fresh fruit.

A survey conducted by Mr. Hasler in 1964 had indicated that the bulk of the Michigan processed apples were sold either as applesauce or frozen slices. Of all the processed apples sold, 58 percent was marketed in consumer packs, usually under an A&P, Kroger, or other private label, and 42 percent in institutional packs.

More than 75 percent of the consumer-packed processed apples were in the form of applesauce. From time to time as funds permitted, the Commission had advertised at the consumer level to promote the sale of ready-to-serve applesauce. In addition to the spot radio or magazine ads which had been used in the past 10 years, the Commission also included displays about applesauce in some of the point-of-purchase materials it sent on request to retailers in its market area.

Of the 42 percent of all processed apples sold in institutional packs, 80 percent went to the wholesale market in the form of frozen slices. These could be shipped, stored, and put through many different final processes to appear in a large variety of consumer products, chiefly apple pies, TV dinners, frozen cakes, apple strudels, turnovers, and so on. The frozen slices were not promoted at the consumer level, since the consumer never saw the product in this form. They were, however, advertised to the food industry in the two leading monthly trade magazines, *Institutions* and *Cooking for Profit*.

branding of fresh apples

Growers generally sold fresh apples, shipped in large wooden boxes, to packagers who sorted and graded the fruit before placing it in plastic bags, containing from 3 to 20 pounds. These were the packages that the consumers would ultimately find in their retail food stores. Because the Commission's marketing activities were less highly organized than many similar groups, fresh Michigan apples were not always marketed under a uniform brand name as are some other fruits, for example, California "Sunkist" citrus fruits. A few large Michigan growers attached their own trademark stickers to the crates of apples they sold; but the trademarks used by these growers were not the same from one grower to the next, and the practice was not widespread. The name "Michigan Flavorbest Apples" had been adopted by the Commission for promotion, and it was later registered as the Commission's trademark. But "Flavorbest" was not applied to all apples and apple products, nor was it used by as many growers and processors as the Commission desired. Information indicating what portion of the Commission's growers were actually using the Flavorbest trademark was not available.

While the Commission's registered trademark might be applied to the boxes of apples which were shipped from the producers to packagers, the trademark was primarily designed for use at the consumer level. Sometimes the packagers were permitted to use standard plastic bags printed with the trademark, "Michigan Flavorbest Apples." But many large purchasers demanded that apples be in their own bags displaying their own brand names. Both Jewel Tea and Kroger had specially designed bags, for example, and this precluded the use of the "Flavorbest" trademark on the package. Other retailers, however, allowed the phrase "Michigan Flavorbest Apples" to be used on the bag under their own brand name. In this way they could tie in with any point-of-purchase and consumer advertising promotions which might be sponsored by the Michigan State Apple Commission in their local area.

More and more frequently the Commission had been asked to drop the "Michigan" from the trademark in some of its promotions of processed apple products. This would mean that customers who bought fresh apples or frozen slices to reprocess would be free to obtain their apples from sources other than Michigan if necessary. In the interest of improving relationships with its members' large customers, the Commission had in some cases acceded to these demands.

1967–68 promotional program

By July 1, 1967, the promotional program and the budget for the 1967–68 fiscal year had been approved and put into effect, with the principal objectives of furthering the demand and sale of Michigan Flavorbest apples.

The Commission's fiscal 1967–68 budget totaled nearly $245,000. Funds were allocated roughly as follows:

```
Rebates to growers requesting exemption.............................$ 25,000
Salaries and operating expenditures.....................................  40,000
Marketing Information Services (Michigan Apple Council)...............  35,000
Merchandising, advertising and promotion:
    Fresh apple promotion......................................$49,000
    Processed-apple programs.................................  12,000
    Merchandising services:
        To National Apple Institute........................$29,000
        Two merchandising representatives and P-O-P
            materials........................................  45,000
                                                                    74,000
                                                                             135,000
Budget reserve.........................................................  10,000
        Total 1967–68 Michigan State Apple Commission
            Budget.........................................................$245,000
```

The first three items listed in the 1967–68 budget were considered to be very nearly fixed from year to year, although if the new assessment proposal were to pass, it would eliminate the approximately $25,000 in rebates which the Commission would have to pay out in the next year. There was little change from one year to the next in the salaries paid to the Commission's headquarters personnel or in its operating expenditures.

The Commission's marketing information service, which was called "Michigan Apple Council," was established in 1960 to provide growers, packagers, and processors with market information which would be useful as a guide to marketing decisions. Three biweekly reports were issued: (1) a storage report, showing the stocks of the various kinds of apples which were available at that time; (2) a bulletin telling of new promotions and marketing activities which might be of importance to the Commission members and their customers; and (3) a voluntary traffic association service for members, whereby sales people exchanged price and movement information for various grades of apples.

The really volatile portion of the Commission's budget, and the segment which was by far the largest, was the $135,000 allocated for merchandising, advertising, and promotion. By relying on these funds to absorb the fluctuations in income which were the result of basing assessments on annual sales, the Secretary-Manager could retain the personnel necessary to ensure continuity of operations at headquarters and the continuation of the marketing information services rendered by the Commission.

Of the $135,000 which had been allocated to merchandising, advertising, and promotion during the 1967–68 fiscal year, $49,000 went for trade advertising, display contests, sales incentives, point-of-purchase materials, and other special promotions for fresh apples. Nearly 70 percent of the $49,000, roughly $34,000, represented some form of point-of-purchase promotion, while the remaining $15,000 went for trade advertising. Three publications carried this trade advertising: *The Packer,* weekly trade newspaper; *Supermarket News,* a weekly tabloid; and *Produce Marketing,* a monthly magazine. Out of this $135,000, the Commission also continued its financial assistance to Michigan State University for the study of apple storage and maturity problems, co-sponsored the Michigan Apple Queen contest, participated in numerous national and state conventions, meetings, and seminars, and sponsored exhibits at trade shows and at the Michigan State Fair stressing Michigan Flavorbest apples.

Of the $12,000 allocated to programs promoting processed apples, $7,000, went for point-of-purchase material, while the remaining $5,000 was expended for trade advertising of frozen apple slices in *Institutions* and *Cooking for Profit,* the two leading monthly trade magazines distributed to the food industry. In prior years advertisements in these two magazines had produced many inquiries from buyers regarding institutional packed apples.

The final category in the promotional budget represented $74,000 worth of promotional expenditures labeled merchandising services. About $29,000 of this amount constituted the Michigan State Apple Commission's annual contribution to the National Apple Institute, of which the Michigan Commission was a member along with similar groups in New England, Virginia, New York, and another in western New York. The remainder of this $74,000 was used for point-of-purchase materials and to compensate the two merchandising representatives for their full-time work in the field to promote Michigan apples and reinforce the Commission's point-of-purchase efforts at the wholesale and retail levels.

The point-of-purchase kit, which was continued through the 1967–68 fiscal year, consisted of two display pieces. First was a large 14-inch by 18-inch die-cut display hanger in four colors, showing four big red apples and a bunch of green apple leaves, with "Michigan Flavorbest Apples" printed in white letters across the top. Any number of these die-cut pieces could be used together in the same display.

The second display piece was an 11-inch by 14-inch price card. The retailer could use this card to show the price of the apples in his display. Enough additional space was provided to accommodate the word "special" or some similar announcement. This display card came in eight different designs to allow a variety from which the retailer could select one suited to his individual needs. For example, one presented the idea of fresh apples as an "Instant Dessert—Just Polish 'n Serve!" Another might emphasize processed apples with a picture of applesauce and fresh sliced apples to make an attractive four-color display. All eight price cards suggested different uses for Michigan apples.

The 1968 display contest took place between January 15 and February 29 and was open to all retailers in the Commission's mid-American apple market. Entries consisted of a photograph taken in the contestant's retail store in which displays of Michigan apples were combined with the "Michigan Flavorbest Apple" point-of-purchase display material issued by the commission. Contest photos were judged on sales appeal, originality, and appearance, and the first-place winner received a 1968 Chevrolet Camaro. Ten color-pack Polaroids were awarded to the runners-up. This program was aimed at getting produce managers to sell more apples in their stores; it was reasoned that most all the apples sold as a result of this regional contest would be Michigan apples.

consumer advertising

As a result of budgetary restrictions, the Commission had found it impossible to do any consumer advertising during the past three fiscal years. In earlier years, when available funds permitted, the Commission had done some consumer advertising but only to promote fresh apples. Spot radio was the medium for most consumer advertising of fresh apples because of this medium's tremendous flexibility and the ease with which local retail stores could tie in with a tag line telling consumers where "Michigan Flavorbest Apples" were locally available. Spot radio had generally been used either to stress one variety of apple, such as Delicious—especially when the particular variety was in excess supply—or to give apples an extra push in some locality where sales had been sluggish or an oversupply had occurred. Blanket advertising had rarely been attempted by the Commission because it was much more economical to concentrate promotional effort in such larger cities within the market as St. Louis, Kansas City, Chicago, or Detroit. In addition, competition varied from region to region, and the Commission did not wish to advertise in regions where Michigan apples were particularly underrepresented and any benefits of the advertising might well accrue to producers and processors from apple-producing regions outside of Michigan.

Besides using its own taped radio jingle, the Commission had placed ads in regional editions of national magazines, including *Life, Ladies Home Journal, Women's Day,* and *Family Circle,* which were available in almost every market segment in the part of mid-America where Michigan apples were sold. Spot advertisements on color TV had also been considered for consumer advertising at one time, but they had never been used because of their high cost and the limited funds at the disposal of the Commission.

The planning for a consumer advertising campaign began with a meeting in March or April between the Commission and its advertising agency. After a consideration of alternatives and an estimate of the appropriation which would probably become available, a campaign would be in final shape about the end of June and completely locked in by the second week in July. The process of estimating the Commission's budget was made much easier by the U.S. Department of Agriculture's July 1 report on estimated production in September, October, and November. In February, 1968, it was tentatively estimated that production in the 1968–69 fiscal year would surpass the previous year's 12 million bushels.

promotional plans for the 1968–69 fiscal year

In laying plans for the 1968–69 fiscal year, which was to begin July 1, 1968, Mr. Hasler intended to continue putting major emphasis upon point-of-purchase materials and to assure that they would have a strong push from the Commission's two field merchandising representatives. The point-of-purchase materials were to be designed to attract attention in the retail stores. This appeal to retail customers appeared especially important in view of reports from recent surveys showing that most women did not use a shopping list but made their selections as they moved around the supermarket.

To complete the promotional picture in 1968–69, Mr. Hasler hoped the proposed assessment would pass so that the Commission could do as much consumer advertising as he felt was necessary to get the customer into the store to buy Michigan Flavorbest apples. The main emphasis would again be placed upon fresh apples; but each year processed apples had been getting a slightly larger share of the promotional budget, and for the first time in the Commission's 28-year history some consumer advertising would undoubtedly promote processed apple products.

The proposed revisions in the assessment would raise the rate to 8 cents per hundred pounds of apples sold for resale as fresh apples and 6 cents per hundred pounds of apples sold for processing. The apples which had been going for juice, cider, or vinegar, 25 percent of the total tonnage, would bear an assessment of 2 cents per hundred pounds of apples sold for these uses. Finally, producers could no longer exempt themselves from paying the assessment; eliminating this provision would save rebating the payment of the $25,000 which had been refunded to growers who claimed this exemption in the preceding year.

The current assessment had provided the Commission with an average over the past five years of about $17,500 per million bushels of apples sold for all uses, or 1.75 cents per bushel. It was anticipated that the new proposal would yield $23,300 per million bushels of production, or 2.33 cents per bushel, if it were passed for the 1968–69 fiscal year. Mr. Hasler estimated that if the 1968–69 crop were the same as in the prior year, the new rate would bring in an extra $60,000. This could be devoted almost entirely to consumer advertising in the coming fiscal year if the increased assessment passed. It seemed probable, in fact, that the crop would be larger than the 12 million bushels produced during 1967 and that even more than $60,000 additional funds would become available for consumer advertising in 1968–69.

The following excerpt from the provisions and regulations of the proposal which was to be voted on in the March referendum provides the complete statement made by the Commission in its new assessment proposal regarding the objectives of its intended expenditures for advertising, promotion, and publicity:

> The Committee will carry on or cause to be carried on such advertising, promotion and publicity programs as it may believe will create new markets for apples and for apple products or maintain present markets. Monies collected under this program shall be expended exclusively to advertise and promote and publicize the apple industry in fresh, processed and juice programs with a reasonable amount allotted to each.

One of the chief objectives of the Commission's consumer advertising, when it could afford to do any, had always been to get local retailers and chains to tie in with their own advertising and displays, and the Commission had merchandised its consumer advertising to the retailers throughout its market. Through such effort in the past, large chains had been persuaded to feature apples in their retail stores to coincide with consumer advertising placed by the Commission. If the assessment passed and additional funds became available for consumer advertising, Mr. Hasler hoped that the Commission's consumer advertising could be successfully merchandised to the retailers in its market area. In this way the benefit which might be realized from a very limited consumer advertising appropriation would be substantially increased.

In case the proposed assessment passed, Mr. Hasler was investigating the possibility of placing some four-color consumer advertisements in a large number of newspaper Sunday supplements to promote the increased use of fresh Michigan Flavorbest apples. As an alternative he was also thinking of using consumer advertising funds to purchase some spot radio time, as the Commission had done three or four years before. Flexibility would have to be the first consideration because of the impossibility of forecasting accurately in July the size and composition of the apple crop that would be harvested in September, October, and November.

Mr. Hasler hoped the assessment would pass. He felt that the Commission had fallen below the level of even its 1955 campaign because of inflation, a demand for more services by the growers, increased competition from organizations promoting other commodities as well as from others within the apple industry, and the increasingly large assessments levied against the Commission by the National Apple Institute. If the new assessment passed in March, the Commission planned to meet with its advertising agency to decide what might be done in newspapers or radio, or both, since each was capable of a different kind of promotion.

QUESTIONS

1. a) Was there a profitable opportunity to stimulate the demand for Michigan apples through consumer advertising? Explain.

   b) In the light of your analysis, had the Commission been wise in giving primary emphasis to the encouragement of point-of-purchase promotion in its past selling efforts? Why?

2. If you were an important apple grower in Michigan would you vote to approve the proposed increase in assessment? Explain.

3. If you were retained as a consultant by the Commission, what recommendations would you make as to an appropriate promotional strategy for Michigan apples?

4. Did the Commission follow a sound approach in determining the promotional appropriation for Michigan apples? If your answer is negative, what approach would you recommend? Why?

case 5–3

RICHARDS, INC.*

review of basic sales strategy

The executives of Richards, Inc., a manufacturer of small electrical appliances, decided to add a food warmer (electric trivet) to their line of products.[1] After the technical developmental work was completed, the president and sales manager faced the task of developing a marketing program which would achieve a national distribution and complete market coverage in as short a time as possible.

background

The president of Richards, Inc., had established this small manufacturing plant in Urbana, Illinois. He engaged the services of two vice presidents, who were responsible for engineering and product development, and a third executive, who assumed responsibility for the production and procurement functions. The sales and promotional aspects of the new enterprise were under the direct supervision of the president.

One of the president's prime assets was an unusual sensitivity for gauging the promotional possibilities of various consumer items. Once he sensed that a particular item had considerable profit potential, he consulted his fellow executives to discuss the feasibility of designing, producing, and selling such an item.

At the time of the decision to produce a food warmer, Richards' product line included *Bug-Kil,* a vapo-electric insect destroyer for the home, retail priced at $2.98; *Bug-Git,* a somewhat similar item for continuous automatic insect control in commercial establishments, retail priced at $13.95; and also a black wrought iron *Bird Cage Planter* with a brass or copper planter pot, retail priced at $2.98. The company officers expected to concentrate on small consumer electric appliances that had plenty of promotional sales appeal. They felt that a well-designed, smartly priced food warmer would be a desirable addition to their product line.

As an initial step in planning the marketing program for the new product,

---

* Written by Thomas J. Forgacs, Research Assistant, Bureau of Business Research, Graduate School of Business Administration, The University of Michigan.
[1] The location and identifying names have been disguised.

the name "Williamsburg" was chosen as the family brand for the food warmer and for any of their future consumer electric appliances. The Williamsburg food warmer was manufactured in the *Norfolk* and *Suffolk* styles, as well as the *Clock* style. Each of these was constructed of black wrought iron with a stainless steel heating unit and a vented heat design to protect the table finish. The first two, however, were authentic colonial reproductions, while the latter was a definitely modern design. Each food warmer was packaged in an attractive gift box, the top of which folded back into a handsome self-selling display unit.

At that time about a dozen or so food warmers were on the market, but none of them had achieved a significantly dominant position in the field. Most were priced at about $4.95. While some unbranded food warmers were priced less than $2, there were branded ones selling as high as $9.95. These prices did not include appliance cords.

introduction of food warmer

Richards, Inc., started producing food warmers in July, and was shipping them by September of that year. The Fair Trade price was set at a highly competitive $2.98, excluding a 6-foot cord at $0.69 or an 8-foot cord at $1. In addition to the price advantage, Williamsburg food warmers had tarnishproof stainless steel heating plates, while competitors used copper. This was felt to be an important advantage to the consumer in that the steel was easier to keep clean than copper and also matched the housewife's silverware on the table.

The tarnishproof stainless steel heating unit provided a long duration of sales appeal without tarnishing on the dealer's shelf as well. Although Richards' executives believed that this was important in appealing to dealers, they hoped that the Williamsburg food warmer's lower price and handsome design would make the item a fast seller anyway. Thus, they hoped that the product's sales results would obviate any long storage periods on dealer shelves.

Seventeen manufacturers' representatives across the country were selected to distribute the Williamsburg line. These organizations had experienced a successful spring selling season with Richards' Bug-Kil and Bug-Git and were impressed with the salability of the company's product line. These manufacturers' representatives called on three types of outlets, namely, department stores, headquarters of chain stores and mail-order houses, and jobbers.

The schedule for discounts for the food warmer and appliance cords was quite involved. It is presented as Exhibit 1.

In order to achieve fast and broad market coverage in a large metropolitan area, the manufacturer's representatives called on the two leading department stores in the community and did everything but ring up sales on the cash register for them. The representatives set up window displays and point-of-sale displays and even guaranteed the sale of all of the Williamsburg merchandise. In addition to this, three newspaper advertisements were placed in

Exhibit 1. Schedule of discounts, electric food warmer.

List price $2.98 (does not include cord), Fair Traded; U.L. Approved
Packaging   Packaged individually in gift box; 24 gift boxes to a corrugated shipper
Shipping
weight   45# per case of 24 units . . . Freight allowed on 6 dozen or more units

	Discount	Unit Cost	Cost/Doz.	Cost/4 Doz.	Cost Gross
Retailers	Less than case lots, 33⅓%	$1.986	$23.83		
Retailers	Case lots, 40%	1.788	21.46	$85.82	$257.47
Chain stores	Case lots, 50%	1.49	17.88	71.52	214.56
Jobbers	Case lots, 40–25%	1.341	16.09	64.37	193.10
Terms of sale	2%/10 E.O.M.				

U.L. Approved Appliance Cord* Important: Read Note Below
(Junior Plug)

List price   (A) Cord 69 cents   6-foot cord U.L. Approved
List price   (B) Cord $1   8-foot special cord U.L. Approved
Packaging   48 to a carton—individually packaged
Shipping   (A) 6 foot   15# carton of 48
Weight   (B) 8 foot   18# carton of 48

	Discount	Unit Cost	Cost/Doz.	Cost/4 Doz.
Retailers	Less than case lots 33⅓%	A0.46	$5.52	$22.08
		B0.667	8.00	32.00
Retailers	Case lots 40%	A0.414	4.97	19.87
		B0.60	7.20	28.80
Chain stores	Case lots 50%	A0.345	4.14	16.56
		B0.50	6.00	24.00
Jobbers	Case lots 40–25%	A0.3105	3.73	14.90
		B0.45	5.40	21.60
Terms	2/10 E.O.M.			

* We recommend units be purchased without cords. If you buy cords, we recommend 25 cords per 100 food warmers.

the local papers, with the first ad being slightly greater than a half page in size. The advertisements for the Williamsburg food warmers designated the two leading department stores as the retail outlets within the area. The total advertising space in a given locale often amounted to a full page, the cost of which was borne entirely by Richards.

Local jewelry stores, hardware stores, and gift shops were quick to place their orders for the Williamsburg line from their local jobbers. The bellwether prestige of the leading department stores was exploited, and a jobber virtually had no choice but to stock Williamsburg food warmers so that he could fill orders from smaller retailers.

Concurrent with this sales effort, a two-month national consumer advertising campaign was run in *House and Garden, House Beautiful, Better Homes*

& *Gardens, Life,* and *Sunset* magazines. This series of quarter-page advertisements was used primarily as a merchandising tool in encouraging jobbers and retail outlets the country over to merchandise the Williamsburg line actively. In addition to the national consumer advertising, consistent trade advertising was placed in *Housewares* and other trade magazines.

A cooperative advertising allowance to department stores and jobbers played a key role in Richards' promotional plan. In fact, 80 percent of the company's food warmer advertising expenditure was accounted for by cooperative advertising. The allowance available to jobbers was equal to 5 percent of their gross sales. An advertising allowance equal to 25 percent of the net amount of the first order of one gross or more was available to all department stores. On orders less than a gross, the allowance was not to exceed 10 percent of the initial order. Richards split the cost of advertising done on reorders on a 50–50 basis, provided that Richards' liability would not exceed 10 percent of the invoice. For example, if a department store that reordered $1,000 worth of merchandise placed a $200 advertisement for Williamsburg food warmers in the local papers, Richards would reimburse the store for $100. If the store placed a $300 advertisement, Richards would still pay only $100, since the company's liability was not to exceed 10 percent of the invoice amount.

Reimbursement was made only if the advertising appeared in the local newspapers and Sunday supplements. Advertisers were required to submit tear sheets to the company for proof of insertion.

A switch in the sales appeal from a "gift" item to an "everyday" item for keeping coffee, stews, soups, and rolls warm on the table, made after the Christmas season, was found to have decidedly more sales impact as measured by retail sales in given areas. Thereafter, this sales message was incorporated into the company's newspaper mat service. Richards offered free newspaper mat service of tested selling appeals, envelope stuffers, mailing pieces, mobiles, counter cards, and consumer recipe booklets to all their distributors whether they received the advertising allowance or not.

The liberal advertising allowances served as a whip in Richards' hand to help maintain its retail price. Any retailer who advertised or sold at less than the $2.98 price immediately lost any cooperative advertising allowance to which he might have been entitled. He was also subject to legal suit by Richards, Inc., for violation of contractual terms.

Any small retailers who cut the suggested retail price were also subject to suit, and thereafter the jobber would refrain from distributing to them. Richards merchandise had not yet found its way into discount houses, though some of its department store outlets were noted for their extensive discount policies. These retailers had not seen fit to cut below the Fair Trade price of $2.98, and there was no Fair Trade litigation pending by Richards, Inc., at the end of the product's first year on the market as of June. Retail price maintenance was policed for Richards by the Advertising Checking Bureau.

The Advertising Checking Bureau Report on food warmer advertising for the last three months of the introductory year indicates how effective the cooperative allowance had been in stimulating retailers to advertise the Williamsburg line. This report is summarized in Exhibit 2. The Advertising Checking Bureau reported that it had never seen another instance where one brand had so completely dominated the field as the Williamsburg food warmer had done.

results of first years efforts

At the end of the first year of marketing effort, the president and his associates surveyed the results of their introductory efforts. As of that date the Williamsburg line was being handled in every major department store, hardware store, and gift shop in the United States. It accounted for roughly 50 percent of Richards' total sales volume of $1 million and yet had been on the market for only 12 months. In this short span, Williamsburg had become the nation's fastest selling food warmer as well as the nation's leader in sales volume.

Exhibit 2. Retail advertising linage and cost reports (all daily and Sunday newspapers in all cities).

Brand	Current Month, 12/1 through 12/31			Cumulative (2½ months) 10/14 through 12/31		
	Ads	Lines	Cost*	Ads	Lines	Cost
WILLIAMSBURG................311	79032	$22,334		606	158015	$46,739
Electra-Tile...................... 12	1258			25	3440	
Enterprise.........................				1	92	
Hotrivet..........................				3	217	
Kenmore......................... 27	1172			33	1440	
Liberty........................... 4	1515			5	1771	
Paragon.......................... 40	3814			59	6590	
Peco.............................. 6	928			7	1096	
Raymor...........................				2	178	
Salton............................ 1	115			3	356	
Thermoflex.......................				1	98	
Timely............................ 1	30			1	30	
Triv-a-Tric........................ 1	30			4	520	
Unbranded.......................341	20288			647	45127	
	744	108182	$22,334	1397	218127	$46,739

* Cost on Williamsburg trivets only calculated at 65 percent National Line Rate.

plans for future

The company officers did not intend to be lulled into complacency by reviewing their past successes. They felt that perhaps a change in basic marketing strategy was in order for the campaign of the second year, since they now faced a somewhat different marketing problem than in the introductory marketing phase of a year previous. They had pretty well achieved national distribution for the Williamsburg food warmer now and were concerned with increasing their brand's share of the market during the coming year.

With this objective in mind, accordingly, Richards' executives turned to the problem of defining the basic sales strategy to be followed in marketing the Williamsburg food warmer during the coming fall and winter season.

QUESTIONS

1. Evaluate the promotional strategy used during the first year that the food warmer was on the market.
2. What basic promotional strategy would you recommend for the coming fall and winter season? Why?

case 5–4

HAROLD F. RITCHIE, INC.*

development of promotional mix for Brylcreem

Harold F. Ritchie, Inc. is a subsidiary of Beecham Group Limited of London, a very successful international organization, operating in the toiletry, proprietary medicine, soft drink and food products fields. Brylcreem, one of its items, is the number one hairdressing in many parts of the world.

Ritchie, Inc. markets Brylcreem, Scott's Emulsion, Scott's Emulsion Capsules, Eno, Silvikrin Shampoo, Beecham Pills, etc. in the U.S.A.

Brylcreem history began in 1928 when it was first marketed in England. Shortly after introduction it became an outstanding seller in that country and distribution was soon expanded to many countries around the world. It was not until 1936 that it was first introduced in the U.S.A.

Years in the '30's and '40's were not particularly kind to the new product. Brylcreem could not make headway against the established American brands.

This situation continued until the early '50's when H. G. Lazell was appointed Managing Director of the parent company, Beecham Group Limited.

Mr. Lazell was of the opinion that Brylcreem's fine acceptance around

* Reprinted from "Brylcreem: A Little Research'll Do Ya," *Nielsen Researcher,* Vol. 17, No. 8 (August, 1959), pp. 3–8.

the world could be a big item in the U.S.A. But, how to get a foothold in the big men's hairdressing market . . . ?

A market by market approach seemed to be the best means of establishing the new product's reputation. Accordingly, in 1952, work was begun on this approach with Nielsen's index services providing information on progress.

At this time, Maurice Bale was brought in from the Beecham Canadian subsidiary as Executive Vice President–General Manager to head up the new effort. Thinking here centered around the belief that results which the parent company had been able to achieve around the world should be repeated here. The man they chose to lead the program was eminently qualified.

With a 15-year background of experience in marketing drugs and toiletries, Mr. Bale's decisions would be based on much more than guesswork. He had been responsible for sales and marketing with Harold F. Ritchie & Company, Ltd. (Beecham Canadian subsidiary) for a number of top grocery items (Ritchie handled grocery items in Canada—Dole items, Sunmaid, etc.) together with Brylcreem, Eno's "Fruit Salt" and other items in the proprietary and toiletry field.

In the initial stages the executive staff was quite small. Working with Mr. Lazell and Mr. Robert Alexander (Ritchie Canada President) a three-year plan was established, the base of which was Sectional Merchandising.

Fifteen salesmen and one sales manager were on hand to execute the plan.

It called for an immediate doubling of the sales force and a division of the U.S. into 65 sales territories. The needs or size of each territory would then be modified or evaluated in the light of developing situations as the regions were being serviced.

The thinking here was that any promotional program that generated consumer demand would call for prompt filling of the distributive pipelines.

The fly in the ointment was that the company could not afford 65 salesmen. They had to cut the planned number of territories down to 35 and finally to 33 to meet budget limitations. Today the number is up to 45.

It became important in these early stages to determine just what direction the campaign might take and what could be reasonably expected in a given amount of time. Also, how big was the market and how much bigger would it grow?

These were the questions that faced Mr. Bale and his executives. His first move was to evaluate what he wanted in terms of total share and the length of time it would take him to reach it.

The figures must be established on the basis of what it would take to run a profitable business. That is, sheer market share or sales without profit could not be tolerated. At that time the total market was estimated at about $40 million in consumer dollars. At the close of 1951, Brylcreem held 1.3% of this nationally.

Mr. Bale studied Nielsen's competitive brand market shares and rates of advertising. He related these expenses to sales and came up with a ratio of sales percentage. For example, if Company D was doing a million dollars worth of business in one territory, the company's advertising expenses of, say, $250,000 were measured, then related to volume which, in this case, was 25%.

By doing this in every market across the country, Ritchie learned approximately how much each advertiser was spending to achieve his proportional share of market.

These various advertising ratios to sales were studied and a set of them was applied in three test areas. It was in the West Central Minneapolis–St. Paul section, where the most satisfactory sales results, in view of advertising expenditures, were attained.

By increasing promotion, spending a higher proportion on advertising than they were doing in other parts of the country, they were able to watch results closely by means of the Nielsen audit.

A projection was finally set up which had as an objective a 10% share of market on a three-year payout basis.

With the background of the West Central region, Brylcreem had a fair idea of how the different ratios might work on sales performance. They carried the Sectional Merchandising program into the East Central, then the Pacific territory. However, the steady growth was not without some problems.

For instance, at one time early in their efforts, Brylcreem management noted an inconsistency in factory shipments to the East Central region. These figures showed a *static* rate while Nielsen audit sales figures showed a *rise* for the same region. Initial reaction was that because shipments were down, sales must be slipping. Such did not turn out to be the case. As in many situations of a similar nature, sales were picking up slowly. The product was merely a little slow in getting into distribution.

Shipping and production records did not show the gradual building up in consumer demand but actual sales and consumer acceptance were growing. Future growth was marked by a careful correlation by management of actual sales and factory shipments with proper weight given to each.

This was but one problem the company faced and successfully met. Another important point in this rise was the close alliance between sales, advertising, production, management and marketing.

Said Mr. Bale:

Of all the many things we were fortunate enough to have happen, I think the most important was our size. We were small enough for all departments to work closely together, carefully using facts in each move.

If one phase had moved too fast for the others I think we would have been much less effective. Unfortunately yesterday's press clippings or sales successes can't buy a bar of soap tomorrow, and we'll have to keep watching each of these phases with the same close eye if we are to maintain our position.

same approach on ads

In building its advertising program, Brylcreem showed the same painstaking attention to detail that they did in sales. Again, the Sectional Merchandising plan was used whereby an idea or concept was tried in one area before expanding it. Nielsen audience analysis and ratings evaluated effectiveness of various media and themes.

Initially, a major radio spot schedule was put into effect with territorial results carefully checked through Nielsen analysis. Results indicated that spot radio, though it increased sales slightly, did not appear to be the most satisfactory vehicle for telling the Brylcreem story at that time. Accordingly, it was decided to establish test areas to determine the most effective advertising medium.

After six months, (three Nielsen rating periods) the results were heavily weighted in favor of the market where television was being used. Taking into consideration all variables, it was decided that a television campaign should be initiated with the least possible delay.

Late night television, especially movies, appeared most attractive in terms of cost, and it would enable high frequencies of repetition to be developed within a particular audience.

Using 106 television stations, a spot campaign was begun with the result, over a five-year period, that sales were increased ten times.

An important factor in this success was the use of commercials that told a convincing story, and continuous use of the now-famous Brylcreem jingle:

> Brylcreem, a little dab'll do ya.
> Brylcreem, you'll look so debonair.
> Brylcreem, the gals will all pursue ya.
> Simply rub a little in your hair.

Later, this same principle of developing as much frequency of repetition as possible in a particular audience group was applied to a network approach in 1958. Here, the Brylcreem message was seen and heard on such network shows as "77 Sunset Strip," "Cheyenne" and "Colt 45." Increased network support is currently being planned.

Even today, the Sectional Merchandising test concept is still being applied to advertising because of the differences in population habits.

From a market share standpoint, the Brylcreem story has been most impressive. The 1951 level of 1.3% climbed to 14.0% with some territories reaching as high as 18.0%.

What are Mr. Bale's reactions to the strong showing of Brylcreem in the past five years? Here is what he says:

We were fortunate in having an outstanding product and a reasonably successful advertising and merchandising approach such as our puppets and jingle. We consider that we are specialists in only one line—the men's hairdressing market. We like to employ specialists in other lines as we need them such as advertising, packaging and marketing.

We use what many people call "investment spending" as does the management of many companies. When we want to expand into other markets we feel the money spent for research into sales potential and advertising effectiveness is just as important as that spent on a new package or a product development.

As for the future, we will shoot for a larger share of the market. Certainly with the top competition in this business, nothing is going to be easy. But we're going to try to use all of our tools to the best advantage. I would say that I don't foresee any great change in our policies or methods of operation.

Research will continue to be a tool. But it is only one factor in making decisions; it is not an answer in itself. If we have the facts though, many times a more successful plan can be projected. Otherwise, we might be guessing.

The confidential nature of the marketing business prohibits the disclosure of any comparative figures. But regardless, the Brylcreem story is one that can stand alone in showing how a company can set its goals on one territory, draw its bead, and execute a program of Sectional Merchandising in a most effective manner.

QUESTIONS

1. In promoting Brylcreem, should the main burden of selling be placed upon consumer advertising, reseller stimulation, or personal selling? Why?
2. What approach did the firm take in determining the advertising appropriation for Brylcreem? Was this a sound procedure? Would you suggest any modifications?
3. Did the firm follow a sound method in deciding upon the main types of advertising media to use? Why?

pricing strategy

The selection of a level of price for a product is but one of several pricing decisions which must be made by marketing management. In many cases freedom to price at levels different from the current competitive level is limited and, therefore, the marketing strategy of the firm emphasizes nonprice methods of attracting patronage. In other instances, however, the decision as to level of price is of special importance. These include, for example, when a price must be set for a new product, when an established price must be changed, and when a price must be chosen for a new addition to an existing line of products.

Once a level of price has been determined, the question becomes one of how to select and administer specific pricing policies. These policies may range from an immediate departure from the established level by means of discounts and allowances to an attempt to maintain a given level of price through resale price maintenance or geographic pricing systems.

The theme of this section is that pricing can be a potent promotional instrument. But successful pricing requires consideration of potential changes in competition, product development, and market acceptance. Thus, pricing decisions cannot be made without considering how these decisions are related to the other marketing strategy variables and to the overall marketing program of the firm.

price
determination

introduction

Although the concept of the marketing mix describes a blending process in which management combines various controllable elements in an attempt to develop an integrated program to achieve stated objectives, there is nothing in the concept which requires that all of the elements be added to the mix at the same time. In fact, quite the opposite is true. Once market targets are defined and environmental constraints considered, marketing management faces decisions in those areas of strategy dealing with the product, its distribution, and non-price promotion. Only after decisions have been made here, which reflect the interrelationships among the variables concerned and which are consistent with the achievement of the specified marketing goals, can management attention be devoted to the remaining element of the mix: that of pricing.

In the decision area of pricing, many different types of questions must be answered ranging from the determination of a price for a new product to the redetermination of a price for an established product. In addition, strategies must be formulated to gain the promotional advantages of varying from an established level of price or, conversely, from preventing such variation by resellers.

Once the decisions have been made with respect to determining a level of price and whether or not to vary from that level, then, of course, these decisions must be integrated with those previously made in the areas of product, distribution, and (nonprice) promotional strategy. Adjustments in all areas are likely to be necessary in order to create a marketing mix which is consistent, integrated, and capable of achieving predetermined goals.

This chapter will consider the first part of the pricing decision, that is, the determination of a level of price for a new product, an established product, or an addition to a line of products. The following chapter will cover those pricing decisions of an essentially promotional nature which enable the seller to adapt better to diverse needs of customers or to competitive pressures. Although these chapters will illustrate the use of various tools borrowed from economics and accounting as aids to decision making, the point must be made at the outset that pricing is more of an art than a science. In the process of making pricing decisions, analytic tools are most helpful, but when the chips are down, the judgments of intelligent, experienced, and highly intuitive human beings are vital.

price versus nonprice competition

Because most marketing managers would be well advised to work out the nonprice aspects of the mix before turning to the questions involving price determination and variation, some attention should be paid to the relative emphasis placed by business firms on price versus nonprice methods of promotion. Although it would be wrong for an individual firm to bias its strategy to conform with the norm of its industry, it is important for the managers of an individual firm to recognize the relative emphasis placed upon price versus nonprice promotion by their major competitors. This recognition would require an evaluation of the firm's position vis-à-vis competitors in terms of products sold and markets served. Only after such an evaluation can the decision be made to follow industry patterns or to deviate from them.

Most firms making such an investigation will find that industry mixes are heavily biased in favor of nonprice methods of promotion. Product differentiation, broad market coverage to provide availability, and considerable personal selling and/or advertising effort to create selective demand seem to be the favored means of gaining patronage. Recourse to frequent or drastic price changes appears to be a less popular strategy in the present-day American economy.

This general emphasis on nonprice promotion, which is reflected in the assignment to price of a lesser role in the marketing mix, is the result of several factors. The increased numbers of consumers with disposable incomes has diversified demand. Consumers evaluate product design and quality, locational convenience of outlets, service, and the availability of credit as well as price. With increased consumer affluence, price, as a major determinant of the purchase decision, has lost ground to the other nonprice factors.

The techniques of influencing buyers have also improved greatly over the years, and sellers find that dollars allocated to nonprice promotion have a greater effect on stimulating sales than a like amount of dollars spent in granting a price reduction. Even if evidence is not available to support the contention that promotional elasticity of demand is greater than price elasticity of demand for their products, many businessmen act as if it were.

First, they habitually underestimate the sensitivity of demand for their output to changes in price.

Second, they are hesitant to risk making a mistake by changing a price, preferring, rather, to engage in nonprice promotion where mistakes are both less noticeable and more easily corrected.

Third, the reliance on nonprice modes of competition appeals to the individual seller because it promises a greater stability of patronage. Customers won on the basis of product design, availability, and service appear less vulnerable to competitive attack than customers gained on the basis of price.

Fourth, competing on a nonprice basis eliminates many of the headaches associated with short-run price adjustments. Nonprice competition does not require as frequent revaluation of reseller inventories, changes in price lists, or renegotiation of contractual arrangements as does competition involving frequent and fairly sizable price changes.

Fifth, and perhaps the most important of all reasons for the predominant bias toward nonprice methods of promotion, is the nature of competition faced by most large firms in the American economy. As will be discussed in more detail later, a few large sellers dominate our leading industries. Autos, rubber, cigarettes, soap, aluminum, and steel are just a few of the types of products produced and sold by a relatively small number of large firms. Essentially we have in these industries a competitive environment which is oligopolistic and in which price changes initiated by one member of the oligopoly result in a fairly predictable set of reactions on the part of the other members of the industry. Thus, in many situations a price move by one seller can result in a severe loss of business by him, a general industrywide price change which is advantageous to all, or an industrywide price change which is disadvantageous to all. Little wonder, then, that most firms in oligopolistic situations shy away from price changes unless there is considerable assurance that industry changes beneficial to all members of the industry are likely to result.

special importance of pricing decisions

It is not too difficult to presume from the preceding discussion that price is not the major concern of the modern marketing manager. Perhaps, greater attention is paid to nonprice means of gaining patronage while prices are held at levels which reflect the product's relative value-in-use as compared with the prices of close substitutes. There are instances, however, when the pricing decision is of special importance. These are: (1) when a firm must set a price for a new product, (2) when the firm wishes to initiate a price change for an existing product, and (3) when a company producing several products with interrelated demands and/or costs is faced with the problem of pricing a new addition to the line. Before these areas are considered in more detail, however, some additional attention must be paid to the influence of the competitive environment upon the pricing decision-making process.

pricing and the competitive environment

In order to understand better the environment in which pricing decisions are made by managers of individual firms, it is helpful to rely on economic theory. Although instances in which economics provides a ready-made answer to the pricing problem are rare, in an ever increasing number of applications economic theory has provided the insight necessary to improve the quality of the pricing decision.

If one would examine the nature of the pricing decision faced by the manager of a small wheat farm, one would find that it was very simple, indeed. All that this "manager" would have to do would be to check with the local grain elevator to see what the going prices were. These prices quoted by the elevator would, in turn, reflect the interaction of industry supply and demand in the grain market at Chicago. The economist would draw the diagram shown in Figure 13–1 to explain the derivation of industry price as well as the price as viewed by the individual firm. In the situation pictured, the farmer would sell quantity Q^* at industry price P^* if his goal were that of maximizing profits in the short run. This is because at quantity P^* the marginal cost of producing another unit is equal to the marginal revenue obtainable from its sale. At this output total profits are maximized.

It is not our purpose to delve into price theory to any great extent, but it is important to recognize that the wheat farmer producing a

Figure 13–1. Price determination in purely competitive markets.

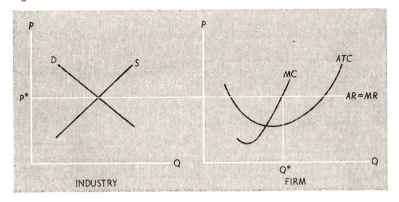

INDUSTRY FIRM

homogeneous product and unable to influence the industry price by dumping wheat or withholding it from the market has no opportunity to set a price for his output. Economists characterize this type of market situation as being "purely competitive." The choices open to the farmer include the decision to sell or not to sell wheat, the decision as to quantity to sell, the decision to effect changes in his farm's cost structure, or the decision to go out of business if the industry price drops below his level of costs. In no event does the farmer have the opportunity to make a true pricing decision.

The other extreme in terms of market environment is illustrated by the situation faced by the owner of an isolated water source in the midst of the Arizona desert country. As far as he is concerned, he is the only firm in the industry, and his picture appears as shown in Figure 13–2.

Figure 13–2. Price determination by a monopolist.

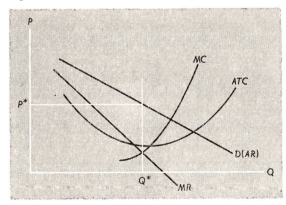

Because he does not have to face competition from others, he takes the aggregate or industry demand schedule as his own. This schedule is simply a curve relating the number of gallons of water that can be sold to the local inhabitants at varying levels of price. Inasmuch as he has no competition, he simply adjusts his output so that he will sell quantity Q^* at price P^*. Given the nature of his cost structure, he maximizes profits at the Q^*, P^* combination. This is the classic monopoly situation in which a single seller can set his price to sell whatever output he wishes to dispose of.

In the world of business we very rarely face either of the above types of market situations. Rather, most pricing decisions are made in market environments having characteristics of both pure competition and monopoly. Such market environments are described as being monopolistically or imperfectively competitive. In these types of markets we find that the firm does not view the industry demand schedule as its own. Depending on the degree of selective demand developed for its output, the firm may view its demand schedule as being somewhat independent of the industry schedule. Of course, the industry demand schedule is still the aggregate of all of the individual schedules of the member firms. The overall view, therefore, is of an industry schedule made up of many segments each of which may tilt or shift as competition or changes in buyer behavior cause changes in demand for the products of a given firm. Figure 13–3 illustrates some of these movements. Remember that this is a diagram of a firm and, as such, it resembles the picture of the monopoly situation. The difference here is that this firm is not alone in its industry but is one firm among many. There is, in addition, relative freedom of entry or exit of firms to or from the industry.

Figure 13–3 indicates the theoretical short-run profit maximization combination of price and quantity which would result if this firm were able to calculate its marginal cost and marginal revenue data at any given instance of time. Profit is indicated by the shaded area and at this combination of P^* and Q^* it is at a maximum.

Several important insights can be gleaned from this theoretical model which are helpful in considering actual problems of price determination. These include:

1. Both the industry demand schedule and the segment of the industry schedule faced by a firm are downward sloping to the right. For the industry, of course, this means that if larger and larger quantities of output are to be sold, the price of this output must be reduced. Shifts in the curve's position come about as a result of changes in

consumer tastes for the industry's product or as a result of interindustry competition. Such shifts in the industry demand schedule may, however, be accelerated by the combined effect of the promotional activities of the individual firms in the industry.

2. Although the individual firm usually faces a demand schedule which is downward sloping to the right, it is not without recourse to certain moves which can improve its profit position. Unlike the farmer,

Figure 13–3. Price determination in monopolistically competitive markets.

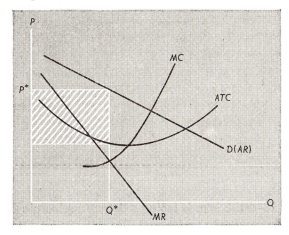

the manager of this type of firm can exercise some control over the prices he charges for his output. He can, for example, select some price other than the established industry price at which to sell his product. The extent to which he can exceed the competitive level of price is a function of the strength of the selective demand that he has been able to create for his output. This demand is, in turn, a function of his product's value-in-use, distinctive features, and general availability. In addition, the ability to price above the market level is related to the effectiveness of the firm's nonprice promotional efforts and the degree of competition faced from producers of substitute products or services.

3. The ability to price continually below the generally accepted industry level is dependent also upon the reaction of competitors. If pricing below the market level is a reflection of the firm's inferior position in terms of product features and/or market cultivation, then some price differential is probably sustainable. If the decision to price lower than competitors is the result of conscious strategy aimed at

increasing market penetration, then competitive reactions of either a price or nonprice nature can be expected.

4. The alternative of nonprice promotion has as its objective the shifting of the demand schedule to the right so that a greater quantity can be sold at a given price. The seller would also like to get a greater slope ("tilt") in his schedule reflecting a lowered sensitivity of his demand to changes in price (especially upward changes).

Figure 13–4. Price and nonprice moves in monopolistically competitive situations.

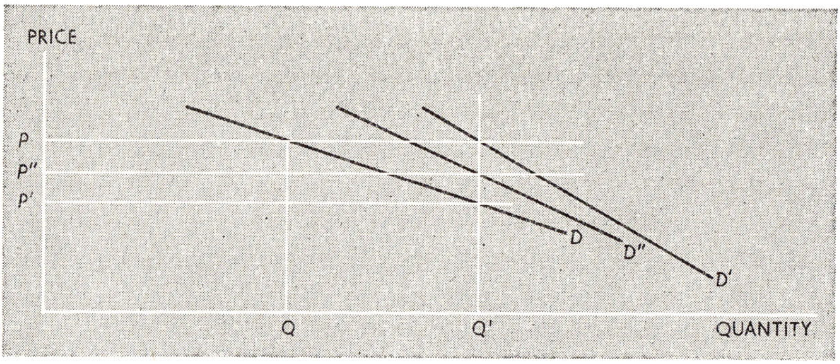

In Figure 13–4 the firm is facing a demand schedule D. With price P, quantity of output Q can be sold. To sell output Q', three actions are possible:

1. Price P can be reduced to price P'.
2. Demand schedule D can be shifted to D' by vigorous nonprice promotion.
3. Some combination of lowered price and nonprice promotion can be selected, for example P'' and D''.

Note that in cases 2 and 3, which involve some shifting of the demand schedule, the "tilt" or slope increases, thus reflecting what economists call greater price inelasticity of demand or less sensitivity of demand to changes in price. (For example, a percentage change in price will cause a smaller associated percentage change in quantity demanded along schedule D' than along schedule D.)

implications

Without becoming too involved in price theory, it becomes evident that the pricing decision is closely interrelated with several other areas both external to the firm and internal to it. Certainly the pricing manager must have a clear idea of the competitive environment in which he operates so that he can estimate the extent of pricing flexibility available to him. Although he will generally be operating under market conditions of monopolistic competition, in an ever increasing number of situations the number of sellers in the industry is few. Then the reactions of rivals become especially important, and the pricing decision area becomes more limited. These problems of oligopoly pricing (pricing when sellers are few) will be discussed in another section of this chapter.

In addition to knowing about the competitive environment, one needs to recognize the legal restraints which limit freedom of pricing action. This area will be covered in the next chapter.

Finally, pricing decisions must be related to the overall objectives of the firm and the marketing strategy designed to reach these objectives. Pricing decisions cannot be made in a vacuum, for they involve one of the firm's "action parameters" by which it seeks to reach its goals in a given market environment.

pricing objectives

In addition to knowledge of the market environment in which prices are to be set, the marketing manager must define clearly those objectives of the firm whose attainment his pricing must further. As a result of a study by the Brookings Institution and an accompanying journal article by one of the principal investigators, some light has been shed on the major pricing objectives in selected large American business.[1]

The major pricing goals pursued by the 20 firms in the sample studied were: (1) pricing to achieve a target return on investment; (2) stabilization of price and margin; (3) pricing to realize a target market share; (4) pricing to meet or prevent competition; and (5) pricing to maximize profits.[2]

It is not the purpose of this text to discuss each of these objectives in detail. It is important, however, to recognize that the major pricing decision, that of setting a basic price for a product, is related not only to the external market environment but also to the goals of the firm.

---

[1] A. D. H. Kaplan, Joel B. Dirlam, and Robert F. Lanzillotti, *Pricing in Big Business* (Washington, D.C.: Brookings Institution, 1958); Robert F. Lanzillotti, "Pricing Objectives in Large Companies," *American Economic Review*, Vol. 48, No. 5 (December 1958), pp. 921 40.

[2] *Ibid.*

Price determination is a means to an end and not an end in itself. Recognition must also be given to the fact that rarely does a firm seek only a single objective. In most cases the goals sought are a combination. For example, a firm might seek maintenance or improvement of its market share while at the same time aiming for a target return on invested capital. Such a combination of goals may well describe the objectives of a large automobile manufacturing company such as General Motors or the Ford Motor Company.

The final goal of pricing, to maximize profits, does require some further discussion because it is rather ambiguous. Perhaps one might generalize by saying that all firms attempt to maximize profits in the long run. That is their basic objective, and all other goals, such as growth, control over markets, and freedom from excessive competition, are corollary objectives which are supportive of the goal of long-run profit maximization. In like manner, the goals of pricing are also supportive of the objective of long-run profit maximization. When, however, the pricing goal is that of short-run profit maximization, the situation is somewhat different. Here we have a goal which is consistent with one of the assumptions underlying the economic models discussed previously. In such a situation the economist's suggestion that short-run profits are maximized when marginal costs equal marginal revenues provides a good basic guide to price determination.

The first step in establishing a price system is, as Stanton notes, "consciously to formulate an objective and state it clearly in writing. Once the pricing objective is agreed upon, the executives can move to the heart of price management—the actual determination of the base price."[3]

setting the basic price for a new product

Assuming that those executives responsible for the pricing decision have a clear understanding of the competitive environment in which they must operate and that the pricing objectives of the firm have been specified, they can now begin to set the basic price for a new product.

Their first task is to find out what the demand schedule for the new product might be like in terms of its location, its slope, and its degree of shiftability. It is not necessary, however, to be concerned with the entire schedule but only with that portion of the schedule which is

---

[3] William J. Stanton, *Fundamentals of Marketing* (2d ed.; New York: McGraw-Hill Book Co., 1967), p. 405.

meaningful in terms of the specific pricing decision under consideration. Figure 13–5 might be helpful.

Price p'' is the ceiling price or estimate of the highest price that
might be charged for the new product. This estimate is based on an
appraisal of the new product's superiority or inferiority as compared to
close substitutes as well as on the need to sell a minimum quantity of
output to cover associated costs. Price p' is the minimum price at which
the firm would be willing to sell given the nature of its future costs.

Figure 13–5. The zone of demand resulting from a range
of prices and a shifting of the demand schedule for a new
product.

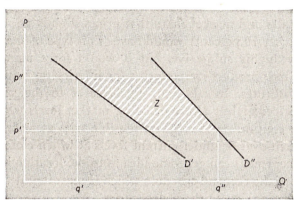

Such a level is generally set by the price of the lowest priced substitute
product, but quite often strategy considerations will result in a price
considerably below that of close substitutes.

D' is the demand schedule which reflects the most pessimistic estimate of consumer acceptance and/or competitive retaliation assuming
little or no non-price promotion. D'', on the other hand, reflects the
most optimistic view of consumer acceptance considering planned nonprice promotional efforts and anticipated competitive response. The
zone of demand relevant to the decision is, of course, Z while the
interval p''–p' is the range of price under consideration, and the
interval q''–q' the range of quantity which might be sold under all
combinations of price and demand within their respective ranges.

demand estimation

Although the preceding discussion has conceptual value in terms of
explaining the reason why an estimation of demand given a set of

prices and assuming various combinations of promotional efforts (both by the firm and its competitors) is vital to the process of price determination, it does little in the way of producing usable data. What is needed is a more concrete evaluation of product utility.

Comparison with close substitutes. If the product is a new version of an established type of product, then, of course, some information is available as to the size of the present market for the generic product type. A careful evaluation of the relative ability of the new product to fill consumers' needs vis-à-vis available substitutes can give some idea of the share of total market the new product might capture over time if it were priced at the current level at which close substitutes were sold. Once this estimate has been made, consideration can be given to the effect upon sales and market share that prices slightly above or below market level (say 10 percent) would have. This type of analysis would, of course, be highly subjective, but it would force management to estimate the new product's superiority (or inferiority) with respect to available substitutes. In addition, estimates as to the sensitivity of demand to prices slightly above or below market levels would have to be made. By continuing to estimate possible sales at prices 15, 20, or even 25 percent over or under current levels at which close substitutes are sold, management can get some idea as to the location and slope of that portion of the demand schedule which is meaningful to the determination of basic price for the new product.

Asking customers. Estimation of demand by managers can often be improved by surveying the more astute members of the reseller organization. Wholesalers and retailers who are in closer contact with the market than are manufacturers develop an instinctive feel for what is a "right" price for a new product. They can evaluate its attributes from the buyer's point of view and reflect the buyer's appraisal of product utility. Such questioning of potential buyers need not stop at the reseller level but may well include questioning end users by means of consumer panels or personal interviews with selected individuals. It has been suggested that in those cases where the new product is so unique as to rule out the use of a similar type of product as a basis of comparison, the concept of the "barter equivalent" be applied.[4] In this approach the new product, surrounded by a diversity of other products whose uses and prices are well established, is placed in front of a consumer panel. The members of the panel are then requested to match up the new product with another product of roughly equivalent

---

[4] Joel Dean, "Pricing Policies for New Products," *Harvard Business Review,* Vol. 28, No. 6 (November, 1950), p. 30.

value. By such means insight can be gained as to how the consumer might value the new product without the opportunity of comparing it with close generic substitutes.

Test marketing. As the process of estimating demand at various prices proceeds, there comes a point where an actual market test is required. Only in this way can consumer response to a price level (or a variety of levels) be measured in a realistic manner. The market test allows demand response to be viewed under actual purchase conditions, with controlled nonprice promotional inputs, and in the face of real competition. The disadvantage of such testing is that the surprise effect of the new product introduction upon rivals is blunted. In many situations, however, where a wrong pricing decision could be most costly, market testing is desirable even if it alerts competitors to the introduction of a new product.

Capitalization of cost savings. The steps in the process of estimating demand which have been discussed briefly have a very strong consumer product orientation. This is not to say that a producer of a product for sale to the industrial market would not find the comparison of his product with close substitutes useful in terms of aiding him to set a basic price. Moreover, he would also find his distributors most helpful in appraising the salability of a new product at a given price or over a given range of prices. What is important to note, however, is that the value-in-use of industrial products is easier to measure than is product utility in the consumer market. This is because industrial buyers can measure cost savings which are likely to accrue from the use of a new product. These cost savings (which may differ by application) when capitalized over the life of the new product indicate the ceiling price which may be charged for a new product when used in a specific application. It is evident that if cost savings associated with the use of a new industrial product have a present value of $1,000, the purchase price must be somewhere below this figure unless some other technical factors are involved.

Derived demand. Because the demand for industrial goods as inputs to an industrial process is derived from the demand for the output of the process, it is less sensitive to price changes than is consumer demand. When demand for the end product is stable or falling off, sales of capital equipment are limited to the replacement market and prices must reflect the cost savings which the new machine can offer over continued use of the old. In viewing the economics of replacement, it is found that a rather large price reduction would be required to cause a replacement sale to be made in the absence of technologically induced cost savings. On the other hand, when end product sales are rising, prices of new machinery can be raised above the level of capitalized cost savings with little effect on quantity demanded.

Price sensitivity of demand for industrial goods varies with respect to the type of good being considered. Moving from capital equipment to accessory equipment, component parts, and operating supplies, one finds increasing price elasticity of demand. But in almost all cases such sensitivity is less in the industrial market than in the consumer market.

implications

The purpose of demand analysis is to provide some estimates of the market's evaluation of product utility or value-in-use. In addition to discovering the location of the demand schedule, some information as to its probable slope and shiftability is also needed. The end result of demand analysis, therefore, is the delineation of a range of prices acceptable to the market and the achievement of some idea of sensitivity of demand to various prices within this range. The top of this range is the demand "ceiling." The next step in the pricing process is to relate demand over the acceptable range of price to the cost of producing output. As demand sets the ceiling on price, costs set the floor.

the role of costs

Although costs may be viewed as setting a floor to price while demand constraints set the ceiling, those persons responsible for the pricing decision must recognize that there are several cost floors from which to choose. In any summation of costs for floor determination, the questions arise as to the type and amount of cost to be included in the buildup. Should overhead costs, for example, be allocated on the basis of standard volume? Over how long a period of time should research and development costs be amortized? Should estimates of future costs be used rather than past or present costs?

In attempting to wend their way through the maze of costs and the various methods by which costs can be allocated to products, the pricing executives must keep two points in mind. First, in most cases, over the long run an individual product should and must bring in revenues which cover fully allocated costs and provide a reasonable profit. The second point is that because there is little or no causal relationship between cost and price in the short run, for the individual firm a price that fails initially to cover "full costs" may be a good price.

Cost-plus pricing. Because of the confusion of short- and long-run goals, businessmen often engage in the cost buildup process and add to the cost floor thus obtained some amount of "plus" in order to arrive at a price. The plus is either described as providing a certain percentage return on invested capital associated with the introduction of the new product or, in a more general sense, as an attempt to guarantee that with each sale the firm will receive a predetermined margin of profit. In retrospect, however, such an approach is not as easy as it appears to be, nor is it a really safe one. The question arises as to what costs are to be used for the base. Should the price setter consider past costs, present costs, or future costs? How large should the "plus" be?

Regardless of how sophisticated the approach, one thing is evident: cost-plus pricing which ignores the demand aspect of the pricing problem involves circular reasoning. Because price influences volume to be sold and volume affects unit costs, it is obvious that costs are determined factors in the pricing process rather than determining factors. Although the "plus" is management determined, it is often set without a clear understanding of the consequences. Too large a "plus" can result in too high a price, too low volume, and too high unit costs. Thus, a hefty "plus" aimed at improving gross profit per unit may prove very disappointing if the resulting price fails to fit in with the market's evaluation of product utility or fails to consider alternatives offered potential customers by competitors.

The tier concept. A clearer understanding of what a cost floor actually is and how its definition is relevant to the pricing decision may be gained by examining the "tier" concept. This is merely a way of looking at the cost floor in terms of the layers of cost which make up its foundation. Visualize a cost floor consisting of three tiers. The first tier is composed of indirect costs or overhead items which are fully allocated to units of output. The second layer it made up of direct costs of a noncash nature, such as depreciation expense directly associated with producing a unit of the product. The third layer is composed of unit direct costs, commonly called out-of-pocket costs, which represent cash outlays for items such as labor and materials.

We see in Figure 13–6 that there are two subfloors in addition to the full-cost floor. If the demand ceiling were sufficiently high, the full-cost floor could be covered by price. This type of situation is illustrated by Figure 13–7.

If the demand ceiling were below the full-cost floor as illustrated in

Figure 13–8, the price setter would have to consider whether or not he could set a price below the full-cost floor but above subfloor No. 2 representing the direct-cost floor.

Such a decision to price below the full-cost floor would be feasible only if the firm produced other products which could be sold at prices sufficiently high to make up for the lack of contribution to overhead resulting from pricing this product at less than full-cost levels. Another possible reason for initially pricing below full cost would be that such

Figure 13–6.   Tiers or layers of cost with associated subfloors.

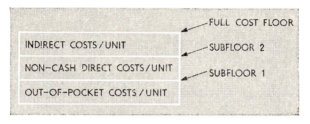

Figure 13–7.   Demand ceiling above full-cost floor.

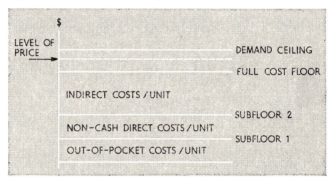

Figure 13–8.   Demand ceiling below full-cost floor.

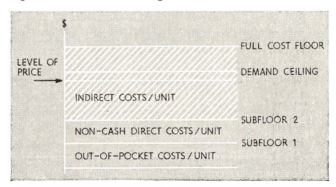

a price would, in time, bring in sufficient volume to cause a reduction in full-cost levels per unit as illustrated in Figure 13–9.

Thus, the cost floor which the price setter uses may vary with the competitive situation faced, with the behavior of costs over time as volume changes, and with the need to have a full line or family of products. The revenues from all the products sold must, of course, cover full costs in the long run. In the short run, however, when single products are being priced the full-cost floor is not an absolute barrier to lower prices.

Figure 13–9. A dynamic view of the cost floor–demand ceiling relationship.

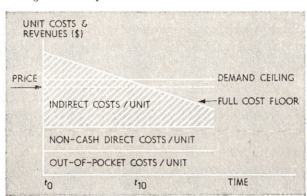

Costs and pricing strategy. In addition to setting the floor (or floors) to price, costs also enter into pricing strategy decisions. Knowledge of one's own costs, for example, provides insight into the nature of the cost structures of competitors and thus enables one to estimate better the reaction of rivals to pricing moves. Evaluation of costs also can help answer the question of whether or not a pricing proposal will invite competitors into the market or whether it will discourage their entry. Finally, knowledge of costs can help the firm decide whether to make a component or to buy it on the outside.

There will be a further discussion of pricing strategy a little later on. At this point, however, it is advisable to examine an approach in which demand and costs are considered together.

the interactive approach

It is far safer to view the pricing process as the interaction of cost and demand. If the firm starts with costs and tests various cost buildups against demand, the dangers associated with a purely cost-plus approach may be averted. In like manner, starting with demand and working back to costs is a more desirable approach than straight cost-plus pricing. Of course, in recommending the interactive approach, it is assumed that the pricing decision is concerned with manufactured goods which, although new, are not totally unknown (in a generic sense) to the market. In those cases where the product being sold is a highly specialized custom-built item purchased by a single buyer, cost-plus may be the only feasible way in which a price can be set.

break-even analysis

In using the interactive approach to price determination, some method of visualizing the relationship among fixed costs, variable costs, volume, and price and the effects of these relationships on profit is almost a necessity. Break-even analysis is such a method. It calls attention to the various types of costs involved, such as those which are fixed over the range of output, those which vary with output, and those which vary with executive decisions. The analysis also allows management to visualize a series of preliminary prices which are then evaluated in terms of volume possibilities.

With known or estimated costs and a series of possible prices, the volume requirements to break even for any given price proposal are identified.

Break-even analysis also shows how rapidly profits can be increased if volume above the break-even level can be secured. In like manner, the analysis shows management the size of the loss at volumes below the break-even level.

In Figure 13–10 those costs which remain fixed over the range of output to be considered are estimated to be $10,000. Those costs which vary with output are zero at zero output and $10,000 at 500 units of output. They are $20 per unit in this illustration where variable costs are assumed to vary directly with output. This assumption is not necessary for the analysis, as costs which vary with output on a nonlinear basis could be portrayed by an appropriate curved line. In similar manner fixed costs which change abruptly at different levels of output could be illustrated by means of a step function.

The last element of the cost buildup is that which represents costs associated with specific executive policies relating, for example, to nonprice promotional efforts. In Figure 13–10 they are shown as being constant over the range of output and of the magnitude of $5,000.

Thus, from zero to 750 units of output, total costs vary from $15,000 to $30,000.

Looking now at the revenue side of the picture, one sees three revenue lines each associated with a price proposal. The first price suggested is $100 per unit, the second $75 per unit, while the third proposal is $50 per unit. Each revenue line indicates the extent of gross income (price times volume) forthcoming from the associated price

Figure 13–10.   A break-even chart.

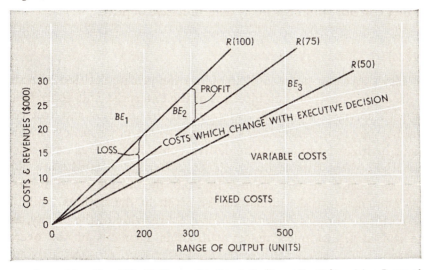

Source: Adapted from Wilfred J. Eiteman, *Price Determination* (Report No. 16 [Ann Arbor: Bureau of Business Research, Graduate School of Business Administration, The University of Michigan, 1949]).

proposal. Note that some estimate of the demand schedule for the product over the price range of $50 to $100 per unit is required before these revenue lines can be drawn.

The volume requirements needed to cover costs (or to break even) for each price proposal are clearly seen to be 200 units at $100, 300 units at $75, and 500 units at $50. Profits are shown by the vertical distances between the total costs and the revenue line to the right of the break-even point. For example, at a price of $100 per unit, break-even occurs when 200 units are sold. If 300 units are sold, profits would be about $8,000 as shown by the line segment labeled "profit." Losses are shown by vertical distances between total costs and revenues to the left of a given break-even point. For example, at a price of $50, break-even occurs when 500 units are sold. If only 200 units are sold, the loss is approximately $8,000 as shown by the line segment labeled "loss."

Value and limitations of break-even analysis. Break-even analysis is a useful technique in balancing demand and cost factors in the process of determining price. It requires of the pricing executive estimates of demand at different levels of price, and then it indicates the behavior of costs at various levels of output associated with different price proposals. Of course, the quality of the analysis can be no better than the quality of the cost data and demand data inputs, but the very nature of the approach forces a consideration of the interaction of demand and costs. As such, break-even analysis indicates well that neither cost nor volume is solely determinative of price.

pricing strategy

Having a clear understanding of how the pricing decision is related to the achievement of the objectives of the enterprise and being familiar with a range of possible prices given the demand and cost constraints, the pricing executives can then consider those strategies which might be followed to attain the desired goals. In this area of decision, executives often share feelings held by military officers who are planning an assault on the enemy. In both the business and military environments, consideration must be given to the options available, the resources at one's disposal, the possible reaction of the enemy, and the consistency of one's moves with other elements of the overall program. Thus, pricing strategy like military strategy is uniquely associated with available opportunities and the means on hand for their exploitation.

It is senseless to talk of strategy unless some alternatives are available. Assume, for example, that the pricing executives face a situation in which the price they can set is limited on the high side by competition and on the low side by the full-cost floor. If the distance between the floor and the ceiling is fairly wide, the executives have some discretion as to whether to price near the ceiling or the floor or somewhere inbetween the two extremes. If the floor and the ceiling are closer together, the discretionary range is smaller. It may even be nonexistent if the floor and ceiling coincide or if the floor is above the ceiling.

Let us look at examples A, B, and C in order to see what strategies might be available in each case. In situation A, where the range of discretion is fairly wide, the price might be set up near the demand ceiling. This would be called a "skim" type of strategy in which a high initial price for a new product would be set to "skim the cream" off of the market. Such a strategy could be expected to work over a period of time only if the product were protected from competition because of its technical or design uniqueness. If such were the case and the demand ceiling held at its original level over time, a skim pricing strategy accompanied by heavy nonprice promotion would offer considerable advantage.

Certain other attributes of a situation might suggest a skim strategy. Limited production facilities, need to recoup research and development expenses, and unclear nature of demand all would indicate that a high-price, limited-volume strategy would be best for the beginning. Such a strategy would be even more effective if the market could

Figure 13–11. Illustration of three floor-ceiling combinations.

DEMAND CEILING D	DEMAND CEILING D	FULL COST FLOOR c_f
RANGE OF DISCRETION	RANGE OF DISCRETION	
	FULL COST FLOOR c_f	DEMAND CEILING D
FULL COST FLOOR c_f		
		SUBFLOOR c_s
A.	B.	C.

be divided into segments and promotion could be directed to those segments where demand was relatively insensitive to price.

The advantages of a skim strategy are great when product uniqueness provides protection from competition, thus allowing a high initial price to provide for new product introduction by means of generous trade margins and nonprice promotion. There are, however, situations in which a strategy of a low initial price might be called for. If, for example, the new product were of a type generally known to the consumer, if competition were a strong threat, if demand were estimated to be sensitive to price, and if sizable economies of production were associated with volume, then a low initial or "penetration" price might be superior to a higher one. It would allow the product to gain a mass market quickly, thus moving in ahead of competition. The low price would not allow for much nonprice promotion or for wide trade margins, but because of the sensitivity of demand to a low price, nonprice promotional efforts could be kept to a minimum. Finally, although price were set at the full-cost floor, over time, as production economies took effect, the floor would be lowered thus producing greater profits.

Situation B in Figure 13–11 is a variant of situation A. In this second example the floor and the ceiling are much closer together and the range of discretion more limited. In situation C the demand ceiling (D) is actually below the full-cost floor (C_f). This means that the product's value-in-use is less than the producer's full costs of manufacturing and marketing or that competitors offer close substitutes at prices lower than the producer's costs. In this type of situation the manufacturer faces the alternative of either not introducing the product or of placing it on the market at a price under the present full-cost floor but above a cost subfloor such as the one representing direct costs. A strategy of pricing below full costs might be indicated when cost reductions are anticipated with volume or when the product is an essential part of a line and must be placed on the market even if its price will only cover part of its cost of production and marketing. If the price can cover direct costs, some contribution to overhead may be forthcoming. Placing a new product on the market at a price below its present full costs may be a profitable move, especially when the new product is viewed as a member of a family of products each making different sized contributions to overhead and profit.

Strategy over time. The discussion of pricing strategy to this point has been essentially in static terms or at the very best has dealt with pricing in the short run. The concepts of demand ceiling or cost floors, although helpful in determining the range of discretion open to the price setter at the time of new product introduction, can be dangerously misleading if not viewed in a dynamic context. Demand ceilings change over time as do cost floors, and the price setter must be aware of these changes and anticipate them by changes in strategy.

We have already spoken of the case in which the price of a new product is set high to tap those segments of the market where demand is relatively inelastic and where the need is great to bring in revenues quickly. We have also looked at situations in which the initial price might be set close to the full-cost floor or even below it. There are strategies, however, where future product and/or market changes are considered. One such strategy has been called "sliding down the demand curve."[5] The firm following such a strategy starts with a high initial price emphasizing value more than cost in an attempt to skim the cream from successive market segments. However, the firm anticipates competition and reduces price faster than is required by the market. Thus, potential competition is forestalled, and the firm be-

---

[5] D. Maynard Phelps and J. Howard Westing, *Marketing Management* (3d ed.; Homewood, Ill.: Richard D. Irwin, Inc., 1968), p. 326.

comes an established volume producer over time with a price approaching the level that a penetration pricing strategy would have required initially.

Because new products age in that they lose their aura of uniqueness or face increasing competition from substitutes, pricing strategies suited to the introductory stage of the product's life cycle must be amended over time. As competition increases, prices are forced down, and price becomes the dominant element in the promotional mix. When brand preference weakens and private brands enter in force, there is little left to do but to reduce prices promptly to forestall private brand competition. This is merely the acceptance of the fact that in the mature stage of the product life cycle, competition is largely on a price basis.

price redetermination

In addition to the problem of determining a price for a new product, marketing executives are often faced with the problem of changing the price of an established product. This process is called "price redetermination," and the problems arising from it differ somewhat from those associated with the determination of initial price. Essentially, these differences are an outgrowth of the aging of the product. The problems of pricing in the competitive or mature stages of product life are less involved with uncertainty than are those dealing with setting the price for a product in the introductory stages of its development. In the competitive stage, for example, more is known about demand. The degree of sensitivity of demand to changes in the producer's promotional mix, to actions of competitors, and to variations in the overall economic environment is understood with greater clarity. In like manner, the producer has a clearer picture of his production and marketing costs with an established product than with a new one.

motivation for redetermination

Management may decide to change a price for several reasons. It may be necessary to raise or lower a price to reflect a modification in the market's valuation of a product. On the other hand, the change may be the result of variations in costs of production, distribution, or promotion. Or the price move may come about to increase market share or to gain some other competitive advantage. Finally, a price change may be defensive to meet price or nonprice moves of rivals.

Change in market valuation. If demand for a given product slackens over time and if there have been no overt changes in the producer's promotional mix or the actions of competitors, then it is quite obvious that changes have taken place in the market. Perhaps the market segment composed of prospects who placed a high value-in-use on the product has been saturated. Or, perhaps, the novelty aspects of the product have worn off, and consumers have turned elsewhere to spend their money. Regardless of causation, the producer must readjust his promotional mix to conform to the realities of the marketplace. Usually, such a readjustment entails a reduction in price to enable the producer to tap segments of the market where demand is more sensitive to a price reduction than to additional nonprice promotion.

Changes in costs. Although demand is usually the controlling factor in the pricing of fabricated goods, cost changes can have a motivating or triggering effect on price redetermination. For example, cost reductions associated with volume production may allow price reductions which will either help maintain current volume levels or increase them. Price redetermination which is associated with a declining cost floor has several strategic implications which will be discussed shortly.

In contrast, product cost increases associated with (1) declining volume, (2) rising labor and/or material costs, or (3) both factors, may force consideration of higher product prices. The decision to raise price is, of course, influenced by the general sensitivity of demand to price and the possible reaction of competitors. Thus, it is quite evident that although cost changes might motivate price changes for established products, whether or not such changes are made depends on the demand factors, that is, on how consumers value the product and what substitutes are available to them.

Changes in strategy. Price redetermination, especially in the downward direction, may be used to implement a new marketing strategy. As was noted earlier, a desire to "slide down the demand curve" requires frequent evaluation of the competitive situation and correctly timed price reductions. Through these reductions the firm hopes to tap successive layers of demand which vary in price sensitivity. Timing is crucial, as the reductions must be made sufficiently early to dissuade competitive entry or to catch those rivals already in the market off guard.

Price increases as part of a process of redetermination also have strategic implications. For a firm with a highly differentiated product, a move to a higher level of price may reflect product superiority. The higher price may well bolster the quality image of the line. Such upward moves are, of course, easier to sustain when the nonprice promotional efforts have created a strong selective demand for the product. Price redetermination on the upside may reflect a decision to pursue a high price, limited-volume strategy by reblending the marketing mix to give price a lesser role in relation to the other elements.

Changes in competition. Price changes, either upward or downward, after initial introduction of a product may be necessary to adjust to the actions of competitors. Such changes become especially necessary when the number of sellers in a given industry is few.

Let us start with a market situation in which there are many sellers in the industry and selective demand for the products of individual sellers varies from weak to strong. In this type of environment the firm which had developed the strongest demand for its product would have the greatest degree of flexibility in dealing with competitive change of a price or nonprice variety. The firms with weak selective demand would find that demand for their products would be very much affected by price or nonprice moves of rivals. Because of lack of product differentiation or other reasons which have denied them strong selective demand, the response of these "weak demand" firms is very much limited to changes in price. Thus, for a very large number of sellers in markets which are monopolistically competitive, price is the major vehicle by which they adjust to competitor-invoked change.

Price redetermination when sellers are few. The problem of price redetermination becomes especially complex when the number of sellers in the industry is few and the degree of product differentiation is slight. The economist would call such a market situation an example of a nondifferentiated or pure oligopoly. In such an environment a firm would have to be very careful about redetermining its prices because such a redetermination could under certain conditions result in a redetermination of the *industry* price level and the industry marketing mix. As the degree of product differentiation increases when sellers are few, the extent of price differences among them may also increase. There still comes a point, however, when a price move by one firm will cause an industrywide reaction.

Perhaps some idea of the price behavior of firms in oligopolistic industries in the short run may be gained by viewing the "kinked" oligopoly demand curve.

In Figure 13–12, p is the industry price or the modal value of the cluster of industry prices. If a firm in the industry raises its price to p 1, one of two responses can be expected. If the rest of the firms in the industry feel that strength of demand or pressures of cost suggest an upward readjustment of industry price, they may follow the first firm up to price $p+$. In this case the operative demand schedule for the initiating firm would be the segment of D'' above the intersection with D'. This segment is relatively inelastic because all suppliers of close substitutes also have raised their prices.

On the other hand, if the other firms do not follow the initiating firm, a great deal of the initiator's patronage will shift to other firms in

Figure 13–12. Kinked oligopoly demand curve.

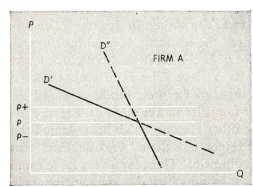

the industry who offer lower prices. Thus, in this situation the demand curve which is operative for the initiating firm is the segment of D' above the intersection with D''. It is highly elastic, for demand falls off rapidly for the firm which raises its price above the industry level but does not have the degree of selective demand to support the differential in price.

Looking at the downside we see a similar pattern of behavior. If the initiating firm drops its price to $p-$ and the rest of industry is forced to follow, schedule D'' from the intersection with D' becomes operative. It is relatively inelastic for the initiating firm because all firms in the industry have matched the move. An important question to raise here, however, is, What effect will a lower industry price level have on industry demand?

If the initiating firm lowers its price and is not followed, then, of course, it will gain a great deal of patronage at the expense of its rivals. In this case the demand schedule D' from the intersection with D''

downward would be operative. Because rivals would react quickly, this highly elastic segment would not be operative for long, if at all.

It can be seen from this brief discussion that price redetermination when product differentiation is weak and/or sellers are few is quite a touchy task. This is because price moves by the firm are closely related to reactions by rivals. In like manner, price moves by rivals have an important effect on any firm in the industry. In many situations, therefore, price redetermination by a firm is forced upon it by competition. When a firm itself initiates a price change, especially in an oligopolistic industry, it is actually proposing a readjustment of the relative importance of price in the *industry's* marketing mix.

pricing a new addition to the product line

The problem of pricing a new product is compounded when the new product is to be part of an existing group or line of products. The products involved may be physically distinct or they may be physically similar but sold under different demand conditions reflecting value-in-use, seasonal, or life cycle variations.

cost interdependence

In many situations prices for new additions to the product line are made on the basis of costs. Dean reports that common policies include, among others, setting price proportional to full cost, setting price proportional to incremental costs, or setting price to provide profit margins proportional to conversion costs.[6]

Using cost as the sole basis by which to set the price for a new addition to the line can be dangerous. Many of the costs of producing and marketing the new product are overhead costs or joint costs. Allocation or separation of these costs may be impossible and, therefore, any attempt to determine the full cost floor for the new addition will require that costs be applied on an arbitrary basis. Even if direct or incremental costs are used too great an orientation to the cost side can cause management to lose sight of the reasons for the introduction of the new product. Cost pricing by ignoring variations in demand or in competition faced may cause the firm to forego opportunities for market segmentation.[7]

---

[6] Joel Dean, "Problems of Product Line Pricing," *Journal of Marketing*, Vol. 14 (January, 1950), pp. 519–20.

[7] C. N. Davisson, "Pricing the Product Line," unpublished technical note, Business Administration Library, The University of Michigan.

demand interdependence

The main economic question raised when a new product is added to the line is not usually concerned with costs. It is, rather, a question of the nature of demand interdependence. Is the new product a complement or a substitute? Can the new product be used as an instrument for market segmentation and/or price discrimination? The answers to questions such as these, which have a strong demand orientation, are useful in finding the "right" price to be placed on a new addition to an established line.

In much the same way that the pricing decision for an individual new product must be an outgrowth of overall strategy, so must it be when pricing a new member of the product line. Is the goal of the firm to increase its penetration of specific market segments? Does the firm wish to favor certain items in the line over others? Is the firm committed to a policy of "full-line" pricing in which the goal is to set an array of prices for members of the line so that the total contribution of the line is a maximum?

Given a clear understanding of the goals of the firm for the longer run, the pricing decision in the short run assumes a strategic as well as purely economic character. Perhaps a view of two diverse situations will offer a better view of the nature of the problem.

A substitute product. A large manufacturer of industrial chemicals had developed a nontoxic solvent for degreasing metal parts. The basic chemical in this product was produced as a by-product of another process and thus carried a low cost burden. The new solvent was superior to carbon tetrachloride, the currently used chemical. The manufacturer of the new solvent was one of the largest producers of carbon tetrachloride. It sold about 20 percent of its output to the solvent market and 80 percent as a raw material for the subsequent manufacture of chlorinated hydrocarbons.

The new chemical was clearly a substitute for the established product in the solvent market. If the new product were priced somewhat higher than the old, it could displace carbon tetrachloride in those applications where toxicity was a major problem. If the product were priced equal to, or slightly under, carbon tetrachloride (as the cost floor readily allowed), considerable displacement would occur. In fact, preliminary market research indicated that if priced at the level of carbon tetrachloride, the new product would almost completely take over the cold-cleaning solvent market.

The question which faced the manufacturer was whether or not a relatively low price on the new product and its subsequent penetration of the cold-cleaning market would invite competitors to cut their prices on carbon tetrachloride. If this were to happen, the gains in revenues from an increased share of the solvent market would be more than counterbalanced by losses in revenues in those markets where carbon tetrachloride was purchased as a raw material.

Thus, the issue facing the manufacturer in pricing the new addition to the line concerned the cross-elasticity of demand not only between items in the line but also between the market segments served by the firm and its rivals.

A complementary product. In another situation a manufacturer of home traffic appliances found that he was losing business to competitors because his line did not include a small portable mixer. To remedy this weakness he developed a new mixer which on the basis of cost estimates would have to be sold at a price 10 percent above the price of competing products, that is, if the new product were to make an average contribution. Careful evaluation indicated that product superiority was not sufficient to warrant the price premium, and the decision was made to price the new product at competitive levels. It was felt that although the product was somewhat better than competing items, it would be sold at the price which would guarantee market acceptance even if revenues received barely covered direct costs. The manufacturer reasoned that the new product would stimulate sales of the rest of the line and that total contribution was more important to the firm than was the contribution of any one item in the line.

Dual relationships.[8] In addition to a product being a substitute or a complement, it well may be both. For example, in the case of the solvent manufacturer we viewed the new product as a substitute for the old. If, however, the addition of the new product enabled the manufacturer to attract new customers, to strengthen his distributor organization, or to gain fuller coverage for his line, the demand interrelationship between the new product and the rest of the line would be one of complementarity. In similar fashion, if the portable mixer developed to fill a gap in the line of the home appliance manufacturer shifted sales away from the standard mixer, then a substitute relationship would exist.

implications

If a new product is added to a line to implement the firm's marketing strategy, as is usually the case, the demand factors must dominate the pricing decision. The degree of flexibility open to management is,

[8] *Ibid.*

however, limited by the extent of demand interdependence between the new product, existing products in the line, and products of competitors.

As is the case with individual products, costs set the floor for the price of an addition to a product line. Management does have considerably more discretion in defining the cost floor when adding a product to an existing line than when introducing a single product. This flexibility arises from management's ability to apportion revenues received across the line to the coverage of direct and indirect costs.

While gaining some flexibility on the cost side, the firm probably loses some on the demand side as has been noted above. As demand is probably the prime determinant of price, in most cases there is a net loss in flexibility when setting a price for a new addition to a line. This loss in flexibility, however, need not prevent a price setter from tapping specific market segments on the basis of price. Market opportunities are always present, and only a constant appraisal of demand will make their exploitation possible. A continuing process of demand appraisal is especially important when demand interrelationships change over the product's life cycle to such an extent that price redetermination might be necessary.

conclusion

In this chapter we have considered the role of price in the marketing mix and three areas in which the pricing decision is of special importance. Attention has been paid to the need to understand the nature of the competitive environment in which the firm must set its prices as well as to the role that price determination plays in implementing the overall strategy of the firm.

questions

1. Why is it generally suggested that the nonprice aspects of marketing strategy be determined before the pricing decision is made?
2. What is the value, if any, to a pricing decision maker of the economist's models of price determination in diverse market situations?
3. Can a firm have differing pricing objectives in the short run as opposed to the long run? Can a firm have more than one pricing objective for the same time period? Explain.
4. Why is demand estimation so vital to the process of price determination? How might one go about estimating demand for a new consumer product? A new industrial product?

5. What is meant by "cost-plus" pricing? What are the advantages and limitations of such an approach?
6. Define what is meant by a "cost floor." What is the "tier concept" and its pertinence to pricing decisions.
7. "Break-even analysis cannot determine a price." Comment on the preceding statement, and if you agree, indicate the value, if any, of such analysis to the pricing decision maker.
8. Describe those characteristics of a situation which would indicate the use of an initial strategy of pricing near the demand ceiling; of pricing near the full-cost floor; of pricing below the full-cost floor.
9. Can cost floors change over time? Explain.
10. Why must prices be redetermined on a periodic basis?
11. Union Carbide Corporation is a large producer of ethylene glycol, a chemical used as an antifreeze. It supplies this product in bulk to private labelers and packagers. Union Carbide also sells large quantities of ethylene glycol under its well-known Prestone brand.

    Wyandotte Chemical Company, which supplies ethylene glycol antifreeze only in bulk to private branders announced an increase in price from $1.24 per gallon in truckload lots to $1.345 per gallon.

    The Wall Street Journal reported that Union Carbide as well as Olin Mathieson and Allied Chemical Company, other producers of ethylene glycol, were studying Wyandotte's move.

    a) How should Union Carbide Corporation executives reason before deciding whether or not to raise ethylene glycol prices to the level set by Wyandotte?

    b) How should Union Carbide Corporation reason if, contrary to the above situation, Union Carbide contemplates assuming the role of price leader by initiating an increase in ethylene glycol prices with Wyandotte's reaction being uncertain?
12. How does the problem of pricing a new addition to a product line differ from the problem of pricing a single new product?
13. Does each product in a product line have to cover its full costs in the short run? In the long run?

price policies

Introduction

This chapter will discuss certain policy alternatives open to those in management responsible for the administration of prices. These alternatives range from immediate departure from the established price to the maintenance of the level of price over the longer run. The discussion, therefore, will cover such topics as price variation, discounts and discount policy, geographic pricing, and resale price maintenance. In each of these areas attention will be focused on the marketing significance of the policy as well as those legal constraints which are likely to be encountered.

A central theme of this chapter is that price policies, whether aimed at price variation or maintenance, are promotional instruments and should be considered as means by which the firm attempts to implement its overall marketing strategy.

basic policies

The administration of a price or a set of prices may be guided by certain basic policies. These include (1) the single-price policy, (2) the nonvariable price (one-price) policy, and (3) the variable price policy.

Under a single-price policy, there is but one price for all buyers regardless of the timing of the purchase, quantity ordered, or other aspects of the transaction. Such a policy may be highly discriminatory in an economic sense but, as will be discussed later, not illegal.

A nonvariable price (one-price) policy is one under which the seller charges the same price to all buyers who purchase under similar conditions. This policy should not be confused with the single-price policy, under which there is one price for *all* buyers. Under the non-variable price policy, different prices are charged. These differences, however, reflect variations in quantities purchased, in timing, and in other pertinent conditions of purchase. Under a nonvariable price policy, terms of sale are known and are administered uniformly. Although utilizing price differentials, a nonvariable price policy may be nondiscriminatory in both an economic and a legal sense.

A third type of basic policy is that of variable pricing. Under this policy the price arrangement between the seller and each buyer is the result of direct negotiation or other means of reflecting relative bargaining power based upon the buyer's evaluation of the product's value-in-use and the availability of alternate sources of supply.

The use of a single-price policy appeals to firms selling to small customers. The policy is easy to administer and permits the emphasis of nonprice appeals over price by salesmen and in advertisements. The policy is not likely to appeal to large buyers who believe that their volume purchases entitle them to a price reduction. The large buyer feels that a single-price policy discriminates against him, and unless the seller has built a very strong selective demand for his product, the buyer will seek a source which will vary price in this favor.[1]

Because the U.S. market is so large and diverse and because a single-price policy usually limits patronage to small customers, most sellers vary their prices. The question is, therefore, not usually one of choosing between a single-price policy and a variable price policy. It is, rather, deciding what kind of a variable price policy to follow.

variable versus nonvariable price policies

Under a variable price policy, prices are changed when such an adjustment is indicated by the nature of market conditions. These adjustments, either upwards or downwards, may reflect a change in competition, the differing elasticities of demand among potential buyers, and differing costs of production and/or marketing accruing to the seller.

The major advantage of a variable price policy is its speed and flexibility of adjustment. Competitive moves can be counteracted almost immediately. Desires for bargaining can be accommodated. The relative emphasis upon price versus nonprice promotion can be changed to suit the needs of a particular situation. In all, a variable price policy is a powerful promotional device.

---

[1] D. Maynard Phelps and J. Howard Westing, *Marketing Management* (3d ed., Homewood, Ill.: Richard D. Irwin, Inc. 1968), pp. 361–62.

The policy is not without its disadvantages. These include: (1) the need to delegate pricing authority to sales managers or to salesmen, thus requiring them to be skilled in negotiation; (2) the increased cost of selling due to the time taken up by the bargaining process; (3) the loss of centralized control over prices; (4) the customer ill will caused by different prices even though conditions of sale are similar; (5) the weakened sales effort caused by the substitution of price cutting for intensified personal selling; and (6) the legal complications growing out of the Robinson-Patman Act.[2]

The advantages of a nonvariable price policy include ease of administration, simplification of the selling process, and a general recognition that such a policy is, "fair to all buyers regardless of their ability to bargain or of the competitive situation surrounding the transaction."[3] In addition, a nonvariable price policy avoids many of the previously noted disadvantages of a variable price policy. Although a nonvariable price policy has been found most often in the United States at the retail level, manufacturers appear to be recognizing the advantages of such a policy and, "seem to be adopting a one-price [nonvariable price] policy to a far greater extent in recent years than in the past, although considerable price negotiation between manufacturers and their customers still takes place."[4]

price variation

Regardless of whether the firm follows a nonvariable or variable price policy, the act of charging different prices for essentially similar products or services is one of price variation. The reasons for such variation are generally, but not exclusively, to advance the promotional strategy of the firm. Individual companies may use differential pricing to achieve goals unique to themselves. There are, however, several commonly sought after objectives, which are noted in the next section.

goals of price variation[5]

Change of purchase pattern. Sellers use differential prices to influence or change patterns of purchase. Lower prices may be granted to induce customers to buy in larger quantities, to buy in anticipation

---

[2] Donald V. Harper, *Price Policy and Procedure* (New York: Harcourt, Brace, & World, Inc., 1966), p. 174.

[3] *Ibid.*, p. 175.

[4] *Ibid.*

[5] See Joel Dean, *Managerial Economics* (New York: Prentice-Hall, Inc., 1951), p. 515, and Phelps and Westing, *op. cit.*, pp. 358–59.

of future need, or to concentrate their purchases among fewer sources of supply. Higher prices may be charged certain customers to discourage them from carrying the line, thus reducing the intensity of competition in certain markets.

Market segmentation. Price variation can be used to tap segments of a market which differ in price elasticity of demand. These differences in sensitivity to price may come about because of differing values-in-use among various classes of buyers and/or differing competitive situations facing the seller.

Market expansion. By offering lower prices to customers who have lower values-in-use, the market for a given product or service may be expanded. Such expansion may also be accomplished by offering lower prices to present customers to gain new applications of the product or service where prior price levels made such applications uneconomic.

Utilization of excess capacity. Differential prices which gain additional volume may utilize excess productive and/or marketing capacity. If such capacity exists, a price differential which makes a sale possible and which covers direct costs may contribute to the total profits of the firm.

Implementation of channel strategy. Differential pricing is a major device by which a firm attempts to implement its marketing strategy with respect to channels of distribution. Price variations may reflect differences in marketing tasks performed by various types of resellers or differences in the competitive environments in which they operate. Price differentials may encourage certain channels to engage in vigorous promotion of the line, or they may be used to gain representation of the line in diverse channels. On the other hand, differential pricing may discourage certain channels of distribution when such a policy is deemed useful in the furtherance of overall strategy.

To meet competition. Price variation is, of course, a device which can be used to meet competition. As previously discussed, the price ceiling for a given product or service is set by the value-in-use or utility offered the buyer as well as by the alternatives open to the buyer with respect to other sources of supply. In many situations, although the utility offered is high, the options available to the potential customer are numerous. Under such circumstances, the varying of a price in favor of the buyer may induce him to become a customer. In other situations, where the seller is disadvantaged because his production facilities are located far from the potential buyer, a price differential may be used to make the delivered price competitive with that of a seller located closer to the potential customer.

implementation of price variations

A variation in price from the established level may be the result of direct negotiation between the seller and the buyer. In many situations the transaction may reflect economic costs to the seller and economic values to the buyer better than would be the case if the sale was made at established prices. On the other hand, where the economic power or bargaining skill are markedly unequal, equity may better be served by an established price rather than by one which is negotiated.

When using established price variations, a schedule may be developed showing net prices charged to various customers or to all customers who buy in specified quantities or at special times. A more common approach, however, is to develop a schedule of discounts from the established level of price. These discounts reflect the extent of variation in price offered to those who represent a given class of customer or who buy under certain specified conditions.

Whether or not prices are stated as net, or gross less a discount, some variation from the established level must be specified. If discounts are used by a seller to implement his policy of price variation, they must not only offer the price concession needed to attract patronage but they must operate in a manner consistent with the overall marketing strategy of the firm.

discount policy

The discounts most commonly used to implement a policy of nonvariable pricing include quantity discounts, trade-functional discounts, and promotional discounts and allowances. Cash discounts, although widely used for financial purposes or because they have become trade practice, will not be discussed here. Discounts in the other three categories will, however, be examined in some detail in terms of how they are used to achieve certain marketing goals as well as the degree to which specific discounts reflect cost savings accruing to the seller. This latter point is especially important when considering the defensibility of a particular discount in terms of the Robinson-Patman Act.

quantity discounts

The quantity discount is the most widely used instrument for establishing price variations among customers. There are two types of quantity discount: the cumulative and the noncumulative. Each has different purposes and different capacities to reflect seller cost differentials.

Noncumulative quantity discounts (NCQD). This type of discount provides a reduction from the established or the list price for those customers buying in specified quantities. An NCQD is applied on a per order basis, and the principal goal of the user is to effect some change in the purchase pattern of the buyer. This change may be in the direction of larger but less frequent orders, buying in anticipation of demand, and purchasing the full line.

Figure 14–1. Relationship between buyer and seller costs as order size increases.

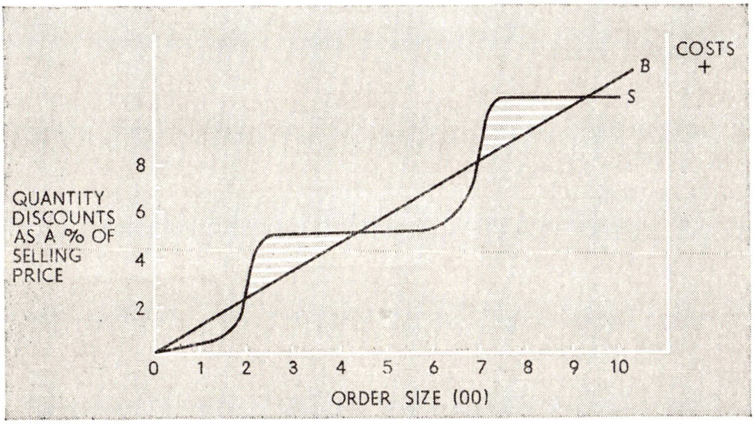

B represents increased buyer inventory holding costs with quantity purchases.
S represents seller's cost savings with quantity sales.

Source: Adapted from J. L. Heskett, Robert M. Ivie, and Nicholas A. Glaskowsky, Jr., *Business Logistics—Management of Physical Supply and Distribution,* p. 238. © 1964 The Ronald Press Company, New York.

Larger, less frequent orders allow more efficient scheduling of production and provide economies of scale with respect to billing, physical distribution, and selling activities. Cost savings, therefore, do accrue to the seller who can gain such orders through the use of NCQD's. Whether these savings are sufficient to cover the revenues foregone by the discount is one question. Another question, and one which appears to be more important from the marketing point-of-view, is whether or not the discount offered is large enough to compensate the buyer for the increase in his inventory holding costs occasioned by his purchasing in larger quantities. Given today's legal environment, the second question cannot be considered alone. Figure 14–1 graphically indicates how the two questions pertaining to the use of NCQD's are interrelated.

The shaded areas in the above illustration show that there are certain instances when the discount required to induce buyers to purchase in larger quantities can reflect the sellers' cost savings. In other cases (unshaded areas) seller cost savings are insufficient to fully reflect the discounts needed to change buyer behavior.

Although NCQD's are used primarily to implement marketing strategy by getting customers to buy in larger quantities, they may have a secondary application. An NCQD can be used to satisfy the demands of larger buyers for price concessions without the need to identify these customers by trade status, industry grouping, or other criteria. NCQD's can thus be used to reflect variations in price elasticity of demand among firms of varying size and bargaining power without regard to arbitrary and often difficult classification procedures. The discount approach essentially attempts to formalize price adjustments which might be brought about by interfirm bargaining and negotiation.

Cumulative quantity discounts (CQD). This variant of the quantity discount is also used to change purchase patterns. The CQD differs from the NCQD, however, in that it is granted on the basis of total purchases over a specified period of time. For example, a discount of 2 percent might be granted a buyer purchasing at least 100 units per year.

The basic marketing goal of a CQD is to tie the customer more closely to the seller. By granting him a price concession on the basis of total volume of sales per period of time, the buyer can be induced to concentrate his purchases to as great an extent as is consistent with his needs to maintain multiple sources of supply. Although the CQD is used to "tie up patronage," it does a rather poor job of reflecting cost savings. There are, of course, some reductions in selling costs if a seller can count on continued patronage from his customers, but such savings are hard to quantify. Under a CQD policy, there is no penalty to the buyer who purchases frequently and in small quantities. Therefore, such may be the case, and the seller's costs of producing and distributing may well increase. Thus, in many instances, sellers use NCQD's and CQD's together to gain the advantages of each without the disadvantages which might arise from the use of a CQD by itself.

Regardless of the behavior of seller's costs in any specific case, CQD's can never be easily defended on the basis of cost savings. This is what might well be expected, because the objective in using a CQD is not to save on per unit production and marketing costs but rather to hold on to customers. When the pressure for justification of discounts is great, the seller is on much firmer ground with a noncumulative rather than a cumulative quantity discount.

trade discounts

A reduction in price given to a buyer because of his position in a channel of distribution is called a trade discount. If the discount is granted to compensate customers who are resellers for their performance of certain marketing functions, perhaps a better name for the trade discount would be a "trade-functional" or "functional" discount. If the trade discount were granted to gain entry to a channel or to stimulate the resellers in the channel to provide promotional support for the product, a better name for the trade discount would be a "competitive-functional" discount.

Trade-functional discounts. As noted above, this type of discount compensates resellers for performing such marketing functions as holding inventory, engaging in sales promotion, and offering credit. Because so many resellers today have mixed trade status; i.e., wholesalers who engage in retailing and vice versa, the concept of paying resellers on the basis of functional performance has become more meaningful than paying them on the basis of their trade classifications. If the seller's objective in using a trade-functional discount is to compensate for functions performed by channel intermediaries, variations in discounts offered to customers in competition with one another may be defensible under the Robinson-Patman Act. This is especially true when variations in discounts offered reflect variations in the cost savings accruing to the seller because of customer assumption of a greater part of the marketing task.

Competitive-functional discounts.[6] When a seller is desirous of gaining entry into a channel of distribution or wants a certain level of marketing effort from his resellers in established channels, he finds that compensation for functional performance is not enough. The discounts which he offers must also take into account the competitive pressures under which the resellers operate. These pressures include the rivalry faced from other sellers for channel support, the rivalry which resellers face from other resellers within their own channels, and the competi-

---

[6] For a more complete discussion of competitive-functional pricing, see Charles N. Davisson, *The Marketing of Automotive Parts* (Ann Arbor: Bureau of Business Research, Graduate School of Business Administration, The University of Michigan, 1954), pp. 910–17.

tion among all resellers for patronage in the end market. Thus, an effective discount policy needed to gain channel access or support requires that payments be in excess of that required to compensate resellers for their functional performance. When such payments are made, the seller is said to be "buying distribution." Under such a discount policy, payments reflect the competitive as well as the functional needs of resellers and thus the name competitive-functional discounts. Unfortunately, these discounts which are used to buy distribution do not reflect variations in the seller's costs of serving different customers except by coincidence and are, therefore, difficult to defend under current price discrimination legislation.

trade discount strategy

The development of a trade discount structure to implement marketing strategy is not a simple process. The objectives of the seller may vary, the needs of resellers are diverse, and competition impinges unequally on different parts of the distribution structure.

If the seller's objective in using trade discounts is to pay for functions performed by resellers, his discount structure must be oriented to the costs incurred by these resellers in providing a given level of functional performance. Discounts must be set sufficiently high to gain the support of those marginal resellers whose costs are higher than average but who are needed in each geographic area to provide the intensity of distribution required by the seller. Finally, the discount schedule must reflect the seller's cost of using alternate channels of distribution (including the direct channel) to reach the market.

If the seller's strategy is aimed at buying distribution, the demand factors become more important. Questions to be considered include: (1) the discount structure of competitors, (2) the value of gaining entry to a new channel or of getting increased promotional support from an existing channel, and (3) the ability to sell to market segments of varying price elasticity of demand.

Trade discount schedules set to implement overall marketing strategy are usually discriminatory in that they favor some customers over others. Yet, these discounts are means of engaging in price competition and, as such, are of economic value to our society. From the seller's point of view the use of varying trade discount schedules, although resulting in different net prices from customers in different channels, increases total revenues and, hopefully, total profits.

promotional discounts and allowances

Price reductions or payments granted by sellers to buyers in return for promotional services rendered by the buyer are called promotional discounts or allowances. An example of such a discount is one in which a buyer is offered a 2 percent discount on his purchases if he will give prominent window display space to the seller's product for a specified period of time. An example of an allowance is a payment to a buyer for the services of an in-store demonstration program featuring the seller's product. Other types of promotional discounts or allowances may be made to support a cooperative advertising program or to furnish incentive payments to sales personnel.

The marketing objective of these discounts or payments is to gain the promotional cooperation of the reseller. Variations in these discounts or allowances among customers may represent differences in seller's costs, but as will be noted later, a cost defense is not generally applicable when discrimination is charged on the basis of seller's use of varying promotional discounts or payments. When promotional discounts or allowances exceed the costs of services performed by buyers, they may be considered to be disguised quantity discounts or just simple price variations.[7]

price variation—legal issues

Whether implemented by negotiation or a discount policy, price variation is a form of price discrimination. The object of price variation is to adapt price to the requirements of a given market situation. In some cases prices may be lowered to reflect a lower value-in-use in a specific application. In other cases price may be raised to reflect increased costs of serving a customer and/or the absence of a competing source of supply. Regardless of why a price variation is used, it is almost inevitable that two or more customers will pay different prices for essentially similar products or services. When such a practice occurs, it is price discrimination, and the legal constraints relating to such discrimination must be noted by those responsible for pricing policy. Further consideration of the legality of specific price variations must await a brief discussion of the Robinson-Patman Act, which is the principal federal law relating to price discrimination.

---

[7] Phelps and Westing, *op. cit.* p. 370.

the Robinson-Patman Act[8]

In 1936, Section 2 of the Clayton Antitrust Act of 1914 was amended by the Robinson-Patman Act. The amended section dealt with price discrimination, and the amendment sought to strengthen its provisions and extend its jurisdiction. At this time (1969), the Robinson-Patman Act has survived almost 33 years of administration by the Federal Trade Commission and continuous judicial review by the federal courts. To understand the act, which is the major legal constraint facing those sellers who use differential prices, is not an easy task. This is because the Robinson-Patman Act is not in the form of a traditional antitrust law. It is, rather, a law which attempts to redress imbalances in economic power. It is a creature of the depression years of the 1930's—a politically motivated response to the growing power of the corporate chain stores in relation to the smaller and economically weaker independent wholesalers and retailers.[9]

The Robinson-Patman Act itself is composed of six sections. Because it amended Section 2 of the Clayton Act, these sections are denoted as 2a through 2f. Sections 2a and 2b deal with price discrimination and certain defenses available to those charged with the offense. Section 2c deals with allowances in lieu of brokerage commissions, sections 2d and 2e cover the granting of promotional services and allowances, and section 2f holds that buyers accepting or inducing illegal price reductions are in violation of the act together with the grantor of the discriminatory price.

Injunctive or punitive action under the act may be initiated either by an FTC examiner or by a private complainant. If the presumed violation is one of price discrimination under Section 2a, a prima facie case must be shown to exist. The elements which must be present to make such a case should be fully understood by pricing executives. They include: (1) a sale at different prices, (2) by a seller engaged in interstate commerce, (3) to two or more competing customers, (4) of commodities of like grade or quality, (5) with a tendency to injure competition.

---

[8] This discussion is very much condensed and the intent of its presentation here is to give the reader a general overview of the act and its marketing and legal implications. Three sources which explain the act in greater detail are: Brian Dixon, *Price Discrimination and Marketing Management* (Ann Arbor: Bureau of Business Research, Graduate School of Business Administration, The University of Michigan, 1960); Phelps and Westing, *op. cit.* pp. 386–400; and W. David Robbins, "A Marketing Appraisal of the Robinson-Patman Act," *Journal of Marketing*, July, 1959.

[9] See Joseph C. Palamountain, *The Politics of Distribution* (Cambridge, Mass.: Harvard University Press, 1955).

Faced with such a case, the respondent may avail himself of several defenses. These include: (1) that not all of the elements of a prima facie case were actually present as charged, (2) that variations in prices charged competing customers reflected seller cost differentials in producing, selling, or delivering goods to these customers, (3) that a price reduction was granted to one customer "in good faith" to meet the lower price offered the customer by a competitor, and (4) that there was a change in market conditions or in the goods being sold which required a distress sale at lower prices.

The respondent may avail himself of these defenses, and if he is not satisfied with the findings of the FTC in his case, he may appeal the Commission's findings to the federal courts. If found guilty of a Robinson-Patman violation, the respondent may be required to cease and desist from current pricing activities, to pay a fine, or to be imprisoned for up to one year. Customers or competitors who claim injury by the respondent's price discrimination may sue him for treble damages in federal court.

implications for discount administration

What types of price variations are allowed under the Robinson-Patman Act? What types are patently illegal? Which pricing policies appear safer than others? These are some of the questions for which pricing executives need answers.

First, the act allows price differentials to customers who are in competition to the extent that these differentials reflect the seller's cost differences in manufacturing, selling, and/or delivery to the specific customers.

Second, under the "good faith" defense a seller may lower the price to one customer while keeping the price at former levels to competing customers if such a low price was necessary to meet a price offered the customer by a competitor.

Third, price reductions may be granted to some customers and not to others in response to "changing market conditions," such as deterioration or obsolesence of the commodity being sold or a licensed discontinuance of business by the seller.

The wording and the intent of the act does not seek to outlaw any specific type of discount or discount policy. It only says that price discrimination under certain specified conditions is illegal. A single-price policy, although discriminatory in that it penalizes customers who buy in large quantities, is not illegal under the act because the difference in price, which is the first element of a prima facie case, is missing. Likewise, a nonvariable price policy under which all customers of similar class, or who buy under the same conditions of sale, receive the same discounts is easier to defend under the act than is a variable price policy.

In terms of a cost defense, it is clear that noncumulative quantity discounts reflect seller cost savings better than do cumulative quantity discounts, and trade-functional discounts reflect variations in seller's costs better than do competitive-functional discounts.

The good-faith defense as stated in Section 2b was originally a procedural defense or a rebuttal to a prima facie case. A Supreme Court decision in 1951 in the *Detroit Gasoline* case held that the good-faith defense was an absolute defense.[10] To utilize this defense the seller must be able to prove that a customer was actually offered a lower price by a competitor and that the meeting of said price was necessary to retain the customer. Any use of a lower price to gain a customer, a partial meeting of a lower price, or an undercutting of a competitor's price will invalidate the defense.

Section 2c is concerned with the granting of price reductions to those buyers who perform their own brokerage services. The law simply states that such payments or allowances are illegal. The political basis of this section of the act was the desire to keep the large integrated chain from gaining a price advantage over their smaller and nonintegrated competitors. There are no defenses to the charge that a seller gave a buyer an allowance to reflect nonuse of a broker except proof that such was not the case.

Sections 2d and 2e cover the granting of promotional allowances or the offering of promotional services. These sections were placed in the act to prevent discrimination in the disguised form of supplementary payments or services offered to selected buyers and not to others. Two guidelines govern the use of promotional allowances and services under current FTC rulings.

First, payments or services must be granted on a *proportionately equal* basis. This means that competing buyers can receive payments or services which are roughly proportional to their dollar purchases from the manufacturer. For example, a buyer of $100,000 worth of goods may receive 10 times the dollar value of services and/or allowances from a manufacturer than a buyer whose purchases total $10,000 during the same period.

The second guideline is that all competing buyers must be able to

---

[10] *Standard Oil Co.* v. *FTC*, 340 U.S. 231, 71 S.Ct. 240 (1951).

participate in the manufacturer's program. The concept of participation covers both the informing of all buyers by the manufacturer of the allowances and services available and the designing of a program sufficiently flexible so that all buyers can benefit from the involvement. In other words, the program of the manufacturer must not be tailored solely to the needs of the larger buyers.

There are no absolute defenses to a Section 2d or 2e violation except proof that the allowances and services were properly offered and were distributed in a nondiscriminatory manner. Although in a very few isolated cases defenses available under Sections 2a and 2b have been attempted, the results are inconclusive.

Section 2f, which holds a buyer who knowingly induces or receives a discriminatory price, allowance, or service equally guilty with the grantor, has no specific defense. The best course of action for a buyer charged with a 2f violation is to help the grantor prove that there was no illegal discrimination. Another and more difficult approach for the buyer is for him to prove that he was unaware that the price, allowance, or service received was illegal.

geographic pricing policies

In addition to the development of price differentials reflecting variations in quantities purchased, the trade status of the buyer, and the extent of the marketing job performed by him, the seller must also consider price policies which concern the relative geographic location of the seller and the buyer. These policies range from those under which the seller absorbs the varying costs of transportation to arrive at a uniform delivered price for all customers to those under which the seller passes all freight costs on to the buyer. In between these extremes are other policies which attempt to simplify the administration of price variations imposed by location or which seek to improve the position of the seller when he is faced with competition from rivals located nearer to a customer than is he.

F.o.b. factory. The first policy to be considered is that of "free on board" at the seller's factory or warehouse. Under this arrangement the customer assumes title to the goods when they are turned over to a common carrier and in addition assumes the costs of transport and insurance. The delivered price varies in relation to the distance between the factory and the customer, while prices at the factory net of transport costs are constant for all customers served unless some other type of price variation is operative.

Uniform delivered price. Under this policy the seller assumes all of the costs of delivery in order that all of his customers pay a single delivered price. Such a policy is often called "f.o.b. customer's place of business," "freight allowed," or "postage stamp" pricing. Although the delivered prices which customers pay are equal regardless of their location, the net prices received by the seller at the factory differ in relation to the location of the customer served.

Freight equalization. A seller engaged in f.o.b. factory pricing often discovers that his market is limited geographically because competitors located closer to customers than is he have an advantage in that they can quote lower delivered prices. In order to extend his market, the seller may absorb some of the freight costs, so that his delivered price is equal to or less than that of rivals located closer to the customer. Such a practice is called freight equalization and involves the absorption of different amounts of freight costs resulting in varying net receipts for the seller.

Zone pricing. When the costs of freight are too high to allow a uniform delivered price over the entire market area, the seller may compromise by establishing a uniform delivered price for a given geographic area or zone. In so doing he may gain some of the promotional and billing advantages of a uniform delivered price policy without having to assume all of the freight costs. A policy of zone pricing should not be undertaken lightly by management because of certain associated results of such a policy which may be illegal. Perhaps the following illustration will indicate the nature of price behavior under zone pricing.

Assume the following attributes for the zone system pictured in Figure 14–2: (1) the firm (A) located in Ann Arbor sells a single product with a factory price of $100; (2) delivery costs are linear with distance and are $0.10/mile; and (3) zonal boundaries are 100 miles apart. The problem facing the seller using a system such as illustrated above is how to set the price for each zone. If the price is determined on the basis of factory cost plus delivery cost to the leading edge of the zone (for example, x_1 in zone II), then the delivered price for all customers in zone II will be $100 + $0.10/mile (50 miles) or $105. If the seller sets the price to reflect costs to get to the far side of the zone (x_2 in zone II), then the zone price is $100 + $0.10/mile (150 miles) or $115.

In the first case the seller is absorbing varying amounts of freight costs for customers in the zone located beyond the leading edge; in the second case he is charging customers located nearer to A than x_2 for freight costs which do not exist. This practice results in customers paying what has been called "phantom freight."

If the seller sets his zone prices on the basis of the average cost of delivery to the zone, all customers located before the zonal midpoint will be charged phantom freight, and all customers located beyond the zonal midpoint will have some of their freight charges absorbed by the seller. The legal implications of these happenings will be discussed at the end of this section.

Figure 14-2. A zone pricing system (single firm).

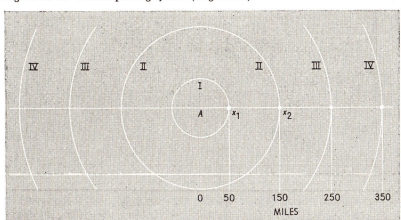

Basing point pricing. The last type of geographic pricing method to be discussed is one in which delivered prices are quoted by adding to the f.o.b. factory price the delivery cost from a specific geographic location to that of the customer regardless of whether or not the shipment was made from that point. The specific location so chosen is called a basing point.

If there is but one location from which all sellers quote delivered prices, the industry is said to use a single basing point system. The steel industry's "Pittsburgh Plus" was the prime example of the use of a single basing point from which to set prices.

When more than one geographic location is used from which to calculate delivered prices (either by a firm or a group of firms in an industry), a multiple basing point system is said to exist. These systems are not illegal per se, but certain attributes associated with their use may run afoul of the law.

In Figure 14-3 a situation is illustrated in which three selling points, S_1, S_2, and S_3, serve three customers, B_1, B_2, and B_3. The prices at S_1 and S_3 are $100 per unit. These locations are designated as basing points while S_2 is a nonbase mill or point of origin. Distances between these points are as noted on the connecting lines.

From an examination of the behavior of individual transactions, it can be seen that when a seller is serving a customer located closer to a base mill than to the seller's mill, freight charges must be absorbed by

Figure 14–3.   A multiple basing point system with two base mills.

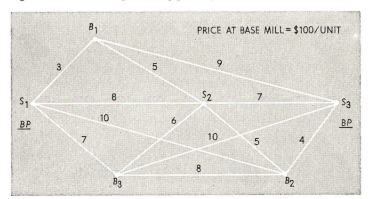

	Price (at Destination)	—	Delivery Cost	=	Factory Net (Price at Origin)
Seller 1 (base mill) sells to:					
Buyer 1	$103		$ 3		$100
Buyer 2	104		10		94
Buyer 3	107		7		100
Seller 2 (nonbase mill) sells to:					
Buyer 1	103		5		98
Buyer 2	104		5		99
Buyer 3	107		6		101
Seller 3 (base mill) sells to:					
Buyer 1	103		9		94
Buyer 2	104		4		100
Buyer 3	107		10		97

the seller. Such absorption occurs when seller 1 ships to buyer 2. Although freight costs are $10, the customer is located sufficiently close to the basing point at S_3, so that the seller must absorb $6 in freight costs.

In other cases the seller is forced to raise his price above that which would be expected based on actual cost of delivery. For example, seller 2 charges buyer 3 $107, although the actual freight costs are $6. The added charge of $1 is phantom freight assessed because the price the buyer pays is related not to the point of origin of the shipment but to the location of the buyer in relation to the nearest base mill. That mill in this case is S_1.

geographic pricing—legal constraints[11]

Many of the geographic pricing policies described above have run into legal difficulties over the past 50 years. In 1921, for example, the FTC complained that the single basing point system used by the steel industry discriminated in price in violation of Section 2 of the Clayton Act. The FTC claimed, in addition, that the "Pittsburgh Plus" method of quoting delivered prices violated Section 5 of the FTC Act. It held that the steel industry was engaged in a collusive attempt to fix prices and that such activity was deemed an "unfair method of competition" under the law. By 1924, the Commission ordered the steel industry to cease using a single basing point system. The industry obeyed without going to court and changed to a multiple basing point system. For the ensuing 16 years, all was relatively peaceful, but in 1940 the FTC opened a new attack on basing points which was to last a decade. The various rulings of the FTC and the subsequent support of the FTC by the courts resulted in a substantial limitation of the use of multiple basing points as a means of implementing a delivered-price policy.

The two major questions raised by the use of basing points are: (1) Is the system a method by which competing sellers attempt to fix prices? (2) Does the system discriminate in price to such an extent that competition is diminished among buyers? At this time (1969), it appears that if a basing point system does not result in price fixing through the systematic absorption of freight, if it does not contain nonbase mills which give rise to phantom freight, and if it does not result in different factory nets being received from competing buyers, then the user has a good chance of avoiding legal difficulties. The design of such a system is so difficult and the assurance that present FTC policy will hold for the future so tenuous that most sellers formerly using basing points have changed to straight f.o.b. factory pricing.

Individual sellers who want to engage in freight equalization on an *ad hoc* basis have had very little trouble with the law. Uniform delivered prices also seem to be quite acceptable to the FTC because under this policy all delivered prices are equal. The irony of the situation is

---

[11] See Phelps and Westing, *op. cit.*, pp. 400–407, for a most complete treatment of this subject.

that in the case of basing points the FTC defines price as mill or factory net. Under a policy of uniform delivered price, the opposite definition prevails: that the price is the amount which is paid at the destination. Legislative change or judicial review is sorely needed to clarify the question of whether price is that which is received by the seller at the point of shipment or paid by the buyer at the point of receipt.

Zone pricing by members of an industry has run into legal difficulties when all members of the industry have used identical zonal boundaries and identical zonal price differentials. The charge was one of violation of Section 5 of the FTC Act. The courts have held that in these cases evidence of collusion is not necessary if the results of a pricing system are the same as if there had been an actual meeting of the competitors or communication among them.

Section 5 is not violated by an individual firm's use of a zone system. Problems can arise, however, when customers located near zonal boundaries who are in competition pay different prices. In these situations the seller may be in violation of the Robinson-Patman Act.

resale price maintenance

As stated in the introduction to this chapter, a seller may choose from pricing policy alternatives ranging from those which entail variation of price from an established level to those which are aimed at the maintenance of such a level. The latter policies are especially difficult to implement when the seller uses independent resellers in his pattern of distribution and when the title to the goods being sold passes to these middlemen.

When the seller decides to follow a policy of resale price maintenance, commonly called RPM, it is because the advantages to be gained from such a course of action outweigh the disadvantages. These advantages are diverse, but like those sought by the user of a policy of price variation, are essentially promotional. They arise out of the ability of a properly executed RPM policy to eliminate or control price rivalry among resellers in the channels of distribution. When price rivalry is diminished, certain benefits may accrue to the seller. These include the following.

Protection of product image. The reduction of price rivalry at the retail level may protect the consumer image of a product or a brand. The stabilization or control of resale price is especially important when the buyer associates quality with price as in the case of a luxury good or prestige item. Stabilization or maintenance of retail price is also of value when consumers purchase the product as a gift item.

Reduce interchannel rivalry. The use of an RPM policy can restrict price competition among different channels of distribution, thus protecting the margins of those resellers in high-cost channels. The promotional advantage sought is the added market coverage gained through the seller's ability to distribute through a variety of channels which differ in their average costs of operation.

Reduce intrachannel rivalry. The use of RPM to reduce price competition among competing resellers in the same channel of distribution is aimed at protecting reseller margins from erosion. If RPM can preserve margins, the seller may be able to gain the support of the resellers in terms of higher levels of nonprice promotion and service to the consumer.

implementing a policy of resale price maintenance

If development of overall marketing strategy indicates that a price maintenance policy is desirable, there are several ways in which such a policy might be implemented. Sellers might, for example, become sufficiently selective in their distribution so that the line becomes important to the reseller. Then a franchise agreement might be negotiated with each reseller, specifying the price and discount schedule which would govern the resale of the product line. Failure to comply with this agreement would be grounds for its possible termination. Where the product line requires more intensive distribution to gain market coverage, the manufacturer's bargaining power is diminished. Selling to specific market segments which do not overlap at prices which reflect elasticity of demand in each segment may keep prices stable both within the segment and among segments. Finally, before turning to legal means of implementing an RPM policy, the seller might consider reducing his discounts so that margins are not so wide that they induce price cutting.

In many situations the only recourse left to the seller is to enter into price-setting contracts with resellers. These contracts are "price-fixing" agreements and, therefore, need federal and state enabling legislation to exist. These laws are commonly called "fair trade" laws, and the policy of engaging in an RPM policy using the contract approach under these laws is called "fair trading." The so called "fair trade" contract to be effective requires a nonsigner clause. This allows a contract made between a seller and one of his reseller customers to be legally binding on all other resellers of the line in the state when they are formally notified of the existence of the original agreement. Because of the controversial nature of the nonsigner clause, many states, including Michigan, have ruled such fair trade laws to be unconstitutional. It has been estimated that at this time (1969) less than 30 of the 50 states have effective fair trade laws.[12]

A recent analysis of methods used to encourage stability of retail prices by manufacturers of consumer goods seems to indicate that the use of fair trade laws, promotional allowances, and moral suasion were relatively ineffective ways of attaining RPM goals. The author of the study suggests that restricting the intensity of distribution, market segmentation, and reductions in discounts and allowances are more effective and less controversial ways of gaining stability of price at retail levels.[13]

Analysis suggests that a policy of RPM is too intimately related to product, channel, and promotional strategy to be applied by law. It appears that successful application of RPM is more dependent on the overall program of the manufacturer (or other seller) than upon the legal environment in the existing market area.

implications

The basic questions to be asked by a seller in attempting to decide whether or not to follow an RPM policy might include: (1) Will the revenue gains from an RPM policy cover the costs of policing the dealer organization? (2) Will most of the resellers stay loyal to the seller's policy in the face of a few recalcitrant price cutters? (3) Are stable and relatively high prices needed to support the prestige image of the product or product line? (4) Does the amount of aggressive selling required from resellers require an RPM policy to protect their margins? If the answer to most of the above queries is positive, RPM becomes a viable policy alternative.

In contrast to a policy of price variation, RPM attempts to reduce the influence of price in the marketing mixes of the members of the reseller organization. Thus, if price variation aimed at gaining greater volume from various resellers results in a mix of both price channels and channels which do not emphasize price in their promotional

---

[12] William J. Stanton, *Fundamentals of Marketing* (2d ed.; New York: McGraw-Hill Book Company, 1967), p. 470.

[13] See Louis W. Stern, "Approaches to Achieving Retail Stability," *Business Horizons* (Fall, 1964), pp. 75–86.

strategies, the seller will have great difficulty in implementing an RPM policy. Price variation and RPM policies appear to work in opposite directions, and the wise manufacturer will decide in which direction he wants to go and will develop a policy which is consistent and which will lead him to his goals. Only if the market is clearly segmented can the seller use both policies with some hope of success. Here an RPM policy may be used in one market segment while a policy of price variation may be used to tap another and more price sensitive market segment.

conclusion

This chapter concludes the sequence on pricing. In the preceding chapter, the discussion centered on the problems of determining a price or a basic level of price. This chapter has attempted to illustrate how variations from the established level or maintenance of levels of price may be used for promotional purposes. The coverage of topics was highly selective and of necessity brief. The purpose of the two-chapter sequence has been to provide an overview of pricing in the context of the marketing mix.

Pricing in all of its various nuances is more of an art than a science. But in the same manner in which an artist improves his work by studying the principles of composition, perspective, and color, the executive can improve the quality of his pricing decisions by under-standing more thoroughly the economic, psychological, and legal forces which impinge upon price determination and administration.

questions

1. Why do most American business firms follow a variable price policy rather than a single-price policy?
2. How does price variation relate to the development of an overall marketing strategy? Specifically, how does price variation facilitate the achievement of product, channel, and nonprice promotional objectives?
3. "Discounts differ in terms of the marketing goals they seek to achieve as well as in their ability to reflect differences in sellers' costs." Explain the promotional and legal implications of this statement.
4. Compare and contrast trade-functional discounts and competitive-functional discounts.
5. What is the difference between a promotional discount and a simple price variation? Is this difference as clearly defined in practice as in theory?

6. What types of price variations are allowed by the Robinson-Patman Act? What types are illegal?

7. What is the "good faith" defense to a Robinson-Patman Act violation? Trace the evolvement of this defense from its initial interpretation to its present interpretation.

8. What is a basing point? A basing point system? Are all basing point systems illegal?

9. In commenting on proposed federal "fair trade" legislation the Council of Economic Advisers to the President said, in a special report:

> "For many types of goods, the total demand by consumers is sensitive to the number of retail outlets which handle them, and manufacturers therefore like to have as many outlets as possible."

How do you reason concerning the outlet coverage implications of a policy of resale price maintenance?

10. What are some of the ways in which a seller may implement a policy of resale price maintenance? What legal restrictions must he be aware of in designing his program?

cases for part six

case 6–1

POP-TENT (B)

pricing a new product*

Some years ago, the management of the Pop-Tent Corporation of Ann Arbor, Michigan, was reviewing the pricing of its basic product, the "Pop-Tent Camper."

The Pop-Tent Corporation was formed to conduct the business of manufacturing and selling camping and outdoor recreational equipment. Among the principal assets of the firm were the inventory of and an exclusive license to manufacture, sell, and to use the trademark "Pop-Tent." The Pop-Tent was based on a new concept of tent design and erection which had been invented and developed by Mr. Henry Stribley and Mr. William Moss of Ann Arbor.[1] The promoters of the Pop-Tent Corporation, Mr. Clifford G. Baker and Mr. Oscar W. Haab, had joined with Messrs. Stribley and Moss after the invention of Pop-Tent to help them produce and market the then existing line. A year later Mr. Baker and Mr. Haab, along with other investors, had bought out the interests of Mr. Stribley and Mr. Moss, both of whom wanted to devote themselves to other activities, and subsequently the corporation was formed.

During the period they were associated with Pop-Tent, Mr. Baker and Mr. Haab had encountered all of the problems of launching and operating a new and inadequately financed business. They had raised funds from friends and other persons in the area. They had established channels of distribution, expanded the line, and had organized and trained a work force to manufacture their basic products.

line of products

At the time the pricing of the product was under review, the firm's line included 22 different items, 11 of which they manufactured, and the remainder of which were produced by other firms but sold by and under the Pop-Tent name.

Of the tents produced by the company, three embodied the design and

* Written by Ross J. Wilhelm, Associate Professor of Business Economics, Graduate School of Business Administration, The University of Michigan.

[1] See Pop-Tent (A), p. 27, for the history of this invention and these products.

mechanical principles of Pop-Tent. These were called "Pop-Tent Camper," which was the basic tent; "Pop-Tent Beach Cabana," a colorful version of the camper designed especially for waterside use; and the "Pop-Tent Sportsman's Shelter," which was a smaller adaptation of the camper and cabana for use as a portable duck-blind or as an ice-fishing shelter.

The other products manufactured and sold by the firm were:

1. "Para-Wing"—A portable, outdoor tarpaulin, supported by two poles and four stakes which was so designed that it could be erected for outdoor shelter without any center poles and without the canvas sagging. This product was designed by Mr. Moss and was manufactured in a 12′ × 12′ size and in two colors: yellow and white stripes and green and white stripes. It was designed to provide shade and privacy for backyard, patio, or picnic use by consumers or for temporary shelter for advertising or display of merchandise.

2. "Wing-Tent"—A large camping tent formed by sewing vertical side panels, together with a sewn-in floor panel, to the "Para-Wing," the enclosure thus serving as a large recreational tent. This was the largest tent sold by the firm.

3. "Para-Wall"—A colorful canvas wall panel, held up by poles and staked ropes for use as protection against wind and to provide some privacy on outdoor picnics or camping trips.

4. "Tour-A-Tent"—This was a tent which was carried on and erected on the top of a station wagon. It was large enough to sleep two adults. To use the tent, the campers climbed up a ladder to get to the top of the wagon and could easily erect the shelter, which provided ample sleeping room although it was not large enough to stand in. A zippered screen door prevented anyone from falling out. Also, an overhead shelter extended out from the side of the tent and provided shelter on the side of the station wagon.

Other items designed, manufactured, and sold by the firm at this time included: car window screens tailored for car or station wagon windows to allow sleeping or sitting in the car on trips or at drive-in theaters, etc.; toy Para-Wing and Pop-Tents large enough for youngsters to play in; a "Breeze-Wing Screened House," which was of the same design as the "Wing Tent" except that the four walls were screened for use as a summer house or for backyard sitting; "Station Wagon Boot," which was a canvas device designed to convert the wagon into sleeping quarters by closing off the windows and back tail gate for privacy.

The other items sold by the firm but not manufactured by them included air mattresses, sleeping bags, various knapsacks, and a line of conventionally designed tents.

During the period December 1, of the year after incorporation, to June 30, the company's sales totaled $188,063.01. These sales, by product, are shown in Exhibit 1.

Exhibit 1. Pop-Tent Corporation, sales by product, December 1–June 30, of the year after incorporation.

Product	Actual Sales	Percent of Total
Pop-Tent Camper................	$ 48,335.07	25.6%
Wing-Tent.......................	29,620.11	15.8
Tour-A-Tent.....................	26,756.36	14.3
Station Wagon Boot.............	25,756.36	13.7
Air Mattresses..................	17,702.74	9.5
Para-Wing.......................	10,270.99	5.5
Screens.........................	8,068.85	4.1
Breeze-Wing....................	5,869.25	3.1
Other...........................	15,683.28	8.4
	$188,063.01	100.0%

The sales of the company by month, during this period, are shown in Exhibit 2.

According to a survey of 8,774 sporting goods dealers who sell tents,

Exhibit 2. Pop-Tent Corporation, sales by month, December 1–June 30.

Month	Actual Sales	Percent of Total
December...............	$ 2,202.59	1.2%
January.................	1,664.29	0.9
February................	1,268.46	0.7
March..................	43,146.21	22.9
April...................	51,270.69	27.2
May....................	44,053.25	23.5
June...................	44,457.52	23.6
	$188,063.11	100.0%

conducted by *Sporting Goods Dealer Magazine,* the breakdown of when camping equipment dealers buy was as shown in Exhibit 3.

Of the dealers surveyed, 72.6 percent bought their stock during the months

Exhibit 3. When do camping equipment dealers buy?

Month of Purchase	Percent of Stock
January...............................	8.6%
February.............................	10.9
March................................	16.0
April..................................	15.4
May....................................	16.6
June..................................	13.7
July...................................	7.5
August...............................	4.7
September...........................	2.2
October	1.5
November............................	1.5
December............................	1.4

of February through June. It was also estimated by another sporting goods trade journal that of 23,974 sporting goods retailers, subscribing to the magazine, 51.7 percent carried tents and camping equipment.

the Pop-Tent Camper

The Pop-Tent Camper was designed to be a light, compact, easily erected shelter. It was made of high-quality canvas in a dome shape that required no poles for its erection and contained no inside poles. The tent was 7 feet in diameter and 58 inches high. It folded into a 30-inch carrying bag which weighed only 13 pounds.

The Camper had a sewn-in floor, a zipper door, and a small rear window, and came equipped with a nylon mosquito netting. The material used was 7.68 ounce twill and was treated with a special dry water repellent. The tent could be erected by anyone in 90 seconds with a few simple movements.

The basic frame of the tent was provided by a fiberglass rod rib frame which could be folded down and whose tension provided the force for the erection. When erected, the tent literally "popped out," and thus the name of the product was descriptive of one of its principal features. The tent was produced in a grey-green color.

The company's list price on the tent in the summer after incorporation was $79, and its discount policy was:

1. 50% discount and freight prepaid on orders of $300 or more retail list.
2. 5% advertising allowance on orders of $1,500 or more retail list (50–5).
3. 40% discount and f.o.b. factory on orders less than $300 retail list.
4. Terms 2/10, net 30.

From the beginning the company had employed manufacturers' agents instead of a sales force, and it had 14 such agents who employed on the average four salesmen each. The company had salesmen in most areas of the country, except for eastern Michigan, where the officers of the firm did the selling. The agents were paid a commission of 10 percent on sales and had exclusive territories.

Initially the firm had attempted to sell through wholesalers to retailers; however, it soon felt that it was not receiving promotional support from the wholesalers. As a result, it had its agents stop attempting to sell to wholesalers and to concentrate on direct sales to retailers, offering them the same discounts as had been originally offered to the wholesalers. After this change the company's sales were highly concentrated among large department stores, mail-order houses, retail chains, and large sporting goods dealers.

The company also had made a large number of sales to Ford dealers, who had bought the Tour-A-Tent, air mattresses, and window-screens in large quantities for use as promotional aids to sell automobiles. The sales of these items to these outlets were not expected to be continuous over time, however, in view of their promotional nature.

The retailers who sold the Camper had a wide variety of initial markups on the retail price. The markups ranged from a low of 20 percent on special sales to 40 percent or more, which were the "traditional" markups on such items. Characteristically, it was the smaller retailers who took the larger initial markups.

While there were no tents on the market at this time which had the same features as the Pop-Tent Camper, the officers of the firm felt that the tent best served the needs of the camper who was traveling on a trip in either a car, station wagon, or canoe and who had to set up and take down the tent a number of times during the trip. The management felt that the tents which were the best alternatives to Pop-Tent for the purchaser who had a need for such a shelter were pup tents, umbrella tents, and lean-to canvas shelters. The firm felt that wall tents better served the needs of the camper who went to one place and stayed there for a period of time and to whom the erection ease and portability were of lesser importance as compared to living comfort in the tent. The Wing-Tent served this need in the Pop-Tent line.

The catalog of one of the major mail-order houses for the spring-summer season of this year listed four umbrella tents which were in the same class (not scouting or children's tents) as the Pop-Tent Camper. This house did not carry nor offer Pop-Tents. These four tents were:

1. 11⅓′ × 11⅓′—four-way ventilation with scwn-in nylon screening 3 feet wide on each side. Material 7.68-ounce drill[2], each side panel and the door having full-length zippers to seal out rain and wind. The tent had a center height of 7½ feet, 6-foot wall height, and a front awning. This tent also had a sewn-in floor, an aluminum frame, and telescoping aluminum canopy poles, which were included along with ropes and steel stakes. The shipping weight was listed at 67 pounds and the retail price was $89.95. Color, forest green.
2. 9½′ × 11′—in either forest green or blue spruce colors. This had three nylon screen windows plus a large nylon screen door. The walls and canopy were of 7.68-ounce drill, all water repellent and mildew retardent. This tent also had a sewn-in floor with zippers on the sides of the windows for a flap, tied at top, and the on-the-door flap had zippers at the sides and top and snaps at the bottom. Its height in the center was 7½ feet at the peak, 6-foot high at the eaves, and it had a front awning. Its shipping weight was 54 pounds, and the retail price was $69.95. There was a 9½′× 9½′ variety of this also, with the same features, and it weighed 52 pounds and retailed for $62.95. Both included poles, ropes, and stakes.
3. 9′ × 9′—with a large nylon screen rear window for two-way ventilation. This tent was made of 6.74-ounce drill (a less expensive material) which was water repellent. The door and window flaps were snap or tie fastened. The tent also included a front canopy, poles, stakes, and a sewn-in duck

[2] 7.08 drill is a less expensive material than 7.00-ounce twill.

floor. This tent differed from the preceding two, however, in that it had an inside center pole and it was 7½ feet high in the center, with a 6-foot wall height. Its shipping weight was 50 pounds, and its retail price was $38.74. There was also a 9′ × 11′ variety with the same other dimensions and features for $44.94. Color, forest green.

4. 7′ × 7′—of 6.74-ounce water-repellent drill with a screened rear window and door-tie flaps, canopy, center pole, sewn-in floor of duck, color forest green, with a center pole and a center height of 5 feet 9 inches, and wall height of 4 feet. The unit included wood stakes, wood poles, wire, and guy ropes. Its shipping weight was 23 pounds, and its price was $18.66.

This same house also offered two-man, screened, pup tents for $25.97.

Canvas and better lean-tos sold for prices from $22.50 and up, depending on size and quality, from other mail-order houses.

While the company knew the total camper market at this time was estimated at 22 million persons and growing, it had no data on the size of the market for the Camper, nor of the sales of tents by sizes, types, prices, or even total sales of the industry.

From an appearance viewpoint the Pop-Tent Camper was generally considered to be more attractive than any other tent type.

Pop-Tent expenses

The company estimated that the direct labor and direct material costs to produce a Pop-Tent Camper (in lots of 100) were:

$$\text{Direct labor}\ldots\ldots\ldots\$ 2.50$$
$$\text{Material}\ldots\ldots\ldots\ldots 17.34$$

The company also estimated that its total fixed expenses for the current year (December 1 to November 30) would be $73,688.

It was estimated that the other variable expenses which could be charged to Pop-Tent production other than materials and direct labor amounted to $6.82 per unit. This estimate was made by summing the other variable costs for the period December through June, of the current year, multiplying this figure by the proportion that Pop-Tent sales were of the total sales for the period and dividing the remainder by the number of units of Pop-Tent which were produced. This figure includes the 10 percent commission to its agents. During the period December through June, the company produced 1,790 Campers. In July, 166 Campers were produced.

Since its inception the company had been plagued by capital problems, and the firm was seriously undercapitalized. This handicap hampered the firm's operations and raised its production costs, since the company was not able to take advantage of cash discounts (around 2 percent) on its purchases, nor was it able to take advantage of excellent material-buying opportunities which periodically were presented on a cash basis.

On reviewing its experience on the cost of producing a Pop-Tent Camper, the company believed that while the material cost would remain the same, the direct labor cost would drop to $1.50 per unit if production lots of 500 units were run.

retail sales at various prices

While the company had no information on the number of units that were sold at the various retail prices in all stores during this period, it did have the experience of the sales through its factory outlet in Ann Arbor, Michigan, to retail customers, as well as some information as to the experience of various large-scale retail outlets which had run the Camper as a sale item during the spring and summer of that year.

The cash sales of the Pop-Tent Camper to retail customers through the factory outlet during the period of January, through August, of the year after incorporation are shown below in Exhibit 4. The units sold through this

Exhibit 4. Retail sales through factory outlet, Pop Tent Camper, January–August, year after incorporation.

January	(Regular retail price $79.95) Sales—None.
February	(Regular retail price $79.95) Sales—Seconds:
	3—$30
	1—$25
	New—None
March	(Regular retail price $79.95) Sales—Seconds:
	3—$63–$68
	1—$45
	1—$32
	New—1 unit
April	(Regular retail price $79.95) Sales—Seconds:
	1—$60
	2—$49
	1—$45
	New—1 unit
May	(Regular retail price $48) Sales—Seconds:
	1—$25
	1—$30
	New—1 unit

outlet included items which were new and which were sold at the regular retail price indicated, as well as returned, worn, and damaged items which were sold at lower prices. The company also ran three advertised sales during this period from its outlet which were at the prices indicated. These sales were advertised in the Ann Arbor newspaper and, while advertised in two cases as "seconds," consisted of new items as well.

During May the company also ran a sale in which it advertised seconds for calo at $29.95. All 11 units which they had on hand at this price were sold out in the first two days. The company also offered its regular (new) units to these customers at a price of $39.95 each, and during the week of this sale it sold 45 units at this price.

June   (Regular retail price $48)
              Sales—Seconds:
                4—$45
                3—$43
                2—$39
                1—$30
              New—11 units

The company also ran a sale on June 30th of its regular units at a price of $44. Five units were sold during this sale.

July   (Regular retail price $48)
              Sales—Seconds:
                3—$46.00
                2—$43.00
                5—$41.00
                4—$29.95
              New—6 units
August   (Regular retail price $48)
              Sales—Seconds: 0 units
              New: 7 units

On August 14–18, the company ran a sale of seconds of which it had a large supply (many of which were for all intents new items) at a price of $29.95. It also offered new items at the $39.95 price. The results of this sale were:

$29.95—54 units sold
$39.95— 2 units sold

During the remainder of the month, it sold five additional units at $29.95 and one unit at $39.95.

experience of other stores

1. A large department store in the western part of the lower peninsula of Michigan ran a sale of the Camper on May 26 at a price of $69.99, the regular price being indicated at $79. The net cost price to this store was $35 per unit. The store had six Campers on hand, and the sale was completely unsuccessful. At the $69.99 price it took this store six weeks to sell the six items.

This same store ran another sale of the Camper at a price of $49.99 on July 23. The cost was $35 per unit again. The store had 25 units on hand and sold them all out during the sale period.

2. A major department store in Cleveland ran a sale of the Camper in early June at a price of $69. The net cost per unit to the store was $47.40. The store had six units on hand, and a Pop-Tent representative reported that the store sold none of the items the first day. The sale was considered unsuccessful.

3. In mid-August a major department store in a large southern Michigan city ran a sale of the Camper at a price of $44.50. It had 68 units on hand at a

net cost of $32 per unit (a special deal). It sold 60 of the units during the four days of its sale.

4. A hardware store in a small southern Michigan town ran a sale of the Camper in early August at a price of $49 each. The net cost per unit to the store was about $36. The store had 10 units on hand and sold 2. A special demonstrator from Pop-Tent was in the store during this sale to sell the item.

QUESTIONS

1. At what price should the Pop-Tent Camper be offered to the trade during the coming season, assuming costs given?
2. How would you recommend your hypotheses and conclusions be tested for verification?

case 6–2

TROLEX SALES COMPANY*

price determination and pricing strategy

A group of several young men in Detroit, Michigan, developed and patented a device called the "Trolex." The device could be used to measure the speed of a boat in water so that a fisherman could select and maintain the proper speed to troll for fish (see Exhibit I).

Trolling is the art of dragging a fishing lure through the water at a slow speed so that the lure resembles a small fish, thus attracting the desired game fish. To be effective the lure must be drawn through the water at an appropriate and constant speed.

the Trolex

The Trolex consisted of a weight on a string, attached to a spring, which in turn was attached to a pivoted pointer. The pointer rotated on the face of a dial. The Trolex was clamped to the side of the boat, and the weight was allowed to drag in the water. The faster the boat moved, the greater was the drag on the string, as indicated by the pointer on the dial. If a constant speed was maintained, there was a constant drag on the line, and the pointer remained on the same number.

---

* Written by Gordon E. Miracle, Associate Professor, Department of Advertising, Michigan State University. Although the general background of the case is essentially accurate, many of the specific facts of the case have been disguised.

Exhibit 1

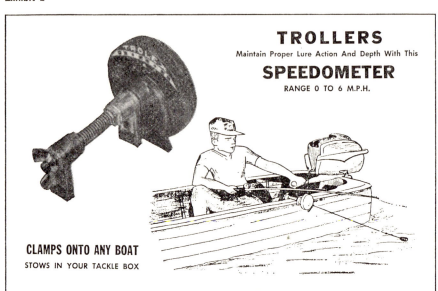

TROLLERS

Maintain Proper Lure Action And Depth With This

SPEEDOMETER

RANGE 0 TO 6 M.P.H.

CLAMPS ONTO ANY BOAT

STOWS IN YOUR TACKLE BOX

INSTALLATION AND OPERATION INSTRUCTIONS

Your TROLEX speedometer comes to you in convenient take-down form for easy carrying and storage in your tackle box. It can be installed on any boat in a matter of seconds.

To Install TROLEX, Follow These Simple Steps.

1. Squeeze two clamp fingers together. Insert bolt head into square hole in dial head. Rotate bolt ⅛ turn to engage internal recess. Release pressure on fingers and engage square end of clamp in square hole in dial head with finger extended straight down from dial.

2. Clamp TROLEX on left side of boat. One or both clamps can be turned end for end on the bolt to accomodate boats having a side thickness from ⅞" to 2⅝".

3. Insert wire strut thru hole in sinker with small end of sinker toward loop. Bend over end of wire to keep sinker from sliding off.

4. Attach one end of line to loop in wire strut. Thread other end of line thru hole on dial assembly marked "L". Adjust length of line so that sinker is approximately 10" below the surface of the water. This is the setting for the average small boat which has sides 10 to 12 inches above the water line.

5. When using TROLEX on larger boats with greater free board, determine correct line length as follows: for calibration purposes power your power up to the highest speed you expect to troll (normally 4 to 5 M.P.H.). Let

out enough sinker line to enable the sinker to remain slightly below the surface of the water at that maximum speed.

Hints for Choosing the Best Speeds for
Trolling Your Favorite Lures

Few manufacturers of artificial bait specify, in miles per hour, the best speed or speeds at which to troll their lures. Many manufacturers, however, do emphasize slow speeds for maximum action. Therefore, the surest plan is as follows:

1. Troll selected lure alongside boat and observe the reading on TROLEX speedometer dial when desired lure action is obtained.

2. Let out line until the desired trolling depth is reached. Then regulate boat speed as necessary to maintain speedometer reading at same value as observed in item 1 above.

This procedure will insure your lure maintaining the desired action and running depth regardless of wind and wave action.

TROLEX SALES CO.
P. O. BOX 53
ANCHORVILLE, MICHIGAN

To make use of the device, the fisherman dropped the lure in the water near the side of the boat so that he could observe it. He then moved the boat at the speed at which the lure made the proper motions, and he noted the position of the pointer on the dial of the Trolex. Then he could let his line out, maintain the proper speed by watching the dial setting, and be sure that his lure was moving in the proper manner and at the desired depth.

Control of the depth and action of the lure was important to the serious troller. Control was particularly important immediately following a strike, when the fisherman wished to get his lure back to the same place as soon as possible. The path of the lure depended upon two factors: (1) the amount of line out, and (2) the speed of the lure. An accurate speedometer such as the Trolex was especially valuable, since a difference of as little as one-half mile per hour could mean that the lure was 4 or 5 feet lower or higher than desired.

forming a partnership

The group of men that developed the Trolex decided that it might be profitable to form a partnership to produce and sell it. They noted that fishermen often spent considerable sums of money on fishing gear and accessories. For example, a rod and reel might cost $20 to $50. A tackle box typically retailed at $8 to $10 and often was filled with $30 to $40 worth of accessories. Lures and baits usually sold in the $0.75 to $2 range. Boat speedometers sold for $8 and up, although they were not a good substitute for Trolex because they usually were inaccurate from 0 to 10 miles per hour. A minnow bucket could be purchased for about $2.50, and a landing net typically cost about $3.75.

The founding group included several engineers and men with business experience. They all held full-time jobs, and each partner expected to spend only a few hours of his spare time monthly on the business unless it should turn out to be highly successful.

Initial cost estimates indicated that the partnership needed a total of about $3,500 for dies, materials, and other "start-up" costs. This amount was easily raised by the prospective partners. Furthermore, one of the members of the group owned a garage which provided suitable space to assemble and pack the Trolex.

The device was simple and inexpensive to manufacture. The cost of materials varied somewhat (see Exhibit 2). Purchased piece parts cost about 30 cents per unit if ordered in lots of 144 or more. The five castings, which could be made by other firms using the partnership dies, cost 64 cents per unit if purchased in lots of more than 500.

On the average it took a man three minutes to assemble one unit and pack it for shipment. The cost of labor, whether performed by the partners or by hired employees, was approximately $2.50 per hour. The package consisted of a plastic box with styrofoam in the bottom. The costs of the packaging materials were included in the material costs shown in Exhibit 2. Shipping costs were about 6 cents per unit in lots of 100 or less and 3 cents per unit in larger lots. The cost of carrying an inventory of materials and finished units was considered to be insignificant. The dies and patterns, which cost about $3,000, were estimated to have a useful life of about three to four years. Rent on the garage in which the Trolex units were assembled was $300 per year.

Exhibit 2. Material costs.

	Quantity Ordered		
Castings	50–100	101–500	501–Up
1—Back plate w/dial, plastic.........	$0.30	$0.24	$0.20
1—Front plate, plastic...............	0.26	0.20	0.18
2—Metal plates.....................	0.32	0.25	0.20
1—Pointer, plastic..................	0.09	0.07	0.06
	$0.97	$0.76	$0.64

	Quantity Ordered	
Piece Parts	12–144	144–Up
1—Stove bolt.......................	$0.10	$0.08
2—Metal washers...................	0.02	0.01
1—Rubber washer..................	0.02	0.01
1—Wing nut.......................	0.11	0.07
1—Spring..........................	0.06	0.04
1—Weight..........................	0.02	0.02
4 foot—String......................	0.01	0.01
1—Plastic box......................	0.05	0.04
Styrofoam..........................	0.02	0.02
Glue...............................	Insignificant	
Paint..............................	Insignificant	
	$0.41	$0.30

The group felt that administrative work could be handled by one of the partners. He would be expected to perform the following duties:

1. Determine the quantity of the product to be produced each month,
2. Order sufficient materials periodically to produce the desired quantity,
3. Inform the others in the group as to when and how long they would be required to work,
4. Keep the books.

It was estimated that for the first year this administrative time would amount to about 80 hours and would be fairly constant regardless of the number of units produced. This time was valued at $5 per hour.

marketing plan

Members of the group felt that the market for Trolex would be large and spread throughout much of the United States, since there were more than 20 million fishermen who purchase licenses, permits, and stamps in the United States (see Exhibit 3). In Michigan alone there were nearly 1 million fishermen (see Exhibit 4).

Although they felt that the market could be reached through sporting goods stores, department stores, hardware stores, and perhaps even drugstores, the partners were not in a position to contact all appropriate middlemen in the country. Therefore, they planned to try to achieve distribution in selected sporting goods stores in locations where fishing was quite popular, such as northern Michigan and Wisconsin. They also decided to take several advertisements in *Field and Stream,* hoping that it would bring in orders by mail.

The partners selected a number of sporting goods stores in Michigan and Wisconsin and sent each of them four free samples of the Trolex. They hoped the item would catch on and generate mail orders. In order to get an idea of the proper price for the Trolex, the partners divided the selected dealers who received the free samples into five test groups. Each group was quoted a different wholesale price. The intention was to try to estimate the total quantity which would be sold at each price. The groups were offered the Trolex at the following prices:

> Group A: $4.75
> Group B: $4.00
> Group C: $3.35
> Group D: $2.65
> Group E: $2.00

Based on the size of the initial orders by the selected retail sporting goods stores, and on the reactions of some of the store owners, estimates were made of the total number of units that would be sold if the price to all retailers in the test groups were set at each of the following levels:

Selling Price to Retailers	Expected Annual Sales (Units)
$4.75	400
4.00	500
3.35	1,000
2.65	1,600
2.00	1,800

Sporting goods stores require approximately a 40 percent markup; thus if the sporting goods store purchased the Trolex at $3, the fisherman would pay about $5.

In the first few advertisements in *Field and Stream,* the Trolex was priced at $7.95. Although the advertisement attracted few orders from ultimate consumers, it did bring in a number of inquiries from sports dealers, and even one from a New England sports broadcaster. In response to these inquiries, a wholesale price of $4.75 was quoted.

Exhibit 3. Summary of the number of paid fishing license holders, license sales and the cost to fishermen, fiscal year 1962.

State	Paid Fishing License Holders*	Resident Fishing Licenses, Tags Permits & Stamps Issued	Nonresident Fishing Licenses, Tags Permits & Stamps Issued	Total Fishing Licenses, Tags Permits & Stamps Issued*	Gross Cost to Fishermen
Alabama...............	413,159	518,284	27,659	545,943	$ 786,820
Alaska................	53,583	42,015	14,783	56,798	343,156
Arizona...............	212,266	245,560	37,265	282,825	807,707
Arkansas..............	456,663	298,841	157,822	456,663	1,183,070
California.............	1,485,809	3,192,002	303,740	3,495,742	6,247,472
Colorado..............	413,525	296,628	120,556	417,184	1,501,931
Connecticut...........	107,545	104,172	3,373	107,545	414,522
Delaware..............	11,141	10,226	915	11,141	18,396
Florida................	502,610	385,704	135,223	520,927	1,068,498
Georgia...............	495,882	484,040	13,241	497,281	588,994
Hawaii................	4,209	4,190	19	4,209	8,824
Idaho.................	239,374	159,730	80,673	240,403	1,007,136
Illinois................	700,654	683,964	21,813	705,777	1,487,023
Indiana...............	754,431	726,290	34,209	760,499	1,013,848
Iowa..................	414,215	405,840	13,688	419,528	963,041
Kansas................	271,362	261,919	9,857	271,776	827,360
Kentucky..............	316,090	247,257	69,713	316,970	1,021,961
Louisiana..............	223,031	202,297	22,304	224,601	272,429
Maine.................	229,019	153,647	76,545	230,192	758,381
Maryland..............	111,741	97,101	14,640	111,741	339,390
Massachusetts.........	183,924	140,957	4,946	145,903	578,165
Michigan..............	927,627	888,508	226,628	1,115,136	2,712,551
Minnesota.............	1,287,947	1,091,131	217,720	1,308,851	2,494,789
Mississippi............	285,898	211,022	81,116	292,138	542,780
Missouri...............	691,005	746,863	137,903	884,766	2,509,597
Montana...............	235,709	183,594	47,544	231,138	459,883
Nebraska..............	221,301	204,919	16,382	221,301	468,054
Nevada................	63,098	49,237	22,845	72,082	227,801
New Hampshire........	121,192	83,029	45,933	128,962	444,981
New Jersey............	138,950	205,850	9,894	215,744	758,056
New Mexico...........	142,168	98,745	46,111	144,856	547,061
New York..............	727,246	678,346	48,900	727,246	2,379,985
North Carolina.........	319,277	433,336	44,067	477,403	933,267
North Dakota..........	72,719	50,194	4,076	54,270	125,411
Ohio..................	821,452	802,427	19,395	821,822	1,683,303
Oklahoma.............	462,695	381,957	83,459	465,416	1,036,088
Oregon................	436,407	636,157	29,826	665,983	1,577,943
Pennsylvania..........	602,323	578,235	24,088	602,323	2,013,633
Rhode Island..........	15,207	21,315	505	21,820	51,555
South Carolina.........	272,192	281,892	21,382	303,274	599,124
South Dakota..........	148,443	109,075	43,226	152,301	293,822
Tennessee.............	649,743	708,714	179,573	888,287	1,128,527
Texas.................	832,913	832,913	...†	832,913	1,790,763
Utah..................	172,762	169,429	16,207	185,636	527,958
Vermont...............	101,028	70,107	32,004	102,111	240,056
Virginia...............	324,165	475,425	32,970	508,395	883,209
Washington............	377,546	358,942	18,679	377,621	1,639,052
West Virginia..........	160,051	238,651	12,497	251,148	555,862
Wisconsin.............	1,060,000	693,615	377,854	1,071,469	3,620,729
Wyoming..............	132,168	70,899	65,655	135,554	679,179
Totals.............	19,403,405	20,015,191	3,069,423	23,084,614	$54,103,153

* A paid license holder is one individual regardless of the number of licenses purchased. Data certified by State fish and game departments.
† Same license issued to both residents and nonresidents.
Source: Michigan Department of Conservation. Compiled by the Bureau of Sports Fisheries and Wildlife from information furnished by the State fish and game departments.

Introduction to marketing management

Exhibit 4. Fishing license sales in Michigan 1948–61.

Year	Resident Fish	Temporary Nonresident Fish	Annual Nonresident Fish	Trout Stamps
1948..........807,911	160,245	121,745	169,498
1949..........819,702	154,740	127,430	182,058
1950..........789,382	136,302	130,376	170,773
1951..........841,913	141,838	140,587	186,138
1952..........848,659	141,007	156,720	193,744
1953..........852,788	142,342	164,795	208,497
1954..........878,668	153,246	156,220	216,774
1955..........876,670	130,379	143,613	226,824
1956..........852,440	128,563	138,654	234,009
1957..........854,775	123,197	131,461	233,417
1958..........837,877	101,547	117,038	202,572
1959..........756,132	94,525	113,816	192,580
1960..........752,806	88,916	111,130	190,246
1961..........739,063	83,413	105,151	187,509

Source: Michigan Department of Conservation, *1895–1961 History of Fishing and Miscellaneous License Sales*, p. 2.

Exhibit 5. Reasons for purchases of outboard motorboats.

Primary Reasons	Percentage of Purchases in 1959
Hunting............................	6.9%
Fishing............................	42.1
Racing.............................	2.9
Cruising...........................	28.0
Water skiing.......................	19.6
Rental.............................	0.2
Commercial.........................	0.3
	100.0%

Source: Outboard Boating Club of America and National Association of Engine and Boat Manufacturers, published in Milton P. Brown, Wilbur B. England and John B. Matthews, Jr., *Problems in Marketing* (New York: McGraw-Hill Book Co., 1961), p. 123. Used by permission.

QUESTION

1. Considering the various aspects of demand and cost, what retail price for the Trolex do you recommend? Explain your reasoning.

case 6-3

MONSON DIE CASTING COMPANY*

pricing policy of a metals fabricator

Monson Die Casting Company (hereafter referred to by the initials MDC) was organized some years ago in Detroit, Michigan, to manufacture zinc alloy die castings. Initially, it produced items for manufacturers in a variety of industries, but as time passed, its customers were primarily from the automotive industry. The company grew steadily, and at the time of this case its annual sales were approximately $2.5 million, and its replacement value was estimated at $1.5 million.[1]

product characteristics

Die casting is a process whereby molten metal is put into a die or form, under pressure. When the metal has cooled, it retains the shape of the form. Die casting is done with nonferrous metals. By far the greatest amount of nonferrous die casting is with zinc alloys, although there is some die casting of aluminum, magnesium, and brass.

Zinc alloy die-cast parts find their greatest applications in the automobile industry, although they are also used in home appliances, plumbing and heating parts, and a variety of industrial machine applications. Zinc alloy parts were first used on autos for interior trim. As techniques improved, applications in dashboard instruments followed. As larger and more intricate shapes became possible, die castings began to be used in a number of decorative hardware items on the exterior of the car: radiator grills, door and trunk handles, and a variety of trim situations, including nameplates and letters.

MDC specialized in the relatively smaller items of automobile trim and had a reputation for being able to cast the more intricate items. The company also built a reputation for filling rush jobs on short notice without sacrificing quality.

Over the span of any one year, the company manufactured approximately

---

* Written by A. R. Krachenberg, Professor of Marketing, Dearborn Campus, The University of Michigan.

[1] These figures have been multiplied by a constant; the name of the company has been disguised.

100 different items. Of these, 75 were usually new items, while 25 were so-called service jobs. Service jobs consisted of rerunning an additional quantity of an item that had been manufactured in a prior year. In the die-casting business it was standard practice for the automobile manufacturers to become the owners of the dies and special equipment necessary for any given job. These items physically remained in the possession of the individual die-casting firm, however. At any time, this firm faced the possibility of being requested to make a rerun on any given job, at which time it would be expected to have the old dies still available or stand the expense of making a new set.

In addition to the storage expense of an ever increasing number of dies, another costly feature of the service job was that it usually involved a relatively small-volume run per month. Nevertheless, being able to rapidly produce a previously manufactured item was an important patronage appeal which most die casters offered to the automobile manufacturers.

A job averaging around 100,000 pieces a month, or approximately 5,000 per day, was considered to be good business. This, of course, was based on a 9-month to 10-month year, since on the average, two months during the summertime were devoted to changeover. Anything averaging 5,000–10,000 a month was considered small. Such runs were relatively undesirable jobs primarily because of the time and cost required to set up and tear down the equipment.

industry competitive structure

The zinc die-casting industry was located primarily in the Detroit-Toledo area, since it depended so heavily on the automobile industry. Approximately 50 companies were active, all of whom were regarded as competitors of MDC in some degree or other. MDC was considered to be a medium-sized company for this field. Only two or three companies were of a larger size, namely Grand Rapids Die Casting with annual sales of about $12 million or $15 million and Doehler-Jarvis with annual sales of about $20 million to $30 million. There were many small companies[2] in this industry with sales averaging less than $1 million annually.

Competition within the industry was keen. It was relatively easy to enter the business, for capital requirements were small (basic capital goods requirements were a manually operated die-casting machine and a small melting furnace). "Alley shops" had very low fixed overhead and thus were able to price low on the smaller, relatively simple items. The major competitive factors favoring the larger companies on these items were their reliability regarding schedules and consistency of quality.

While competition hinged primarily on price, other factors were important. Efficient automobile production required continuous assembly; no parts de-

---

[2] Small firms were frequently referred to as "alley shops," a term used in the industry to denote a small 5- or 10-man operation with work often performed in a garage.

lay was tolerated that could possibly cause a shutdown of a line or a plant. Therefore, reputation for prompt deliveries and for being able to meet an increased delivery schedule when necessary was most important. Also, quality level and consistency of quality were considered in making a source selection.

In addition to competition from other independent die casters, MDC, as others, faced competition from the die-casting shops owned by the automobile manufacturers, primarily those operated by General Motors. GM owned and operated rather substantial die-casting plants which produced a variety of items for use on GM autos. The major GM plants were Bay City Chevrolet and Brown-Lipe-Chapin. These shops provided not only competition for selected jobs but also provided GM buyers with a double check on prices submitted by outside die casters.

While the other automobile manufacturers were not as active as GM in die casting their own parts, there was always the possibility that they might make their own die-cast requirements. Make versus buy evaluations were a never ending process with the automobile manufacturers, and as competitive circumstances varied, as technology improvements took place, present policies could change.

bidding and pricing

Business was obtained by MDC through bids submitted to the automobile manufacturers. The request to bid was obtained either through personal solicitation or, once the reputation and high quality level of the company had been established, requests to bid were automatically sent to MDC from the automobile manufacturers on a variety of selected parts.

The bid requests received from an automobile company usually included the following information: (1) a blueprint and specification sheet of the part needed, (2) the maximum required number of pieces needed monthly, with some indications of possible variations that may be anticipated, (3) what percentage of the total requirements MDC was being requested to bid on, or whether this was a "sole supplier" item, and (4) when the part was needed.

In responding, MDC usually provided the following standard information: (1) the unit price of the article, (2) total charge for special tools, dies, jigs, and fixtures, and (3) a statement indicating ability to meet required schedule or an indication of alternate dates.

Since the company dealt almost entirely with the automotive industry, its work schedule throughout the year was dependent upon that of the new-car manufacturers. By late fall of each year, bids were already submitted on parts that would be used on cars to be introduced in the fall of the following year. Since the automobile manufacturers were usually prompt in awarding contracts, by early December MDC had firm knowledge of the approximate level of operations it would start the new-model year with. Manufacturing operations for the new models started in midsummer at the same time as the automobile assembly plants were switching over to the new models. July and August of each year were rather hectic, then, in that this was the time when the items of last year's model were being finished and the new dies were being tested and parts' samples being sent to the automobile companies for final approval.

pricing procedure

MDC used a standard-volume concept in establishing bid prices, predicated primarily upon the preceding year's volume and costs. In this sense, MDC utilized a form of cost-plus pricing.

When a request to bid was received by MDC, the part's blueprint was studied by engineers, and an estimate of manufacturing cost was prepared. Total cost was estimated on the basis of cost per 100 pieces and developed by estimating separately the cost of each major manufacturing step involved in producing a given part. Exhibit 1 below presents in columns (1) through (6) a cost estimate on a nameplate made by MDC for one of the major lines of automobiles for the current model year. The cost estimate was derived as follows:

1. Column (2): The labor time required to process 100 pieces was calculated for each operation.
2. Column (3): The average prevailing hourly direct labor rate adjusted to anticipate known or considered changes in the future was determined for each operation.
3. Column (4): Total dollars overhead per hour of direct labor, also adjusted to anticipate future changes, was calculated. This overhead included all fixed and variable items for the whole company except selling costs, that is, it was not just factory overhead but included as well administrative and management costs.

   This overhead figure was determined from an analysis of the prior year's activity and was also adjusted to anticipate any changes during the coming year.
4. Columns (5) and (6): The sum of the hourly direct labor cost plus the hourly overhead allocation (column 3 and column 4) was then multiplied by the estimated hours required to produce 100 pieces for each operation. This is presented in column 5. Column 6 presents a cumulative estimated cost figure. In Exhibit 1 the cumulative estimated total cost of the first five operations is $10,801.
5. Metal & dross[3] costs, a scrap factor not included in the overhead calculations, and packing and shipping cost estimates, were then added to the cumulative labor and overhead costs. The result was a total cost includ-

---

[3] Dross is the scum which forms on the surface of metal, especially lead, zinc, and aluminum, when molten or melting. It is due both to oxidation and the rising of dirt and impurities to the surface.

ing all company costs except selling[4]; that is, both manufacturing and administrative. In Exhibit 1 this total estimated cost is $15,436.

A percent was then added to this total cost to arrive at the price quoted to the buyer. The percentage added for profit was not a fixed amount but varied depending on a variety of circumstances. The owners of the company had a minimum desired rate of return on the company's investment, which in turn was translated into a profit margin necessary to meet this standard. To

Exhibit 1. Auto nameplate—estimated and actual costs.

(1)	(2)	(3)	(4)	(5)	(6)	(7)	(8)
					Cumulative		Cumulative
	Direct			Esti-	Esti-	Actual	Actual
	Labor	Direct		mated	mated	Cost per	Cost per
	Hours	Labor	Over-	Cost per	Cost per	100	100
	per 100	Rate per	head per	100	100 Pieces	Pieces	Pieces
Operation	Pieces	Hour	Hour	Pieces			
1. Cast.............0.3333	$2.35	$6.25	$2.866	$	$2.783	$ .....
2. Trim............. .2500	1.70	3.10	1.200	4.066	0.980	3.763
3. Buff............. .1250	3.40	7.25	1.331	5.397	....	3.763
4. Plate............. .340	2.813	1.820	4.973	10.370	3.614	7.377
5. Pack............. .1250	1.70	1.75	.431	10.801	0.273	7.650
6. Metal and Dross...	....	....	3.336	14.137	2.646	10.296
7. Scrap 5%.........	....	....	0.707	14.844	0.515	10.811
8. Carton...........	....	....	0.260	15.104	0.097	10.908
9. Shipping 2.2%.....	....	....	0.332	15.436	0.240	11.148

obtain this required profit margin, the company first estimated a normal rate of production and its attendant standard costs based on the preceding year's actual cost experience. From the (1) desired rate of return, (2) the standard cost data, and (3) capital turnover rates which were also obtained from past experience, there was then no problem to calculate the markup figure needed.[5]

A variety of factors beyond the minimum desired rate of return on investment was also considered. Intensity of competition varied so the company necessarily considered the number of, and the quality of, its competitors on each individual bid. In addition, the time of the season was a crucial consideration, especially in relation to operating level of the plant at any given moment. The particular characteristics of the part being bid on and MDC's past experience with this or a similar item were also noted. Finally, there was the consideration of MDC's past relations with this customer as well as the past competitive experiences in relation to this customer.

A detailed record was also kept of actual costs on all jobs by the com-

---

[4] Selling costs were included in the markup applied to costs when a price was being determined.

[5] See Joel Dean, *Managerial Economics* (New York: Prentice-Hall, Inc., 1951), p. 448, including footnote 26.

pany by the same breakdown as the cost estimate. In Exhibit 1, columns (7) and (8) present the actual cost data for this job. MDC relied heavily on these actual cost records to aid them both in making more effective future quotes on similar items and in establishing a standard-volume cost level for each new year.

special tooling charges

All special tools belonged to the customer. It was standard procedure to submit a total tool charge in a lump-sum figure along with the per piece price of the item. On the first delivery of parts the tooling costs were then paid for in full by the automobile manufacturer. When bidding any job, these tool charges were important for several reasons. First, when the automotive manufacturer's buyer received the bid, the standard practice was to calculate the tool cost on a per piece basis, that is, to amortize the tool charge over the total number of pieces to be purchased from the vendor, coming up with a price per piece which included tool costs. Thus, tool charges were not simply a matter of figuring cost only, or cost plus a fixed percent; rather some degree of latitude existed on the possibility of skimping on cost so as to have a lower total cost per piece.

A second aspect of tool charges concerned the pricing of low-volume jobs. Here the tendency was to "load" tool charges, hence include a factor to cover the nuisance aspect inherent in low-volume jobs. Since the total tools charge was paid for with the first delivery of parts, this would also mean a fast return of cash.

specific product pricing

(1) Ornamental trim item. In late fall of the current model year, MDC was requested to bid on a piece of ornamental trim for one of the more expensive makes of automobiles. The company manufacturing the car was one of the Big Three auto makers and was a major customer of MDC. It had taken MDC some five years to become a regular supplier of this company, becoming so only after having thoroughly proven itself to be (1) an efficient and low-cost producer, (2) a consistently high-quality producer, and (3) a producer capable of expanding production schedules on short notice.

Exhibit 2 presents the cost estimate that was made on this part. In trying to develop a price, MDC officials noted the following factors peculiar to this specific item. They knew that several other companies had also been requested to bid on this part, although they did not know specifically which ones. They knew also that the part involved intricate casting considerations, hence they were certain that the other sources requested to bid would not include alley shops. They felt that since this was a type of part at which they were highly skilled in casting, and had the reputation of being able to handle well, they had some slight edge over their competitors. Finally, it was an item that would give them a fairly substantial volume for 9 to 10 months of the year. All things considered, the bid was submitted at a price of $1.33 each, which was equivalent to a markup on selling price of 24.9 percent.

Within a very short time, MDC was informed by the automobile manufacturer that further negotiations were being initiated on this item, and a rebid was requested from them. Through various trade and industry sources, MDC learned that if they could reduce their price to $1.17 (which is equivalent to a 14.6 percent profit margin), they could have the business.

Exhibit 2.   Ornamental trim piece—estimated and actual costs.

(1)	(2)	(3)	(4)	(5)	(6)	(7)	(8)
	Direct Labor Hours per 100 Pieces	Direct Labor Rate per Hour	Over- head Rate per Hour	Esti- mated Cost per 100 Pieces	Cumula- tive Esti- mated Cost per 100 Pieces	Actual Cost per 100 Pieces	Cumula- tive Actual Cost per 100 Pieces
Operation							
1. Cast.........0.500	$ 2.35	$ 6.25	$ 4.300	$	$ 2.996	$ ....
2. Trim.........0.333	1.70	3.10	1.600	5.900	2.909	5.905
3. Polish......0.500	1.85	1.90	1.875	7.775	2.907	8.812
4. Buff.........0.333	3.40	8.25	3.883	11.658	4.814	12.626
5. Buff.......... ...	...	...	....	....	1.311	14.937
6. Plate.........0.425	11.250	17.080	28.755	40.513	26.429	41.937
7. Paint.........1.250	1.70	3.35	6.313	46.726	5.941	47.937
8. Pack.........2.000	1.70	3.10	9.600	56.326	6.316	53.623
9. Metal and Dross........ ...	...	...	30.300	86.626	19.782	73.405
10. Scrap 5%...... ...	...	...	3.851	90.477	3.788	77.193
11. Special pack.. ...	...	...	2.310	92.787	2.345	79.538
12. Carton........ ...	...	...	5.000	97.787	2.417	81.955
13. Shipping 2.7% ...	...	...	2.151	99.938	1.803	83.758

(2) *Nameplate.*   Late in May of the same model year as above, MDC received a call by phone from one of the major three auto makers saying that a blueprint was on its way by special messenger on a nameplate which spelled out the name of a new-car model in script. The automobile manufacturer wanted a price on this part within two days. It seemed that the auto manufacturer's styling department had made an abrupt decision to come out with a new model and production was to start with all haste. Samples were to be ready within six weeks, whereas the normal lead time averaged four to five months. All overtime required to prepare the job was chargeable to the buyer.

MDC knew here also that they were not the only company bidding, but since it was a rush job, there would probably be no more than two or three bidders. This was an item on which the successful bidder was to be the sole source of supply.

The cost estimate for this job was shown in Exhibit 1. The company submitted a price of 0.1704 cents each, and they were awarded the business. Columns (7) and (8) in Exhibit 1 suggests that the actual costs were much lower than the estimates and that a substantial profit margin thereby resulted.

QUESTIONS

1. Would you have accepted the suggested price reduction to $1.17 and taken the business of manufacturing the trim item? What factors were pertinent to making this decision?
2. Compare and contrast the situation regarding the pricing of the ornamental trim piece (question 1 above) with the pricing of the nameplate. What specific factors were pertinent in reaching a decision in each case?
3. Evaluate MDC's general pricing policy. What are its strengths and weaknesses? Can you justify their approach?

case 6-4

ROBERTSON, INC. (A)*

establishment of trade discounts for original equipment manufacturers and replacement markets

Robertson, Inc., was a corporation with headquarters in Chicago, Ill., engaged in the manufacture of parts for the automotive industry, especially those parts used in automotive engines and chassis. The major items included valves, front-end steering and suspension parts, and engine parts.

background information

Robertson sold to both the OEM[1] market and the replacement market. Total sales were $286,229,000. Of this, sales of $84,603,000 were made to manufacturers of automotive, marine, and industrial products; $172,201,000 went to manufacturers and users of aircraft and aircraft engines; while sales

---
* Written by A. R. Krachenberg, Professor of Marketing, Dearborn Campus, The University of Michigan. The material presented in this case has been based on the following sources: C. N. Davisson, *Marketing of Automotive Parts* (Michigan Business Studies, Vol. 12, No. 1, [Ann Arbor: Bureau of Business Research, Graduate School of Business Administration, The University of Michigan, 1954]) and Brian Dixon, "Price Discrimination and Marketing Management" (Ph.D. dissertation, The University of Michigan, 1959). The company's name has been disguised, and all figures have been multiplied by a constant.

[1] OEM is a term used in marketing meaning original equipment manufacturer.

of $29,425,000 were made to jobbers and others primarily for the automotive replacement market. The company initially was organized as a manufacturer of parts supplied exclusively to the OEM market. Later, it began selling a line of engine and chassis replacement parts to independent distributors throughout the country. Since then, it continuously expanded the range of merchandise which it offered for sale to the replacement market.

At the time this analysis was prepared, Robertson, Inc., had come under considerable pressure to realign its pricing structure for selected automotive parts. This pressure was especially directed to the price differential that existed between the distributor and OEM prices for these parts.

product distribution

OEM products were sold directly by the Robertson manufacturing division responsible for the products' manufacture. The sales were made in bulk and in large quantities and without trademark. No differentiation was made in these products as to whether they were to be used by the OEM for original installation or for replacement sales by the OEM to his distributive organization.

The manufacturing divisions had no contacts whatsoever with the replacement market. All replacement market sales were handled by the replacement parts division which operated as an entirely separate organization within Robertson. A variety of marketing activities was carried on by the replacement division, which was not found in selling to the OEM market. Parts were packaged, boxed, and branded. There was a profusion of catalogs and price lists. The division had warehouse facilities and offices and packaging plants, plus a sales staff which operated solely within the replacement market field selling only to distributors.

This replacement division operated in a sense just like a large wholesale concern. For example, it not only obtained parts from Robertson's manufacturing divisions but it also purchased approximately 50 percent of its product line from other replacement parts manufacturers. It then sold its line to distributors, who in turn sold both to smaller jobbers and to the large retail outlets, such as independent repair shops, garages, filling stations, and to some extent, new-car dealers. Robertson had approximately 2,400 franchised distributors, called Robertson distributors, who in turn sold to about 2,000 jobbers. These jobbers were referred to as Robertson jobbers and had to be approved and franchised by Robertson, Inc., before a distributor could sell to them.

The replacement division offered over 20,000 parts to Robertson distributors. Of these parts, somewhat over 300 were sufficiently similar in character and quality to be classed as parts common[2] with those sold to the OEMs.

---

[2] For our purposes, a *common part* may be simply defined as being an identical part manufactured by Robertson and sold both to the OEM and the replacement markets. There was no difference in its physical or functional characteristics other than the possibility that the replacement market part may have carried a brand name on it. For a description of the

industry competitive structure in the replacement market

In the replacement market for the parts that Robertson handled, the major competitive pressures were on the distributor level.[3] This stemmed from the following basic market considerations. The demand for repairs was tremendously complex. There were over 55 million "on-the-road" vehicles which had to be kept in operation. These vehicles were of a wide variety of makes and grades. Different makes often called for different parts on the same repair job. To maintain and repair these vehicles, there was a variety of repair outlets[4] which were the real market for replacement parts. Since different types of outlets performed different kinds of repairs, their patterns of parts procurements were diverse. Certain segments of the repair market were the natural customers of given distribution channels, but any given channel usually reached more than one area of the repair market. Hence there was a constant and keen interchannel competition.

There was also extensive intrachannel competition in that when a manufacturer like Robertson bought parts from another manufacturer, it was not unlikely that both manufacturers would be distributing the same parts to the same distribution channels. Intrachannel competition also occurred one step further along in that most warehouse distributors were also jobbers who sold to general trade accounts; at the same time, the jobbers who were the WD's customers also solicited GT accounts.

Exhibit 1 suggests in outline form the basic patterns of competition that existed among the various channels. This chart emphasizes the major channels of distribution for hard parts[5] sold to the replacement market. While the channels depicted are the major ones that are used in the industry, the exhibit includes more channels than those specifically dealt with in this case.

As is generally the situation with any highly competitive industry, rivalry for good outlet coverage was strong on all levels of distribution. In this case, however, competitive pressures were particularly strong on the WD or primary level of distribution. There were two major reasons for this keen rivalry. First, the number of truly top-quality wholesalers was limited. Second, by virtue of the heavy inventory requirements due to the breadth of stock and

definition used by the FTC (which is in essence: those parts with a common replacement use where the cost variation between the parts is within 10 percent), see H. F. Taggart, *Cost Justification* (Michigan Business Studies, Vol. 14, No. 3, [Ann Arbor: Bureau of Business Research, Graduate School of Business Administration, The University of Michigan, 1959]), chapter xv, pp. 431–32.

[3] By distributor we refer primarily to warehouse distributors (WD) who were large wholesalers generally carrying inventory in greater breadth and depth than the average automotive jobber. The warehouse distributor usually was franchised by parts' manufacturers and sold in significant volume to other wholesalers. (See Davisson, *op. cit.*, p. 958.)

[4] Seven general types of repair outlets usually could be identified. These were: general independent repair shops, specialist independent repair shops, new-car dealers, gasoline service stations, automotive wholesalers with a shop activity, fleets with an organized repair activity, and private-car owners doing their own repair work. See Davisson, *op. cit.*, p. 4. Aside from the private-car owner doing his own repair work this variety of repair outlets was often referred to by the inclusive term "General Trade," or just simply GT.

[5] "Hard parts" was the trade term frequently applied to engine and chassis parts.

Exhibit 1. Major channels of distribution for hard parts.

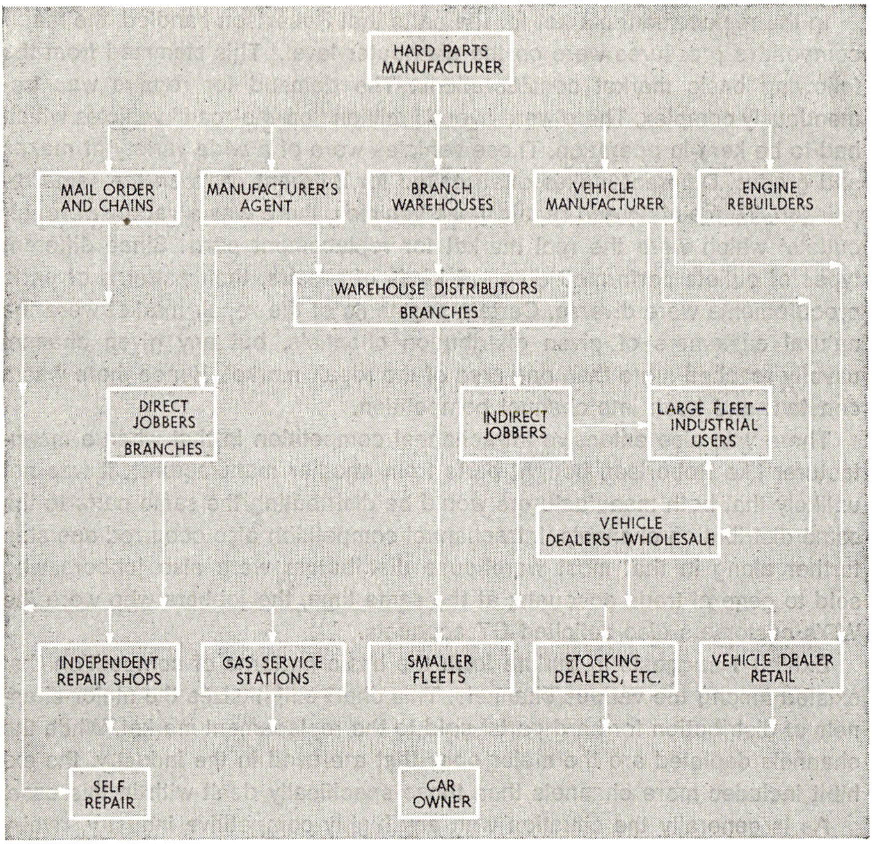

Source: Derived from C. N. Davisson, *Marketing of Automotive Parts* (Michigan Business Studies, Vol. 12, No. 1 [Ann Arbor: Bureau of Business Research, Graduate School of Business Administration, The University of Michigan, 1954], p. 390).

the wide variety of applications, there was a definite tendency for wholesalers to buy from as few sources as possible. As a corollary to this latter point, the inventory requirements were such that the general trade would rarely carry much in the way of stock, depending rather upon the wholesalers and the manufacturer to assume this function for them.

As a result of these factors, there was a rather sharp correlation between a manufacturer's sales success and the strength of his distributor organization. Selling activities of the parts manufacturer were thus primarily aimed at maintaining and holding distributors. In the struggle to obtain and hold distributors, three major competitive weapons were available to the hard-parts' manufacturer. First, as already indicated, there was the natural desire on the part of wholesalers to buy from as few sources as possible and still carry a line of parts which covered a wide range of repair needs. Thus, product line rivalry among manufacturers was a most important aspect of competition.

Second, the closeness of the relationship established between distributors and a source was most critical. Some of the more important items which materially influenced a source-wholesaler's relationship were: technical advice and services offered by the source, amount of advertising and sales support given by the source, how selective the distribution policy of the manufacturer was, and return goods privileges and obsolescence policies of a source. The last point was a most prominent consideration to both wholesaler and manufacturer. In general, the obsolescence policy increased in importance with the depth and breadth of the manufacturer's product line. The policy could be both costly and a source of constant headaches to the manufacturer. For the wholesaler, however, a balanced inventory freed his dollars for the purchase of higher turnover items, thus increasing the manufacturer's sales as well as improving a wholesaler's turnover, and hence his profit and return on investment. Patently these areas of relationship materially influenced distributors in their selection of a source.

The strength of the manufacturer's brand also influenced the distributor in his choice of source. However, in the case of the product line carried by Robertson branding was less important than in the case of other replacement parts such as piston rings, oil filters, and other accessory items. In Robertson's product area there was a tendency for the final customer to accept whatever part the dealer had, since he, the customer, was more interested in the complete repair job than in parts replacement per se. Generally, he had no strongly preconceived ideas as to the most desirable product. This statement must be tempered somewhat by a recognition of the activities of the vehicle manufacturers and their new-car dealers in this area.

The third major facet of a hard-parts manufacturer's competitive strategy was in pricing policy, which is discussed in some detail below.

industry competitive structure in the OEM market

Competition on this level took a substantially different form from that of the replacement market. Here a manufacturer did not provide an inventory service nor did he have such pressing product line problems regarding breadth and variety of application. Rather the manufacturer quoted on specifications supplied by an OEM for a specific part, and usually for a specific quantity to be supplied over a given period of time. If the manufacturer's bid was satisfactory he was awarded the contract. Competition in this market among hard parts suppliers had become essentially a matter of quoting the most acceptable price on the given specifications. Such factors as quality, service, product consistency, and speed of delivery were relatively consistent among the major parts suppliers, and hence they were of secondary importance in awarding a contract.

It is to be noted that obtaining a contract for one model year gave no assurance of the continuance of that contract for the next model year. Indeed the parts manufacturer was under a continual pressure to meet the price competition offered by other potential suppliers of a given part. Moreover, the vehicle manufacturer himself was often among these potential suppliers. As can be readily understood, the vehicle manufacturer was continually conducting "make versus buy" evaluations on all his parts of any consequence (i.e., especially those of high unit value or large volume or a combination of both). The "make versus buy" decision centered around such factors as alternative cost possibilities, available capacity, and such other general criteria as reliability of supply, quality, and so on.

pricing dilemma

Thus, in pricing those parts which were common both to the replacement and the OEM market, Robertson faced a major problem. The nature of the pricing problem is best grasped by referring to Exhibit 1. The company supplied two major channels which were in direct competition with each other, not at one but at several points along the channel. Robertson sold to its regular warehouse distributors, who sold to jobbers, who in turn sold to the general trade. Among the jobbers' potential customers for replacement parts were the new-car dealers. The same Robertson manufactured part, however, was also coming to the new-car dealer via the vehicle manufacturer with his brand on it as a part of his full-line offering to the automobile dealer. So Robertson found its parts competing against each other at this point in the channel. The competition moved also one step further along in that some new car dealers, particularly the larger ones, also performed a jobbing function by supplying the branded parts of the vehicle manufacturer to other segments of the repair trade. Again, Robertson's common parts competed with each other.

This competition of automotive dealer channels with the replacement parts jobber channels was most severe because of two prime considerations. First, approximately 50 percent of the total vehicles registered, hence 50 percent of vehicle repairs, were concentrated in Chevrolet, Ford, and Plymouth. All three of these makes had relatively strong dealer organizations which aggressively sought out the replacement market business not only by providing repair services but also by merchandising these parts to other repair outlets. Second, this competition was particularly strong to the extent that a consumer market existed for branded replacement parts. Over a period of years, the vehicle manufacturers had devoted increasing amounts of consumer advertising to emphasizing original equipment in repair jobs. The stress had been on brand identification, and the use of the "genuine factory built part" when repair work had to be done. There was no question that this appeal had met with some degree of favorable consumer response. The extent of this response was a key consideration regarding the increased competitive pressures put on the replacement market channels by the new-car dealer who could furnish these branded parts.

pricing strategy

Robertson was thus forced to price against the vehicle manufacturer to some extent in order to allow its jobbers to be competitive with the vehicle manufacturers as represented by their dealers. Because the hard-parts manufacturer was also supplying the vehicle manufacturer with common parts, however, his pricing problem became quite complex. It was intensified in that the vehicle manufacturer in some cases made his own parts and was constantly evaluating the possibility of making additional ones.

Since the auto manufacturer bought parts both for use in assembly and for sale to the after market,[6] he attempted to purchase the common part at a price sufficiently low to cover costs of distribution to the new-car dealers and to allow the dealer to resell competitively against Robertson distributors and jobbers. This meant that the Robertson selling price to the vehicle manufacturer had to be low enough to accommodate the packaging, warehousing, distributing, branding, promotional, and sales expenses of the vehicle manufacturer, as well as a payment to the new-car dealer for his performance of the wholesaling function when he competed against Robertson wholesalers for sales to the general trade.

The Robertson distributors also had to be compensated for redistribution parts sales, for example, those purchased from Robertson and in turn resold to Robertson jobbers. These jobbers and the general trade accounts to which they sold also had to realize a margin in reselling the parts.

In addition to the regular wholesaler margin, Robertson also offered additional compensation features to WD's for functions performed. First, the company had a purchase bonus arrangement. This provided for year-end payments to a franchised distributor, the amount of which depended on the distributor's annual purchase volume. The plan, as set out in Robertson's full-line distributors' franchises, provided for a purchase bonus ranging up to 10 percent on annual purchases over $10,000 of connecting rods, engine bearings, and shims, and for a 10 percent bonus on annual purchases over $60,000 on all other products.

A second aspect of additional compensation was that Robertson offered to warehouse distributors an amount equal to 10 percent of the distribution price on all sales made to Robertson jobbers. This allowance was, in effect, a payment to the WD for the expense involved in handling and servicing the jobber accounts, including the vital function of an inventory maintenance service.

Another integral aspect of the warehouse distributors' compensation plan was Robertson's policy of allowing return of unwanted or obsolete parts on which the distributor might otherwise take a loss or continue to have substantial amounts of dollars tied up in slow-moving items rather than in rapid-turnover items. Robertson's policy here followed the industry practice of providing return privileges limited to a given percent of total annual pur-

---

[6] This was a term used to indicate the repair market; it was the market where sales were made for repair and replacement as differentiated from original assembly sales.

chases. Such returns amounted to about 3½ percent of total distributors' sales.

A final item of importance in Robertson's pricing policy was the 2 percent cash discount allowed on all sales to distributors. The importance of this item was such that most jobbers not only took advantage of it but considered it an essential aspect of their continued business success.

A distributor's profit was based upon an accumulation of small margins on many items, none of which could be overlooked. The 2 percent cash discount reduced the cost of the merchandise purchased and had a material

Exhibit 2. Combined operating and performance ratios for general line automotive wholesalers (all ratios expressed as percent of net sales).

Sales Size Group	Up to $250,000	$250,000– $500,000	Over $500,000
Total gross profit................................	31.98%	30.12%	27.91%
Total operating expenses including taxes.......	28.59	26.79	25.33
Net operating profit...........................	3.39%	3.33%	2.58%

Source: Data presented is taken from C. N. Davisson, *Marketing of Automotive Parts*, p. 829.

Exhibit 3. Comparison of OEM and distributor prices of common parts.

OEM Customers	Comparable Sales Value		Difference Favoring OEM	Percent of Distributor Price
	Distributors	OEM		
Chrysler.................$	310,127	$170,379	$139,748	45.06%
Ford....................	297,191	170,074	127,117	42.77
General Motors..........	286,497	167,232	117,265	41.22
All others..............	675,195	443,247	231,948	34.35
Grand Total.......$	1,500,010	$950,932	$615,078	39.28%

effect on profit margins as indicated by the net operating ratios presented in Exhibit 2.

As already noted, of the 20,000 parts which a distributor could purchase from Robertson, somewhat over 300 were sufficiently similar in character and quality to be classed as parts common with those sold to the OEM's by Robertson.

Robertson sold these common parts to 23 OEM's. Exhibit 3 shows a comparison of OEM and distributor prices charged by Robertson on common parts at that time.

On the average, then, it seems that for common parts, the OEM's received a price which was 39.28 percent below the comparable price to distributors. The dollar sales volume of these common parts is far from being of minimal significance. For example, with respect to 77 common parts for Chevrolet, Ford, and select GM lines, the three car manufacturers paid $1,511,480. Had

Robertson distributors purchased a comparable amount, their cost would have been $2,756,105, or a difference of $1,244,625.

An analysis of the operating statement of the Robertson Service Division has developed the data which is presented in Exhibit 4. The data are presented in an attempt to analyze and explain the reason for the OEM-distributor price differential. Thus, after arriving at a net sales figure, all justifiable expenses incurred by the replacement parts division in selling and

Exhibit 4. Costs incurred in selling through replacement parts channels.

	Dollar Amount	Percent of Net Sales
Gross sales......................................	$12,325,000	
Less:		
2% cash discount.............................	249,500	
8% federal excise tax.........................	894,700	
Purchase bonus rebate........................	415,900	
Net sales..	$10,767,900	100.00%
Allowances and expenses		
Franchise discount.............................	286,785	2.66
Transportation allowed........................	124,819	1.16
Special allowances............................	110,588	1.03
Transportation to warehouse...................	173,300	1.61
Warehouse expense............................	2,140,269	19.88
Selling expense................................	715,510	6.64
Catalog and advertising expense...............	231,187	2.15
General and administrative.....................	337,035	3.13
Total allowances and expenses of Robertson Service Division..............................	$ 4,119,466	38.26%
Add factory billing and sales expense applicable to Service Division.............................		0.05%
Deduct selling expenses of sales to OEM's.......		0.16%
Operating cost differential......................		38.15%

servicing Robertson distributors and jobbers have been calculated in dollar amount and as a percent of net sales.

This 38.15 percent operating cost differential is presumably the additional expense justifiably incurred by the division in selling replacement parts to wholesale channels. As opposed to this, the manufacturing divisions selling to the OEM market had no such expenses as listed above.

Thus, if all OEM customers were compared as a group with all distributors, there appeared to be a difference of only 1.13 percent which was unjustified by costs actually incurred. This is obtained by subtracting the 38.15 percent obtained in Exhibit 4 from the 39.28 percent obtained in Exhibit 3.

There was considerable and increasing pressure being brought to bear on Robertson to realign its pricing structure, primarily that which involved the differential between the distributor and the OEM prices. This pressure came from two sources. First, in a similar situation the FTC had ruled such a pricing differential to be illegal under Section 2(a) of the Clayton Act as amended by the Robinson-Patman Act. In addition, major pressure was being exerted by Robertson's distributors and jobbers, who claimed that they were unable to compete with those new-car dealers who were performing a wholesale function by selling branded parts to the general trade. Many jobbers also complained that whereas they at one time had new-car dealers for customers, these dealers were now able to purchase the common parts at a much cheaper price from the vehicle manufacturer. Thus, the favorable price advantages granted to the vehicle manufacturer by Robertson presumably gave a substantial competitive advantage to their franchised new-car dealers. This price advantage gained from Robertson had, in effect, set up the franchised new-car dealer as a powerful wholesaler competitor on these parts in the place of a former actual, or potential, customer of the Robertson distributors and jobbers.

QUESTIONS

1. Did Robertson have a sound price policy with respect to price differential between OEM's and distributors? First, consider the policies only from the standpoint of sound marketing management; second, consider the possibility of conflict with federal price legislation.
2. In what ways, if any, could this pricing policy have been improved?
3. What are the major elements to consider in establishing a discount differential between the OEM and replacement channels? Are there any non-price competitive strategies that might be more forcefully used?

case 6–5

ROBERTSON, INC. (B)*

differential pricing in the replacement market channels of distribution

background information

Robertson, Inc., was a corporation engaged in the manufacture of parts for the automotive industry, primarily those used in automotive engines and

---

* Written by A. R. Krachenberg, Professor of Marketing, Dearborn Campus, The University of Michigan. The material presented in this case has been based on the following sources: C. N. Davisson, *Marketing of Automotive Parts* (Michigan Business Studies Volume 12, No. 1 [Ann Arbor: Bureau of Business Research, Graduate School of Business Administration, The University of Michigan, 1954] and Brian Dixon, "Price Discrimination and Marketing Management" (Ph.D. dissertation, The University of Michigan, 1959)—*Background Information and Channels of Distribution*. The company's name has been disguised and all figures have been multiplied by a constant.

chassis. Along with most firms in the automotive parts industry, Robertson sold to both the OEM and the replacement market. Sales amounted to $286,229,000 of which $84,603,000 were sold to manufacturers of automotive, marine, and industrial parts; $172,201,000 were sold to manufacturers and users of aircraft and aircraft engines; and $29,425,000 were sold to jobbers and others primarily for automotive parts replacement.

While at the time of this case Robertson, Inc., initially manufactured parts sold only to original equipment manufacturers, the company introduced a line of engine and chassis replacement parts sold to independent distributors throughout the country. Since that time it continually expanded the range of merchandise offered to the replacement market; later, it had a wide line of related products comprised of some 20,000 different items. In the sales to distributors, Robertson competed directly with other replacement manufacturers, some of whom offered as complete a line as did Robertson, others who specialized only in selected items or groups of items.

The Robertson manufacturing division making the product sold directly to the OEM market. All replacement parts sales by Robertson however, were handled through its replacement parts division.

This division's operations were similar to those of a large wholesale concern. Parts were packaged, boxed, and branded; and there was a variety of catalogs and price lists. The division had warehouse facilities scattered throughout the country to better service its distributors. The division not only obtained parts from the Robertson manufacturing divisions, but it also purchased approximately 50% of its product line from other replacement parts manufacturers. It then resold all parts to warehouse distributors, and to "direct" jobbers.[1]

Both jobbers and warehouse distributors resold to a variety of repair outlets.[2] These repair outlets were essentially the real market for replacement parts.[3]

Exhibit 1 suggests the overall industry competitive structure in the replacement market.

The demand for automotive repair parts was complex and diverse. Over

[1] Warehouse Distributors (WD) were large wholesalers generally carrying inventories in greater breadth and depth than the average automotive jobber. The warehouse distributor usually was franchised by parts manufacturers and sold in significant volume to other wholesalers. See Davisson, *op. cit.,* p. 958.

[2] The term "jobber" in the automotive parts industry referred to either one or the other of two types. There was the direct jobber to whom a parts manufacturer sold directly, from the factory or from field warehouses. Unlike warehouse distributors, however, direct jobbers seldom sold significant volume to other wholesalers, selling primarily instead to a variety of repair outlets. There was also the indirect jobber (or subjobber or secondary jobber) who bought parts usually from a warehouse distributor for resale to repair trade. The indirect jobber was typically franchised by the WD and the parts manufacturers.

[3] Seven general types of repair outlets usually could be identified. These were general independent repair shops, specialist independent repair shops, new-car dealers, gasoline service stations, automotive wholesalers with a shop activity, fleets with an organized repair activity, and private car owners doing their own repair work. See Davisson op. cit., page 4.

Aside from the private-car owner doing his own repair work, this variety of repair outlets was often referred to by the inclusive term, "general trade" or just simply GT.

Exhibit 1. Major channels of distribution for hard parts.

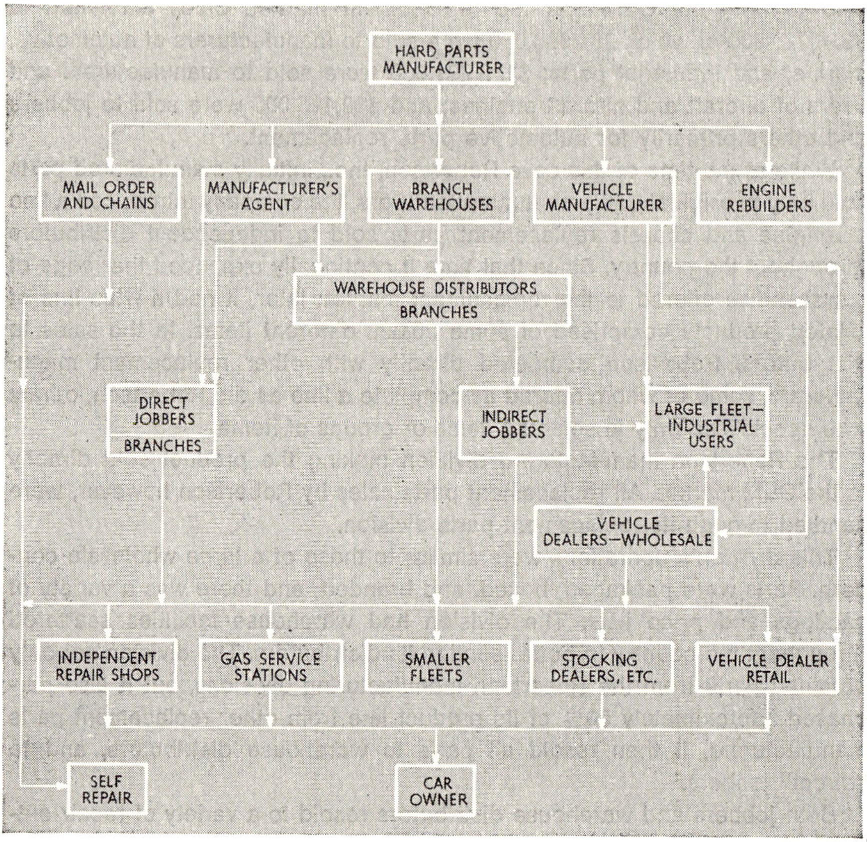

Source: C. N. Davisson, *Marketing of Automotive Parts,* p. 390.

55 million operating vehicles had to be kept in operation; and there were many different makes and models. Different makes called for different parts on the same repair job. Many repairs could not be postponed, and ready availability of parts was required.

The wide variety of repair outlets contributed further to the complexity of the market structure. These different types of outlets frequently performed different kinds of repairs. Hence, their pattern of parts procurement was diverse. Certain segments of the repair market tended to be natural customers of given distribution channels, but any given channel reached more than one area of the repair market. There was keen interchannel competition, as illustrated by the rivalry between the jobber channel and the vehicle manufacturer channel. The vehicle manufacturer's natural outlet was the new-car dealer, while the wholesaler's natural channel was the independent repair outlets, but each invaded the other's market.

There was also intrachannel competition. For example, Robertson bought replacement parts from other replacement parts manufacturers. Many of Robertson's sources distributed the same parts through the same channels as Robertson. Thus, Robertson was a competitor as well as a customer. The fact that a majority of WD's sold to general trade accounts as well as to other jobbers who also sell to GT's is another example of intrachannel competition.

Any one parts manufacturer, therefore, found it necessary to sell to a variety of direct accounts if he was to reach the various segments of the repair market. Market coverage in terms of numbers of distributors and dealers was also important. A rather sharp correlation existed between a manufacturer's replacement market sales and the number of WD's and jobbers that handled his line.

As is the case with any highly competitive industry, the struggle for good outlet representation was constant and sharp. Two basic reasons existed for this rivalry at the primary distribution level. First, there was a limited number of large, high-quality wholesale representatives. There was keen competition among manufacturers for these accounts. Second, there was a tendency for all wholesalers to buy from as few sources as possible consistent with maintaining lines which covered the wide variety of repairs performed by their customers. Many manufacturers stressed the appeal of a broad line which covered all makes and models and thus strengthened their bid for outlet representation. Other manufacturers, handling short lines, might stress price and turnover. In the rivalry to hold and strengthen outlet representation, a hard-parts supplier had at his disposal three major competitive weapons; product line appeal, maintenance of favorable relationships between himself and his distributors, and price and discount structure.

product line appeal

A broad product line appealed to a wholesaler because of his desire for as few sources as possible. In this respect, Robertson was in a most favourable position in that it had a broad line and was ever active in its efforts to broaden its offerings as well as keep them up to date. It is to be noted, however, that there was an effective appeal offered by the specialist parts supplier. He claimed superior technical knowledge and background in a given area.

relations between a source and a distributor

There was a variety of factors of mutual interest to both supplier and distributor, and emphasis on these factors contributed substantially to a supplier's ability to hold his distributors and jobbers. Rival manufacturers emphasized the amount of technical advice and service offered by the manufacturer, the amount of advertising and missionary sales support given, and return goods privileges and obsolescence policies. Robertson executives believed that their policies in these areas were as effective as those of rivals.

price and discount structure

The price at which a distributor could buy merchandise for resale was obviously a key consideration in the distributor's selection of source. Another prime consideration was the extent to which a source's suggested resale prices to various trade levels beyond the WD level were competitive with prices of other sellers. This was most important to the WD (and other wholesalers) in that they were in competition with other channels of distribution. Other elements of the price structure important to distributors included transportation for freight prepayment, volume or per order rebates, and prompt payment discounts.

Since a parts manufacturer had to price against some competitors offering a line as complete and as up to date as his own, and since each manufacturer recognized the importance of establishing and maintaining close manufacturer and distributor relations, price rivalry was a major facet of competition.

Robertson pricing practices

Robertson entered into franchise agreements with certain independent WD's, who were then designated as Robertson Distributors. These distributors in turn, with the consent of Robertson, selected Robertson jobbers who were then serviced by them. Included in the Robertson distributor franchise agreement were all the terms and conditions regarding the basis of payment to a distributor for performing functions expected of him.

For many years the Robertson franchise agreement provided for a purchase bonus to be paid by Robertson to its WD's. This bonus was based upon the distributor's annual volume of purchase of those parts subject to the plan. The purchase bonus provision in the distributor's franchise was applicable to a distributor's purchase of all parts in the franchise line and provided for the nonretroactive schedule of rebate payments shown in Exhibit 2.

The discount was nonretroactive in that the percent for each bracket applied only to the amount in excess of the top quantity limit of the preceding class. Thus, the purchaser of more than $25,000 of goods received only 3 percent on the amount over $25,000 and less than $40,001. The 1.5 percent was applicable to those amounts between $10,001 and $25,000.

Exhibit 2. Purchase bonus plan.

Annual Purchases	Purchase Bonus Percent
Up to $10,000	none
$10,001 to $25,000	1.5%
$25,001 to $40,000	3.0
$40,001 to $60,000	4.5
$60,001 to $80,000	6.0
$80,001 to $100,000	7.5
Over $100,000	8.0

A redistribution allowance was paid by Robertson to each warehouse distributor in the amount of 10 percent of the distributor's cost of Robertson parts resold by it to Robertson jobbers. This is the only extra remuneration received by Robertson distributors from Robertson for soliciting and selling to jobbers. (WD's of course, also made a minimal amount of gross profit on these sales as well as having the sales volume contribute to their total amount of purchases from Robertson which is subject to the purchase bonus plan.)

Robertson also allowed a two percent cash discount to distributors for prompt payment of bills. The importance of this cash discount was such that most jobbers not only took advantage of it, but they considered it to be an essential aspect of their continued business success. The importance of the two percent cash discount is indicated by the following operating data.

Exhibit 3. Combined operating and performance ratios for general line automotive wholesalers (all ratios expressed as a percent of net sales).

	Sales Size Group		
Items	Up to $250,000	$250,000–$500,000	Over $500,000
Total gross profit	31.98%	30.12%	27.91%
Total operating expenses, including all taxes	28.59	26.79	25.33
Net operating profit	3.39%	3.33%	2.58%

Exhibit 4. Purchase bonus plan.

Plan for Connecting Rods, Engine Bearings, and Shims—Nonretroactive Bonus

Annual Purchases	Purchase Bonus Percent
Up to $750	None
$751 to $2,000	3.5
$2,001 to $5,000	5.0
$5,001 to $10,000	7.5
Over $10,000	10.0

All Other Products—Nonretroactive Bonus

Annual Purchases	Purchase Bonus Percent
0 to $5,000	0
$5,001 to $7,000	2
$7,001 to $12,000	3
$12,001 to $18,000	4
$18,001 to $24,000	5
$24,001 to $30,000	6
$30,001 to $36,000	7
$36,001 to $48,000	8
$48,001 to $60,000	9
Over $60,000	10

Finally, Robertson provided for the return of unwanted or obsolete parts. Robertson's policy here followed the industry practice of providing return privileges limited to a given percent of total annual purchases. Such returns to Robertson amounted to about 3.5 percent of total distributor's sales.

After a thorough review of competitive pricing practices as outlined above, Robertson decided to modify the purchase bonus provisions by changing the percents of discount and the quantity required for the various discount brackets. A separate schedule was also provided with respect to two different classes of parts. These new discount schedules are presented in Exhibit 4.

QUESTIONS

1. Ideally, what should Robertson's price structure attempt to accomplish so far as the replacement market is concerned?
2. Evaluate Robertson's price structure, as modified. Are there any further recommendations you would suggest? Are there any nonprice adjustments that could be made?

marketing planning and organization

A firm's overall marketing program is a composite of many bits and pieces. Parts Three through Six of this text treated in depth specific decision areas in development of an overall marketing program. The success of this program, however, is not only a function of the wisdom of these specific decisions but also depends on: (1) how these decisions are integrated into a total program, and (2) how effectively both specific decisions and the overall program are implemented. If these two things are accomplished well, the resultant marketing program will be, in a very real sense, more than the sum of its parts.

Integration is accomplished by many means, but foremost among these is the marketing planning process itself. In developing formal, written marketing plans, integration of many specific decisions is a prime goal. Successful implementation of a marketing program depends heavily upon the existence of an organization structure capable of accomplishing this goal. Part Seven considers the role of marketing planning and the marketing organization in the development of integrated marketing programs.

development of
integrated
marketing
programs

The first chapter of this text provided an overview of marketing and introduced the concept of planning overall marketing strategy. Subsequent chapters went beyond this generalized treatment and considered major decision areas of marketing in substantial depth. This chapter attempts to put these pieces together again into an integrated marketing program. At the same time, it will give us a chance to take a look at some of the practices engaged in by business firms to achieve integrated, and hence more effective, approaches to the market.

synergism and marketing

Synergism is a popular word in business management literature. It is defined by Webster as: "Cooperative action of discrete agencies such that the total effect is greater than the sum of the two effects taken independently."[1] Nowhere in business management is synergism a more important concept than in management of the marketing function. The effectiveness of action taken with regard to one controllable variable depends greatly on what is done with regard to others. For example, the effectiveness of advertising depends on the adequacy of distribution of a product. Even favorable responses to advertising appeals cannot lead to consumer purchase if the product is not availa-

---

[1] *Webster's Seventh New Collegiate Dictionary*, copyright © 1963, by G. & C. Merriam Co., Springfield, Mass.

ble in the marketplace. Personal selling can have its effectiveness blunted if advertising has not been used to lay the groundwork for the approach of the salesman. A price cut may fail to have the hoped-for effect if it is not promoted effectively. In short, the total effect of marketing effort is very much a function of the integration a firm manages to achieve in developing and carrying out its marketing program.

The concept of synergism applies not only to the marketing function but to the total operation of a business. The marketing concept, described in the first chapter, involves the orientation of the entire business to the needs of the consumer. This means, for example, that production must be integrated with marketing requirements and that finance must provide the capital resources required to serve these consumer needs. It is the special role of marketing not only to assure that the marketing function is so oriented but also to guide the other business functions in serving the same goal.

Current trends in business are complicating this integration process. Firms are becoming larger and more complex, thus increasing the magnitude of the task. Product lines are broadening and diversifying, making it more difficult to achieve an optimal overall approach to the market. The growth of so-called "conglomerate" firms represents an extreme illustration of this problem.

Approaches used to achieve synergism in business vary widely. In the small enterprise, important decisions are usually made by one man. This in itself provides some measure of an integrative approach. As a firm grows in size, effective integration usually requires more and more committees and staff meetings. At some level of size, these somewhat casual approaches to integration no longer are adequate, and achievement of this goal becomes a difficult and perplexing thing. In the large firm, achievement of the synergistic effect is accomplished by more formal planning and more attention to the organization structure. Although both planning and organization are important to the small firm, they are indispensable to the large one. In the smaller firm, close interpersonal contact overcomes some defects in organization; ability to change course quickly overcomes some inadequacies in planning.

marketing planning

Marketing planning is a subfunction of business planning. An inevitable result of the complex business environment in which change is the order of the day is the need for both short-range and long-range planning. A business firm, in order to survive and prosper, must know where it is going and how it is going to get there. It needs clearly defined goals and a well-thought-out course of action to achieve these goals. Without these two things efficient employment of resources is not possible.

A business firm may have many goals, either implicit or clearly stated. It may choose to maximize long- or short-range profits, to achieve steady but not necessarily maximum growth, to provide maximum security for management personnel, to maximize dividend payments to stockholders, and so on. The merit of these or other goals is not at issue here. What is at issue is the fact that these goals must be known before marketing planning can proceed. Planning for marketing activities must be consistent with the overall goals of the company.

The role of marketing planning is a special one in overall business planning. Marketing is the major link between the business firm and its environment. In order to achieve the orientation of the business firm to its market, marketing must study and interpret consumer needs and then guide the firm in serving those needs. In a rough sort of way, a marketing plan can be thought of as a company's battle plan. It surveys the environment, isolates marketing opportunities, and states the courses of action to be followed in taking advantage of those opportunities. Other parts of the overall business plan (for example, those relating to production and finance) are more in the nature of support plans—things which must be done to carry out the marketing plan which has been agreed upon. Obviously, however, no part of the overall plan for a business is independent of the other parts.

Because the marketing plan must be consistent with and serve a particular company's objectives, the marketing planning process and the resultant marketing plan will differ from one firm to another. Nonetheless, an in-depth look at the marketing planning process in one company that has adopted the marketing concept will reveal some practices that have general applicability.

the marketing planning process

The marketing planning process as it is carried out in the General Electric Company is outlined in Figure 15–1. The process as a whole is visualized as beginning with and ending with the customer. The whole process rests on the study of the customer, as carried out through marketing research activities. Such research activities are the first step undertaken to determine who and where the customer is; what he

Figure 15–1.   The General Electric marketing planning process.

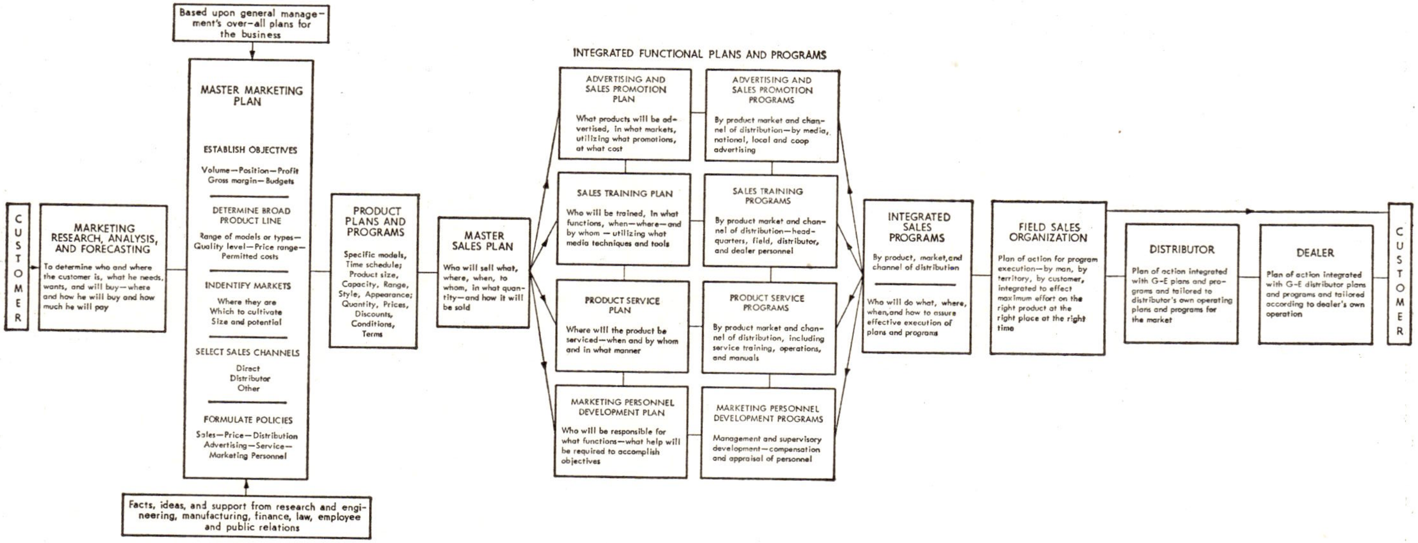

CUSTOMER

MARKETING RESEARCH, ANALYSIS, AND FORECASTING

To determine who and where the customer is, what he needs, wants, and will buy—where and how he will buy and how much he will pay

MASTER MARKETING PLAN

ESTABLISH OBJECTIVES
Volume—Position—Profit
Gross margin—Budgets

DETERMINE BROAD PRODUCT LINE
Range of models or types—
Quality level—Price range—
Permitted costs

IDENTIFY MARKETS
Where they are
Which to cultivate
Size and potential

SELECT SALES CHANNELS
Direct
Distributor
Other

FORMULATE POLICIES
Sales—Price—Distribution
Advertising—Services—
Marketing Personnel

PRODUCT PLANS AND PROGRAMS
Specific models,
Time schedule,
Product size,
Capacity, Range,
Style, Appearance,
Quantity, Prices,
Discounts,
Conditions,
Terms

MASTER SALES PLAN
Who will sell what,
where, when, to
whom, in what quan-
tity—and how it will
be sold

INTEGRATED FUNCTIONAL PLANS AND PROGRAMS

ADVERTISING AND SALES PROMOTION PLAN
What products will be ad-
vertised, in what markets,
utilizing what promotions,
at what cost

SALES TRAINING PLAN
Who will be trained, in what
functions, when—where—and
by whom—utilizing what
media techniques and tools

PRODUCT SERVICE PLAN
Where will the product be
serviced—when and by whom
and in what manner

MARKETING PERSONNEL DEVELOPMENT PLAN
Who will be responsible for
what functions—what help will
be required to accomplish
objectives

ADVERTISING AND SALES PROMOTION PROGRAMS
By product market and chan-
nel of distribution—by media,
national, local and coop
advertising

SALES TRAINING PROGRAMS
By product market and channel of distribution—head-
quarters, field, distributor,
and dealer personnel

PRODUCT SERVICE PROGRAMS
By product market and channel of distribution, including
service training, operations,
and manuals

MARKETING PERSONNEL DEVELOPMENT PROGRAMS
Management and supervisory
development—compensation
and appraisal of personnel

INTEGRATED SALES PROGRAMS
By product, market,and
channel of distribution

Who will do what, where,
when,and how to ensure
effective execution of
plans and programs

FIELD SALES ORGANIZATION
Plan of action for program
execution—by men, by
territory, by customer,
integrated to effect
maximum effort on the
right product at the
right place at the right
time

DISTRIBUTOR
Plan of action integrated
with G-E plans and pro-
grams not tailored to
distributor's own operating
plans and programs for
the market

DEALER
Plan of action integrated
with G-E distributor plans
and programs and tailored
according to dealer's own
operation

CUSTOMER

Based upon general management's over-all plans for
the business

Facts, ideas, and support from research and engineering, manufacturing, finance, law, employee
and public relations

Source: Courtesy of General Electric Company.

needs, wants, and will buy; where and how he will buy; and how much he will pay. The next step is formulation of the master marketing plan. Note that this plan is based upon general management's overall plans for the business. This means, of course, that the master marketing plan must be consistent with the short- and long-range goals of the company as a whole.

The company objectives must be translated into marketing objectives. These are indicated in Figure 15–1 as being stated in terms of volume, position (market share), profit, gross margin, and budgets. Then, and only then, can the product line to be offered by the company be determined. This clearly implies, as recommended in the first chapter of this text, that the product line is considered as a controllable variable —something that can be manipulated in order to achieve agreed-upon objectives. At this stage in the planning process, products are specified only in very broad terms, such as the type of product, the overall range of models, the general quality level, the price range, and permitted costs. The details are to be worked out later.

The next step in formulating the master marketing plan is seen as identifying markets. This step is a logical outgrowth of the previously made market studies and the decisions which have been made about the product line to be offered. Given these two types of information, markets can be identified as to where they are, which to cultivate, and their size and potential. Knowing the markets to be served, distribution channels can be selected. It is now possible to formulate basic policies concerning sales, price, distribution, advertising, service, and marketing personnel. Again, these are broad in concept and are to be refined later with regard to specific products.

Now that the master marketing plan has been structured (or, in a sense, now that the company has decided what business it is going to be in), it is time to construct plans and programs by products. Decisions must be made as to specific models, time schedules, product size, capacity, range, style, appearance, quantity, prices, discounts, conditions, and terms. In essence, these are the product strategy decisions discussed in Chapters 5 and 6.

The next step in the General Electric Company's marketing planning process is to develop a master sales plan (a subplan of the marketing plan) to determine how the things it has been decided to produce are to be sold to the markets that have been discovered. This, in their words, means deciding "who will sell what, where, when, to whom, in what quantity—and how it will be sold." The master sales plan is now broken down to its several integral parts—advertising and sales promotion, sales training, product service, and marketing personnel development. These plans are then converted into concrete programs, which in turn must again be put together into an integrated sales program to achieve the desired synergistic effect. The plans must now be implemented through the field sales organization, distributors, and dealers. As a result of this planning process, the customer is more likely to receive the product he needs and wants, and the company is more likely to achieve the profit it seeks.

anatomy of a marketing plan

There is an important distinction to be made between marketing planning and a marketing plan. Marketing planning is a continuous function and is never completed. A marketing plan is an expression of the output of the planning process as of a particular moment for a particular period of time. Our discussion to this point has emphasized the planning process, with particular emphasis on the steps involved in that process. We shall now shift our attention to the structure of a marketing plan.

There is a trend in business toward formal, written marketing plans. Usually both long-range and short-range plans are prepared. The appropriate time span for marketing plans will vary with each industry, but the long-range plan should cover the longest predictable period ahead for which objectives can be defined. Short-range plans must be in harmony with the long-range plan. They are steps on the way to achieving the long-range objectives.

Although no one plan structure is necessarily the best, there are certain things which must be encompassed in any marketing plan. The structure discussed below incorporates these things. It is built around the controllable and uncontrollable marketing variables utilized in Chapter 1. These are integrated with other factors to form a plan structure that has wide applicability.

general structure of a marketing plan

An appropriate skeletal structure for a marketing plan might appear as follows:

I. Situation Analysis
    A. Demand
    B. Competition
    C. Distribution structure

D. Marketing law

E. Non-marketing cost

II. Problems and Opportunities

III. Marketing Strategy

A. Objectives

B. Methods

1. Product strategy

2. Distribution strategy

3. Price strategy

4. Advertising strategy

5. Personal selling strategy

IV. Marketing Tactics

1. Who

2. What

3. When

4. Where

5. How

the situation analysis

Basic to marketing planning is an understanding of the environment in which marketing effort is to be expended. The environment determines not only what must be done, but what it is possible to do. Situational variables are multitudinous in number. One useful way of classifying them is the one suggested in the outline. It will be noted that this classification system is the same as that used for the uncontrollable marketing variables in Chapter 1.

The purpose of the situation analysis is, in a sense, to take a picture of the external environment for marketing planning. It cannot, however, be a still picture that merely depicts what exists at the time it was snapped. It must be a moving picture that reveals trends and helps us to forecast what the environmental situation will be throughout the planning period. It is really the future situation in which we are most interested.

Demand is the most significant situational variable because it is least known and least predictable, yet has the greatest effect on what can or cannot be done in marketing. This means that marketing research is a very important tool in the marketing planning process. Demand must be understood both quantitatively and qualitatively. We need estimates of total potential demand, the distribution of demand, and so on. In addition, the marketing plan should include information on buying motives, buying practices, and the like. The other situational factors included in the outline (competition, distribution structure, marketing law, nonmarketing cost) must be similarly analyzed and the pertinent information recorded.

problems and opportunities

The next phase of the marketing plan is a listing of problems and opportunities which are uncovered by distilling the information gleaned from the situation analysis. Sometimes it is hard to tell which facts constitute problems and which facts constitute opportunities. In the early 1960's, automobile manufacturers noticed that economy compacts that had been introduced several years earlier were not selling well. However, compact cars with sporty features, such as bucket seats, were doing well. For example, the sporty Monza model of the Corvair line went from 4.8 percent of total Corvair sales in 1960 to 71.5 percent in 1962.

Marketing research conducted as part of a situation analysis by Ford Motor Company revealed several important changes taking place in the automobile market. First, a major change was occurring in the age makeup of the population of the United States, as shown in Figure 15–2. In the 1960–70 decade, there would be a tremendous increase in

Figure 15–2. Population count and percentage change by age groups, 1960 to 1970.

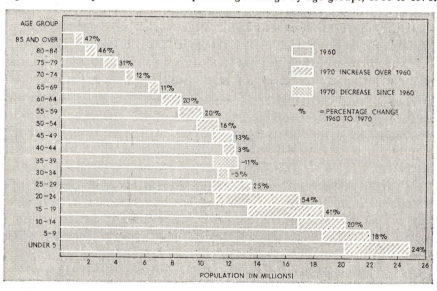

Source: U.S. Bureau of Census, *Current Population Reports*, Series P–25, No. 241 (January 17, 1962), Series II Estimates.

the 15–19, 20–24 and 25–29 age groups, while the over 30 age group would grow much more slowly. Younger buyers could therefore be expected to be a more potent factor in automobile demand in the future than in the past. Younger buyers have different tastes in automobiles, these tastes tending more toward the sporty than the staid models.

A second significant market fact bearing on automobile demand was the anticipated growth in college enrollment, which was expected

Figure 15–3. New-car buying rate increases with educational level.

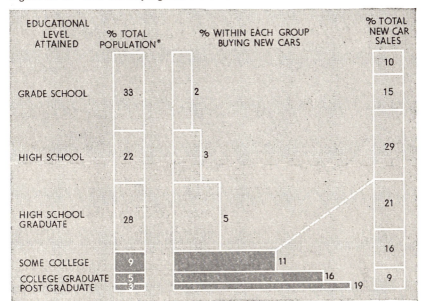

* 14 years and older.
Source: Courtesy of Ford Motor Company.

to almost double in the 1960–70 decade (from 3.6 million to 7 million). People who have attended college behave differently in the purchase of automobiles from those who have not attended college. For one thing, they buy more automobiles. The 17 percent who have attended college account for 46 percent of total new-car sales, whereas the 83 percent with a high school education or less account for 54 percent (see Figure 15–3). Furthermore their tastes are more sophisticated and tend more towards sporty vehicles. Most sports cars, domestic and imported, are purchased by people with some college education.

A third important market fact was the trend toward multiple car

Figure 15–4. Multiple car owning spending units, January, 1949–65.

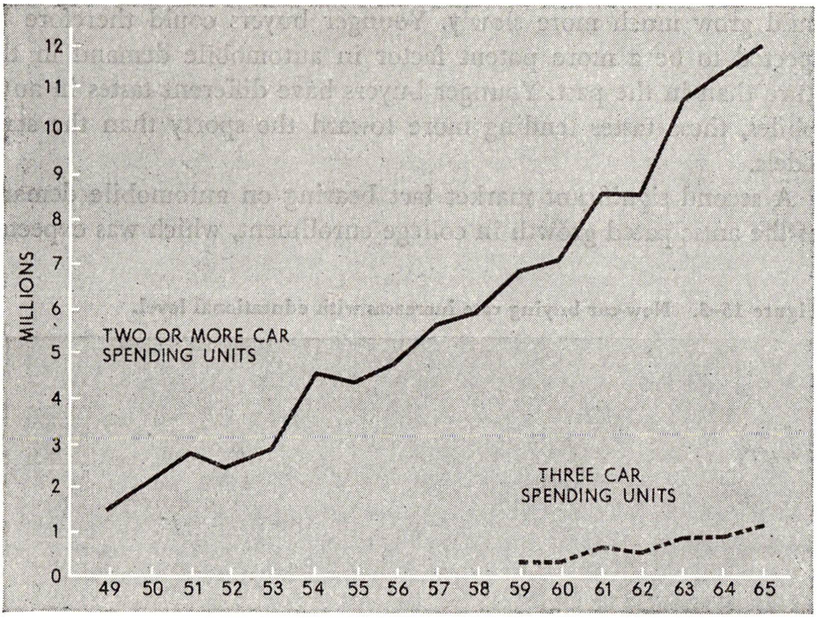

Source: Courtesy of Ford Motor Company.

ownership (see Figure 15–4). This trend reduces the domination of the all-purpose family vehicle and opens a market for more "personalized" transportation.

These three facts about the market uncovered in a situation analysis were dominant factors leading to introduction of the Mustang by the Ford Motor Company. The success of this new car entry is well known.

marketing strategy

The planning of marketing strategy consists of making decisions about the use of controllable marketing variables to achieve predetermined goals. If goals have not been clearly established, there is little point to planning. If you don't know where you are going, any road will take you there, and there is no meaningful basis for choice between one route and another. Therefore, the first step in planning marketing strategy is to establish goals.

In order to be useful, goals should be reasonably specific, and performance in achieving them should be measurable. A goal of maximizing profits does not fit these criteria when the achievable maximum is not known. Growth is not a meaningful objective unless expressed as a specific growth rate which is either achieved or is not. The most common ways of stating marketing strategy objectives are: (1) sales volume, expressed in either dollars or units; (2) market share, expressed as a percentage of the total market for a product or service; and (3) profit, expressed as a return on investment. These objectives are concrete, and the degree to which they are achieved can be calculated.

The heart of the marketing plan is the section on methods of strategy. Here decisions are made about the manner and extent of use of each controllable marketing strategy variable and how these variables should be meshed together into a total strategy. The way of doing this was discussed in Chapter 1. Again, decisions should be reasonably specific and should be consistent with the kind and amount of resources available. Plans must be consonant with budget considerations, and often must be modified to fit budget constraints.

marketing tactics

A marketing strategy program still is not an action program. Many details remain to be worked out. Specific responsibility for carrying out individual portions of the strategy must be assigned. Those to whom responsibility is assigned must be instructed as to just what they are to do. Time schedules must be planned and carefully integrated. Decisions must be made about the allocation and sequencing of marketing effort. Specific procedures must be agreed upon. This is the tactical part of the plan. Although not very glamorous, it is essential to the successful implementation of the marketing program.

marketing organization

A business firm is a combination of men, money, plant, and equipment so coordinated that they can fulfill an economic objective. The active ingredient in this combination, of course, is people. The other resources are inert and are effective only if people make them so. Basically, therefore, company objectives are accomplished through people. In order to achieve these objectives, the activities of people must be coordinated. This is the function of organization planning. An organization is simply a means for carrying out tasks necessary to achieve a predetermined goal. In the case of a marketing organization, the goals are those incorporated in the marketing plan.

Marketing planning and marketing organization have something of a chicken and egg relationship. As stated, a marketing organization is a means for carrying out the marketing plan. Therefore, the plan should determine the organization structure. On the other hand, an organization is needed to carry out the ongoing marketing planning function. Most marketing planning is, in fact, done within established organization structures. The answer to this dilemma, as usual, is that the marketing plan and the marketing organization must reflect and adapt to each other. The result is that they are more or less simultaneous activities, and each is continually prompting changes in the other.

implications of marketing concept

Implementation of the marketing concept is intended to achieve customer orientation of the business firm. This objective is simple in statement, but to accomplish it is far from easy. Such accomplishment requires a proper state of mind on the part not only of top management but also of all key executives. It requires a concern with ends external to the company, such as service to consumers, rather than allowing internal considerations to dominate decision making. It requires an organization that makes possible effective coordination and integration of all business activities.

Organization is a key factor in implementation of the marketing concept, and implementation of this concept is a key factor in overall business success. A consequence of these basic facts is an increasing concern with organization structures, particularly for marketing. Much experimentation has been going on in regard to organization for marketing in recent years. There is a strong feeling among students of marketing that while the perfect answer has not yet been found, improvements have been made.

To illustrate the nature of the changes that have been taking place in marketing organizations and to suggest the reasons for them, let us take a look at a hypothetical pre–marketing-concept organization of a typical marketing department and compare it with what such a department might look like today. Of course, the appropriate organization structure varies widely by type of industry. Therefore, let us assume we are talking here about a company in the consumer packaged-goods field—a food company, say. For such companies, marketing tends to be the dominant business function. This adds piquancy to their problems of marketing organization.

pre–marketing-concept organization

Until relatively recently a typical organization structure for a food company was likely to have some resemblance to the organization depicted in Figure 15–5. Sales was recognized as a major function and was likely to be headed by someone with the title of sales manager. If the company sold both through retail stores to ultimate consumers and to the institutional market (hotels, restaurants, and so on), there might be a separate sales organization for each of these markets. Advertising was a separate and distinct function from sales and probably was headed by an advertising manager, an executive on a par with the sales manager. The director of marketing research reported to neither the sales manager nor the advertising manager but operated

Figure 15–5. A pre-marketing-concept organization structure.

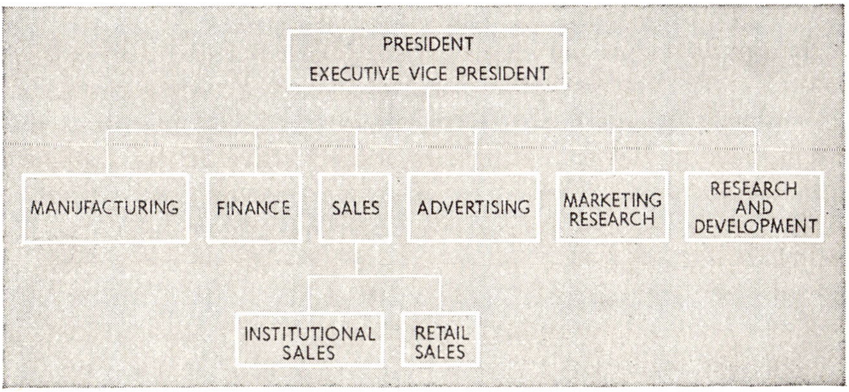

independently of both. Manufacturing, finance, and research and development were separate functions and had no direct ties to marketing activities.

Several things in particular should be noted about this type of organization structure. There is no provision in the marketing structure per se for integration of marketing activites. Sales, advertising, and marketing research are seen as separate activities. If there is to be integration, it must come through the actions of top management or through informal contacts of the executives heading each activity. If top-management people have marketing backgrounds, a fair measure of integration might be achieved. If they do not, such a result is unlikely.

There is no provision in the organization structure itself for coordination of marketing and nonmarketing activities. If production reflects marketing requirements, this is again a result of action by top management. Likewise for finance and research and development. There is no clearly defined route for information about the environment to be processed and translated into a marketing strategy. Again, this must happen by chance or through the coordinating efforts to top management.

There is nothing about this organization structure to assure achievement of a synergistic effect. The several business functions are fragmented and insulated from each other. If there is any marked degree of achievement in implementing the marketing concept, it is in spite of, not because of, the organizational structure.

a post–marketing-concept organization structure

It is probably presumptuous to talk about any particular organization structure as being typical of the post–marketing-concept era. Organizational structures vary tremendously both by industries and within the same industry. Still, to be fully effective, an organizational structure must make provision for achieving a synergistic effect, and to do this certain common traits are beginning to emerge. The organization chart in Figure 15–6 incorporates these traits, but this does not rule out alternative approaches to the same end.

Chief marketing executive. Note that the chief marketing executive is designated Vice-President, Marketing. Under the old system the chief marketing executive usually had the title of sales manager. He may have been a vice president, but often he was not. Marketing is a much broader function than sales, and the change in title reflects a recognition of the breadth of the marketing function in the modern company. The vice president status typical of chief marketing executives today reflects an upgrading of the marketing department within the corporate organization.

The shift from a sales management to a marketing management concept increases substantially the scope and complexity of the chief marketing executive's job. He must be capable of thinking, planning, and administering in all phases of the marketing function. He can no longer concentrate on sales, let others worry about other aspects of marketing, and then rely on top management to bring all these loose ends together. Planning and coordination have, in fact, become his major responsibility.

Figure 15–6. Hypothetical post–marketing-concept organization structure.

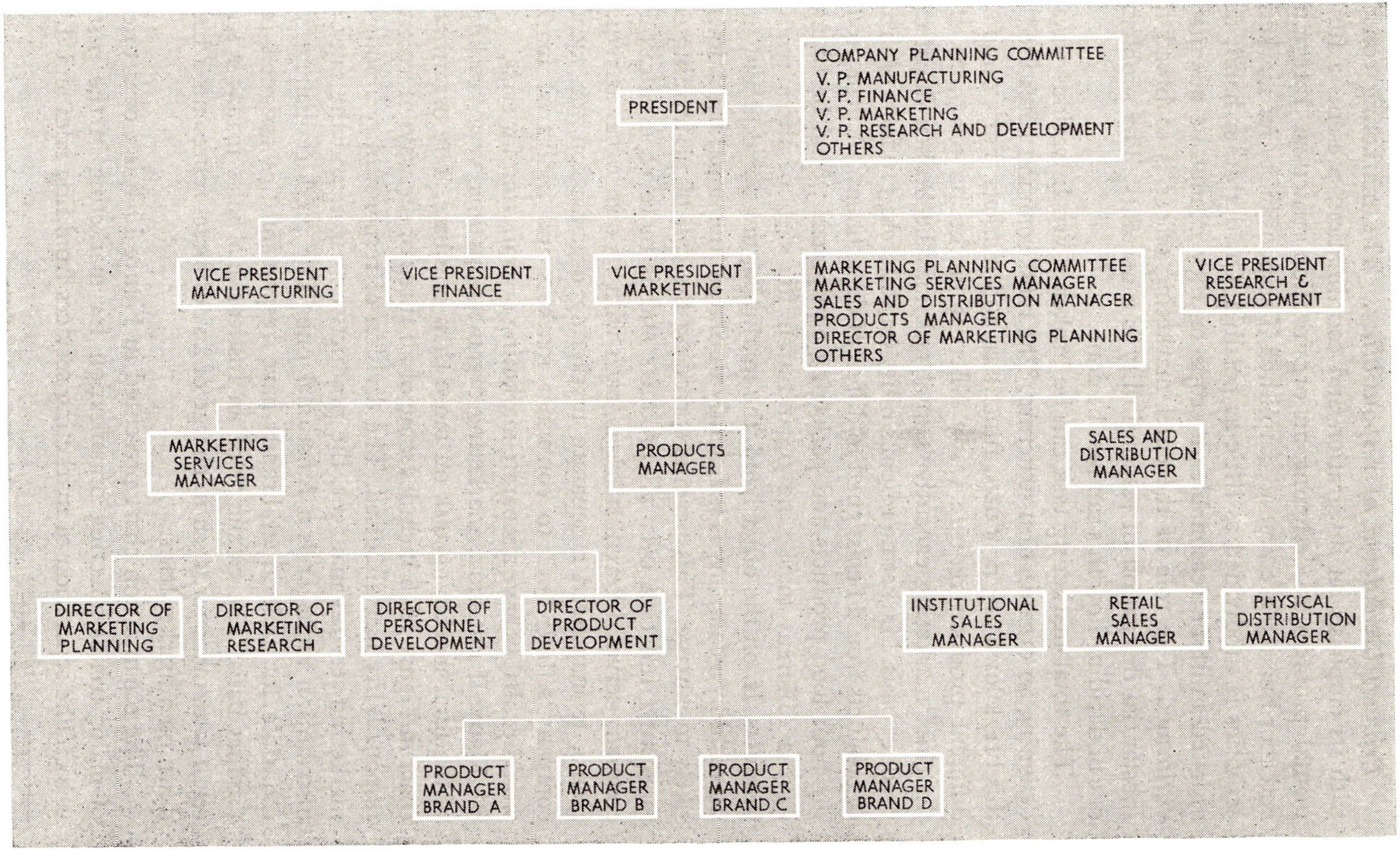

COMPANY PLANNING COMMITTEE
V. P. MANUFACTURING
V. P. FINANCE
V. P. MARKETING
V. P. RESEARCH AND DEVELOPMENT
OTHERS

PRESIDENT

VICE PRESIDENT MANUFACTURING

VICE PRESIDENT FINANCE

VICE PRESIDENT MARKETING

VICE PRESIDENT RESEARCH & DEVELOPMENT

MARKETING PLANNING COMMITTEE
MARKETING SERVICES MANAGER
SALES AND DISTRIBUTION MANAGER
PRODUCTS MANAGER
DIRECTOR OF MARKETING PLANNING
OTHERS

MARKETING SERVICES MANAGER

SALES AND DISTRIBUTION MANAGER

PRODUCTS MANAGER

DIRECTOR OF MARKETING PLANNING

DIRECTOR OF MARKETING RESEARCH

DIRECTOR OF PERSONNEL DEVELOPMENT

DIRECTOR OF PRODUCT DEVELOPMENT

INSTITUTIONAL SALES MANAGER

RETAIL SALES MANAGER

PHYSICAL DISTRIBUTION MANAGER

PRODUCT MANAGER BRAND A

PRODUCT MANAGER BRAND B

PRODUCT MANAGER BRAND C

PRODUCT MANAGER BRAND D

Primary breakdown of responsibility. The marketing concept, with its emphasis on integration and coordination, presents a fundamental problem in designing an organization structure. Integration and coordination are best accomplished if responsibility for marketing activities is subdivided as little as possible. On the other hand, tasks assigned must be reasonable in scope or they cannot be adequately performed. The role of the chief marketing officer is so broad that substantial delegation of responsibility is a necessity. The problem is one of deciding how this can best be done.

The total marketing task can be broken down in various ways in designing an organization structure. The most common bases used for this breakdown are products, functions, and markets. For example, if different products require vastly different marketing programs, then the chief marketing executive's total task may be broken down on a product basis. Marketing responsibility for different products or groups of products would be assigned to different departments. A firm producing both food products and packaging equipment would be likely to have a different marketing organization for each of these types of products. If, on the other hand, the marketing task for different products sold by a company is sufficiently similar, a functional breakdown is likely to emerge. This permits spreading the cost of performing each marketing function over all products and is more economical. If a company serves different markets, each with its own peculiar requirements, it may need a separate marketing organization for each. A company selling both to consumer markets and industrial markets would probably have a separate marketing organization for each.

Many, if not most, marketing organizations involve a breakdown of the total marketing task on more than one base. The organization chart in Figure 15–6 includes some of all three of the ways of assigning responsibility just discussed. The division of responsibility among the marketing services manager, the products manager, and the sales and distribution manager is a functional one. The product managers responsible for individual brands have responsibilities assigned on a product basis. The existence of an institutional sales manager and a retail sales manager, each in charge of a sales force, represents a breakdown on a market basis.

The organization chart presented in Figure 15–6 is a consequence of major trends affecting organization for marketing in the past 15 years.[2] The separation of marketing services from line sales and distri-

---

[2] For a detailed discussion of these trends and their effect on the marketing organization, see Henry Bund and James W. Carroll, *The Changing Role of the Marketing Function* (Chicago: American Marketing Association, 1957).

bution activities is a way of focusing more attention on these service activities and improving performance in regard to them. Grouping them together under a marketing services manager who is responsible for their integration and coordination reflects a recognition of the need for synergism in marketing. The use of product managers has become a major approach to assuring that there is integration of all marketing activities associated with a particular product. How each of these departments operates to further the accomplishment of an integrative marketing program will now be explained.

Sales and distribution manager. The closest thing to the general sales manager of the pre–marketing-concept era included in Figure 15–6 is the sales and distribution manager. He is responsible for all field sales operations. His duties are complex, including all aspects of sales force management: recruitment, selection, training, supervising, and so on. These duties have here been broadened further to include physical distribution (discussed in Chapter 9). There is logic in combining responsibility for these two functions. The service that salesmen can render customers is very much a function of delivery dates, adequacy and location of inventory, means and times of transportation, and so forth. The physical distribution system must be so designed that it gives full support to sales requirements.

This organization chart, assumed to be for a food company, includes separate sales forces for institutional and retail sales. This separation may or may not be justified. It is based on the assumption that the sales requirements for these two markets are substantially different, that the salesmen who call on one type of customer would not be effective in making calls on the other. Because these customers overlap geographically, this involves duplication in market coverage and adds to costs. If the increased revenues generated by this specialization of salesmen does not justify this cost increase, then a common sales force would be preferable.

Marketing services manager. It was rare to find a position such as marketing services manager in a pre–marketing-concept organization. Staff functions in marketing were often organized on a helter-skelter basis, and no overt attempt was made to provide for integration and coordination. Today, this position is commonplace in marketing organizations. Its existence is evidence of a determined effort to develop integrated marketing programs. The specific marketing functions assigned to the marketing services manager vary widely, and usually the number is greater than the four included in Figure 15–6. Only the most common are shown there.

Marketing planning is and should be a top-management function.

The chief marketing executive has overall responsibility for marketing planning and probably spends the better part of his time on this function. The role of the director of marketing planning is to assist in this activity and to put together the detailed long- and short-range marketing plans. He accepts the goals and broad strategy which have been agreed upon by top management and designs a detailed marketing plan consistent therewith. He coordinates the planning activities of all marketing organization units, particularly the product managers, and attempts to assure integration and consistency in the plans they devise. In short, the marketing planning department is concerned with the mechanics and coordination of marketing planning; it is not a policy-making unit.

Marketing research is a key function in a market-oriented firm. It is the basic tool for obtaining the information about demand essential to the planning and execution of marketing strategy. Without the information it provides, goals cannot be set and choices among different strategies cannot be made. To obtain, process, and disseminate this information is the assignment of the director of marketing research. He is also usually charged with the task of measuring market performance, providing the feedback of information essential to modification and restructuring of marketing strategy. The information-gathering role of the marketing research department is important to all organizational units within marketing, and all of them can be expected to utilize its services. The director of marketing research must work closely with the directors of marketing planning and product development. The product managers need marketing research information for decision making. The sales and distribution manager requires data on market potential in order to assign salesmen, set quotas, and allocate stock. It is not surprising that marketing research departments have been growing faster than any other unit in the marketing organization.[3]

Responsibility for personnel development on a companywide basis is likely to be centered outside the marketing department. However, there is usually a personnel development department within marketing as well. Its role is the initial and continuing development of all marketing personnel. In a changing environment, nothing is more crucial to a company's long-run success. One of the implications of the marketing concept is the need for broad-gauged marketing personnel. Narrowly trained personnel greatly complicate the task of developing and executing integrated marketing programs.

---

[3] *Ibid.*, p. 9.

Chapters 5 and 6 described the product development function and the important role of marketing with regard thereto. Even if a company has a "new products" division organized separately from marketing, the marketing department is likely to require a director of product development. His role is concerned with the marketing aspects of product development and liaison with the nonmarketing departments also involved in product development. In a consumer packaged-goods company, particularly a food company, product development is often more a marketing task than a technological one. In such a case, the basic function of the product development department is to translate consumer wants into a product that adequately serves those wants. Then, its role becomes one of assuring that the product keeps pace with changes in the market.

Products manager. Although a few companies have employed the product manager concept for many years, there has been a great surge in its popularity since the advent of the marketing concept. The use of product managers is an attempt to cope with the complexities of modern marketing through the use of decentralization.

The product management concept is simple. A product manager is assigned to each product or group of products. It is his task to plan for the marketing of that product and to see that his plans are implemented. In so doing he works closely with other organization units. He draws heavily on the staff services available in the marketing services department and works with and through the sales and distribution department in implementing his plans. The products manager who oversees the work of product managers for specific products integrates and coordinates their activities.

The product management concept is too new for uniformity in its application to have been achieved. There seem to be three basic types of product management organization.

1. Product managers with primarily advertising and sales promotion orientation. This type predominates among consumer companies, such as Procter & Gamble, where advertising is a large and critical part of the marketing program. Product managers work directly with advertising agencies. There is probably no separate advertising department in the firm.
2. Product managers with primarily customer service and customer relations responsibilities. This type is most common among firms selling to the industrial market.
3. The most comprehensive (and most rare) kind of product manager can probably be more correctly called a general manager. He is

found in large companies in charge of a product division. He is responsible for all manufacturing as well as marketing, with supervision from above.[4]

The product managers in Figure 15–6 are the first of these types. It is for this reason that advertising does not appear as a separate function under marketing services. This is not to imply that the job of these product managers is limited to advertising and promotional strategy, but only that this is the major part of what they do. They are concerned with marketing planning for their products in the broadest sense. It is just the nature of things that marketing strategy for consumer packaged goods involves heavy emphasis on advertising and promotion.

The status of product management in marketing organizations is ambiguous. *Printers' Ink* makes the following comment about the product manager:

How does he operate? Some of the confusions about the PM system can be laid to the lack of sufficient experience with it. For example, 60 percent of the consumer companies choose to designate their PMs as line executives, when in fact some of them exercise little line control and actually perform planning and advisory duties usually designated as staff. Probably the most realistic approach to the question of line or staff designation is offered by those two out of ten consumer companies that reported they make no distinction—for they most clearly suggest the fluidity of the situation.[5]

If the status of product managers is unclear, the objective sought by companies who use this organizational concept is not. They hope by this means to assure integrated and coordinated marketing planning and strategy for each product and for the company's entire product line. Although the concept originated among consumer packaged-goods companies, it has now spread to companies of all types.

Marketing planning committee. The hypothetical marketing structure of Figure 15–6, as discussed to this point, reflects a heavy emphasis on the achievement of integrated and coordinated marketing effort. In spite of this emphasis, there is a strong likelihood that this goal will have been less than perfectly achieved. To aid in its accomplishment, the establishment of a marketing planning committee is suggested. The purpose of the committee is twofold: (1) to aid the marketing vice president in the formulation of broad marketing policy and strategy, and (2) to improve coordination among the several

---

[4] "Why Modern Marketing Needs the Product Manager," *Printers' Ink*, Vol. 273 (October 14, 1960), pp. 25–30.

[5] *Ibid.*, p. 30.

organization units which make up the marketing department. It is a way of achieving a two-way flow of information, both up and down the organizational ladder, on a face-to-face basis. Each executive is kept aware of what others are doing and thinking, and why.

The makeup of the marketing planning committee will vary greatly from firm to firm. Almost invariably, however, it will include the executives who report directly to the vice president and are in charge of major marketing functions. The director of marketing planning should be included because of his detailed knowledge of the marketing plan and his need fully to understand company goals and overall strategy. Others can be brought in when their knowledge is relevant to the topic under consideration.

Company planning committee. The purpose of the company planning committee is to coordinate companywide efforts to achieve the company's goals. The marketing concept specifies customer orientation of the entire business, not just of the marketing department. This is one approach to stimulation of coordinated effort toward this end.

review and modification

No amount of planning is likely to produce the perfect marketing program, nor is any organization likely to implement it faultlessly. Perhaps this is particularly true of marketing programs because of the rapidly changing environment in which they operate. There is need for continuous review and modification. It is the rare marketing program that achieves its full measure of success from the beginning. Rather, most successful marketing programs become such through evolution over time. Therefore, a marketing program must have built into it procedures for review of performance.

What should be reviewed? The nature of marketing is such that anything short of an all-encompassing review is likely to be unsatisfactory. The success or failure of a marketing program depends in large part on the interaction of activities and people. Hence a review of any one part of that program is likely to be inconclusive even though it might be helpful in a limited way. A full-scale review must reconsider goals, strategy, and tactics as well as the organization structure.

review of goals

Perhaps the best place to start a review of company and marketing goals is with a determination of whether or not they were achieved.

Failure to achieve stated goals may be the result of one or more of the following: (1) the goals were unrealistic, (2) the wrong strategy was employed, (3) the right strategy was employed, but not successfully implemented. Marketing goals are usually stated in terms of sales volume, market share, or profit contribution. It is possible that specific goal choices did not properly anticipate demand conditions, competitive activity, actions of government, changes in production capacity, and so on. Should this be the case, goals must be revised before marketing strategy performance or organizational effectiveness can be determined.

Unfortunately, if goals are achieved or exceeded, the correctness of the stated goals is not proven. Goals can be set too low as well as too high. The stated goals, even though achieved, may not be the ones most important to a company's long-run success. Many corporation executives have recently come to the conclusion that they have placed too much emphasis on the profit goal and have not been sufficiently concerned with their total contribution to society. This has led them into programs to recruit and train the underprivileged, help secondary schools upgrade vocational education, and undertake other public-spirited activities even at the expense of immediate profits. It is not clear, however, that such moves are necessarily inconsistent with maximization of long-term profit.

review of strategy and tactics

A review of marketing strategy and tactics can only be done on the basis of originally stated or revised goals. But here again attainment of goals doesn't prove correctness of the strategy. For example, a high-cost strategy may have been employed when one of lower cost would have been equally successful. In this case attainment of goals stated in terms of sales volume or market share is an insufficient measure of strategy performance.

The measurement of specific elements of marketing strategy is a difficult one for two reasons. It is difficult because integration of marketing activities in order to achieve a synergistic effect makes it hard to measure the effect of any one activity by itself. The end result achieved is always a function of total marketing strategy. It is also difficult because of the inadequacy of measurement tools. For example, the effectiveness of advertising is very hard to gauge. We measure exposure to advertising, recall, and so on, but not net contribution to sales success. Quotas used in the measurement of salesmen's performance are far from perfect, often being based on inadequate data. Hence, a lot of judgment must be used in evaluation of marketing strategy and tactics.

review of marketing organization

The same limitations on evaluation in terms of goal achievement mentioned in connection with marketing strategy apply to reviewing the effectiveness of the marketing organization. Another complication exists in the fact that goals stated in the marketing plan are too broad for use in evaluation of specific organization units. The sales manager (or products manager, etc.) is not by himself responsible for achieving a specific share of market. This is the function of the entire marketing department. Therefore, the sales manager must be judged against some sort of subgoal. These subgoals might be such things as number of new accounts gained, increase in average order size, sales against quotas which take into account other marketing effort, and so on. A major problem exists in setting subgoals which are fully consistent with, and whose achievement leads to, accomplishment of the more general goals.

the marketing audit

Auditing of accounting and financial operations is traditional in the business world. Some marketing experts are now suggesting that a similar formal, periodic review and evaluation be made of marketing operations.[6] Probably this is a good idea, but many questions remain about appropriate procedures, measurement tools, scope of the investigation, and so on. In essence, this would merely be a more formal review and evaluation than the one discussed above. Such an audit would be a far more difficult task than are audits of accounting and financial operations. Quantitative measures in marketing are both less developed and harder to apply. Judgment would be an extremely important ingredient.

Oxenfeldt describes the marketing audit as follows:

A total evaluation program for the marketing effort can be termed a marketing audit. The term is employed here to denote a systematic, critical, and unbiased review and appraisal of the basic objectives and policies of the marketing function, and of the organization, methods, procedures and

---

[6] See A. Shuchman, "The Marketing Audit: Its Nature, Purpose, and Problems," American Management Association Report, No. 32 (1959) ; R. Ferber, and P. J. Verdoorn, *Research Methods in Economics and Business* (New York: Macmillan Co., 1962) , chap. ii.

personnel employed to implement those policies and to achieve those objectives. Clearly, not every evaluation of marketing personnel, organization, or methods is a marketing audit; at best, most such evaluations can be regarded as parts of an audit. The total audit includes six separate aspects of marketing activities that should be appraised: (1) objectives, (2) policies, (3) organization, (4) methods, (5) procedures, and (6) personnel.[7]

Whether it is called a "review" or a "marketing audit" is not important. What is important is recognition that integrated marketing programs evolve into success stories out of such careful attention.

conclusion

Successful marketing depends on more than effective product policy, distribution policy, advertising policy, personal selling policy, and pricing policy. It requires that these controllable variables be so integrated that the overall result is more than the sum of its individual parts. This, in turn, is made possible by (1) marketing planning that achieves a synergistic effect and (2) effective implementation of the marketing plan through a vital and viable marketing organization. In the last analysis, success of a free enterprise economy depends on its ability to out-perform other economic systems. High performance of a free enterprise economy depends, to no small degree, on efficient marketing.

questions

1. The planning and execution of marketing strategy has been described as a "synergistic" process. What does this mean?
2. What is the relationship between marketing planning and corporate planning?
3. Figure 15–1 outlines the marketing planning process as it exists in the General Electric Company. Which part of this outline would also be encompassed in General Electric's sales plan? What is the essential difference between a sales plan and a marketing plan?
4. Discuss the role of marketing research in the marketing planning process.
5. Why must a situation analysis precede the planning of marketing strategy?
6. Discuss the ways in which implementation of the marketing concept affects the problem of developing a marketing organization.

---

[7] Alfred R. Oxenfeldt, *Executive Action in Marketing* (Belmont, Calif.: Wadsworth Publishing Company, Inc., 1966), p. 746.

7. The primary breakdown of tasks in planning a marketing organization is sometimes on a product basis (for example, General Motors) and sometimes on a functional basis (for example, Figure 15–6). What determines which type of organization structure is best?
8. The brand management type of organization is rapidly growing in popularity. How do you explain this trend?
9. If a marketing plan fails to achieve its objectives, it should, of course, be reviewed to determine what went wrong. What sequence of steps do you recommend for such a review?
10. Write a job description for the vice president, marketing, in a large consumer packaged-goods company. Reference to Figure 15–6 may be helpful.

cases for part seven

case 7–1

RCA COMMUNICATIONS, INC.*

development of a marketing program

Mr. Val Arbogast, a marketing executive of RCA Communications, Inc. (RCAC) of New York City, the international communications subsidiary of the Radio Corporation of America, was considering what recommendations he should make to Mr. Ludwig Engler, vice president and general sales manager, concerning RCAC's advertising and selling program for 1963. Mr. Arbogast was specifically interested in drawing useful conclusions from a recent "benchmark" survey conducted for RCAC by an independent market research firm. The purpose of the survey was to find out what executives of various types of business involved in foreign operations knew about international communications systems. The survey results, based on responses from 465 different individuals or firms, seemed to indicate that, although RCAC was better known than its competitors in the field, the potential market lacked real familiarity with the scope of services offered by RCAC and the industry as a whole.

THE INTERNATIONAL COMMUNICATIONS BUSINESS

In 1962 the international communications industry in which RCAC operated consisted essentially of three major U.S. carriers that provided a variety of cable and radio transmission facilities from the United States to almost anywhere in the world. The three major carriers were RCAC; Western Union International (WU); and American Cable and Radio (ACR), a complex of subsidiaries of the International Telephone and Telegraph Company. The operating statements of these three carriers for the period 1959–61 are given in Exhibit 1.

The principal international communication services provided by the industry are described below.

* This case was made possible by the cooperation of RCA Communications, Inc. It was prepared by Mr. Derek A. Newton, Research Assistant, under the direction of Professor Martin V. Marshall, as the basis for case discussion rather than to illustrate the effective or ineffective handling of an administrative situation. Copyright © 1963 by the President and Fellows of Harvard College. Revised 1965. Reproduced by permission.

Exhibit 1. Condensed income statements of principal international telegraph carriers ($M—rounded)

	1959			1960			1961		
	RCAC	WU	ACR	RCAC	WU	ACR	RCAC	WU	ACR
Revenues									
Transmission revenue	$24,975	$12,615	$26,871	$27,214	$12,371	$29,952	$28,588	$12,051	$30,340
Leased circuit revenues	3,844	2,540	1,971	4,546	1,137	1,701	5,357	551	2,664
Other revenues	860	185	5,586	783	199	3,634	858	201	3,443
Total revenues	$29,679	$15,340	$34,428	$32,543	$13,707	$35,287	$34,803	$12,813	$36,447
Expenses									
Maintenance expense	$ 1,717	$ 3,028	$ 5,457	$ 2,078	$ 2,311	$ 5,938	$ 2,238	$ 2,434	$ 5,007
Operations and other expense	18,431	9,412	24,494	20,858	9,115	26,652	22,535	9,255	26,614
Administrative expense	2,540	319	1,819	2,731	335	1,942	2,894	344	1,758
Total expenses	$22,688	$12,759	$31,770	$25,667	$11,761	$34,532	$27,667	$12,033	$33,379
Operating income	$ 6,991	$ 2,581	$ 2,658	$ 6,876	$ 1,946	$ 755	$ 7,135	$ 780	$ 3,068
Other income, net	(18)	249	785	633	(284)	331	735	13	222
Net income	$ 6,973	$ 2,830	$ 3,443	$ 7,509	$ 1,662	$ 1,086	$ 7,871	$ 793	$ 3,291
Provisions for F.I.T.	$ 3,375	$ 900	$ 1,300	$ 3,451	$ 850	$ 175	$ 3,390	$ 400	$ 810
Transferred to earned surplus	$ 3,598	$ 1,930	$ 2,143	$ 4,058	$ 812	$ 911	$ 4,481	$ 393	$ 2,481

Source: FCC.

overseas telegrams[1]

The use of a telegram (also called cable, wire, or radiogram) is well known. The sending of a telegram in the United States is simple:[2] the sender supplies Western Union with his message and it is transmitted by wire through the use of a typewriterlike machine known as a teletype or teleprinter.

When sending a message overseas, however, the process is more complex. All international telegrams are sent overseas from one of three so-called gateway transmission and reception points in the United States, namely, New York, Washington, or San Francisco. Because all carriers do not operate direct circuits to all countries, it is desirable that the sender specify the overseas carrier in order to obtain speed and reduce the chance of error caused by transfers and reprocessing at exchange points. If a carrier is not specified, messages are distributed among the carriers by quota rather than by the most direct routing.

Over the years specific routings have been honored by all telegraph companies operating in the United States, and WU, as the domestic telegraph company, has accepted routed messages anywhere in the United States and delivered them to the specified carrier at the gateway city. By the same token, all incoming messages destined for areas outside the gateway cities or to areas where no international carriers operated offices have been delivered by the international carriers to WU. The exception to this was when the message was sent from or delivered to a gateway city. All U.S. carriers could accept and deliver messages direct in a gateway city.

Rates in 1962 for telegram service to and from selected overseas points are given below:

	Ordinary Telegrams	Letter Telegrams	
Destination	Rate per Word (7 Word Minimum)	22 Word Minimum	Each Additional Word
Argentina	$0.31	$3.41	$0.15½
Ceylon	0.27	2.97	.13½
Germany	0.25	2.75	.12½
Iran	0.34	3.74	.17
Japan	0.34	3.74	.17
Scotland	0.21	2.31	.10½
Trinidad	0.21	2.31	.10½

Source: FCC.

---

[1] Telegraphy: a system of communications between two or more points in which electric impulses are transmitted and received as signals in accordance with a code. The transmission of these electric impulses can be through a wire system—generally a cable—or through wireless radio. The basic instruments involved are a sending key and a sounder. An impulse from the sending key activates a magnet which, by energizing an armature on the sounder, produces clicks. In modern systems these senders and receivers were essentially teletypewriters which converted messages to impulses directly or via perforated tape and converted the impulses at the receiving end to a printed message.

[2] Since 1943, WU had had sole monopoly of domestic telegraph messages. It had become apparent at that time that there was not enough business to support both WU and the Postal Telegraph Co., an ITT subsidiary, which was also engaged in this activity. Through an FCC ruling the Postal Telegraph Co. sold its assets and operations in telegraph service to WU, thus establishing a government sanctioned monopoly.

The participation of the major carriers in overseas message telegrams revenues for 1959–61 is given below:

Carrier	1959	1960	1961
RCAC.........................	31.3%	32.0%	32.6%
ACR..........................	46.1	45.7	45.0
WU...........................	18.1	17.5	17.1
Others.......................	4.5	4.8	5.3
	100.0%	100.0%	100.0%
Total revenue ($MM)..........	$64.25	$65.08	$64.30

Source: FCC.

international "telex" service

This service afforded two-way teleprinter communication between two or more correspondents in foreign countries. Business firms with a sufficient volume of international telegraphic communications could have sending and receiving equipment installed in their offices at a minimum billing charge of $10 monthly. Since anyone who could type could easily operate a teleprinter, this machine was provided for business usage in the firm's own offices and connected by direct wire to the telegraph office of one of the carriers. Much of this equipment was automatic—that is, the signals were transmitted and recorded by the machines without an attendant. The receiving machines printed messages, either in page form or perforated tape as soon as received and even while the machines were unattended, for instance, after the close of the business day. On a telex call the teleprinters at both ends were directly connected by means of an overseas cable or radio channel and charges were based on the length of time the connection was maintained. There was a three-minute minimum charge for all connections; additional time was charged by the minute. The following is an example of telex transmission savings which could be realized on lengthy messages when the minimum telex charge was $9:

Telegram Rates		Number of Words Telex Becomes More Economical Than	
Full Rate	Letter Telegram	Full Rate	Letter Telegram
$0.34	$.17	27	53
0.31	.15½	30	59
0.27	.13½	34	67
0.25	.12¼	37	73
0.21	.10½	43	85

In addition to economy, the direct contact between customers afforded them immediate reply, a written record of the transaction, and the opportunity to clear up misunderstandings on the spot. Telex machines in most overseas countries were each equipped with an automatic device which identified the machine to which it was connected, even when the machine was unattended. As a result, it was possible to transmit overseas one-way after business hours in the country of destination. The messages thus were in the correspondent's office awaiting his attention at the start of the next business day.

Domestic teleprinter Exchange Service (Telex) was offered by WU and the Bell Telephone system (TWX). International telex was inaugurated by RCAC in 1950. ACR adopted the service in 1955 and WU followed in 1960. The participation of the major carriers in overseas telex revenues for the years 1959–61 is given below:

Carrier	1959	1960	1961
RCAC.....................	74.1%	70.0%	64.3%
ACR.......................	25.9	29.0	32.6
WU........................	...	.7	2.5
Other.....................	...	.3	.6
	100.0%	100.0%	100.0%
Total revenue ($MM).........	$ 5.39	$ 7.54	$10.00

leased channel service

This service, introduced commercially by RCAC in 1948, afforded 24-hour, seven days a week telegraph communication with an overseas correspondent by means of a private channel. Since the points were continuously connected, subscribers benefited from immediate service and had complete control over message traffic at all time. The channel was leased from one of the carriers but operated by the customers from their offices. The basic equipment consisted of a keyboard machine used to prepare perforated message tapes; an automatic transmitter into which tapes were fed; a teleprinter which made page copy of messages as they were transmitted; and a receiving teleprinter. This service was particularly attractive to those firms having a considerable volume of traffic to one overseas point. Charges were generally monthly, running around $4,000 a terminal depending on transmission speed of the equipment. The potential capacity, for a normal seven-hour day, was 41,000 words for a 100 wpm channel; 25,000 words for a 60 wpm channel. The participation in overseas leased channel revenues of the major carriers for the years 1959–61 is given below:

Carrier	1959	1960	1961
RCAC.....................	41.0%	53.1%	56.2%
ACR.......................	21.0	21.6	26.0
WU........................	37.9	24.0	14.2
Other.....................	.1	1.3	3.6
	100.0%	100.0%	100.0%
Total revenues ($MM)........	$ 9.37	$ 8.56	$ 9.54

other services

Other communication services offered by the major carriers were photo transmission, data communications, and unilateral press transmission. Photo transmission was used to transmit overseas material that could not be sent in telegraph form: material such as blueprints, legal documents, or a language in a non-Roman alphabet. The increasing use of computers in both government and industry had brought about the inauguration of data transmission. Although this service in 1962 was relatively undeveloped, RCAC had begun operating "Datatelex" service between New York and London, and expected to provide the service to other countries in the near future. Datatelex was capable of transmitting data overseas at the rate of 1,200 bits a second or the equivalent of 1,500 words a minute. Unilateral press transmissions were transmissions which were broadcast to an area or overseas point with the reception the responsibility of the subscriber. Its appeal was limited mainly to press and government usage where large quantities of messages were continually being sent to a single point.

BACKGROUND ON RCAC

RCA was organized in 1919 as a result of suggestions by the U.S. Navy that this country needed an American-owned communications company. The subsequent growth of RCA in other areas besides point-to-point communications made it desirable to organize RCA Communications, Inc., as a separate, wholly owned subsidiary in 1929. As of the middle of 1962, RCAC operated a global network consisting of more than 600 radio and cable channels providing message telegraph service between the United States and 71 countries; telex service to and from 81 countries; and radiophoto service with 48 foreign terminals. RCAC operated the terminals of 14 radiotelephone circuits in the Pacific area and provided two-way program transmission service for broadcasters with almost any point on the globe. In addition, it maintained extensive facilities for communications with ocean-going vessels and ships plying U.S. inland waterways.

RCAC officials endorsed a corporate strategy which involved four main points. First, they believed it was necessary to maintain technical and production superiority both as a competitive necessity and as a desired corporate image. Second, they desired to continue to acquire foreign outlets and channels so as to provide more opportunity for developing their services. Third, they desired to improve customers' awareness of RCAC in terms of its industry leadership, scope of activities and services offered, and as a standard of reliability. Fourth, they desired to stimulate usage of all types of overseas communications, particularly with emphasis on the business sector.

To meet anticipated growth in traffic, RCAC officials had embarked upon a program designed to provide them with the necessary capacity to meet this challenge. They intended to acquire additional coaxial cable channels as these new cables were laid down and expected to obtain additional radio channels utilizing communications satellites.

Exhibit 2. RCA Communications, Inc., marketing department

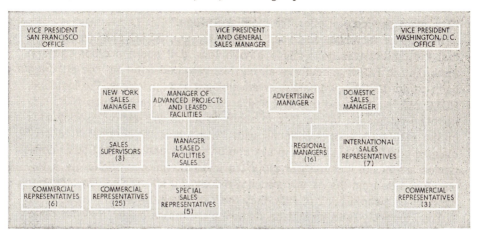

The last two points in RCAC's strategy were the particular domain of the marketing executives. Insofar as possible, it was their responsibility to identify prospects and to educate prospective and current customers as to the scope and quality of RCAC services. Exhibit 2 gives a partial and simplified organizational chart of the marketing department.

MARKETING

In 1962 the three major carriers were aiming at a relatively narrow market, namely, those private individuals, business firms, and government agencies who had a need to communicate overseas. Private individuals were becoming a smaller factor in the telegram business as the total volume of business grew. Business and government usage was, on the other hand, causing the boom.

For the purposes of this case, government usage was not a factor in RCAC's marketing plans. RCAC and the other carriers were engaged in vigorous competition for business with private firms. Since all rates were uniform, competition had to be based on the quality and type of service. Quality could be gauged by reliability, i.e., service free from errors or avoidable delays, as well as speed of message delivery. This speed depended upon the capacity of the route (the number of messages that could travel at the same time) and the directness of route (the number of transfers from carrier to carrier that were necessary in the message relay). The directness of the route also affected the quality of service since most of the errors and delays were generated, as indicated, at the transfer points from carrier to carrier.

The competitive importance of the type of service offered could be illustrated by RCAC's introduction of telex in 1950. Some industry officials believed that it would reduce message telegraph revenue. Public reaction was typically: "What do I need it for? I use cables or overseas telephone." Once business started using it, however, the speed and convenience of the new service made it seem indispensable to its users. As one RCA official put it, "The more service you offer, the more the usage."

In spite of technical advances in recent years, RCAC officials believed that the market was generally apathetic toward it and the other carriers. According to RCAC executives, all carriers provided good service although each carrier had its own particular advantages and limitations. For instance, RCAC officials believed that WU had a great advantage because of its monopoly on domestic telegraph operation; its name was almost synonymous in the minds of most Americans with "wire" and "telegram." "Indeed," claimed one RCAC official, "the average layman is unaware that other companies are in this business at all. WU's international operations get a tremendous ride from the parent company's domestic advertising. On the other hand, when people think of RCA they think of television sets."

The monopoly held by WU on domestic telegrams meant that the other carriers lost control at the message source because most people failed to specify carriers, due to apathy or ignorance concerning the carrier offering the best connections to specific destinations. Compounding this was the aforementioned fact that anyone receiving an overseas telegram at any point in the United States that was not a gateway city received the message on a WU telegram form. RCAC officials believed that it was unlikely that the receiver would notice the carrier initials printed in the routing directions as part of the delivery address. As a result, RCAC received less than 20 percent of its telegraph volume from personal messages and less than 30 percent of its telegraph volume from areas outside its three gateway cities.

RCAC's overseas message telegraph volume, in terms of messages transmitted from the United States, broke down approximately as follows: Originating in New York—50 percent; San Francisco and Washington—20 percent; "Hinterland" (the remainder of continental United States)—30 percent.

RCAC officials attributed much of the success of ACR in certain areas to aggressive personal selling efforts and strong control over its foreign terminals, many of which were in key locations. In many countries ACR had set up its own offices permitting direct dealings with its customers. In many instances this meant better service and more reliable delivery. RCAC chose instead to rely on government-operated offices wherever possible. The reason for RCAC's decision was the belief that eventually the nationalization of all foreign offices would come about as nations increased in their desire to control all their communications facilities. Thus RCAC preferred to assist foreign nations to operate their own international communications instead of competing with them at the foreign end of the terminal.

prospects

Almost every business which had any occasion to communicate overseas soon requested a cable address. This enabled any firm or organization to save words on its address. (For example, the Harvard University Graduate School of Business Administration, Soldiers Field, Boston 63, Massachusetts, was simply: HARBUS.) The over 30,000 registered cable addresses contained, for all practical purposes, the total market for overseas communication as far as the gateway cities were concerned. (For the purposes of the case, press and government usage was not being considered.) These cable addresses were registered by a central agency and supplied to all carriers every month. These addresses were studied by all carriers as a possible source of new business.

As a further refinement to the cable address lists, RCAC's research department analyzed all traffic handled by RCAC lines. Although the department did not have access to information regarding customers who used competing carriers, the research staff could often evaluate a customer's outgoing traffic and determine opportunities for telex or leased channel sales from this pattern. For instance, telex transmission reduced telegraph costs when the time required to transmit a given number of words by telex cost less than the telegram charge for the same number of words.

By the same token, an analysis of incoming traffic could be similarly rewarding. As an example, a particular firm might be receiving a large volume of service via RCAC from Tehran. A check might reveal this firm was not using RCAC to Tehran and so either RCAC was losing business to another carrier or no replies were being sent, which was probably unlikely.

From these and similar activities RCAC was readily able to identify prospects in the gateway cities. In the hinterlands the problem was somewhat more difficult since many firms did not register their cable addresses with the central agency in New York. WU did, however, keep records on these approximately 20,000 firms and charged other carriers 25 cents a name to supply them with addresses. The problem of whom to request cable address information on was solved, in part, by studying traffic flow as in the case of the gateway firms. Certain industries also gave indication of good potential. The bulk of overseas communication was done in 1962 by banks, stockbrokers, import and export firms, insurance, and transportation firms.

RCAC personal selling—gateway cities

The prime duties of the sales representatives were to analyze customer needs and to outline to prospective buyers the advantages of using RCAC. Salesmen were selected mainly from current employees, such as radio operators, branch (customer service) office clerks, and other office personnel. After being interviewed and tested they were assigned to a sales supervisor. New salesmen were likely to be in their thirties with probably two years of college education. In selecting salesmen, emphasis was placed on knowledge of the communications business as well as ease of manner and articulate speech. Salary levels for such salesmen, depending on results and experience, ranged from $6,000 to $10,500 a year. In addition, a group

Exhibit 3.   Direct telegraph circuits of major carriers (partial list)

Country	RCA	ACR	WU	Country	RCA	ACR	WU	Country	RCA	ACR	WU
Afghanistan		x		Formosa	x	x		Morocco	x	x	
Argentina	x	x		France	x	x	x	Netherlands	x	x	x
Australia	x			Germany	x	x	x	New Zealand	x		
Austria	x	x		Great Britain	x	x	x	Norway	x		
Azores		x	x	Greece	x			Pakistan	x		
Barbados	x		x	Greenland	x			Panama	x	x	
Belgian Congo	x			Guam	x			Peru	x	x	
Belgium	x	x	x	Guatemala	x	x		Philippine Rep.	x	x	
Bermuda	x	x		Haiti	x	x		Poland	x		
Bolivia	x	x		Hong Kong	x			Portugal	x	x	x
Brazil	x	x	x	Hungary	x	x		Puerto Rico	x	x	x
Bulgaria	x	x		Iceland	x	x		Rumania	x	x	
Caracas	x	x		India	x	x		Saudi Arabia	x	x	
Chile	x	x		Indonesia	x			Spain	x	x	x
China	x	x		Iran	x			Sweden	x		
Colombia	x	x		Iraq	x			Switzerland	x		
Cuba	x	x	x	Ireland	x			Syria	x		
Czechoslovakia	x	x	x	Israel	x	x		Thailand	x		
Denmark	x	x		Italy	x	x	x	Turkey	x		
Dominican Republic	x	x		Jamaica	x	x		U.S.S.R.	x	x	
Ecuador	x	x		Japan	x	x	x	Uruguay	x	x	
Egypt	x	x		Korea	x			Venezuela	x	x	
Ethiopia		x		Lebanon	x			Yugoslavia	x		
Finland	x			Liberia	x						

Source: RCAC.

incentive based on market share penetration in words transmitted could add from 4 percent to 6 percent to the base salary.

Salesmen submitted daily reports on those accounts which involved sales activity, i.e., a telex installation; monthly reports were also submitted by salesmen which summarized all account activity. Each sales office kept a Kardex file which showed billing records on all accounts. By matching the date of the salesman's call to telegram activity of the account, the supervisor could determine the relative effectiveness of account coverage. Each salesman was responsible for keeping close track of the total number of messages sent and received by his accounts and for developing sound recommendations for directing more business through RCAC channels. Salesmen in the New York office averaged 10 calls a day.

The salesman's job when calling on established accounts was to remind the firm's personnel of the benefits of using RCAC services. For instance, the firm might be using RCAC to Europe and another carrier to the Middle East. The salesman attempted to point out the advantages of using RCAC to that area also. He also attempted to get the U.S. company to ask their foreign correspondents to use RCAC for messages to the United States. For this purpose the salesman provided his customers with printed routing request forms which the salesman attempted to get the customers to fill out and send to their overseas correspondents. At a given level of communication volume, the salesman might recommend the installation of an RCAC teleprinter. (As previously mentioned, this equipment carried a $10 minimum monthly billing charge.)

In calling on new accounts the salesman attempted to get RCAC "Desk-Fax"[3] equipment, or a call box,[3] installed in the prospect's office. Since a call box was free to the customer, RCAC attempted to place it only if it thought future traffic would warrant the installation. RCAC officials believed that other carriers were not always this selective and tended to place this equipment in as many places as they could. There was a $10 minimum monthly billing charge for a "Desk-Fax" installation. It was generally believed that the presence of a carrier's equipment in an office tended to channel most of the telegram business to that specific carrier. Whether or not the RCAC salesman succeeded in placing RCAC equipment in the prospect's office, he attempted to explain to the prospect the advantages of using RCAC direct overseas communication facilities. Exhibit 3 gives company data comparing RCAC direct routes with major competing carriers.

---

[3] "Desk-Fax" was a small facsimile telegraph-sending machine. The message could be typed on a "Desk-Fax" blank, and placed on a revolving drum which submitted the typed message to a "scanner" which translated this printed matter to electrical impulses. This signal was then transmitted to a central telegraph office where it was connected to the destination point and automatic transmission began. A call box was a signaling device which indicated to the carrier that a customer wished to transmit a message. A messenger was sent to collect the message from the customer.

RCAC personal selling—hinterlands

It must be reemphasized that RCAC could only transmit and receive overseas messages in the three gateway cities. The problem in the hinterlands, therefore, was to persuade prospective users of overseas communication facilities to specify that telegrams or telex calls be placed "via RCA." This could be done by dialing the RCAC number and then requesting the overseas connection. In the case of TWX calls, RCAC absorbed the local TWX toll for these calls by having the customer call RCAC collect; if WU equipment was used, RCAC did not absorb the cost of the domestic portion of the routing. RCAC was able to provide leased channels to customers in the hinterlands, but had to charge these firms for the control lines into the gateway offices.

It was felt that personal selling efforts should only be directed toward companies with substantial overseas communication requirements. Personal selling in the hinterlands was done by the regional managers covering, by themselves, fairly large territories. For example, the regional manager in Boston covered all of northern New England. These regional managers were senior salesmen who were left pretty much on their own. They received higher salaries than the commercial representatives, plus travel expenses, but the selling job was similar, as was the analysis and record keeping.

problems in personal selling

Identifying the right man to see within a company was usually not a serious problem. Large companies often had communications managers; smaller operations generally delegated this function to an office manager. Top executives were not often involved in deciding a choice of carrier but could and often did become involved in decisions regarding use of telex or leased channels. (Leased channel sales were handled by special representatives. Since this was a "big ticket" item involving much analysis and groundwork, negotiations quite often took a year or two before final arrangements were consummated. Commercial representatives would often "bird-dog" leads for the leased-channel salesman, receiving a spot bonus of from $100 to $300, depending on the facilities, when the final sale was made.)

Overseas telegram business was not stable within a company. In the opinion of RCAC officials, many companies made a practice of "sharing the wealth," dividing their business between carriers in order to enjoy the facilities of more than one carrier. To many companies such overseas telegram activity was a small-cost item though the monthly bills could be very substantial. Sometimes subsequent costs could be a determining factor in the decision of an executive not to use one or another of the services. Errors and delays, for instance, in overseas communication could lead to a loss of revenue. An individual user might not be aware of such a possibility until faced with a problem such as missing the deadline for placing a bid. All of the carriers, often through no fault of their own, lost business from time to time due to errors and delays. One "foul-up" could set a carrier back seriously in the eyes of the customer. Quite often a carrier was blamed for bad service on incoming messages due to mishandling at the point of origin. A carrier's liability for damages arising from error or delay was limited by law to $500; foreign carriers had no liability. In addition, FCC disallowed payments for "goodwill."

advertising and promotion

The RCAC advertising program was designed to inform the business community about RCAC services, make the RCAC name synonymous with industry leadership, and supplement RCAC's personal selling efforts. According to RCAC officials, ACR did little advertising, depending mainly on personal selling, while WU International received a "big ride" from the WU domestic advertising.

RCAC's advertising budget was set at approximately one half of 1 percent of next year's estimated sales. In addition to a limited budget, about $165,000 for 1961, there were other problems. Media selection appeared difficult because the 20 percent of RCAC's customers which produced 80 percent of the business were in many different industries. Copy also was a problem because educational efforts could easily get tied up by the technicalities of the service. As one official put it, "Try to print up some literature advising a customer how to send overseas messages on a TWX Teleprinter." (TWX teleprinters had different characteristics from those supplied by the international carriers. For instance, a TWX teleprinter allowed two more characters per line than did standard overseas teleprinters.)

Appeals also seemed difficult to present. Mr. Arbogast said, "Why should a businessman in Detroit care which carrier he uses? That is, until he gets 'burned.' People don't always understand that the more a message gets transferred from one carrier to another the slower and more dangerous, in terms of accuracy, it's going to be. A New York to Tokyo message might possibly be routed via Ceylon by one carrier, as opposed to San Francisco on a more direct routing by another carrier. The price is the same to the customer and there's not much money involved. For this reason it is hard to create interesting copy."

The major portion of RCAC's advertising budget was devoted to direct mail. Lists were prepared from cable addresses and mailings were sent to one or more individuals specified by the salesman as being responsible for the account. Approximately 10 mailings were made each year to about 47,000 names. The majority of the mailings were couponed, but coupon returns were negligible because, according to Mr. Arbogast, customers expected the salesman to call anyway.

Testimonials were a favorite direct mail inclusion. Exhibit 4 gives a typical example of the approach used which, according to Mr. Arbogast, "allows us to give a standard sales message while maintaining variety in our story."

Exhibit 4. A centerfold layout for a direct mail advertisement

M-20

DROUGHT DESTROYS GRAIN IN ARGENTINA...
INSECTS CAUSE HEAVY CROP DAMAGE IN
MIDDLE EAST...TWO VESSELS COLLIDE
IN ST. LAWRENCE RIVER...

These are more than just news headlines. They are vital pieces of intelligence that have immediate repercussions all over the world.

For example, drought in Argentina may cause a sudden and drastic reduction of that country's feed-grain exports. As a result purchasers of Argentine grains must now look elsewhere. Within minutes, U.S. grain exporters like Bunge are racing the clock to deliver a quotation.

Insect damage in the Middle East leads to smaller barley and cotton crops. Again buyers need quick replacements and Bunge specialists rush to fill the gap.

Two vessels collide in the St. Lawrence River. One of the vessels carrying wheat to a flour mill in London will be laid up for weeks. The miller must have immediate replacement to keep his mill in operation. A rapid exchange of overseas telegrams between Bunge, the miller, the captain of the ship, and the ship owners, answers the buyer's urgent need without loss of time.

Speed, speed, speed. This is the essential ingredient in the grain trade. News must reach the exporter almost as quickly as events happen. Communications between buyer, seller, and shipper must be swift, accurate, and dependable.

DECISION MAKERS — Bunge commodity traders and freight experts confer daily to coordinate trade activities and decide on the selling offers to be made to buyers overseas.

Round Table Conference Shot — Angle Down

A COMPANY OF STATURE

Established in 1923, Bunge Corporation today ranks as one of the foremost commodity exporters in the U.S. — a nation that leads the world in volume of farm production and exports.

According to estimates based on recent Department of Agriculture statistics, Bunge annually handles approximately one tenth of all U.S. exports of grains, oil seeds, oils, and fats.

Its global network of 110 offices in 80 countries is staffed with farm-marketing experts and foreign trade specialists who provide a diversity of world-wide services: buying, selling, storing, grading, freighting, trucking, barging, shipping.

Bunge operates a nation-wide system of offices in most major U.S. farm centers, and grain storage and handling facilities in major U.S. grain-producing areas.

BUNGE USES RCA

Recently a Bunge specialist in New York received a message containing a bid for a cargo of soybeans from Bunge's Antwerp office. In Belgium it was nearing four p.m. Very little time remained to complete the transaction before European offices closed.

There were other complications, too. Soybean prices are among the most volatile in the agricultural trade. Many factors affect the soybean crop and cause frequent wild price fluctuations. There was also the risk of a sharp change in market price during the time interval between Bunge's reply and the buyer's answer.

The Bunge specialist went right to work. First, he called Chicago and checked the market price of soybeans. Then he cabled London, a world freight market to locate a ship of the right size available for the desired loading period. Next, Bunge's man calculated the freight and insurance rates. After compiling all this information, the offer was sent directly to Bunge's Antwerp office via the company's private RCA telegraph channel — this circuit connects Bunge's headquarters in New York with their Antwerp office 24 hours a day.

A few minutes later the answer came — awarding the bid to Bunge.

Transactions like these are all part of a day's work at Bunge — soybeans to Antwerp, corn to Norway, barley to Germany, wheat to Venezuela, tallow to South Africa, cottonseed oil to Pakistan. These are just a few of the many thousands of transactions that flash back and forth between buyer and seller around the world — around the clock — via RCA Communications.

GRAIN TRAFFIC CONTROL — These Bunge traffic men keep the wires humming as they stay on top of each grain shipment up to final moment of delivery.

Shoot Down Long Row of Desks

"Bunge relies heavily on RCA leased channels, telex, and overseas telegraph not only because these facilities enable us to communicate at high speed, but also because they furnish a written record of each transaction for future reference.

"For over 40 years this Company has been highly satisfied with the caliber of service provided by RCA Communications. We appreciate how much RCA has contributed in helping us to attain our present position of leadership in the competitive world of commodity trading."

Show Head & Shoulders

WALTER C. KLEIN, PRESIDENT OF BUNGE CORPORATION—

RCA SERVES COMMERCE AND INDUSTRY

RCA Communications acknowledges with pleasure the complimentary remarks made by Mr. Walter C. Klein, President of Bunge Corporation, regarding the quality of RCA service to Bunge.

Today, modern global communications are becoming increasingly important not only in the conduct of the export business, but also in the growth of many other fields of commerce and industry. Airlines, automobile manufacturers, international bankers, shipping companies, and stock brokers, to name but a few, rely heavily on the world-wide services of RCA Communications. RCA offers all five services: overseas telegraph, telex, dataplex, leased channel, and radiophoto. If overseas communications are essential in your business, we invite you to consult your nearest RCA representative — or direct your inquiries to the Manager of Commercial Research.

RCA AT WORK — This battery of teletypewriter machines puts Bunge specialists in constant touch with buyers and sellers around the globe via RCA telex and leased channels.

BUSY NERVE CENTER (front cover) — Commodity board in Bunge's New York offices automatically posts prices as changes occur at Chicago and Kansas City commodity exchanges.

Printed in U.S.A. B155-962

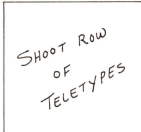
Shoot Row of Teletypes

RCA COMMUNICATIONS, INC.
66 Broad St., New York 4
812 M. St., N.W., Washington 6, D.C. ■ 135 Market St., San Francisco 5

(RCA) THE MOST TRUSTED NAME IN COMMUNICATIONS

The advertising department kept close watch on the mailing list and reminded regional managers and commercial representatives to maintain accurate records. Once a year a mailing was made by first class, from which the advertising department was quickly able to verify "dead wood."

Direct mail was supplemented by a print-media advertising program in *The Wall Street Journal* and the *Journal of Commerce.* Exhibit 5 gives some typical ads used in these media. Mr. Arbogast was uncertain as to the value

Exhibit 5. Examples of advertisements used in newspapers

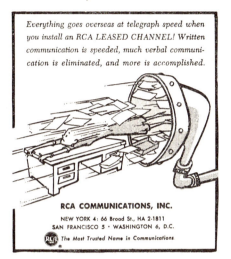

Exhibit 6. Layout of an advertisement to be used in a trade journal

RCA'S MODERN HIGH-SPEED COMMUNICATIONS

enable the Overseas Division of First National City Bank to maintain contact with the world's principal banking centers as well as remote areas of the globe ...faster, easier and more efficiently than ever before

Recently, a ship built in Japan was sold to a buyer in Norway. First National City financed the transaction from New York, while the principals remained thousands of miles apart. The time was 8 a.m. in Norway ... 4 p.m. in Tokyo ... 2 a.m. in New York when the principals gathered in their respective cities. They completed all arrangements, including the transfer of millions of dollars from New York to Tokyo and the registration of the ship in Norway, quickly and easily, right on the spot — via long-distance RCA Telex.

There was a time when an overseas banking transaction consumed, not minutes, but hours — sometimes days.

After World War II, however, came a steady expansion in world trade, accompanied by a mushrooming in the volume of overseas banking that has continued to the present day.

And what happened in international communications has been equally dramatic and progressive. For international banking requires communications systems that are constantly growing and becoming more diversified.

SPEED, VOLUME AND DIVERSITY

Goods move quickly, so must money.

Today at First National City in excess of 1200 overseas messages are handled each working day in New York alone.

Hundreds of thousands of banking transactions a year, handled by First National City, mean volumes of overseas communications, ranging from the transfer of money to the issuance of commercial letters of credit — the routine to the complex.

Eighty-six First National City branches in 30 foreign countries are staffed by over 7,000 people who have more than 27,500 years of combined experience in international banking. The Bank, together with its correspondent banks in the world's leading cities, today serves the economic needs of the international business community.

COMMUNICATIONS AT FIRST NATIONAL CITY BANK

Nerve center at First National City is the Telegraph and Cable Department located in the Bank's Uptown Headquarters, 399 Park Avenue, New York.

This large deceptively quiet room houses batteries of teletypewriters which, by means of modern communication circuits, are constantly in touch with branch offices, banks, and customers around the world.

In the Cable Department an automatic conveyor system adds to the efficiency by whisking messages between personnel stationed at the far ends of this huge communication center.

The department is in continuous operation. Messages in an impressive volume pour through it enroute to and from all parts of the world — 24 hours a day, the year 'round.

FIRST NATIONAL CITY BANK SAYS:

The Bank has always been aware of the important role international telegraphic communications play in the conduct of international banking. In our opinion, modern communication services which feature fast, accurate customer-to-customer connections are essential to the conduct of international trade.

The advent of modern telegraphy, telex, leased channel and radiophoto services has provided those of us engaged in international commerce and trade with communications tools ideally shaped to meet our specific requirements.

With this in mind, First National City is pleased to state that the scope and quality of the service provided by RCA Communications for more than three decades is completely satisfactory. The bank's position as a leader in the field of international banking has been helped immeasurably by modern, accurate communications.

SHOT OF OFFICE AREA

FILING DEPT.— SHOW SORTER

LONG SHOT OF TELETYPES

V.P. STANDING BY WALL MAP

The Europe, Africa, Middle Eastern District is housed in this huge area in the Bank's Overseas Division, Park Avenue Headquarters Building, New York.

A single day's messages, more than 1200 in all, are prepared for filing in the Bank's Cable and Telegraph Department.

The Bank's busy communications center is in constant touch with branches, banks, and customers around the world — 24 hours a day.

Walter B. Wriston, Executive Vice President, in charge of the Overseas Division of First National City's world wide banking system, at desk showing operations of First National City 'world wide' operations.

of space advertising and, in addition, he believed that the budget did not allow for the constant, repetitive, adequate-size advertising he believed to be necessary.

Foreign trade magazines were continually soliciting him to buy space. Typical of these was the *German-American Trade News* with a circulation of 13,500, of which 5,000 was in New York, New Jersey, and Pennsylvania, and a full-page, black-and-white rate of $300. He felt that if he took one of these magazines he would be pressured to take all. He had likewise considered using industry trade journals but felt that the problem in these was that the potential was so broad, that with a limited budget RCAC would have to restrict itself to a handful of magazines from the scores of effective ones available. Almost every industry served by RCAC had its own trade journal but none was viewed as important enough percentage-of-saleswise to justify the expense of advertising. The only exception to this was a three-times-a-year insertion of the "First National City Bank" piece (Exhibit 6) or something similar as a centerfold in the *International Trade Review* and *Export and Shipper*.

RCAC also spent some money each year on conventions and trade shows in the gateway cities. Publicity was hard to place, according to Mr. Arbogast, because interest in the industry was limited. Radio spots on the NBC station in New York were tried during 1961. The spots, twice daily on Saturday and Sunday, were used over a three-month period and "plugged" telex and RCAC credit cards. RCAC officials believed that radio advertising proved to be too expensive since the percentage of potential RCAC customers in the listening audience was very small.

RCAC advertising expenditures for 1961 broke down as follows:

Direct mail (including preparation)...............$110,000	
Space	
Wall Street Journal..............................	5,000
Journal of Commerce............................	4,000
International Trade Review, Export and Shipper,	
and miscellaneous.............................	13,000
Conventions and trade shows.....................	5,000
Sales promotion items, instruction pamphlets,	
directories, sales presentations, etc..............	28,000
Total..	$165,000

Of this dollar amount, approximately 30 percent featured message telegrams, 60 percent featured telex service, and 10 percent featured leased channels.

THE MARKET SURVEY

It seemed to Mr. Arbogast that the Market Survey, which had cost RCAC $5,000, contained information regarding RCAC's current position that might be useful in developing the marketing plan for 1963. He was open to any reasonable suggestions as to how the survey data should be interpreted. In particular, he was interested in any analysis of the data which might contribute to the formulation of the 1963 marketing plan.

The Appendix gives the first 12 pages of the report to RCA Communications by the independent market research firm on "International Overseas Communication Survey—1962," together with the questionnaire.

APPENDIX: INTERNATIONAL OVERSEAS COMMUNICATION SURVEY— JUNE, JULY, AND AUGUST, 1962

preface or purpose of study

This study was conducted to develop information on:

a) Knowledge—familiarity with companies providing international overseas communications.
b) Concepts or impressions about overseas communication services and the companies providing these services.
c) Procedures used by overseas communication companies to keep business and industry informed about their services.
d) The position or title of people controlling the selection of companies or services used for overseas communications.

method and scope of study

This study was conducted by three different methods: personal interview, telephone, and direct mail.

The interviewers did not know the identity of the company for which the study was being conducted, and all direct mail material was on [our] letterhead.

The interviews, by the three methods, were confined to the list of firms and individuals in the New York City area having registered codes (approximately 30,000).

Preparatory to the main study, the questionnaire and procedure was developed and tested in actual production.

The personal interview phase involves 128 contacts, which resulted in completed interviews—refusals to cooperate were a low percent.

Firms and individuals contacted in the personal interview phase of the study were selected from the 30,000 list, but were confined largely to the following classifications of business:

Brokers	Chemical firms
Banks	Drug firms
Importers, exporters, shippers	Airlines
News media	Insurance (marine)

(Large manufacturers and prestige firms, as institutes, etc.)

(A random tabulation of the 30,000 list showed the name of a person on 37 percent, with 63 percent showing only firm names.)

The study is presented in the following manner: (1) a general summary and analysis, covering highlights; and (2) the complete tables for the various questions.

summary and analysis

First—Familiarity of the firms and individuals with overseas communication services and the companies supplying these services. Every effort was made not to assist the respondents in reporting their knowledge or familiarity with companies and/or services.

R.C.A. was predominantly identified by those three letters. Western Union was reported, in most cases, in this manner or as W.U. American Cable and Radio was reported as A.C. & R., Mackay, All American, Globe, Commercial, and in a few instances as I.T.&T.

Generally, R.C.A. seems better known in the overseas communications field than Western Union, or A.C. & R. French Cable is known in a limited way, but seems highly regarded.

From the standpoint of knowledge of services provided by overseas communication companies, some services are well known and some are practically unknown.

In response to the question: "Please list/report the names of companies in the overseas communications service" (Question 1):

88% reported R.C.A.

71% reported Western Union.

65% reported A.C. & R. (49% A.C. & R., 12% Mackay, 11% All American, 3% Commercial, 5% Globe—adds to more than 65%; some reported more than one A.C. & R. Division.)

21% reported French Cable.

Opinion on services provided by the respective companies (Question 2):

	R.C.A.	Western Union	A.C. & R.
Leased channel service	17%	14%	12%
Telex	37	19	27
Data transmission	10	4	3
Marine telegraph service	17	6	13
Program transmission service	5	2	2
Photo service transmission	12	5	5
Overseas telegraph service	48	41	39
Night letter	60	52	46
Full rate	62	50	46
Others	7	5	5

Percentages based on total number of respondents—465.

Services used by the respondents showed the following.

Night letter. 83
Overseas telegraph service. 57
Full rate. 85
Telex. 33
Marine telegraph service. 10
Leased channel service. 9
Photo service transmission. 3
Data transmission. 1
Program transmission service. 1
Other services. 8

Average number of services used by respondent—3.

The above table indicates percent of respondents reporting that type of service—not necessarily
relative volume of types of services.

*Second—Concepts or impressions about overseas communication serv-
ices and the companies providing these services.* The section of the study
and report covers impressions of the respondents on several factors, and
they are handled as sub-headings of the above.

Company or carrier which has done the most to develop new services for
the international businessman (Question 3): About one third of the respondents reported they did not know. R.C.A. received more mentions than the
other carriers combined. (Some reported for more than one company.)

41% reported R.C.A.

11% reported Western Union.

13% reported A.C. & R.

International carrier having the largest global communication network
(Question 4): Here again, about 4 out of 10 reported they did not know.

39% reported R.C.A.

9% reported Western Union.

12% reported A.C. & R.

At this point we believe it valuable and interesting to present the results
of question 16 which states: "What company provides the best service to
Europe, the Far East, and South America?" The table below shows those
reporting each of the three.

	Europe	Far East	South America
R.C.A. 42%	37%	24%
Western Union. 20	7	10
A.C. & R. .20	13	30

Carrier which introduced international leased channel service (Question 5): In answer to this question, about two thirds (68%) reported they did
not know.

20% reported R.C.A.

10% reported Western Union.

3% reported A.C. & R.

Carrier which first inaugurated international telex service (Question 6): Approximately 6 out of 10 reported they did not know.

27% reported R.C.A.

8% reported Western Union.

5% reported A.C. & R.

Opinion—whether night letter service is always the cheapest way to telegraph overseas (Question 7): Most of the respondents had an opinion on this. The opinion was fairly evenly divided between "yes" and "no."

43% reported it is the cheapest way.

47% reported it is not.

10% did not know.

Opinion—if respondent had a considerable volume of overseas communication to one overseas point, which of the three services (overseas telegram, telex, or private leased channel) would they use? (Question 8): The majority had an opinion on this, but it varied considerably. (This is a hypothetical question, hinging on the factor if they had considerable overseas communications to one point.) Overseas telegram was stated by 35%; telex by 28%; private leased channel by 22%; the balance (15%) was not sure.

Furthermore, the respondents did not seem to differentiate between the carriers according to the aforementioned three services. R.C.A. received more mentions than either of the other companies, but respondents did not associate any one company with a particular service, except Western Union showed up low on telex.

	Overseas Telegram	Telex	Private Leased Channel
R.C.A.	47%	63%	59%
Western Union	25	14	27
A.C. & R.	24	28	23

Which carrier would be called if respondents wished to send a blueprint or document in a non-Roman language overseas (Question 9):

54% reported they wouldn't know.

31% reported R.C.A., 10% A.C. & R., 8% Western Union.

The same pattern of response held true for telephone, personal, and direct mail phases.

Third—procedure and effectiveness of carriers in keeping business and industry informed about advances or improvements in the communications industry. This section of the study indicated A.C. & R. is doing a more aggressive job than seemed to be reflected in the sections of the study on "knowledge or familiarity with overseas communications carriers," or in the section on "concepts and impressions."

Carrier which keeps respondents best informed on advances or improvements (Question 10): The majority of the respondents had an opinion on this. (Some mentioned two companies.)

22% reported they didn't know.

47% reported R.C.A.

21% reported A.C. & R.

13% reported Western Union.

Methods used to keep business informed (Question 10a): This is analyzed by the three companies in the following table, and is based on the reporting of each company in the preceding analysis. Note many respondents reported more than one method.

	R.C.A.	Western Union	A.C. & R.
Personal call...................54%		59%	76%
Advertising—trade papers, newspapers........29		28	21
Direct mail...................81		75	68

The above table is based on number reported each company keeps them informed, not on the total number of interviews. Example, percentages under R.C.A. are based on those reported R.C.A. keeps them best informed. Note the relatively high per cent on A.C. & R.

Have noticed advertising on overseas communication services (Question 11): 32% reported they have seen advertising on overseas communication services. Some answered yes to the question, but did not report or recall the company.

12% reported R.C.A.

9% reported Western Union.

4% reported A. C. & R.

These percents were based on number recalling advertising of each company.

	R.C.A.	Western Union	A.C. & R.
New York Times..............14%		26%	13%
Wall Street Journal...........11		18	31
Journal of Commerce......... 7		3	6
New York Herald-Tribune...... 7		8	13
Business Week............... 9		8	6
Time magazine.............. 7		8	—
All others....................11		8	19
Not sure where it was seen....48		38	50

The above represents total for telephone, personal, and direct mail.

Publications read regularly by the respondents (Question 11*b*): The business section of *The New York Times* showed first, and *The Wall Street Journal* second in number mentioning each publication. Of those interviewed by personal call, 77% reported the business section of *The New York Times,* and 54% *The Wall Street Journal.*

Publications read regularly (based on total respondents—374)

```
Business Week.....................................37%
New York Times....................................75%
New York Herald–Tribune...........................37%
New York World–Telegram & Sun.....................40%
Journal of Commerce...............................33%
U.S. News & World Report..........................25%
Wall Street Journal...............................44%
All Others........................................21%
```

Respondents on the factor of receiving direct mail outlining services on overseas communications (Question 12): 63% reported they receive direct mail. Of those receiving direct mail:

76% reported from R.C.A.

32% from Western Union.

43% from A.C. & R.

Company which provides the most helpful items, such as reference books, rate computers, time charts, etc. (Question 13):

36% reported they didn't know.

37% reported R.C.A.

10% reported Western Union.

21% reported A.C. & R.

(Some reported more than one company.)

Company in the international overseas communication field which gives the best personalized service (Question 14):

42% reported R.C.A.

13% reported Western Union.

24% reported A.C. & R.

26% were not sure.

(Some respondents reported more than one company.)

Examples of what they like about the services of the respective three companies, and services which they consider unsatisfactory are presented in verbatim form. However, what they like is promptness on service and repair of equipment, and reporting on delay in message. Contrariwise, they dislike not being informed of delays, and laxness on service or repairs.

If selection had to be narrowed down to using one company in the overseas communication field, which carrier would you choose (Question 17): The response to this question did not vary much from answers to other questions or preferences of service of the three companies.

43% reported R.C.A.

14% reported Western Union

19% reported A.C. & R.

21% reported they were not sure which company they would choose. (Some reported two or more companies.)

Interest in sending and receiving computer produced data internationally (Question 18): Of the total respondents:

6% reported they are interested in sending and receiving computer produced data.

85% reported "no."

9% were indefinite.

Title or position of people controlling the selection of international communication services (Question 15): The response to this question indicated that the major decision on company and type of service used is decided, in most instances, by a top executive: President, Vice President, Owner-Partner.

The manager, or assistant manager, or supervisors of communications are important in the largest companies using international communications services to a large extent, but in the medium and small company, it is someone at the executive or managerial level who makes the decision. (For example, 54% of those exerting a major influence are in the executive group.)

```
Executive group.............................54%
Managers of departments (general)...........14%
Managers—supervisors of communications....10%
Clerical, secretary..........................9%
Foreign department...........................5%
All others..................................11%
Difficult to say............................17%
```

(Some mentioned more than one position or title. Minor influence was negligible, 69% reporting no minor influence.)

brief discussion and summary of the study

Generally, the three companies—R.C.A., Western Union, and A.C. & R.— are well respected and services are satisfactory.

R.C.A. is known by more respondents as inaugurating new services and seems to be generally regarded as the leader in this field in practically every phase except one.

A.C. & R. is regarded by more respondents as giving better service to South America than R.C.A. or Western Union.

Sales effort is comparable, although A.C. & R. seems to be doing a very aggressive sales contact program.

All three companies are doing an aggressive direct mail program on folders, rate computers, time charts, etc.

Publication promotion has made little impact.

There was more criticism of the service of Western Union than of the other two companies.

The decision of the company to use the service(s) is largely up to the people at the executive or managerial level.

INTERNAL OVERSEAS COMMUNICATION SERVICE SURVEY
(Please fill in without referring to any reference material.)

Familiarity with companies in the international or overseas communication service and services provided.

1. Please list the names of companies which provide international overseas communication service.

_____   _____   _____

_____   _____   _____

2. Which overseas communications companies offer or provide the following respective services?

a) Check (V) if used by your company.

List of Services	*Which Companies Provide These Overseas Services*	*Check (V) if Used by Your Company*
Leased channel service	_____ _____ _____	( )
Telex	_____ _____ _____	( )
Data transmission	_____ _____ _____	( )
Marine telegraph service	_____ _____ _____	( )
Program transmission service	_____ _____ _____	( )
Photo service transmission	_____ _____ _____	( )
Overseas telegraph services	_____ _____ _____	( )
Night letter (LT)	_____ _____ _____	( )
Full rate (FR)	_____ _____ _____	( )
Other services	_____ _____ _____	( )

Concepts or impressions about overseas communication services and the companies providing services.

3. Which U.S. carrier, in your opinion, has done more to develop new services for use by the international businessman? _____

4. Which U.S. international carrier has the largest global communications network? _____

5. Which U.S. carrier introduced international leased channel service in this country? _____

6. Which U.S. carrier first inaugurated international Telex service?
_____

7. Is night letter service always the cheapest way to telegraph over-seas? Yes ( ) No ( )
   Comments: _____
   _____
   _____

8. If you had a considerable volume of overseas communications to *one* overseas point, which of the following services would you use? (Please check)
   Overseas telegrams ( )
   Telex ( )
   Private leased channel ( )
   a) Which carrier would you contact to get the information about this service? _____

9. If you wished to send a blueprint or a document in a non-Roman language overseas, which carrier would you call? _____

   Procedure(s) in keeping business and industry informed on overseas communications.

10. Which carrier keeps you best informed on advances or improve-ments in the communications industry? _____
    a) How do they keep you informed? (Please check)
    ( ) Personal call
    ( ) Advertising (trade papers and newspapers)
    ( ) Direct mail (letters and brochures)
    ( ) Others: (Please describe) _____

11. Have you noticed any advertising by U.S. telegraph companies on overseas communication services?
    Yes ( ) No ( )
    a) If "yes," in what publications and for what company? _____
    _____ _____ _____
    b) Will you check which, if any, of the following publications you read regularly?

Business Week	( )	*Journal of Commerce*	( )	
N.Y. Times (Business Section)	( )	*U.S. News & World Report*	( )	
		Wall Street Journal	( )	
N.Y. Herald Tribune (Business Section)	( )	Others: (Please list) _____		
N. Y. World Telegram & Sun (Business Section)	( )	_____ _____		

12. Do you receive any direct mail from U.S. telegraph companies out-lining or explaining their services?
    Yes ( ) No ( )
    a) If "yes," from what companies? _____ _____
    _____ _____ _____

13. Which company, in your opinion, provides the most helpful items, such as reference books, rate computers, time charts, etc.?

_____ _____ _____
_____ _____ _____

14. Which company in the international overseas communication field gives the best personalized service? (This refers to the everyday operation in terms of attention, courtesy, and servicing of your organization.) _____

a) Will you please give an example or examples of service which you thought were good?

_____
_____

b) Any example of service which you consider unsatisfactory?

_____
_____

General

15. Will you list the business titles or positions in your company that exert a major or minor influence on the selection of international communication services (e.g., president, vice president, official manager, secretary, etc.)?

Titles or Position of People Who Exert a Major Influence	*Titles or Position of People Who Exert a Minor Influence*
_____	_____
_____	_____
_____	_____

16. Generally, what company, in your opinion, provides the best service to:
Europe _____, The Far East _____,
South America _____?

17. If you had to use only one carrier for your international communications, what carrier would you choose? _____

18. Are you interested in sending and receiving computer produced data internationally?

Yes (   )   No (   )

19. Do you have any suggestions for improvement of overseas communication service?

Comments: _____
_____
_____

Your type of business (mfg., broker, exporter, etc.): _____

Thank you.

case 7–2

MERRILL, INC. (A)*

marketing program for a new product

Merrill, Inc., of Syracuse, New York, one of the world's largest manufacturers of circuit breakers for aircraft and other electrical appliances, developed Mini-Breaker, a household circuit breaker that could be screwed into a fuse socket.[1] Although there appeared to be a profitable potential market for Mini-Breaker, sales and promotional efforts during the first three years were not successful. In the fall of the third year, accordingly, the sales manager faced the task of diagnosing reasons for failure and of working out a marketing program which would result in a profitable sales volume.

DEVELOPMENT OF PRODUCT

Some years ago, W. H. Bell, president of Merrill, Inc., engaged a very able engineer named J. W. Trask. His job was to devise a product which Mr. Bell, with his long business experience and great skill, could manufacture and develop into a profitable item. In carrying out his assignment, Mr. Trask experimented with a new principle for a circuit breaker that would make it possible to design the mechanism in a size small enough to be contained in a regular screw-based fuse case. It was thought that such a device would have certain outstanding advantages. Heretofore, it was necessary to have an electrician rewire the house in order to install one of the many types of circuit breaker boxes then on the market. In contrast, the home owner merely had to screw Mr. Trask's device into each receptacle in his fuse box in order to convert to "push to reset" circuit protection for the life of the home. The breaker, as visualized, would interrupt service on any overload and could be reset to restore service when the overload had been removed by merely pressing a button. This could be done over and over again without damaging the device in any way.

Experimental work proved Mr. Trask's new principle to be sound. Since

* The Merrill, Inc., (A), (B), (C), and (D) cases were written by Peter A. Repenning, Research Assistant, Bureau of Business Research, and James D. Scott, Professor of Marketing, Graduate School of Business Administration, The University of Michigan.

[1] The location and identifying names have been disguised

there was a more pressing need for such a mechanism in aircraft than in the home, company officials decided to produce first for the aviation market. This was done, and after six years Merrill, Inc., had secured a substantial portion of the aircraft circuit breaker business and was a highly successful company. After 10 years, Merrill Inc. had captured an even larger proportion of the aircraft circuit breaker business, and had developed a large business in original equipment circuit breakers which were installed on heavy appliances to protect house lines from overloads originating in these appliances.

After six years of developing the industrial market, the success achieved by the company gave Mr. Trask more time to improve his original development—the household circuit breaker that could be screwed into a fuse socket. He set about to develop such a device, and when he had a working model, he took it to Underwriters' Laboratories, Inc. for approval. There he found that his idea had been far from unique. Many people had tried the same thing, and Underwriters' Laboratories, Inc., officials had been plagued with a constant stream of inventors asking them to test such inventions. The technicians took his sample and put it to the initial test—a 5,000-amp., 125-volt direct current short circuit. As with all other such screw-based circuit breakers tried in the past, the Trask model exploded violently.

Mr. Trask then went back to his laboratory and undertook further developmental work. Some time later he returned to Underwriters' Laboratories, Inc., with 12 new model household circuit breakers. This surprised the technicians, since no inventor, faced with the results of the rugged initial test, had ever tried again. The first circuit breaker not only did not blow up, but it adequately interrupted the circuit. Further, it did not set the cotton wrapped around it on fire. It did not work thereafter, but because of the violence of the test, continued operation was not a requirement to pass the test. While the first of the 12 had passed the initial test, Underwriters' Laboratories, Inc. men, in their disbelief, went through the other 11 samples and to their surprise, all 12 passed the test. Mr. Trask was then sent home to make more samples while the testers thought about what kind of test they would give next. Previously it had not been thought necessary to develop further tests, since no applicant's device had ever passed the first one. After considerable argument as to what classification should be given the device—i.e., whether the device was considered sufficiently good not to require further tests while using the U.L. label on a tentative basis—full approval was finally given, and Mini-Breaker was ready for marketing.

Ten years after Mr. Trask began his developmental work, Merrill, Inc., had many models of circuit breakers on the market for industrial uses. For household use they had, however, only one type of Mini-Breaker in four values—10, 15, 20, and 30 amps. When qualification was imminent, the standard for fuses was introduced. To comply necessitated additional length and because of this, fuse boxes containing Mini-Breakers could not be closed. This was not a drawback if all fuse receptacles contained Mini-Breakers, but if Mini-

Breakers were to be used only on trouble circuits, electrical codes in most cities required that boxes be closed to protect against flash from any of the old type fuses that might blow. Utilities were interested in the product but would not endorse it. Later, Mr. Trask redesigned the Mini-Breaker short enough to be accommodated in any fuse panel with the cover closed. After this development the short Mini-Breaker that allowed fuse box doors to be closed was the only model being manufactured.

During the initial distribution of the product, Sears, Roebuck became interested in having Merrill, Inc., supply the device for distribution under the Sears private brand. Because Merrill, Inc., executives wished to exploit the consumer market themselves, they wanted all prestige from sales to accrue to their own brand name, Mini-Breaker. They were very much against manufacturing under any but their own brand.

INITIAL MARKETING PROGRAM

Before the product had gotten final U.L. approval, the Hawley Advertising Agency was retained to help promote it. The Hawley agency was a very small one, but it had had good experience in the promotion of electrical goods. Mr. Hawley's first move was to prepare an editorial for the McGraw-Hill trade journal *Electrical World.* Soon after that, he prepared two full-page spreads on Mini-Breaker for the same magazine. The response to these two advertisements was excellent, and in a market which is not usually inquiry minded, it was phenomenal. There were hundreds of replies and many sample orders. Because of delay in getting a final decision on the proper U.L. classification for Mini-Breaker, however, it was some time before advantage could be taken of the interest shown in the product by those sending in inquiries.

Many of the inquiries were from manufacturers' agents wishing to represent Merrill, Inc., in their areas. At first, C. P. Jacobs, who preceded O. W. Greaves as sales manager of Merrill, Inc., was against the use of manufacturers' agents in the distribution of Mini-Breaker. Mr. Hawley, however, convinced him that with a single-item line of low unit value, it would be unwise for Merrill, Inc., to set up its own sales organization as a means of getting distribution. In spite of the initial rebuff, manufacturers' agents were still very anxious to get a franchise for their areas. Accordingly, after U.L. approval, 24 agents located throughout the United States were selected to handle the sale of Mini-Breaker.

These agents sold to hardware and electrical supply houses primarily, although some of the agents sold directly to industrial users in large lots.[2] The aim of Merrill, Inc., was intensive distribution in all retail outlets where consumers would think of buying a fuse. After three years, however, only

[2] It was found that industrial users liked Mini-Breaker because a workman could restore his machine to service without violating electrical union rules by replacing a fuse without the aid of an electrician. A minor disadvantage was the pilferage of Mini-Breaker units which resulted because of the ease with which they could be removed.

spotty distribution had been achieved in hardware stores and appliance shops throughout the country. Most hardware stores could produce a Mini-Breaker from some hidden shelf if they were asked to do so. None of the agents attempted to sell Mini-Breakers to utilities.

The initial price of Mini-Breaker was set at $1.50 to the consumer, $1 to the retailer and 75 cents to the wholesaler because of manufacturing cost and distributor and dealer markups. The wholesaler was also allowed a 2 percent cash discount. From the remainder was deducted a 5 percent commission to the manufacturers' agents. After three years of experience with this price schedule, the commission of the manufacturers' agents was increased to 10 percent. This was done in order to induce greater push by the agents. Eight months after the change, however, there was no evidence that the increase in commission had had any effect upon sales.

At this time, after discounts, the company received $0.66 per Mini-Breaker sold. At this figure there was available considerably less than $0.05 per unit for administration and promotion expense.

In planning the initial promotional strategy for Mini-Breaker, the Hawley Advertising Agency recommended only a modest consumer advertising program, but suggested that real effort should be directed to utilities which have free fuse replacement service. Toward this end, Mr. Hawley designed an animated cartoon figure of a girl with a Mini-Breaker body. This, it was hoped, would be used along with "Reddy Kilowatt," the trade character already featured in the promotion of many utilities. All utilities watch the advertising of others to see how they may effectively use this figure, and it was thought that if one utility could be induced to use the two figures together, all would soon take notice of it.

Mr. Hawley's recommendations were not accepted by the executives of Merrill, Inc. They were more interested in selling to consumers than to utilities. As a means of introducing Mini-Breaker to the consumer market immediately in a big way, company executives considered buying a 26-week participation in Arthur Godfrey's radio program. Approval was given to show filmed commercials on television in New York, Chicago, and Syracuse. Even these programs were canceled after three weeks of broadcasts when it became apparent that the distribution pattern was not sufficient to warrant such expenditure. Later, the representative of a national magazine bypassed the Hawley agency and sold Merrill, Inc. some expensive advertisements.

Neither of these attempts was successful in building a profitable consumer demand for Mini-Breaker. Late in the first year after U.L. approval, field contacts with jobbers and manufacturers' agents provided Mr. Hawley with evidence that these middlemen were becoming dissatisfied with the apparent unpopularity of Mini-Breaker and with what they believed to be inconsistent and faulty sales policies of the company. Influenced by these findings, and by the fact that few of his suggestions were followed by Merrill, Inc., executives, Mr. Hawley resigned from the account in December of that year.

ANALYSIS AND RECOMMENDATIONS OF JOHNSON AND BAKER

In May of the following year, the executives of Merrill, Inc., appointed Johnson and Baker as the advertising agency to handle the promotion of Mini-Breaker. Johnson and Baker was a large, well-known advertising agency located in Chicago. In accepting the appointment, Johnson and Baker emphasized the need for three to four months to study the market, existing distribution methods, basic sales appeals, and other important factors before any plans were submitted for consumer advertising.

preliminary report

On August 6, after six weeks of preliminary research and study, Johnson and Baker submitted the following preliminary report dealing with four major topics: the product, sales management and distribution, promotion, and research. Under each of these broad categories, Johnson and Baker presented a brief analysis of existing conditions, including both favorable and unfavorable factors. Recommendations then followed.

The Product

Positive factors:
1. It is a quality, precision-made product.
2. It eliminates "fussing with fuses."
3. It has the approval of Good Housekeeping and Underwriters' Laboratories, as well as many utilities.
4. When properly used, it is practically never defective—it carries a lifetime guarantee.
5. It appeals strongly to people who are uncertain and a little afraid of electricity, as well as those who like convenience and lack of trouble.
6. Its built-in "time-lag" feature is excellent for larger appliances.
7. It is unique in its field, well protected by patents.

Negative factors:
1. Although it meets code requirements in a strict sense, it has been attacked by fuse manufacturers for two reasons: (a) some fuse box doors won't close properly. This is being corrected. (b) Lack of tamperproof characteristic. Easily fixed, if necessary, by liquid solder.
2. The price to consumers at $1.50. This is not necessarily a bad feature. The Mini-Breaker is a quality item, and people appreciate the fact when its advantages are explained to them. The price seems high when people are introduced to the product because the Mini-Breaker has the outward appearance of an ordinary fuse. The prospect instinctively compares the Mini-Breaker with a fuse, and then compares their prices. He thinks of the Mini-Breaker as a fuse rather than as a circuit breaker or circuit protector.
3. The name itself is confusing to many people. It is, of course, a diminu-

tive for "miniature circuit breaker" (although strictly speaking it is not a circuit breaker). While the name has been used effectively with an animated figure, it still does not get across quickly the product's primary function, which is to protect electrical circuits.

4. The Mini-Breaker unit is poorly packaged, and externally there are some minor criticisms of the unit itself. (a) The line around the plunger which shows when tripped, is hard to find. (b) The labels are crowded and cluttered with textual matter. (c) When the labels become dirty, sun-faded, or defaced, there is no easy way to determine amperages.

Recommendations:

Obviously, the good characteristics of Mini-Breaker greatly outnumber the bad. We are all agreed that this is a very fine product, well designed and well manufactured. Tentatively, we would offer these recommendations:

1. Keep the present unit price until more evidence that it is too high is forthcoming . . . we believe people will always claim the price is too high, because they compare Mini-Breaker with a fuse. People must be sold on its advantages . . . on "you can't afford *not* to have a Mini-Breaker." With respect to price, we must face the fact that soon a new, improved Mini-Breaker will be ready, and that there are still hundreds of thousands on dealers' shelves. The raising of the price for the new model to about $1.69, therefore, merits consideration. It would permit more money for promotion and discounts. There is some evidence to the effect that the item could be priced higher without affecting sales adversely. Lowering of the unit price with the appearance of a new model is also a possibility, although it is difficult to see that it would increase sales volume appreciably.

2. We don't advise changing the Mini-Breaker name, but we do recommend that the designation of the item, "circuit-protector," and its functions, "ends fuse problems forever," be given greater prominence.

3. We are currently still studying the packaging of Mini-Breaker, along with point-of-sale material. We intend to recommend a packaging consultant at a future date.

Sales Management and Distribution

Positive factors:

1. The client is well established in the airplane circuit breaker market and its product is of unquestionable quality. So is its companion product, Mini-Breaker.

2. The client enjoys an excellent reputation as a soundly financed business concern with high credit rating.

Negative factors:

1. The sales and distribution problems involved in the marketing of a primarily consumer product are vastly different and more complex than

those encountered in a captive market such as the aircraft industry.

Apparently no established overall sales policy exists. The product is sold through various channels of distribution ranging from house accounts (Sears, Roebuck), manufacturers' agents, and direct distributors to house-to-house retail salesmen.

2. The sales department currently consists of a sales manager and a secretary. The very nature of such a diversified program makes it impossible at present for the sales department to cover all the facets adequately.

3. The client is interested in the widest possible distribution ranging from hardware and electrical retailers to department stores, tobacco stores, country stores, drugstores, food chains, and gas stations. The leading manufacturers' agents (Chicago and New York) maintain that servicing their established wholesale accounts (primarily hardware, electrical, and housewares, selling in turn to their retail outlets) takes a great percentage of their time and thus they cannot go farther afield. Additionally, most want exclusive rights in their territories. The wholesalers are dissatisfied with "spread distribution," and many maintain they will not exert extra effort as long as this condition exists.

4. Utility cooperation in the marketing of such a product is vitally important. Even if the utility does not actively merchandise it, approval is almost mandatory. In some instances utilities have given the impression they did not receive the utmost in cooperation.

5. There does not seem to be close enough liaison between the factory and field representatives. It is not easy to master-mind a nationally distributed product operation from a single office. Experienced representatives on the local scene, familiar with changes in buying attitudes, distributive methods, etc., can be most helpful to the manufacturer, if given encouragement, and reasonable attention paid to his suggestions.

6. Though it is difficult to maintain "fair-trade" prices, there are evidences of price cutting by door-to-door salesmen, by dealers dissatisfied with the slow turnover of their stocks, and, of course, by Sears, Roebuck.

7. Wholesalers are discontented with the client's freight policy of charging freight on shipments of 1,000 units or less. One quoted Bussman's policy of shipping orders of $60, minimum freight prepaid.

Recommendations:

1. We suggest that the client settle upon a definite sales policy and maintain it. Whatever this policy turns out to be, if the manufacturer stays with it, the field represenatives, distributors and dealers will develop greater confidence in the future of Mini-Breaker and their stake in it. This policy should include advertising and promotion activities. In order to build and maintain the confidence of the sales team (distributors and dealers), any proposed promotion program should be carried through to completion.

2. To strengthen sales management, we recommend more assistance for the sales manager.
   a) Appoint an assistant sales manager to relieve Mr. Greaves of much routine detail.
   b) Begin the establishment of a group of regional sales managers (four to eight) who will report to Mr. Greaves and will maintain close contact with the manufacturers' agents, direct distributors and wholesalers in their respective areas.
3. We agree in principle with "spread distribution." We agree that Mini-Breaker should be sold wherever fuses are sold. Today, the hardware and electrical wholesalers (via the manufacturers' agents) seem to be the strongest link in the sales chain. Though the number of their retailers is much smaller than the potential, this method seems to be best in view of the relatively short time the product has been on the market. It would appear that the soundest procedure, in the long run, would be to build upon this base and later strengthen the overall distribution picture with other types of outlets. Summarizing the distribution problem and possible solution, we recommend retaining the present manufacturers' agents, adding to them and gradually replacing those who stick to one or two fields of distribution with established agents who will aggressively increase the distributive channels.
4. The client should do more and more to make the manufacturers' agents a part of the first-string sales team. As this group is developed and strengthened, the small direct distributors should be absorbed or dropped. We have given a good deal of thought to all methods of distribution. We do not believe that a product such as Mini-Breaker can be sold in sufficient volume by mail. We do not feel that bypassing the wholesaler is the answer either. The problems of contacting, shipping, and credit checking on dealers would offset the cost of wholesaler's discount.
5. Price cutting should be policed and every effort made to stop it.
6. The discount structure should be carefully reviewed. There have been complaints on the present structure. Discounts within a trade should be in line with the discount structure of other comparable lines. Otherwise, the client's sales staff will be spending time selling the discount structure—time which could be more profitably spent selling the product and the client behind it. We recommend quantity discounts be given on orders of 5,000 units and up.
7. House accounts should be eliminated in favor of the aforementioned regular channels of distribution. The subject of house accounts includes a discussion of private labels. Sears and one or two direct selling organizations have requested private labels. We are opposed to this policy for several reasons. No customer will furnish guarantee of *continued* business. The client *cannot* control the price factor. The loss of national

recognition of the trademark (M–B) is an important consideration. The only possible reason for resorting to private label would be to reach a channel of distribution, that could not otherwise be reached and that would not conflict with present channels. Sometimes, too, manufacturers use this procedure to pick up slack in production—but it seldom proves profitable.

Potential Market for Mini-Breaker

This investigation has revealed that a sizable market exists for Mini-Breaker. This potential may be divided into five classifications: (1) original equipment, (2) utility free fuse replacement market, (3) industrial and institutional market, (4) new construction market, and (5) the residential replacement market. While a brief evaluation is made below of each of these markets, our research efforts have been concentrated on the residential replacement market.

I. *Original equipment market*

Reliable figures show that the size of the original equipment market is nearly 6 million fuses per year. Further, this market exhibits a long-term growth pattern.

II. *Utility free fuse replacement market*

It is known that a sizable number of fuses are replaced free each year by certain utilities. It is not believed, however, that the free fuse replacement policy in operation by certain utilities will reduce materially the potential market for Mini-Breaker. There are indications that more and more utilities are educating their customers in how to replace fuses and thus eliminate insofar as possible the service call.

III. *Industrial and institutional market*

The industrial and institutional market consists of factories, stores, office buildings, hospitals, schools, and similar buildings. Relatively little evidence has been obtained to indicate the size of this market. It is, however, believed to be much larger than the new construction market.

IV. *New construction market*

Evidence obtained from contractor supply houses, publishing houses and utilities suggests that approximately 80 percent of homes *currently* being erected are equipped with fuse boxes. It is unlikely that contractors can be sold Mini-Breaker for original installation of residential circuit breakers. It should be noted, however, that all new homes which are built with fuse boxes do enlarge the residential replacement market for Mini-Breaker. To illustrate, this year there will be 1.5 million new homes constructed, and 1.2 million (80 percent) will be equipped with fuse boxes. With an average of four fuses per home, the ultimate potential for Mini-Breaker has been increased by 4.8 million.

New industrial construction is not an important market for Mini-

Breaker. Practically all new construction of this type is using circuit breaker installations.

V. *Residential replacement market*

A. *Market potential*

The purely theoretical potential residential market for Mini-Breaker equals household replacement fuse consumption. No precise figures have been obtained to show the exact size of this market. However, the following carefully considered estimates are offered.

(1) Sears, Roebuck claims that its sale of 6 million fuses annually equals 5 percent of the total replacement fuse market. On this basis, the total market would be 120 million fuses.

(2) The consumer survey in Springfield, Ohio, revealed that the average household contacted replaced 2.85 fuses in the past 12 months. When this figure is multiplied by the total number of households (47.5 million) the total fuse replacement market annually would equal 135,375,000. This estimate is based, of course, on an extremely limited sample.

(3) There is strong evidence to suggest that the primary market for Mini-Breaker is in *owner-occupied residences.* Since there are 27 million such residences with an average of four fuses per home, the theoretical potential among home owners would be 108 million. The above computations do not consider the present percent of homes equipped with residential circuit breakers which has been authoritatively estimated at less than 2 percent.

B. *Summary of market potential*

On the basis of the above conservative estimates, the potential for Mini-Breaker would seem to exceed 100 million. This figure would be slightly reduced when homes served by direct current and by utilities offering free fuse service are considered. More important, the estimated figure may be reduced more significantly when consideration is given to the number of circuits in each home which are completely trouble free. Our later research might reveal, for example, that 25 percent of the electrical circuits account for 75 percent of fuse consumption. If this *hypothetical* case were true, the potential for Mini-Breaker would be reduced considerably.

C. *Characteristics of the ultimate consumer market*

On the basis of the consumer interviews conducted in Springfield, Ohio, the following facts have been tentatively established:

(1) The average urban home has four fuses installed. Farm homes, however, tend to have a larger number of fuses as more electrical circuits are needed.

(2) Men do most of the fuse buying and installation. This situation may not be entirely true on farms as farm women are apparently more self-reliant in this regard.

(3) People are accustomed to buying fuses in boxes of four or five. Relatively few persons buy fuses individually.

(4) Consumers are unaware of what brand of fuses exist and therefore exhibit no brand preference.

(5) Few people have an intelligent appreciation of fuse prices. Estimates ranged from 5 cents to 50 cents. Farmers were more precise in their estimates of fuse prices.

(6) When shown Mini-Breaker, approximately one third of the respondents expressed sincere interest.

(7) From the nature of the comments made, tenants are not an important market for Mini-Breaker.

(8) Estimates given with reference to the price people would be willing to pay for Mini-Breaker ranged from 25 cents to several dollars. $1, $1.50, and $1.98 were suggested several times.

Recomendations:

1. Further research should be sponsored in connection with the residential replacement market to expand and verify information gained from consumer interviews conducted in Springfield, Ohio. Specific points which warrant considerably more investigation include:

a) The relative importance of men versus women in making the Mini-Breaker buying decision.

b) The characteristics of the farm market for Mini-Breaker.

c) The best retail outlets for Mini-Breaker.

d) General fuse buying and installation practices and their relation to the sale of Mini-Breaker.

e) The extent to which one or two circuits in the average home tend to cause most of the fuse trouble.

Such research should be conducted on the basis of a carefully constructed nationwide sample which includes an adequate proportion of farmers and urban residents, and high-, middle-, and low-income groups. It is recommended that personal interviews be used to obtain this information and that the actual investigation be made by a national survey organization such as Market Opinion Research, Inc., or A. J. Wood, Inc. A minimum of 5,000 interviews should be conducted to make the findings reliable. Approximate cost of this undertaking will be $15,000. Actually, this will be a very economical measure, for on the basis of the facts uncovered, selling appeals and advertising media can be selected much more carefully with the result that the entire sales effort will be more effective.

2. Additional research is needed to determine with more precision the trend and regional sales pattern of circuit breakers versus fuse box installations in new home construction. This will be extremely helpful in predicting the long-run market potential for Mini-Breaker.

3. It is recommended that carefully planned and controlled research be used to determine the effects of the first advertising campaigns which

were discussed elsewhere in this report. Such rsearch will enable the agency to determine more clearly the nature of the advertising to be used in national or regional sales campaigns.

Promotion

Our preliminary Investigations indicate very little organized and *sustained* promotional effort has ever been put behind the product. Consequently, we can draw no real conclusions from either the previous trade paper or consumer advertising or from sectional promotions such as that started by Sears in Chicago.

To date our research indicates that Mini-Breaker is a sound product with good sales potential. However, we have no reliable basis on which to judge just how effective *real* advertising support of the product can be . . . to what extent we can arouse interest, create consumer demand, increase sales, and facilitate distribution.

An important consideration we cannot overlook is that, at present, Merrill, Inc., has a national sales organization operating entirely without advertising support. Some sales literature, mailers, countercards, displays, ad-mats, etc., are available, but no direct consumer or trade advertising is working for your sales organization to help build consumer demand and trade support.

A limited amount of such advertising was done at one time, but this apparently was done without the full support and cooperation of your sales and distributor groups and was more a sectional than a national promotion. In a few instances we know that there was strong resentment on the part of a few distributors because they were not fully informed of these sectional promotions . . . what they would consist of, when they would start and stop, and how tie-ins could be used effectively.

For these reasons we believe it absolutely essential that we start at once on a limited, but national, advertising program which as a minimum, would be a token advertising program supporting your sales and distributor groups. Such a program would immediately start building consumer interest and demand for Mini-Breaker (urgently needed) and would be a moral and physical encouragement for your agents, distributors, and dealers to renew their enthusiasm and sales efforts.

This national program should be built around small space ads in both consumer and trade publications, maintained on a regular schedule, and fully merchandised to your sales agents, wholesalers, and dealers.

For maximum effect we believe this national program should be carried out over a 12-month period. Estimated costs would be between $35,000 and $50,000, or roughly, $4,000 monthly.

To help determine what this national effort should be, we recommend that several localized, carefully controlled sales promotions be given serious consideration. If carried out effectively, these promotions would be fairly accurate yardsticks by which we could measure consumer acceptance; distributor and dealer cooperation and the most effective distribution channels; importance of TV versus newspaper and radio as Mini-Breaker advertising media; the type of sales tools most useful; the most logical Mini-Breaker prospects; etc. In other words these local promotions would indicate who we want to sell, how we should try to sell them. By projecting these results we could estimate our national market and what it might cost to sell it.

Conclusion

On the previous pages we have condensed our findings, and given you recommendations. These can be summarized as follows:

1. *Strong sales management is necessary*

   Additional personnel should be provided; regional managers methods for getting maximum out of these personnel must also be provided. A program for utility sales should be set up.

2. *Consistent sales policy is necessary*

   This includes determining the best distributive channels and protecting and encouraging them. It includes decisions on pricing, discounts, and house accounts.

3. *Consumer advertising is necessary*

   This includes a modest but consistent magazine campaign, which will later be expanded. It also includes a definite cooperative advertising program for use as desired. Additionally, individual markets should be tested and their results carefully noted.

4. *Packaging and point-of-sale material should be expanded*

   Our advertising must be carefully carried to the point of ultimate purchase. The product must be displayed, and a sales message given.

5. *Continued market research is necessary*

   At the earliest possible time, we should obtain a definite, realistic figure on the market potential. We should learn more about our prospects, and how to fit our product to their buying habits.

If Merrill, Inc., agrees to these recommendations, we are ready to serve you.

QUESTION

Should the management of Merrill, Inc., accept the recommendations of Johnson & Baker? Why or why not?

case 7–3

MERRILL, INC. (B)

advertising and promotional program

Johnson and Baker, an advertising agency, took over the Mini-Breaker account in May of the second year after this product had received approval by Underwriters' Labortories, Inc. In August, after six weeks of preliminary research and study, the agency submitted a series of recommendations outlining a program designed to develop a market for this new product.[1]

After thorough analysis and discussion by the management of Merrill, Inc., the preliminary report was approved. Johnson and Baker then continued its survey of the product, its market, and its distribution. Later in August, Merrill executives agreed that the appearance of the new model Mini-Breaker, which was shorter, would provide an excellent opportunity to change the product's price, packaging, external appearance (label, etc.), discount structure, and to perfect advertising and merchandising plans. Executives of Merrill, Inc., also agreed that sales management should be strengthened and improved as an indispensable part of retail selling.

In September of this same year, Johnson and Baker submitted a second report making definite recommendations for the advertising and promotion of Mini-Breaker during the last quarter of the current year.

A condensed version of this report is reproduced below:

I. National Consumer Magazine Program

Agency previously recommended a limited, but national advertising program which, as a minimum, would be a token advertising effort to support your sales and distributor groups. This program is to start as soon as possible (earliest editions are November) and will begin to immediately build consumer interest and demand for Mini-Breaker (urgently needed) and will encourage your agents, distributors and dealers to renew their enthusiasm and sales efforts.

---

[1] See Merrill, Inc. (A) for this report.

Recommendations:

1. *Good Housekeeping* (circ. 3,000,000)

   One of the best read and circulated shelter books, but selected primarily for the merchandising value of the "Good Housekeeping Seal of Approval." We suggest minimum space necessary to obtain the Seal and use it over a 12-month period.

   6⅓ col. B&W ads @ $22.27 line*.......................................$6,413.76

2. *Household* (circ. 2,250,000)

   A popular, young and relatively inexpensive "home" magazine which claims the largest "home owner" readership of all the shelter books. Primarily a female audience but with appeals to both sexes. Has large farm circulation.

   12⅓ col. B&W ads @ $15.75 line†.......................................$9,072.00

3. *Better Homes & Gardens* (circ. 3,780,000)

   The largest and best accepted shelter book with home ownership almost equal to *Household* but with primarily an urban audience.

   12⅓ col. B&W ads @ $21.50 line.......................................$13,674.00

4. *True* (circ. 1,750,000)

   Largest selling man's magazine. Audience median age, 33.3 years; median income, $8,690. Selected for strictly male audience.

   12⅓ col. B&W ads @ $14.70‡.......................................$8,467.20

5. *Popular Mechanics* (circ. 1.5 million)

   Selected for the "do-it-yourself" audience and also on the basis of previous good returns from ads and publicity in this book. Primarily male readership.

   12⅓ col. B&W ads @ $8.93 line.......................................$4,072.08

6. *Rotarian* (circ. 275,000)

   Economical space, read by good prospects, with excellent ad visibility. A fraternal magazine selected primarily for good circulation at minimum costs. High home ownership probable.

   12⅓ col. B&W ads @ $3.45 line.......................................$1,945.80
   (Alternate space, 6½ col. B&W ads)

7. *Moose* (circ. 850,000)

   Selected on the same basis as *Rotarian* but with slightly different class readership.

   12⅓ col. B&W ads @ $4.00 line.......................................$2,256.00
   (Alternate space, 6½ col. B&W ads)

Total Space Costs	$48,510.84
Total Preparatory Costs	2,000.00
TOTAL	$50,510.84
Total Circulation	13,809,778

* Effective February next year, $24.50/line.
† Effective February next year, $17.00/line.
‡ Effective January next year, $16.00/line.

Agency will contact all magazine representatives and make arrangements, if possible, for photos and description of Mini-Breaker to be used in "new product" or "retail selling" columns or sections of these magazines.

As important as the ads themselves is a *sustained* advertising program that is continued without interruption for the 12-month period. An incidental benefit is reduced space rates, but more important is the fact that we *consistently* show our product, tell our sales story, and point out the benefits of having Mini-Breaker in the fuse box. This is particularly true of small space advertising where we benefit largely from cumulative effect of repeated exposure to our sales story and where our objective is slow but progressively increasing sales to a national market.

II. Localized Promotions

Several localized, concentrated promotions were included in our previous recommendations. We believe these promotions should still be carried out, but in view of our recent findings in New York and Atlantic City, we highly recommend Atlantic City and Rockford, Illinois, as the promotion cities. If carried out effectively, they would be fairly accurate yardsticks for measuring consumer acceptance; distributor and dealer cooperation and the most effective distribution channels; importance of TV versus newspaper and radio as advertising media; the types of sales tools most effective; the most logical Mini-Breaker prospects, etc. By projecting the results from these two cities we can better estimate our national market and what it will cost to sell it.

1. *Atlantic City, New Jersey* (44,500 families). Recommendations (for promotional program): (1) Continuing spots on radio station WOND on present basis of six times daily, five times a week, for six weeks. (2) Adding spots on radio station WMID for six times daily, five times a week, for six weeks. (3) Place fractional page ads in Atlantic City Press to tie in with radio spots and reach new audience. (4) A close check of distribution and promotional efforts will be made by agency representative with evaluation of results at frequent intervals. Total (estimated expenditure) $1,697.00.

2. *Rockford, Illinois* (34,900 families). We propose different distribution and different advertising media in Rockford, in order to contrast results with Atlantic City procedures. Whereas in Atlantic City all "fuse selling" retailers are used, we suggest distribution in Rockford only through normal hardware and electrical retail outlets, and services through their normal wholesalers. As advertising media, we recommend the use of TV alone for the first three weeks, with small newspaper ad tie-ins and support for the balance of the promotion. As in Atlantic City, we believe close agency check of the promotion will be necessary. Recommendations: (1) Distribution to be effected and support of local utility to be solicited before promotion gets under way. (2) Station WREX–TV (CBS–ABC Network) four spots daily, five days a week, for three weeks. (3)

Place small space ads in Rockford Star and Register-Republic to tie-in with TV for the first three weeks and to carry promotion alone for another six weeks after end of TV promotion. Total (estimated expenditures) $4,505.00. Both the Atlantic City and Rockford promotions should be started as soon as practical. . . .These promotions should include every effort to push the product at the point of purchase.

III. Newspaper Ads and Dealer Ad Mats

Newspaper ad mats should be made available for dealers, or distributors, or for use by Merrill, Inc., in any localized promotion in a metropolitan area. Layouts are included with this presentation, and proof sheets of mat ads should be made available to distributors, dealers, and agents. An opportunity to determine how well this material will benefit us is available right now in Pittsburgh. This city has been developed to a point where it needs consumer promotion. . . .We therefore recommend that $1,000 be allocated for consumer newspaper advertising in Pittsburgh during the remainder of the current year. Most of this will be cooperative, although some may be factory advertising. Increase in number of outlets and sales volume will be carefully watched. The advice of the manufacturers' agent will be solicited.

IV. A Trade Campaign

A limited trade campaign is recommended to help attract new dealers and distributors and to remind the hardware and electrical trade that Mini-Breaker is a very active high-profit item that shouldn't be overlooked. Primary purpose is to attract new dealers and encourage new dealer enthusiasm. . . .Recommendations: Hardware Age (circulation 34,861), Hardware and Housewares (circulation 46,871), six one-half pages in black and white in each publication, estimated total cost $3,110.

(The second report also contained a suggested advertising by direct mail campaign to be tested in Rockford, Illinois, and Atlantic City, New Jersey, at an approximate cost of $900 and $450 respectively. Suggestions were also made for continued marketing research.)

V. Conclusion

Let's briefly review the recommendations made in this report to Merrill, Inc., and what we think they will accomplish. We have chosen five basic media—magazines, both consumer and trade; radio; TV; direct mail; and newspapers, both co-op and direct factory.

A minimum of point-of-purchase material (window streamers) and a revision of the present convention booth are also recommended. Other media, transportation and outdoor advertising, for instance, have been considered but are not recommended at this time.

We have proposed limited national campaigns, and localized promotions in several areas with these media. An estimate of their costs for the balance of the current year is as follows:

Consumer magazines	$ 8,000*
Trade magazines	1,100†
Radio	1,100
TV	3,000
Direct mail	1,100
Newspapers	3,700‡
Point-of-purchase	750
Display booth	825
Total	$19,575

* 3-month share of 12-month schedule.
†3-month share of 12-month schedule.
‡ Atlantic City, Rockford and Pittsburgh.

The object of this advertising is to encourage the existing sales force (agents, wholesalers, retailers), to increase distribution and to learn more about our problems with specific relation to announcement of a new model next year.

Very importantly, the localized promotions should help us determine the cost per unit of promotion. Checks should be maintained in Atlantic City, Rockford and Pittsburgh, as well as our direct-mail locations, on promotion costs versus sales. This should be of great value in determining a price for the new model.

Work on this new model must be carried on this fall. For this reason, a continuing research program should be begun and a packaging consultant retained. We estimate the costs of these activities to be $4,000 and $5,000 respectively.

Adding $7,000 for contingencies, travel expenses, etc., we recommend that Merrill, Inc., budget approximately $37,000 for promotion and allied research in the last quarter of the year. This total presupposes that we will use existing literature, displays, and TV commercials. It does not include production work on items which will be used with the new model. From time to time, during the balance of the year, we may make other recommendations. The $37,000 is a basis point only.

Once approval is given to this interim program of research, national advertising, and localized promotion, it is our intention to develop point-of-sale material for the new model. This will include packaging, unit redesign, counter cards, streamers, decals, cartons, etc. All of our other material, advertisements, literature, sales aids, commericals, display booth, etc., will then be integrated with the point-of-sale material.

As soon as the skeleton framework of the consumer promotion for next year is set, and work begun on its details, we should begin development of integrated campaigns aimed at the important groups which influence the ultimate consumer. These influence groups include utilities, the REA's, the electrical inspectors, the contractors, and various trade associations. Methods of reaching them will include motion pictures, slide film and flip chart presentations, special ads, booth displays, publicity stories, etc.

Much care must also be given to the launching of the new model with the maximum impact on the public and on the trade. It is anticipated that this will take place in January. Once the new model is on the market, we can take up other problems, namely, commercial and industrial sales, the original equipment market, the cartridge breaker, and the motor protector.

This, then, is our basic blueprint for Mini-Breaker promotion in the months ahead. We hope that affirmative action will be taken on our immediate recommendations. But we reiterate that advertising and promotion will not achieve the desired results unless the sales organization is strengthened and the distribution improved. If necessary, we are willing to defer our fourth-quarter activities to accomplish this. Once begun, the timetable will be difficult to change, and Mini-Breaker cannot afford a false start. Once begun, everyone must be in complete agreement with our program.

QUESTION

Should the executives of Merrill, Inc., approve the advertising and promotional program recommended by its advertising agency? Why or why not?

case 7–4

MERRILL, INC. (C)

strategy for long-range market development

During September of the second year after Mini-Breaker had received Underwriters' Laboratory approval, the Johnson and Baker advertising agency submitted recommendations for an interim program of advertising and promotion to carry the product through the last quarter of that year. This was the second report submitted to the management of Merrill, Inc., and the proposals that it contained were based upon preliminary studies just completed.[1]

action taken on recommendations

After considering the agency's recommendations, the executives of Merrill, Inc., authorized Johnson and Baker to go ahead with the national adver-

---

[1] See Merrill, Inc. (B) for information on these recommendations.

tising campaign in the magazines recommended. These advertisements ran for 12 months, at which time they were not renewed. Merrill, Inc., officers also authorized the agency to conduct a test campaign in Rockford, Illinois. The test campaign was personally supervised by Mr. Greaves, sales manager of Merrill, Inc. Under his direction a more efficient distribution system was set up for the test, and missionary salesmen were hired to help get intensive distribution in the area. Advertising and promotion were carried out on the basis recommended by the agency. While window streamers were available to be placed in stores which carried Mini-Breaker, difficulty was experienced in getting store owners to make use of such material. They were not willing to take window space for signs promoting a $1.50 item when there were many higher priced, higher profit items which they wished to promote in the same space. Sears, Roebuck did not take part in the campaign, but at the end of the eight-week test the local Sears store had sold 59 Mini-Breakers, more than any other retail store in Rockford.

Not only were results of the Rockford test campaign discouraging but also there was no noticeable effect during the last quarter of the current year from any of the consumer advertising which was undertaken.

recommended promotional program for third year after U.L. approval

By December of the second year after U.L. approval, Johnson and Baker had completed its research on possible advertising themes and on the potential market for Mini-Breaker. Accordingly, a presentation was made to Merrill executives on December 3, entitled "The Outlook Today for Mini-Breaker." The essential points from this presentation are outlined in the following pages.

What We Are Selling

Mini-Breaker stands alone in: (1) Personal safety . . . no danger of injury. (2) Household security . . . real protection against fires. (3) Convenience . . . simple, quick way to restore power. (4) Home efficiency . . . household duties resumed quickly, no need to wait for husband or serviceman. (5) Modernization . . . simplest, most economic way to modernize electric panel systems. (6) Economy to utilities . . . Mini-Breaker can eliminate three out of five service calls.

Potential Market

How big is the market for Mini-Breaker in American homes? Of the 45 million homes in America, 90 percent, or 40,500,000 have fuse boxes. Of those with fuse boxes, surveys indicate that 72 percent, or 29,200,000, would be interested in Mini-Breakers, 60 percent of this number or 17,500,000 would replace existing fuses 100 percent with Mini-Breaker units. The remaining 11,700,000 or 40 percent would partially replace existing fuses on selected trouble circuits (see Exhibit 1).

markets during the coming year, involving an additional $250,-
g budget would need a production volume increase next year
4,000 on top of current production.

:

ing, exclusive product . . . "The one white pea in a pod."
ous residential market potential.
portunity through electric utilities.
stic, aggressive, persistent, determined belief in the ability of
uct to succeed.
y market approach . . . 12 during the coming year.
tribution . . . heavy trade relations activity in each market.
al consumer advertising in next year: $250,000.
al production in next year: 650,000 units.

t is ready, the market is ready, the plan is ready. Your OK is
ded.

the sales manager of Merrill, Inc., would you accept the goal
million units per year for five years as an attainable objective?

approve the proposed three-pronged approach to each of the
which the agency proposes to develop during the coming year?

approve an additional advertising appropriation of $250,000 as
e program of developing 12 additional markets during the com-
Vhy or why not?

5

L, INC. (D)

isal of marketing strategy

of the second year after U.L. approval, the Johnson and Baker
ency completed its research on the potential market for Mini-
n possible advertising themes. Representatives of the agency

The 40,500,000 homes with fuse boxes average 5.7 fuses per home . . .
therefore they hold 231 million fuses. The 72 percent of the homes interested
in Mini-Breaker hold 167 million fuses. Those likely to replace existing fuses
100 percent with Mini-Breaker units hold 100 million fuses. Partial replacement of fuses among the 11,700,000 interested homes might be expected to
add another 12 million units to the immediate potential thus giving a total of
112 million Mini-Breakers (see Exhibit 2).

In addition to the immediate potential, it is estimated that partial replacement homes plus noninterested homes provide a long-term potential market
of an additional 119 million Mini-Breakers.

Exhibit 1. Potential market for Mini-Breaker (number of homes).

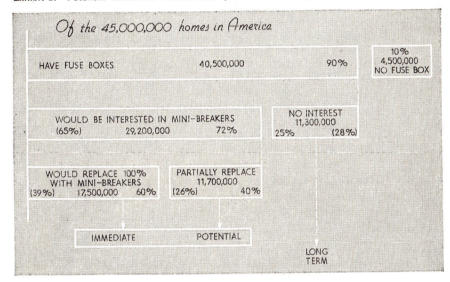

What does this mean in relation to (the established sales goal of) 25 million Mini-Breakers in five years? The immediate potential of 112 million units
plus one sixth of the long-term potential of 119 million units, or 20 million
Mini-Breakers, adds up to a total potential for the next five years of 132 million units. The sales goal of 25 million units in the next five years is 18½ percent of the very real potential calculated above.

In addition, there are 1,300,000 new homes with fuse box protection sys-
items being built each year. This building rate will increase rather than
decrease during the next five years. At current building rate, new home construction will add an annual demand of approximately 7,500,000 fuses. If each
new home were to install just one Mini-Breaker it would add another 6,500,-
000 in the next five years.

We couldn't be more enthusiastic about the immediate opportunity for the
expansion of Mini-Breaker sales. The goal of 5 million is:

. . . Only 4 percent of the estimated Mini-Breaker potential based on expressed interest for buying Mini-Breaker.

. . . Only 2.1 percent of the estimated fuse population.

. . . Only one Mini-Breaker cash register sale in every 33 fuse purchases
(based on current total industry production estimate).

. . . Only one fuse in every seven homes that have an interest in Mini-
Breaker (based on expressed interest for buying Mini-Breaker).

Twenty-five million in five years? Five million per year? Yes, definitely.

Recommended Marketing Program

What must we do to sell 5 million units per year? The most practical approach is a market-by-market development. Hitting few markets at a time . . .
building distribution and consumer recognition. Then moving to the next
group of markets.

We suggest a three-pronged approach to each market: (1) building distribution, (2) cultivation of electric utilities, (3) building consumer recognition
and demand.

Utilities play a fantastic part in the fuse business. Two thirds of residential
electric meters are serviced by electric utilities without charge. Three out of
five utility service calls require only the replacement of a fuse. The average
utility service call costs $2 to $3. Utilities replace over 4 million fuses annually.

Exhibit 2. Potential market for Mini-Breaker (number of Mini-Breaker units).

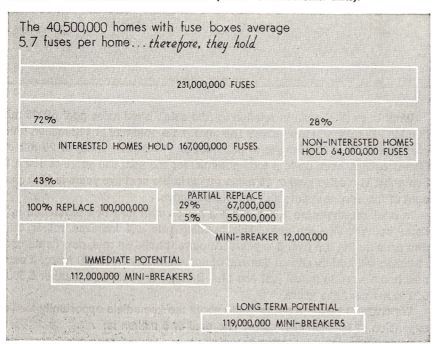

Why should electric utilities be interested in Mini-Bre
real economic pressures working in our favor to have
standard replacement in fuse trouble calls by electric u
standards of product are exclusively in keeping with th
ties. (Only utility objection has now been eliminated.)
household security are in common with the major ele
lations purpose. And . . . of major importance to us
small number of utilities handle the lion's share of th
electric utilities, 200 or 6 percent service 75 percent

The electric utility is potentially Mini-Breaker's nu
tivation of electric utility is a very important second
plan.

Prong No. 3 in the market plan: The tremendous
just been shown for Mini-Breaker is conclusive evi
of immediate expansion of the program to other
pansion, market by market, is currently being to
Rockford. We are uncovering in these two cities
will be encountered as new markets are added.
increase the rate of advertising that has been esta
rate of $8 per $1 million of consumer buying po
were to have national distribution this would m
$1,950,000. However, we cannot build national
is one of the basic reasons for city by city rec
mend the development of 12 markets during th
tional advertising expenditure of $250,000. We
plan start immediately in six more markets. T
markets as there are several other combinat
using media that need testing. Such as . . .
selling in printed media to compensate for in
and/or radio selling for the same reason.

The cost of this advertising should be ad
price. We see no indication that this increas
the goal of 25 million Mini-Breakers in five
available to us on Mini-Breaker costs, the
ing price would look like this:

Current manufacturer's selling
Cost of advertising (Atlantic City
Total manufacturer's selling pri
Manufacturers' Agents commis

Wholesaler's mark-out (20%)..

Retail mark-up (37½%)......
Consumer selling price......

then presented recommendations to executives of Merrill, Inc., identifying an objective of selling 5 million units of Mini-Breaker per year for five years and proposing a three-pronged strategy for achieving this goal. A key recommendation involved establishing an advertising appropriation of $250,000 for the coming year.[1]

action taken on agency recommendations

In reaching a conclusion on the foregoing recommendations, the officials of Merrill, Inc., kept clearly in mind the fact that the firm was already obligated to continue the magazine advertising campaign previously approved until the completion of the schedule in the fall of the coming year (a nine-month period). Moreover, at the time Johnson and Baker's recommendations for the coming year were under consideration, there was no evidence that the advertising program of the last quarter of the current year was producing any results at all. Accordingly, Merrill, Inc., officials were reluctant to approve the additional expenditure of $250,000 on the recommended advertising program. The magazine advertising was the only promotional effort which continued, and even this was canceled in June of the third year after U.L. approval.

introduction of models MP–252 and MP–600

Due to the discouraging results from previous efforts, management and sales officials had agreed in March of the third year after U.L. approval that all marketing effort should be directed to the new MP–252 and MP–600 models of Mini-Breaker, which were designed primarily for use on electric ranges, built-in ovens, and automatic washers and dryers. This effort proved fruitful. In less than nine months, 28 original-equipment manufacturers were using the MP–252 or MP–600 models.

results of the 12-month campaign

By August of the third year after U.L. approval, it had become clear to the executives of Merrill, Inc., that the attempt to develop a consumer market for Mini-Breaker was a complete failure. Sales of Mini-Breaker units had not increased during the 12-month campaign starting in September of the second year after U.L. approval. Indeed, sales volume remained at about the same level as when no advertising was being done. By this time only 8 of the original 24 manufacturers' agents were still handling Mini-Breaker. Only spotty distribution had been achieved in hardware stores and in appliance shops throughout the United States.

diagnosis of reasons for failure

In view of these disappointing results, both Mr. Greaves, the sales manager, and the representatives of the Johnson and Baker advertising agency,

---

[1] Refer to Merrill, Inc. (C) for this report.

faced the problem of diagnosing the causes for the lack of success and/or working out a program which would result in a profitable sales volume in the future. In the discussions which followed, David Hunter, the head of the research department of Johnson and Baker, argued that the difficulty could not properly be traced to the product. He pointed out that several major concerns were interested in the product from a functional standpoint and presumably because of the undeniable success Mini-Breaker was bound to enjoy. Sears, Roebuck was very much interested in the product and had initially made an attempt to get Merrill, Inc., to produce it for Sears exclusively. Moreover, the ease of getting manufacturers' agents to handle the product when it was first introduced was attributed by Mr. Hunter to its very great appeal. As evidence of the promise of Mini-Breaker, he pointed out that 80 percent of the homes in the United States had inadequate wiring as of the current year and that in the next five years the average home would have a $5,000 investment in electrical appliances as compared with the current figure of $1,300.

In Mr. Hunter's opinion the reason for the failure of the product, in spite of its appeal, was that Merrill, Inc., had not followed through on any consistent plan of promotion which it had begun. The Rockford test campaign, for example, was permitted to continue for only eight weeks, and Mr. Hunter argued that this was not a long enough period to provide a fair test of the promotional program. Moreover, he pointed out that the television spots were also discontinued after only a few weeks of broadcasting. In fact, he said, only the magazine advertising had been done consistently for any period of time.

Jack Ross, assistant to the head of the Johnson and Baker research department, held a somewhat different view from that expressed by Mr. Hunter. While Mr. Ross admitted the high quality of Mini-Breaker, he did not believe that there was any strong appeal available which could satisfactorily be used to sell it. Mr. Ross admitted that the findings of the consumer research seemed to run counter to his opinion. Thus, it had been found that of the families living in homes with fuse boxes, 72 percent had expressed an interest in, and a definite desire for, Mini-Breaker. (See Exhibit 1 in Merrill, Inc. [C].) Careful analysis of this survey, however, had led Mr. Ross to question its validity. Thus, he pointed out that of the homes with a fuse box under the control of the inhabitant, 45 percent were rented, and renters are not interested in buying permanent fixtures for the homes they occupy. Although renters may be interested in the product, Mr. Ross argued, they are not likely to become buyers.

Analysis of the nature of the need for Mini-Breaker, furthermore, had convinced Mr. Ross that the product could be better characterized as a necessary evil (as are ordinary fuses) rather than as a product in which consumers can be expected to develop a strong interest. As evidence to support this point of view, Mr. Ross cited the consumer response to an attempt to get consumers to fill out questionnaires giving their reactions to Mini-Breaker. This study involved two parts. In the first, a coupon and a questionnaire were enclosed in 500 Mini-Breaker packages. An offer was made to refund 50 cents of the purchase price to the consumer if the enclosed coupon were returned with a completed questionnaire. Of 500 offers made, only 50 were returned. In the second part of the study, 500 questionnaires were enclosed in Mini-Breaker packages with a request that they be filled out and returned, but in this case the company did not offer any compensation for cooperating with the request. Out of 500 questionnaires enclosed in the packages, none was returned by consumers.

With reference to the appeals which had been used in the advertising campaign, Mr. Ross argued that none was strong enough to stimulate a profitable volume of sales. The only emotional appeal that could be used was to personal safety, but Mr. Ross believed that the strength of this appeal was doubtful, since those who are afraid to replace a fuse were getting fewer and fewer in number. Except in rare cases where chronic trouble was experienced on an electrical circuit, he argued that the benefits to be derived from using a $1.50 Mini-Breaker were not great enough to justify its purchase as compared to a 7-cent ordinary fuse.

Mr. Greaves, the sales manager, took a somewhat different view from those expressed above. He claimed that the benefits of using Mini-Breaker were great enough so that he could sell the product door-to-door without the slightest difficulty. Indeed, he explained that six national direct selling organizations, who maintain 100 to 150 salesmen, were handling Mini-Breaker currently. These salesmen sold lighting fixtures, lamps, starters, fuses, etc., direct to industrial and commercial establishments for their own use, not for resale. As of the current year, these six groups had sold more Mini-Breakers than the 1,200 wholesalers distributing the product. According to Mr. Greaves, this indicated that the product could be sold if its advantages were explained to the customer through personal contact. (These firms had maintained that even larger sales would result if they were given larger discounts and if they were permitted to distribute under private labels.) Mr. Greaves went on to say, however, that he was only too aware of the fact that Mini-Breaker looked very much like an ordinary fuse. When the consumer saw the two side by side, the ordinary fuse priced at 7 cents and Mini-Breaker priced at $1.50, he was likely to take the 7-cent item unless he was acquainted with the advantages of the more expensive one. In the opinion of Mr. Greaves this indicated the necessity for consumer advertising.

Then, too, Mr. Greaves argued that consumer advertising was made necessary by the impossibility of getting middlemen to give aggressive support to Mini-Breaker. Thus, Mini-Breaker was sold to 1,200 hardware and electrical supply houses by manufacturers' agents. In Mr. Greaves opinion, the reasons for their failure to market Mini-Breaker in greater volume included (a) retail price too high, (b) lack of consistent consumer advertising, and (c) discount of 25 percent of selling price too low to stimulate interest in the item. Wholesalers of this type carry thousands of items, according to Mr.

Greaves, and they could therefore only be expected to serve as order takers. To expect aggressive sales help from such firms is futile, in Mr. Greaves opinion. Thus, if retailers are to stock Mini-Breakers, the pressure of consumer demand must be such as to lead them to ask specifically for the item when ordering from supply houses.

Moreover, in Mr. Greaves opinion, aggressive selling was not to be expected from hardware stores and appliance outlets under normal circumstances. Experience had indicated that it was difficult indeed to get dealers to push Mini-Breaker when sales might occur only once a month and when the gross margin per unit was less than 50 cents. Competing with Mini-Breaker for the retailers' sales support were items worth several hundred dollars on the floor which carried a relatively large dollar gross margin. Experience had shown that to get such a dealer to make room for a Mini-Breaker counter display was indeed a triumph.

Subsequent to March of the third year after U.L. approval, during the introduction of models MP–252 and MP–600 to original equipment manufacturers, Mini-Breaker promotion was dormant. By the fall of that year, only eight manufacturers' agents were still handling the product. Except for two of the agents, there was very little sales activity on the part of these firms. All advertising of Mini-Breaker units had been stopped in June of that year. Nevertheless, Mini-Breaker sales continued, increasing during August, September, and October. In the opinion of company officials, this proved that the complaints of manufacturers' agents and wholesale distributors were merely excuses for poor performance rather than real reasons for failure.

At the same time, Mr. Greaves was aware of the fact that sales of Mini-Breaker by Sears, Roebuck and Company had been consistent and profitable to that firm. Sears officials, however, continued to press Merrill, Inc., for permission to sell the product under the Homart private label and for a buying price which would permit Sears to retail the item at 98 cents.

Although Mr. Greaves could see that the situation appeared to call for consumer advertising, he had serious doubts as to whether such advertising could be done cheaply enough to result in a profitable sales volume on Mini-Breaker. At the current volume of 25,000 units a month, Mr. Greaves estimated that the margin available for sales and administrative expenses was somewhat less than 5 cents per unit. It was estimated that if sales volume could be increased to 500,000 units per month, a modest profit could be made with a $300,000 per year advertising budget. But Johnson and Baker had recommended an advertising appropriation for national coverage based on a volume of 500,000 per month of six times $300,000, or $1,800,000. Thus, even though consumer advertising through mass media seemed to be highly desirable, it did not appear to Mr. Greaves that Mini-Breaker could support an advertising appropriation large enough to accomplish the necessary task.

The problem involved in developing the consumer market profitably led Mr. Greaves to consider the alternative of selling through public utilities. Mr.

Hunter, of Johnson and Baker, quoted figures indicating that Mini-Breaker could save public utilities a substantial sum of money on free fuse replacement calls. Mr. Ross, however, expressed some doubts as to the appeal of this proposal to public utility managers. First, the expense of replacing fuses with Mini-Breakers in boxes served by public utilities would be sizable. Second, such replacements, together with the time which would be required to educate consumers in the operation of Mini-Breaker units, would require a great deal of time on the part of servicemen. On balance, therefore, Mr. Ross was of the opinion that public utilities would not save money by installing Mini-Breakers.

In spite of the negative arguments of Mr. Ross, Mr. Greaves was beginning to favor the suggestion of selling Mini-Breaker through the public utilities market. By this time, Mini-Breaker had been shortened to comply with electrical codes, and thus would meet the original objections which public utilities had to the substitution of Mini-Breaker for the ordinary fuse. Moreover, it appeared that profitable volume of business could be secured through the public utilities without incurring large selling expenses. Since Mr. Greaves believed that all other alternative approaches to the development of a market for Mini-Breaker had been adequately tested, he felt that sales through public utilities was the only promising path which was open to him.

QUESTIONS

1. What is your diagnosis of the failure of the marketing program for Mini-Breaker?
2. What further marketing action, if any, should be taken by executives of Merrill, Inc., to develop a profitable sales volume for this product?

indexes

index of cases

subject index

Bourne, Francis S., 65
Bowman-Stewart formulation, 345–46
Bradford, G. A., 425
Brand name defined, 187
Brand policy, promotional methods, influence upon, 383
Brand preferences, attitude of consumer in relation to, 46–48; *see also* Attitudes
Brand-shifting behavior, probabilistic process, 54
Brand strategy decisions
  company name combined with individual brand, 456–57
  distributors' brands, 461 ff.; *see also* Distributors' brands
  family brands versus individual brands, 443–56; *see also* Family brands versus individual brands
  issues involved, 443
  manufacturers' brands, 461 ff.; *see also* Manufacturers' brands
  promotional implications of brand-quality-price relationships, 457–60
  "trading down," 457
Branding of products, 226–31; *see also* Brand strategy decisions *and* types *of brands*
  basic objective of, 188
  definitions of terminology used, 187–88
  generic name, 189
  importance of, 187
  infringement, 189
  marketing research used for, 232–46
  protection of, 189
  registration of, 189–91
    benefits gained by, 190
  requirements for, 188–89
  selection, 188–89
Brands
  defined, 187
  types, 187–88
Bread, marketing strategy profile of, 18–19, 21
Break-even analysis, 532–33
  value and limitations of, 534
Break-even chart, 533
"Breakdown method" of demand forecasting, 113 n
Brokers, 251
Brown Shoe Company case, 298
Buildup method of demand forecasting
  defined, 113
  established industrial goods, 125–26
  Go-No Go decision, 123
  new consumer products, 123–24
  new industrial products, 124–25
  sales force composite method, 125–26
  steps in, 113
  test marketing, 123–24

Business, basic purpose of, 4
Business conditions, forecast of, 114
  categories of, 126
  econometric models, 127
  four percent method, 127–28
  gross methods of, 127–28
  labor productivity method, 128
  multiple-correlation analysis method, 129–30
  projection procedure, 128–29
  regression analysis, 129–30
  statistical methods of, 128–31
  techniques for, 126–31
  time series analysis, 130–31
"Buyclasses," 102
Buyer behavior; *see* Consumer behavior
Buying decisions; *see* Consumer behavior
Buying motives; *see* Motives *and* Needs
Buying patterns, channels of distribution selection, 279–81
Buying situations, types of, 102
"Buyphases," 97, 99, 102
By-products, utilization of, 158

C

Cake-mix marketing, 268
Case studies
  American Motors Corporation
    selective distribution through dual agencies, 363–69
  The Buhr Machine Tool Company
    wisdom of substituting company salesmen for manufacturers' agents, 358–62
  Ford Motor Company Special Products Division
    naming a new car, 226–31
  Holmes Manufacturing Company
    decision to offer a new product, 207–13
  Johnston, Robert
    consumer behavior: purchase of ammunition loading equipment, 141–43
  Lincoln-Mercury Division
    marketing research used to aid in making brand name and styling decisions for new car, 232–46
  Merrill, Inc. (A)
    marketing program for a new product, 667–79
  Merrill, Inc. (B)
    advertising and promotional program, 680–85
  Merrill, Inc. (C)
    strategy for long-range market development, 685–90
  Merrill, Inc. (D)
    reappraisal of marketing strategy, 690–95

D

Dealer promotion
  advertising used in conjunction with, 400–401
  considerations in use of, 398–400
  factors considered in selecting proper methods of, 402
  interior displays, 400
  main emphasis on, 398–400
  methods of encouraging, 402
  methods of use of, 398
  nature of, 397
  personal selling, use in conjunction with, 401–2
  persons who would use, 397
  window displays, 400
Dean, Joel, 429
Decision areas of marketing; *see* Strategies
Decision-making process, consumer, 36
Decision matrix
  marketing resources, utilization of, 164–65
  production resources, utilization of, 158–60
  resource utilization aided by, 165–66
Decision-theory approach to mixed brand policy
  choice, 470–74
  evaluation of, 474, 476
Deep South, 57
Definitions
  advertising, 386
  agent middlemen, 250
  brand, 187
  brand name, 187
  buildup method of demand forecasting, 113
  communication, 378
  consumer goods, 35
  culture, 55
  demand, 111
  demand forecasting, 111
  distribution strategy, 247
  distribution structure, 249
  family-brand policy, 443
  goals, 37
  industrial goods, 25
  learning process, 53
  market potential, 114
  marketing, 3–6
  motives, 37
  personal selling, 391
  price redetermination, 537
  product, 147
  product development, 174
  product service, 193–94
  projection, 128
  reference groups, 61

Definitions—*Cont.*
  retailers, 250
  sales potential, 115
  sales quotas, 119
  social class, 57
  social group, 63
  synergism, 611
  top-down method of demand forecasting, 113
  warranty, 191
  wholesaler, 250
Demand
  channels of distribution selection, 277–79
  defined, 111
  estimate of, 152
  marketing strategy variable, 7–8, 20–22
  price determination for new addition to product line, 542–43
  qualitative and quantitative approach to; *see* Consumer behavior *and* Demand forecasting
Demand analysis
  buyer behavior; *see* Consumer behavior
  consumer behavior; *see* Consumer behavior
  forecasting; *see* Demand forecasting
  price determination for new product, 525–28
Demand assortments, 259
Demand estimation, 152
  price determination for new product, 525–28
Demand forecasting
  basic approaches to, 113–26
  buildup method of, 113, 122–26
  defined, 111
  importance of, 111–12
  marketing goals set by, 112
  short-term versus long-term, 112
  steps in, 113
  top-down method of, 113–22
Department stores, 253
Depth interviews, 41–42
Derived demand, price determination for new product, 527–28
"Detail men," 392–93
Detroit Gasoline case (*Standard Oil* v. *FTC*), 558
Differential pricing; *see* Price variation
Direct evaluation method of demand forecasting, 113 n
Discount houses, 253
Discounts
  legal constraints, 557–59
  policy of using, 550
  price variations implemented by, 550
  promotional, 555
  quantity, 550–53

	Expected Payoff (000)
Acts	
A_1—Ignore the request.....................	$\$-73.0$
A_2—Counteroffer.........................	-265.2
A_3—Reduce price.........................	$-1,337.0$
A_4—Accede..............................	-260.7
A_5—Adopt price differential system.........	$+125.2$

S₁₁ Z SUPPLIES BLUE AND OTHERS (.05)	-225.7
S₁₂ Z SUPPLIES BLUE ONLY (.05)	-225.7
S₁₃ A OR C SUPPLIES BLUE (.05)	-188.1
S₁₄ BLUE ACQUIRES BAKERY (.05)	-370.5
S₁₅ BLUE WAITS, HARASSES B (.30)	-75.0
S₁₆ BLUE WAITS (.50)	0

S₂₁ Z SUPPLIES BLUE AND OTHERS (.02)	-225.7
S₂₂ Z SUPPLIES BLUE ONLY (.03)	-225.7
S₂₃ A OR C SUPPLIES BLUE (.01)	-188.1
S₂₄ BLUE ACQUIRES BAKERY (.01)	-370.5
S₂₅ BLUE WAITS, HARASSES B (.01)	-75.0
S₂₆ BLUE WAITS (.02)	0
S₂₇ BLUE ACCEPTS A AND C FOLLOW SUIT (.90)	-275.1

S₃₁ Z SUPPLIES BLUE AND OTHERS (.03)	-225.7
S₃₂ Z SUPPLIES BLUE ONLY (.04)	-225.7
S₃₃ A OR C SUPPLIES BLUE (.02)	-188.1
S₃₄ BLUE ACQUIRES BAKERY (.01)	-370.5
S₃₅ BLUE ACCEPTS, A AND C DO NOT MEET (.05)	-456.0
S₃₆ BLUE ACCEPTS, A AND C MEET, B RETAINS ADVAN. (.10)	-1249.2
S₃₇ BLUE ACCEPTS, A AND C MEET, RETURN TO ORIGINAL SHARE (.75)	-1554

S₅₁ Z SUPPLIES BLUE AND OTHERS (.05)	-225.7
S₅₂ Z SUPPLIES BLUE ONLY (.05)	-225.7
S₅₃ A OR C SUPPLIES BLUE (.05)	-188.1
S₅₄ BLUE ACCEPTS, A AND C FOLLOW SUIT (.60)	0
S₅₅ BLUE ACCEPTS, A AND C REDUCE PRICES (.25)	+628.5

$$
\begin{array}{ll}
\text{Direct labor} & \$\ 2.50 \\
\text{Material} & 17.34
\end{array}
$$

(1)	(2)	(3)	(4)	(5)	(6) Cumulative	(7)	(8) Cumulative
Operation	Direct Labor Hours per 100 Pieces	Direct Labor Rate per Hour	Over- head per Hour	Esti- mated Cost per 100 Pieces	Esti- mated Cost per 100 Pieces	Actual Cost per 100 Pieces	Actual Cost per 100 Pieces
1. Cast.............0.3333	$2.35	$6.25	$2.866	$	$2.783	$ .....
2. Trim.............. .2500	1.70	3.10	1.200	4.066	0.980	3.763
3. Buff.............. .1250	3.40	7.25	1.331	5.397	....	3.763
4. Plate............. .340	2.813	1.820	4.973	10.370	3.614	7.377
5. Pack............. .1250	1.70	1.75	.431	10.801	0.273	7.650
6. Metal and Dross...	....	....	3.336	14.137	2.646	10.296
7. Scrap 5%.........	....	....	0.707	14.844	0.515	10.811
8. Carton...........	....	....	0.260	15.104	0.097	10.908
9. Shipping 2.2%.....	....	....	0.332	15.436	0.240	11.148

(1)	(2)	(3)	(4)	(5)	(6)	(7)	(8)
	Direct Labor Hours per 100	Direct Labor Rate per	Over- head Rate	Esti- mated Cost per 100	Cumula- tive Esti- mated Cost per	Actual Cost per 100	Cumula- tive Actual Cost per
Operation	Pieces	Hour	per Hour	Pieces	100 Pieces	Pieces	100 Pieces
1. Cast.........0.500	$ 2.35	$ 6.25	$ 4.300	$	$ 2.996	$ ....
2. Trim.........0.333	1.70	3.10	1.600	5.900	2.909	5.905
3. Polish.........0.500	1.85	1.90	1.875	7.775	2.907	8.812
4. Buff..........0.333	3.40	8.25	3.883	11.658	4.814	12.626
5. Buff.......... ...	...	...	....	....	1.311	14.937
6. Plate.........0.425	11.250	17.080	28.755	40.513	26.429	41.937
7. Paint.........1.250	1.70	3.35	6.313	46.726	5.941	47.937
8. Pack.........2.000	1.70	3.10	9.600	56.326	6.316	53.623
9. Metal and Dross........ ...	...	...	30.300	86.626	19.782	73.405
10. Scrap 5%...... ...	...	...	3.851	90.477	3.788	77.193
11. Special pack.. ...	...	...	2.310	92.787	2.345	79.538
12. Carton........ ...	...	...	5.000	97.787	2.417	81.955
13. Shipping 2.7% ...	...	...	2.151	99.938	1.803	83.758

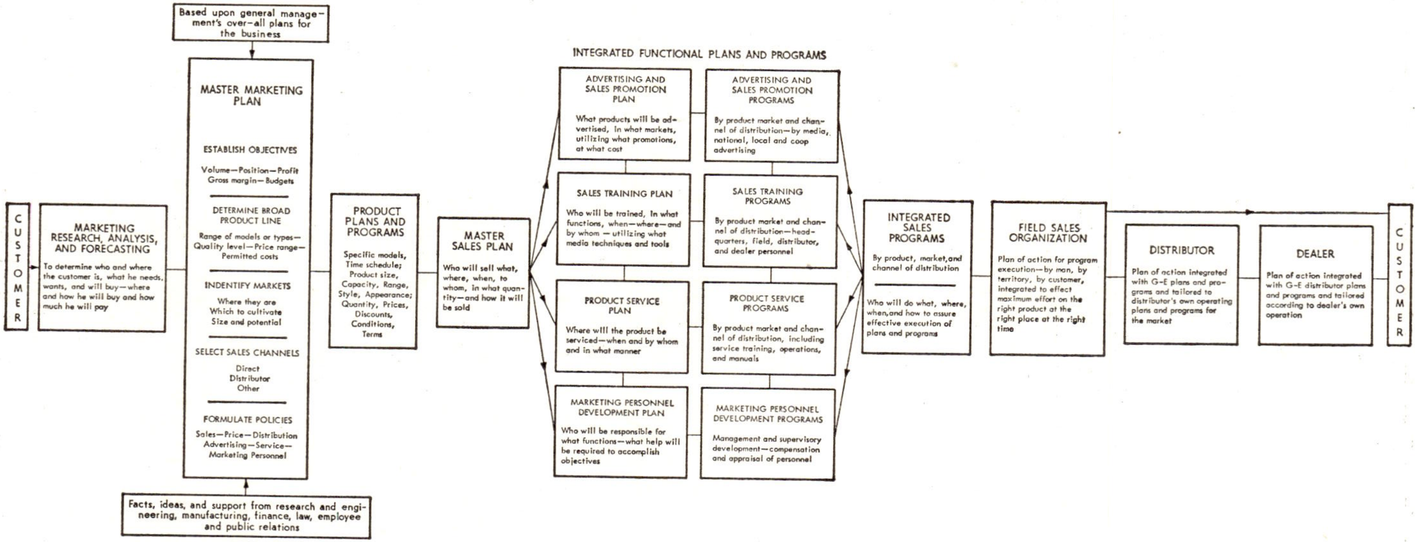

Based upon general manage-
men's over-all plans for
the business

introduction to marketing management

Country	RCA	ACR	WU
Afghanistan	x	x	
Argentina	x	x	
Australia	x		
Austria	x	x	
Azores		x	x
Barbados			x
Belgian Congo	x		
Belgium	x	x	x
Bermuda	x	x	
Bolivia	x	x	
Brazil	x	x	x
Bulgaria	x	x	
Caracas	x	x	
Chile	x	x	
China	x	x	
Colombia	x	x	
Cuba	x	x	x
Czechoslovakia	x	x	x
Denmark	x	x	
Dominican Republic	x	x	
Ecuador	x	x	
Egypt	x	x	
Ethiopia	x	x	
Finland	x	x	
Formosa	x	x	
France	x	x	x
Germany	x	x	x
Great Britain	x	x	x
Greece	x		
Greenland	x		
Guam	x		
Guatemala	x	x	
Haiti	x	x	
Hong Kong	x		
Hungary	x	x	
Iceland	x	x	
India	x	x	
Indonesia	x		
Iran	x		
Iraq	x		
Ireland	x		
Israel	x	x	
Italy	x	x	x
Jamaica	x	x	x
Japan	x	x	
Korea	x		
Lebanon	x		
Liberia	x		
Morocco	x	x	
Netherlands	x	x	x
New Zealand	x		
Norway	x		
Pakistan	x		
Panama	x	x	
Peru		x	
Philippine Rep.	x	x	
Poland	x		
Portugal	x	x	x
Puerto Rico	x	x	x
Rumania		x	
Saudi Arabia		x	
Spain	x	x	x
Sweden	x		
Switzerland	x		
Syria	x		
Thailand	x		
Turkey	x		
U.S.S.R.	x	x	
Uruguay		x	
Venezuela	x	x	
Yugoslavia	x	x	

case 7–1 / RCA Communications, Inc.

The Europe, Africa, Middle Eastern District is housed in this huge area in the Bank's Overseas Division. Bank Avenue Headquarters Building, New York.

Nerve center at First National City is the Telegraph and Cable Department located in the Bank's Uptown Headquarters, 399 Park Avenue, New York.

This large deceptively quiet room houses batteries of teletypewriters which, by means of modern communication circuits, are constantly in touch with branch offices, banks, and customers around the world.

In the Cable Department an automatic conveyor system adds to the efficiency by whisking messages between personnel stationed at the far ends of this huge communication center.

The department is in continuous operation. Messages in an impressive volume pour through it enroute to and from all parts of the world – 24 hours a day, the year 'round.

FIRST NATIONAL CITY BANK SAYS:

The Bank has always been aware of the important role international telegraphic communications play in the conduct of international banking. In our opinion, modern communication services which feature fast, accurate customer-to-customer connections are essential to the conduct of international trade.

The advent of modern telegraphy, telex, leased channel and radiophoto services has provided those of us engaged in international commerce and trade with communications tools ideally shaped to meet our specific requirements.

With this in mind, First National City is pleased to state that the scope and quality of the service provided by RCA Communications for more than three decades is completely satisfactory. The bank's position as a leader in the field of international banking has been helped immeasurably by modern, accurate communications.

[handwritten layout notes:]
SHOT OF OFFICE AREA

FILING DEPT.— SHOW SORTER

LONGSHOT OF TYPES OF TELETYPES

Why should electric utilities be interested in Mini-Breakers? (1) There are real economic pressures working in our favor to have Mini-Breaker be the standard replacement in fuse trouble calls by electric utilities. (2) Quality and standards of product are exclusively in keeping with the aim of electric utilities. (Only utility objection has now been eliminated.) (3) Personal safety and household security are in common with the major electric utilities' public relations purpose. And . . . of major importance to us is the fact . . . a very small number of utilities handle the lion's share of the business. Out of 3,300 electric utilities, 200 or 6 percent service 75 percent of the meters.

The electric utility is potentially Mini-Breaker's number one salesman. Cultivation of electric utility is a very important second prong in the marketing plan.

Prong No. 3 in the market plan: The tremendous market potential that has just been shown for Mini-Breaker is conclusive evidence for the opportunity of immediate expansion of the program to other markets. The plan for expansion, market by market, is currently being tested in Atlantic City and Rockford. We are uncovering in these two cities many of the problems that will be encountered as new markets are added. So far we see no reason to increase the rate of advertising that has been established in Atlantic City . . . rate of $8 per $1 million of consumer buying power in the market area. If we were to have national distribution this would mean an advertising budget of $1,950,000. However, we cannot build national distribution overnight. (This is one of the basic reasons for city by city recommendation.) We do recommend the development of 12 markets during the next year entailing an additional advertising expenditure of $250,000. We strongly recommend that the plan start immediately in six more markets. These markets should be small markets as there are several other combinations of media and methods of using media that need testing. Such as . . . eight-second TV spots; coupon selling in printed media to compensate for inadequate distribution; direct TV and/or radio selling for the same reason.

The cost of this advertising should be added to the manufacturer's selling price. We see no indication that this increase will in any significant way affect the goal of 25 million Mini-Breakers in five years. Based on the information available to us on Mini-Breaker costs, the composition of the *consumer selling price* would look like this:

Current manufacturer's selling price	$0.70
Cost of advertising (Atlantic City plan)	.39
Total manufacturer's selling price	$1.09
Manufacturers' Agents commission (10%)	0.11
	$1.20
Wholesaler's mark-out (20%)	0.24
	$1.44
Retail mark-up (37½%)	0.54
Consumer selling price	$1.98

A plan of 12 markets during the coming year, involving an additional $250,-000 advertising budget would need a production volume increase next year of 650,000 or 54,000 on top of current production.

In summary:
1. Outstanding, exclusive product . . . "The one white pea in a pod."
2. Tremendous residential market potential.
3. Great opportunity through electric utilities.
4. Enthusiastic, aggressive, persistent, determined belief in the ability of the product to succeed.
5. Market by market approach . . . 12 during the coming year.
6. Build distribution . . . heavy trade relations activity in each market.
7. Additional consumer advertising in next year: $250,000.
8. Additional production in next year: 650,000 units.

The product is ready, the market is ready, the plan is ready. Your OK is all that is needed.

QUESTIONS
1. If you were the sales manager of Merrill, Inc., would you accept the goal of selling 5 million units per year for five years as an attainable objective? Explain.
2. Would you approve the proposed three-pronged approach to each of the 12 markets which the agency proposes to develop during the coming year? Explain.
3. Would you approve an additional advertising appropriation of $250,000 as a part of the program of developing 12 additional markets during the coming year? Why or why not?

reappraisal of marketing strategy

In December of the second year after U.L. approval, the Johnson and Baker advertising agency completed its research on the potential market for Mini-Breaker and on possible advertising themes. Representatives of the agency

Communication—*Cont.*
  response to, 380
  source, 378
Company goals, 631–32
Company name, brand name combined
    with, 456–57
Company planning committee, 631
Competition
  marketing strategy variable, 8–9
  price redetermination because of changes
      in, 539
  price versus nonprice, 516–18
  price variation to meet, 549
Competitive-functional discounts, 553–54
Competitive markets, price determination
    in, 518–23
Competitive-parity approach, promotional
    appropriation determination, 422–26
Competitor, removal of, 167–68
Complementary product, price determina-
    tion, 543
Component parts, industrial buying of, 101
Consumer behavior
  advertising, effect of, 87
  attitudes, 44–50; *see also* Attitudes
  awareness, levels of, 40–41
  brand-shifting behavior as probabilistic
      process, 54
  cognitive dissonance, 50–53
  cultural influences, 55–57
  decision-making process, stages in, 36
  defined, 35
  environmental factors, 36–37
  environmental influence upon, 54–72; *see
      also* Influence of environment
  factors influencing brand choice, 68–69
  family brands versus individual brands;
      see Family brands versus individual
      brands
  family influence, 68–71
  family life cycle, 69–71
  habitual brand choice, 36
  individual's needs and attitudes, 37–50
  industrial market, 94–107; *see also* Indus-
      trial consumer behavior
  learning process, 53–54
  marketing strategy as function of, 35
  models of, 78–94; *see also specific model
      by name*
    Du Pont, 85–88
    Howard-Sheth, 88–93
    Morgan, 78–85
    Nicosia, 93–94
  motivation research in, 40–43
  motives, 37–43; *see also* Motives *and*
      Needs
  needs, 37–43; *see also* Motives *and* Needs
  problem solving and, 36

Consumer behavior—*Cont.*
  purchase of ammunition loading equip-
      ment, 141–43
  reinforcement, 53–54
  relation between individual and environ-
      ment, 36–37
  relevance for marketing decision maker,
      72
  social class, influence of, 57–62; *see also*
      Social class
  social group influence, 63–71; *see also* So-
      cial group influence
  values, 44–50; *see also* Attitudes
Consumer durables, high-priced, marketing
    strategy profile of, 13–15, 21
Consumer goods; *see* New products *and*
    Product
Consumer panels and juries, 179
Consumer products; *see* New products *and*
    Product
Consumer promotions, 403–6
  considerations in determination to use,
      404
  objectives, 403
  short-run benefits, 405–6
  types of, 403
Consumer surveys, 179
Continuum of feeling, 50
Controllable variables, marketing strategy,
    10–12; *see also* Marketing strategy
Cost floor, 528–31
Cost-plus pricing, new product, 529
Cost savings, price determination for new
    product, 527
Costs
  development, capitalization of, 168–69
  estimates of, 154
  marketing, 257–58
  nonmarketing, marketing strategy varia-
      ble, 10
  physical distribution, 309, 311
  physical distribution system, components
      of, 321
  price determinations
    new addition to product line, 541
    new product, 528–31
  price redetermination because of changes
      in, 538
  pricing strategy and, 531
  sunk, 181
Coulson, John S., 68
Cultural influences, 55–57
Cultural patterns, 55–57
Culture defined, 55
Cumulative quantity discounts (CQD),
    552–53
Customer service level (CSL), 328–30

Mixed brands—*Cont.*
  decision-theory approach to choice of, 470–74
    evaluation of, 474, 476
  gains in production efficiency, 463–64
  improvement in working capital position, 463
  marketing considerations, 464–67
  policy of selection, 461–76
  recognition of profit opportunities in production of private brands, 463
  reduction in average collection period, 463
  relative profitability of different brand policies, 469
  risks of, 467–69
  Robinson-Patman Act restrictions, avoidance of, 465–67
Models of consumer buying behavior, 78–94; *see also specific model by name*
  Du Pont, 85–88
  Howard-Sheth, 88–93
  Morgan, 78–85
  Nicosia, 93–94
"Modified rebuy," 102, 104
Monopolist, price determination by, 519–20
Morgan, J. M., 78–85
Morgan's model of family decision making, 78
  ability to exert power, 81–82
  combining individual preferences, 81–83
  criticism of, 83–84
  evaluation of, 84–85
  expectation as to outcome, 80
  factors determining individual preference, 78–80
  incentive values of the outcome, 79–80
  innovation of, 78
  limitations in scope of theory of, 78
  needs, 78–79, 81–82
  steps in development of theory of, 78
  uncertainty, element of, 80
Motivation research, 40–43
  criticisms of, 43
  depth interview method, 41–42
  direct questioning, 43
  free association, 42
  incomplete sentences, 42
  projective techniques, 41–42
  social long-distance telephone calls, 135–41
  Thematic Apperception Test, 42
  word association, 42
Motivational theory, 37–43; *see also* Motives *and* Needs
Motives
  awareness, levels of, 40–41
  defined, 37

Motives—*Cont.*
  differences in purchase, 40
  preconscious level, 41
  unconscious level, 41
Movement inventories, 336
Multiple channels of distribution, 268–71
Multiple-correlation analysis method of business conditions forecasting, 129–30
Multiple-facility location, 344
Multiple influence groups, industrial consumer behavior, 97–102
Myers, 50

N

National brands, 188
Needs; *see also* Motives
  basic, 38
  belongingness, 38
  cognitive, 38
  esteem, 38
  hierarchy, 38–39
  love, 38
  Morgan's model of family decision making, 78–79, 81–82
  physiological, 38
  safety, 38
  self-actualization, 38
New products
  brands chosen, factors influencing, 450–56
  consumer, 123–24
  decision to offer, 148 ff.; *see also* Product choice decisions
  external acquisition of, 167–69
  family brand versus individual brand, choice of; *see* Family brands versus individual brands
  Go-No Go decision in consideration of, 123
  ideas for, 178
  industrial, 124–25
  internal development of, 166, 169–71
  life cycle of, 148–50
  marketing program for, 27–29, 667–79
  organization for development of, 199–201
  price determination for, 524–31; *see also* Price determination
  steps in conversion of idea into new business, 176
  which to offer, 150–66; *see also* Product choice decisions
New products division, 629
  organization and functions of, 199–201
"New task," 102, 106
Nicosia, Francesco M., 93–94
Nicosia model of consumer decision-making process, 93–94
Nielsen Company, A. C., 432–38

Noncumulative quantity discounts (NCQD) , 551–52
Nonprice promotion, 516–18
Nonvariable price policy, 546–47
 advantages of, 548
 disadvantages of, 548

O

Objective-and-task approach, promotional appropriation determination, 426–28
"Old families," members of, 58
Organization inventories, 336
Organization for marketing; see Post–marketing-concept organization structure
Organization for product development, 199–201
Osgood Semantic Differential, 50
"Overall forecast approach" to demand forecasting, 113 n
Oxenfeldt, Alfred R., 633, 634 n

P

Packaging
 containment function, 183
 development of, 183
 diverse effects of decisions involving, 184–85
 functions of, 183
 importance of, 184
 legal constraints on, 185–87
 promotional requirements, 183
 role played in marketing mix, 183
 soft-drink industry, changes in, 184–85
 weights and sizes, 186
Packard, Vance, 197
Paired comparisons, 50
Past sales indexes, 119
Patents, acquisition of, 158
Payoffs, 472
Perceived incongruity; see Cognitive dissonance
Percentage of sales approach, promotional appropriation determination, 417–20
Perishables, channels of distribution, 264
Personal selling
 advertising and, 391
 dealer promotion, use in conjunction with, 401–2
 defined, 391
 "detail men," 392–93
 elements of, 391
 factors influencing use of, 393–95
 kinds of, distinguished, 391–92
 main emphasis on, 395–96
 management problems involved in, 394–96
 marketing strategy variable, 12

Personal selling—Cont.
 missionary salesmen, 392–94
 purpose of, 391
"Phantom freight," 561, 563
Physical capacity, utilization of, 157
Physical distribution
 audit, 322–24
  marketing requirements and, 323–24
 cost components of system of, 321
 cost-saving potential, 309–10
 costs of, increase in, 309, 311
 customer service level (CSL) , 328–30
 design of a system of, 320–24
  alternate, 324–35
 factors involved in question of, 308
 implications of, 311–12
 inventory management, 335–40
 location decisions, 340–48
 managing function of, 348–49
 number of distribution points, 325–28
 optimization of total system, 334–35
 promotional potential, 310–11
 renewed interest in, reasons for, 309–12
 selective stocking, 332–34
 systems analysis or approach to, 312–20; see also Systems analysis
 total logistics concept, 312; see also Systems analysis
 traffic analysis, 322–23
 traffic department concept, 311
 transportation concept, 311–12
 warehouse replenishment time, 330–31
Physical facilities, utilization of, 163
Physiological needs, 38
"Pittsburgh Plus" pricing method, 561, 563
Planned obsolescence, 197
Plant capacity, utilization of, 218–25
Plant equipment, industrial buying of, 100
Platten, John H., Jr., 99
"Poor but honest workers," 58
Post–marketing-concept organization structure, 624–25
 chief marketing executive, 624
 company planning committee, 631
 marketing planning committee, 630–31
 marketing research department, 628
 marketing services manager, 627–29
 new products division, 629
 primary breakdown of responsibility, 626–27
 products manager, 629–30
 sales and distribution manager, 627
 sales manager, 624
 vice-president, 624
"Postage stamp" pricing, 560
Power over another person, sources of, 81–82
Preliminary evaluation, 178–79

Product—*Cont.*
  industrial
    channels of distribution, 265–66
    defined, 35
    demand forecasts of, 125–26
    service problems of, 198–99
  marketing strategy formulation
    comparisons, 12–19
    variations, 19–22
  marketing-strategy variable, 11
  price determination of new addition to
    line of, 541–44; *see also* Price deter-
    mination
Product advertising, 386; *see also*
  Advertising
Product choice decisions, 213–17
  ancillary factors; *see* Ancillary product
    decisions
  basic, 147
  cost, estimates of, 154
  demand, estimate of, 152
  estimates
    cost, 154
    demand, 152
    life cycle, 154–55
    price, 153–54
  external acquisition, 167–69; *see also*
    External acquisition of new
    products
  high cost factor, 148
  high failure rate, 148
  internal development, 166, 169–71; *see*
    also Internal development of new
    products
  life cycle
    estimates of, 154–55
    new product, 148–50
  marketing resource, utilization of, 161–
    65; *see also* Resource utilization
  net revenue expectation, 155
  new product offering, 148 ff.
  "newness" determined, 150–51
  price, estimates of, 153–54
  production resources, utilization of, 157–
    61
  profit maximization, objective of, 151
  profitability formula, 151–52
    compound, 155–56
  public policy and, 171–72
  resource utilization, 156–66; *see also*
    Resource utilization
  risk involved, 148
Product decisions
  ancillary; *see* Ancillary product decisions
  choice of product; *see* Product choice
    decisions
  development of product; *see* Product
    development decisions

Product development decisions, 207–13
  ancillary factors; *see* Ancillary product
    decisions
  basic objective of, 5
  cautious process, 177
  characteristics of product development,
    175–77
  concurrent marketing and, 175–76
  Go-No Go decision, 181–82
  interdependence of marketing and, 176–
    77
  marketing plan, 182–83
  marketing research used for, 232–46
  new product ideas, 178
  organization for, 199–201
  preliminary evaluation, 178–79
  pretesting, purpose of and methods used
    in, 179–80
    limitations of, 180
  process span, 175
  selection of product; *see* Product choice
    decisions
  steps in, 178–83
  test marketing, 180–81
    limitations of, 180
  "total" product involved, 177
Product development
  defined, 174
  process; *see* Product development
    decisions
Product improvement, 175
Product innovation; *see* Product choice
  decisions
Product life cycle, 148–50
  estimates of, 154–55
Product management
  organization, types of, 629–31
  status of, 630
Product quality, interrelationship with
  service, 197–98
Product service
  defined, 193–94
  dissatisfaction of consumers with quality
    of, 194
  exchange versus, 198
  industrial goods, special problems for,
    198–99
  interrelationships with quality, 197–98
  problem area for manufacturers, 194
  role in marketing strategy, 194
  strategies, 194–97
    competitive weapon view, 196
    factory service view, 196
    limited obligation view, 196
    natural agent view, 195–96
    negative view, 195
    optimum quality view, 196–97
    personal service, 197
    "public be damned" attitude, 197

R

Rank order, 50
Reduction of uncertainty, 167
Reference-group influence, 64–68
Registration of trademarks and brand
    names, 189–91
  benefits gained by, 190
Regression analysis, 114, 119
  business conditions forecasting method,
    129–30
Reinforcement, 53–54
Replacement component, marketing
    strategy profile of, 15–16, 21
Replacement markets
  price variation in channels of distribu-
    tion, 602–8
  trade discounts for, 593–602
Replenishment inventories, 336–40
Resale price maintenance (RPM), 564–66
  implementing policy of, 565–66
  implications of, 566–67
  protection of product image, 564–65
  reduction in interchannel rivalry, 565
Research; see Marketing research and
    Motivation research
Research-objective approach, promotional
    appropriation determination, 426–28
Resident buyers, 251
Resource utilization
  decision matrix, aid of, 165–66
  marketing resources, 161–62
    decision matrix, 164–65
    distribution channels, 163, 165
    goodwill, 162
    marketing know-how, 162–63
    physical facilities, 163
  organization of, 169
  plant capacity, 218–25
  production resources, 157
    by-product factor, 158
    common raw materials, 158
    decision matrix, 158–60
    hypothetical new product, 159, 161
    labor skills, 158
    physical capacity, 157
    technical know-how, 158
  relationship to product planning, 156–57
Restricted distribution, 288
  advertising, 292–93
  benefits of, 288–91
  legal constraints, 294–305
  limitations of, 291–94
  specialty goods, 292
  wisdom of, 288–94
Retail selling, 391
Retailers, 253
  defined, 250
  types, 253

Return-on-investment approach, promo
    tional appropriation determination,
    428–30
Reynolds, 50
"Right-to-buy" laws, 294
Robinson-Patman Act, 9–10, 465–66, 548,
    553, 556–57
  good faith defense to, 557–59
  price variation, implications for, 557–59

S

Safety needs, 38
Safety-stock inventories, 336–40
Sales
  forecast, 115–16
    revision of, 120
  geographical distribution of, 116–19
  past, indexes of, 119
  percentage of promotional appropriation
    based upon, 417–20
  potential, 114–15
  quotas, 119–20
Sales agents, 251
Sales and distribution manager, 627
"Sales force composite method" of demand
    forecasting, 125–26
Sales forecast, 115–16
  revision of, 120
Sales management, shift to marketing
    management concept, 624
Sales Management Survey of Buying
    Power, 117–18, 124
Sales manager, 624
Sales potential, 114–15
  defined, 115
Sales promotion; see Promotional strategy
Sales quotas, 119–20
  defined, 119
Scaling techniques, attitude measurement
    by, 49–50
Seasonal inventories, 336
"Seconds," 262
Selected distribution, 286–88
Selective stocking operation, 332–34
Self-actualization, need for, 38
Selling
  aggressive; see Aggressive selling
  personal; see Personal selling
Selling mix; see Promotional mix
Semantic generalization and family brand-
    ing, 447–49
Service; see Product service
"Service marks," 187
Sherman Act, 295, 298, 300
Sheth, Jagdish N., 88–93
Single-plant relocation, 341–44
Single-price policy, 546–47
Single-warehouse decisions, 345–46
Situation analysis of a market plan, 617–18

*This book has been set in 11 and 10 point
Baskerville, leaded 2 points. The part numbers are in 30 point Helvetica Medium;
part titles, chapter numbers, and chapter
titles in 18 point Helvetica Medium. The
size of the type page is 28 x 44½ picas.*